I07124467

ALSO BY JAMES GAVIN

Intimate Nights: The Golden Age of New York Cabaret

Deep in a Dream

Deep in a Dream

The Long Night of CHET BAKER

James Gavin

ALFRED A. KNOPF
NEW YORK
2002

12

THIS IS A BORZOI BOOK
PUBLISHED BY ALFRED A. KNOPF

Copyright © 2002 by James Gavin

All rights reserved under International and Pan-American Copyright Conventions. Published in the United States by Alfred A. Knopf, a division of Random House, Inc., New York, and simultaneously in Canada by Random House of Canada Limited, Toronto. Distributed by Random House, Inc., New York.

www.aaknopf.com

Knopf, Borzoi Books, and the colophon are registered trademarks of Random House, Inc.

Library of Congress Cataloging-in-Publication Data
Gavin, James.
Deep in a dream : the long night of Chet Baker / James Gavin.—1st ed.
p. cm.
Includes index.
ISBN 0-679-44287-1
1. Baker, Chet. 2. Jazz musicians—United States—Biography. I. Title.
ML419.B14 G38 2002
788.9'2'165092—dc21
[B] 2001043379

Manufactured in the United States of America
First Edition

FOR CINDY BITTERMAN,
WILLIAM CLAXTON,
AND
ROBIN SWADOS

If it weren't for you
this would never have happened

"We gotta go and never stop going till we get there."

"Where we going, man?"

"I don't know but we gotta go."

—JACK KEROUAC, *On the Road*

CONTENTS

Deep in a Dream

PROLOGUE

Saturday, May 21, 1988
Inglewood, California

Graveside funerals dotted the rolling hills of the Inglewood Park Cemetery, in a residential black neighborhood on the outskirts of L.A. White canopies shielded mourners from the sun, but couldn't block out the rumble of planes, which zoomed in and out of the nearby Los Angeles International Airport. All through the cemetery, the foul smell of jet fumes hid the scent of freshly cut grass.

Two days earlier, a passenger flight from the Netherlands had carried the badly decomposed body of a trumpeter recalled as one of the handsomest men of the 1950s. Chet Baker had died a mysterious, drug-related death in Amsterdam on Friday the thirteenth. Now, after years in Europe, he was back in Southern California, where he had first known glory, to be laid to rest alongside his father. A former Oklahoma farmboy, Baker had filled people's heads with fantasies from the time he was born. Everything about him was open to speculation: his "cool" trumpet playing, so vulnerable yet so detached; his enigmatic half-smile; the androgyny of his sweet singing voice; a face both childlike and sinister. The melody that poured from his horn had led Baker's Italian fans to dub him *l'angelo* (the angel) and *tromba d'oro* (the golden trumpet). Marc Danval, a writer from Belgium, called his music "one of the most beautiful cries of the twentieth century" and compared him to Baudelaire, Rilke, and Edgar Allan Poe. In Europe, even his longtime addiction to heroin worked in his favor, making him seem all the more fragile and precious.

But in America, his death didn't arouse much sympathy. Baker's *New York Times* obituary, which listed the wrong age (fifty-nine instead of fifty-eight), portrayed him as a faded heartthrob whose "phenomenal luck" had "turned sour" due to drugs. "Some critics said he might have been overrated at the beginning," the paper noted of a musician once proclaimed the Great White Hope of jazz trumpeters. Despite announcements in the *Los Angeles Times* and the *Hollywood Reporter,* only about thirty-five people showed up at the funeral. "It was sad, it was not a celebration," said clarinetist Bernie Fleischer, Baker's high-school bandmate. "But nobody expected him to last this long anyway."

Few of those gathered knew much about his life abroad, and now, as they stared at a closed coffin, they were even more puzzled by his death. At about 3:10 in the morning, Dutch police had removed his body from a sidewalk below the window of his third-floor hotel room near Amsterdam's Central Station. Steps away was Zeedijk, a winding side street notorious for the most blatant drug dealing in Holland. Officers dumped the anonymous corpse at the morgue, assuming they had found one more unlucky dope fiend. The next day, Peter Huijts, Baker's Dutch road manager, identified the body. The death was ruled either a suicide or a drug-induced accident.

But contradictory evidence abounded. The window of his hotel room opened only about twelve inches, making it impossible for him to have fallen out involuntarily. Drug paraphernalia was found all over the room, yet a police spokesperson announced that Baker's blood showed no sign of heroin. In recent months, Baker had told several people that someone was out to get him. His English widow, Carol, living in Oklahoma with their three children, seized upon the same notion. "It wasn't suicide; it was foul play," she insisted. Pianist Frank Strazzeri, who had played for Baker not long before, took her suspicion a step further: "I'm looking down at the coffin and I'm saying, 'What the hell happened, man? What did you do? You fool, man, you burned another cat for bread. They finally killed you.' "

It was just like Baker to keep everybody guessing, even in death. He was a man of so few words, and notes, that each one seemed mysterious and profound. British writer Colin Butler had noted a similar quality in Jeri Southern, a melancholy singer-pianist of the fifties whose neuroses had led to a nervous breakdown and a refusal ever to sing again. "It was as though she had looked into the heart of some American dream and seen the outlines of a nightmare that was never ever to be discussed," Butler wrote. Baker had lived inside some unnamed torment of his own, and drawn from it such lusciously sad, lyrical music that people clung to him for years, determined to uncover his secret. To Hiro Kawashima, a young Japanese trumpeter, Baker was like Buddha: "He taught me about life itself, and I look up to him as the 'master of life,' so to speak." Singer Ruth Young, Baker's girlfriend of ten years, was so entranced by her "Picasso," as she called him, that she smuggled dope across borders for him and once even helped him drag a dead body out of a European apartment and dispose of it.

Baker had unleashed a similar mania in photographer Bruce Weber, who paid for the funeral. From 1986 through 1989, Weber had reportedly spent a million dollars of his own money to make the documentary *Let's Get Lost,* an orgasmic fantasia about a man whose fifties look had helped inspire Weber's homoerotic ads for Calvin Klein underwear. His camera lingered just as rapturously on the Baker of the late eighties, a figure whom film critics called a "singing corpse" (J. Hoberman, the *Village Voice*), a "withered goat" (Julie Salamon, the *Wall Street Journal*), a "hollow-cheeked, toothless, mumbling, all but brain-dead relic" (Charles Champlin, the *Los Angeles Times*), an "unreliable, conniving heroin addict" (Lee Jeske, the *New York Post*), a "bloodsucker" and "drug-ravaged ghost" (Chip Stern, *Rolling Stone*). All this of a man whose solos were regarded as models of heartfelt expression, as graceful as poems.

Each person at the funeral had his own fascination with Baker. At around 2 p.m., mourners started drifting into the cemetery. They passed the coffin, which was placed on a gurney beside the grave, and sat in a cluster of folding chairs. Everything had been planned by Emie Amemiya, the young woman who had coordinated the shooting of *Let's Get Lost.* There in the cemetery, Amemiya saw, for the first and only time, the trumpeter's second wife, Halema Alli, who had refused to participate in the film. In 1956, Alli had posed shyly with a bare-chested Baker for a coolly erotic portrait by photographer William Claxton. Four years later, she wound up in an Italian jail, howling in anguish while awaiting trial as an accomplice in her husband's biggest drug bust. Diane Vavra, Baker's lover for years, attended the funeral but stayed at the back of the crowd, as far as possible from the front row, where Carol, the three children, and Baker's mother, Vera, were seated. Baker and Vavra's mutual obsession had raged so intensely that she called it a "sickness." The trumpeter couldn't live without her, yet his abuse had finally made her run for her life the previous February.

Only now was it safe to return, or so she had thought. Even before the service began, Baker seemed to be present, stirring up the same jealousy and paranoia he had aroused in life. Baker's daughter, Melissa, began taunting Vavra in her hillbilly twang: *"We don't like you! We don't want you here! We want you to leave!"* Vavra recalled seeing a "really evil smile" cross Carol's face with every harangue. Many wondered why Carol had stayed with Baker for twenty-eight years, given his continual absence, violence, overt relationships with other women, and financial neglect. She loved him, she explained. Years after his death, royalties from his CD reissues earned her more money than he himself had ever made from his albums. Yet she kept selling Chet Baker T-shirts, homemade CDs, and photos on the family Web site, seemingly determined to earn every cent, and more, of the cash he had denied her.

Melissa's outbursts shook Ed Hancock, a boyhood acquaintance of Baker's. He walked up to her, put his hands on her shoulders, and said, *"Not now!"* Amemiya motioned nervously for the eulogies to start. Bernie Fleischer reminisced about the teenage Baker: "I just couldn't believe the way he played! Everything was such a struggle for me, and it was so easy for him, like a bird singing." Peter Huijts quoted some words allegedly spoken to Dizzy Gillespie by Charlie Parker, the father of bebop, who had used Baker in his band in 1952: "You better look out, there's a little white cat who's gonna eat you up!" There were tributes from bassist Hersh Hamel, another early pal of Baker's; Russ Freeman, who played piano in his famous quartet of the midfifties; and Frank Strazzeri, his accompanist in *Let's Get Lost.* Then Chris Tedesco, a young West Coast trumpeter who worshipped Baker, stepped forward. Holding back tears, he played an a cappella version of "My Funny Valentine," Baker's theme. When he cracked a note—just as Baker had on his first recording of the song in 1952—Fleischer felt a chill, as if his old friend were truly haunting the proceedings.

Amemiya witnessed an even stranger moment. She had brought a huge bouquet of white roses to distribute among the guests, and had placed the vase on the ground in front of Carol and Melissa. What happened couldn't be blamed on the sun, which was bright but not blazing. Suddenly the vase shattered, Amemiya said, strewing flowers and broken glass at their feet.

As the funeral ended, Melissa placed a rose on her father's coffin, then joined the other attendees as they filed out. Diane Vavra trailed behind. Melissa turned around and hissed: *"I'd kick your ass right now but I'm not dressed for it!"* Years later, Vavra tried to be philosophical about that "awful" day. "Well, she's just a little kid," she said of Melissa, who was nearly twenty-two when Baker died. "Her father didn't treat her very well. Never was around."

Tedesco was one of the last to leave the gravesite. He stopped at the coffin, which was still aboveground, and laid a note, handwritten on musical staff paper, atop the lid: "Dear Chet, you were the first jazz trumpet player that I ever heard and studied. You touched my life so many times with your solos and your singing. Farewell."

Whatever horrors they may have faced in their pursuit of Chet Baker, most of the mourners shared Tedesco's sentiment. "After all is said and done," felt Amemiya, "Chettie was so gifted and so magical that what he gave out he could never, ever get back." But Gudrun Endress, a German broadcaster and publisher who had known Baker for years, saw things less romantically. "Chet can hurt people even after he's dead," she warned. "Remember that."

1

The Christmas season of 1929 arrived just weeks after the stock market had crashed. But that December, nineteen-year-old Vera Baker got the gift of her dreams. In her little Oklahoma house, she gazed down at the infant in her arms, an angel with alabaster skin and hazel eyes. When he smiled at her, she saw magic. The child would surely lift her above the cold realities of marriage to a frequently unemployed alcoholic; more than that, he would bring meaning to her life, supplying all the tenderness and excitement that were missing. He was named Chesney, after his father. But with his chubby cheeks and dark hair, the child seemed like a tiny replica of herself. From the time of his birth, "Chettie," as she called him, was the center of Vera's universe.

Her obsession with him, and his father's response to it, had a darker effect on Chet Baker than he ever acknowledged; even he probably didn't understand it. Years later, he told Lisa Galt Bond, his collaborator on an unfinished memoir, "I had a very happy childhood; no problems." The tendency to keep things hidden had been ingrained in him from an early age. In 1954 he brought his French girlfriend, Liliane Cukier, to his parents' home during the first national tour of the Chet Baker Quartet. She observed the Bakers for three weeks. "This was a family where nobody hollered, didn't say what they had in their hearts or in their minds," she noticed. "Everyone was just trying to be cool."

Cukier recalled Chesney and Vera as "Oklahoma peasants, ordinary white people from way in the center." Starting in 1946, Chesney drove a yellow cab, the only job he had held on to for more than a couple of years. For a while in the twenties, he had lived his dream by touring as a guitar and banjo player. He worked mainly in hillbilly bands, but according to his son, Chesney had a feeling for jazz: he could whistle the licks of his hero, the Texas-born trombone master Jack Teagarden, while improvising on guitar.

Then came the Depression and the birth of his child, and he was forced to quit music and take a series of dreary survival jobs. He rarely mentioned his frustration, but it showed on his face: by his thirties he looked old and haggard, with crow's-feet spreading down his cheeks, pointing to a mouth that rarely smiled. He kept his sandy hair combed back, exposing a deeply furrowed brow. That prematurely ravaged look was inherited by his son, whose facial decay in later years would be commonly blamed on drug abuse. Chesney, though, aged far less strikingly. Bernie Fleischer recalled him as "very bland-looking," a man who faded into the background: "He was one of those shadowy figures who was always away somewhere." In the forties, Chesney surfaced occasionally to brag to his son's musician friends about a night when the great Teagarden had come to the house to jam with him. Some of them would later suspect that the fabled meeting had never happened at all.

Liquor helped Chesney dull the truth, including memories of a grim childhood. His family had moved from Illinois, where he was born on January 24, 1906, to Snyder, Oklahoma. Life in Snyder seemed cursed—not just by the tornado and fires that had plagued the small town, but by domestic strife. Vera later explained that Chesney's father, George Baker, had deserted his mother, Alice, and their five children for another woman. Alice went on to marry "Grandpa Beardsley," as the family knew him, a farmer with a bad leg and a nasty temper. Grandpa Beardsley seemed to hate his stepson on sight; Chesney told Vera that the older man beat him with his cane and badgered him to leave the house and never come back. Alice tried to protect her son, but Chesney fled before he was eighteen. For the rest of his life he hated his father and stepfather. Even after the latter had suffered a stroke and needed two canes to walk, Chesney had no sympathy; he grumbled to Vera that he wouldn't cross the street to see his stepfather even if the old man were on his deathbed.

It was in his teens that Chesney first found solace in the infant art of jazz. An improvisational music born of gospel, Negro spirituals, blues, and ragtime, jazz was all about letting the imagination take wing, molding split-second flights of fancy into personal statements of the heart. Chesney needed escape, and jazz seemed like the perfect vehicle. Besides Teagarden, whose ability to play trombone with endless invention defined the form, one other star fascinated Chesney: Bix Beiderbecke, a cornetist with a rich tone, spare delivery, and a poignance seldom found in early jazz, which tended to sound like party music.

Chesney taught himself to play banjo, a popular instrument in traditional jazz, and thus wrote his own ticket out of Snyder. The still-tiny jazz circuit seemed out of his reach, so he joined a series of country-western bands that entertained at dances throughout Oklahoma and other Midwestern states. It was a hand-to-mouth existence, but never had he known such joy: he lived each day for music, then unwound at night by drinking and smoking reefer, just like his heroes.

In 1928, Chesney passed through Yale, Oklahoma, a small oil town between Tulsa and Oklahoma City. Yale was so marginal that, in years to come, many state history books failed to mention it. The city's only claim to fame was Jim Thorpe, the American Indian whose 1912 Olympic triumphs in football and track had won him the title "World's Greatest Athlete" and inspired a Hollywood movie, *Jim Thorpe: All American,* starring Burt Lancaster. During the twenties, most of Yale's 2,600 other residents worked in the town's oil fields and refineries or as farmers.

One of the latter was Salomon Wesley Moser, a native of Iowa. In 1889, he had joined the legendary Oklahoma Run, in which white settlers charged in on horseback to drive Indians off the fertile land and claim it for themselves. Moser took eighty acres and started a farm. Around that time he met and married Randi, a young blind woman from Norway. The couple had seven children, who tended the farm. The next-to-youngest, Vera Pauline, was born there in May 1910. Vera grew into an unglamorous teenager. Short and stocky, she wore her mousy brown hair hanging down and parted in the middle. Her deep-set eyes were surrounded by little lines, deepened through years of exposure to the Oklahoma sun and dry winds.

At eighteen, Vera went to a Saturday-night barn dance where the young men and women of Yale gathered to find mates. She and the visiting guitar player, Chesney Baker, caught each other's eye. "He was such a handsome fellow!" Vera recalled. After a brief courtship they were wed by a justice of the peace, and found a cozy house at 326 South B Street in Yale. But any dreams Vera may have had for married bliss crumbled when Chesney skipped the honeymoon to go on tour, leaving her in Yale. Rather than live alone, she went back to her parents' farm, where she waited almost a year for her husband to return.

Their estrangement ended abruptly in October 1929, when the stock market crash wiped out people's entertainment budgets, along with Chesney's modest career. Just before Christmas, he came home broke and bereft of prospects to find his wife seven months pregnant, which only compounded his worries. On Monday, December 23, Vera gave birth to Chesney Henry Baker, Jr. Suddenly the disappointments of her marriage didn't seem to matter. Vera refashioned her life around Chettie. She bought a Brownie box camera and began obsessively photographing her beautiful son—one way she could possess his every move. She documented his infancy in a photo album called *The Dear Baby.* Under the heading "Baby's Most Cherished Playthings," she noted the odd combination of a doll and a Tinkertoy car, a portent of the sexual ambiguity for which he eventually became known. When Chettie murmured "I ov u," she wrote it neatly under "Some of Baby's First Sayings."

Vera's infatuation with her newborn son couldn't erase her fear of a bleak future. She fretted over how they would survive with no income. When Chesney finally found work, it was bitterly removed from the guitar strumming he loved: he smashed up old boilers with a sledgehammer in an oil field for twenty-five cents an hour. But even that job vanished as the Yale refineries fell victim one by one to the Depression. Life there seemed hopeless, and when Chettie was about a year old, his parents took him and headed for Oklahoma City, the state capital. Purely by chance, the town had escaped the worst effects of the crash: just months before, an oil well had been drilled there, setting off a thriving petroleum industry. Several public-works projects were launched, and out of them came the Oklahoma Arts Center and the Oklahoma City Symphony. All this cultural activity made Chesney think he might be able to play again.

He and Vera rented a small house downtown, on a street lined with shops and factories. Compared with Yale, Oklahoma City felt like a big-time metropolis. Pedestrians stared up in awe at the state's first "skyscraper," twelve stories high; they streamed in and out of the First National Bank building, the Biltmore Hotel, the YWCA, and other modern structures. Steam trains puffed white clouds as they chugged along the Rock Island and Frisco railroad lines, which ran through the center of town. The city's sparkle filled the Bakers with hope. Vera found a job in an ice-cream factory, while Chesney joined a band at radio station WKY, opening the broadcast day at 6 a.m. with a half-hour of hillbilly music. Fiddle players, a drummer, and guitarist Chesney huddled around a stand-up microphone in blue jeans and vests, stomping out a backbeat with their cowboy boots as they played. Often Chesney brought his son, then looked after him at home until Vera returned, bearing quarts of ice cream. On weekends, the band gathered at the house and jammed all night. For Chesney, life was complete again.

According to Vera, jazz and swing played on the radio for just an hour a day. During that time, she said in *Let's Get Lost,* Chettie would climb onto a stool and listen with the burning concentration that one day would mark his playing. Sometimes she romanticized the memory by claiming that her two-year-old son used to jump off the chair and play songs on the trumpet; in fact, he didn't touch a horn for another decade. But he was already absorbing the music, and in 1980 he told Lisa Galt Bond that he learned his first tune, "Sleepytime Gal," from his father before he was two.

As he also revealed, music wasn't the only thing Chesney exposed him to. In a 1960s tabloid article, "The Trumpet and the Spike: A Confession by Chet Baker," he recalled lying in bed late one night and hearing his father gab with his buddies from behind the closed door of the living room. Curious, the child toddled over and peeked through the keyhole. His description of the event bordered on the surreal. "My old man and his pals were lying back in their chairs with their eyes closed," he said. "They've gone to sleep, I thought, and they're dreaming strange, wonderful dreams. The room was filled with white smoke and its pungent smell reached me through the door and made me feel sick." One man, he recalled, wasn't smoking; instead he sat with his mouth wide open, inhaling smoke from the air. "They were almost in ecstasy," Baker said. "I didn't say anything to my father, nor to my mother, feeling that those gatherings were something secret, forbidden. After that first evening I spied a lot of other times on my father and his friends from the keyhole, more and more impressed and frightened."

Once he became known as a junkie, rumors spread that Baker used to smoke pot with his parents. "I don't know how that story got invented and circulated," he declared angrily to journalist Jerome Reece in 1983, after years of turning his life into a fantasy for reporters. "My father would smoke with other musicians a few times a week at the house, but I was very young at the time. What a ridiculous story—my mother was very strict and she was against all that."

For the rest of his life, Baker defended his father stubbornly, even though he had reason not to. Their relationship took a harsh turn when Chesney lost his radio job. He never played professionally again. A failure as a musician and, increasingly, as a breadwinner, he started drinking heavily. Chesney sat around the house with the radio on, hearing others play the music he no longer performed; his frustration festered until it exploded. His son was usually the target. Chesney started raising his hand or belt to Chettie anytime the boy made too much noise or wouldn't finish his dinner. "His father used to beat the shit out of him," said Sandy Jones, a woman with whom the trumpeter shared heroin, sex, and some rare revelations in 1970.

Baker seldom mentioned those childhood beatings to anyone. Even Ruth Young, who drew the deepest confidences out of him, knew only the outlines of his early paternal relationship. "Chet always wanted to be close to the father, but he was afraid of him," she said, adding: "They were divided by the mother's rein." Until Chesney died in 1967, Baker longed for his father's approval; with his own career seemingly finished by that time, he empathized all the more with the older man's pain at having to give up music.

Diane Vavra got an insight into Chesney's violence in 1986, when Baker took her on a visit to Oklahoma to see his mother. In a moment alone with Vera, Diane confided that Baker had been beating her. Vera was sympathetic. "My dear, why would you stay with a man who hit you?" she asked. "Let me tell you a story." She went on to recall a day early in her marriage when she and Chesney were in the car, with him at the wheel. He started accusing her of flirting with another man, and worked himself into a fury. The angrier he got, the more wildly he drove, until he made a bad turn and flipped the car over on its side. "After that," said Vera, "I never felt the same way about him again."

Vera couldn't have imagined that this abusive streak, passed down from Grandpa Beardsley to her husband, would appear in her son as well, but eventually she found out firsthand. Vavra remembered hearing Baker snarl to her in the early seventies that he had just hit his own mother. That admission was echoed chillingly in Vera's comment, made in *Let's Get Lost,* that Chettie was "exactly like his father."

Even in hard times, Vera kept up appearances. Despite her new full-time job as a saleslady at F. W. Woolworth, she maintained an immaculate, well-ordered home. To her son's friends she seemed ever calm and maternal, with a doting smile. Nearly everyone described her as "sweet," although when Bernie Fleischer met her in the forties, he saw a "very used, washed-out, thin little lady."

Her little boy remained her salvation. Every morning before he left for kindergarten and she for work, she dressed him fussily in clothes she had bought with her employee discount, including a sailor suit with a big white pointed collar. She made him stand still as she plastered his hair back and tied his shoelaces. Small for his age, he resembled a little doll as he walked to school along the railroad tracks.

Photos kept filling up the family albums: Chettie on his bicycle, Chettie playing ball, Chettie with his dog, Chettie in the backyard or on the porch. By seven or eight he was an eminently handsome child: his baby fat gone, he revealed high cheekbones, flawless skin, and thick, dark blond hair. Already, he knew how to pose for the camera: which way to turn to catch the light in the most striking fashion, how to hold his body in a relaxed yet controlled way. Photographed on his bicycle, Baker looked strong and confident—shoulders back, eyes focused coolly into the distance. Even when he stared straight at the camera, the boy seemed detached, unattainable.

Certainly Vera reminded him constantly of his appeal. Some thought it odd that she had only had one child, for in that age of primitive birth control, many wives stayed serially pregnant for years. But given her frosty relationship with her husband, their sex life had probably dwindled; in any case, Vera smilingly explained that Chettie was enough. She had no doubt that he favored her over his father. "I think he was closer to me," she declared in *Let's Get Lost.* As an adult, Baker remembered how uncomfortable he had felt when Vera put her arms around him and told him he had to stick by her forever: " 'Yes, mother, I will always stay near you,' I answered. Now I understand her. I represented for her, in so much poverty and pain, the only reason for living." But Vera seemed oblivious to the fact that her fixation on Chettie was driving a growing wedge between herself and her husband, that her son would come to hate her smothering, and that she was nurturing in him a lifelong pattern of narcissism and self-involvement.

For now, she had more urgent concerns. The family was struggling to survive on her small salary and Chesney's sporadic paychecks, so his sister, Agnes, and her husband, Jim, invited the Bakers to move into a spare room in their house on the fringe of Oklahoma City. Chettie later called his aunt and uncle the kindest people he had ever known. As a soldier stationed in Belgium during World War I, Jim had suffered permanent lung damage from inhaling mustard gas dropped by the Germans. He needed fresh air, and through the WPA he found work as a gardener and caretaker with the Oklahoma parks department. His wartime ordeal had also left him sterile, so the childless couple were thrilled to help raise such a handsome, polite, energetic boy as Chettie.

The WPA hired Chesney as a timekeeper, which involved clocking man-hours on work sites for payroll purposes. The Depression was hardly over—Chettie heard Jim talk about people coming to the parks and eating grass and leaves off trees—but with three employed adults in the house, the family was spared its worst effects. Still, with Chesney, Vera, and Chettie crammed into one bedroom, life grew so claustrophobic that the boy was sent to the Moser farm in Yale for several summers. Vera usually joined him at some point, pleased, no doubt, to spend time away from Chesney and alone with her son. Sixty years later, she recalled her pride at watching him roam through the big red barn filled with horses and pigs, climb peach trees, wander along a stream on the property, and play in the watermelon fields. "How that boy could run!" she marveled. "Oh, I couldn't keep up with him!"

But he also showed a tendency to withdraw—especially when his father began sending him to Snyder in the summertime. Given Chesney's hatred of his stepfather, it seemed cruel of him to expose his son—maybe on purpose—to the old man's tyranny. By now a stroke had nearly crippled Grandpa Beardsley, leaving him no patience for a rambunctious little boy. Chettie stayed outdoors as much as possible, scampering on a hillside chasing lizards.

Back in Oklahoma to resume grade school, Chettie was confronted anew with his parents' strained relationship. Night after night he watched his father come home drunk, then launch into "dreadful quarrels" with Vera; increasingly the boy couldn't stand being home. Chesney had often played guitar around the house for pleasure, but now the instrument lay untouched. "He would never admit he was a failure as a musician, and always blamed the 1929 Depression," said Baker in a rare moment of candor about his father. With the romance between Chesney and Vera long dead, their son developed a distorted notion of what men and women could mean to each other, especially physically.

He became even more confused in 1939, when the family left Agnes and Jim and moved into an apartment over a restaurant in the heart of Oklahoma City. Years later, he told Lisa Galt Bond about an incident that unnerved him deeply. One Saturday afternoon as he stood on the back porch, nine-year-old Chettie heard moaning sounds below. Curious, he hung from the railing and peered through a crack in the restaurant wall. He spied a naked woman spread-eagled on a table with one of the two young restaurant owners on top of her. The child stared, bewildered, as the man ground against his partner furiously until he went limp. Lifting himself up, he wiped his and her genitals with tissues. At that moment, Chettie lost hold of the railing and fell several feet with a crash. Heart pounding, he ran and hid in a vacant lot until it was safe to go home.

Baker recalled that early vision of sex with a mixture of prurience and distaste, and it left its mark on him. Far into his adult life, he "made love" as roughly and mechanically as the man in the restaurant. It was a dismaying counterpart to the sensitive ballads he sang.

Chesney Sr. had lost all sense of romance, if he'd ever had any. His life was a failure in most regards, and soon after moving to Oklahoma City, he was out of work again. He responded by doing what his son would do whenever the pressure got too intense: he hopped in his car and fled. Leaving his family in Oklahoma, Chesney drove and drove. This time he never came back. He ended up in Glendale, a Los Angeles suburb in the southeastern tip of the San Fernando Valley. Chesney landed a job at Lockheed, a huge manufacturer of jet components, as a parts inspector. He rented a small house, where he lived alone for months before sending for his family.

In 1940, Vera and Chettie embarked on a 1,428-mile bus trip that lasted nearly two days. They took a direct ride on the "Main Street of America": Route 66, the highway that spans the whole United States. As a hotshot jazz star, Baker would drive that road hundreds of times. Bobby Troup, a West Coast Jazz pianist and songwriter, made it seem like a hipster's paradise when he wrote the 1946 hit "(Get Your Kicks on) Route 66." Years before Jack Kerouac's *On the Road,* Troup extolled the wonders that might occur when a free spirit hit the open road.

As the bus sped west along Route 66, mother and son moved through the pastures and prairies of Texas, breathed the arid desert air of New Mexico and Arizona. Towns Vera had barely heard of whizzed by: Amarillo, Santa Rosa, Albuquerque, Flagstaff, Needles. Finally they reached Glendale. Chettie stared out the window at vineyards and orange groves; at the woodsy hills and blue-tinged mountains that surrounded the city on three sides; at the glistening concrete sidewalks and sunny streets lined with eucalyptus, palm, and pepper trees. Relaxation was in the air, mingled with the sweet fragrances of flowering greenery. After the turmoil of Oklahoma, he and Vera thought they had found heaven.

The new family home stood in a quiet, residential neighborhood surrounded by hills and canyons. Each day Chesney drove to Lockheed in his newly acquired 1936 Buick, while Vera rode the bus to the downtown L.A. branch of W. T. Grant, the five-and-dime where she now worked. Vera was a model of motherly efficiency on the sales floor, her hair now cropped short and pushed back, a cardigan draped around her shoulders. She beamed when anyone asked about her son, who seemed like a dream child: his grades were good, he didn't make trouble, and the teachers liked him. In the move from Oklahoma to California, Chettie even jumped a term ahead.

But he wished he hadn't. Still small, he looked even more undergrown among his older classmates. They started making fun of him, which stirred up an anger he had never shown before. The humiliation drove Chettie to prove he was faster and better than any of them. He raced to school on roller skates, then went after class to the YMCA, where sports became his passion. Whether in swimming, basketball, or track, he met every physical challenge without trying. Trumpeter Jack Sheldon, who became his friend later in the forties, was awestruck by Baker's stamina. Sheldon was a superb athlete, especially in swimming and diving, but he could hardly keep up with Baker. "He was so very special," Sheldon said. "I remember we played tennis once. I was real good at tennis. He'd never played before, he told me, and I just barely beat him."

Chettie's prowess didn't end with sports. Since learning "Sleepytime Gal" as a child, he hadn't pursued music much, but when he found an old upright in the basement of the Y, he began pecking out tunes by ear. At home, he sang along with the radio. His voice had yet to change, and it sounded as high and neutered as a choirboy's. Vera found it irresistibly pretty, and it gave her one more excuse to show him off. In 1942, she started to "drag" him (as he later put it) to Clifton's, a popular restaurant near W. T. Grant's that held kiddie talent shows. Competing against fledgling accordionists, tap dancers, and yodelers—all towed by their own fawning mothers—twelve-year-old Chettie crooned some rather mature love songs. Vera had taught him her favorite tunes from the Hit Parade: Cole Porter's seductive "You'd Be So Nice to Come Home To"; "I Had the Craziest Dream," a woman's plea for a princely lover, made famous by singer Helen Forrest with Harry James's orchestra; and "That Old Black Magic," a hit about the "tingle" of sexual attraction, popularized by the teenage singer Margaret Whiting. "Maybe some kind of Oedipus thing was going on," said Diane Vavra, "because his mother taught him all these very erotic lyrics." Baker looked slight and fey as he sang them; years later, he confided to pianist Jimmy Rowles that some of the children had laughed at him, calling him "sissy" and saying he sounded like a girl. The taunts infuriated him, but typically, Vera romanticized those contests by claiming that Chettie had always won first place. Baker said he never did, although he came in second once to a little ballerina who did a split.

Having a "pretty" son with a feminine singing voice wasn't too pleasing to Chesney, and he took steps to recast the boy in a manly image. In 1943, he stopped at a pawnshop on his way home from the factory. With Jack Teagarden in mind, he bought a trombone and gave it to his son. It was an insensitive choice: with the slide extended, the horn was almost as long as Chettie, who couldn't possibly manipulate it. Begrudgingly, Chesney exchanged it for a trumpet. He brought it home and coldly set it down, not even handing it to the boy. For the rest of her life, Vera claimed that it took her son only two weeks to learn how to play along with Harry James's lightning-speed solo on "Two O'Clock Jump." Most musicians learn their craft through a combination of practice and study of the intricacies of technique and theory, but that wasn't Chet Baker's approach to music or life. "You gotta realize, Chet was not that intelligent," said Ruth Young. "He did not know what he was doing, on that level, *ever.* He just did it."

No sooner had he shown all this musical promise than disaster struck. As he played in the street after school with his neighborhood pals, one of them threw a rock at a lamppost. It ricocheted and hit Chettie in the mouth, breaking off his left front tooth. Chesney flew into a rage, shouting that the boy would never be able to play his horn again. Chettie couldn't understand the fuss; he didn't know it was almost impossible to control the flow of air into a wind instrument with a missing front tooth. He practiced with such tenacity that he made the dental gap a part of his technique. The lost tooth limited his range, but he didn't care; high notes were just for showing off, he decided, and once he reached twenty he wasn't interested in that. Vera took him to the dentist and got him a removable tooth, but he seldom wore it. Instead, he hid the space by keeping his lips closed in public, creating the Mona Lisa half-smile that made him look so inscrutable.

At Glendale Junior High, the teenager signed up for a basic instrumental training course, but it bored him. He mastered each exercise in moments, and had no patience for studying a textbook. It struck him as a waste of time to memorize dots and curly lines on staff paper; why bother when he could pick up a song by hearing it once or twice? Playing in the school dance band, he learned the Sousa marches by ear, then pretended to read the scores. At home, he learned the pop tunes of the day from radio or from Vera's 78s. His favorite musician was trumpeter Harry James, whose dance band had zoomed to the top of the charts with a sentimental old ballad from 1913, "You Made Me Love You." James played the trumpet with a honey-dripping tone, decorating songs with a frilliness that most of the budding beboppers found corny. But Baker loved James's big, bright sound, and studied the bandleader's solos until he could copy them almost exactly.

With James's soaring expressions of love in his ear, Baker lost his virginity at fifteen. The experience, as he described it to Lisa Galt Bond, was even tawdrier than his first voyeuristic glimpse of sex in Oklahoma City. Baker had made friends with Bennett and Leo Little, two brothers who lived with their mother in a residential hotel in downtown Glendale. According to Baker, Mrs. Little's full-time job at Thrifty Drugs left her sons to their own devices after school, and the boys divided their free time between a tree house and a pit they had dug behind the hotel. Baker remembered vanishing with them into one place or the other and talking naïvely about how it would feel to have sex with a girl.

They soon found out. Baker knocked on their apartment door one day, he said, to find Leo and Bennett inside with a fifteen-year-old girl named Barbara. She announced her willingness to take on all three boys. Afraid that Mrs. Little would come home and catch them, Baker and the brothers took Barbara out to the tree house, which was hidden behind two adjoining signboards. As she lay on her back, Baker—the best-looking boy—went first. Barbara was obviously no virgin. Naked beneath her dress, she lifted the hem and guided him inside her as Leo and Bennett watched. Baker was so overwhelmed that he climaxed in seconds, then stumbled dizzily to his feet as the brothers laughed. Instead of exhilaration, he felt nauseated and shaken, and ran out the door thinking, "Never again, never again." The recollection—apocryphal though it may be—so traumatized Baker, he claimed, that for a time he didn't want to go near another girl. In 1980, he described that initiation into lovemaking as "my first pussy," a phrase that reinforced his general attitude toward sex.

The end of World War II in August 1945 brought an economic boom and a rush of job opportunities for returning servicemen, but not for Chesney Baker. After coming to blows with his boss at Lockheed, he once more found himself out of a job. Now almost forty, he was far less employable than the young ex-GIs, especially with a work history that marked him as trouble. In the months he spent searching fruitlessly for a job, Vera's dime-store salary was stretched to the limit.

The Bakers were rescued by two old friends from Oklahoma, Bob and Tillie Coulter. They let the family move into their house in Hermosa Beach, California, a seaside town bordering the larger community of Redondo Beach. In a replay of their experience with Jim and Agnes, the Bakers uprooted themselves and took over a spare room at the Coulters'. With her spotless employment record, Vera obtained a transfer to the W. T. Grant's store in nearby Inglewood. With no other options, Chesney started driving a cab.

The bedroom in the Coulter house became a pressure cooker. Thrown into such close quarters with her sullen, brooding husband, Vera grew even more obsessed with her son, who at sixteen started to rebel. Desperate to get away from her, he took a job as a pinsetter in a bowling alley, heading there straight from class and working until midnight. His grades sagged; all he cared about at school was playing in the band. To that he added two new passions: the beach and cars. Taking along the Coulters' son Brad, now his best friend, Baker went drag-racing in his father's Buick. Since he had no license yet, his parents were furious. But Jack Sheldon was dazzled: "He drove like a race-car driver—very fast, and he'd go into places I would never drive."

A devious side of Baker started to show as he became a whiz at stealing gas. He would insert one end of a hose into the tank of some stranger's car, suck the air out of the other end to create a vacuum, then insert it into his own tank. Sometimes he sniffed the gas—his first experience of getting high. Baker recalled weekends of skin-diving, bodysurfing, and mountain climbing with Brad in Palos Verdes, whose cliffs tower above L.A.'s South Bay. They found a cave and hid there at night, he said, building a fire and sprawling on blankets to a soundtrack of crashing waves.

The boys were having a ball, but Vera panicked. As she watched her son turn into a juvenile delinquent, she agonized over where she might have gone wrong. But Chettie, like his father, craved escape. He found it when he saw a military recruitment poster with Uncle Sam pointing a finger, inviting him to "join the army and see the world." Impulsively he decided to do just that.

A heartsick Vera had to agree that there was no other answer. On November 5, 1946, a few weeks before her son reached the legal age of seventeen, she signed him into the army for an eighteen-month stint. On his last night at home, Baker—now a licensed driver—borrowed his father's car to take a girl named Gloria on a date. At the end of the night, he found a hidden parking spot near her home and beckoned her into the backseat, where they hastily made love. Afterward, he recalled, she dashed out of the car, explaining that she had to wash herself out to avoid getting pregnant.

The encounter was only a trifle more dignified than the one with Barbara, but to Chettie, having sex in a car seemed a lot cooler. Over time, his memory of that date took on a dreamlike glow: Gloria gave him a picture of herself, he said, then kissed him and ran from the car, her golden hair reflecting the moonlight. Just as he discovered how to seduce the camera lens into depicting him in make-believe terms, he learned to glamorize the truth into a fairy tale of romantic intrigue. Baker drove home that night and went to bed, eager to start the life of an independent man.

Lake Wannsee, Berlin, Germany, 1947. Photo by Howard Glitt

2

A few days after his enlistment, Baker stepped off a train at Fort Lewis, a huge army post in Washington state, to start two months of basic training. He and a herd of equally callow-looking youths lined up to have vaccination needles jabbed into their shoulders. As the ache set in, they strapped on seventy-pound backpacks and headed for the forest to practice marching, digging foxholes, and aiming their rifles. Every morning they did a battery of sit-ups and push-ups designed to turn them into rock-solid defenders of their country.

The effort seemed a little pointless. World War II had ended thirteen months earlier, leaving America the preeminent world power, with a rosy future of financial ease and domestic security. The government vowed to guard that vision from any more Japanese or German attacks. It kept recruiting soldiers, while refining and testing the atomic bomb that had devastated Hiroshima and Nagasaki at the close of the war. The image of a gray mushroom cloud of death, shown and reshown in movie newsreels and later on TV, spread a chilling unintended message: that America could accidentally incinerate itself at the touch of a button. Soon the Beat Generation would argue that it was idiotic to plan ahead for a future that might not exist; better to spend each moment as if it were your last. By the late fifties, Chet Baker was living that philosophy more hazardously than almost any Beat.

At Fort Lewis, though, rebellion wasn't an issue; most of the enlistees were just biding their time while they tried to figure out what to do with their lives. Right after New Year's Day of 1947, Baker and his barracks mate, Dick Douglas, sat together on a bus to Camp Kilmer, New Jersey, where they would embark for Germany. In the dead of winter, hundreds of frightened boys filed up the gangplank of a huge ship. They sailed past the Statue of Liberty, then out to sea. For ten days, said Baker, they "lived like packed maggots." Some vomited from seasickness and fear; others tried getting drunk on Aqua Velva aftershave. When the ship docked at the German seaport of Bremerhaven, they fought their way through the snow to a bulletin board that posted each man's destination. Baker was disappointed: both he and Douglas were slated for Berlin, but while Douglas's high IQ had earned him an assignment to manage the Western Theater, the center of military operations, Baker—whose recent school grades were mediocre—got the dull job of clerk-typist.

The next morning, a train took them to Berlin, where they beheld the capital of the Third Reich, reduced mostly to debris by the Russians in response to the German invasion of the Soviet Union. American and Soviet forces had divided up the city, occupying the apartment buildings left standing. Russian women shuffled through bombed-out areas, picking up bricks and shoveling dirt. Baker never forgot the images of hopelessness and destruction; they made the future seem like a grim place.

He wandered around the Onkel Tom, an unravaged district of northwest Berlin where the American troops were headquartered. His spirits rose when he heard an orchestra playing from inside the ground floor of an apartment building. Opening the door, he found the fifty-six-piece 298th Army Band finishing its afternoon rehearsal. He begged the first sergeant to let him join. The next morning, Baker auditioned with the Martin horn he had brought from America and won the last seat in the trumpet section.

At his first rehearsal, he was handed march arrangements he couldn't read. He knew certain songs, like "When Johnny Comes Marching Home," from his Redondo band days, and bluffed his way through the others. During the initial run-through of a piece, he pretended to play while listening closely to the other trumpeters. The second time he executed the march almost perfectly. He learned the band book so quickly by ear that his interest wandered. There wasn't much for the orchestra to do, anyway, besides greet the rare visiting dignitary. Some of the musicians spent their free time practicing, but Baker couldn't see the point of laboring at something he found so easy. Instead, he auditioned for the smaller army dance band, in which he really wanted to play. The conductor and lead alto player, Howard Glitt, was amazed at how bold and strong the seventeen-year-old trumpeter sounded; already he soloed with the confidence of a star. Glitt was sure he had found a sight-reading wonder.

But even the dance band posed no great challenge, and Baker amused himself by hanging out with Dick Douglas, who was fast becoming his hero. Years later, in his autobiographical writings, Baker recalled watching in awe as the cocky Douglas mounted a set of parallel bars, gliding into a perfect handstand. Then Douglas would swagger to his office, fitted out with two German secretaries, a bar, cases of schnapps, a sofa, a film projector, and some French porno films that he used to seduce nurses. "My kind of guy," Baker said. One day when a taller, burlier man shoved him aside while leaving the mess hall, Douglas whirled around and knocked him unconscious. Baker was even more impressed to see Douglas, a high-ranking administrator, get away with running a lucrative black-market business, selling coffee, soap, cigarettes, and other rationed items under the counter. Douglas was casually macho, physically superior, and afraid of no one. For Baker, who had been beaten down by his father and babied by his mother, his buddy's cool masculinity was enviable. The trumpeter spent hours doing calisthenics in his room to make himself as strong as Douglas.

When summer came, Baker, Douglas, and a couple of their friends took a train to Lake Wannsee, at the southwest edge of Berlin, and rented a sailboat. Douglas brought his transistor radio, which picked up crackly broadcasts from the Armed Forces Radio Service (AFRS). Baker heard a new wave of jazz that sounded a lot hipper than Harry James. The most controversial new bandleader was Stan Kenton, an intellectual young maestro from the West Coast who seemed to view himself as the jazz Toscanini. Kenton played his share of silly novelties ("His Feet Too Big for De Bed"; "And the Bull Walked Around, Olay") to appease his record label, Capitol; he had to, no doubt, to offset the weak sales of such pseudo-symphonic pieces as "Concerto to End All Concertos." Kenton sat at the piano and pounded out grandiose accompaniment, rising occasionally and waving his long arms to conduct. Pompous as it could seem, his band was full of raw power: trumpets blared in the high register, trombones thundered in the low; the saxophones added a chill that made the music feel like a wintry blast.

Baker's colleagues in the army dance band were dazzled by Kenton, who signaled big, exciting changes in jazz. *Down Beat* and *Metronome,* the top jazz magazines of the day, carried stories about all the Kenton sidemen who were becoming celebrities in their own right: trumpeters Shorty Rogers and Al Porcino, saxophonists Art Pepper and Bob Cooper, trombonist Kai Winding, drummer Shelly Manne, arranger Pete Rugolo. Baker stayed tuned to AFRS to hear other groundbreaking sounds from bandleader Woody Herman, whose arrangers, Ralph Burns and Neal Hefti, were using complex harmonies and tone colors to create an ambitious form of concert jazz.

One musician fascinated and confused Baker above all others: Dizzy Gillespie, a Manhattan-based black trumpeter who was helping trigger what Phil Leshin, a young bassist on the scene, called "a complete revolution—socially, personally, certainly musically." Gillespie and a small core of New York players—alto saxophonist Charlie Parker, pianists Bud Powell and Al Haig, drummers Kenny Clarke and Max Roach—were taking the simple harmonic and melodic language of swing and turning it inside out with dissonant chords, bullet-fire chromatic solos, and rhythms so tricky they made the head swim. The music was called bebop, and few had the ears to understand it, much less perform it. "If you were a young musician at the time and wanted to play jazz, suddenly your ears were opened up to a whole new way of doing it," said Leshin. On standards like "What Is This Thing Called Love?" and "I Got Rhythm," beboppers tossed out the melody and "ran the changes," improvising so wildly over the chords that only the sharpest ears could identify the songs. Baker had never heard a trumpeter like Gillespie, who skittered through eighth- and sixteenth-note runs with a thin, steely tone that climbed into a piercing upper range. The notes flew by maniacally; like his peers, Gillespie seemed to connect to some higher consciousness as soon as he pressed his horn to his lips.

The music intimidated even Louis Armstrong, the father of jazz, who bitterly denounced it in *Down Beat.* Gillespie made bop seem even kookier by adopting a far-out French bohemian look—horn-rimmed glasses, goatee, beret—that lots of beboppers copied. Negro slang became their coded vocabulary, whether they were white or black.

Their whole lifestyle, which included the reckless use of hard drugs, mocked every value—money, security, planning for the future—that obsessed America in the wake of World War II. Beboppers starved for their art while reveling in noncommercialism. In the article "Remembrances of Bop in New York, 1945–1950," published in a 1963 issue of his underground magazine *Kulchur,* poet and bop devotee Gilbert Sorrentino remembered glorying in his sense of alienation:

> Be-bop cut us off completely, to our immense satisfaction. It was even more vehemently decried as "nigger music," but even to the tone-deaf it was apparent that it (the music) didn't care what the hell was thought of it. . . . It was probably, more than at any other time in its history, including the present, absolutely non-popular: and its adher-

ents formed a cult, which perhaps more than any other force in the intellectual life of our time, brought together young people who were tired of the spurious.

Bop was nothing like the lyrical playing that would make Chet Baker famous. But he plunged fully into the culture surrounding it: the burning drive to keep moving, the pleasure in shocking people, and later, the compulsion to self-destruct. He admired how Gillespie had rejected every convention of trumpet playing in order to create his own sophisticated voice. Baker studied the Gillespie solos he heard on AFRS, trying to follow the strange lines. "Everything changed for me," he told reporter Les Tomkins years later. "I found myself getting further and further away from the 'sweet' Harry James style of playing, and trying to phrase things in, I guess—for lack of a better word—a 'hipper' way."

But neither Sousa marches nor army dance tunes gave him much of a chance to sound hip. In those days, Baker struck most people as a corn-fed innocent. He didn't smoke or drink, spoke in a high country-boy twang, and looked closer to twelve than seventeen. Most people called him Chettie; not until 1952, when he joined the Gerry Mulligan Quartet, would he adopt the more rugged-sounding "Chet." Pianist and arranger Bob Freedman, who met Baker while both were soldiers, recalled him as "just non-threatening—his looks, his demeanor. He had this wide-open face."

In his wallet he carried a picture of Gloria, his Glendale girlfriend, and another of his mom and dad. But he avoided showing his vulnerable side, thinking, perhaps, that it wouldn't seem cool to be seen pining for a girl or the comforts of home. Baker paid a German artist in rationed cigarettes to create oil portraits of the two photos, then hid the canvases under his bunk. His army and band buddies couldn't recall his ever writing to his folks; yet when they weren't watching, he sent Vera numerous letters, enclosing pictures of himself looking handsome in his khaki pants, olive-brown belted army jacket, and cloth cap. She proudly displayed the photos to her co-workers at W. T. Grant's as proof of what a good and loyal son she had.

Baker didn't have to strain for secrecy, though, for he spent much of the summer of 1947 alone. While his friends went into the French-occupied sector of Berlin to look for prostitutes, he sailed Lake Wannsee in a tiny motorboat and daydreamed of his ideal woman.

Those lazy excursions on the lake inspired one of his favorite stories about his young self, and one of the most revealing. One afternoon as he drifted on the water, he said, the sky went dark and thunder started to pound. Turning toward shore, he spotted the exact girl of his fantasies, a twenty-two-year-old blonde beauty, wading with the hem of her skirt held in her hands. He asked if she wanted to go for a ride. According to one of his accounts, she answered "I'd love to" in perfect English, giving her name as Gisella. In another version she spoke only German, and he used sign language to beckon her into the boat. As the storm raged they sailed past a deserted cabin, climbed inside, and made love for hours.

Forever after, he recalled Gisella as the love of his young life. But their fairy-tale romance was doomed. The young woman lived with her family, and money was tight; soon, Baker said, he found that she and her sister were virtual whores, cozying up to soldiers in exchange for cash, gifts, and a hoped-for marriage proposal from a solvent GI. "She didn't really care for me," said Baker in 1963. "I was just the best prospect at the time." After Gisella learned he couldn't meet her requirements, she turned cool. One night when he came by her house, her parents informed him, falsely, that she had wed a Russian officer. In fact, as he bitterly informed Lisa Galt Bond around 1980, Gisella had married a GI buddy of his, a lousy trumpet player from the same army band.

Whatever the truth of that episode, its theme—that the woman to whom he had opened his heart had turned out to be a liar and a phony—permanently marred his attitude toward love. In future relationships he would veer between a need for mothering and a paranoid mistrust, all the while seeing himself as the victim. He revealed his double standard in 1948, after an emergency appendectomy had ended his first stay in the army. Baker went home and sought out Gloria, only to find she hadn't waited for him. She was married and fat, far from the glowing goddess he remembered. Another woman had let him down. Never mind that he himself had had an affair that, while it lasted, had made him forget all about her. He gave Gloria the painting from Germany and, he declared, never thought of her again—except on all the occasions over the next forty years when he told that tearful story.

In January 1948, Baker moved back in with his parents, who now had their own place in Hermosa Beach. Life had settled down for the couple: Vera had been promoted to floor supervisor at W. T. Grant's, while Chesney had hung on to his job as cabdriver, maybe because there were no coworkers or supervisors with whom he could clash. The Bakers had saved enough for a down payment on a modest two-bedroom house at 1011 Sixteenth Street; its hilltop site overlooked the Pacific Coast Highway and the beach. On a clear day they could see the resort island of Catalina from their tiny front yard.

Once home, Baker was thrust back into the suffocating atmosphere that had driven him away in the first place. "He didn't want to be there," said bassist Hersh Hamel, his teenage friend. Vera, though, was grateful to have her Chettie back, and his return to school offered hope that maybe his delinquent days were over.

Baker enrolled at Redondo Union High School, a huge institution in nearby Redondo Beach. Redondo High was said to have the number-one high school football team in America, and one of the top concert bands. Within days of his arrival, Baker showed up at band practice with his army trumpet and a mouthpiece he had made in the school machine shop. He had learned the effects of different-sized mouthpieces on a trumpeter's sound: a wide, deep one produced just such a tone; a shallow one with a smaller opening created a pinched, high-flying wail like Gillespie's. For now, Baker wanted the latter. The band's conductor, George Cather, tested Baker by sitting him in the trumpet section and calling for the band to play "Ruslan and Ludmilla," a big, flashy overture by the Russian composer Glinka. Baker knew nothing about classical music, and still had little ability to read a score. Afterward, Bernie Fleischer, who played clarinet in the band, asked the first trumpeter, Gene Daughs, for a report. "It's the most incredible thing I've ever seen," Daughs said. "The first time through, the guy hardly played a note. The second time he cut my ass. But the worst thing is, he never once pushed the right valves down."

"He's not better than you, is he?" asked Fleischer.

"Bernie, this guy's in another world."

If his virtuosity confounded the other players, it was his looks that entranced the female students. Seated among a lot of pimply-faced boys in white shirts and bow ties, Baker got most of the attention with his invitingly remote manner and the thatch of dark-blond hair that coyly veiled his handsome face. A fellow student, Jane Thompson, recalled her first look at him: "I just remember this cute boy in the midst of all these square-looking guys. My girlfriends and I couldn't hear what he was playing, but we didn't care. We all said, 'Who's that?' "

Those same delicate features made him a target for campus bullies, who called him "pretty boy"—the worst jeer in those days, when men were supposed to be super-masculine at all times. The remark hit such a nerve in Baker that he nearly went crazy. "If you insulted Chet, he'd kill you," said Fleischer. "He got into fights all the time." On one occasion Baker and

Fleischer were walking on the campus of the upscale, snobbish Beverly Hills High. Baker wore his outfit from the Redondo Variety Show: a facsimile of a zoot suit, the flashy getup of swing-era hipsters. Its big padded shoulders, pleated trousers, and low-hanging tails were now out of fashion, and the outfit looked especially silly on the small, wiry Baker, then eighteen. Four football players passed by and made some snickering comments. In a flash, Baker lunged at the biggest jock, who pounded him so viciously that Fleischer and the other players struggled to separate them. By the time they did, Baker was a bloody mess, and his suit hung in shreds. "That was standard practice," Fleischer said. "Chet used to get beat up all the time. The other guy would start with an insult, and Chet would start the physical stuff. I guess it was wounded pride and ego."

These sudden outbursts would worsen as the years went on, to the point where his rages terrified people. At Redondo High, though, he learned to affect a cool air much of the time. If he couldn't look as tough as a football player, he could arm himself by acting aloof and fearless. The next year, pianist Jimmy Rowles noticed Baker's confident walk: shoulders thrust back, eyes down, a glance that revealed nothing.

It worked for him in the fall of 1948, when he entered El Camino Junior College, a two-year free university, filled with ex-servicemen, in nearby Torrance. Baker was welcomed into Kappa Theta, an exclusive fraternity populated by football players. His music professor at El Camino was Hamilton Maddaford, a twenty-three-year-old ex-GI. Maddaford taught sight-reading and harmony, the traditional foundation for any aspiring musician. His most conspicuously bored student was Baker, who slouched at his desk in the back of the room and rarely, if ever, raised his hand. "I could tell he wasn't really happy there," said Maddaford. "He didn't have a bit of interest in book learning."

Baker came to life only when he joined Maddaford's El Camino College Warrior Band. Sometimes the professor let him solo. Maddaford recalled him as talented but unformed: "He wasn't a virtuoso, but he had a good tone." But Bernie Fleischer was awestruck: "The stands would quiet down just like it was a jazz concert. We'd get as much applause as the football team sometimes."

At home, Fleischer and Baker sat around the Victrola and spun the latest bebop 78s. Baker couldn't contain his joy at hearing Dizzy Gillespie or Don Byas, a fat-toned tenor player, race through phrases that made the Redondo band marches seem like nursery rhymes. Jumping out of his chair, he would shout: "What was that? How'd he do that? Play it again!"

In 1949, Baker and Hersh Hamel were visiting their friend Ian Bernard, an aspiring bop pianist. Bernard's family had a disc-cutting machine that made noisy transcriptions on 78s. The three boys gathered around the bulky contraption and made a two-sided record for fun. It still exists. Even with the music on that old disc worn down to a rumble, Baker's trumpet cuts through with so much brashness and spirit that it's easy to hear why he caused a stir. Compared with his refined delivery of the fifties, Baker's work here is unrecognizable: he blusters through two standards, "All the Things You Are" and "Get Happy," with a hard, pinched tone and lots of notes, many out of tune. In "All the Things You Are," he hurries past Jerome Kern's lilting melody and tears into a bebop chorus, trying hard to ride Bernard's wild chords and mostly succeeding. "Chet was burning," said Bernard. "Even then, he had the most incredible sense of time. You couldn't lose him."

Hungry to learn new songs, Baker began showing up on the doorstep of Jimmy Rowles, who played piano for Billie Holiday, Peggy Lee, and other great jazz singers. Rowles was known for his encyclopedic repertoire, and once Baker met him in L.A. he wouldn't leave him alone. On his mornings off from school, Baker drove to Rowles's house in Culver City and rang the bell until he woke him up. He waited impatiently for Rowles to make coffee, light a cigarette, and come to the piano. Baker listened intently to each song Rowles played, then tried to copy it on trumpet. "I was just astounded at his talent," the pianist said. "He grabbed things so quick." Rowles's restrained, spacious touch made Baker understand the power of simplicity. But he was still a fiery trumpeter, and when Rowles took him to jam sessions, Baker was noticed. "People kept saying, 'Where the hell did you get this guy?' " said Rowles. "Nobody had ever heard of him, and he was up there blowing these guys out." Phil Brown, a bop drummer, first heard Baker in that period. "Chet didn't sound like he did in the fifties," Brown said. "He had a more aggressive, black-sounding style then. He got whiter later."

In either case, Baker's friends marveled at how easily everything came to him. His gifts seemed heaven-sent, the kind no amount of practice could bring. "When Chettie was young, he was like an eagle," said Jack Sheldon. "He would do anything. We would go to Palos Verdes and climb around on the cliffs. One time we were climbing and I was following him. I was scared to death, and he was climbing like a goat." Baker liked talking about music but could only discuss it "in the most simple terms," said Walter Norris, a pianist from Arkansas who became a mainstay of West Coast Jazz. The trumpeter's comments, Morris said, were "mostly about feeling, the soulful part of music." He could be quite arrogant about the rest. Bob Neel, soon to become his roommate and drummer, couldn't believe Baker's nerve. "When I was a teenager I thought, eventually I'm gonna be the best drummer in the world," Neel said. "Probably by twenty-five I realized, well, maybe I won't be the best, but I'll be in the top ten. Then pretty soon . . . maybe the top hundred. But I don't think Chettie ever thought of himself as anything but number one."

His guts didn't end with his playing. In the dead of night, after a gig in Hermosa Beach, he and Bernie Fleischer walked along the Esplanade, a cement pathway along the ocean. They passed a catamaran docked on the beach. "Wanna go to Catalina?" asked Baker.

"Not tonight, I don't!"

"Well, I'm going!" declared the trumpeter.

"I helped him drag this boat that he was swiping down to the water," said Fleischer. "He got on it in his gig suit and sailed to Catalina. That's twenty-six miles, open water! He scared me to death."

The word almost everyone used to describe Baker was "cool," the quality all jazzmen coveted. "You had to be cool," said pianist Russ Freeman, who in 1953 became the maestro of Baker's first quartet. "It wasn't cool if you weren't cool! Somewhere, somehow, young jazz musicians started to see themselves as separate from other people. And it's true—they *are* separate from other people." Cool was a sound, but it was also a way of life. "It means you get done in a sentence what somebody else would take a paragraph for," explained pianist Paul Bley. "You edit your behavior."

No one felt more alienated or superior than Miles Davis, the black trumpeter whose spare, edgy playing defined cool as a mask for violent emotions. In 1949, Baker heard a set of Capitol 78s that starred Davis. Known as *Birth of the Cool,* these records, made by an interracial group of New York players, had a studied sophistication and an icy intellectual aura that were copied widely in white West Coast Jazz. Lyrical as it sounded, Davis's playing bristled with an undercurrent of anger, and Baker—whose own rage, centered on his parents, was brewing—connected with that style so passionately that he felt he had found the light.

Davis had numerous chips on his shoulder. Like Baker, he had lost several talent competitions as a boy; his opponents, though, weren't little girls in tutus but white trumpeters. He later told *Playboy:* "In high school, I was the best in the music class on trumpet. I knew it and all the rest knew it—

but all the contest first prizes went to the boys with blue eyes. It made me so mad I made up my mind to outdo anybody white on my horn."

He was no starving waif. Born to a well-to-do family near East St. Louis, Davis had advantages known then to few blacks, and even attended the prestigious Juilliard School of Music in Manhattan. But as he said in *Miles: The Autobiography,* cowritten in the late eighties with Quincy Troupe, he had grown up in a town still reeling from a 1917 race riot in which "those crazy, sick white people killed all those black people." His exposure to racism infuriated him almost from birth; it also helped give him a burning drive to succeed.

As a rising musician in New York, he became friends with Freddie Webster, another young trumpeter. Webster's solo on a 1946 Sarah Vaughan disc, *If You Could See Me Now,* thrilled Davis with its "big singing sound," devoid of the mania of bebop. By the time he recorded with Charlie Parker in 1947, Davis's style was mostly in place: melodic, vaguely sinister, and harmonically advanced, offering one note for every ten of Parker's. That year, Davis lost Webster to a heroin overdose; he also saw Parker start to self-destruct on alcohol and dope. Rather than shy away, he launched a four-year heroin habit of his own.

In the throes of addiction, Davis perfected the ethereal sound of cool. It grew from his love for the music of Claude Thornhill, an ambitious swing-era pianist and bandleader. Thornhill's arranger, Gil Evans, had created a shimmering, cloudlike texture through his unusual combination of reed instruments, led by the French horn, whose mournful tones were heard mostly in classical music. Davis joined Evans, pianist-arranger John Lewis (later famous for leading the Modern Jazz Quartet), and Gerry Mulligan, a brainy young saxophonist, arranger, and composer, to launch a nine-piece band that included French horn and tuba. Their brand of jazz had such unheard-of refinement that Ross Russell, Charlie Parker's white record producer, told the press that Miles Davis might be "founding the next school of trumpet playing."

Davis showed no gratitude. "White people back then liked music they could understand, and that they could *hear* without straining," he explained in his book. Unlike bop, he said, which "didn't come out of them," *Birth of the Cool* "was not only hummable but it had white people playing the music and serving in prominent roles. The white critics liked that."

So did Baker, who spun those 78s until the shellac turned gray. "Chet and I worshipped those records," said bassist Bob Whitlock, who became his roommate in 1949. For a while, Baker came to jam sessions with a French horn he had borrowed from the El Camino music department. But what he really wanted was to capture Davis's ideal choice of notes, his bell-toned lyricism. "I didn't really get locked into what I wanted to do until I found Miles," he told interviewer Leonard Malone almost forty years later.

Baker also loved Davis's aloofness, which implied control, and he kept crafting a "cool" façade of his own. His peers were working on theirs. "A cool guy wasn't a corporate type; he was laid-back, hip," said Phil Brown. "This stuff has always been tied up with drugs." Baker remembered seeing his father's cares vanish under the influence of pot—the substance that jazzmen had used for decades to create a buffer zone between themselves and the world, out of which the music could flow freely. The trumpeter learned more about marijuana's mind-altering magic from Andy Lambert, a bass and tuba player in the El Camino band. Having lost a leg in the war, Lambert hobbled around on a wooden peg, yet insisted on marching with the other musicians at football games. Baker was impressed by his nonchalance, especially onstage. Lambert played bass in a trio at the High Seas, an oceanside jazz club in Hermosa Beach, and he let Baker sit in. As Baker wrote in his memoir and elsewhere, Lambert smoked pot with his band every night before and after work, and he invited Baker to join them. "I readily agreed—did I want to be taken as a square?" Baker "liked the stuff" immediately, for reasons he could only articulate years later. "Everything becomes beautiful and pure, serene and pleasant. . . . The nerves are relaxed, worries fade away. . . . Time takes on new meaning. There's no need to worry because the hours, the days, the years are all for you, at your service . . . everything is easy, everything is possible."

Soon he was smoking pot from the minute he rolled out of bed until he went to sleep. "No matter what Chettie did he did it all out, one hundred percent," said Hersh Hamel. "He was so determined, so competitive, and so impulsive."

That wasn't true in school, though. He managed only low passing grades in English (his minor), psychology, and political science, and while he excelled in band, he floundered at sight-reading despite the simplicity of Maddaford's course. "You had to really goof off to get anything less than a B," the teacher said. Baker still thought that learning to read music was pointless, and his homework was sloppy and incomplete. "If you're going to be a professional," Maddaford warned him, "you've got to have a grounding in these fundamentals." The teacher finally gave him an F.

Enrolling for the fall 1949 semester, Baker signed up only for music appreciation and orchestra. Midway through the term, Maddaford came to class to find Baker's chair empty. For many years, the trumpeter grumbled bitterly that Maddaford had told him he would never make it as a musician, but eventually he admitted he just couldn't handle the study. "I wanted to do things by ear," he later told Mike Nevard of *Melody Maker.* "To me, if it *sounds* right it *is* right. Maybe this rule stuff is all right for those who have no ear or creative ability."

Free of school at last, he could get the education he wanted. Baker was hired to play in a Latin band at a hotel in downtown L.A. There he made friends with the only other white member of the group: Bob Whitlock, a talented bassist from Utah. With his dark, wavy hair and boyish face, Whitlock looked just as innocent as Baker, but he had already started experimenting with drugs. At eighteen, Whitlock had married and separated from his high school sweetheart, whose parents had pushed her to divorce him so she "could live a life of quality and respectability," he noted sardonically.

Baker invited Whitlock to move into the family house in Hermosa Beach. Although the trumpeter was now too grown-up to hit, Chesney Sr. was still strict; when Chettie wrecked his father's car, he was forced to get a job and keep it until he had paid for the repairs. Chettie found part-time work in a rivet factory and spent every moment he could away from home. He and his friends lay on the beach, swam, sailed, took flying lessons, and hunted—Baker ran through the hills shooting birds and watching them fall from the sky, feathers flapping madly as they let out a deathly screech. "There was just a kind of openness and wildness about him then," said Whitlock. "He had a fantastic sense of humor, and maybe the most infectious laugh I've ever heard. He was a very funny guy when he was young, believe me."

Even at twenty, Baker had so much star quality that he acquired a pack of adoring followers. They included Hersh Hamel, Bernie Fleischer, Ian Bernard, Bob Neel, pianist Gordy Swain, and Jack Sheldon, most of them still undeveloped musicians. Sheldon, who was two years Baker's junior, had moved in the midforties from Jacksonville, Florida, to his aunt's home in L.A. He was almost as sweetly handsome as Baker, but not as skillful. "We wouldn't let Jack play with us in those days because he was so lousy," said Bernard. "He couldn't stay in the chord." Sheldon practiced day and night, and by the late fifties he had become an accomplished bandleader and studio musician. Until then, he lived in the shadow of Chet Baker. "Chettie was everything I would like to have been," Sheldon admitted. "He was always in command, so hip, slick, and cool. I was like Forrest Gump. I'd be struggling away to play the trumpet."

Throughout his life, Baker rarely hung out with his equals; he needed to be the best, and no one in his "pack" doubted his stature. "Chet was a superior being to most of us," acknowledged Whitlock. "He was a leader." With Baker at the wheel of his latest car, a bulky Pierce-Arrow from 1936, his pals crowded in and sped to jam sessions, which were bursting forth all over L.A. Hundreds of young musicians were home from the war and longing to play real jazz instead of army band music. Invading bars, restaurants, clubs, garages, basements, and studios, they jammed around the clock. Music was a drug, and they couldn't get enough.

When Baker heard about the Showtime, a San Fernando Valley club that held the most elite sessions in town, he raced there, disciples in tow. Those in the backseat were in charge of rolling joints while the whole group chatted hiply about the "cool" saxophonist Stan Getz's latest record or some trumpeter's new mouthpiece. No one delved into anything deeper; showing your feelings just wasn't cool.

Baker kept his eyes on the road. By now his car was like a shiny second skin; it meant speed, sovereignty, freedom. With no freeways yet in L.A., the drive from Hermosa Beach to Encino, where the Showtime was located, took about forty tedious minutes. Baker drove as though the car were a bomb about to explode. The speedometer crept past eighty miles an hour, yet no matter how high he was on pot, he handled the wheel as deftly as he fingered his horn. Hamel never forgot the way Baker pulled into a parking lot near the Showtime: "Chet comes racing in, and there was a big wall there, and he skids about two feet before the wall and stops. Boy, that's the way he was!"

From 1949 through 1952, the Showtime's Monday-night jam sessions were the top incubator of West Coast Jazz talent: trumpeters Maynard Ferguson, Shorty Rogers, and the brothers Pete and Conte Candoli; saxophonists Herb Geller, Dave Pell, Art Pepper, and Bob Gordon; pianists Andre Previn, Russ Freeman, Lou Levy, and Paul Smith; bass players Red Mitchell, Joe Mondragon, Monte Budwig, and Harry Babasin; drummers Alvin Stoller and Shelly Manne. Despite the occasional presence of such black West Coast jazzmen as the saxophonists Wardell Gray and Teddy Edwards, the Showtime was "practically one hundred percent white," according to Phil Brown. "You had more affluent musicians in that area." Baker offered his own explanation to Lisa Galt Bond: Why would black musicians drive so far only to be kept off the bandstand?

The L.A. of those years was shockingly racist; musicians were even segregated into the "white union" or the "colored union." In the thirties and forties, the city's answer to Harlem was Central Avenue, a thoroughfare that ran through the black district of South-Central Los Angeles. Entertaining in the clubs there were such black luminaries as Duke Ellington, Fats Waller, Lena Horne, and Art Tatum, who created a far more partylike atmosphere than the white West Coast Jazz artists of the fifties. Art Pepper recalled the Central Avenue scene in his autobiography, *Straight Life,* cowritten with his wife, Laurie: "The women dressed up in frills and feathers and long earrings. . . . Most of the men wore big, wide-brimmed hats and zoot suits . . . and you could smell powder and perfume everywhere. And as you walked down the street you heard music coming out of everyplace." Such white swing stars as Harry James, Artie Shaw, and Buddy Rich flocked to Central Avenue, hungry to learn from the black innovators; Pepper went night after night to an after-hours spot, the Ritz Club, to smoke pot and sniff Dexedrine with his idol Dexter Gordon. On Mondays and Wednesdays, Chet Baker drove to the all-night sessions at Jack's Basket Room, where Charlie Parker worked several gigs.

Some black players had a bitter sense that their styles were getting "borrowed" and commercialized for the masses. They saw young whites copying their language, their clothes, their mannerisms. "The white people, they learned from us and took what we knew and went on," said trumpeter Harry "Sweets" Edison in *Blues for Central Avenue,* a 1986 documentary directed by Lois Shelton. In the same film, reed player Buddy Collette remembered how the white union had the clout to grab all the best-paying jobs for its members.

More blatant racism came from the L.A. police. Collette traced the decline of Central Avenue in the fifties to officers "who didn't like the idea of some people, especially the young white ladies, coming down and mingling in the clubs." Driving into South-Central, Phil Brown was pulled over and strip-searched by cops who clearly thought he was there either to buy or sell drugs. "I imagine black people going to the San Fernando Valley were subject to the same harassment," he said. As the West Coast Jazz movement grew nationally prominent, the black players' resentment rose. Soon, much of it would be aimed at Chet Baker.

The first substantial buzz around him started at the Showtime. The sessions there were organized by Herbie Harper, a trombonist who, at twenty-nine, seemed like an old man to the college-age musicians present. True to the meticulous, premeditated quality associated with West Coast Jazz, even jam sessions were planned ahead. Using a rhythm section of his own strict choosing, Harper assigned soloists to each forty-five-minute set, picking from dozens of eager youngsters. "It was run like a business," said Jack Sheldon. "Getting on the session was a real prestige thing. The place would be packed." The first time he was allowed onstage, Sheldon was soon asked to leave. Bernie Fleischer didn't fare much better. "I was never good enough to sit in there," he said. "Those guys probably wouldn't have let me anyway; it was a real snobbish kind of thing."

Baker had to come several times before he got to play. Once he did, Harper put him onstage every Monday without delay. The trombonist wasn't thrilled with Baker's friends, though, who struck him as a bunch of druggies desperate to look as cool as their leader. "Chet had a tendency to play with his horn pointing at the ground," said Harper. "Jack would point it a little farther at the ground." Hersh Hamel, whose real name was Herschel Himmelstein, plucked his bass like a cartoon of a bebopper: head hunched over and bobbing with the beat, eyes half-closed, as if he were in a musical trance that only the hippest of the hip could dream of entering. Ian Bernard was just as anxious to stand out. "I was so fucking cool, the beat was nine yards ahead of me and I didn't care," he said. By the midfifties, Bernard had given up jazz to conduct for such "square" pop stars as Vic Damone and Al Martino—singers his hipster buddies would have laughed at.

Harper was amused at the whole spectacle. "In my band," he said, "we weren't afraid to say, 'Hey, man, that sounded good!' But the guys in Chet's group wouldn't think of saying that. It was a sign of weakness. They just looked down at the ground." Baker himself spoke only in monosyllables: "Hey, man." "That's cool." Harper couldn't recall ever having a conversation with him: "He didn't really look at you. Hard to make a connection."

Yet Baker got attention wherever he sat in. In 1949, he discovered Esther's, a Mexican restaurant in Manhattan Beach where Matt Dennis, the grinning, wavy-haired composer of such swing-era hits as "Will You Still Be Mine?" and "Let's Get Away from It All," played piano and sang. Of all Dennis's tunes, Baker was the most taken with "Everything Happens to Me," a 2 a.m. saloon song in which the gods conspire to reduce an innocent man's life to a grind of "catching colds and missing trains." Baker made Dennis sing it again and again; he loved the victim sentiment, and wallowed in it by singing the song himself until the end of his life.

Certainly it echoed his feelings about the sad love story between himself and Sherry, a timid teenager he recalled meeting at Esther's. Baker cajoled her into his car, after which she became pregnant. In his memoir, Baker claimed a willingness to marry her, even though he knew he couldn't afford a wife. Since Sherry was afraid to break the news to her father, Baker brought her home to Chesney and Vera. They responded, he said, by finding an abortion doctor. Afterward, they pressured their son into breaking off the relationship. "I sure missed having her around," he said wistfully.

The episode made him more impatient than ever to escape his parents' control. By the end of 1949, he and Bob Whitlock had rented the guest cottage of a mansion in Redondo Beach. Even with a parade of roommates, including Bob Neel, they could hardly afford the tiny rent. But they were on their own, and life was sweet. "We would wake up and have a bowl of corn flakes and start playing," said Whitlock. "We could be sound asleep at four in the morning, then three or four people would drop by after work and we'd all get up and play again."

The cottage had thick concrete walls, allowing them to jam as loudly as they wanted. But they didn't make much noise. One of the regular guests was Jimmy McKean, a drummer whom Hersh Hamel considered a pioneer of the low-key West Coast style. "He played with the ultimate finesse on brushes," Hamel said. "This was a time when drummers were playing with great big cymbals, dropping all kinds of bombs."

Baker admired McKean's playing, but liked his cool attitude even more. While most of the scuffling musicians Baker knew drove any old wrecks they could afford, McKean cruised L.A. in a flashy MG sports car. Baker also knew the drummer's reputation of having "one of the biggest whangs west of the Sierra Madres"—a blessing that the modestly endowed Baker couldn't help but envy. McKean's true claim to fame, though, was his outrageous drug use. According to Jack Sheldon, the drummer went to all lengths to get high, including shooting formaldehyde. "Even I wouldn't do this, and I was ready to do anything," Sheldon said. "Because if you missed the vein, your whole arm would swell up."

Drugs, and drug users, held a growing allure for Baker. Another frequent visitor to the guest cottage was Manuel Vardas, a pot dealer who sold to Baker and his friends. A "spaced-out guy," as Baker recalled him, "whose main object in life seemed to be to find out how much grass he could smoke up before the second coming of Christ," Vardas enjoyed a no-strain, off-the-books income that made Baker jealous. The trumpeter had drifted through a series of part-time blue-collar jobs—fixing flats in a gas station, working as a stockboy at the Lincoln-Mercury dealership—but like his father, he couldn't stand holding down a "real job" in which he had to report to a superior. Soon he and Bob Neel began selling marijuana themselves—"just so we could have some," Neel said. Hamel saw them in action: "They'd be rolling joints, measuring the pot with the Prince Albert can and putting it in bags. And the penalties at that time were very severe." Before long, Baker had a marijuana fetish. "He loved to clean the pot, to play with it," observed Jack Sheldon. "He'd roll, like, five hundred joints."

Whitlock had already started "chippying," or dabbling in heroin. Working in a musical field that required spontaneous, brilliant invention every night, he noticed how heroin seemed to unlock the magic in his idols, notably Charlie Parker and Billie Holiday. Years after he had kicked his own habit, trumpeter Red Rodney told historian Ira Gitler that heroin was the "badge" that made beboppers "different from the rest of the world. It was the thing that said, 'We know. You don't know.' " The drug seldom improved anyone's music, but it did numb their pain: "the pain of non-recognition, of not having any money," said Phil Leshin. "And whatever money you had you pissed away on junk, which was very expensive."

The perils only made it more enticing. "Almost every one of us had a friend who had died from an overdose," Leshin said. He never forgot his shock at hearing of the demise, in 1947, of Sonny Berman, a promising young trumpeter known for his solo on the Woody Herman recording of "Sidewalks of Cuba." At twenty-two, Berman died in New York, supposedly in the arms of bebop saxophonist Allen Eager. Freddie Webster was only thirty-one at the time of his OD. Another prominent trumpet player, Fats Navarro, had died of tuberculosis at twenty-six, his body ravaged by heroin.

Whitlock admitted "turning on" Baker for the first time: "I told Chet, 'Hey! You gotta try this!' " It happened not at the Redondo cottage but at a friend's house in San Pedro, California. Years after, Baker recalled the pain of that first injection, his "fear as the liquid flowed little by little out of the syringe and went inside me." He had the typical reaction to a first heroin fix. "Chet was strictly a weedhead at the time, and he got violently ill," Whitlock said. "I figured, well—he's safe. He'll never try that again." Baker described the episode to critic Rex Reed in 1973: "I threw up for hours, and it took me another year before I tried it again. I figured, hell, we're only here once, I gotta find out what's happening."

Scouting out jam sessions, going to the beach, selling pot, and smoking it compulsively didn't leave Baker much time to date. According to Ian

Bernard, that was typical among their circle of musicians. "I guarantee that every one of us would rather have played jazz than dated a girl," he said. After the sting of his letdowns with Gloria, Gisella, and Sherry, Baker seemed finished with love, at least for now. "Chettie wasn't very much interested in girls then," confirmed Bob Neel. "They'd gravitate to him, but he was mostly fighting them off. He didn't seem to care about anything except playing his horn."

Baker was certainly capable of treating women like pieces of meat, as he proved when he drove to Santa Barbara with Sheldon, Hamel, and Neel for a hotel gig. After work, Sheldon and Baker stayed overnight at the home of their friend Bill Perkins, a young tenor player. There they encountered the girlfriend of Gene Roland, a Stan Kenton arranger. Roland was known as a voracious pot smoker and sex fiend, and his girlfriend matched him in the latter category, as Sheldon found out when she turned up in his bedroom. "She was up there in Santa Barbara for some reason, so I started fucking her," he explained. "Chettie came in, and I moved down and he started fucking her. It was so dark, I don't know if she even knew the difference. Now Chet used to fuck 'em real fast, like a rabbit. I think he thought this was real sexy. He didn't have an idea about sex, really. He finished up, and I started fucking her again. She was a friend for life after that."

In 1950, at a Sunday-afternoon jam session at the Lighthouse, a Hermosa Beach jazz club, Baker caught the lustful eye of Charlaine Souder, a twenty-year-old who lived with her parents in Lynwood, just south of L.A. He later described her as a slender, "sharp-looking blonde, well-built and very self-assured," who had "been around." Busty and aggressive, Charlaine had a taste for musicians, and she set her sights on Baker. "I think all that was something of a challenge for Chet," said Whitlock. "He was probably used to more passivity in girls." The trumpeter bought her a drink, then she took him for a ride in her father's new Buick. Soon they were parked atop Palos Verdes, a midnight mecca for amorous young couples. "We had this joke in high school," said Bernie Fleischer, "that Palos Verdes was getting smaller every day because guys kept going up and knocking off a piece."

Baker's memories of Charlaine were hardly romantic. "She loved being screwed and I loved screwing her," he bragged. "Once in front of her house in Lynwood we made it nine times in three hours." He took her everywhere, flaunting her like a new set of wheels. According to Charlie Davidson, a clothier from Cambridge, Massachusetts, who began a long friendship with Baker in 1954, the trumpeter's idea of sophistication leaned closer to redneck than hipster. "I know he had a picture in his head of the coolest jazz musician in the world, who pulls up in a nice car, a gorgeous chick gets out, he walks in, she sits down front while he plays."

Baker and his new "chick" became inseparable, but they had little to share besides sex. Clearly Baker was no Prince Charming; some found him downright menacing. "Here was this saintly-looking son of a bitch," said Davidson, "but you also knew that right behind that was a pretty dangerous little bastard." Fleischer knew it too, and gradually he cut off their friendship. "I got very frightened by Chet's lifestyle," the clarinetist said. "After a while he always had enough grass with him to get us in trouble. In those days, if you got arrested with marijuana, you could be in jail for twenty years. And he drove so fast, I figured he was gonna kill us." Jack Sheldon was just as scared. When Baker siphoned gas from other cars, Neel and Hamel pitched right in, but Sheldon cowered in the backseat. His friends called him a sissy. "Chettie was already into a little larceny then," said Sheldon. "I gave him a fluegelhorn that I had checked out of City College, and he never gave it back. It was like stealing gas—he thought it was all right to do that."

The "pack" looked like troublemakers, and police sometimes stopped the car to search them. Nervous as he was, Sheldon wanted desperately to fit in, and he stayed at Baker's side. One night the two trumpeters were driving home after scoring a bundle of pot. Sheldon had foolishly left a rifle in the backseat. His timing couldn't have been worse: inadvertently he and Baker drove through the site of a robbery, and cops were searching for suspects. Two officers signaled Baker to pull over. Sheldon hurried to stuff the marijuana down a crack in the front seat, but he couldn't hide the gun. The policemen ordered them to drive to the station, then handcuffed them together and took them inside. "We know who you are," one officer told Baker. "We had your father in here."

After questioning, they were cleared, and one of the cops escorted them back to the car. "He had his face right over the pot that I had shoved down in the seat," said Sheldon. "I was sweating bullets. Chettie didn't seem intimidated at all."

But eventually Baker's luck ran out, and by the end of 1950, he was a soldier again. "I don't know what made me go back in the army," he claimed years later. According to Fleischer, though, the police had busted him for pot, and his cool mask proved no defense. "The judge gave him a choice of reenlisting or going to jail," said Fleischer. "This was during the Korean War, and the judge probably thought he was giving Chet a death sentence."

3

Though back in the army as punishment, Baker wound up living the life of his dreams, free of responsibility besides playing the trumpet. He was assigned to the 6th Army Band at the Presidio, the military base in San Francisco, whose charms included a lush backdrop of pine trees and a view of the Golden Gate Bridge. Thousands of young soldiers were facing a grimmer sight on the battlefields of South Korea, which had been invaded by Communist forces of the north. Directed by President Harry S. Truman, the United States began sending troops to South Korea's aid. Over the next three years, 34,000 American servicemen would be killed and 103,000 others wounded.

But at the Presidio, Chettie Baker was having a ball. He woke at dawn and blew reveille, his new silver trumpet gleaming in the sun. Baker rehearsed with the band all morning, ate lunch, got high on pot, joined his friends for a game of pinochle, practiced some more, then closed the day by playing a mournful chorus of taps to mark the burial of the latest Korean War casualty. Then he hit the road with his horn, combing San Francisco for jam sessions.

Letters flew between him and Charlaine, whom he missed more than he would have expected. Vera's doting had left him permanently dependent on the caretaking of a woman, even one as flighty as Charlaine. Having finally split from her other boyfriend, she was now free to accept a hasty proposal from Baker. He left the Presidio on a weekend pass and met her in Las Vegas, where they were wed by a justice of the peace. As a married man, Baker could live outside the Presidio as long as he reported there for duty.

He and Charlaine drove back to San Francisco and set up a one-room love nest.

Their immature union had less to do with love, though, than with conquest. Baker had tamed another wild blonde; Charlaine had nabbed the cute trumpeter all the girls wanted. But she was more interested in jazz musicians than in jazz, and any semblance of romance faded from their marriage as Baker gave priority to his trumpet. Coming home from the Presidio at dinnertime, he would have sex with Charlaine before rolling over and sleeping until midnight. Then he would get back into uniform and turn the key in his car's ignition, horn at his side. At first he brought Charlaine along, but she wearied of his midnight outings; increasingly she stayed home after a screaming argument about his neglect. She couldn't face the fact that any relationship with Baker would be on his terms alone. "This man was going to be the way he was," said Ruth Young after their decade-long affair. "And if you didn't like it, as he once said, then get the hell out."

The marriage deteriorated into a childish war of jealousy ploys and head games. "She was constantly doing things to aggravate him," said Bob Whitlock. "I think they were ways to keep his interest up, to keep him guessing." Once when he and Baker were playing at a frat dance, Charlaine waltzed past the bandstand in the arms of another man. Baker stared coolly until the end of the night, whereupon he hurled his horn against a radiator with such fury that he mangled it. No wonder pianist Donn Trenner, who had met Baker at a jam session, saw him as "a little boy in a man's uniform."

Music was his only focus. A regular stop on his nightly treks was the Black Hawk, San Francisco's top jazz club and the launching pad of such stars as Johnny Mathis. Headlining in 1951 was a quartet led by the young West Coast pianist Dave Brubeck, whose scholarly jazz had made him a college idol. With his horn-rimmed glasses and unruly hair, Brubeck looked like a conservatory geek. He played like one, too, his touch heavy with harmonies learned from his professor Arnold Schoenberg, the father of atonal composition, and French composer Darius Milhaud. Bop musicians and their fans called Brubeck arty and unswinging; when his LPs, notably *Dave Digs Disney* and *Jazz Goes to College,* began selling like pop albums, they jealously dismissed him as a sellout. Brubeck had defied the jazz underground by making jazz "respectable," an intellectual pursuit in line with the wholesome values of the Truman and Eisenhower fifties. *Time* magazine even chose the white pianist over Charlie Parker, Dizzy Gillespie, and Max Roach for a cover story on the "new jazz."

Baker's only interest in Brubeck centered on his alto saxophonist, Paul

Desmond, whose rainwater tone and billowy lyricism excited Baker far more than the macho excesses of bebop. In 1960, Desmond played the cool lead solo on "Take Five," Brubeck's top-forty hit, written in a tricky 5/4 meter. "He had such a delicate way of playing, so melodic," Baker told writer Les Tomkins. It was the sound the trumpeter aspired to, and he kept showing up at the Black Hawk and sitting in—against Brubeck's wishes, he claimed; Desmond had to go to bat for him every time.

From there, Baker moved on to two black after-hours clubs, Jimbo's and Bop City. He sat in with tenor saxophonist Frank Foster (later a fixture of the Count Basie orchestra); Parker disciple Norwood "Pony" Poindexter; and Kenny Dorham, a bop trumpeter who combined a fierce attack with a flair for creating long, tuneful lines. Hot and cool were coming together in Baker's playing. He strove for the clear, vibratoless tone and emotional reserve of Desmond and Miles Davis, but according to his army bandmate Bob Freedman, "every now and then Chettie could do a burst of fire that would just blow you off the chair."

Even in the loudest dive, Baker's music was a profoundly internal process. "Most guys, if they run out of ideas, will start playing a whole lot of notes, hoping that some will make sense," Freedman explained. "Chettie did the opposite. If he got to a point where he didn't know what to play, he stood there for ten or twelve or sixteen bars without playing a note. He would look very serious, as though waiting for the message to come, then continue as if he'd been playing all along."

After a year of this daily routine, Baker grew bored, and he hated being in the army. In his memoir, he recalled seeing fellow band members faking insanity to get discharged. One of them, he said, fell into such a convincing "trance" that he was carried out of the barracks by his shoulders and feet, flat as a board, without a stretcher. A flutist told the master sergeant that a little man inside his instrument was screwing up his playing.

For the rest of his life, Baker boasted in great (and possibly apocryphal) detail of having plotted his own release. According to his story, he met with the post psychiatrist and explained that he was too shy to use the unpartitioned toilets in the latrine; instead he had taken to defecating in a clump of bushes across the street. Asked to interpret a set of ink blots, he likened them all to sex acts or genitalia. He mentioned his obsessive pot smoking, and when the doctor gave him a multiple-choice exam written to detect sexual deviants and other "undesirables," Baker exploited his delicate looks and voice to pose as a homosexual. Asked his preferred career—mechanic, forest ranger, or florist—Baker circled the most effeminate choice. The ploy seemed rather hypocritical for a man whose later homophobic outbursts struck Ruth Young and others as evidence of repressed gay tendencies. Yet Baker stopped at almost nothing to get what he wanted.

This time it didn't work. An army official had started to suspect that many in the band were untutored slouches, and he demanded that all of them be tested for sight-reading abilities. Baker, of course, failed. Instead of getting a discharge, he was banished to Fort Huachuca, a military base near the Mexican border. A desert ghost town, Fort Huachuca felt like the middle of nowhere; the men stationed there called it the Asshole of America. Baker was placed in the 77th Army Band, whose members were mostly rejects from other orchestras, marijuana violators, and similar delinquents.

Perhaps because they were considered lost causes, discipline was low; in between grinding out Sousa marches at occasional military functions, they endured only light calisthenics, which left plenty of time for other diversions. On weekends, Baker and his bandmates drove into Mexico and returned with duffel bags full of "dynamite grass," as Baker called it. By day he sat blissfully stoned in the barracks, playing along with Miles Davis records; at night he and Bob Freedman drove around Arizona looking for bars and clubs where they could sit in. Freedman noticed how cunning his baby-faced comrade could be: "Chet was aware of how handsome he was. He always made sure his hair was cool, and one time he gave me advice on how to roll up the sleeves on my short-sleeve shirt so it would be more attractive to women. He'd say, 'You know, that's a really nice shirt, man, but if you roll it up this way the chicks will like it more.' "

The ability to manipulate through charm while giving an impression of utter innocence was the key to Baker's seductiveness. He certainly won Freedman over: "The outstanding thing about Chettie was how nice he was. He was just a sweet guy. He had this wide-open face, and he trusted everybody. He got a reputation for being standoffish, but that might have been a protective device." Baker looked so vulnerable, said Freedman, that "the leeches were after him even then." The leeches, in this case, were Fort Huachuca's resident drug pushers: "Big John," a tall Italian rumored to have mob connections; and Henry, a slick-looking, wavy-haired clerk. After his discharge, Henry bragged of having hooked Judy Garland on pills again after one of her several attempts to quit.

According to Freedman, both Henry and Big John teased Baker with drugs. Henry "never let his hooks out of Chet. He'd tell him how great he was, how great he looked, how great he was gonna be. I know that once

Chet left, Henry sought him out and did his act on him, trying to get him to do drugs."

For now, there was no proof that the trumpeter had gotten hooked on anything but pot. But if Baker, in his interview with Rex Reed, correctly calculated the time of his second experiment with heroin, it would have happened in this period. By 1951, several of his favorite musicians had OD'd. But that didn't deter him, nor did memories of his traumatic initiation into heroin. He felt its forbidden pull, and kept trying it periodically.

After a few months at Huachuca, all he wanted was out. He remembered that a sympathetic psychiatrist at the Presidio had advised him to go AWOL for a month, then turn himself in; the same doctor would "evaluate" him as unstable and grant an honorable discharge. With this in mind, Baker fled Huachuca. He hitchhiked to Lynwood, where Charlaine had moved into a bungalow behind her family's home and gone to work in a dress shop.

A month later, he went back to the Presidio, only to find that his psychiatrist friend had been transferred. Finally Baker had to pay for his misdeeds. In his memoir, he told of getting thrown into the stockade with other insubordinates and being subjected to punishing calisthenics and the threatening glares of shotgun-wielding guards. Some inmates were so terrified, he claimed, that they tried getting high by sniffing a gasoline-soaked rag, which left them glassy-eyed and reeling.

Baker recalled sitting on a bench, traumatized. He shut his eyes and entered a state so trancelike that it looked as though he had suffered a nervous breakdown. He was carried out, he explained, and thrown into the psychiatric ward, where he heard the screams of men receiving shock treatment and the moans of others who had been sedated. Baker told of sharing a room with a shell-shock victim who kept bursting into seizures, leaping out of bed and swinging his fists at some imaginary foe.

Baker remained paralyzed, stone-faced. Had he really had a breakdown, or was he faking, as he could do so well? He received three weeks of testing, after which a doctor pronounced him mentally unstable and gave him an honorable discharge: "unadaptable to army life." Finally, he had gotten his way. Early in 1952, Baker went home to Charlaine to resume his "normal" life.

The Southern California to which he returned was a breeding ground of unreality. Every day was summer; people on the street posed and preened as if they were on a movie set. "Hermosa Beach in the summer of 'fifty was jumping," Baker recalled. "There were hundreds of beautiful young things lying all over the place, and the guys were always walking up and down the strand, flexing their muscles and talking hip, flaunting their stuff like a bunch of male peacocks."

Jazzmen throughout L.A. tried to make music with the same glossy perfection—to show how smart they were, how cool. For the West Coast pianist Joe Castro, "cool" meant "having the perfect intonation, the great execution, everything clean and neat." As drummer Shelly Manne informed *Metronome:* "Four out of five musicians are writers; among the more modern, each is studying Bach, atonality, etc. and it comes out in the playing. . . . Training is the thing." Sight-reading expertise opened the door to an abundance of studio work. In one day, a musician could go from playing in the orchestra on a Peggy Lee or Frank Sinatra album to recording a movie soundtrack to working in the house band on a TV show. This routine spared them from having to eke out a living by playing dives on the road, shacking up in bad motels, surviving hand-to-mouth—toils that gave East Coast jazz a lot of its grit and urgency.

The music of Shorty Rogers, king of the West Coast jazzmen, reflected cleverness and craft, not life experience. One of the highest-paid trumpeters and arrangers in L.A., Rogers (born Milton M. Rajonsky in Great Barrington, Massachusetts) led The Giants, a band that dispensed, according to the liner notes of one of its albums, "a buoyant California feeling" teeming with "fresh air and sunshine." Rogers's cutely titled originals—"Powder Puff," "Bunny," "The Pesky Serpent"—seemed casual and breezy but were in fact heavily scripted, with not a note out of place. That style defined so-called West Coast Jazz—the prevailing sound, though by no means the only one, to come from the Southern California jazz scene of the fifties. "The jazz out of the East was heavy and black and out of the West light and white, that's the way it sounded," said the L.A.-based saxophonist Teddy Edwards in *Cadence.*

The more famous it grew, the more West Coast Jazz was attacked by musicians in New York, who called it fey and bloodless, "the same old clichés all the time," as Max Roach once said to Miles Davis. Embarrassed to be thought of as sissies, many L.A. musicians denied they belonged to any "school," or that one even existed. "I have never understood that whole 'West Coast Jazz' business—I think the term was something created by a writer," declared pianist Russ Freeman, whose rugged, boppish playing didn't fit the mold. Ralph J. Gleason, jazz critic of the *San Francisco Chronicle,* assured readers that West Coast players could "get pretty funky"—especially, as Shelly Manne had explained, if they'd roughed it up by eating "in those all-night hamburger joints."

Such remarks annoyed black musicians on both coasts, who viewed the West Coast sound as a symbol of white affluence, devoid of pain or struggle. Teddy Edwards complained to Bob Rusch that the black "hard-hitters" of L.A. jazz, including Sonny Criss, Wardell Gray, and himself, had been ignored by the big record companies "for mostly a racial thing." Certainly those musicians went underrecorded, while several independent West Coast labels—Nocturne, Mode, Trend, Pacific Jazz—sprang up to capture the "white" fifties sound that Chet Baker would soon embody. "Chet's music was not the fast-lane New York bebop," said Hersh Hamel. "It was relaxed, super-cool. It sounded like Southern California, the sun, the beach."

All these elements came together at the Lighthouse, a Hermosa Beach club that stood a half-block from the ocean. From 2 p.m. to 2 a.m. every Sunday, live jazz spilled out of the Lighthouse's open doors while salty sea breezes wafted in. In summer, patrons wandered in wearing bathing suits, sand crunching beneath their feet on the floorboards. Attractive young men and women filled the club's long picnic-style tables, or stood at the bar in front of groupies with sun- or peroxide-bleached hair.

Music was almost incidental to the scene, and many people talked through the playing of the Lighthouse All-Stars, a rotating ensemble who jammed the day and night away. They sat in Hawaiian shirts on a bandstand decorated with sheets of woven bamboo, fake palm trees, and coconuts. Kitschy as it seemed, the Lighthouse gave a boost to nearly every up-and-coming L.A. jazz star of the day. These included clarinetist and saxophonist Jimmy Giuffre, who went on to write ambitious orchestral works and to arrange for Anita O'Day and Sonny Stitt; flute and sax player Bud Shank, the winner of *Down Beat*'s 1954 New Star award; and ex–New Yorker Stan Levey, whom critic Leonard Feather called "one of the first and most important drummers of the bop movement."

Despite these men's talents, and the occasional galvanizing presence of Miles Davis or Max Roach, the group became known to some as the Lightweight All-Stars. In their weekly marathons they tried to capture the spark of a Manhattan jam session, but their albums capture mostly ragged ensemble work and generic solos. Even Baker's efforts in that setting, recorded more than once, are rough and strained. "There were pretty solid musicians there, but no one super-exciting as a soloist," said Bob Whitlock, an early participant. Bassist Howard Rumsey was in charge. A better businessman than artist (other musicians called him Howard Clumsy), he nonetheless took the proceedings quite seriously, calling those seaside sessions "jazz concerts." Teddy Edwards was mainly disgusted as he watched one black player after another be phased out: Sonny Criss was replaced by Art Pepper, drummer Larance Marable by Larry Bunker, a white percussionist. Edwards himself was dropped as white alumni of Stan Kenton—Rumsey's idol and ex-boss—gradually took over. "I was beginning to get the message," Edwards said.

At the time, Chet Baker was scuffling as much as any of his black colleagues. His former roommate Jimmy McKean had found work in a Dixieland band, and although Baker hated the old-fashioned "oom-pah" beat of traditional jazz, he was so hard up that McKean recommended him to his boss. The trumpeter drove to nearby Seal Beach to meet Freddie Fisher, a clarinetist and burlesque-style comic. Onstage, Fisher's band, the Schicklefritzers, played "When the Saints Go Marchin' In," after which the leader took off his shoes and socks, rolled out a foam-rubber mat that simulated a bed of red-nippled breasts, and walked all over it as he told dirty jokes. Baker, who normally made a show of attacking the redneck humor and lowbrow tastes he had known in Oklahoma, thought the act was hilarious, and he joined Fisher immediately. The music bored him, though, and he switched to a new band led by Vido Musso, a Sicilian tenor saxophonist whose schmaltzy, overwrought solo on Stan Kenton's hit record "Come Back to Sorrento" had given him a flash of fame.

But in the spring of 1952, all talk in the L.A. jazz world shifted to the arrival of the master who brought every modern jazzman to his knees: Charlie Parker had come west for a short tour. This was his first trip to Los Angeles since the midforties, when a disastrous drug-and-alcohol binge had sent him to a mental hospital in Camarillo. Parker wove his brush with death into an upbeat blues called "Relaxin' at Camarillo"; thereafter he resumed playing with such speed and inspiration that many musicians compared him to God.

Yet this voice from heaven was anything but soothing. It sounded manic and harsh, implying a search for truths that weren't pretty. Between gigs, the charming and erudite Parker slept on friends' floors, borrowed horns and hocked them for dope, and cheated people in countless other ways to feed his all-consuming habit. "He was an extremist, he did more of everything than anybody," said Teddy Edwards, whom Parker called Teddy Bear. "He'd drink more whiskey, take Benzedrine tablets like popcorn, just chew 'em." He paid the price: at thirty-one he looked bloated and grandfatherly; he would die three years later. In his short life, he gave beboppers a dream of what incredible heights of expression they might reach. He also set a dangerously romantic example, self-destructing as he created the greatest art they had ever known.

Myths surrounded him, and after Parker's death Baker used the Bird legend to mythologize himself. Sometime in the sixties, Baker started telling an apocryphal tale about his "discovery" by Parker, a story he honed for the rest of his life. One day in April 1952, claimed Baker, he found a telegram stuffed under his door. Dick Bock, his future record producer, wanted him to know that Parker was auditioning trumpeters at 3 p.m. that day, at the Tiffany Club in Hollywood. Baker went. Entering a "pitch black" room, he found himself standing among "forty trumpet players . . . all the trumpet players in L.A.," as their hero jammed onstage. After just five minutes, Parker—who must have heard all about him beforehand, Baker supposed—abruptly stopped playing to ask if Chet Baker were present. "Yeah, Bird, I'm here," said the trumpeter, who strode up to join Parker on one tune, then another. With that, Bird sent all the others home; he had found his man.

Baker related this with such sincerity that interviewers bought every word of an account that Bob Whitlock termed "bullshit." Years later, Donn Trenner, the pianist on that Tiffany Club engagement, was startled to hear Baker's version of how he had been hired. "None of that sounds like anything connected with the truth," Trenner said.

Just before Bird's arrival, Trenner, a studio pianist and musical director for such singers as his wife, Helen Carr, had been asked by an agent to put together a band for the musician, who was booked at the Tiffany for two and a half weeks. Trenner hastily lined up Larance Marable and a bassist, Harry Babasin. Asked to hire a trumpeter, too—Parker liked having a front-line sidekick—Trenner called Chet Baker. They all met for an afternoon rehearsal at the club. Neither Trenner nor Marable recalled an audition; Jack Sheldon, whom Baker named as one of the multitude of trumpet players at the club, had no knowledge of any such incident either: "I don't remember a lot of guys auditioning. I just remember him being the one." But it wasn't enough for Baker to have landed the job that any young trumpeter would have all but killed for; he had to weave his "discovery" into a Cinderella fable that anointed him The Chosen One. "Oftentimes, reality wasn't quite satisfying to Chet," said Whitlock. "He loved drama. If there wasn't something in the air, he'd get bored." It amused him to manipulate people, and facts, as if they were the little wooden kings and queens on a chessboard. He was an expert at both games.

On May 29, 1952, the Charlie Parker quintet opened at the Tiffany. The first-night crowd was full of musicians eager to worship at the feet of Bird, and to hear his curious choice of partner. They saw the wasted Parker looking warm and gracious; his young white cohort aloof, humorless, face and horn as usual pointed down. Baker had no other defense against all the jealous and disapproving looks. On a bootleg recording of him and Parker, made a few weeks later at the Trade Winds jazz club in Inglewood, he sounds painfully out of his league. Alongside Parker and guest Sonny Criss, he flounders in fear, missing entrances and struggling to stay in tune.

Throughout the run at the Tiffany, photographer William Claxton heard angry whispers that Baker was nothing but a Miles Davis wanna-be. Art Farmer, a widely respected trumpeter with a similarly lyrical style, seemed especially bitter: years later he told saxophonist Bob Mover of how he and his brother, bassist Addison Farmer, had lodged Parker in their Los Angeles apartment, only to be passed up for the job that went to Baker. The fact that Bird had apparently chosen a white upstart over one of "his own" incensed some black musicians, who felt he had sold out. Only a few people saw Parker and Baker's union as a statement of the interracial unity L.A. lacked.

Parker spotted the frightened young man's potential. "He treated me sorta like a son," recalled Baker, who had never known such loving patience from his own father. "I can see now how helpful and understanding he was. He stayed with the tunes I knew well, and he avoided the real fast tempos he used to like so much." Talking later to Claxton, Parker praised Baker's work as "pure and simple," a reminder of the Bix Beiderbecke records he had heard while growing up in Kansas City. "I remember him being absolutely dazzled by Chet's ear," said Whitlock, who subbed for Harry Babasin a couple of times. "He was amazed that Chet could do what he did without the harmonic training a lot of players had." Parker "sort of nurtured him along," according to Larance Marable. "He told Chet what notes to hit on the ends of tunes, how to play a cadenza—everything."

Baker repaid him by driving him around town to show him the sights, including the cliffs at Palos Verdes. Parker stood on the cliffs gazing at the waves, utterly at peace, it seemed. But each day he sought out the balm of dope. Baker watched him "snorting up spoons of stuff and drinking fifths of Hennessy," then going on to play with complete ease, care wiped from his face.

Finding drugs was no problem. Wherever they worked—at Billy Berg's in Hollywood, the 5-4 Ballroom at Central Avenue and Fifty-fourth, the Say When club in San Francisco—dealers circled like vultures, waiting for Parker to leave the stage. Russ Freeman described them as "creeps, hangers-on who were strung out themselves and selling in order to support their own habits." But when they started whispering to Baker, Parker pulled him aside. "You got nothin' to say to him," the saxophonist said tersely. "Don't fuck with these guys."

For now Baker heeded the advice, yet Parker's "do as I say, not as I do" posture only made heroin all the more tantalizing for Baker and countless others. By the end of their mini-tour, the relationship, according to Jack Sheldon, had taken a disturbing turn: "I remember Chettie would score for Bird."

The Chet-and-Bird saga wrapped up on another mythic note. Parker, it was said, went home to New York and phoned Dizzy Gillespie, Miles Davis, Lee Morgan, and other black trumpeters to announce: "You better look out, there's a little white cat on the coast who's gonna eat you up." Baker loved to quote those words, though their real source—he himself, perhaps?—was vague.

In any case, this "pronouncement from God," as Whitlock called it, made Baker a jazz celebrity overnight. Musicians were gossiping, and sometimes maligning, his musical skills, but it was his looks that fascinated William Claxton, a twenty-four-year-old photographer from Pasadena. Six-foot-five, gangly, and shy, Claxton had been entranced since childhood by Duke Ellington, Billie Holiday, and other jazz stars. As an adult, he spent his nights driving to this club and that theater. In a fuzzy voice that seemed stuck in the back of his throat, he asked permission to take pictures. Charlie Parker was his idol, and Claxton crouched around the pillars of the Tiffany Club snapping photos, camera straps and extension cords dangling from his neck.

Late that night, in a darkroom he had set up in his family's house, Claxton had an epiphany. Staring at the print in the developing tray, he watched Baker's face appear "like magic." He called that moment a "dream." In a documentary about Claxton, *Jazz Seen,* by filmmaker Julian Benedikt, Claxton said that he had never known the meaning of "photogenic" until he took those first pictures of Baker. "Without the photograph," explained Claxton, "Chet was sort of a nice-looking, athletic guy; he kinda looked like an angelic prizefighter. He had one tooth missing, so he looked a little dopey, and a sort of fifties pompadour in his hair, but then you put him in front of a camera and he became a movie star. He knew instinctively what to do . . . he could concentrate on his music and still turn into the light, away from the light and all that, knowing that he was being photographed. So I think he was very, very shrewd."

As much as any recording, Claxton's photos created the Baker image. Word about Baker reached one of the forces behind *Birth of the Cool:* baritone saxophonist Gerry Mulligan, whose arranging and composing for those sessions had made him known as the wonder boy of modern jazz. Though not handsome, Mulligan had a memorable look of his own: he was tall, lanky, and pimply-faced, with a reddish crew cut and bangs that reminded a *Time* magazine reporter of Jerry Lewis.

But he took himself with deadly seriousness. Joyce Tucker, whose father, Jack, owned the Tiffany Club, told writer Donald Goddard that Mulligan "thought he had the voice of Christ in his horn"; the circles under his weary green eyes revealed the burden. They also betrayed his heroin habit, which he had moved west in 1951 hoping to break.

Early the next year, Mulligan had begun assembling his own band. He hired Bob Whitlock, who in turn recommended Baker. The trumpeter auditioned at Cottage Italia, a club in the San Fernando Valley where the saxophonist liked to rehearse. Baker wasn't about to bow to Mulligan's authority, and moments after walking through the door he warmed up with a series of ear-splitting trumpet shrieks. "DON'T EVER DO THAT AGAIN UNDER MY ROOF!" shouted Mulligan. Any pretense of coolness vanished as the two men screamed at each other like mean little boys. Finally Baker threw his horn in its case and stormed out, slamming the door as he yelled behind him, "GO FUCK YOURSELF!"

No one could have seen that meeting as a new "birth of the cool," or foretold the almost psychic musical rapport that Baker and Mulligan would come to show. As the lead players of the soon-to-be-formed Gerry Mulligan Quartet, they were perfectly matched: rarely did they let even a hint of vulnerability peep through the glossy surface of their music.

In fact, Mulligan seethed with resentment, although he kept it out of his work; for him, it seemed, music was about notes, not feeling. Born in Queens, New York, in 1927, he grew up in a Catholic household with a tyrannical Irish father, an industrial engineer. The elder Mulligan kept uprooting his wife and four sons as he took a series of jobs in different cities. Ultimately they settled in Philadelphia, but for Gerald Joseph, the youngest child, the damage was done. "No sooner did I get to know children in one town, than we'd move someplace else," he told writer Martin Abramson in 1959. "I became very insecure in my relations with other people as a result."

Gerry inherited his father's disciplinarian streak, and applied it most harshly to himself. As a boy, he had learned to play piano and clarinet, compose tunes, and write rudimentary arrangements while steeping himself in

Bach, Prokofiev, Stravinsky, and Ravel. By twenty-one, he had arranged for several prominent bandleaders, including Eliot Lawrence, Gene Krupa, and Claude Thornhill. Even his earliest charts showed the trademark Mulligan style—breezy, yet compulsively ordered and precise—that defined West Coast Jazz. He adopted as his main instrument the baritone sax, a big, unwieldy, grainy-toned horn that he played with elegance but little depth. To Baker, he was more of an arranger than a soloist, even though he played a "nice solo" once in a while.

Usually, though, Mulligan's mind was far from clear. No sooner had he moved to New York in 1946 than he was busted on a marijuana charge. Subsequently he got hooked on heroin, and his cherished self-discipline crumbled. "The junk had such a sedative effect on me I just couldn't finish anything that I sat down to write," he told Abramson. Mulligan was "rescued" by his new girlfriend, Gail Madden, the first in a series of controlling mother figures to whom the supposedly iron-willed artist gave full rein over his life. Madden promoted herself as a pianist, an arranger, and the first player of jazz maracas—efforts championed by Mulligan, who unpopularly called her a genius. She "believed she could help addicts with the power of suggestion," Abramson explained, and with her aid Mulligan got back to work.

The two became co-eccentrics. Identifying with the "strange, enchanted" Nature Boy of Nat King Cole's then-current hit, Mulligan walked the streets of Manhattan with a parrot on his shoulder. His behavior grew even weirder when Madden brought home a copy of Ayn Rand's celebrated 1943 novel *The Fountainhead.* It tells the story of Howard Roark, an architect whose revolutionary vision is met with rejection and misunderstanding—except by Dominique Françon, a painfully sensitive art critic. Mulligan and Madden so identified with the book's main characters that they seemed to metamorphose into them. "I never could tell if I was talking to Gerry or Howard Roark," said Bob Whitlock, "and with Gail there was always a bit of Dominique."

Around 1950, Mulligan began carting his sax to the Red Door, a rehearsal space in a midtown Manhattan walk-up. There he experimented with the concept that would make him famous: a rhythm section with no piano. He credited the idea to Madden. "To have an instrument with the tremendous capabilities of the piano reduced to the role of crutch for the solo horn was unthinkable," he declared. The new format gave him more room to improvise, for it freed him from following a pianist's strict chord progressions. According to Phil Leshin, Mulligan assembled his first pianoless quartet at the Red Door. It featured Leshin, drummer Walter Bolden, and trumpeter Tony Fruscella, an overlooked pioneer of the pared-down style adopted by Baker and Miles Davis. As he tried out other musicians, Mulligan slowly went broke; any funds he had he shot into his arm. When he hocked his sax, he knew he had to get out of New York.

In the fall of 1951, just months after Jack Kerouac had detailed his own cross-country quest for truth in a first draft of the Beat bible *On the Road,* Mulligan hitchhiked west with Madden. Reaching L.A., the strung-out musician kept scuffling, playing jam sessions and writing arrangements while doing his best to pose as a hotshot. In 1952 he walked into the Haig, a tiny jazz club in L.A.'s residential Wilshire district. Inside, jazz pianist Erroll Garner, the café singer-pianist Bobby Short, and others played without amplification in what had been a one-room bungalow. From outside, the Haig looked like a dollhouse amid tall apartment buildings, palm trees, and open sky. It was overshadowed further by the palatial Ambassador Hotel across the street, whose Coconut Grove supper club splashed the names of its headliners—FRANK SINATRA or LENA HORNE or DEAN MARTIN & JERRY LEWIS—across its marquee. In contrast, a modest banner hung over the entrance of 638 South Kenmore Avenue: THE HAIG DINNER COCKTAILS.

Borrowing another horn, Mulligan guested at one of the club's Monday-night jam sessions. Soon he took them over, using those nights to audition local players for his own group. His abortive encounter with Chet Baker had soured him on the trumpeter, but after Baker's run with Charlie Parker, Mulligan had a change of heart and invited Baker to sit in at the Haig. The saxophonist saw him as an idiot savant. "I've never been around anybody who had a quicker relationship between his ears and his fingers," Mulligan told Les Tomkins. "I believe Chet was kind of a freak talent. There's no figuring out . . . where he learned what he knew."

While the relentless complexity of Parker's music didn't suit him, Baker found the right partner in Mulligan: a player who loved melody as much as he did, and who saw a solo as a work of architecture, not as an excuse to blow. Most horn-playing duos took turns soloing, then competitively traded "fours" and "eights" (four- and eight-bar phrases), but Baker and Mulligan checked their egos and looked for ways to complement each other. They played in unison or harmony, broke into effortless counterpoint. "We could always anticipate what the other was going to do," Mulligan said.

Baker sat in with Mulligan for several Mondays. Listening in wonder in the back of the room was Richard (Dick) Bock, the Haig's balding, bespectacled young host. A frustrated horn player, Bock worked for Discovery, a small jazz label in Hollywood, but he dreamed of starting his own company. Bock organized a makeshift record date for Mulligan at the Hollywood Hills cottage of Phil Turetsky, a studio engineer. On July 9, 1952, Mulligan, Baker, Jimmy Rowles, and bassist Joe Mondragon gathered there. Bock, acting as producer, positioned the one microphone and turned on the Ampex recorder.

Mulligan had picked "She Didn't Say Yes," a Jerome Kern show tune, and "Dinah," a Dixieland favorite that he slowed to an easy pace. Rowles's piano dominated the group, and Mulligan vowed again to drop the instrument. ("The only piano player Gerry likes is himself," Baker told Bernie Fleischer.) That summer the baby grand at the Haig had been moved to the basement to make room for vibes player Red Norvo, and when Bock suggested renting a cheap spinet for Mondays, Mulligan said, "Oh no, you won't!"

By now he had filled out his Monday-night band with Bob Whitlock and Chico Hamilton, a handsome, light-skinned black drummer who used mallets, brushes, and his fingers so suavely that he suggested Sammy Davis Jr. doing a tap dance. Few people paid much attention except Claxton, who stood on the sidelines with his camera, and Bock, who recorded the shows on a portable reel-to-reel deck. With two thousand dollars of his own and another two thousand from Roy Harte, who owned a successful Hollywood drum shop, Bock founded Pacific Jazz Records. He could afford to release only one 78-rpm single of two songs, the Mulligan original "Bernie's Tune" and a standard, "Lullaby of the Leaves." That disc, plus a good word from Dave Brubeck, got the group their first big break: a week opposite Brubeck at the Black Hawk.

Whitlock was busy, so Baker recommmended Carson Smith, a bassist from San Francisco who idolized Mulligan and had come to L.A. hoping to meet him. On the morning of Tuesday, September 2, Mulligan and Baker drove to San Francisco, happy as larks, singing their own arrangements all the way.

It was a charmed trip. Fantasy, Brubeck's label, immediately hired them to record. Circled around a single standing microphone, they made four quick sides. Mulligan had seen Fred Astaire and Ginger Rogers perform the Latin-style dance tune "The Carioca" in the film *Flying Down to Rio,* and he wrote a chart that had the airy, gliding quality of Astaire's singing and dancing. He and Baker sailed through the melody, lifting each other up with witty little fills; the low gravel tone of Mulligan's sax set off Baker's cloudless trumpet playing, and vice versa. Chico Hamilton added gentle Latin touches, while Carson Smith tied it all together with his unfussy bass playing. Without ever raising the volume or rushing, they made their statement in two and a half minutes.

Mulligan named two originals after local DJs: "Line for Lyons" was dedicated to Jimmy Lyons, "Bark for Barksdale" to Don Barksdale. "Gerry wasn't above kissing a little ass when it was convenient," said Carson Smith with a laugh. Decades later, Peter Schickele, a distinguished classical conductor and musicologist, would rave in the *New York Times* about the "fantastically clear three-part counterpoint" the group achieved without piano. Only one of the four tunes moved into darker territory. Mulligan felt they needed a ballad, so Smith recommended an obscurity by Richard Rodgers and Lorenz Hart, written in 1937. The bassist had found it in an old songbook and couldn't get it out of his head.

By the sixties, "My Funny Valentine" was a pop cliché, with hundreds of versions on the market. But in 1952 only Margaret Whiting and a couple of other singers had recorded it. In *Babes in Arms,* the show from which it came, "My Funny Valentine" was a girl's vow of unconditional love to a scoundrel named Valentine. None of Smith's bandmates knew it, so he scrawled out the chords, then sang them the melody. Rodgers had stated a haunting theme in the first phrase, then explored it over and over, changing it subtly each time. The melody kept ascending, creating a tension that built to a soaring climax under the words "Stay, little valentine, stay!"

Mulligan and Smith threw a chart together that spotlighted Baker. Here the trumpeter had no clever arrangement to hide behind, so he played the tune as written, stretching out its slow, spare phrases until they seemed to ache. His hushed tone drew the ear; it suggested a door thrown open on some dark night of the soul, then pulled shut as the last note faded. Smith countered the rising melody with a descending line of quarter notes, ominous as a clock ticking in the dark. He ended by mistake in a minor key instead of the major one in the sheet music, giving the record one last chilling touch.

The song fascinated Baker. It captured all he aspired to as a musician, with its sophisticated probing of a beautiful theme and its gracefully linked phrases, adding up to a melodic statement that didn't waste a note. "Valentine" became his favorite song; rarely would he do a show without it, or fail to find something new in its thirty-five bars. At the same time, the Baker mystique—a sense that "cool" was a lid on an explosive jar of emotions—had its roots in that performance.

"After Fantasy released those records," said Smith, "everybody knew that this new voice of Chet Baker was the thing. All of a sudden everybody was talking about Chet." People kept comparing him to the honey-toned Bix Beiderbecke, an influence denied by Baker, who said he had hardly even heard Beiderbecke. Yet *Metronome* raved of how Baker had blended "a sound reminiscent of Bix and a style owing much to Miles to an effect little short of surpassing beauty." His delivery got much of its "cool" languor from his conscious manipulation of pitch. "I wanted to play on the dark side, a little bit under the center of tonality," he told interviewer Leonard Malone in 1988. "Not really flat, but just on the underneath side."

Mulligan was deified on local radio, thanks in part to his shrewd dedications to Jimmy Lyons and Don Barksdale. In *Down Beat,* Ralph J. Gleason anointed him the new genius of jazz. The quartet's "fantastic, fugue-ish, funky, swinging and contrapuntal sound" had every musician in town "shaking his head in wonder," the critic reported. As for Baker, once he figured out how "to project his personality to the audience and not rely on the music completely," Gleason wrote, "he should be sensational."

Later in September 1952, the group returned to the Haig as headliners. The scene looked like a jazz club sequence in some low-budget film noir. Mulligan and Baker stood side by side on the rim of a platform in the corner, dressed in dark business suits and ties yet looking barely old enough to enter a nightclub. One mirror hung on the wall behind them, another at an angle overhead, giving views of them from various angles. Well-dressed Hollywood couples were crowded around tiny tables in a space not much larger than the average living room. The customers sat puffing on cigarettes and looking self-consciously blasé.

But no one could be cooler than Baker or Mulligan, who offered up their music and nothing more. Baker stared at the floor; Mulligan nodded sleepily to the beat with half-closed eyes as he fingered a lumbering instrument that reached from his lips to his knees. They looked sexy, and sounded like nothing musicians had ever heard. There on several nights was an aspiring L.A. trumpeter, Herb Alpert, then seventeen and years from his huge success as leader of the Mexican-style pop band the Tijuana Brass. "Chet could play with lightning speed, those even eighth notes," Alpert noticed. "It was mystifying to most trumpet players, because we all got the feeling he didn't really practice. You'd hear these stories that he couldn't play a C chord, he was just doing this by instinct and by ear."

Arlyne Brown, who went to the Haig often before wedding Mulligan in 1953, saw a side of the duo's relationship that few people glimpsed: "They would come off the stand flushed and glowing, and look at each other and practically fall into each other's arms. They were just so joyful and in love with playing together." But they never let the audience see it. "To show enthusiasm was not cool," explained jazz singer Mark Murphy. "You had to act like you didn't care—can you dig it?"

Acting like you were interested only in the fix of the moment was a radical statement at a time when the future meant everything. Americans were supposedly in the midst of a hard-earned dream. The key was mass conformity—the stubborn belief that a family-oriented suburban life, ruled by God, was all anyone needed for happiness. Driving to the Haig, one heard star-kissed song lyrics on the car radio, filled with words like "forever" and "always." Doris Day warded off boys looking for no-strings fun by firmly telling them: "When I fall in love, it will be forever." In his number-two hit "I Believe," Frankie Laine promised, like a minister from the pulpit, that God would watch over Americans for eternity, while trees and flowers bloomed in endless splendor.

Amid all this sunshiny optimism came the first heroes of a defiant new youth culture: Marlon Brando, Montgomery Clift, and James Dean, all of whom symbolized disgust with every false hope infecting America. Onscreen, these actors were bundles of raw nerve endings, quivering with inner turmoil and mumbling semi-coherently, as if their rage were too dark to express. The stance allowed them to dramatize their sensitivity; it set them apart by implying depths that few people possessed. In his controversial 1957 essay "The White Negro," Norman Mailer glorified "the American existentialist—the hipster," who identified so deeply with the minute-to-minute hazards of black life that he fancied himself an honorary Negro. Hipsters knew that conformist America was headed for doom, either by atomic incineration or by the smothering of "every creative and rebellious instinct" that made the soul breathe. The only answer, then, was "to live with death as immediate danger, to divorce oneself from society, to exist without roots, to set out on that uncharted journey with the rebellious imperatives of the self."

That was the path taken, in their cool way, by Mulligan and Baker. They made it clear they weren't about to pander to anybody; all they cared about was themselves and their music, not you. A few observers were hip enough to know that much of this detachment came from drugs. What kind almost didn't matter, for most people were still so naïve on the subject that anything from marijuana to heroin seemed like an express train to hell. Every few years some theater revived *Reefer Madness,* the 1936 exploitation film about the evils of pot-smoking. Eventually it became a camp classic, but in the fifties, the movie's message—that marijuana led to violence, hallucinations, the use of harder drugs, and perhaps death—was commonly accepted as truth. Shock waves had greeted the 1948 arrest of film star Robert Mitchum for possession of grass—as if the surly, brooding actor with the hooded eyes couldn't possibly have ever smoked a joint. In dime stores, mothers yanked their children away from the spinning racks of such pulp novels as *Junkie: Confessions of an Unredeemed Drug Addict* and *It Ain't Hay.* The cover of the latter showed a skeleton rowing a coffin-shaped boat, head resting on a giant marijuana cigarette.

Author Richard Lamparski, who moved to Hollywood the year Mulligan's quartet debuted at the Haig, saw the taboo attached to pot. "It wasn't just that people were afraid of using it because it was addictive; it was highly illegal," he said. "It was a very messy bust. If you used grass in Hollywood at that time, it was a lot like being involved in S&M. It was something you would quickly get a name for."

Baker's reputation as a "pothead" went public in late 1952. On December 23, a policeman caught him and Bob Whitlock smoking weed in Baker's car between sets. Searching the automobile, they found a whole can of marijuana under the front seat. The musicians landed in jail for the night. Baker was very lucky: he took the rap and received only three months' probation.

Word of the incident must have escaped *Time,* which on February 2, 1953, profiled Mulligan and his supposedly upstanding young colleagues. "In comparison with the frantic extremes of bop," the reporter explained, "his jazz is rich and even orderly, is marked by an almost Bach-like counterpoint." The leader portrayed himself as a genius of Bach's order: "Mulligan is extremely serious about his music. As early as he can remember, he was inventing tunes of his own on the piano—'I hate to play other people's.' "

That article packed the tiny Haig as never before. Lines formed down South Kenmore Avenue; fans stood three-deep at the bar. Electricity peaked on the nights when limos pulled up outside, depositing Mitchum, Jane Russell, or Marilyn Monroe at the greenery-lined entrance. Mitchum played the band's records "morning, noon, and night," according to his friend Russell. "I think it's fantastic, the things they do with no arrangement whatsoever," she raved to *Down Beat.* But Jeffie Boyd, a cocktail waitress at the club, saw another reason for the group's success: "They were good-looking white musicians. In L.A., white was good. Black, people weren't so sure how to take."

The Haig's owner, John Bennett—formerly John Bernstein of Toledo,

Ohio—"tried to maintain a snob appeal for the place," according to saxophonist Herb Geller. Bennett spouted trivia on opera or Art Tatum while wearing ties full of crumbs and soup stains. The club itself was far from chic. "If you saw it in the daytime, you'd hesitate to go there at night," said Carson Smith. "There were cracks in the wall, the carpet was coming up, there were cockroaches and spiders that you didn't see in the dark." William Claxton recalled the tacky décor: "Everything was painted terrible peach. They had some dreadful art on the walls."

Nothing could hide the fact that the Haig was a gin mill like any other. But to Mulligan, anywhere he played was Carnegie Hall, especially now that he had been lionized by *Time.* His cool veneer burst in midsong as he stopped to scold customers who talked, laughed, or clinked their glasses. "You're here to listen to my music!" he announced, informing the squirming crowd that they were lucky to be there, and if they didn't agree, then he wished they would leave. "It was so ridiculous," said Boyd. "Gerry got irritated quite easily."

Mulligan's haughtiness helped shift attention to Baker, who already commanded the eyes of female customers and the ears of other musicians. "He had a sound that could be like candy—just gorgeous," said Jack Sheldon. Walter Norris called him a "young god," adding: "When Chet was about twenty-two, he was on fire! The notes were magic." Smith chalked it up to magic as well: "I heard Chet night after night, and I very seldom heard him repeat himself. I don't know where it all came from." Baker offered no clues. When asked what he thought about onstage, he said enigmatically: "The next pretty note." He seemed unfazed when the group was hired to play a birthday party for Anne Baxter, who had recently costarred with Bette Davis in *All About Eve.* "These glamorous people would come wanting to talk to Chet, and he didn't want anything to do with them," Smith said. "He could never even hold up a conversation. He'd just sit in the corner and listen to the records. I could see, years later, why he went into hard drugs. He was always trying to escape reality."

Indeed, Baker found it almost impossible to relate to others directly and honestly. He dealt with most people by withdrawing from them, using them, or disappointing them. His actions recalled a comment made by Arlyne Brown about all the musicians she had known who were "very sensitive to music and completely insensitive to the rest of the world." Years later, Ruth Young would term Baker a psychopath—a species explored by Robert Mitchell Lindner in his 1944 book *Rebel Without a Cause: The Hypnoanalysis of a Criminal Psychopath.* "The psychopath is a rebel without a cause, an agitator without a slogan, a revolutionary without a program," wrote Lindner. "In other words, his rebelliousness is aimed to achieve goals satisfactory to himself alone; he is incapable of exertions for the sake of others. . . . The psychopath, like the child, cannot delay the pleasures of gratification."

Living with him, Young would see the root of Baker's behavior: "Chet was miserable! He was the most insecure person you'll ever meet. And he buried those insecurities the best way he could."

One of these ways, according to Bob Whitlock, was to play the star, at least for a moment. The bassist remembered seeing him flaunt a flashy new topcoat at the Haig: "I thought, Jesus Christ, he thinks he's Clark Gable or something. A lot of people were blowing smoke up his butt, and he really ate it up." Sheldon compared him to "a leading man in the movies: he always had a convertible, a big dog, and a girl."

For a time, the female interest went to his head. "It was girls, girls, girls for him," said Larry Bunker, who had replaced drummer Chico Hamilton in the quartet. "He was fucking everything in sight, treating Charlaine like a piece of shit, balling chicks on the ten-minute break out in the car while Charlaine was sitting in the club. That was his style. He was gorgeous and he knew it."

Others recall him focusing on one girl at a time. For part of 1953 it was Joyce Tucker, the sexy daughter of Jack Tucker, who owned the Tiffany. Briefly a child actress in films, Joyce now worked as a camera girl at the Coconut Grove, which stood just between the Haig and the Tiffany. Tall, slender, and obsessed with jazz musicians, Joyce was out for kicks, and she found plenty. Along with her husband, a clarinetist named Marvin Koral, Joyce frequented the Haig to see the Mulligan Quartet—more specifically, Chet Baker. The trumpeter was struck by her long auburn hair and big brown eyes that "bored into you"; she stared at him so intensely, he said, that he couldn't imagine Koral didn't notice. Joyce began coming to the Haig alone, and soon, Baker said, he was spending intermissions with her in his car, parked behind the Ambassador Hotel.

For months they carried on like naughty children, making little secret of their affair: a peril, since both were married. Russ Freeman recalled seeing them at a gathering held at a friend's house. While the guests chatted, Baker lay silently in the middle of the floor. Suddenly he shouted at the top of his voice: "I WANNA FUCK!" Everyone knew he was referring to Joyce, who giggled. "I think it was a show of his masculinity, showing off to everybody how he could do or say anything he wanted and it didn't matter," Freeman said.

If Baker delighted in stirring up trouble, Mulligan was anxious to set his life in order, drug habit notwithstanding. Having broken up with Gail Madden, he impetuously proposed to Jeffie Boyd, a smart, vivacious brunette in her early twenties. Jeffie had grown up in New York, and to her, L.A. was an intellectual vacuum. Mulligan's brains and "leprechaunish" sense of humor attracted her. They eloped to Mexico, then honeymooned in "Palm Springs or someplace," she said, where the saxophonist announced his plan to quit heroin. "I was supposed to help him," she explained. "I was such a moron, what did I know? I said, 'Oh sure, I'll be happy to help you.' So I locked him in the room and went and lay by the pool. He started screaming for the doctor, and I kept saying, 'No, you can't have the doctor.' I left him there for three or four days. When we went home, he returned to being a junkie."

He struggled to project whatever air of normalcy he could. Mulligan wrote outside arrangements to help finance his drug use, while trying to keep his habit discreet. "Gerry functioned at a very high level," said Larry Bunker. "He took command of the situation." The saxophonist let no one, including Baker, see him shoot up, and hid his heroin and drug paraphernalia ("works") under the back porch of the house he rented at 1818 North Harvard Boulevard, near the Haig. Yet Baker had known enough addicts to spot the telltale signs. He found Mulligan "tense and jittery; extremely high-strung"; onstage, he spotted the leader's hands shaking as he fingered his saxophone.

As far as their friends knew, the two men had never had a heart-to-heart talk about drugs or anything else. Apart from their music, they seemed unable to connect—a problem that became obvious when the Mulligans invited the Bakers to share their house. "We all sort of went our own way," said Jeffie. "I don't remember us ever really communicating, even having a meal together. Strange." Mulligan stayed so aloof from his sidemen that Bunker felt he hardly knew him. But he treated most people that way: even Jeffie realized that she and Mulligan had practically nothing in common. "The thing was over before it began," she said.

The same could almost be said of the Gerry Mulligan Quartet. As their Pacific Jazz records piled up, the group's format of airy counterpart and harmony, wrapped into neat little three-minute packages, began to wear thin. Despite the promise of "My Funny Valentine," they seemed trapped behind their wall of cool; even in such rueful ballads as "Darn That Dream" and "I Can't Get Started," they kept a rigid distance. For all its supposed spontaneity, Mulligan's music was controlled with an iron hand. Jeffie remembered him drilling bassists like a marine sergeant, forbidding them to leave his house until they had memorized their parts. Mulligan had dropped Whitlock—"I mean, I was out of line, I was using, it was one of the worst periods of my life," the bassist admitted—and replaced him with Carson Smith. Thereafter, he kept firing Smith—"You're just not playing the way I want you to play!"—and rehiring him. He reduced Larry Bunker's role to that of a faceless timekeeper. "You did as you were told," said Bunker. "I think I reached the point where I didn't even have a pair of drumsticks. It was all brushes—that's all he wanted."

Meanwhile, the saxophonist spent almost all day, every day at home, rehearsing and writing. "Everything was music," said Jeffie, and Mulligan had no patience with anyone less disciplined. A *Down Beat* headline screamed: "Says Gerry Mulligan: GET RID OF THE AMATEURS!"

It was sometime in 1953 that he started resenting Chet Baker, whose popularity was surpassing his own, through no apparent effort on Baker's part. While Mulligan labored at his desk, Baker lay on the beach or flew kites in the hills; where the saxophonist approached music as a draining intellectual process, Baker simply put his trumpet to his lips and out it flowed.

Everything about him started to annoy Mulligan: his habit of driving "a hundred miles an hour down the Hollywood Hills in his Jaguar, switching back roads, making these tight corners"; his "pack," who hung around the house sprawled on the floor and the sofa, squirting one another with water pistols. To Mulligan, it was unthinkable for Baker to spend so much time skiing, swimming, and hiking, then playing at the Haig without even warming up. Forty years later, he groused that Baker was so exhausted, and his lips so chapped from the sun and cold mountain air, that he was cracking notes—a problem Jeffie couldn't recall. "We the audience never noticed that," she said. "Chet was wonderful all the time." Mulligan was even more disgruntled to see audiences treating Baker like the star of the group: "Chet liked to be king of the hill. Well, with the quartet *I* was king of the hill. Of course," he added, "Chet never had any problems with that. He accepted my leadership, and that was that."

Baker had his own complaints. "Gerry used to make these claims that he had discovered Chet and that Chet was his protégé," said Bob Whitlock. "It used to get under Chet's skin something fierce, and Chet would take every opportunity to rebel." Instead of confronting Mulligan, he griped to *Melody Maker,* a British jazz magazine. "Gerry Mulligan is a great musician," he said. "But too many people have been telling him he's a genius. . . . Gerry now walks around thinking he is the greatest thing that ever happened to jazz. . . . Maybe it's all right for Gerry to give the customers lectures about keeping quiet while he's playing. But when these lectures last fifteen minutes or more it gets a little embarrassing for the rest of us on the stand—to say the least. Gerry shouldn't keep knocking other musicians, either."

But apart from their initial blowup at Cottage Italia, neither man felt free enough to air his grievances to the other. Chico Hamilton recalled nights onstage when "Gerry would be facing north and Chet would be facing south," but the other band members were mystified at reports of friction.

That relationship, like others in Baker's life, was a bomb waiting to burst. He had continued seeing Joyce Tucker while maintaining the pretense of a friendship with her husband. One night Baker gave Carson Smith and the Korals a ride home from the Haig. Baker and Marvin Koral sat up front, with Joyce in between; Smith sat in the back, his bass sticking forward between Marvin and Joyce. "Marv's looking out the window, and Joyce and Chet are necking," said Smith. "I thought, hey, wait a minute, this is getting a little dangerous here. This guy's supposed to be a friend of his."

It was more than a little dangerous, and the game exploded with a hysterical call from Joyce, reporting that her husband had snapped. "A half-dozen of us drove over to the Korals' house," Smith said. "She opened the door, and Marv had trashed the entire place. He had dumped the refrigerator over, torn up the stove, ripped open the sofa, cut open the mattresses on the bed, broken all the windows. It was unbelievable. He'd gone absolutely nuts."

Baker found just as violent a foe in John Edward O'Grady, head of the Hollywood Narcotics Detail and the scourge of the L.A. jazz world. From 1948 through 1958, O'Grady led a squad of detectives on a frightening witch-hunt that he loftily termed "the dream of my life . . . protecting society against the creeping menace of drugs." O'Grady's typically fifties crusade was to save an imaginary pristine ideal of L.A. from its sordid underworld. "Mine was not to reason why addicts took drugs, mine was to bust their asses," he wrote in his 1974 memoir, *O'Grady: The Life and Times of Hollywood's No. 1 Private Eye.* His self-righteous savagery mirrored that of Joseph R. McCarthy, the U.S. senator who had just begun his anti-Communist rampage.

O'Grady's mission stemmed from a little-known vendetta. He had dreamed of starring in films; having failed at that, he terrorized entertainers, thus getting his name and sometimes his picture in the papers. He groomed himself into an unconscious parody of a B-movie detective. Six-foot-three and two hundred pounds, O'Grady wore a flattop crew cut and dark glasses and strutted along Hollywood's Sunset Strip with a pearl-handled revolver on his hip. He called himself "ball-busting Sergeant O'Grady, the big-time Big O . . . the most feared cop in the city." His methods included storming homes without a search warrant, threatening musicians on the street, even smashing out the teeth of a dealer who had tried to hide the dope in his mouth. One of his henchmen, a big, swarthy Hispanic detective named Rudy Diaz, was "the meanest-looking man you ever saw in your life," according to Mel Bartfield, a jazz lover who had his own run-ins with O'Grady's pack. "Even to see him would scare you."

O'Grady amassed what some called the biggest narcotics-arrest history in LAPD history: an estimated 2,500-plus suspected junkies and pushers, many innocent. His main targets were jazz musicians, whom he considered the dregs of society. "I set out to destroy that crowd and damn near did," he wrote. The "crowd" included Stan Getz, Billie Holiday, and jazz fan Lenny Bruce. "I ran Charlie 'Yardbird' Parker, the great saxophonist, out of town," O'Grady bragged. "I could have nailed him. His arms were covered with track marks from heroin needles. But he was too old and too drunk and I decided it wasn't worth wasting the time nailing Parker just so the City of L.A. could pay for his keep."

Drug gossip had dogged Mulligan and Baker for months, and one night in April 1953 they looked down from the stage to see O'Grady and his partner Dick Hill glaring at them from a ringside table. The surveillance went on for several nights. "It turned into a plague," said Mulligan, who put the blame on Baker: "O'Grady used to love to come around and bait Chet, and Chet always had a smart rejoinder, so this guy was after him." Mel Bartfield confirmed it: "O'Grady hated Chet." And vice versa. In 1955, on a trip to Worcester, Massachusetts, Baker and Bill Loughborough—a drum maker who became his lifelong friend—met two gypsies who offered to help them cast a spell against O'Grady and Hill. Trekking into the woods at night, they lit a fire, sat around it in a circle, and murmured incantations against the policemen while fondling clay dolls with pins stuck in them. Years later, Baker claimed the curse had worked: not only had O'Grady been ejected from the narcotics squad, but Hill, Baker heard, had been badly injured by a bottle thrown at his head.

The witchcraft came too late to save them in April 1953, when O'Grady and Hill plotted to bust the two young musicians. On the thirteenth, while the band was at work, the detectives drove an unmarked car to North Harvard Boulevard, where Jeffie and Charlaine were home alone, and parked across the street. Spotting Jeffie's sports car out front, O'Grady locked bumpers with it to feign a parking accident. Then he knocked on the door. When Jeffie answered, O'Grady explained that he wanted to give her his insurance number to arrange payment for the "damage." As she opened the door to peek at her car, he shoved her aside and barged in as backup cops leaped from the bushes. Charlaine bolted into the bathroom to flush a can of marijuana. O'Grady pounded on the door until she emerged. Looking into the toilet, he spotted a few leaves in the water—sufficient grounds for arrest. Angry as mad dogs, he and Hill ransacked the house for heroin.

Finding none, they arrested the two women for marijuana possession and took them to the Haig. There the detectives ordered the quartet into the back office and made them roll up their sleeves. Only Mulligan revealed an arm covered with tracks. "Look at that—fresh marks!" hissed O'Grady. Mulligan's iron shell crumbled. "Gerry broke down, almost started to cry," said Carson Smith. "He went like a rag doll. Chet was just standing off to the side, watching."

Ordering the Bakers and the Mulligans back to the house, O'Grady demanded that Mulligan surrender his dope. Trembling and teary-eyed, Mulligan stumbled to the back porch, where he pulled out a set of hypodermic needles, burned teaspoons, cotton, and a small amount of heroin. "I've been on the stuff for a long time," he moaned, too shattered to realize he had done himself in: had he not succumbed to O'Grady's bullying, the detective could have only charged him with having track marks, a sign of heroin use but not necessarily possession.

Minutes later, the couples sat huddled together at a police station in downtown L.A. As charges were filed, two wall panels parted, and out jumped a throng of paparazzi. "Flashbulbs were going off all over the place," said Jeffie. "I was scared to death."

The next day's *Los Angeles Mirror* blared: "HOT LIPS BOPSTER, AIDE AND 2 WIVES JAILED; NAB DOPE." A photo showed four supposedly cool youngsters in shock: Jeffie glanced at the camera tearfully; Charlaine tried to hide her face in her coat; Mulligan looked pathetically defeated; Baker stared out with wide, uncomprehending eyes, unable to react. The article made Mulligan sound like a joke, calling him a "real cool sax player, whose crazy recording of 'Bweebida Bobbida' has the cats slipping their scalps." All except him pleaded not guilty. Mulligan took the blame for not only the heroin but the pot, which had belonged to everyone. "He was wonderful," said Jeffie.

Her mother posted his bail, and the couples went free. Mulligan's trial was set for June.

The scandal brought more business to the Haig than ever. But Mulligan took another blow when his early champion, Ralph J. Gleason, scathingly reassessed his quartet as "the most overrated small band in jazz" in *Down Beat.* The group's shallow, overstyled approach, he wrote, was "boring me silly. . . . Mulligan with or without a piano and with or without his pretentious explanations of what he's doing, is still a child when racked up against men like Duke."

Mulligan said nothing about the review to his bandmates. He seemed sure that in June, after he had received his acquittal, everything would go back to the version of reality he had so painstakingly crafted.

Los Angeles, California, 1954. Photo by William Claxton

4

With his career in limbo and his private life a shambles, Mulligan more than ever needed a guiding hand. Jeffie wasn't equipped to be his savior, nor did she care to be, and they parted just after the arrest. Weeks later, on May 8, 1953, he married an old girlfriend, Arlyne Brown. She was the daughter of Lew Brown, who as part of the thirties songwriting team of DeSylva, Brown, and Henderson had penned such frothy hits as "The Best Things in Life Are Free." That was hardly Arlyne's sentiment, though. A blunt, aggressive businesswoman, she became Mulligan's manager as well as his wife, and set out to raise his price above the $1,200 a week his band earned at the Haig. Mulligan happily granted her complete authority, and until they divorced in 1957, his standard reply to every request was "Aw, I don't know, man, talk to Arlyne."

The situation didn't bring him and Baker any closer. Arlyne considered the trumpeter a talented imbecile; he found her abrasive and pushy. But Jeffie was grateful to let Arlyne inherit the burden of Mulligan, and when the two women met in the ladies' room of the Haig, Jeffie blurted out: "Oh, thank God you've come! Take him, he's yours!"

Soon after the breakup, she moved back to New York, where she stepped into a bigger mess by marrying "Crazy" Joey Gallo, a soon-to-be-notorious bisexual mobster and murderer. Gallo shared Mulligan's verbosity and love of books, but not his professional smarts. During the sixties he served a long term at Sing Sing for a botched extortion attempt, and in 1972, after he and Jeffie had divorced, Gallo was gunned down at a restaurant in New York's Little Italy. "How much more déclassé can you get?" Mulligan would snicker to Arlyne. "He's not even a *successful* criminal."

Neither, as it happened, was Mulligan. In September 1953, he appeared in court. The judge, Charles W. Fricke, was a nationally acclaimed scholar of criminal law and an expert on everything from forensic chemistry to growing orchids. More erudite than Mulligan, he was also tougher: the saxophonist later heard that Fricke had put his own son in San Quentin for joyriding, and that the youth was murdered there in a brawl. But Fricke earned his true claim to fame in 1955, when he sent accused murderer Barbara Graham, a heroin addict and ex-prostitute, to the gas chamber—a historic judgment immortalized in the film *I Want to Live,* starring Susan Hayward.

Though known as the Hanging Judge, Fricke treated Mulligan kindly. When the saxophonist testified that the household pot was all his, the judge leaned over and whispered, "Son, you don't want to say that." He ended up ignoring the marijuana charge but gave Mulligan six months in prison for possession of heroin—a light penalty, given the harshness of L.A.'s drug laws. As guards led him off in chains, Mulligan seethed with a bitterness that would last for decades. Along the way, he rewrote history to cast himself as the victim. "Chet got a good lawyer, I got a stupid lawyer," complained the musician, who also told a few friends that Baker had informed on him. He accused the "Hanging Judge" and the LAPD of treating him savagely. "But Gerry handed them the junk," said Arlyne. "He confessed. What did he want the judge to do?"

Mulligan was sent to the Sheriff's Honour Farm, an L.A. jail. Placed in an isolation cell to kick heroin, he suffered the agonies of cold turkey—and, perhaps, the anger of feeling betrayed and defeated.

Thanks largely to Mulligan, other people's dreams were taking wing. With profits from the first Pacific Jazz LP, *The Gerry Mulligan Quartet,* Dick Bock had moved his label into its first office. In the winter of 1953, he dragged a desk, a file cabinet, and a couple of chairs into a corner of Drum City, a Hollywood shop co-owned by his partner Roy Harte. The space stank so badly from the chemically cured animal hides used to make drums that Dot Woodward, Bock's new secretary, insisted they move to a small room upstairs. Once settled, she faced such a tight budget that she did the bookkeeping in Bock's college notebook. "But we were all so young, and eager to do well, that it seemed like a dream to us," she said.

Bock stayed poised and cheerful, thanks in part to his immersion in Eastern philosophy and meditation. He was a devout member of Hollywood's Vedanta Society, along with novelist Christopher Isherwood, scientific and mystical writer Aldous Huxley, and Bock's wife, Kay, granddaughter of the twenties pop evangelist Aimee Semple McPherson. Bock's faith could be obsessive, as he showed on a pilgrimage to Big Sur, a vacation spot on the California coast where he went to meditate. Hearing that the Maharishi Mahesh Yogi, the Hindu religious leader, advocated sun worship, Bock sat cross-legged on a hill, removed his glasses, and stared at the sun until it nearly blinded him. His digestive system was also in an uproar due to compulsive macrobiotic dieting.

His mania would pay off. In 1956 he signed Ravi Shankar, the Indian sitar player who became a flower-power icon in the sixties, when George Harrison of the Beatles studied with him. As Indian culture grew into a hippie sensation, Bock's stable of Eastern artists—Shankar; the Maharishi, who recorded spoken-word albums; and Ali Akbar Khan, composer and player of the twenty-five-string sarode—would keep his label afloat at a time when straight-ahead jazz was floundering.

But in 1953, Bock sensed a gold mine in Chet Baker. Even before Mulligan's arrest, Bock had tried to convince the trumpeter to leave Mulligan and start his own quartet on Pacific Jazz. Baker resisted. Running a group and making decisions came naturally to Mulligan, but Baker wanted no part of any responsibilities. "Chet and I were just hanging around waiting for Gerry to get out of jail," said Carson Smith. "It was kind of a dark period." Months earlier, when Mulligan ran off with Jeffie, Baker had been left in charge of the band at the Haig. He managed to call the tunes, but whenever Smith and Herb Geller, Mulligan's sub, asked, "What key?" Baker stared blankly. "I don't know," he would say.

When *Melody Maker* inquired about his plans, Baker offered the aimless reveries of a beach boy. Because he had bad teeth and gums, he said, he planned to give up the trumpet in two years, whereupon he would buy a boat and "see things I've never seen. . . . I want a fifty-foot sailboat to travel on and write music, heavier things. . . . I've had coastal sailing experience around L.A., and I intend to start studying navigation." He added that he would "definitely rejoin" Mulligan upon his release. But the saxophonist's jail term dragged on without a call, card, or visit from his partner. Baker shifted the blame back to Mulligan, grumbling that in all his months in jail, the leader hadn't written him once.

That year, another musician came along to make sense of Baker's career. Russ Freeman had moved from Chicago, his birthplace, to L.A. at five, but the languor of California life hadn't mellowed his piano playing. Freeman loved Bud Powell and Joe Albany, two hard-bop pianists, and adopted their choppy, percussive style. Leonard Feather would later praise him for creating an "incisive, swinging" sound of his own. Freeman was most inspired by Charlie Parker—"the greatest musician who ever lived," he declared—and he was ecstatic when he got to accompany his hero at an L.A. gig in 1947. Freeman followed Parker to New York, staying almost a year.

There he absorbed the sounds and the lifestyle of bop. Already on five years' probation for a marijuana bust, he got hooked on heroin. Two fellow Parker disciples "turned him on": saxophonist Dean Benedetti, who earned a place in jazz history by trailing Parker with a disc-cutting machine and recording hundreds of his solos; and trombonist Jimmy Knepper.

Freeman learned the ritual known to every junkie—a procedure that Chet Baker would enact untold thousands of times. The first step was to place a small chunk of heroin—usually sold in pasty blocks resembling brown sugar—in a teaspoon or square of aluminum foil. A little water was added, then a match or lighter was held underneath, cooking the dope into a clear, bubbling liquid and releasing "the scent of burning earth and metal," as Jerry Stahl, a former TV writer, described it in *Permanent Midnight,* a memoir of his own heroin addiction. A rubber hose, necktie, belt, or shirtsleeve was bound around the upper arm to make the veins on the forearm pop out. With the other arm, the user grabbed a syringe, squeezed the little rubber ball at the end—syringes with sliding valves came later—and sucked up the melted heroin. The needle was plunged into a vein, the ball squeezed again. Then came a warm, euphoric glow as the dope passed through the heart and spread to every corner of the body. "You don't exactly hallucinate on smack," Stahl explained. "But you do see, when the first, fast rush courses north to glory, the smiles of all the unseen beings in the world nodding in the shadows. All the benevolence hidden in the universe makes itself known. The spirits reveal themselves, because they know, when the rushing stops, and the gush wears off, you'll forget all about them. You'll see the world then in a different way: as an awful, hateful place, where every breeze that blows is like the hateful breath of Moloch on your flesh."

Freeman began four frightful years of dependency. "When you get really strung out, it's a twenty-four-hour-a-day job," he said. "You don't worry about anything except scoring. That's your life." He recalled working in a quartet with Art Pepper at Facks, a San Francisco club, around 1950. Jazz audiences in those days were used to seeing musicians scratching themselves and nodding off, two tics of the heroin user. But Pepper's group took junkiedom to another level. "Three of us were so strung out, it was ridiculous," Freeman said. "We were on the bandstand falling asleep against our instruments. When you're in that state, your playing is nothing, because you don't care."

Freeman perfected "jacking off," the junkie equivalent of masturbation. It involved pinching the rubber ball repeatedly with the needle in the vein, sending a mixture of heroin and blood in and out. "Every time you do that, you get a huge jolt," he said. "Whoooo! It's as close to sex as it gets." Especially since, for most addicts, "smack" wiped out the libido, and sometimes the erectile capacity.

In time, Freeman started copping (buying dope) with money "borrowed" from his wife, Marion Raffaele, a former camera girl at the Famous Door, the West Fifty-second Street club where he had played intermission piano. The cost of his habit rose when he got hooked on "speedballs," a combination of heroin and cocaine that later became Baker's favorite high. The coke triggered an electric flash, while the heroin made things mellow. Speedballs, said Freeman, are "so addictive, it's just nuts. You can do it every half hour. I used to sit at this little dressing table in my bedroom with all this paraphernalia laid out. People would be coming in and we'd be talking. I'd be sitting there fixing, cleaning everything, sticking the little wire in there to get the blood out of the syringe so it didn't clog. Crazy, totally crazy." Inevitably, he OD'd: "I remember sitting in a chair, and I could feel my breathing starting to stop. I panicked. I got my wife and said, 'Stay here, keep me awake, shake me, do something.' I was that close to going under."

After about three years, Freeman knew he was headed to the grave or at least to jail, like so many of his friends. He kept trying to quit and failing as heroin demolished the remains of his self-discipline: "One time, with nothing better to do, I sat and counted ten or twelve different symptoms that my body was going through at the same time—yawning, stretching, sweating, eyes running, depression, couldn't sleep at all, just lay there. I felt like I wanted someone to pull my legs all the time. Once I went two weeks without having a bowel movement. It turns your insides to cement. The worst part of withdrawal lasts about five days, then you have another couple of days that are not too good. You're left like a rag doll."

In 1952, he finally found the strength to quit for good. His vices from then on were pot and cigarettes, and music resumed its central role in his life. Hearing Baker at a jam session, Freeman was so "captivated" that he knew he had to get close to him. His marriage had split up in early 1952, so he and the Bakers pooled their funds to rent an old two-bedroom house on Hollyridge Drive, high in the secluded Hollywood Hills. The foundation had sagged with age, leaving the floors so tilted that when Baker tossed a ball to his collie, Honey, it rolled back across the floor by itself. The three youths set up a West Coast version of Bohemia, with few books, clothes, or other possessions. "We were only interested in playing music and smoking a lot of pot—I mean, constantly," said Freeman. He spent hours at his upright piano; Charlaine halfheartedly took on the role of housewife. Baker wandered around in an undershirt and jeans, sprawling on the living-room floor to play with Honey or lying on his bed smoking pot and staring at the ceiling.

The household revolved around his whims. "He was like a spoiled little boy," Freeman explained. "You accepted him for that, or you didn't accept him. He didn't talk a lot, so when he said something, people had a tendency to listen. It isn't that the things he said were ever very profound; they certainly weren't. When he would say, 'Let's go to the beach now,' everybody said, 'Hey, great idea! Let's go to the beach!' " As for practicing his horn, why should he, he felt, when he was in full command of the instrument as soon as he walked onstage? "I practice, I play every night," he later said.

At the moment he needed work but avoided asking for it; that wouldn't have sounded cool. "Chet would never hustle for anything," said Charlie Davidson, the Boston clothier who soon became his longtime pal. "It was against that code of his. If a club owner said, 'I like the way you play, come on back,' fine. He was not one to help himself."

Bock was anxious to record him as a bandleader before Mulligan got out of jail. With three hundred dollars borrowed from Roy Harte, Bock scheduled the first recording dates of the still-unformed Chet Baker Quartet. Baker left the legwork to Freeman, who picked the tunes, arranged them, then called Baker to the living-room piano to teach them to him. Freeman chose a combination of elegant standards (Rodgers and Hart's "Isn't It Romantic?"; Harold Arlen and Johnny Mercer's "This Time the Dream's on Me"; "The Lamp Is Low," based on a theme by Ravel) and his own catchy originals, with cute titles like "Russ Job" and "Happy Little Sunbeam." Baker could read the melody lines from the sheet music but not the chords, which he learned by ear after Freeman had played the songs once or twice. "If it was a song he hadn't played before, he would say, 'What note does it start on?' " recalled the pianist. "I would say, 'Let's do this on the intro, then you play the melody, play a couple of choruses, I'll play a couple of choruses, we'll do something with the bass and drums, then we'll take it out, let's do this with the ending.' He'd say, 'OK.' "

That July at the Gold Star Studios, the dates proceeded haphazardly. Throughout four sessions the group changed bassists (first Red Mitchell, then Bob Whitlock) and drummers (from Bobby White to Larry Bunker). The first session yielded only one usable track, "Isn't It Romantic?" Decades later, neither Freeman nor Bunker remembered what had slowed things down, but according to Dick Bock, Baker had spoiled so many takes through nerves or inexperience that Bock had to splice his solos together from bits and pieces.

When the British journalist Brian Case asked Baker about this in 1979, the trumpeter launched into a tirade against the producer who had launched his solo career: "He's full of shit. I never had any solos spliced. The only credit that man deserves is that he was able to borrow three hundred dollars from Roy Harte, who had a drum shop there in Hollywood, to rent the studios and pay the union wages for the record date. He knows nothing about music whatsoever in any way." But in the nineties, when record producer Michael Cuscuna unearthed the Pacific Jazz master tapes for reissue, he found them riddled with splices.

Bock was certainly known for making bumbling use of the splicing block in order to achieve his own conception of the perfect take. "Sometimes he left out beats, or you could hear the edit on the record," said Russ Freeman. "I did some splicing myself on Chet's solos. My rationale was, recording is very difficult. Go into a studio, and somebody points a finger at you and says, 'OK, make magic.' "

Yet magic is what a lot of people heard in those early singles, which emerged as polished little packages of California cool. The time restriction of the 78-rpm—three minutes and twenty seconds—left no room for long-winded arrangements. Baker offers brisk opening and closing choruses, between which Freeman solos in his punchy, energetic way; often they trade some fours or eights. The trumpeter plays with a confident swagger yet stays in the middle range, never showing off with high notes, screeches, or other displays of musicianly ego. His tone is always lovely, each note a model of poise and restraint. "To me," said Art Farmer, "what was impressive is that he had a way of playing that seemed effortless, without any pressure or strain. That's not what the trumpet is about. You're supposed to play like you're calling the troops."

Unlike the beboppers, Baker started with the melody, then improvised with a lyricism unsurpassed even by Miles Davis, whose technical prowess took him down more complicated paths. "Miles knew everything about polytonality, so he could play notes against chords and make them work," said Freeman. "Chet could not do that. He heard music very melodically, very linearly, because he didn't know any chords." The only thing those gracefully crafted solos lack is a hint of vulnerability. Passionate ballads like "Long Ago and Far Away" become light up-tunes, while the wistful "Imagination" is stripped of feeling. "What Chet did was different from Miles in that way—it was smoother, prettier," said Jack Sheldon. "Miles was pretty too, but it was kind of dark. Chettie played like an angel."

Down Beat was delighted with the records, and gave five stars to one of them, *Maid in Mexico,* praising the "charming theme, wonderful beat throughout, and Chet's great time and ideas on his horn." On August 12, the quartet made its earliest known live appearance in a concert at L.A.'s Carlton Theater. But not everybody trusted Baker to stand on his own. With Mulligan still in jail, John Bennett had paired Baker with Stan Getz, another baby-faced wunderkind whose feathery, cascading solos, even more detached than Baker's, had made him a fellow prince of West Coast cool. Getz had won the 1952 tenor polls in *Down Beat* and *Metronome* by a landslide, while Baker still ranked low in the trumpet categories. The two addressed each other politely enough, but they loathed each other almost on sight, as their live duo recordings suggest: the counterpoint sounds like a traffic jam, with each man racing toward his next solo. At the Haig, Getz glared out with a sneer while Baker, typically, looked at the floor.

Some of the friction involved drugs. Despite his own experiments with heroin, Baker could still show a moralistic disdain for addicts, and he considered Getz a slob of a junkie. The saxophonist had visited Baker and Freeman on Hollyridge Drive, and after bragging to the scuffling roommates about all the money he was making, Getz went to the bathroom and OD'd, as he would on several occasions. Baker and the pianist had to dump him in the bathtub and hold him under cold water to revive him.

In another story Baker liked telling, Getz came to a party thrown by the trumpeter at his subsequent home a year or so later. The sax player closed himself in the bathroom for almost an hour. Finally Baker and a friend forced the door open. There lay Getz in the corner, bright blue and not breathing, with a needle hanging out of his arm. They worked on him for over a half-hour, pressing cold rags to his neck and using artificial respiration. Finally Getz made a choking sound. Opening his eyes, he muttered angrily: "You guys messed up my high!"

In October 1953, when he opened a monthlong run with Getz at the Black Hawk, Baker's own attraction to the drug seemed to be growing. To save money, he and Getz roomed together—an episode with disturbing results, according to Bill Loughborough. "Stan was always trying to get him to shoot up heroin," he said. "Chet chippied some with him at that time. I always thought Stan was the main instrument in changing him from a viper to a junkie."

The Black Hawk gig fell apart in two weeks, destroyed mainly by jealousy. Bock had gathered eight Baker singles in the ten-inch album *The Chet Baker Quartet,* and *Down Beat* gave it a five-star rave: "Our suspicions that the 23-year-old trumpet man from Yale, Okla., was a major star are confirmed by this LP, which is a gasser from start to finish. The lad had the style, the sound, the command of the horn. . . . To the names of Dizzy, Miles, Joe Newman, Shorty Rogers and Clark Terry must now be added an extra finger on the hand: Chet Baker has arrived."

Baker became the star of that engagement, and as Carson Smith reported, "Stan couldn't bear having the spotlight taken away from him." At the close of the first week, Getz flew back to Los Angeles, then phoned the club's owner, Guido Caccianti, claiming he had caught a virus. Baker stayed on until a few nights later, when he showed up late for work and found the band playing without him. He stormed off and sat in the corner, refusing to play. Finally Caccianti—"a little annoyed at modern music's problem children," as *Down Beat* said—fired the whole group.

Back in L.A., Baker continued his rise. In November, he reunited with Charlie Parker and the Dave Brubeck Quartet for a ten-day all-star package tour, mostly of colleges in California and Canada. The students got their first glimpse of Baker and one of their last of Bird, whose drinking and drug use were ruining his health. Jimmy Rowles, the pianist on that tour, recalled the tension backstage: after stepping off the bus in each town, Parker vanished, leaving everyone to worry until the last minute if he would show up for the second half, when he made his entrance. He always made it, playing so well that people were thrilled to see that the great Bird, age thirty-three, still "had it." At the end of the show, Baker joined him onstage, and Parker's pride in his "discovery" was clear.

Talking with Bernie Fleischer, though, Baker showed a surprisingly cocky attitude toward his mentor. It passed quickly, but Fleischer never forgot it. "He once said that Bird couldn't blow his nose, he was just an old junkie," the clarinetist recalled. "He talked about what an old fart he was. And Bird thought Chet was the greatest." Later Baker told *Melody Maker:* "Naturally I liked the opportunity to work with Parker. Of course, he hasn't changed at all in his playing really for ten years. Also, he is on this 'worship' kick like Gerry Mulligan. This must affect a guy's playing."

While Baker was making tactless comments about his past employers, Dick Bock scrambled to record as much Baker product as possible before

Mulligan came home from jail. The album *Chet Baker Ensemble* presented Baker as the star of a septet that played the music of Jack Montrose, a composer-arranger in the Mulligan mold whose group played Monday nights at the Haig. With its intricate themes and four-horn counterpoint, the album had the feel of a diligently assembled puzzle. *Down Beat* called it "cool, clever, and bloodless."

Yet in "Goodbye," a gloomy ballad by the forties composer-conductor Gordon Jenkins, Montrose simply let Baker play, and out came a poetic construction of spare, aching lines and weighty silences, mournful as the version of taps he had offered for the returning dead at the Presidio. "Goodbye" caught the sound that made him famous—a tone as smooth and clear as glass, with a glimmer of pain and mystery flickering below the surface, sealed off from closer scrutiny.

But Baker wasn't at all mysterious when it came to getting what he wanted, especially from Bock. He had the producer "by the balls," as Carson Smith said, for it was no secret that Bock was hanging his dream—a hit label—on Baker's success. The trumpeter could certainly see that more and more people wanted a piece of him, and that he could get plenty in return. For now, though, his requests of Bock were fairly modest. Standing in front of the producer's desk once or twice a week, he would announce in his pubescent-sounding Oklahoma drawl: "Hey, man, I've been thinking . . ." Then he would ask for an "advance" of twenty-five or fifty dollars—no small sum for Bock at the time—pleading a busted transmission or a sick mother. The funds went toward buying pot, fixing up his car, or simply paying the bills.

He made a much larger demand when he insisted that Bock produce an expensive album with strings for him, just like the one Charlie Parker had made a few years earlier on the Mercury label. Since that landmark release—which yielded "Just Friends," the closest Parker ever had to a hit single—the phrase "with strings" had a sacred ring for jazzmen. It meant that a record company considered them worthy of a big investment, one that might bring them a wide audience and maybe put an end to their struggles. In those early days of the LP, "mood music" albums of gooey orchestral sounds ("for dining" or "for relaxation") sold in the millions—musical wallpaper for the happy fifties home. And that's how most jazz-with-strings albums sounded. As George Avakian, who headed the jazz department at Columbia Records, recalled: "So many musicians told me proudly, 'I'm gonna do an album with strings.' Then it would be lousy."

Bock couldn't afford single-handedly to grant Baker's wish, so he struck up a coproduction deal with Columbia, whose jazz catalogue was normally reserved for the likes of Duke Ellington, Louis Armstrong, and pianist Erroll Garner, a huge favorite. "Gerry was the one I really wanted," said Avakian. "People talk about what a big star Chet was in those days, but I'd say that eight thousand records over a couple of years would have been a big seller for him then." Nonetheless, the deal gave Bock enough of a budget to hire several arrangers—Shorty Rogers, Johnny Mandel, Marty Paich, Jack Montrose—who aimed for a pop audience by honey-coating such old favorites as "What a Diff'rence a Day Made" and "I'm Through with Love." Russ Freeman and the "cool" saxophonist Zoot Sims played cautious solos.

Aside from a new ballad by Freeman, "The Wind," to which Baker brought the eeriness of "My Funny Valentine," the charts gave him little room to do anything but stick to the tune. "I find strings very inhibiting, you know," he later told DJ Paul Fisher. "It's hard to really stretch out and get into any really complicated kind of playing when you've got the strings going on behind you." Mandel recalled the album with embarrassment: "You could hear something like this anytime in the supermarket or the elevator."

But many trumpeters, including Herb Alpert, considered *Chet Baker with Strings* a beautiful album. Zuza Homem de Mello, an important Brazilian music producer, broadcaster, and historian, heard it at the time in São Paulo. "I was astonished!" he said. "I thought, 'Is that really a trumpet? I think it's a saxophone. I've never heard that sound before!' My conception of trumpet had to have vibrato like Louis Armstrong or Harry James. Because Chet played mostly in the low notes, he sounded closer to Lester Young than Louis Armstrong. I listened to the whole record, and it was like no sound I had ever heard in my life. It was like a door opening."

On the day of the first session, *Down Beat* had published the winners of its 1953 Readers' Poll. Baker was named number-one trumpeter over Armstrong, Davis, and Gillespie. On February 1, 1954, while headlining at the Haig, he was profiled in *Time.* Unlike the super-articulate Mulligan, Baker came across as a barely literate hipster, brainless but magically gifted. His goal in jazz, he explained, was "to get away from the obvious. We try to play different things that fit together. . . . When I'm up there blowing some new conceptions and I see the audience likes it, it's a gas."

Feeling more like a star than ever, Baker knew he no longer needed Gerry Mulligan. On a stroll through Hollywood in the winter of 1954, he ran into his former boss, accompanied by Arlyne Brown. Now heroin-free, Mulligan had been released after serving half of his six-month sentence. Yet he was as angry as any ex-con as he faced the "protégé" who had deserted him to find greater glory alone. More than Baker, Mulligan blamed Dick Bock. "Dick defended himself by saying that Chet and Russ insisted he record them," Mulligan said. But as Bock told writer Will Thornebury: "It was apparent that Chet was going to have his own thing. He wanted it, and if I hadn't recorded it he would have gone someplace else."

There on the street in Hollywood, the Gerry Mulligan Quartet with Chet Baker came to its official end—due not to Mulligan's resentment but to Baker's request for a raise from his $125-a-week salary. In 1995, Mulligan gave his version of the "reunion": "Instead of two musicians throwing their arms around each other and saying, 'Oh, man, I'm glad to see you, pal,' forget it, man! Before he says hello or Merry Christmas or anything, he says, 'Listen, I've been thinking about it, and I gotta have more money.' He asked me for three or four hundred dollars. Well, considering that we were getting twelve hundred a week, out of which I had to pay commissions, a couple of other musicians, expenses, hotels, transportation, taxes, I don't know where the hell he thought the money was coming from. I just laughed. It was like a scene out of a bad movie."

Hotels and transportation weren't an issue at the Haig, and if the band had toured, Arlyne would have likely asked for more money. But naturally, she saw Mulligan as the injured party. "I think there had been more love between Chet and Gerry, possibly, than in any affair Gerry had with a female!" she said. "All of us, including me—and I think I was the most serious of the lot of Gerry's women—were incidental. Music was the real love. I think that's why Gerry was so hurt."

Baker went on to denounce Mulligan as a tightwad. "Gerry's so pissed off because I've been able to make it on my own, without him," he told writer Jerome Reece in 1983. "He can't hack that. I was supposed to be his trumpet player for life, I guess. And at ridiculous wages. . . . He wouldn't give me a raise, and I'd just been voted the best trumpet player in the world."

Soon after their confrontation, Columbia released *Chet Baker with Strings. Down Beat* dismissed it as "largely soporific," adding: "Mr. Baker, as Dorothy Parker once said of the young Katharine Hepburn, runs the gamut of emotions from A to B." But William Claxton's cover photo was so dreamy that record shops all over the country put the LP on display. Claxton showed Baker at his peak of beauty, staring out wistfully at the session, cheek resting against his horn's mouthpiece. George Avakian, who wasn't expecting much of a hit, was surprised to see about thirty-five or forty thousand copies sold over the next year. That made *Chet Baker with Strings* the biggest recorded success Baker had in his lifetime. Many of the buyers were young women with little interest in jazz, who bought the LP for its cover. They were surprised to hear music as pretty as Baker was.

By now, William Claxton's pictures had made him the poster boy for West Coast Jazz. They typified Claxton's fashion-influenced work: a body of impeccably composed, beautiful images of Southern California as a Shangri-La of warm ocean breezes and life without care. For one of his more famous shots, he placed six of the Lighthouse All-Stars on the beach with their instruments, then drew the group's name in big letters across the sand. Claxton showed Zoot Sims, Jack Sheldon, and Baker in white T-shirts, looking like wholesome college athletes. Nearly everyone he photographed appeared happy and cool, as if the creative act were the most effortless thing in the world. Such pictures seemed a world away from the New York scene, where Francis Wolff, the photographer for Blue Note Records, caught intense glimpses of jazzmen in smoky basements, struggle etched on their sweaty faces.

But in L.A., a town preoccupied with healthy living—even pot was thought of as "the natural high," said Joyce Tucker—Claxton withheld any shots that didn't show his subjects looking fit and attractive. "There was a lot of health consciousness going on out here," he explained. "People were going to health-food stores and exercising. The young guys who were writing music in a so-called West Coast mold were out of universities; they were more sophisticated musically and didn't want to be strung out." Many were, of course, as Claxton knew. Yet even though Baker was numbing his senses mainly with pot, the photos show a young man feeling nothing. "Everything's perfect, the jawline, the hair," said Mark Murphy. "Then you see the eyes, and they're cold and dead."

All the same, it was his looks, more than his music, that the Hollywood crowd cared about. "Editors of magazines, all these other people jumped on the bandwagon and wanted to shoot him," said Claxton. "They thought, wow—here's a hot new guy."

By now Mulligan had said a bitter goodbye to California. "I was thoroughly pissed off with Los Angeles and Los Angeles musicians," he said. He recalled phoning his trombonist friend Bob Brookmeyer in Manhattan and saying, "Bring me a couple of guys from New York. Let's finish the gigs I've got lined up and get the hell out of here."

In the nineties, Ruth Young reflected on Baker's charmed road to success. "People gave him his identity," she said. "The mystique was born out of other people telling him what to do. Chet wasn't that person. Chet was Chet. But nobody challenged that he was any different from his aura or his outward appearance. Nobody asked."

They were so anxious for him to become a star that he had little choice in the matter. "Everybody was talking about Chet Baker," said Carson Smith. "But Chet was still hesitant. He didn't want to have to deal with people, and certainly not with finances." Eager to capitalize on his investment, Dick Bock set Baker up with Joe Glaser, president of Associated Booking Corporation, one of the most powerful jazz booking firms in the country, with offices in Chicago, New York, and Hollywood. A short, homely ex-gangster from Chicago, Glaser had turned his tough-guy wheeling and dealing in the twenties to the task of managing Louis Armstrong, then an underpaid musician who suffered the same racist mistreatment as any black performer. Glaser took Armstrong to the zenith of pop stardom, earning them both a heap of money in the process. From there he built a staggering client list, including Duke Ellington, Billie Holiday, Lionel Hampton, and Anita O'Day, whom he informed with typical crudeness: "Anita, you've got a million dollars' worth of talent and no class."

Glaser set up Baker's first national tour, to start in Detroit on March 3, 1954. Meanwhile, the trumpeter continued at the Haig, the Tiffany, and other L.A. clubs. Anyone could see what a hot property he was, as girls flocked around to ogle the dreamboat they had seen in Claxton's pictures. Baker took such advantage that many people didn't even know he was married. "He always had a different girl with him," said Dot Woodward. Russ Freeman remembered how offhandedly he treated them: "It was almost like: you want me, come and get me. I don't remember seeing him pursue anybody—they always pursued him."

Claxton recalled driving home from a San Diego concert with Baker and a lovestruck groupie named Cindy. On the way they stopped at a motel room to eat hamburgers and smoke pot. Baker was less concerned with Cindy than with the safety of his car, which he kept eyeing through the open door. "Tell me something, Chet, what are the most important things in the world to you?" asked Claxton. "Oh, I don't know for sure, Clax," he said. "I guess my horn, and my new caddy—and—well, of course, my music. I guess that's about it." Cindy was enraged. "Well, thanks a lot, *Mister* Baker!" she hissed. She stormed out, punching the car bumper with her fist. "Chet looked at me and shook his head and smiled," said Claxton. "Then he shouted out into the parking area, 'I forgot to mention my dog!' "

Only one woman kept an iron grip on Baker all his life: his mother. Baker knew that Vera, like Dick Bock, had pinned her dreams on him, and that he had disappointed her before; until he died, he regarded her with a dizzying mixture of resentment, dependency, and guilt. Starting in 1943, when she began teaching him her favorite love songs, Baker's sweet voice had meant more to her than his trumpet, and she badgered him to sing more. Her fetish wasn't shared by Baker's friends, notably Marion Raffaele, now the girlfriend of Bob Neel, whom she later married. Marion had heard Baker's adenoidal tenor on car trips. "It used to crack me up," she said. "He wished he could sing in tune."

In the winter of 1954, he called Bock and insisted on making an album of vocals. The producer hated the idea, thinking, no doubt, of Baker's amateurish singing job on two sides made the previous October. Crooning the ballads "I Fall in Love Too Easily" and "The Thrill Is Gone," he displayed wobbly pitch, hillbilly vowels ("thuh" for "the," "wull" for "well"), and a habit of taking breaths in the middle of words. He sounded like a painfully sensitive farmboy, and therein lay the charm of his singing. "People really loved it or they hated it," said Baker.

The year before, Claxton heard him sing at Falcon Lair, the Beverly Hills estate of tobacco heiress Doris Duke. Built in the twenties by Rudolph Valentino, the hilltop house was later bought by Duke to share with her lover Joe Castro, a boyish Mexican-American jazz pianist who led a trio at Hollywood's Mocambo nightclub. Duke had built him a plush music room with two Steinway grand pianos, and the gifted Castro used it to hold candlelit midnight jam sessions.

One night Baker put down his horn to sing with June Christy, the petite blonde jazz singer who had left the Stan Kenton orchestra to go solo. Christy had just recorded the song that became her trademark: "Something Cool," the dark monologue of a woman at a bar, telling a stranger glamorized tales from her past. "Something Cool" echoed the delusion and self-aggrandizement of Hollywood, where such scenes were played out nightly on the Sunset Strip. Christy's record anointed her one of the queens of the "Cool School" of fifties jazz singing. But there was nothing "cool" about Christy, who suffered from agonizing stage fright and insecurity over a voice that many critics attacked as strained and flat. Eventually she drank away her career and her health.

In 1953, though, she seemed like a springtime breeze, with her pigtail and bangs. As Baker pecked out chords on the piano, he and Christy crooned the Cole Porter ballad "Ev'ry Time We Say Goodbye." Christy's husband, saxophonist Bob Cooper, noodled in the background. To Claxton, Baker and Christy "sounded like two angels singing," and he recalled the stillness that fell over the room. He, Christy, and other guests urged Baker to sing on his next album.

In February 1954, the trumpeter made the ten-inch LP *Chet Baker Sings* in Hollywood. Russ Freeman picked a repertoire full of worldly songs of despair, including the Gershwins' "But Not for Me," Hoagy Carmichael's "I Get Along Without You Very Well," and Baker's first vocal version of "My Funny Valentine." Bock listened in alarm as he struggled to sing on key, pushing the session into overtime. "He must have had a hundred takes on every tune," said Dot Woodward. "He'd get through part of the tune, then he'd have to go back and do it again."

Baker's dogged persistence didn't impress the musicians, who were reduced to near-invisible accompanists, tiptoeing behind his fragile efforts. "I thought it was bullshit," said Freeman. "Louis Armstrong and Jack Teagarden sang like jazz singers. This was ballads. Totally meaningless." Carson Smith walked away thinking, "Why is he doing this?"

Claxton, whom Bock had hired as art director and chief photographer for Pacific Jazz, took a cover picture that showed Baker looking like a jazz angel. There he stood in his white undershirt at the microphone, mouth open in song, the photo so grainy he seemed about to dissolve in the air. His singing had the same wispy quality. Later he learned to improvise as confidently with his voice as he did with his horn, but in the fifties he clung timidly to almost written note. His fragile tone implied deep sensitivity, yet as he murmured tales of shattered romance—*"They're writing songs of love, but not for me"*. . . *"I fall in love too terribly hard for love to ever last"*. . . *"The nights are cold, for love is old"*—his delivery was emotionless. "None of these songs had any meaning for him, truly," said Ruth Young. "He could have been singing Charmin commercials. He was coming from a musical place, and the words were mere notes to him."

But as people stared at the cover and listened to Baker's blank slate of a voice, they projected all kinds of fantasies onto him. They imagined a wounded child in need of mothering, a seductive devil luring them into trouble, a dark prophet of doom, or the ultimate soulful male. Baker could sound as intimate as if he were whispering in someone's ear, or so distant that he might as well have not been there at all.

Gerry Mulligan brushed off the mystique of Baker's voice: "That's just the way he sang; he didn't know any other way to sing." Yet Liliane Cukier saw that sound go "to the hearts of the girls in a very seducing way." It had the same effect on a hip cult of gay men, who connected Baker's winsome looks with the sexual ambiguity of his sound and drew their own conclusions. With *Chet Baker Sings,* Baker became the first jazz musician to attract a strong homosexual following. "All the gay boys who were into jazz at all were into him," said Cherry Vanilla, who assisted Bruce Weber in the making of *Let's Get Lost.*

Baker emerged in a deeply homophobic age, with sexual roles rigidly defined and no deviance allowed. His pop-music colleagues were paragons of manhood: Frank Sinatra, with his finger-snapping machismo; the rugged western-style belter Frankie Laine of "Mule Train" fame; the Four Lads, a group of clean-cut guys-next-door who scored a big hit with a Frank Loesser show tune, "Standing on the Corner [Watching All the Girls Go By]." In jazz, where macho stereotypes were even more extreme, singing musicians were typified by crooner-bandleader Billy Eckstine, whose booming bass-baritone sounded like a cartoon of virility; or Louis Armstrong, who hid his vulnerabilities behind a comically bearish growl.

Then came Baker, whose androgynously sweet tenor, light as the breeze, made many jazzmen squirm. Hearing one of Baker's early records, pianist Richie Beirach, who played for him in the seventies, snarled in disgust: "He sounds like a *girl*!" Critics began calling him "fey" and "effete." He told reporter Richard Williams in 1973: "There was a very mixed reaction when I started singing. In the first place, a lot of people thought—foolishly so—that because of the way I sang I, y'know, *liked fellars* or something. I can only say that that's a lot of bullshit." Cool as he tried to act, Baker overcompensated in his haste to show how manly he was. He always flaunted his latest "chick" and new set of wheels; the word "faggot" was in his vocabulary.

It wasn't his sexuality that concerned Marion Raffaele; she simply found *Chet Baker Sings* painful to hear. "We loved him," she said, "but I used to cringe when they played it on the radio." Mimi Clar would later savage his "abysmal vocal deficiencies" in *Metronome:*

> Criticizing Baker's "singing" is as unfair a game as commenting on a four-month-old baby's lack of coordination because he can't walk. How can one speak critically of an anemic voice which sounds like a boiled owl trying for out-of-reach high notes . . . and which doesn't come within an ice-age mastodon's tusk of most of the notes aimed for? . . . Any musician giving a performance on an instrument equivalent to Baker's vocal daubs would not remain two minutes on the stand, let alone be allowed to record.

In fact, out-of-town clubs were clamoring for him. As their tour drew near, Freeman realized that Baker hadn't a clue as to how to manage a band, or any intention of learning. The pianist appealed to Phil Turetsky, who taught him the basics of on-the-road finance: setting up a bank account for the musicians, withholding taxes from their paychecks, keeping a weekly accounting log. "Otherwise none of it would have happened," said Freeman. "Chet wanted to play, but he wouldn't put himself out to do anything else. Consequently I was stuck with it. I did everything but sweep the floors."

Larry Bunker had declined the tour, preferring to stay in L.A. and work in the comfort of the studios. He was sick of "pussyfooting around" on drums the way Mulligan had demanded, and that Baker wanted too: "I kept thinking: I wanna play like the guys in New York are playing. I wanna bash! Not play all those carefully crafted arrangements. But that was the work, so that's what I did."

As a replacement Baker called upon Bob Neel, who planned to take Marion along. Carson Smith would travel with his new wife, Joan, Baker with Charlaine; only Russ Freeman, for the moment, was single. Freeman broke the lease on the Hollyridge Drive house, using the tilted foundation as an excuse. In the last days of February, he, Baker, and Charlaine packed up their minimal possessions, leaving some behind, and prepared to lead the nomadic lives of traveling musicians. From that point on, said Freeman, "we were homeless people."

5

On the morning of March 1, 1954, Russ Freeman, the Smiths, Bob Neel, and Marion Raffaele piled into Marion's Pontiac and prepared to tour America. Conspicuously absent was their leader, who had already left town to play a gig without them. His friends made their own exit from a balmy Hollywood, instruments and other possessions crammed into a little trailer hooked to the car. The women tingled in anticipation of seeing the landscape unfold; the men couldn't wait to spend every night blowing jazz in cellars and back rooms. "What could be better than being on the road?" asked Neel.

With Freeman at the wheel, they headed for River Rouge, a suburb of Detroit, to play the Rouge Lounge, a combination jazz club and bowling alley. An hour into their trip, the Pontiac's cheap retreads started to fall apart, and the group had to turn back and replace them. Racing above the speed limit to make up for lost time, Freeman was slapped with a ticket by a California patrolman. The trip resumed smoothly until they reached Oklahoma, where they drove through a sandstorm so violent that red dust pelted them through the dashboard. Fifteen miles from Detroit, the car ground to a halt in a blizzard, and they were forced to hole up in a roadside motel for the night. The next morning the men dug out the car, and finally they hit River Rouge, tired and disillusioned.

They were joined that afternoon by Baker, who strolled into the Rouge Lounge, cool as ever, with Charlaine at his side. The club, said Freeman, was "a funky little place with a bad spinet piano. Just because Chet was a poll winner, it didn't mean we didn't play some real toilets." But once they eased into their first set, the music—along with the grass they smoked before each show—made their spirits soar. They knew they were living out their dream, and for the next nine months, no distance was too far, no annoyance too great, if it got them back onstage. "I thought this was an ideal existence," said Neel. "Sure, it's not as glamorous as it seems—cheap hotels, bad food, and everything. But all we cared about were those four hours on the stand."

Decades later, in her essay "Beat Culture: America Revisited," Lisa Phillips wrote of what an exhilarating high the road held for the blossoming fifties counterculture: "This was a generation searching for some kind of ecstasy, some marvelous vision of God—and drugs, jazz, and relentless mobility were all ways to get there." Russ Freeman made it more than once in 1954. "I'm not a religious person at all," he said, "but a few times I actually had an out-of-body experience while playing. I was next to or behind myself, watching myself play, totally oblivious to everything around me. And I knew at those moments that the magic was happening."

That December, Baker would report proudly to *Tonight* show host Steve Allen that he had driven twenty thousand miles since March, zigzagging from Boston (Storyville) to Philadelphia (the Blue Note) to Chicago (the Streamliner) to New York (Birdland) to St. Louis (the Glass Bar) to Toronto (the Colonial Tavern) to San Jose (San Jose State College) to Providence (the Celebrity Club) to Washington, D.C. (Olivia's Patio Lounge) to Baltimore (the Comedy Club).

For audiences everywhere, Baker's quartet *was* California. People saw four tanned, fresh-scrubbed young men in no hurry, breezing through tunes like "Happy Little Sunbeam" and "Lullaby of the Leaves." Every sound was pleasing: not a honk or squeal marred the pearly tone of Baker's horn, while Neel's drumming evoked a graceful soft shoe. "I was like the slave," he said. "Chettie wanted somebody that would just keep time and stay out of his way, and that's what I did." Baker and Freeman bounced phrases between them as casually as two beach boys playing kickball on the sand. The trumpeter stayed poised even while sprinting through "Winter Wonderland," in which he fired off sixteenth-note runs without effort. "I would sit there listening to him play," said Freeman, "and I'd think, where did that come from? You mean I have to play a solo after *that*?"

With the blessing of such a powerful tool of the establishment as *Time,* Baker got exposure most jazzmen only dreamed about. Millions saw him on TV's *Today* and *Tonight* shows, while student trumpeters memorized his every note from a book of transcribed solos, *The Trumpet Artistry of Chet Baker.* Everywhere he went, officials welcomed him like visiting royalty. "They gave him the keys to their little cities and took him to dinners they

Today show studios, New York City, 1954. Photo by Carole Reiff; © Carole Reiff Photo Archive

wanted him to attend," said Marion. John McClellan, host of a series of broadcasts from Boston's Storyville club, introduced Baker as reverently as if Arthur Fiedler had raised his baton in front of the Boston Pops. "This young man's rise to popularity has been little short of phenomenal," confided McClellan in a hushed voice. Baker took the mike and drawled in the flat, nasal tones of a grade-school violinist at a school recital: "For our next tune, we'd like to play . . ."

If he never approached the superstardom of Louis Armstrong, Baker at least had the makings of an upstanding fifties role model. A middle-American farmboy, he had served his country in the army twice, then flown to fame on the wings of his trumpet, whose sound was purity itself. Surely he was nothing like the burnout Kirk Douglas had played in *Young Man with a Horn,* the 1950 film about an alcoholic, abusive trumpeter who ruins the domestic dreams of his wife, played by Doris Day. Nor was he a kooky hipster like Dizzy Gillespie, who danced around the stage in his beret. Baker still avoided cigarettes, drank tall glasses of milk, and dressed neatly in a suit onstage. His name suggested a college football jock at a time when many jazzmen were called "Buck and Lockjaw and Peanuts and Dizzy," as screenwriter Lawrence Trimble noted in *Let's Get Lost.* "And here was this name Chet, which is kind of a soft sound. . . . The way he played, what he looked like, his name—it all went together."

A whitewashed version of his story appeared on school bulletin boards in the form of a comic-strip poster, "Successful Careers in Music," issued by the Martin Band Instrument Company of Indiana. It starts at the Baker family table, where Chesney Sr. and Jr. sit in dinner jackets; there, Father hands happy Chettie his first trumpet. Baker launches a high-school dance band, diligently composes at the piano, then enrolls in college, leaving early to join the army. Triumph comes when Charlie Parker and Gerry Mulligan make him a star. The tale ends with an image of Baker's head—a square-jawed, dimpled replica of the heroic youth shown on the Wheaties cereal box—floating before the issues of *Metronome* and *Down Beat* that had crowned him America's top trumpeter.

For now, most people accepted the cartoon as the truth. That spring, Baker and his companions stopped in suburban Nassau County, on New York's Long Island, to visit Joan Smith's family. The group's arrival thrilled Jim Coleman, Joan's thirteen-year-old cousin and a student trumpeter who worshipped Baker. But he couldn't figure out why all the guests kept going into the bathroom. "My mother thought someone had been burning rope in there," he recalled. "I went in and said, 'Yes, it smells like someone's been burning rope.' That's how naïve we were about drugs, even pot, in Nassau County in 1954."

Less gullible was Charlie Davidson, who owned the Andover Shop, an upscale men's haberdashery with stores in Cambridge and Andover, Massachusetts. Davidson's true love was jazz, and he prided himself on dressing Gerry Mulligan, Miles Davis, and the Modern Jazz Quartet. But none of them fascinated him more than Baker, and on opening night at Storyville, he studied the musician's ambiguous manner. "He had that beautiful face," said Davidson, "and what you wanted to interpret as that totally vulnerable side."

They met at intermission. "I said, 'Chet, I just want to tell you, I think you're great.' He said, 'Hey, thanks,' in that cool way of his. He asked me what I did, and when I answered, he said, 'Oh, yeah? I like clothes.' He didn't, really. He was trying to act cool, but deep down I think he was in stark terror. I think his luck had gone behind anything he could deal with. But I also knew this was a pretty dangerous little bastard. He was gonna have his way and that was it."

Every time Baker got his hands on a steering wheel, his bandmates saw how menacing he could be. Fixing a frozen stare on the road ahead, he slowly pushed down the gas pedal; soon the car was zooming along the highway so fast it threatened to take flight. "He looked possessed," said Carson Smith. "It was like he had to find some way to let the pressure out or he'd explode." The scenario would be much the same when he shot heroin. Speed and risk were like drugs to Baker; he also seemed to feed on his passengers' terror. But frightened as they were, his friends were amazed at how he wove through traffic and turned sharp corners as deftly as a racecar pro.

Still, there was always the chance of Baker meeting the fate that awaited James Dean, another wild but ultimately less lucky driver. Other brooding doomsday prophets of the fifties were flirting with self-destruction. Montgomery Clift was known to hang from the balcony of his hotel room in Florence, Italy, just to "challenge the edge, [to see] how close to danger he could come," said his friend and fellow actor, Kevin McCarthy, in a Clift documentary. Jack Kerouac announced his intention to drink himself to death, which he finally did in 1969, at the age of forty-seven. Like them all, Baker was abundantly gifted with looks, talent, and celebrity, yet he was ready to risk them all, as if the future meant nothing.

Few people dared think that way at the time. "If you didn't grow up then, you can't imagine how square America was in the fifties," said Stephen

Holden, a film and music critic for the *New York Times.* "Words like 'abortion' and 'gay' were almost never heard. Women were expected to stay in the kitchen. Everything was wrapped up in Christian values. If you voiced political opinions that were even slightly to the left, you could really get in trouble."

Still, as Howard Goodkind, a book publicist of that era, observed to David Halberstam: "You had the feeling that pressure was building up, something was gonna explode." The company he worked for, Julian Messner, published a monumental best-seller of the fifties: *Peyton Place,* housewife Grace Metalious's scandalous novel about covert sexual intrigue in a staid New England town. The poster for a 1953 film, *The Wild One,* showed a surly Marlon Brando in a leather jacket, riding a motorcycle—a warning that the nation's youth was about to run amok. And it did, as the first strains of rock and roll glorified the black culture Middle America feared.

Jazz had done the same thing for years, but since it was still considered a fringe music, it seemed to pose less of a threat. Then came Chet Baker, and a cult of restless youngsters had a new hero. In *Let's Get Lost,* Lawrence Trimble recalled how he and his friends were "just obsessed" with Baker, at a time when "antisocial role models" were hard to find. How, they wondered, could such idyllic music come out of a guy who was clearly up to no good?

Female admirers in bobby sox and penny loafers filled every club he played. They sighed collectively during "My Funny Valentine," when the princely trumpeter assured his plain-looking sweetheart: "You're my favorite work of art." It seemed so romantic, yet his faraway stare withheld darker secrets. What was he thinking about? Like Pandora's box, the mystery kept drawing people in. "Because of his natural reticence, people deemed him to be what they wanted," said Ruth Young. "It was only because he didn't resist that he confused everybody."

Baker hardly saw himself as a social symbol. "He was just a kid who wanted to go out and jam and drive a car," said Charlie Davidson. To Young, the spell he wove was deceptive: "I don't think Chet's music was for anybody but him. He got tipped off early on to the effect and ran with it."

The tip-off was unmistakable when girls lined up backstage with copies of *Chet Baker Sings* clutched to their powder-blue or pink sweaters. "Mr. Baker, I just love your music," they'd say, giggling and blushing. "Thanks," he would answer coolly, staring over their shoulders.

"Can I have your autograph?" "Sure." He'd sign their albums in neat schoolboy penmanship: "To Claire—thanks, Chet Baker," "Annette—all the best." Bassist Jimmy Bond, Carson Smith's successor in the band, recalled nights when twenty or thirty girls crowded around Baker: "Some of the women who chased after Chet were gorgeous, unbelievable. He would leave with three or four."

Baker's youthful womanizing made his friends wonder if he had any romance in him at all. None remained in his marriage to Charlaine, which had so deteriorated that they were using their only link—sex—as a weapon against each other. "It was a sordid relationship," said Bob Whitlock. Baker flaunted a parade of girls at clubs and record dates, calling them "baby." "After a while you didn't even ask, you just accepted who was there next," said Neel.

Charlaine retaliated by sleeping with several of his best friends. One day Jack Sheldon came to visit, and with Baker in another room, she lured Sheldon into the bedroom. "Chettie tried to get in, and we were in bed, naked," he said. "We didn't unlock the door. He didn't say or do anything, but it must have been very painful." Another time, Charlaine spotted Whitlock at a table in the Haig, and sat with him while Baker was onstage. Before the show ended, she and the bassist left together and checked into a hotel room in Malibu. "I knew she had made it with Art Pepper, so it wasn't like I was invading some sacred territory," said Whitlock.

When he brought her home at dawn, Baker merely glared, unable to vent his rage. "If looks could kill, I would have been dead," recalled Whitlock. "Cool" as they may have seemed, Baker and his friends were a bunch of children courting big trouble.

With the trumpeter at peak celebrity, Dick Bock recorded him at every opportunity—maybe too much. Baker made eight albums in his first year and a half as a leader. Little care or planning went into his career; it appeared as if he and Bock were just looking to cash in while they could. In some ways, the scheme backfired. Years after Baker had left Pacific Jazz, Dot Woodward estimated that Baker had sold well under ten thousand copies per title. That was a respectable figure by jazz standards, yet according to Columbia producer George Avakian, some Dave Brubeck albums sold seventy-five thousand or more; Erroll Garner's famous live album *Concerts by the Sea,* also on Columbia, soon reached the half-million mark. Pacific Jazz was an independent label, of course, and couldn't match Columbia's distribution. "But Chet spread himself too thin," said Avakian. "He didn't have that much of a basic appeal anyway. He was a special taste."

By late 1954, critics were already losing patience with Baker. Reviewing

Jazz at Ann Arbor, a live album made at the University of Michigan, a *Down Beat* reviewer said: "He lacks the ability to create deeply driving emotions, he doesn't flow or create memorable climaxes, and his sense of dynamics is very limited."

But to all appearances, Baker was getting the glory—and, one assumed, the money—that his finest young peers, particularly the black ones, were denied. In the industry, the most beloved was Clifford Brown, the bebop trumpeter who won *Down Beat*'s 1954 New Star award. A baby-faced black man one year Baker's junior, "Brownie," as he was called, thrilled musicians with his big, clarion tone and electric delivery. Writer Nat Hentoff proclaimed him a giant in 1954: "Brownie has really arrived; now let's hope he can get some steady gigs."

That was the rough part. Along with his bandmate, drummer Max Roach, Brown hit the road in his car, trying to become more than a struggling critical favorite. By 1956 he had recorded for Blue Note, Prestige, and EmArcy, three important jazz labels, but his slow ascent came to a halt on June 26. Driving to Chicago to join Roach on a club date, Brown sped over an embankment on the Pennsylvania Turnpike. He and his passengers—pianist Richie Powell (the brother of pianist Bud Powell) and Powell's wife—were killed.

Suddenly the road seemed no longer a symbol of America's boundless potential but a dead-end path where so many superior artists faced hopeless odds. To Max Roach, blacks had it the worst. "If conditions had been more just and equitable in this country, we wouldn't have been jumping all over the country in cars, trying to make a living," he told Barbara Gardner in *Down Beat.* "We would have been able to work and be paid according to our contributions." Brown, said Roach, "was aware of Chet Baker . . . and the recognition and the money he was making. . . . Brownie realized what was going on, and in his way, he resented it." Apparently, so did Roach. "I remember Max and Miles Davis coming into the Haig one time when we were playing there, and they were ice-cold," said Russ Freeman.

In fact, Baker was hardly getting rich; the quartet's salary averaged a thousand dollars a week, which had to feed, lodge, and transport seven people. But he was able to work five or six nights a week in the better jazz clubs while guesting occasionally on big TV shows and recording often. Some black musicians mockingly called him "The Great White Hope," the upstart who had clobbered Miles, Louis, Brownie, and Dizzy in the polls. At the time, whites were topping almost every category, a situation Art Farmer recalled sadly: "It seems like the music is not really accepted until a white person comes along and can do it. They called Benny Goodman the King of Swing—but a lot of other bands were swinging like hell before he did. Well, that's the world."

Baker took the brunt of the resentment, for he was seen as someone who, by virtue of his looks as well as his color, had never had to struggle for anything, and whose "cool" sounds reflected that ease. Nat Adderley, the cornetist who played often with his brother, saxophonist Julian "Cannonball" Adderley, attacked "that Chet Baker ballyhoo" in the British jazz magazine *Crescendo.* Adderley called Baker "a ridiculously poor imitation of Miles," adding: "They were saying he was so great and Miles was starving at the time. It's downright repulsive to think of it. Though I must say there was something about the way he played 'My Funny Valentine.' Had he been channeled right and if he had some chops it might have been another story."

The veteran swing trumpeter Roy Eldridge had his own bitter complaints. "About Chet Baker, I can't say anything because he's number one in the polls," Eldridge told *Down Beat.* "Well, I guess I will have to commit myself anyway. I don't dig that type of trumpet player. It's too mild or something. . . . Baker plays right in a straight line, no ups and downs, soft or loud. I don't think it should be like that."

Not all black players shared his feelings; trumpeter Kenny Dorham, pianist John Lewis, and bassist Oscar Pettiford all praised Baker in the same pages. But many were eager for him to fail, and Baker knew it. "It puts a pressure on your ass you wouldn't believe," he told Rogers Worthington of the *Detroit Free Press* years later. "You've got musicians coming in to hear you, sitting there waiting for you to play something trite or to flub."

And in May 1954, a fall seemed inevitable. That month Baker made his New York debut: a full month at Birdland, the "Jazz Corner of the World," in a pair of double bills, first opposite Dizzy Gillespie, then Miles Davis. The booking made perfect sense to his agent, Joe Glaser: after all, Baker was a lot more popular than Gillespie or Davis. But Baker was scared. A few months earlier, Davis had met the poll-winning sweetheart of the trumpet at the Lighthouse, and he saw Baker's discomfort. "Both him and me knew that he had copied a lot of shit from me," Davis said in his autobiography. Subsequently, Davis went home to his father in St. Louis to kick a four-year heroin habit. He returned to New York in February 1954. Without the numbing effects of dope, his playing sounded darker than ever. In his book, he raged against the club owners and critics who had treated him like "dirt" when he was hooked: "I was just cold to the motherfuckers; pay me and I'll play."

He had even less respect for the "cool jazz" played by whites in L.A. "I guess it was supposed to be some kind of alternative to bebop, or black music, or 'hot jazz,' which in white people's minds, meant black. But it was the same old story, black shit was being ripped off all over again." To him, the worst culprit was Chet Baker. It was bad enough, he said, that critics had crowned Baker "the second coming of Jesus Christ," but Davis couldn't excuse the comparisons between him and a man who played "worse than me even when I was a terrible junkie."

The Birdland gig represented a fight to the death between East and West—"the big black guys versus the little white guys," as Marion Raffaele called it. "The big black guys" in Davis's band were four bebop titans: tenor saxophonist Lucky Thompson, pianist Horace Silver, bassist Percy Heath, and drummer Kenny Clarke. Marion wondered how they "could possibly be as good as our boys, these California sunshine athletic wonders."

But California sunshine had no place in Birdland, a midtown cellar where the spotlights cut gray beams through a cigarette haze. Only the most assured (or stoned) musicians could keep from getting the jitters on the stage of that two-hundred-seat room, whose walls were lined with paintings of the greats who reigned there, including Count Basie, Duke Ellington, Sarah Vaughan, and Charlie Parker, for whom Birdland was named. At a long bar on the left, jazz stars mingled with whores, pimps, and groupies; near the bar, in a nondrinking section of benches called the "bleachers," fresh-faced college kids stared in awe at their idols. On the right was a higher-priced section of banquette seating; the center area was jammed with tables.

In May 1954, the audience consisted largely of girls who adored Chet Baker, along with a few beboppers—Art Farmer, Lee Morgan, Art Blakey—who were there to watch the showdown between Baker and Davis. The first half of the month passed smoothly; if the easygoing Gillespie was annoyed by the double bill, he didn't show it, and in the seventies he would play a crucial role in lifting Baker out of oblivion.

Then Davis took over as the opening act, and tension rose. In tunes like "Blue Haze" and "Blue 'n' Boogie," he introduced a hotter version of cool: a slow, insinuating form of bop, full of midnight atmosphere and steeped in the blues. "One passionate note from Miles Davis seemed to imply a whole complex of passionate sound, and three notes a ravishing melody," wrote critic Martin Williams. The group oozed confidence: Silver with his funky piano, saxophonist Thompson with his beefy tone.

The reception was polite. Then Baker's group came on, and the squeals from their female fans were little comfort. "We were scared to death," said Carson Smith. "It was like the boys coming to play next to the men." Now, songs like "Happy Little Sunbeam" didn't seem so clever. After hearing Kenny Clarke, Bob Neel "started to feel inadequate back there," he admitted. "I began to think that maybe we weren't the greatest jazz band in the world. And I didn't like it when Chettie sang." For the first time anyone could remember, Baker looked terrified. "He can't be that afraid of Birdland!" said a bassist to Nat Hentoff, who covered the event for *Down Beat.*

Offstage, the group felt a chill from Davis's band: the leader ignored Baker, while Smith recalled getting the brush-off from Silver, who later excoriated West Coast Jazz in *Down Beat.* "I can't stand the faggot-type jazz—the jazz with no . . . no guts," he told Hentoff. "And the discouraging part is that the faggot-type jazz is getting more popularity than the jazz with real soul. The groups that play with a lot of guts are not making as much loot."

Sy Johnson, a young pianist-arranger who went on to join bassist Charles Mingus, was there in the Birdland audience. The Baker band, he recalled, "seemed pale by comparison, and Chet knew it. The worst part is that two thirds of the audience had come to see Chet Baker and didn't know. But Chet knew." As Johnson left the club, he was astounded to hear people chattering about how Davis stole everything he knew from Baker. "You'd want to shake them and say, 'You fucking stupid shits!' "

Hentoff did just that in his review, a scathing attack on Baker's quartet. Compared to Davis's "wholly alive, stimulating voice," he wrote, Baker sounded "rather frail, and, I'm afraid, a little dull." Smith and Neel, said Hentoff, "could take lessons from Heath and Clarke," while Freeman's playing was "pallid," his tunes "underdeveloped sketches of small thematic strength." He found the group's brand of cool closer to bland indifference: "If they deeply enjoy what they play, it is not at all apparent."

Freeman saw how badly the engagement shook Baker. "For a while he got more into Miles's bag than his own," said the pianist. In his more candid moments, a middle-aged Baker would reflect humbly on his heyday as a poll winner. "I really wasn't ready for all that," he told Rogers Worthington. "Maybe I didn't feel I really belonged there." Pianist-singer Andy Bey, who met him later in Paris, recalled how guilty Baker felt. "And he shouldn't have," Bey said. "But no matter how big a lot of the white musicians become, they always want to feel that black respect, to know that the brothers appreciate them."

Long after most of the "brothers" had stopped caring, Baker felt the sting of their early rejection, and he never stopped resenting them for it. In 1980 he complained to Lisa Galt Bond that the "young black cats who play music . . . are filled with such hatred for the white person." Yet even Charlie Davidson had to agree that the early fuss over Baker was exaggerated: "Half of it was physical attraction. I mean, what right did he have to be winning *Down Beat* polls over Miles and Dizzy and Clifford Brown? Everything was getting so out of proportion."

As Baker ascended, a master was hitting bottom. Visiting Birdland on another night in May, Sy Johnson encountered a bloated-looking black man at the ticket window a few steps below the entrance, greeting customers like a barker at a sideshow. "Young man, you're really going to enjoy the show tonight!" he announced in a deep, resonant voice. "This young man Chet Baker is wonderful, and you're going to love hearing him." Taking his seat in the bleachers, Johnson was stunned to realize he had just seen Charlie Parker, whose drug- and drink-induced hell-raising had gotten him banned from the club that bore his name. Sensing that Parker wanted someone to buy him a ticket and escort him in, Johnson ran upstairs, but the saxophonist was gone, perhaps ejected forcibly.

It was one of the saddest declines he could remember. By his early thirties, said Miles Davis, "Bird was all fucked up—fat, tired, playing badly." Everything was closing in on him: his beloved two-year-old daughter had just died of heart failure, while he had developed his own heart condition, along with bleeding ulcers. He killed his pain the only way he knew how. In an interview with the British jazz writer Steve Voce, Parker's pianist Walter Bishop Jr. recalled his boss's words: "I go to this heart specialist and he treats me but it don't do no good. I go to this ulcer man and give him seventy-five dollars to cool my ulcers out and it don't do no good. There's a little cat in a dark alley and I give him five dollars for a bag of shit—my ulcer's gone, my heart trouble is gone. Everything is gone."

Music seemed to be the only thing keeping Parker alive, but heroin had cost him his cabaret card, a musician's legal permit to work in New York clubs. His habit had also alienated many of his friends, including Davis, who was tired, he said, of finding Parker's dealers at his door, announcing that the saxophonist had sent them there for payment. One of Parker's last resorts was his former protégé, Chet Baker. During the trumpeter's first engagement at Birdland, Parker would sneak behind the building, walk through a back alley lined with trash cans, and knock on a door that opened into the dressing room. Baker or Carson Smith would let him in, and he and Baker would play chess until showtime. Then Parker would sit alone, keeping the door ajar so he could hear the music.

The experience brought them closer together, and when Baker's army pal Bob Freedman came to town, the trumpeter proudly took him to meet the great Bird. "He was all excited about introducing us," said Freedman. "We got to this hotel room, and there was Bird stretched out across the bed, barely able to breathe. He turned his head toward Chet and said, 'Did you get that chick for me?' Then he passed out. Chet was kind of embarrassed. We just left. I don't think we even discussed it."

Later in 1954, when Baker returned to Birdland, Parker began showing up almost nightly at the Hotel Bryant and asking to sleep on his couch. "Bird was sick, he had no work, no money, and few places to go," said Liliane Cukier, who by then had started an affair with Baker. Parker was her hero, and for three weeks she had the thrill of cooking for him and hearing him tell stories about his early days and the jazz greats he had known. "He was well-spoken and polite, he had poise and dignity, and to me he just looked very intelligent," she said. It was a shock, therefore, when the couple awoke one morning to find him gone, along with the money from Baker's trouser pocket. The trumpeter forbade her from confronting Parker; instead of feeling angry, he felt only compassion. "He wasn't gonna make a fuss about a few dollars that Bird needed," Cukier said. It was a response similar to the empathy he felt for his father, whose anger and abusiveness came from a frustration Baker could understand.

The saxophonist died on March 12, 1955. An autopsy listed the cause as lobar pneumonia. Viewing the body, the coroner mistook Parker, then thirty-four, for a man twenty years older. Ironically, his life ended in luxury. At the time, he was staying with the Baroness Pannonica de Koenigswarter, a wealthy patron of jazz musicians, in her suite at the fashionable Stanhope Hotel on Fifth Avenue in Manhattan. His memorial, attended by the royalty of East Coast jazz, was held at Carnegie Hall. Baker was appearing at Basin Street, a jazz club a few blocks south. During his break, he rushed to the tribute, only to be stopped at the stage door. "Chet Baker? Who's that?" said the guard.

In May 1954, the exotic young woman at the Birdland bar certainly knew who Chet Baker was. As she watched him play, her looks drew plenty of their own attention. She wore a tight, off-the-shoulder black dress and a dark crew cut; her eyes were outlined in black, raccoon-style. As she sat coolly, pimps hovered around her; Dizzy Gillespie even made a pass at her, which she declined. "She likes the white trumpet player better," he said.

Liliane Cukier was a twenty-one-year-old French Jew. Two weeks earlier, she had sailed from Paris, her hometown, where she had just appeared in the chorus of *Ah! Les Belles Bacchantes,* a hit revue. She couldn't sing or dance, but her magnetism was undeniable, and years later she put it to use by becoming an acclaimed film actress in Paris. But in 1954 she had other intentions. "My father hoped that I would establish in New York and find a nice husband or something," she explained. "But I was not on my way to establish. I was on my way because I was crazy about jazz. And I figured in New York I'd have all the jazz I wanted."

Between choruses, Baker fixed her with the same probing glance he might have given a shiny foreign sports car in a showroom window. At intermission he came over. "Chet fell in love with me on sight," she said. "And strongly." Baker admitted it: "She was different. Not exactly beautiful, but attractive, intelligent, and sexy in the French way. . . . We hit it off immediately." Once more, though, romance seemed far from his mind as they consummated their attraction in the backseat of his Mercury. "He was very surprised that I didn't hesitate first," she said. "But I didn't even know if I was gonna see him the next day. I was just living in the moment."

They plunged into a two-and-a-half-year affair. To Baker, she was a sexy trophy, the kind an Oklahoma boy dreamed of showing off at the drive-in. "I think Chet just couldn't believe how non-American I was, and I think he loved that," she said. Photos of the couple show him gazing at her in wonder, with as much of a smile as he ever mustered. He was still married to Charlaine, of course, but avoided the subject, mentioning only that they "weren't getting along" and that he planned to leave her. Liliane wasn't too concerned. "Everybody knew they were quarreling a lot," she noted. "I had nothing to do with it." Soon after they met, Baker started leading her around by the hand and introducing her as his wife, a deception she didn't discourage.

Nobody foresaw the near-fatal consequences. Leaving the Bryant one night to meet her husband at Birdland, Charlaine spied him in his car, entangled with Lili between sets. The young blonde exploded. Storming back to the hotel, she grabbed a handgun Baker had given her to protect herself from big-city troublemakers. Then she headed for Birdland. With Baker onstage, Lili walked inside to find herself eye to eye with a hysterical wife shakily pointing a gun at her. "Do you know what a German Mauser is?" Charlaine hissed, as though trying to erase one foreign threat with another. Taking a cue from her new lover, Lili stayed cool: "I just stood there. I didn't believe she would do anything."

Lili escaped harm, for Charlaine had another target in mind. She headed down the stairs to the main room, on the way passing George Avakian's brother Al, whom she had met. *"I'm gonna kill that son of a bitch!"* she sputtered in his ear. Somehow Al persuaded her not to, and she left; but later, back at the Bryant, Bob Neel had to wrestle the gun from her to keep her from trying again.

Once more, Baker was the quiet eye of a tornado of jealousy and hurt. He put his wife on a plane to California, but she didn't vanish as quickly as he hoped; for about two years she delayed a divorce by asking an alimony settlement Baker didn't care to pay. It seemed like a vengeful move, but when Carson Smith saw her at a party in Hollywood, he found her depressed. "I still miss my old man," she said.

Baker hit the road with the new "Mrs. Baker," who took to the role eagerly. When a parade of Baker groupies followed her into the ladies' room of an Atlantic City nightclub, she enjoyed their envious questions: "Did I wear a brassiere? I didn't. Why didn't I wear lipstick? Was I married to Chet or not?" She made it known that Baker was hers, and as the tour continued she saw little reason to mix with the other musicians and their ladies. "I wasn't so hot about the West Coast and the ways of the people there," she admitted. "They looked too easy, too rich, too cool, too white." The band, in turn, called her "Frou-Frou" behind her back. "We thought, why does this woman have to go into the bathroom to redo her black eyeliner every half-hour?" said Marion. "We didn't even know about black eyeliner."

Lili was greeted just as suspiciously by Vera and Chesney Baker, whom she met that summer when Chet brought her to the family house in Hermosa Beach for a two-week rest between gigs. The young lovers shook up a domestic scene that had grown ice-cold and robotic. The love of Vera's life remained her son, and in his absence she had continued to pour all her attention into her job as floor manager at W. T. Grant's. Chesney still drove a cab. Musical dreams long dead, he blotted out their memory with alcohol.

Vera was thrilled to have "Chettie" home, but she and her husband mistrusted his girlfriend on sight. To Vera, an unsophisticated farmgirl, Lili looked like a prostitute. "They could never figure out that this little Jewish girl from Paris was not after their son's money and fame," Lili explained. Vera maintained her motherly veneer, yet made it subtly clear that Baker was hers. She doted on him as if he were a little boy home from school, and he treated her like his loving mommy. Weeks later, William Claxton did a portrait of the trumpeter and Lili at a Pacific Jazz record date. Claxton photographed him nestled in Lili's arms, head snuggled to her breast, looking utterly docile with closed eyes and mouth hanging open. In his left hand he clutches his other love, his trumpet. Lili stares at the camera with a glance as protective as Vera's.

As months went by, she was startled to see how volatile her angel-faced beau could be. "He could switch, just like that, from sweetness to violence," she said. "He was not physically violent, but he introduced such a tension." Communication was almost impossible: "Chet was so rigid. He didn't speak about himself, we didn't discuss the world, we didn't discuss music. Everything was just held in."

Yet they shared a taste for trouble. Baker's tour took them to St. Louis, a still-segregated town with water fountains and public toilets marked FOR COLORED ONLY. Lili caused a stir when she made friends with some young black people, and took them back to her and Baker's room in a chic white hotel to party.

And for her, partying often meant drugs, sometimes heroin. "I touched everything you can name, and didn't get hooked on anything," she insisted. Baker confirmed it in his memoir, as did Bill Loughborough, but the quartet members worried about her influence on Baker. Lili vehemently denied that Baker had any drug problem during their affair, and Carson Smith agreed: "I was fooling around with heroin a little bit, and I could never get Chet to come near me then. He told me he was deathly afraid of needles and didn't see any reason to get on that shit."

But Baker's compulsive pot-smoking pointed to an addictive personality, and many of his friends, including the Neels and Russ Freeman, were sure that Baker was easing into a heroin habit as early as 1954. That view was shared by his ex-bandmate at the Presidio, Irving Bush, who went with a group of army friends to hear Baker at the Tiffany that summer. "You could tell he was totally out of it at that time, and it wasn't just pot," said Bush. "He was so blotted he could hardly talk. We just couldn't believe it. Then he got up and played. He didn't sound great, but we were amazed that he could play at all."

True or not, his reputation as a heroin user had spread as far as Chicago, where Baker worked at the Streamliner, a popular jazz club. He and Lili stayed at a favorite hotel of visiting musicians, and for three weeks the couple's suite served as a stopover for junkie jazz artists, who went there to fix, apparently confident that they were among their own. Lili recalled the nightly gatherings in that Chicago hotel room: "They were all lying around, and some people took forty-five minutes to find a vein, and it was bloody. I said, 'Chet, this can't go on!' " Yet Baker watched silently, noting his guests' blissful expressions the moment they found a "hit."

He still seemed like a picture of carefree life. Clearly he didn't care about stretching himself artistically. In September he made the album *Chet Baker Sextet,* in which saxophonist Bud Shank and trombonist Bob Brookmeyer joined him in playing arrangements by Jack Montrose, Bill Holman, and Johnny Mandel. With its multilayered counterpoint, the album covered familiar ground; Baker sounded as agile and as distant as ever. *Down Beat* called the performances "tightly constructed and thematically shallow."

Expert as he was at mastering intricate music, he still had no idea how to hold a band together, and his was falling apart. Freeman acted as the group's unpaid manager and accountant while Baker went drag racing and cavorting with Lili. The pianist considered his boss a spoiled brat, and one incident in particular disgusted him. Before leaving his parents' home, Baker had taken back the dog he had left with them; according to Freeman, Baker had decided he could care for it on the road. But he tired of the burden, and took the easy way out: "When we left one of the towns, he just left the dog behind," Freeman said.

Life on the road had worn thin for the women, who longed for the comforts of home. A pregnant Joan Smith returned to L.A., and Carson was eager to join her. The Neels wanted to leave too, but for a different reason: they were sure their employer was using heroin, and as ex-users they wanted to stay far away from hard drugs.

For Freeman, the end came in October, an hour after the band had finished its third engagement at Birdland. One day he answered a knock on the door of his suite at the Bryant to find his ex-wife Marion standing there. "Mr. Baker would like the checkbook," she announced icily. "I thought, that's just fine!" Freeman recalled. The next day Baker took the three-hundred-dollar balance and found himself a Jaguar convertible, dark green and slick as a hot rod. Freeman gave his notice. "I was pissed off, and I was fed up," he said. Soon the group began to fill up with heroin addicts, a sign of things to come.

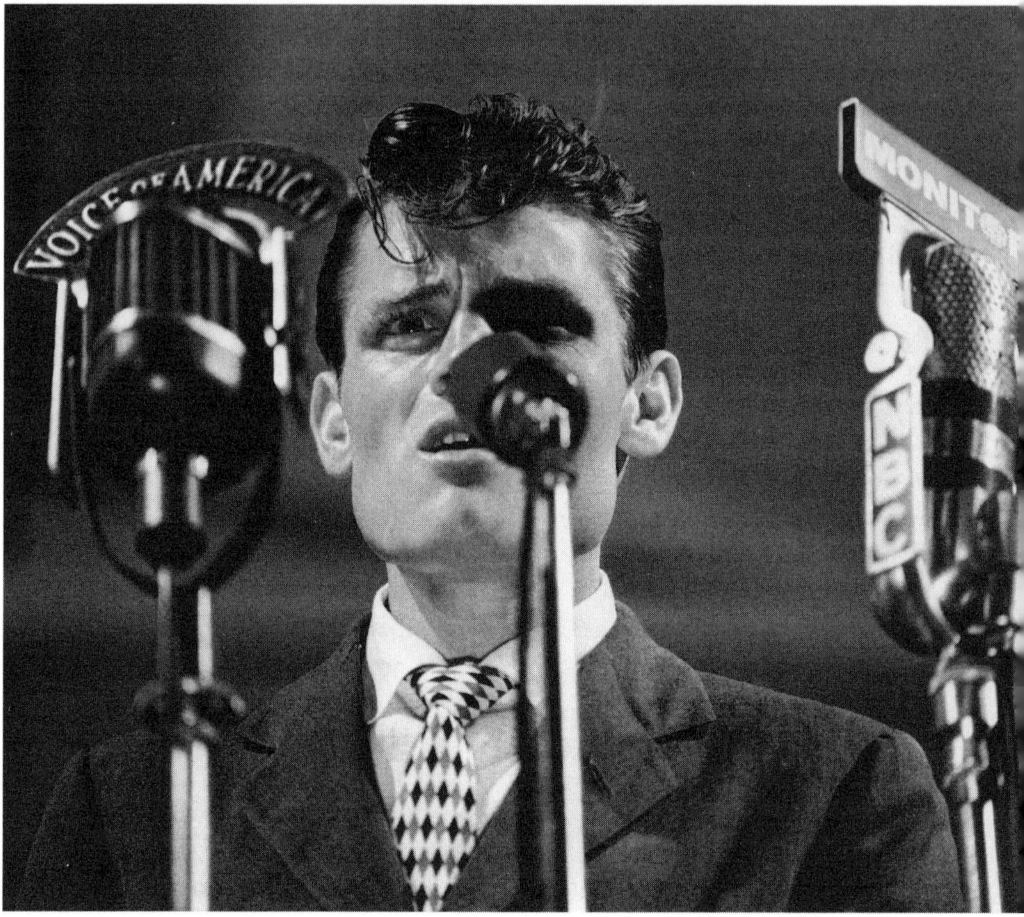

Newport Jazz Festival, Newport, Rhode Island, July 16, 1955. Photo by Herman Leonard

6

Without the steadying hand of Russ Freeman, Baker floundered. Several replacement pianists, including Charlie Parker's former accompanist, Al Haig, came and went before Baker tried forming his own pianoless quartet. In the Gerry Mulligan role he cast Phil Urso, an Italian tenor player from Jersey City, New Jersey, who had worked in the big bands of Jimmy Dorsey and Woody Herman and, briefly, for Miles Davis. Then twenty-nine, Urso had a dopey charm to match his baby face; with his slicked-back, coal-colored hair and mustache, he looked like a young Italian barber. But he played with the feathery lyricism of his idol, Lester Young, and when his debut album, *The Philosophy of Urso,* won five stars in *Down Beat,* Urso's bright future seemed assured. Unfortunately, Carson Smith, who played with the pianoless quartet briefly before leaving Baker, recalled it as a disaster: "It sounded like a jam session. It was terrible."

As 1955 began, though, Baker was still America's top trumpeter. In the new *Down Beat* Readers' Poll he won 882 votes, far surpassing Dizzy Gillespie (661), Miles Davis (128), and Clifford Brown (89). He scored a similar triumph in *Metronome.* Evidently not content with these honors, he would claim in years to come that he had tied Nat King Cole for fourth place in the male vocalist category; he never even came close.

In a Pacific Jazz marketing survey, Dick Bock found that most of Baker's fans were girls who wanted to hear dreamy crooning, not jazz. With them in mind, Bock produced *Chet Baker Sings and Plays with Bud Shank, Russ Freeman and Strings,* recorded in L.A. that February. William Claxton designed a cover that looks like a collage pinned to a schoolgirl's bedroom wall. It gathers a sexy shot of a T-shirted Baker, a torn photo of him and Lili, a rose, and his initials in a heart. The song titles are spelled out in words cut from magazines. A pink cupid points its arrow at Baker, who seems to stare at it blankly while clutching his horn.

With unvarying detachment, he sings of yearning ("I Wish I Knew," "Someone to Watch Over Me"), giddy young love ("Let's Get Lost"), undying bliss ("This Is Always"), and farewell ("Just Friends"). The mood darkens in "You Don't Know What Love Is," a warning to the romantically inclined, murmured in a voice that sounds deadened to all feeling:

> You don't know how hearts burn
> For love that cannot live, yet never dies
> Until you've faced each dawn with sleepless eyes
> You don't know what love is

His seeming indifference to the words came, in part, from struggling just to stay in tune. Liner-note writer Bill Brown hinted at the problem when he mentioned the "overwork" of "these long sessions," explaining: "See if you don't have a feeling of personal achievement as Chet 'makes it' through some of the difficult vocal passages." Bock worked overtime at the editing block, turning out his sloppiest production to date, full of obvious splices and inconsistent volume levels.

Chet Baker Sings and Plays gave the jazz community one more excuse not to take Baker seriously. In *Metronome,* Bill Coss panned his "anemic singing" with its "weird phrasing" and "uneasy intonation." *New York Times* critic John S. Wilson charged him with a "flat, dead voice that is even more despondently formless than his trumpet work."

Their attacks didn't stop Hollywood from calling. Prior to making the album, Baker was cast as a trumpet-playing GI in *Hell's Horizon,* a Korean War drama made for a small subsidiary of Columbia Pictures. It starred John Ireland, the rugged B-movie leading man. Finally, it seemed, Baker had the chance to move from cult stardom to the real thing. But *Hell's Horizon* was a low-budget quickie, filmed in ten days between the two sessions for his album. The project bored him completely, and he complained to Carson Smith about what a "drag" it was to get up at 6 a.m., then sit around for hours waiting for his scenes to be shot.

Upon completing the film, he went on tour with Dave Brubeck, singer Carmen McRae, and Gerry Mulligan, who was now in the humiliating position of playing second fiddle to his former sideman. Mulligan had hit a slump. He had abandoned his last pianoless quartet (featuring trumpeter

Jon Eardley, an early Baker imitator) to spend more time composing and arranging, only to reach a paralyzing writer's block. Needing the work, he had agreed to appear as Baker's guest. "It was sick, very sick," he said. "I didn't know what else to do with myself. To go back and play with Chet Baker's group was just frustration."

The tour opened that March with a concert at Carnegie Hall in New York. *Metronome* sent vibraphonist Teddy Charles to review it. Panning the "watered-down Miles and Zoot sounds from Chet and tenor Phil Urso," Charles decided that Baker's "whole group lacked conviction and direction. . . . Chet has a genuine melodic gift. His lack of creative growth is all the more sad." But in England's *Jazz Journal,* Douglas Hague rose to his defense: "Chet is above Miles in execution and taste and I have never heard the beautiful work shown by Chet on slow numbers exhibited by Davis. . . . The audience was the most quiet and intense that I have ever witnessed at Carnegie Hall."

Dominating the proceedings was Baker's new drummer, Peter Littman, a nineteen-year-old from the Boston area. Normally, Baker hated Littman's kind of playing. The young man idolized Art Blakey and Philly Joe Jones, two hard-core beboppers, and tried to copy their thunderous rhythm by pounding out a heavy, relentlessly swinging beat. He had his fans, notably Daniel Humair, a celebrated Swiss drummer, who believed he had "figured out the modern drumming before anybody else."

But Russ Freeman, who had rejoined Baker part-time, considered Littman "a sycophant, a young punk, sort of creepy," and it alarmed him to see the interest Baker showed in his new discovery. Freeman knew, as did everyone else, that Littman was a full-blown junkie. He had already done time at the U.S. Public Health Service Hospital in Kentucky, a rehab center where Sonny Rollins, Red Rodney, and countless other musicians went to kick heroin. The treatment hadn't helped Littman, who was already physically impaired: a childhood illness had left him with only one lung, which he abused by smoking.

But he didn't expect to live long anyway, and he seemed determined to burn out as explosively as he could. Littman frightened his peers by flaunting dope at jam sessions, as though daring the cops to bust him and everybody else. Recording and rehearsing with Baker, though, he was sneakily covert, whispering to the trumpeter and ignoring the others. "There was always something going on that you didn't know about," said William Claxton, who couldn't stand him.

What Freeman didn't know is that Littman was pestering Baker to hire the drummer's best friend and needle buddy, Dick Twardzik, a twenty-four-year-old pianist whom many Boston jazzmen—as well as Charlie Parker, with whom he had worked—considered a genius. "The other piano players in Boston lived under his shadow," said Herb Pomeroy, a trumpeter who led a big band there. But Twardzik was scuffling, partly from having to support a heroin habit that had begun in his teens. Few noticed his first album, *Richard Twardzik Trio,* on Pacific Jazz—a record produced, ironically, by Freeman, one of his greatest fans. In later years, the handful of musicians who knew that album declared it a masterpiece. "If he had lived, he would probably have changed the whole course of jazz piano," said Marc Puricelli, a pianist and composer who came of age in the seventies.

Twardzik was a forerunner of Bill Evans and Keith Jarrett, both of whom brought a rich knowledge of classical harmony and an orchestral fullness to the keyboard. Poring over every phrase as though possessed, Twardzik cross-referenced blues, boogie-woogie, and the avant-garde harmonies of Thelonious Monk with strains of Bach, Brahms, and Chopin. "His playing had an intellectual heat to it," said Bob Freedman, one of his best friends. "He was never satisfied, always trying to find the next thing." Performing his own pieces, like "A Crutch for the Crab" (named after his hero, Artur Rubinstein, whose hands, Twardzik felt, looked like crabs on the keys), he evoked instruments ranging from timpani to bass. All the while, said Pomeroy, "he could swing as hard as anybody in the history of jazz."

What lifted Twardzik above mere virtuosity was his soulfulness, an eagerness to drown in the melancholy or euphoria of the moment. Both qualities lit up a slow, probing version of "Bess, You Is My Woman" from George Gershwin's opera *Porgy and Bess.* Twardzik interpreted the romance of two lovers from Catfish Row, a black ghetto in 1920s South Carolina, as a halting, troubled journey. He shifted in and out of tempo, switching from weighty silences to a heavy, metronomic touch that implied the ominous passing of time. The solo burst into an orgasmic coda, as if Porgy and Bess were finally consummating their love.

Littman persuaded Baker to let Twardzik sit in with them in Boston, and the trumpeter responded more passionately than he had to any woman. "He was a genius," he would say repeatedly to Ruth Young, gazing wistfully. Twardzik reminded Bob Zieff, a Boston-based composer, of "someone you'd see on the streets of Vienna in the twenties." His sunken cheeks, high cheekbones, and slight build gave him the look of an artist sequestered in a garret. Often he hid his somber eyes behind tinted glasses to conceal pupils reduced to pinpoints by heroin. With the drug to guide him, he entered a trance as he played, climbing higher and higher into his inner world of strange beauty.

Twardzik wasn't a melodist like Baker, but his mastery of harmony created its own poetry. For Baker, who rarely surrendered to his heart, the feeling that flowed out of Twardzik was intensely moving. Perhaps he saw the pianist as the dark obverse of himself. Their association lasted just a few weeks, yet Baker romanticized it all his life, implying that they were the closest of soulmates. "Chet just worshipped the guy," said Carson Smith. "You could see it on his face every time Dick was near him." But according to Twardzik's girlfriend, singer Crystal Joy, the bond was mostly in Baker's head. "Dick thought it was a wonderful musical experience, but I don't think he knew Chet very well," she said. "He never talked about him as a person."

Clearly Baker's fascination transcended music, and it fueled Ruth Young's theory that he harbored a sexual confusion along with his other repressions. "I think it's very possible that he was in love with Dick," she said. "If you're looking at the subliminal angle of where his latent homosexual nature was apt to go if it had been let loose, then it makes perfect sense to me." In 1987, Cherry Vanilla came to the same conclusion after hearing Baker rhapsodize about Twardzik in an interview she conducted for *Let's Get Lost.* "Maybe Chet loved him in a way we don't even know about," she said. "That's something he never told."

Baker may have seen in Twardzik unshakable proof that getting high was the only way to reach that place of purest, most eloquent creativity. Obviously Twardzik felt that way, and even though he had nearly died of several ODs, the needle kept drawing him back.

It brought him a comfort he had never known at home. His Polish father, Henryk, was a stained-glass-window artist; his mother, Clare, a scientific illustrator at the Massachusetts Institute of Technology. The couple also raised prize German shepherds and conducted public tours through their huge historic home in Danversport, Massachusetts. The house would have had a macabre effect on any young imagination. Herb Pomeroy recalled it as "dark and spooky, with weird back stairways that had doors leading off them." Visitors who ascended one flight of steps were confronted by a chillingly lifelike mannequin dressed as a Colonial matriarch. As strangers trudged from room to room, they heard eerie, dissonant chords resounding from behind the closed door of Dick's bedroom.

His parents, remote and wrapped up in their own interests, were almost as foreign to him as their guests. "Dick was like an intruder," said Crystal

Joy. "I know they didn't approve of him much, with all his talent." His bedroom was his sanctuary. There he sat practicing at his spinet piano or studying records by Monk, Earl Hines, Erroll Garner, Art Tatum, and Artur Rubinstein. When his parents were out, he curled up on the living-room sofa to read avant-garde art magazines and French fiction and to smoke pot. His tolerance for drugs was so low that he was known to pass out after only one joint of marijuana.

Twardzik craved new highs, though, and during high school he began slipping away late at night to the black section of Boston, rife with dealers. Soon he was a junkie, and joined with Littman, the rising young saxophonist Serge Chaloff, and other buddies in a fraternal ritual of getting high, then playing jazz. At the time, estimated Pomeroy, about a third of the jazz players in that supposedly straitlaced town were hooked. "The drug scene in Boston was hot," confirmed Crystal Joy. "Narcotics people were all over the place. Musicians were paranoid about getting caught."

Twardzik's career hadn't gone far, but he never doubted his superiority. After working at Boston's Hi-Hat club with Charlie Parker, he told Bob Zieff: "Bird does pretty well, you know. He can follow most of the key changes." "Dickie," as friends called him, could be surprisingly happy-go-lucky. "When he walked down the street," said Pomeroy, "he danced, he strutted"; some mistook him for a flamboyant homosexual. But overall, said Liliane Cukier, "Dick was a sad person. He was sweet, but very secret and isolated. I never heard him laugh." Pomeroy worried over what lay in store for his friend: "His life experience hadn't taught him how to handle all the things that were going on inside him. I kept thinking, something's gonna explode."

That was also the worry of Crystal Joy, his young black girlfriend. A talented singer-pianist, born in Montreal, Joy played intermissions at Storyville and other clubs. Later in the fifties, Steve Allen presented her on his national TV show. Joy had a warm, dusky voice, but tended to be shy, and hid her plump body in clothes she laughingly recalled as "Early Boston Public Library." Playing the Hi-Hat in 1953, she saw a fragile-looking young man walk across the stage "like a zombie" and sit at the piano. She was enamored at once. Friends warned her that Twardzik was a drug addict, but, as she explained, "I was so naïve then, I couldn't conceive of anybody being so bad who played so well."

Twardzik was equally entranced with Joy's unassuming sweetness and passion for jazz. "He found me exotic, I found him different," she said. They began a romance so idyllic at first that not even its bold interracial aspect caused them much trouble; amazingly, Joy persuaded her parents to let him move into their home. Twardzik had denied having a drug problem, but the danger he epitomized was probably seductive to her. Joy got a rude awakening a few weeks later when he made plans to pick her up in front of the Stables, a Boston club. Stepping into his car, she watched him collapse at the wheel from an overdose. Terrified, she ran inside the Stables and found Serge Chaloff, who walked the pianist up and down the street until he regained consciousness. Then Joy, who had no license, drove him to her family's house. They promptly threw him out. From then on, both her parents and Twardzik's, who disapproved of Joy for their own reasons, were dead set against the relationship. Joy struggled to steer him away from drugs, and from the destructive circle of friends who nurtured his habit. But she came to the painful realization that he didn't want to quit.

Eventually she convinced him to go to a rehab hospital outside Boston. There he endured the torture of cold turkey, largely on her account. He poured out his heart to her in a letter: "Honey, please never lose faith in me. I love you. . . For once in my life I'm not hiding a bit. Let's get MARRIED!!! (I'm sober, honey)." Upon his release they reunited, but Joy doubted he would stay clean for long.

As Twardzik sank under the weight of addiction, Baker kept ambling along aimlessly. On July 16, 1955, he worked the second annual Newport Jazz Festival in Rhode Island, backed by Freeman, Littman, and bassist Bob Carter. "It was a pain in the ass—bad sound, screaming mobs, too many musicians milling around," said Freeman. "It wasn't a place for creating good music—most jazz festivals aren't." Battling the din, Baker delivered strained, sour-toned solos full of clams. The finale, "Tea for Two," brought together Dave Brubeck, Paul Desmond, Clifford Brown, Gerry Mulligan, and Baker in a musical traffic jam; only Brown rose above the chaos with his bold, bravura playing.

The New York critics continued tearing down the West Coast wonder. Reviewing Baker at Basin Street, Bill Coss of *Metronome* called the show "disastrous," explaining: "His trumpet was weak, his singing almost insipid." Baker merely froze when he saw the bad notices. But as with Twardzik, the pressure inside him was mounting, and it began to erode his relationship with Lili, with whom he quarreled nastily.

He found temporary escape in Sausalito, a quaintly scenic town outside San Francisco where a Bohemian group of artists and writers dwelled. There Baker visited the house on a barge, accessible by gangplank, of Bill Loughborough, a Texas-born electronics and recording engineer. Loughborough shared his floating mini-commune with jazz guitarist David Wheat (known as Buck Wheat) and Gerd Stern, a poet. "They were hippies before their time," said Lili. "These people were not hanging around Chet to grab something. They had their own thing. Chet adored them." He especially liked Loughborough's home-baked marijuana brownies. Pleasantly stoned, the friends enjoyed the gentle rocking of the houseboat as they played the "boobams"—an instrument invented by Loughborough that consisted of small bamboo drums, bound together in sets and tuned to play on pitch.

Later the houseboat acquired two new tenants: Marguerite Angelou, soon known as Maya, and her young son, Guy. Angelou had yet to become a grand lady of letters; for now she performed in San Francisco clubs, dancing and singing calypso while jiggling her breasts to a tribal drumbeat sometimes provided by Loughborough. In her 1981 memoir, *The Heart of a Woman,* Angelou brushed off her foray into the "beatnik brigade," writing of her former housemates: "Had they been political (which they were not), [they] would have occupied a place between the far left and revolution."

One night she went to hear Baker and Loughborough in a club, and they gave her a ride home. "We smoked a little pot," said Loughborough. Months later, he offered her a joint. "No, I quit," she said.

"What happened?"

"Remember that night that Chet Baker drove me home? I promised God that if I got through it alive I would never smoke pot again!"

Much as he liked the tranquillity of Sausalito, Baker craved his two nonchemical highs: his trumpet and the road. On a moment's notice he told his host to pack up the Jaguar with boobams and join the band; Loughborough could sell his drums from town to town and appear with him on TV, which would probably make him a celebrity, Baker informed him. They raced to New York with Lili stretched out on the ledge behind the Jaguar's two seats.

Once in town, they appeared on the *Tonight* show, joined by Freeman, Carson Smith, and Bob Neel. Playing "Night in Tunisia," Dizzy Gillespie's wild Afro-Cuban bebop standard, Baker tore through the song with a hard East Coast edge, as if he were out to avenge anyone who had called him "fey" or "vapid." "Chet was out to kick some ass," said Carson Smith. "He knew how many of those New York guys hated him. He was burning." When Baker returned to Birdland in the same period, Art Blakey and Thelonious Monk visited him at the Bryant; later they sat with Lili at the show. "I didn't know this muthafucka could play like that!" said Blakey.

His acting abilities were another matter. In the summer of 1955, *Hell's*

Horizon died a hasty death. The eighty-minute black-and-white potboiler veered between tedium and camp, with "special effects" sequences of model airplanes in flight alternating with stock footage of air battles. Set in Okinawa in 1952, it tells the story of an air force captain (John Ireland) ordered to bomb a bridge near Manchuria. The Baker character seems autobiographical, but more likely it was a knockoff of Robert E. Lee Prewitt, the moody army bugler portrayed by Montgomery Clift two years earlier in *From Here to Eternity.* Baker's brooding introvert sits in a corner of the barracks blowing his trumpet. "Without that horn he's stuck for an answer when you say hello," grumbles one of his bunk mates. "Man, you're a real sad drag," Baker whines.

He shows hints of a compelling screen presence, playing as effortlessly to the movie lens as he did to the still camera. Called upon to express anything beyond cool deadpan, though, Baker is lost. In the ludicrous climax, when the airborne crew are sprayed with gunfire for twenty minutes before crash landing, Baker can muster only the same uncomprehending look he wore in moments of real-life crisis. Audiences giggled to see his character shot in the head to the complete indifference of his fellow fliers. After the plane goes down in flames, Ireland drags Baker's corpse to the ground, taking the trumpet mouthpiece out of his clenched fist and placing it on his chest.

A press campaign pandered to his teenage fans—"Chet Baker's playing can be used as the basis of a contest to find the best trumpet player in town"—but no one cared. Two other splashy Korean War movies—*The Bridges at Toko-Ri* with William Holden and Grace Kelly and *Strategic Air Command* with James Stewart and June Allyson—buried *Hell's Horizon* at the box office. There was another reason Baker's film debut as a rebellious heartthrob couldn't have been more mistimed. Just three months earlier, *East of Eden* had turned James Dean into a monument of raging teenage angst. There was nothing really "cool" about Dean, who quivered onscreen like a ticking time bomb. But his brooding sidelong glances, dark silences, and sullen fatalism gave him a strong resemblance to Baker. Around that time, Dean was shooting a scene for his next film, *Rebel Without a Cause,* that could have come from Baker's life. In it, a teenage Natalie Wood eyes Dean as he gears up for a hazardous drag race. "What's he like?" she asks his best friend, Sal Mineo, motherliness and lust mingled in her voice. "Oh, I don't know," says an equally smitten Mineo. "You have to get to know him. He doesn't say much, but when he does, you know he means it."

There is no evidence that Dean had much awareness of Baker, nor that they had ever met, although they came close. One day Lili had stood outside the Bryant with Joe Napoli, Joe Glaser's house publicist, who later took over as Baker's agent. "There was this young guy walking all around Chet's Jaguar, examining it," said Lili. "Joe said to me, 'Meet Jimmy Dean, he's gonna be a very big star!' And I didn't even look at him!"

Months later, Dean was dead in his own demolished sports car. From then on, Baker was called the "James Dean of Jazz," despite having emerged years ahead of Dean. Ignoring the failure of *Hell's Horizon,* a couple of producers offered him Dean-like roles in cheap, teen-oriented films. Baker said no. "Chet couldn't have been less interested in making movies," said Jimmy Bond, who became his bassist that year. "He thought it was unhip."

In the summer of 1955, he was more concerned with the fact that Lili's visa had expired, necessitating her return to Paris. The only solution, Baker decided, was for Joe Glaser to send him to Paris on a European tour. Glaser booked him to play France in September, followed by Holland, England, Denmark, Germany, Italy, and Iceland. Pleased as he was to be reuniting with Lili, Baker was even more excited when Dick Twardzik agreed to join him overseas.

Twardzik was happy too, but Crystal Joy shuddered at the news. Her boyfriend had left rehab drug-free, but she doubted he would stay that way in Baker's company. "Dick and I both loved Chet's music; that wasn't the issue," she said. "Chet liked the people who were hanging out with him to get high."

To Joy's alarm, Baker had hired Peter Littman for the tour, too. There was only one stable figure in the band: Bond, a Juilliard-trained bassist from Philadelphia. At twenty-two, he had already played with Charlie Parker, Lester Young, and Clifford Brown, and his brains and reliability were well respected. "Jimmy Bond was as clean as a hound's tooth," said Phil Urso.

Bond was glad to have the job, but misgivings set in when he saw the circle he was entering. His new colleagues, though only in their twenties, all showed a constant need to sedate themselves against life. Twardzik's and Littman's reputations preceded them; Loughborough too, he found, "stayed spaced most of the time." Lili's relationship with Baker, he said, was "a battle every day. They fought about everything: which road he should take to a city, what restaurant to go to." Baker, said Bond, "was a child whenever he stepped down from the bandstand. But a destructive one."

Near the end of the Baker-Mulligan-Brubeck tour, the trumpeter had gone to the Stables, where Bob Freedman was playing. "Gerry wants me to get him some drugs," he whispered to Freedman. "Do you know anybody?" Mulligan had been basically clean for over a year. "This was no longer

Chettie—this was now Chet Baker," said Freedman. "He was tougher-looking, with that paranoia that goes along with trying to do a drug deal, and knowing that if you got busted, you'd go to jail, so you don't trust anybody."

Except his junkie friends, it seemed. In a Boston hotel room, Loughborough watched Littman share his heroin with Baker. The drummer, whom Lili had to revive one day after an OD, shot dope with a gluttony Baker would eventually match. Twardzik, for his part, had made a disturbing revelation to Herb Pomeroy: having suffered through cold turkey, he would kill himself, he said, if he ever got hooked again. Yet Pomeroy suspected that his friend was already sliding back into the habit.

In September 1955, Twardzik and Littman boarded the *Ile de France,* a ship bound for Paris. Baker had left a week earlier to meet Lili; Jimmy Bond also traveled separately, preferring to keep his distance from all of them. The pianist and drummer had a going-away bash in their stateroom. Joy arrived to bid Twardzik goodbye and found him and Littman crowded into their tiny cabin with several female groupies. "They were all out of their heads already," she said. "Everybody was, like, too cool for words. So phony, so false. I said, uh-oh—bad scene. Dick shoved me out of there as fast as he could." Twardzik promised her he had cleaned up for good, adding that as soon as he got settled in Europe he would send for her. But Joy doubted it would ever happen. "I had a chill," she said, "like I was never going to see him again."

7

On September 10, 1955, Lili met Baker at the airport in Paris, then enjoyed a weeklong reunion with him before his first concert in Holland. Judging by his reaction to Paris, he might as well have been in Pittsburgh or Detroit. "He didn't look especially excited to be here," Lili said, "but the French musicians were delighted. I don't think he expected such a reception." When he showed up for a jam session at Caméléon, a club in the Latin Quarter, fans crowded around him, clutching Gerry Mulligan albums and gazing at him in awe. To them he was "cool" itself, the prince of a far-off land (California) filled with horn-toting young men who lived for sun, surf, and jazz. All their farming made him very nervous. Herman Leonard's cover photo for a new French magazine, *Jazz,* showed Baker holding his hand against his chin, fingernails chewed to the quick.

The trumpeter's photographic image didn't seem too rooted in the truth, as Peter Huijts—a young Dutchman who would become his road manager in the eighties—saw for himself. Huijts was part of a crowd of teenagers who saw Baker that month in Holland. "Chet was our hero," he said. "We liked this kind of music, and we thought he was just like James Dean. Then he came out in this brown three-piece custom suit. Beautiful guy to see, but he looked like an office clerk."

For Miles Davis, Kenny Clarke, James Moody, Don Byas, Bud Powell, and other American beboppers, the place to be was France, where the fascination with Negro and African culture included a reverence for black jazz musicians. Commercially, though, bop was dwarfed there by a Dixieland revival led by Sidney Bechet, the grandfatherly black clarinetist and soprano sax player from New Orleans. Bechet's playing, with its thick vibrato and showy vaudeville mannerisms, enthralled the same audience that loved Edith Piaf and Maurice Chevalier. But to Paris's budding modern jazzmen, Bechet sounded corny and primitive. "People like simple music and songs, and Bechet played well this way, so why not?" said pianist René Urtreger, who won France's Django Reinhardt Prize (named after the great Belgian Gypsy guitarist) as the most promising musician of 1961. "But there was this war between old times and us."

Unfortunately, many in the new breed had discovered heroin, a drug whose popularity grew with every visit by an addicted master. Urtreger recalled a night when two of his friends, bassist Jean-Marie Ingrand and drummer Jean-Louis Viale, showed up to play a concert at the hallowed Salle Pleyel auditorium in Paris. Climbing a back stairwell, they passed a drug dealer selling to a Bohemian-looking black man. "Hello, you are Thelonious Monk?" they said to the buyer. "We are going to play with you tonight." Urtreger estimated that by the midfifties, 95 percent of the modern jazz players in France—himself included—were hooked. "Young people all over the world, they imitate their idols," he said.

That fall, the Chet Baker quartet launched a punishing series of one-nighters throughout Europe. Baker logged his travels in a set of letters to *Down Beat.* Except for some carping about London ("Sorry, but I don't dig this climate. It's supposed still to be summer here but you'd never know it. Can't compare to California"), his reports were both effusive and evasive. "We're packing them in everywhere!" he exclaimed. "You have no idea how well we went over. Just can't get over it." He raved about the reception in Milan ("Just love this crazy town!"), Rome ("too, too much!"), Frankfurt ("A ball!"). A reviewer in the same magazine commented: "We could have used some better information about what happened in Europe between those press agent lines." The truth is that Baker played many half-filled halls on a tour marred by misguided booking and personal chaos.

It began impressively enough. He played his first European concerts at two prestigious Dutch halls, the Concertgebouw in Amsterdam and the Kurhaus in Scheveningen. Writer Pieter Sweens reported the "thunderous ovation" that greeted Baker as he walked onstage at the Concertgebouw. Sweens was surprised at the West Coast hotshot's timidity; Piet Pijnenborg, another reporter, called Baker "a bit nervous and absent-minded" as he played a repertoire of bebop standards borrowed from Miles Davis, pretty ballads ("My Old Flame," "These Foolish Things"), and lots of vocals. But the newspaper headlines were rhapsodic: "Chet Baker, Trumpet Wonder," "Modern Music from a Golden Horn," "Jazz Poetry by Chet Baker." While the critics accused him of imitating Miles Davis on trumpet, they loved the dreaminess of his singing. "Perhaps it's his mournful loneliness that makes such an impression, the sense that Baker really is 'lost in the wood,' " wrote Pieter Sweens, quoting from the Gershwin song "Someone to Watch Over Me," also in the show.

On September 22, Baker headlined the first concert of the season at Paris's Salle Pleyel, an event as grand as opening night at the opera. On a bill with several shining young stars of European jazz—the Belgian flutist and sax player Bobby Jaspar; the celebrated guitarist René Thomas, also from Belgium; the award-winning Algerian pianist Martial Solal—Baker "opened up with full force and inspired everyone," said Jimmy Bond. Dick Twardzik shook him out of his "cool" complacency by throwing him tricky, sometimes dissonant chords that kept him on the edge. In a speedy arrangement of a ballad from 1919, "Indian Summer," Baker blazed through some phrases and sounded so wispy in others that his fragility tugged at the heart. One wondered if his seeming uninvolvement of the past had come from playing in settings that didn't challenge him enough.

But his singing, noted *Jazz* magazine, was greeted coldly. The French, like many other Europeans, seemed uneasy at hearing a supposedly manly jazz musician sound like a choirboy. "CHET'S VOCALS NOT WANTED!" shouted a *Melody Maker* headline. "Chet Baker was given the bird when he sang at the Salle Pleyel Tuesday night," reported Henry Kahn. "But it was only a moderate 'bird.' The fans on the whole were kind to what was really a grueling and rather lamentable performance. Someone should tell Chet to stop singing." Baker was so stung that he barely sang for the rest of the tour. He replaced many of the vocals with hard bop like "C.T.A.," written by the East Coast sax player Jimmy Heath. His playing became more steely and blunt, as if he were out to show how tough he was.

But Jimmy Bond thought his employer was perilously weak as bad influences threatened to drown him. "When we went to Europe, that's when Chet really went crazy," Bond said. "I think he was terribly disturbed." Baker met a whole new circle of addicts, including René Thomas and another Belgian, bassist Benoît Quersin. "They were so hip and funny, and beautiful musicians," said Lili. "But I must say they helped turn Chet to drugs." Meanwhile, Crystal Joy's fear had come true: Twardzik lapsed deeper into heroin than ever. A year earlier, the pianist would have spent his days combing the local museums and libraries; now he and Peter Littman searched the streets for dope, then lay stoned in the hotel until it was time for work.

Professionally, at least, Twardzik and Baker drew closer when Nicole Barclay, a French jazz impresario, began recording Baker voraciously on Barclay Disques, the label she had founded with her husband, Eddie Barclay. A voluptuous, bisexual brunette, Barclay was entranced by American jazz stars, and made albums with Lester Young, Thelonious Monk, singer-pianist Blossom Dearie (then Bobby Jaspar's wife), and the Modern Jazz Quartet, among others. She promoted their efforts in *Jazz* magazine, which she published. "These people knew they had a friend when they came to Paris," said René Urtreger.

Baker's first album for Barclay, *Rondette,* was a project far too arcane for any American producer. Twardzik had sailed to Europe with a bundle of music by his Boston composer friend Bob Zieff, who was nearly starving in his attempt to sell his avant-garde, classically inspired jazz pieces. Dick Bock used to cringe at the sight of the gaunt, rag-clad Zieff, who carried works like "Piece Caprice," "Mid-Forte," and "Pomp" under his arm in the futile hope of getting them recorded on Pacific Jazz. Twardzik felt that Europe would appreciate Zieff's work, with its allusions to Debussy and Alban Berg and its ambitious use of dissonance. Baker found the music lovely in its eccentricity, but its heavily composed themes left little room to improvise, and required more than a good ear to master. Baker stayed true to form by underrehearsing, and his performances sounded labored and tense. That wasn't the case with Bond, who bowed and plucked with cello-like sonority; nor with Littman, who shaded the music with imagination and subtlety. But Twardzik fumbled some of his parts, while Baker played too self-consciously to evoke much magic.

Given the condition of the band, it was a wonder they could focus at all. "Every night," said Bond, the only clean member, "someone was passing out because they were getting so stoned. I think what they were ingesting in Europe was so much stronger than anything they had ever had in their lives." Drummer Daniel Humair, then a teenager, took a train from his hometown of Geneva, Switzerland, to see his West Coast hero's quartet in concert. "It was like the Night of the Living Dead," said Humair. "Dark suits, gray faces, stoned out of their minds. Everything sounded strange to me, unhealthy. They were playing the music of the dead. I decided if I'm gonna be a jazz musician, I'm not gonna be like that."

Jimmy Bond was sure Twardzik had a death wish. Having revived him from an overdose in Holland, Bond kept checking up on him in his hotel room and finding him unconscious. "He wasn't friendly when I woke him up, either," said the bassist. "He'd still have the needle in his arm." In October, Twardzik phoned Crystal Joy in Boston. The connection was so poor that his voice kept fading in and out. "It sounded like he was under the waves," she said. "I could hear him saying 'I love you' and 'I'm clean, I'm straight.' It was a crock. He sounded stoned."

The denouement came on Thursday, October 20, a crisp fall night in Paris. The band had returned to record some more for Barclay, and on the eve of the session Baker, Twardzik, and Littman went to a midnight jam session at Tabou, a cellar boîte on rue Dauphine in the Latin Quarter. When word got out that Baker was there, local musicians excitedly carted their instruments out of the nearby Hôtel du Grand Balcon, the home of many jazzmen, and descended the twenty stone steps to Tabou. One of the first to arrive in that smoky cave was Urtreger, then a uniformed soldier. "For us it was fantastic to meet Chet," he said. "Most of the time his group was playing together, but sometimes we could sit in."

Twardzik sat at the piano with an Arabian fez tilted over his brow as he floated in his own world. Benoît Quersin and an Indonesian bassist, Eddie de Haas, played in place of Jimmy Bond, who hadn't come, mindful, perhaps, of the next day's recording. By the time the jam session broke up, bluish morning light bathed rue Dauphine. Urtreger walked Twardzik out of the club, gushing over him. The Frenchman left him at Grand Balcon. Twardzik was actually staying at another hotel, the Madeleine; it was later believed he had stopped at Grand Balcon to meet a drug connection.

The next morning, Baker, Bond, and Littman gathered at Pathé Studios on rue Magellan, near the Champs-Elysées, and began setting up. Twardzik didn't show. "Usually I looked after Dick," Bond said, "but this day, for some reason, I didn't. I thought, 'I can't keep babysitting for you.' " After an hour, though, Bond was worried, and he phoned the Madeleine and said there might be an emergency. The manager went up to Twardzik's room and knocked, but no one answered. "He had to break down the door," Baker later told Rogers Worthington. "Dick had locked it from the inside. And the thing was still in his arm. He was bright blue."

The manager called the police, who arrived in minutes. With Twardzik lying dead, they ransacked the room for evidence, gathering up his "works," a small amount of heroin, and letters from Crystal Joy. Baker, Littman, and Bond were summoned to the station. Bond was "petrified," he said, as the police fired out questions about Twardzik. Baker sat in a daze, hardly able to respond. "Chet had a way of having a blank stare, not knowing how to react to anything," said Bond. "He was certainly distressed, but I don't think he was really in touch with what had happened. I was devastated. Despite the pain in the ass that he was, I liked Dick a lot. And his music was something else. I felt responsible. It would have taken me a few minutes to stop by his room and bug him again. But this was just waiting to happen." Soon after, the disgusted bassist flew home to America.

A report went out over the wire services that Twardzik had died of a heart attack—proof of the scandalousness of a drug overdose in the fifties. The French state department notified Clare and Henryk Twardzik of their son's death. They requested cremation. The couple arranged a service at the cemetery down the road from their new home in West Newbury, Massachusetts. Serge Chaloff, Herb Pomeroy, and dozens more Boston musicians gathered around a thin bronze tombstone bearing the words RICHARD HENRYK TWARDZIK, 1931–1955 and a quotation from the Thirty-third Psalm:

Make a new sound upon the earth
Play skillfully with a loud noise

Pomeroy noticed a curiously serene look on Henryk's and Clare's faces. "I felt they were relieved," he said. "They didn't say anything to that effect, but Dick had given them so much grief that it seemed like a burden had been lifted from their shoulders."

A week later, Chaloff broke the news to Crystal Joy by phone. She was devastated. He claimed he hadn't wanted to upset her earlier, but Joy was sure that Twardzik's family hadn't wanted her at the funeral. "I was in such a state of shock for so long, I didn't know what hit me," she said. The death set off a campaign of recriminations that tore apart many of the people who had loved Twardzik. Baker and Littman had a violent argument, after which the drummer went back to America. Years later, Eddie de Haas was sure that Twardzik and Littman had gotten high together on that fateful early morning. When Twardzik OD'd, de Haas believed, Littman made a cursory attempt to revive him, but it was too late, and the drummer fled.

Chaloff also held Littman responsible, as he showed in a notorious confrontation at the Jazz Workshop in Boston. Shouting that Littman had killed Twardzik, Chaloff punched him in the face so hard he fell to the floor. Littman didn't fight back. But after briefly rejoining Baker in 1956, he started spreading his own version of Twardzik's last minutes. It was Baker, he said, who had left the Madeleine in a panic after shooting up with Twardzik and watching him OD. "A lot of people blame Chet for Dick's death, especially in Boston," said pianist Hal Galper, Baker's accompanist in the sixties. "Pete told us the story."

And Crystal Joy believed it. "Peter and Dick were like brothers," she said.

"I can't believe he wouldn't have tried to save Dick. He knew how to do it. Chet, on the other hand, had his career to think about, and his name, and he'd be the first one to split, in my opinion." Amazingly, Baker and Littman would reunite as bandmates and needle buddies for a few months in 1956.

The damage to Baker's reputation was already done. "There was a lot of talk that I was responsible for Dick's death," he admitted later in *Today,* a British tabloid. *Metronome* seemed to echo the suspicion in a memorial to Twardzik: "With Chet he went to Europe. His ashes returned recently." Clare and Henryk seethed with hatred for Baker, too, and wrote him blistering letters accusing him of killing their son. Herb Pomeroy wondered if "Dick's parents needed to put the blame on somebody to take it away from themselves."

Yet Baker's accounts of the tragedy and the events preceding it are so convoluted that they hint at some kind of deception. "Practically from the first night we got to Europe I think that Dick and Peter started to take drugs," he told the BBC's Peter Clayton in 1981, admitting no prior awareness of his sideman's habit. "I was, of course, clean at that time, and very naïve, and knew very little about what was happening." Considering his friendships with numerous addicts (Parker, Mulligan, Whitlock), his own experiments with the drug, and his romance with a woman who had dabbled with heroin, the claim was hard to accept. Yet Baker insisted he didn't learn the truth about Twardzik and Littman "for several months," until a concert in late September—one that occurred less than two weeks after the band had arrived in Europe. Onstage he heard a crash, he said, and turned to see Twardzik passed out on the floor. "Of course he was all right," said Baker, "and I found out, at that time, what was happening."

He had changed his tale since 1963, when he told *Today* that before the first concert in Amsterdam, Twardzik had asked his permission to "turn on," or shoot up. "I let him," said Baker. "I told him he was a grown man and had to decide for himself. I warned him not to let it become a daily ritual." Crystal Joy found the story laughable, as did Ruth Young. One night in the late seventies Baker invited a drug dealer into their Austrian hotel room to fix, and the guest OD'd. Young was stunned at her lover's hair-trigger response: to dump the body as fast as possible. "It was just like—oh my God, we burned the eggs," she said. "That's how matter-of-fact he was."

The mystery of Twardzik's death was never solved, but for the rest of his life Baker was haunted by the loss. "Dick's overdose totally destroyed me," he told Jerome Reece in *Jazz Hot.* Lili stood by him: "Chet didn't push Dick into anything. And he suffered very much from his death." His pain went on public show a few days later at the Stoll Theatre in London. Because of a British union ban on American instrumentalists, he gave an all-vocal recital with local players. The 2,900-seat hall was only half-full, and tension swelled as Baker walked out in a funereal charcoal-gray suit and took a stiff bow. "His first words were a shock," reported Mike Nevard in *Melody Maker.* "White-faced, he clenched the microphone and announced that his pianist was dead." He eulogized Twardzik with a string of yearning love songs—"This Is Always," "My Funny Valentine," "Someone to Watch Over Me," "But Not for Me"—delivered to an audience frozen in silence. "He sang as though to himself, eyes closed, face screwed tight in concentration," wrote Nevard, who called the concert "morbid rather than poignant." After fifteen minutes Baker left the stage, "too grief-stricken to continue," according to *Jazz* magazine.

It seemed as though Baker was finally confronting his feelings, yet thereafter he squelched them even further. The next day he returned to Paris to record for Barclay. Ending the sessions with a piece by Bobby Jaspar, "In Memory of Dick," he gave one of his coldest performances ever.

Only six weeks into the tour, Baker had lost his band, his "heroic" American reputation, and whatever optimism his Dutch successes had given him. Most of his forthcoming bookings had vanished too. "Before we left the States," said Jimmy Bond, "the page was black with concert dates. And they faded along the way. Maybe we were playing one or two a week."

In the meantime, Baker needed to form a new group quickly. He hired two fine musicians: Eddie de Haas and Jean-Louis Chautemps, a French tenor saxophonist with the cool lyricism of Zoot Sims and Stan Getz. But the new group was hampered by the addition of pianist Raphel (Ralph) Schecroun, an Erroll Garner disciple—he later called himself Errol Parker—who played in only two keys; and Charles Saudrais, a raucous teenage drummer. In a broadcast from Copenhagen that December, the mood was mainly angry. Baker's playing—harsh, choppy, often out of tune—was unrecognizable. He chose a lot of tough bop that required no vulnerability; even his sole ballad, "Darn That Dream," had a hostile edge, aggravated by Schecroun's wrong chords and Saudrais's bashing. The trumpeter knew he was floundering. "We're a little bit too far apart," he announced apologetically. "We're used to playing all bunched up. Get a better feeling that way."

With so few concert and club dates ahead for Baker, Joe Napoli had booked him at American military bases throughout Europe. Most of the time, the band was greeted indifferently by men who wanted only to laugh and forget their troubles. In December the group traveled to Ruislip, a base in Middlesex, England. They played in a huge gymnasium with basketball nets on all four walls and chairs scattered on a floor covered with canvas sheets. Lacking a stage, they set up beneath the scoreboard and performed in the glare of four overhead spotlights. Mike Nevard described the show in *Melody Maker:* "In a hall big enough to hold two thousand British fans, he blew for a few hundred U.S. servicemen. Some of them got up and left during the first number. Others stood about and talked during the eighty-minute concert. By the finale, some thirty or forty had left the hall." Baker gave them a cold shoulder of his own. "The poignant trumpet that echoed from the Gerry Mulligan records exists today only in fleeting glimpses," wrote Nevard. Baker, he said, "doesn't doodle so much; he blows out, at times almost viciously."

When Baker visited the airbase at Keflavík, Iceland, during Christmas week, "cool" took on a surreal new subtext. Stepping off the plane into a blizzard, the band hurried aboard a freezing army bus. Eddie de Haas peered out the frost-covered window and saw the vehicle enter a long white tunnel, not unlike the one described by people who are brought back from death on the operating table. Eventually Baker and his group were deposited at the entrance of their hotel. Once in his room, de Haas looked out the second-story window to see about ten feet of snow piled to the ledge. That's when he realized the "tunnel" was a huge channel dug through the snow to let traffic pass.

Apart from a friendly Christmas dinner at the home of a young promoter and his family, they were left to their own devices in a place that Lili likened to another planet. As they walked the streets on the holiday weekend, she noticed that everyone in sight was drunk. Later she had to fend off an officer's inebriated wife, who insisted on giving her a bracelet. Getting to work required a three-hour drive to the base. "We raced on a deserted road under the moon," Lili recalled. "It was a moonlike landscape with lava on the sides, kind of violet. It was unreal. And very beautiful."

The long trip didn't reach a comforting end. Arriving at an American military canteen, the musicians were treated like a party band by an audience of small-town soldiers who cared nothing about jazz. Uniformed men milled around, carrying plates of cafeteria food and shouting over the music; from the back of the room came the clatter of pinball machines and yells of "BINGO!"

The New Year brought a glimmer of hope. Baker would be spending January in Italy, a country that eagerly awaited him. According to Adriano Mazzoletti, an Italian broadcaster, journalist, and promoter who spent much of that month with Baker: "In 1952, when the first Gerry Mulligan records arrived in Italy—ah! It was fantastic for the Italian people. Italians at the time loved the white musicians, the sound of California. Chet was a real revelation. He played strong but sweet, and Italians were also fascinated by his singing. The girls were very interested."

But not the customers of the Taverna Room in Milan's Hotel Duomo, where Baker opened a two-week run on New Year's Eve. One of the poshest hotels in Milan, the Duomo catered to an old-money clientele who considered jazz a bizarre foreign language. Photographer Francesco Maino recalled the gig as a disaster: "People were there to celebrate, dance, and get drunk. After a while the audience booed Chet, and finally the proprietor threw him out. Apparently Chet was very depressed."

The response wasn't much better in Perugia, an ancient city on the Tiber River, where Mazzoletti had booked the band to play on January 29. Earlier the promoter had fought to organize a concert there for Louis Armstrong, known as "Ambassador Satch" for his use of jazz as an international goodwill tool. The managers of the old theater shuddered. "No black musicians!" they declared. Mazzoletti persisted, and finally Armstrong gave the town its first jazz concert, to great success. Thus vindicated, Mazzoletti presented Baker. But he had overestimated the trumpeter's popularity, and only about a hundred people came. Later the management sent Mazzoletti a telegram advising him that Baker wouldn't be welcome there in the future.

At loose ends for the next week, Baker stayed in Perugia with Mazzoletti, who found him racked with frustration. Baker confided a neurotic mistrust of Lili, whom he suspected of flirting with other men; his disgust with Charles Saudrais, whose drumming he hated; and most of all, his agony over the death of Twardzik, although he avoided details. But this emotional upheaval was smothered in a televised appearance at the RAI (Radio Italia) studios in Rome.* His group played three songs, including "You Don't Know What Love Is." Baker's rapport with the camera was gone; singing of the agony that comes when "you've loved a love you had to lose," he looked and sounded eerily robotic.

As his visit with Mazzoletti wore on, Baker started exhibiting flu-like

*The RAI footage, seen in *Let's Get Lost* and other documentaries, is mistakenly identified as a performance at Italy's famous San Remo Festival.

symptoms that his host assumed to be heroin withdrawal. "In 1956, nobody in Italy knew about drugs," Mazzoletti explained. "All the people were clean. Chet had no more heroin, and he had many health problems." Through a doctor friend, Mazzoletti obtained a bottle of morphine. He gave it to Baker at three o'clock one afternoon. By eight, the trumpeter had finished it and wanted more. Moving on to Genoa, he combed the streets with Lili in search of a dealer, and ended up scoring opium.

The tour petered out in March with a sparse lineup of German concert dates. It closed in unexpected triumph on March 31, when a triple bill of Baker, Gerry Mulligan, and Stan Getz drew twelve thousand fans to Berlin's Deutschlandhalle, the massive auditorium that had once served as a platform for Hitler. Yet this success couldn't offset all the trouble that had preceded it, and Baker longed for California. At the start of April, he flew back, leaving Lili behind. "I was sad," she said, "because I was afraid I was gonna lose him."

A few weeks later, she found a letter from Baker in her mailbox. He informed her tersely that he had married a girl named Halema. In photos that William Claxton took of the couple, the new Mrs. Baker looked so much like Lili that many assumed they were one and the same. "I cried a lot," said Lili. "All along, I was just living in the moment. I never thought, 'How am I gonna keep Chet here?' or 'How can I get back to the States?' The marriage I never had, never tried to have, she had. Well, I didn't give a shit about marriage."

Nevertheless, a few years later, she wed Gilbert "Bibi" Rovère, a French bassist. She went on to have affairs with Dexter Gordon, Milt Jackson, and other favorite musicians of hers while establishing herself as an actress in France. But even in her sixties, the sight of Baker in old photos would leave her dewy-eyed.

Claxton had a different response when he saw some pictures he took of Baker at a 1956 record date in Hollywood. Standing in his darkroom, he was jarred by the sight that emerged in his developing tray: the face that had once captivated him with its sweetness had hardened into a stony mask.

8

At the time Baker returned to America, jazz there had hit a peak of respectability. Magazines like *Esquire, Life,* and *Playboy* were treating the music like high art; more and more of its stars were moving into major concert halls and recording for big labels. Texaco and Timex sponsored flashy jazz spectaculars on TV; the masters of the swing era—Benny Goodman, Lionel Hampton, Red Norvo—were hailed as grand elder statesmen. Younger players saw their own work as far more than entertainment.

A prime example was the Modern Jazz Quartet, who had swept the polls since their debut in 1954. Pianist John Lewis, bassist Percy Heath, vibraphonist Milt Jackson, and drummer Connie Kay focused on Lewis's semiclassical originals, playing them with the unsmiling dignity of a chamber group. Gerry Mulligan viewed jazz in the same lofty terms. He considered nightclubs an insult to his art, and was fighting, with some success, to remake himself as a concert artist. At the same time, he craved pop stardom, and he took small roles in a number of films—notably *Bells Are Ringing,* whose star, Judy Holliday, was one of his several celebrity girlfriends.

Meanwhile, Miles Davis and arranger Gil Evans were making a series of ambitious orchestral albums, including *Sketches of Spain* and *Miles Ahead,* that were welcomed as reverently as any symphonic work by Leonard Bernstein or Aaron Copland. "I always had a curiosity about trying new things in music," Davis told *Playboy.* "A new sound, another way to do something."

But Chet Baker rarely thought beyond the next gig, and by 1956 he seemed like yesterday's heartthrob, one the jazz world was happy to forget. While he was away in Europe, he had dropped below Davis and Dizzy

Gillespie in the polls. Baker's harshest opponent, critic Martin Williams, charted his continuing crash. "The history of the performing arts in America is certainly strewn with highly promising, immature talents which are overpraised, exploited, and often, never fulfilled," wrote Williams of Baker in *Down Beat.*

West Coast Jazz itself was becoming a quaint anachronism. As clubs like the Haig, Zardi's, and the Tiffany folded, many L.A. players sought the lucrative option of studio work. Sales at Pacific Jazz were falling off, leading Dick Bock to rename his label World Pacific and to shift its roster toward world music and black artists. Bock hadn't given up yet on Chet Baker, but both he and Joe Napoli agreed that the trumpeter needed to toughen up his American image—hence *Chet Baker and Crew,* an attempt, in July 1956, to make an East Coast jazz album in the West.

Instead of love songs, Baker played gritty originals by Al Haig, Al Cohn, and other New York musicians. The charts left room for fiery solos by Phil Urso, Peter Littman (whom Baker had rehired for a few months), and Bobby Timmons, a funky blues-based pianist from Philadelphia who had joined the group in April. Baker's thin, metallic tone sounded more like Miles Davis's than ever. "This may well be Baker's best LP so far," wrote Nat Hentoff in *Down Beat,* noting his newfound "virility" and "cheering diminution of wispiness."

There was nothing remotely "wispy" about tunes like "Chippyin'," a new song in Baker's repertoire, whose title referred to casual heroin use. Having once led a "cool" band, he now had a "hot" one: junkie lingo for addicted, which all of them were, except for Bond. Baker's account of his downfall was designed to elicit maximum sympathy. In 1963 he told *Today* magazine that upon returning to the States, he was walking down Broadway in New York when an "attractive colored girl," Dick Twardzik's girlfriend, slapped him hard across the face. "That's for what you did to Dick," she said tearfully. This was the "final turn of the screw," he claimed. "I hailed a cab and went to see an addict I knew in Harlem. He kept his own habit going by scoring for others. I gave him a twenty-dollar bill and asked for four bags. Fast. That was the start. Whereas most people start by sniffing, then skinning,* and finally mainlining, I started on vein injections straight off. I was hooked."

Crystal Joy, who denied ever seeing Baker again after he left for Europe,

*Injecting under the skin, not into a vein, for a milder high

found the tale ridiculous. "Oh, so it's my fault," she responded. "Well, at least he said I was attractive."

It mystified his "clean" friends to see him follow in Twardzik's fatal path, but to Baker, this may have been the ultimate way to bond with his imagined soulmate. Asked about it all his life, he would answer that when he saw his friend die for the love of heroin, he just had to find out what the drug was all about. But in 1961, as he sat in a Tuscan jail cell awaiting trial for several drug-related crimes, Baker spoke more candidly to the Italian magazine *L'Europeo.* "It is always a terrible moment for me, that moment when I have to appear with my instrument in front of the public," he revealed. "It grabs me by the throat, an inexplicable terror, an unreasonable fear. . . . I suddenly see myself exposed to failure, to shame. Only the drug can help me overcome this terrible moment. I return to being the master. I feel calm. The public stops being an enemy, a hostile bunch of adversaries ready to strike me down with their whistles. I don't have anyone in front of me anymore. I am alone with my trumpet and my music."

Ruth Young took his explanation one step further. "Why is it that every jazz musician just happened to get bent out of shape?" she said. "Is that just an accident? What you have to go through to bare your guts—it's so fundamentally obvious. In order to really, genuinely be a participant in that world, you had to find a poison to let you look in the mirror." And for Baker, she thought, the reflected image was terrifying.

In clubs, even casual observers of his band knew they were seeing a group of users. Littman sat slouched over the drums, eyelids drooping. One night he set up about eight cymbal stands (rather than the two or three most drummers used), and one of them was scratching Bond's bass. "Move the cymbal, man!" Bond whispered. "Awww, *mannnn*!" drawled Littman, too high to care. The usually cool-headed Bond lost his temper and swung a fist at the drummer, who fell off the stage.

Bobby Timmons had more discipline, and went on to become a valued member of the Art Blakey and Cannonball Adderley bands. But for all his talent, Bond said, "he destroyed himself—drugs, alcohol." Meanwhile, recalled Bill Loughborough, Urso's recklessness threatened to get them all arrested. On drives from town to town, Urso stopped at gas stations to fix, and one day he strolled out of a toilet sucking blood off the crook of his arm. Loughborough was furious. "Awww, these people don't know anything about this shit!" muttered Urso.

Loughborough, whose own drug use stopped short of the needle, had lost patience. Baker had left him in charge of road-managing the band and transporting them in his van; that gave the trumpeter time to hunt for drugs. He carried everyone's payroll in his pocket: a wad of hundred-dollar bills that might be traded at any time for a new car or dope. Finally both Bond and Loughborough quit. "I don't want to be around to watch you kill yourself," the latter told Baker.

That was one of the fears of Halema Alli, whom Baker had met in April 1956 and married in May, when she was just twenty. Onstage at the Rouge Lounge in Detroit, Baker had locked eyes with a dark-skinned, short-haired young woman at the bar. Halema lived in town with her East Indian family; she had no foreign accent, but her exotic look attracted him just as Lili's had. Yet Bob Zieff would later call her "a quiet, sweet homegirl, and probably fantastically naïve." She had never had a boyfriend, nor even been to a jazz club before. Baker's forbidding sexiness must have titillated her, while her reserve intrigued him. "She looked like a mirage," he told his friend Jack Simpson years later. "She was so beautiful. A little bit timid, especially with men, but very intelligent, very sensitive and sweet."

Halema was overwhelmed when Baker started bombarding her with calls from other cities, and even more startled when, after so little time in her company, he proposed. Baker picked her up in Detroit and drove her to St. Louis, where they were wed by a justice of the peace. Littman served as witness. It all occurred so quickly that she barely grasped what was happening. "I ran away from home," she said. "I just left one day, don't ask me why. Nobody knew I was leaving. A girlfriend who helped me leave called my parents to tell them so they wouldn't worry about me, and after I got married, then I told them."

Thus began a marriage that, within a month, would turn into a hellish roller-coaster ride; forty years hence, she still didn't want to talk about it. The couple never had their own home; they roomed with friends and strangers, crashed in hotels and motels. But things began romantically enough as Baker tried to make his best impression on the shy young woman. He took her with him everywhere—on helicopter rides and deep-sea diving trips, to gigs all over the United States—and bought her presents, including a brand-new Thunderbird for her twenty-first birthday.

Baker introduced her to all his musician friends; she hardly said a word because they scared her. Perhaps sensing that, they went out of their way to be nice to her. Phil Urso wrote a song called "Halema," which Baker recorded; Peter Littman was on good behavior around her too. Littman had been on drugs but he wasn't anymore, Baker assured her. She had no reason to doubt him. "I didn't even know what a junkie was," she recalled. At first she didn't even seem aware of her husband's habit. "Chet never, ever used drugs in front of me," she insisted. *"Ever."* During their whole marriage, she claimed, they argued only once.

Baker was still in control in the fall of 1956, when he made a new round of albums for Dick Bock. One of them, *Playboys,* teamed him with Art Pepper, the celebrated West Coast alto saxophonist. Aside from his movie-star looks, not unlike Tyrone Power's, Pepper shared with Baker a talent so natural he barely had to think about what he was doing. In his 1979 memoir *Straight Life,* Pepper discussed his music little, focusing instead on the thrills of copping, getting high, and doing jail time. His playing, though sometimes pretty, sounded hardened and cold; so did Baker's as his habit grew. *Playboys* was a blowing contest, with long, leathery solos by the two stars. On *Quartet: Russ Freeman and Chet Baker,* made a month later, Baker played a new ballad by Freeman, "Summer Sketch," that rivaled "The Wind" and "My Funny Valentine" in its stark beauty. His other solos were impeccably shaped, but short on feeling.

William Claxton photographed Baker in the studio that autumn. "He was looking very paranoid, sinister," said Claxton. "In my naïve way, I finally woke up and thought, 'There's something wrong with him! I wonder if he's on some drug.' And of course, he was totally stoned." Baker snapped at Claxton's every request: "What do you mean by that?" "Why should I do that?" Near Thanksgiving, Halema gave Baker some unwelcome news. He was going to become a father—a job he was in no way equipped to handle.

The pressure inside him kept building, as Claxton saw when he took Baker's picture for the cover of *The Blues,* a Pacific Jazz anthology album. Claxton had picked as unbluesy a setting as possible: a vacant house in Redondo Beach, sun-drenched and painted white. Halema was with her husband, and in her sleeveless summer dress she looked so seductive that Claxton used her in the shot. Posing them in a window seat, he asked Baker to take off his shirt. Then he gave directions: "Put your leg up here, Chet . . ." Suspicious of the manipulation, Baker blew up. The photographer tried to calm him down—"Chet, just relax!"—so they could proceed. The contact sheet showed Baker scowling at the camera, wearing bangs that made him look like a nasty juvenile delinquent.

Out of that tense session, Claxton ended up with his most famous photo, a classic of cool sensuality. Wearing only khakis, Baker stands in profile before the window, arm resting on his knee. Halema sits with her head against his hand, gazing out soulfully. Soft light streams in from behind them, yet the couple are enveloped in shadows, as though they were carrying their own dark cloud.

Albert "Tootie" Heath, Baker's new drummer, got caught in it. A twenty-one-year-old from Philadelphia, Heath was the younger brother of bassist Percy Heath and saxophonist Jimmy Heath, both of whom had worked with Baker. Tootie didn't touch drugs, and as soon as he joined the band, his mother phoned Bill Galletly, Baker's new manager, in a panic: "My baby is going out on the road with Chet Baker—can you assure me he's gonna be all right?"

Heath's initiation came on a nightmarish drive from Manhattan to the Rouge Lounge near Detroit, where the group was set to open that night. Baker held up the departure for hours while he prowled for drugs, a pregnant Halema in tow. "She was a beautiful woman, and she followed this guy around like a dog," Heath said. "He was in serious control of her." Finally they set off. Baker hit the Pennsylvania Turnpike in a rainstorm and drove "like a maniac," said the drummer, in an attempt to make up for lost time. "I was a nervous wreck by the time we got there," admitted Heath. "The people were so glad to see us, because we were late." Baker still had the drawing power to get away with such behavior, and he "really worked it," according to Heath.

The addicts in the group—Baker, Urso, Timmons—stuck together, and Heath felt ignored. They fixed before the first set, and the results were all too obvious. Sometimes Baker was so unsteady that he had to sit in a chair onstage; this became his custom. "But the audiences loved him, so he could do no wrong," Heath said. "He could sit there and sleep, and people thought that was cute." In a few months, Heath quit.

A national audience got their last glimpse of the strong, healthy Chet Baker of old in February 1957, when he accepted *Playboy's* All-Star Jazz Award on the *Tonight* show. Baker had placed second in the trumpet poll to Louis Armstrong. That night he announced his spot in "Birdland Stars of '57," a four-month tour set to begin that weekend. Baker would share the stage with some of the biggest names in jazz, including Count Basie, Sarah Vaughan, Bud Powell, and Lester Young.

Narcotics agents trailed him from the start. On February 19, during the first week, Baker and Urso arrived at Philadelphia's distinguished Academy of Music. At intermission, two plainclothesmen slapped them with a search warrant. Urso tried flushing his drugs down the dressing-room toilet, but the officers caught him; then they seized a bag of heroin from his saxophone case and a stash of pot from Baker's glove compartment. The musicians were handcuffed and brought to the station. Baker claimed he hadn't touched drugs in six years, but both he and Urso tested positive for heroin and were thrown into adjacent cells for the night. The next day Joe Glaser arranged their bail, and they were released, with the warning that they faced ten to twenty years in prison if caught again. Reports of the bust went out on the wire services, and the two were fired from the tour.

That winter, Baker hired Joseph "Philly Joe" Jones, a bebop drummer whose explosive rhythms were matched by his reputation as one of the most outrageous junkies in jazz. Jones had won fame as the drummer in Miles Davis's midfifties quintet, which featured saxophonist John Coltrane. For all Jones's talent, his habit was so out of control that he sometimes had to leave the stage to vomit. Davis had suspected Jones of feeding Coltrane's own addiction, and in March 1957 he fired them both. Strapped for funds and willing to work cheap, Jones accepted an offer from Chet Baker.

With Davis's ex-drummer to spur him on, Baker was "playing his ass off," according to Don Friedman, a young pianist who joined them that summer. "Chet at that time sounded like Miles," said Friedman. "He had chops, power, he was playing fast and furious." More than sharing music, though, Baker and Jones loved getting high together. "They were hitting themselves in the foot because the veins in their arms were so messed up," Friedman explained. For them, as for most needle buddies, fixing together was a ritual of bonding. "It was like a homosexual thing," said an addicted bassist. "You saw a guy you hadn't seen or played with for a while, and you'd say, 'Hey man, let's get together, I know a good connection, let's go someplace and get high.' "

Paying for the "stuff" was usually a hassle, though. "You don't have money, you gotta have money, you get it wherever you can," the bassist said. "You have no conscience. You rob your brother, your mother, your wife." Or your employer. For a time Baker was using two cars on the road, one of which he entrusted to Jones, along with a gas station credit card. Only later did the trumpeter learn that Jones was stopping at every other gas station to charge tires, which he sold at alternate stations for cash.

He ended up firing Jones, but Baker was growing just as deceitful. The change in him was all too clear at Peacock Lane, a short-lived Hollywood jazz club where he worked for two weeks in July 1957. Baker's fans saw an embittered junkie, his once-golden tan replaced by a gray pallor. He kept arriving late, infuriating the owner; once there, he lashed out at everyone around him. Early in the run, he fired his whole band. Baritone saxophonist Pepper Adams and bassist Doug Watkins stayed to work out the two-week notice he gave them, but for much of the run he had no drummer, and he used up a series of pianists. Having appropriated Miles Davis's trumpet style, Baker mimicked his hero's hostile stage manner as well by turning his back on the audience. Watkins had a solo in Baker's vocal version of "This Is Always," and one night, before the bassist was through, Baker grabbed the mike stand from him and dragged it across the stage to sing his final chorus.

John Tynan's scathing review in *Down Beat* alerted readers everywhere to Baker's Jekyll-and-Hyde transformation. "Judging by his behavior onstage, the only performer who mattered at all was Baker," observed Tynan. "The leader's governing attitude is surly, unfriendly, strictly don't-give-a-damn. . . . Chet Baker, Established Star, is much less refreshing than Baker, Boy Trumpet Player. In the latter context he still has something of value to say—when he bothers to care."

In the second week, Baker brought in Don Friedman. Then twenty-two and a graduate of Dexter Gordon's band, Friedman was just starting a durable career as a bandleader and pianist with trumpeters Clark Terry and Ornette Coleman, among others. Having grown up in L.A. during Baker's "cool" heyday, Friedman was shocked at the trumpeter's current behavior. "He was a scary guy—never around, always running off to score, very nervous," Friedman said. "He drove like a maniac on Hollywood Boulevard, like he was on the Indianapolis Speedway." Still, Friedman was in awe of his new colleagues. "These people were my idols, like Philly Joe, who had been playing with Miles, who had my favorite band at that time. And Pepper Adams was a monster."

"The kid," as they called him, was desperate to fit in, and soon he was "chippying" as well. "I wanted to be accepted," he said. "The drugs helped ease my mind, made me feel less frightened. I was risking my life every time I shot shit, but I never even thought about it at the time." Nor did his bandmates discourage him, even when he kept nodding off on the stand. More than once, audiences saw his head hit the piano keys.

The group's recklessness backfired near the end of the run. Driving to work with Halema—now eight months pregnant—in the passenger seat, Baker stopped to score, then drag-raced to Peacock Lane in the futile attempt to arrive on time. Pulling up to the curb, he spotted John O'Grady and Dick Hill, his drug-avenging foes from the LAPD, outside the club. They were examining the arms of Friedman and Larance Marable, the fourth drummer in the engagement. Baker parked up the street and snuck inside Peacock Lane. Late for work again, he found the manager blocking his way to the stage. The trumpeter walked out the door and crept to his car, where Halema waited. As soon as he drove off, Hill and O'Grady began chasing him in an unmarked car.

Baker outraced them, and once they were in a safe place, he sent his wife home in a cab. Then he drove to Balboa Bay, where for over a week he hid out on a boat owned by an ex-junkie friend. Back in L.A., Baker learned that Hill and O'Grady had threatened to throw Friedman in jail unless he signed a statement admitting that Baker had given him the dope. The frightened young pianist had no choice but to cooperate.

Now Baker had to leave town. He told Halema to meet him in San Francisco. There, on August 7, 1957, their son was born. She christened him Chesney Aftab Baker, the middle name a Pakistani word for the sun. But the child's twenty-one-year-old mother felt mostly gloom as she realized she was married to a man who couldn't even care for himself. "I don't think Chet was father material to begin with," she said. "He was the type of person that wanted all the attention, and wanted somebody that could go wherever he went. And with a child you can't do that."

In his memoir Baker brushed over his first fatherhood without a hint of sentiment. "The next couple of years were difficult, with a continuous change of personnel in the band," he wrote. Eventually he told Jack Simpson and others that Chesney had been born slightly retarded, a condition he blamed on insanity in Halema's family. But friends wondered if parental drug use might have affected the child's genes. Whatever the cause, Halema vowed to protect him from Baker as they headed for a new life in Manhattan. "My son never knew his father," she said. "I did my best to keep them apart."

Times Square, New York, 1958. Photo by Carole Reiff; © Carole Reiff Photo Archive

9

Baker reached New York in August 1957 with no place to live, no money, and few prospects. Aside from a few Harlem drug dealers, hardly anyone cared about his arrival. Most local musicians had brushed him off as a second-rate clone of Miles Davis, who already lived in Manhattan and had just released the most talked-about new album in jazz, *Miles Ahead.* History was unfolding at the Five Spot club in east Greenwich Village, where John Coltrane and Thelonious Monk were playing a long duo engagement. According to Nat Hentoff, Coltrane had burgeoned from a fine tenor saxophonist into "one of the most persistent, relentless expanders of possibility . . . in jazz history," and no one seemed to disagree. Jazzmen packed the Five Spot to see the future of their music, and the vision didn't include Chet Baker.

The trumpeter came to town at a dangerous time of anti-dope crackdowns—another attempt, on a local scale, to restore fifties society to an illusion of purity and goodness. On May 28, 1957, 160 narcotics officers had gone on a citywide twenty-four-hour sweep, arresting 131 people, including the bop alto player Jackie McLean, on drug raps. Two years later, the *New York Post* would devote pages to the downfall of Billie Holiday, who died at forty-four in Harlem's Metropolitan Hospital. Police had arrested her on her deathbed for possession of heroin. *Time* magazine sounded an alarm to the nation by calling Manhattan "a city where 'pushers' peddle their wares almost as casually as sidewalk balloon vendors, where children sniff heroin even in classrooms, where an innocent-looking drugstore or cafeteria may be an addicts' hangout."

Unquestionably, New York was the drug capital of America. By the late fifties, a fix of heroin cost only a few dollars, and it was easy to find, especially for jazz musicians. They bought from dealers with names like Blond Ray, Slim, Dirty Nick, and Johnny E: sleazy hoods who sold in jazz-club toilets, in doorways along Lenox Avenue, and, in the case of Slim, out of a car on a Harlem side street, with a tire iron at hand to settle price disputes. In midtown, a favorite place to score was Hansen's Drugstore, a hipster hangout at Fifty-first and Seventh where the addicted comic Lenny Bruce held court in a rear booth.

Baker would become a familiar figure in all these places, but first he had to get himself and his family a place to live. Francy Boland, a Belgian pianist who had played for him in Europe, came to the rescue. Boland had just taken a large apartment on the Upper West Side. Struggling to support his wife and two small children, he had rented a room to Eddie de Haas, who was also new in town. Boland invited the Bakers to share the rent too. Once the family had settled into a spare room, Baker focused not on reviving his career but on finding junk. Every few hours he emerged from behind the closed door of his bedroom, unshaven and expressionless, and went downstairs to hail a cab for Harlem. Back home, he used Boland's phone to ask everyone he knew for "loans" of five, ten, twenty dollars. He claimed he needed the money for baby clothes or food, and few had the heart to refuse. Dick Bock kept sending him advances, but Baker's record sales were down, and the producer knew that their winning partnership had died.

Eddie de Haas, the only steadily employed member of the household, found himself supporting seven people plus himself on a paycheck of ninety-seven dollars a week. Every time he stocked the refrigerator, the food vanished before he could touch it. For a while he tolerated the situation for the sake of the children, but finally he moved out.

Halema and Chesney Aftab (or Chetty, as they called him) were the next to go. Everyone could see how frightened and heartsick the young woman was, especially over the welfare of her son. His father's arms and feet were full of bloodied "tracks," and he was losing weight. Halema's parents were horrified at the marriage and insisted she come home. Bundling up her infant son, she went back to Detroit.

Soon afterward, Baker was ejected from the apartment. Temporarily homeless, he slept in his car, then moved in with one of his dealers. "He was all but in the snakepit," said Bob Zieff, who now lived in an apartment in the West Sixties. Learning of her husband's whereabouts, Halema phoned Zieff from Detroit and begged him to take Baker in. "She said, 'If he stays with you, I know there'll be some chance of him being straight,' " Zieff recalled. Against his better judgment, he agreed to her naïve request, but Baker's actions didn't change. "I didn't even bother to blow my horn much," he remarked later. "I just pumped dope into me and dreamed my life away."

For Baker, such "tragic" admissions had a romanticized ring. But his self-esteem was undoubtedly crumbling as the gift he had always taken for granted—his music—slipped way. A loud, indifferent audience in Newark, New Jersey, jarred him out of his haze. "If Gerry Mulligan were here, he would yell at you," said Baker angrily into the mike. "But I'm here, and I don't understand why, if you can get a drink across the street in the bar for one third the price, you're in here making noise while I'm trying to play."

Baker felt so alone in New York that he found a psychiatrist. Halema later learned the doctor's prognosis: that Baker was using drugs to "punish himself" over the guilt he felt about Dick Twardzik. No amount of therapy could soothe him, so in his desperation he reached out to his father, whose approval he still longed for. Rarely had the older man ever offered a word of praise, and when the trumpeter sent his albums home to Hermosa Beach, it was Vera, not Chesney, who wrote back proudly.

Nonetheless, when Baker landed a few out-of-town jobs, he asked his father to come on the road as the band's driver and manager. Once they reunited, all their past resentments surged up again. They began arguing in Philadelphia, and Chesney threatened to drive home to California in one of his son's two cars. The trumpeter threw a tantrum, like a child whose toy was about to be snatched away. "You take that car and I'm gonna call the police and tell them it's stolen!" he shouted. The tension exploded into violence, to which son, like father, resorted all too readily. The blowup occurred before a roomful of people, including Zieff, Baker's pianist at the time. "They were circling around the room with clenched fists. Finally I said, 'Does this have to happen?' They both fell apart and started crying."

After that, Zieff caught a strange glimpse into the hearts of both men: "Chet started calling him Daddy all the time. It was the two of them against the rest of us, and the rest of the world was evil. Everybody was trying to misuse them." In Chesney Sr., Zieff saw a blueprint for much of the trumpeter's behavior. With the older man at the wheel, Bakers junior and senior drag-raced down the highway, both of them "screaming like the Dukes of Hazzard," Zieff said. "He was Daddy's Little Boy for that moment, at least." Baker laughed as his father yelled bigoted remarks—*"You foreign-looking bastard!"*–out the window.

But soon Chesney went home, and his son slipped back into full-time self-destruction. The band played a nightclub near Minneapolis for a two-week run that Zieff recalled as torture. "Chet would pass out on the bathroom floor and come out hours later," he said. "We'd be three or four hours late to the gig."

By now most club owners considered him poison; increasingly, so did Zieff. Home in New York, the composer feared trouble from the police or from Baker's drug connections. Finally he insisted that Baker leave. Baker "got very belligerent," he said, storming out in a huff and checking into a hotel. A freezing New York winter was approaching, and this latest "rejection" gave him one more excuse to feel victimized. He resumed crashing with drug dealers, on friends' sofas, or in the backseat of his car.

He had but one hope in sight: Dick Bock, who had phoned him at Zieff's to propose some new recordings. "Dick was awfully good to Chet," said Jimmy Bond. "He really believed in him, and he tried to help him. He put up with a lot of shit." Groping for a way to save Baker, Bock asked another of his artists, singer David Allyn, to intervene. A respected pop-jazz balladeer, Allyn was trying to salvage his own life from years of heroin addiction and imprisonment. He had just made an acclaimed album of Jerome Kern songs for World Pacific, and was working as a drug counselor. But Allyn knew that unless Baker wanted to help himself, nothing could be done, and clearly the trumpeter had no desire to quit. Asked by Jack Simpson why he did junk, Baker answered: "Jack, that's where I want to be. If I could get in a sailboat, sail around the world, and have all the shit I wanted, that's all I'd want."

What he really wanted was to shirk every responsibility and avoid the cost. After pestering Bock into letting him record several complicated Zieff pieces, Baker came to the studio two hours late, leaving Zieff and a chamber group waiting nervously. Baker didn't know the music, and went on to deliver stiff performances that Bock—no fan of Zieff's to begin with—wouldn't release.

After Zieff and the classical players had left, Baker stayed behind with the bassist, Ross Savakus, and David Wheat, a guitarist he had met on Bill Loughborough's barge. They lingered late into the night, smoking Wheat's bottomless stash of pot and recording sentimental ballads from his repertoire. Several mourned the death of love: "There's a Lull in My Life," "The Night We Called It a Day," "Little Girl Blue" (a woman's torch song whose gender Baker left unchanged). Even in the triumphant "They All Laughed" by the Gershwins, he played the prophet of doom. Baker had hit a turning point: for the first time on an album, he had completely dropped his façade of cool. There is no happy ending, he seemed to be saying, just sinking despair over promises broken.

Most of his chances had perished by his own hand, but it was Dick Bock who delivered the fatal blow to this album. Finding it depressing, he shelved it. Only after Baker's death would it surface under the title of one of its songs, *Embraceable You.* A review by British jazz critic Clive Davis echoed Bock's opinion: "That little-boy-lost persona has its charms but, over the course of an album, the impression is one of oppressive melancholia. But for many that is the essence of his appeal."

Bock was more excited about a project that re-created the Gerry Mulligan pianoless quartet (with bassist Henry Grimes and drummer Dave Bailey). But on *Reunion,* as the album was called, the magic was gone. Two horn lines that had once intertwined rapturously were now like oil and water; arrangements of "Star Dust" and other standards were filled out with lackluster solos. Mulligan couldn't hide his contempt for Baker, whose performance was one more sign of a "life of undiscipline," as the saxophonist called it. "Music requires discipline, and he once had it," Mulligan said. "He was serious about it, and he worked hard. And heroin is the opposite of that. Heroin is giving yourself up to whim, immediate sensation, immediate gratification. That has nothing to do with the quality required to be an artist."

On an album made at the same sessions, featuring jazz singer Annie Ross with the same quartet, Baker confirmed Mulligan's low opinion of him. Midway through the recording, recalled Ross, Baker "went to the loo and never came back." He was replaced with Art Farmer, and the album came out under the title *Annie Ross Sings a Song with Mulligan.* Days later, Baker phoned Ross to ask for a loan. "He told me his transmission had fallen out," she said. "I didn't even know what a transmission was. But I could tell that it was Chet being Chet."

As Baker fell off the jazz ladder, his old rival Stan Getz—whose messy drug overindulgences he snickered at—was on the rise; in 1964, Getz's single of "The Girl from Ipanema" would become a top-ten hit. His sound was candy to the ears of a mass audience, who in the polls had voted him number-one tenor player by a landslide. But he and Baker still shared the same weakness. In the winter of 1958, they stood together in front of Manhattan's Brill Building, the midtown headquarters of many top songwriters and music publishers, and shivered in overcoats and gloves as they awaited their connection. He was Donald Frankos, alias Tony the Greek: a tall, ruggedly handsome dealer employed by Jimmy Spano, the preeminent supplier of heroin and coke for New York entertainers. Frankos later switched to freelance assassination for the mafia—a career detailed in his 1992 memoir, *Contract Killer,* in which he confessed, convincingly, to the unsolved murder of Jimmy Hoffa, the mob-connected former head of the Teamsters labor union. Even in 1958 Frankos had illustrious contacts, naming among his clients Bobby Darin, Miles Davis, Thelonious Monk, Anita O'Day, Lenny Bruce, and the rock star Dion. To Frankos, Baker was just another customer, but the trumpeter's neurotic look stayed in his mind forty years later. "He was pencil-thin," said Frankos. "He seemed alert and scared—scared of getting arrested."

Baker was just as afraid of running out of dope money, and when he and Getz were in Chicago that February, they jumped at the chance to make some quick cash. Norman Granz, president of Getz's label, Verve, booked them to make a duet album, *Stan Meets Chet,* in one hasty session. *Metronome* termed it a "fiasco." As Getz and a local rhythm section set up, Baker lay woozily on a sofa. Roused just before the tape ran, he sounded weak and disoriented, opening "Autumn in New York" with a note so flat it would have made any reputable producer call for a retake. Granz didn't bother. The album was savaged by the press, especially Martin Williams: "When it isn't downright fumbling, most of Baker's playing on this record sounds like that of a man almost stalling until his solo time is up," wrote the critic in *Down Beat.*

Outside the studio, Baker was speeding, not fumbling, toward disaster. As he drove from Chicago to a gig in Milwaukee, his once-gleaming Jaguar was a wreck: a window had been smashed in a scuffle with a dealer, who had also kicked a big dent in the side. When Baker passed through Waukegan, Illinois, a policeman spotted the broken glass and ordered him to pull over. Obviously stoned, Baker couldn't produce a driver's license. The officer searched the car and found heroin under the front seat.

Baker was thrown in jail for four days, until Halema helped arrange for bail. A trial was set for August 1958. Days after the Illinois bust, he was arrested in Harlem. This time he was sure he'd have to do time, but a junkie friend suggested a way out. Baker drove to Lexington, Kentucky, and checked into the U.S. Public Health Service Hospital. The ploy worked: from his room he wrote the judge in Waukegan and explained what he had done to help himself, and the charges were dropped.

Baker endured the Lexington "cure." Doctors weaned him off heroin with synthetic opiates, then placed him in the convalescent ward (the patients called it "Skid Row") and finally in population, where he would learn how to reenter "normal" society. But for Baker, the only normal part of that prisonlike setting was the presence of lots of jazzmen, who had come either voluntarily or because the federal authorities had sent them there for drug infractions. At Lexington, Baker met Tadd Dameron, a pioneering bop arranger who had written "If You Could See Me Now," one of Baker's favorite torch songs. Now serving four years on a drug rap, Dameron led the all-star hospital orchestra, which included pianist Kenny Drew and saxophonist Sam Rivers, a honking, squealing star of the free-jazz movement to come.

Promising as the Lexington cure seemed, by one estimate 85 percent of the patients went back to drugs. Because the hospital was free, many junkies kept returning for free lodging and food while hiding dope in their rectums or swallowing heroin-filled balloons, which they later excreted—unless the rubber broke internally, causing a fatal OD. Visitors had no problem smuggling in drugs to their friends. The resident psychologists were no match for most of the patients, who were expert at staying high no matter what. In the *New York Post,* one Lexington regular identified the population there as "the most devious people this earth has ever spawned."

Baker was starting to qualify for that description, but his ticket out of Lexington came through no deceit of his own. He told *Today* magazine the story. On the thirty-eighth day of the recommended four-month cure, claimed Baker, he met Joyce, a pretty blonde groupie who had made a pass at him at the Rouge Lounge. Informing him that she had checked into Lexington because she knew he was there, Joyce promised to take good care of him if he came to live with her in New York.

They left Lexington that day, drove to New York, and settled into her Fifty-seventh Street apartment. There, apparently, she embarked on a fantasy drug spree with her idol. Any romantic delusions she may have had were entirely one-sided, though. "After two weeks I began to tire of the situation," Baker explained. "Besides, we'd gone through every cent of her fifteen-hundred dollars."

Worse sordidness followed—although with no one to corroborate his stories, it's impossible to tell if Baker was spinning another glamorized fable of his misdeeds. After leaving Joyce, he said, he moved in with a prostitute, Pixie, and her companion, Bob, a "sharp hustler" who had left his wife to live off Pixie. After Bob went home, Baker dipped freely into the hundred dollars a day she earned on the street. "I had all the money I wanted to get high with," he said.

Record producer Bill Grauer couldn't have picked a worse time to sign Baker to his label, Riverside. Based in offices just north of Times Square, Riverside specialized in tough bebop played by Cannonball Adderley, Philly Joe Jones, Thelonious Monk, and other East Coast giants. Grauer thought Baker still had selling power, and he asked Dick Bock if the trumpeter was available on loan. Bock happily consented, as long as Riverside footed all of Baker's future financial demands.

Grauer's partner, Orrin Keepnews, smelled trouble. Decades later, he recalled Baker's twelve-month stay at Riverside as a black mark on the label's history. "Forget any concept of Chet Baker as a romantic figure," Keepnews said. "He was an evil junkie and a whining, devious young man. I was against signing him to begin with. I had never been a Chet Baker fan. I was a hard-bop man—that whole goddamned West Coast thing always left me cold. What bugged me was that I saw Chet being used as the comfortable white equivalent of Miles."

He and Grauer tried tapping into Baker's fading heartthrob appeal by producing a vocal album, *It Could Happen to You,* in August 1958. They hired Kenny Drew, a tunesmith with a vast repertoire, to pick songs, write quartet arrangements, and play piano. Baker came to the session stoned, and Keepnews was repelled to hear him slurring the lyrics almost unintelligibly. Yet despite the state of his chops, Baker had grown into a true jazz singer, capable of vocalizing with the flowing inventiveness of his best playing. Many musicians were surprised by the superior scatting—his first on record—in "Do It the Hard Way," an overlooked song from the Rodgers and Hart musical *Pal Joey.* Even when he delivered the tune "straight," as he did in "I'm Old-Fashioned," he inflected the rhythm with the unmistakable pulse of jazz. But by the end of the session, he could barely mouth the words. Keepnews stormed out, snapping at Grauer: "This was your brilliant idea—*you* finish it."

The reviews gave devastating proof of how the jazz world had turned on him. Once more, Martin Williams led the attacks, awarding the album just one star in *Down Beat:*

> Can you carry a tune? Is your time all right? Sing! If your voice has hardly any range, hardly any volume, shaky pitch, no body or bottom, no matter. If it quavers a bit and if you project a certain tarnished, boyish (not exactly adolescent, almost childish) pleading, you'll make it. A certain kind of girl with strong maternal instincts but no one to

> mother will love you. The way you make it may have little or nothing to do with music, but that happens all the time anyway.
>
> And if the whole thing frustrates, there's the trumpet. If you have a talent for lyric variations, use it a bit. . . . And you can borrow someone else's style. Of course, you may not develop your own talent or even discover what it's like, but that goes on all the time too. Anyway, you've got a large following and you've won a lot of polls, so who needs to develop his talent?

The jazz and blues singer Dinah Washington, who spoke as saltily as she sang, laughed at Baker's version of "Old Devil Moon" in a *Down Beat* Blindfold Test: "Is that a singer or someone just kidding? I don't know who it is, but the diction is terrible. At the end it sounded like he said, 'That old bubble moon.' . . . It sounds like he had a mouthful of mush. . . . I can't rate this. I thought it was the Velvet Fog [Mel Tormé] for a minute, but I can't imagine who it was, unless it was Chet Baker."

For the next album, *Chet Baker in New York,* Keepnews surrounded the trumpeter with an all-star bop quartet: Charlie Parker's former pianist Al Haig; two Miles Davis alumni, Philly Joe Jones and bassist Paul Chambers; and Monk's tenor player Johnny Griffin. "I thought, cover him over cosmetically with the best supporting cast, try to bury him," Keepnews explained. Indeed, Baker played so little on the record, and so weakly, that only the title made it clear who the star was. Baker's third Riverside LP was his own idea: *Chet Baker Presents Johnny Pace,* a collaboration with "this cockamamie singer," as Keepnews called him, whom Baker was mysteriously championing. Along with Baker, Pace—a shaky-voiced baritone—turned in an unmemorable performance.

Keepnews tried to salvage the dates by having the band make a quick ballad album during the last session. One night before New Year's Eve of 1958, some of the most elite young jazzmen in the city—pianist Bill Evans, guitarist Kenny Burrell, Pepper Adams, Paul Chambers, drummer Connie Kay, and Herbie Mann, who wrote loose charts—recorded the bulk of *Chet,* Baker's ultimate "make-out" album. In that company, Baker wasn't about to embarrass himself. He acted "pretty businesslike," said Mann, as he played with the smoldering "junkie beat" that became his trademark: each phrase in slow motion, suspended in air like a curl of cigarette smoke. The whole band fell under his spell, especially in "Alone Together," where Adams's sax and Mann's flute circled sinuously around his solo.

Chet won a kind reception. In the *Daily News,* Douglas Watt heralded the return of the trumpeter's "superb lyricism"; even *Down Beat* softened its anti-Baker stance: "Baker picks his way here with less certainty than he once did, but the sensuous personal tone and the carefully wrought countermelodies are still in evidence and worth hearing."

Yet, like all his recent albums, *Chet* earned little for its producers, a problem compounded by Baker's persistent demands for cash. Keepnews reported paying artists advances of up to one thousand dollars per disc, but even those sums didn't last long in the hands of an addict, and the label's many junkie artists kept coming back for more. Writer Chris Albertson, who worked at the Riverside offices in the late fifties, never forgot finding Baker, Evans, and Jones sitting side by side on the reception-room sofa, all waiting to ask for what Keepnews called "the absolutely necessary advance because their grandmother in Keokuk needed an operation tomorrow." He and Grauer tried a practical solution by employing some of their needier artists as shipping clerks in the company "warehouse"—a floor in a brownstone opposite the label's headquarters on West Forty-sixth Street. "I used to look out the window of my office and see Philly Joe and others walk out with mysterious bulges under their coats," Albertson said.

The bulges were albums, which they sold in Harlem on the street or at the Lone Star Barber Shop, where stolen jazz records went at bargain prices. Pianist Junior Mance told Albertson of a day when Cannonball Adderley came to the Lone Star for a shave. Reclining in a chair with his face covered in hot towels, Adderley suddenly heard the voice of Jones. "Come and get 'em, gentlemen!" the drummer announced. "Got the latest Cannonball album here!" Adderley sat up, yanked off the towels, and said, "Damn! No wonder I ain't getting' my royalties!"

But Keepnews recalled Baker as the most insidious thief in Riverside history. The trumpeter knew Keepnews hated him, and in keeping with a junkie rationale he employed his whole life, he decided that anyone he didn't respect, or who didn't respect him, was fair game to rip off. He began by stealing three blank checks from Keepnews. Forging Grauer's signature, he took them to the Garden Pharmacy on Fifty-second Street, which offered check-cashing privileges to musicians. But it was known there that Keepnews, not Grauer, signed the checks, and as Baker waited nervously for his cash, the owner stepped into the back and phoned the record company. Keepnews rushed over, but by the time he arrived, Baker had fled.

His next crime succeeded. One night, as Keepnews and his wife stood in a theater lobby during intermission, his father came rushing toward them frantically. Keepnews's parents had been home baby-sitting when the police called, reporting that a break-in at the Riverside warehouse had triggered the alarm. The intruders had escaped. But in the days that followed, Keepnews learned that the culprit was Baker, who had enlisted some friends to help him steal a truckload of LPs.

Keepnews and Grauer were livid but didn't prosecute; Baker owed them one more album, and then they would be done with him. In any case, punishment was in store for Baker. By the start of 1959, he had left Pixie and returned to the streets, living with junkies and pushers. In his memoir, he recalled visiting the squalid apartment of Dirty Nick, a junkie dealer who took dope with him. Waking from a nod, Baker said, he found his face crawling with cockroaches.

He always ended up in Harlem, sometimes joined by the bebop trumpeter Lee Morgan. They grew to hate each other. "If you turned your back for a second, he'd shoot up all the stuff," grumbled Baker. The still baby-faced musician showed no qualms about loitering on those streets after midnight. "You wanna talk about a death wish?" said Keepnews. "Chet would go to a fairly famous drug corner like 116th and Lenox, where he would be the only white person visible, and certainly the only one looking for 'the man.' He may not have consciously thought, 'Come and bust me,' but my God, he made it so fucking obvious."

At 1:30 a.m. on February 20, 1959, reported the *Daily News,* police found Baker standing in a courtyard at 210 West 147th Street, shivering and smoking a joint as he waited for his connection. Handcuffed and taken to the station, he used one of his aliases, Henry C. Baker. Grauer generously paid his bail, yet Baker kept returning to the same place to score. "He was asking for it," said Jack Sheldon. Two weeks later, he was busted again. Baker pleaded not guilty. Noting his eight previous arrests, the judge sentenced him to six months at Rikers Island, the huge detention facility across Manhattan's East River.

That March at Rikers, Baker was welcomed like all other new inmates. Wardens made them strip and bend over so they could check for drugs hidden inside the rectum. Burning insecticide was sprayed over every inch of their bodies, including their faces, to kill lice. Baker was handed a prison uniform and led to a cell with a dirty sink and two metal cots. One of these was occupied by Donald Frankos, his former dealer. Baker spent his first days at Rikers suffering through withdrawal. He lay writhing on a scratchy wool blanket, alternately freezing and bathed in sweat. When the worst symptoms had passed, he entered a prison environment whose pervasive odor, said Frankos in *Contract Killer,* was "a devil's mix of shit, urine, and disinfectant." The daily menu consisted of "garbage not fit for the rats who ate most of it." Sometimes, claimed Frankos, he heard "the screams of inmates being beaten, knifed, or killed."

Strangely, the trumpeter would recall his stay at Rikers as one of the happiest times in his life. In 1984, a wistful Baker told Jack Simpson that he wished he could go back there for just twenty minutes. At night he played poker, bridge, and chess; by day he taught in the music department, where he met a parade of musicians whom he had either worked or scored with. They included bassist Curly Russell and trumpeter Howard McGhee, two once-prominent beboppers whose habits had stunted their careers. Tap dancer Baby Laurence, whose rhythm had inspired Charlie Parker, entertained in the cellblock, fellow prisoners cheering him on.

Aside from teaching, Baker spent hours playing basketball and working out at the gym. "I was fighting fit," he said. He had to be. As a soft-looking California "pretty boy" thrown in with thousands of black and Hispanic street toughs, he was constantly endangered. In a letter written from prison in 1995, Frankos recalled Baker as "open prey to 'Booty Bandits' . . . rough homosexuals who rape and prey on weaker inmates." According to Frankos, sodomy was a constant at Rikers; he remembered how the showers smelled of semen.

Baker knew how to play it cool, and he strode the hallways in silence, stone-faced and making no eye contact. But he needed protection, and one day Baker informed Frankos he was moving into the cell of a black inmate. "He told me he knew the convicts wouldn't like it, but that he knew this guy and they had a lot in common," Frankos said. Soon Baker and his new companion were eating together in the black section of the cafeteria.

Given the racial violence that broke out in that segregated prison, the move was risky. But the trumpeter's cellmate guarded him even as they drew angry looks and comments. "The gossip was that Chet Baker was sucking this guy's dick, and that Chet was a fag," recalled Frankos. "A few guys asked me if Chet tried anything with me. I almost went to blows because of that. Now, one day in the main yard when all the blacks were outside getting some sun, there was Chet with his head laying on this black inmate's lap, and looking up into the black guy's eyes. Everyone said they acted like they were in love." And that was just as Baker described it to Jack Simpson: "He loved me. He would have fuckin' died for me."

When he left Rikers in July—two months early for good behavior—Baker returned to Halema and Chetty. He also resumed buying dope from

Frankos, who had been released as well. Baker had reentered society with the standard Rikers "care package" for freed inmates: a bologna sandwich and a quarter for the subway. He was so disgusted that he made plans to take his family and fly to Europe that month.

First he had to make the album he owed Riverside: *Chet Baker Plays the Best of Lerner & Loewe,* a tribute to the composers of Broadway's *My Fair Lady* and *Brigadoon.* It featured the first recorded work of Clifford Jarvis, a teenage drummer who went on to become a leading light of the sixties avant-garde. English jazz critic John Fordham wrote that Jarvis "could fill a room with the intensity of his sound rather than its volume alone." But Bill Coss of *Metronome* called Baker's playing "lackluster," adding: "Nothing on this album is as provocative as it was obviously planned to be and capable of being. Something interferes mightily."

By now the trumpeter had slipped below Miles Davis and Dizzy Gillespie in the *Down Beat* Readers' Poll, and plummeted much farther down the Critics' Poll. He vanished from the Male Singer category—this after opening the door for many instrumentalists, including his early trumpet inspiration, Kenny Dorham, to make their own vocal albums. In a full-page article for *Metronome,* "Chet Baker: A Major Talent Diminished," Jack McKinney panned Baker's recent records as "stillborn" and "completely exhausted."

All this criticism implied that Baker had let everyone down, dragging an American dream through the mud. "Chet had the world at his feet in the fifties," said Jon Burr, one of his later bassists. "He consciously turned his back on it, and used drugs as a means of doing that. That's what he said about it." Baker made no apologies. "All the attempts through the years to get him off heroin—he didn't *want* to get off heroin," said Gerry Mulligan. "That, of course, is heresy in the modern world. You're supposed to be going, '*Mea culpa, mea maxima culpa,* oh God, help me.' Chet didn't give a damn."

Baker's excuse was simple: "The world sucks." But when Russ Freeman heard about all the trouble Baker had gotten himself into, he had no sympathy. "He did it to himself," Freeman said.

Lucca, Italy, April 11, 1961. Photo by F. Ercolini;
courtesy of Archivio Circolo del Jazz, Lucca/Francesco Maino

10

"CHET EST ARRIVÉ!" (Chet has arrived!) proclaimed the Belgian newspaper *La Meuse* in the summer of 1959, as if the Archangel Gabriel had descended, trumpet in hand, to spread the word of God. But it was his self-destruction, more than anything else, that fascinated the European public. Four years before, only jazz fans had cared about the award-winning trumpeter's presence in Europe. Now, thanks to international reports of his dope scandals, people came to gawk at an infamous American junkie. "They didn't give a damn about jazz," said Amedeo Tommasi, the Italian pianist who joined him that fall. "The reason they were interested in Chet Baker is that he was handsome and a drug addict." Particularly in Italy, Tommasi said, "drugs were still a novelty. They were glamorous."

Many black jazzmen, including Kenny Drew, Bud Powell, Dexter Gordon, and Kenny Clarke, had traded the racism and struggle of the United States for freer lives in Europe, where their artistry was revered and work was plentiful. But none had the cachet of Baker, who was white and beautiful, tortured yet rebellious. He quickly entered the world of celebrity decadence exposed in *La dolce vita,* Fellini's landmark film about a failed novelist (played by Marcello Mastroianni) who sells his soul by becoming a gossip hound for a Roman tabloid. Like other major European cities, Rome had become an industrialized metropolis, fully mended after the ravages of World War II. Rich and carefree, it turned into a playground for movie stars and jet-setters who were bored with their privileged lives and hungry for kicks. Scandal reporters and paparazzi feasted on their excesses, chronicling every wrong move for an audience who, like "Marcello," the Mastroianni character, both scorned and coveted all the lavish emptiness.

Chet Baker fit neatly into what Fellini viewed as a Dante-esque frenzy of moral and spiritual decay. His downfall had a tragic allure for many Europeans, who saw him as an artist with a magical sway over people's souls. All over the Continent he found followers who wanted a piece of him; for the rest of his life he put them to use. "Chet was like the sirens," said Lisa Galt Bond, referring to the mythic temptresses whose singing lured sailors to a dire fate. "He had a seductive, mystical sound that people responded to. But to follow the voice of the sirens was to be held captive, or end up dead."

Where his own country was concerned, he felt embittered, victimized, rejected. When the German broadcaster and editor Gudrun Endress asked him how his music could sound so pure and beautiful after all the self-abuse, he explained that dope hadn't destroyed his soul, only protected it from all the "bullshit" of life. "I saw many people greatly affected by things that had happened to them, and I just kind of had it in my head to try and put that part of me in a sort of unreachable place," he said.

Whatever hopes Baker had, his new European career got off to a shaky start. On July 26, he headlined at the Festival Nazionale del Jazz di Fregene, held at a famous beach town outside Rome. Accompanying him were five boyish musicians from a medieval Tuscan city. They called themselves the Quintetto di Lucca: vibes player Antonello Vannucchi; guitarist Gaetano Mariani; drummer Giampiero Giusti; bassist Giovanni Tommaso; and his brother Vito, a pianist. Promising but not too experienced, they worshipped Baker and longed to make music as beautiful and effortless as his.

But the Quintetto couldn't speak English, and Baker didn't know Italian, which caused problems. *Musica Jazz,* the country's top jazz magazine, called the Fregene concert a mess, adding that Baker should have asked his band if they knew "My Funny Valentine" before he tried to play it. At the hotel afterward, Francesco Forti interviewed him for a new magazine, *Jazz de Ieri e di Oggi* (Jazz of Yesterday and Today). Francesco "Cecco" Maino, a talented young photographer and friend of the Quintetto, took pictures. "The music was still great, but the man had changed," said Maino, who had met Baker in 1956. "He treated the musicians in a very bad manner. He made some nasty remarks and treated his wife very badly in our presence." Maino understood why after Baker excused himself to shoot up, then returned, more relaxed.

Gigs in Belgium and Italy kept him traveling, so he left his wife and son at the Paris home of Peter Broome, a sculptor whose brother, Ray, had played in Baker's high-school band. Peter had known Baker as a cocky, rambunctious teenager; now he saw a lost soul whose ineptitude as a father shocked him. Chesney Aftab, recalled Broome, was a "robust, chubby, curly-haired kid," but he was also semi-retarded, and Baker chose an unfortunate way of dealing with it. "Chet brought the kid to us drunk," Broome said. "He'd given him a couple of shots so he would calm down, but the boy just threw up all over the place."

The trumpeter left Paris to headline Belgium's Festival International du Jazz on August 2, 1959. It was held at Comblain-la-Tour, a tiny village in the Ardennes forest, site of the Battle of the Bulge. As a young soldier, Joe Napoli, Baker's manager, had fought there. While recovering from injuries, he had discovered a vacant football field surrounded by rolling green hills and the most brilliant blue sky and water he had ever seen; now he was back to organize the first of many annual jazz festivals there. Never mind that Comblain-la-Tour was "in the middle of nowhere," according to pianist Francis Thorne; an estimated twenty thousand jazz fans arrived on that cold, rainy day, blankets in hand, to hear a strange grab bag of performers. They included Thorne, a classical musician from Long Island, New York, who supported himself by working in Italian jazz clubs; Romano Mussolini, the piano-playing son of Il Duce; Kenny Clarke, Paris's most revered expatriate drummer; the Roman New Orleans Jazz Band, an all-Italian Dixieland group sporting straw hats and banjos; and Jacques Pelzer, a Belgian flutist and sax player who ran a pharmacy where many musicians, including Baker, would spend a lot of time.

But the draw was Baker, the closing act. When he arrived backstage, all concern shifted to him. Pale and weak from lack of heroin, he looked "just horrible," Thorne said. "He was a wreck. We were all biting our nails, wondering how he'd get through it." By the time he played, stars filled the night sky. He walked onstage in a white sweater, and when the spotlight hit him, he glowed like an angel. He didn't sound like one; aching from head to toe, he emitted a strained, sickly wobble. Yet every solo triggered rapturous applause. It was hard to tell whether the audience was applauding his music or the heartrending sight of a wounded master. Whatever the case, he knew that in Europe he was home.

Throughout the coming months, Cecco Maino saw the untiring kindness Baker was shown in Italy, particularly by the Circolo del Jazz di Lucca, a jazz society whose founding members—including Giampiero Giusti, Rudy Rabassini, and Paolo Benvenuti—treated him like a brother in need. Italian fans christened Baker *l'angelo* (the angel) and *tromba d'oro* (golden trumpet). Trumpeter Oscar Valdambrini compared their first encounter to the moment when "a man . . . meets the woman of his dreams." Saxophonist

Gianni Basso likened Baker to Debussy. In a land where melody was sacred, where the fluid *bel canto* opera style reigned, and the language itself had a musical lilt, Baker's graceful lines and honeyed tone were a feast for the ear. Yet he seemed to be paying a ruinous price for these gifts. As bassist Carlo Loffredo said in Paola Boncompagni and Aldo Lastella's book *Chet Baker in Italy:* "He looked like he was suffering or was about to die."

Baker was undeniably at his weakest, and everywhere in Europe, people wanted to cradle him in their arms. "It was a case of worshipping the self-destructive artist who dies young in a garret full of unpublished music or unsold paintings or something," explained Gerry Mulligan. "It's a Christ-like image of self-immolation. That's something you encounter a great deal in Europe. You don't find it a lot in America. It's kind of foreign to our more mercantile nature. That is the role of the patron, the helpful keeper. Somebody like Chet was so needy, as soon as somebody put out a helping hand, man, he'd swallow the whole person."

But to Enrico Pieranunzi, an Italian pianist who worked with Baker throughout the eighties, any nuisance Baker created was richly worth the trouble. "For American people, Chet was just a drug addict," he said. "Here we felt he was a great artist with a great problem. He was a man who needed help. He found a lot of friends here who felt his fragility, his shyness, his inner drama. He was so sweet when he played, so mysterious. Somehow he was able to express the question mark of life with so few notes. In Italy we're more sentimental, and we felt that very much."

For all this enrapturement, Baker found little work there at first. According to Aldo Santini of the newspaper *Il Tirreno,* the Italian public considered the jazz world "both the haven of vice and the world of the devil." Places offering jazz were called "hot clubs": private spots, forbidden as speakeasies and open only on certain days. Pop-jazz orchestras played for dancing at such semi-decadent nightspots as the River Club in Florence's Palazzo Corsini, a huge palace on the Arno River, with sprawling frescoes, high-priced hookers, and a clientele of old nobility and jet-setters. In such an environment, serious artists like Helen Merrill, an American jazz singer living in Rome, were scuffling. "Things were not so wonderful over there," she said. "But there was something hypnotic about it at the time. I guess we were sort of running away from things."

So was Chet Baker, but the "monkey on his back" needed constant attention. Broke, he accepted an acting gig from Lucio Fulci, an Italian film director recalled today for such gory shockers as *Gates of Hell* and *Zombie.* Fulci hired Baker for a low-budget rock-and-roll movie, *Urlatori alla sbarra* (*urlatori* denoting rock shouters, *alla sbarra* meaning "on trial"). The movie was aimed at Italian youths, who had just discovered the thrills of rock music, leather jackets, and screeching motorcycles. German actress Elke Sommer played a teenager who inflames her father, a stuffy record-company executive, by joining a pack of rock-crazed biker youths. *Urlatori* helped launch two Italian pop legends, Mina and Adriano Celentano. Baker, though, was presented for laughs as a stoned trumpeter (called "Americano" by the other characters) who nods off everywhere: in a bathtub during a party, under a sofa, in an elevator. "We made that film above all to give Chet Baker a hand," Fulci said in *Chet Baker in Italy.* "He was in a bad way . . . he didn't even have the money to live."

But on camera, Baker was in control. The closing scene took place in a sunny park in Rome, where love-struck boys and girls lay under the trees. As violins and flute start to play, Baker cuddles a dark-haired Italian girl to his chest and croons the sentimental "Arrivederci." The breeze flutters a lock of hair on his forehead; the sun flatters every chiseled contour of his face. His magic envelops the park, and soon the couples have fallen into each other's arms. But the camera is drawn to Baker. Lying on the grass with sleepy eyes, like a little boy just tucked into bed, he looks, once more, like an angel: so beautiful, so innocent, so sublimely and naturally gifted that it was easy to see how anyone could fall under his spell.

There was a reason for his languor. In order to make the trumpeter cooperate, Fulci had to keep him high on morphine, opium, any drug he could find. Despite the permissiveness of *La dolce vita,* heroin barely existed in Italy, where it was reviled as a sinful and deadly poison. But Baker found a substitute. Seeing his fragility at Comblain-la-Tour, Jacques Pelzer had told him about Palfium 875, a powerful analgesic created in Belgium three years earlier to wean heroin and morphine addicts. At first it was sold as freely as aspirin, but in 1957 the authorities learned that Palfium was harder to kick than morphine; taken in large doses, it produced a heroinlike high. They listed it in the Registry of Dangerous Drugs, making it available only by prescription. In Germany, however, an equivalent medicine called Jetrium was still sold over the counter.

Pelzer gave Baker some Palfium tablets, and the trumpeter started experimenting. He crushed them into a powder, then dissolved them in water. Filtering the liquid through gauze—or a pillowcase, a handkerchief, his shirtsleeve—he filled a syringe, then shot the contents. The warm wave that swept over him felt no different from that of heroin.

But how to get more? On his days off, Baker donned a big overcoat, grabbed a briefcase, and flew to Munich. There he emptied drugstore shelves of Jetrium, which came in economy bottles of two hundred. He returned to Italy with his pockets and valise crammed with rattling tablets. It was later estimated that in September and October, Baker smuggled in ten thousand pills.

As long as his chemical needs were filled, he fit the mellow image that fascinated the young jazzmen of Italy: a silent, all-knowing Buddha of jazz. "The most reassuring thing was a little smile from Chet," said Carlo Loffredo in *Chet Baker in Italy.* "He was closed up in himself and didn't speak to anybody; neither did he waste his time with compliments." Other musicians watched in envy as he cruised around Italy in his Alfa Romeo, making a flashy entrance at clubs. Screeching to a halt at the curb, he strode inside dressed not in the bland business suit most jazzmen wore but in an open-necked shirt and sports jacket, dark sunglasses, and sandals over bare feet. The latter two items were more a practical consideration than a fashion statement: his pupils, shrunken by dope, needed concealing, while his feet were so swollen from all the needles he had jabbed into them that he couldn't bear tight dress shoes.

His blasé attitude seemed like the soul of cool. Musicians would laugh for years at a story about his first meeting with Romano Mussolini. Greeting the executed dictator's son, Baker allegedly said in a deadpan voice: "Gee, it's a drag about your old man." Decades later, Mussolini couldn't remember the incident at all—"Chet and I never talked about politics"—but Caterina Valente, the French-Italian pop singer with whom Baker performed and recorded in the fifties, claimed to have witnessed it. True or not, it defined Baker as a man in a bubble, oblivious to anything outside.

His first Italian album, *Chet Baker in Milan,* featured a mostly Italian quintet—fronted by saxophonists Gianni Basso and Glauco Masetti—who were so in love with West Coast Jazz that the album sounded like Chet Baker in Hollywood. In neat little contrapuntal arrangements of "Line for Lyons," "Indian Summer," and "Look for the Silver Lining," Baker played with moderate inspiration and little involvement. His solo on "Cheryl Blues," a Charlie Parker original, revealed cracks in his famously glossy tone. Baker's pitch had turned slightly sour, and his flights sounded unfocused, as if his mind were elsewhere.

It was. His new drug regimen caused his body chemistry—and his behavior—to seesaw madly, as Carlo Loffredo saw when he joined Baker's group that fall. "He became somebody else, nasty even, but he didn't care about the others and stayed closed up in his own world," the bassist said.

Baker couldn't have cared less about romance at the time, but no one would have guessed it after hearing *Chet Baker and Fifty Italian Strings,* a sentimental pop album he made in Milan. Here he became the Baker Italians wanted to hear: heroic but tender, bruised by love yet still ruled by his heart. He played slow, tuneful choruses of melody and crooned songs of eternal love and sweet heartbreak: "When I Fall in Love," "Deep in a Dream," "Violets for Your Furs." Waterfalls of strings, sighing woodwinds, and a twinkly harp spun a musical Shangri-La. But the album's charm was lost on *Down Beat* critic Don DeMicheal, who called it "lethargic" and "deadly."

Baker's American crash gained an ironic footnote when MGM began production on *All the Fine Young Cannibals,* the film version of Rosamund Marshall's novel *The Bixby Girls.* Robert Wagner starred as Chad Bixby, a menacingly handsome trumpeter who leaves his Texas family—and Natalie Wood, who loves him—to become a star in New York. He sits brooding in corners, dark blond hair spilling over his eyes, trumpet pointed down as he blows music that breaks people's hearts. The resemblance to Chet Baker was obvious but never acknowledged by the filmmakers; rumors that Baker had been offered the lead were unsubstantiated. Released in 1960, *Cannibals* sank quickly.

Urlatori alla sbarra did better, and Lucio Fulci took Baker around Rome, trying to sell him to supper-club owners. Most were too old and stodgy to know who Baker was. The fashionable Gicky Club agreed to hire him only when he made a far-fetched promise to bring in Gerry Mulligan. That didn't happen, of course, and after a few nights he was fired. Fulci then brought him to Le Grotte del Piccione (The Caves of the Pigeon), where bands played for dancing. But no one could dance to Baker's music, and he lost that job, too.

Finally he found work at the Santa Tecla, a jazz club in Milan. Audiences flocked there to see the junior Mussolini and a famous junkie on one stage, and the engagement was a success. But with Halema still in Paris, Baker felt crushed by loneliness and fear—pains compounded by the withdrawal that came when the trumpeter, unable to fly to Germany, ran out of pills. Through the thin walls of his *pensione* room, he later recalled, neighbors heard him sobbing and moaning. One morning the manager knocked on his door. "Signor Baker, you are sick, very sick," she said with a smile. "You cannot continue to live at this hotel. We are very understanding, but not all of our customers are." Like a child crying for Mommy, he wired his wife in Paris: "Come, I need you."

By now Halema had "left Chet four or five times because of the drugs," she said. But she couldn't make the final break, so she bundled up her son and headed to Milan. Baker found them an apartment, and they tried again to mend their rift. "We lived together, but like two strangers," he said. All the while he kept promising to quit dope.

Instead, he put Halema to use. Baker couldn't leave the Santa Tecla to fly to Germany, so he persuaded her to go there and bring back his "medicine." Later she would claim he had assured her this was legal. It wasn't. Jetrium was the same as Palfium, and to possess it in Italy with no prescription was a crime. If he knew, Baker didn't care. He put Halema on a plane to Munich. He also enlisted his American drummer Gene Victory, a fellow addict, to fly there and score for both of them. By the end of 1959, Victory had smuggled in thousands of tablets.

The abundance of Jetrium whetted Baker's gluttony, and he shot huge quantities at once. His habit, he said, soared to a staggering 250 pills a day. At his worst, he shot up forty times in twenty-four hours. "I was into a *lotta* shit," he would tell Jack Simpson. Baker had looked handsome and healthy in *Urlatori alla sbarra;* now, with little rest and no appetite, he lost weight at an alarming rate. His skin took on a corpselike, grayish pallor; his arms and feet were covered with scabs. He suffered from chills, a side effect of the bad circulation caused by his punctured and clotted veins. Italians stared as he walked the balmy streets of Milan in a wool overcoat. "I lived in a nightmare of eternal anguish, existing from one injection to the other, terrified that without Palfium I would die," he would say later.

Halema and his musician friends persuaded him to see a doctor. He got a grim prognosis: certain death in four to six months unless he straightened out. The news jolted him out of his fog. Baker took a leave of absence from the Santa Tecla, and on December 4 he checked into Milan's Villa Turro, one of the few Italian clinics then equipped to handle the rare and mysterious problem of drug addiction. Afraid to go alone, he talked Gene Victory into signing in too. For seven days they were kept unconscious with an intravenous flow of sleeping medication mixed with vitamins and other nutrients. By the time they awoke, they had bypassed withdrawal. The color in Baker's cheeks had returned, and he was closer to his normal 135 pounds. The treatment lasted six weeks more. On January 30, 1960, the men went back to Santa Tecla. Baker must have seemed strong again, for an Italian filmmaker approached him about making a short film, *Tromba fredda,* showing him and Halema in Italy.

At the Santa Tecla, Baker was welcomed back by one of his most obsessive fans: Laurie Jay, a teenage rock drummer who worked in a variety show at the huge Teatro Olympia in Milan. Jay pestered his fellow cast members, including headliner Shirley Bassey, the Welsh pop singer, to come see this amazing trumpet player. In turn, Jay told Baker about the Olympia show, whose acts were introduced by a quartet of sexy European girls. Baker sped to the Olympia, where he gained backstage entrance so he could ogle all the "scantily clad ladies," as he put it.

One night in January, Jay brought the nineteen-year-old Carol Jackson, a British showgirl from the Olympia, to see Baker's show. A creamy-skinned brunette with big, dark eyes, Jackson was lovely, virginal, and naïve. Her parents, Albert and Gladys, had given her and her two sisters a strict upbringing in Surrey, a suburb of London. Jackson had studied to be a secretary, but her looks won her a local beauty contest. Out of that came a few modeling jobs and a cameo as a bikinied harem girl in an obscure film, *Sands of the Desert.* Now, as one of the four onstage hostesses at the Olympia, she paraded on and off in sexy clothes, introducing acts in her polite English accent.

Striking as she looked, she rarely had much to say, and avoided hanging out with the other cast members. Jackson had little ambition beyond wanting to meet an exciting man, preferably along the lines of Elvis Presley, her idol. But she resisted Jay's invitation to the Santa Tecla, for she had never heard of Chet Baker and had no interest in jazz at all. Finally, though, she agreed to go with Jay and his friends after work.

For decades to come, Jackson gave a fairy-tale account of her and the trumpeter's first meeting at the club. She told of standing at the top of a staircase amid mobs of youngsters eager for a glimpse of Baker, who was playing downstairs. He was completely out of view, she said, but his music was drifting upward, enchanting her. At the end of the set, he ascended the steps, and they instantly locked eyes. After some quick conversation, he invited her, Laurie Jay, and their friends out for a late-night supper, she said. Almost immediately, she claimed, they fell madly in love. Telling that story, Jackson hastened to add that she and Baker slept in separate hotel rooms over the coming months.

Certainly Baker noticed her looks—namely, the resemblance he saw in Jackson to Elizabeth Taylor, an object of his lust ever since he saw the actress spilling out of her bathing suit in the scandalous 1959 film *Suddenly, Last Summer.* "Something was gonna happen—there's no question," said Laurie Jay. But other details of Jackson's account were questionable. Jay couldn't remember ever having seen the club mobbed "in the slightest" for Baker, and Halema had a different memory of her husband's early contact with

Jackson. At Baker's suggestion, Halema said, she and the trumpeter took some young people from the Olympia show—including Jackson and Colin Hicks, a British rock star popular in Italy—to dinner. Halema saw Jackson's interest in Baker; the young Englishwoman even asked to look at pictures of the baby. Soon thereafter, Halema said, her husband didn't come home one night. When he called, he told her they shouldn't appear together in *Tromba fredda,* because their marriage was falling apart. It was Jackson who ended up strolling hand in hand with Baker through the Italian streets while the camera ran. (The footage has never surfaced.)

According to Arnold Weinstein, an expatriate American poet who gave poetry-and-jazz recitals with Baker in Italian cafés, the trumpeter still made a few painful public appearances with Halema. "These hideous paparazzi and reporters would literally run after them," Weinstein said. "One guy from some disgusting rag wanted to know what was happening, which wife had he taken, are you gonna go back with her and the kid, are you gonna leave the child—all that stuff."

Jackson didn't know Italian, but she neatly clipped the articles with her picture in them and carried them in her suitcase. One of her favorites appeared on the cover of *Il Reporter.* It showed her and Baker posed at a nightclub table, with the caption IL VELENO DEL JAZZ. She didn't seem to know the translation: "The Poison of Jazz." No matter; Jackson dressed up and romped through Italy with Baker as though she were Cinderella to his Prince Charming. "Chet was like a snake," said Lisa Galt Bond years later. "He could hypnotize. He was dangerous, but he *was* special, you knew that. You could see why women were so vulnerable to him."

Albert and Gladys Jackson, who had never wanted their daughter to go to Italy at all, were shocked to read in the papers that she was running around with an infamous drug addict. Albert phoned Interpol and demanded that they rescue her. Nothing came of the complaint, and Jackson and the trumpeter continued to show each other off for everyone—including Halema—to see. "As a man, he was a real nobody with an eye only for his own personal interests," said Oscar Valdambrini. "But great artists must be imperfect, you cannot ask them to be honest and generous, because what they've already got is of enormous value as it is."

Early in 1960, Halema finally fled, taking Chetty to another part of Milan. Whatever loss Baker may have felt was clouded by other concerns. Before he had left Villa Turro, a doctor had warned him that it was much easier for a drug user to shed the physical hunger than the psychological crutch. Indeed, Baker was scared at the thought of facing life and music without the calming effect of dope. "Something went wrong with my trumpet playing," he claimed. "I felt lacking in ideas, inspiration, the strength and ability to improvise seriously." Less than two months after his sleep cure, Baker was hooked again. In March, he checked into a clinic in Monza, a small town outside Milan. Once released, he went right back to drugs.

His real troubles started in May. Baker had gotten a job offer that seemed like a dream: a full summer season at Il Bussolotto, a cozy lounge inside La Bussola (The Compass), one of Italy's grandest nightclubs. It stood at Le Focette, a beautiful beach in Tuscany. Bathed in ocean breezes and shaded by palm trees, La Bussola presented a stellar array of performers in its huge ballroom: Marlene Dietrich, Sammy Davis Jr., Louis Armstrong, and years later Diana Ross. Il Bussolotto had charms of its own, including a picture window that faced a crystal-blue sea. The view delighted such artists as Brazil's João Gilberto, a founder of the bossa nova, who played his guitar and sang at Il Bussolotto in a feathery voice inspired by his idol, Chet Baker.

With a June opening ahead, Baker and Jackson moved to the Villa Gemma, a *pensione* in Marina di Pietrasanta, a seaside town next to Le Focette. The innkeeper, a friendly young musician named Giali Giambastiani, delighted in having Baker under his roof, and placed himself at the trumpeter's service. But Giambastiani couldn't fill Baker's immediate need. Palfium was in every pharmacy, but without a prescription it seemed unattainable. Out of his mind with the craving, he found a solution. Learning that Italian doctors were identified by a cross on their license plates and on the shingle outside their offices, he raced through the streets in his Alfa, eyes darting right and left, seeking out the cross like a bloodthirsty vampire in reverse.

Once he found a doctor, Baker gave a better acting performance than any he delivered onscreen. Seated in the office, he clutched his temples and groaned that his head was killing him. Sometimes he lay in bed for days, he said, face pressed to a tear-stained pillow. One of the first physicians he found pressed various spots on his face. Baker flinched. "Sinusitis? Trigeminal neuralgia of the cheek and forehead?" he was asked. Yes, said Baker, explaining that he had broken his nose in two car accidents. Sinusitis and trigeminal neuralgia became his official ailments. Most doctors urged him to see a specialist. Baker agreed, but first, he said, he needed something to ease his agony—and not ordinary painkillers. "I've already tried them, they don't help me," he said weakly. "There's only one medicine that works for me—Palfium."

Some doctors wrote a prescription immediately; others warned him that

Palfium was a narcotic. A few, no doubt, knew they had an addict on their hands. But he got what he wanted. "They put in my hand, with embarrassment, the slip of paper; took from it the few hundred lire for their payment, and accompanied me to the door in silence," he said. In time he became so shrewd at arousing their pity that some wouldn't accept payment.

But most of the prescriptions allowed for just a single box of five tablets—the minimum makings of one fix—and Baker needed lots more. Within weeks, at least twenty-five doctors in Italy, and one across the border in Switzerland, had agreed to write him prescriptions. "I remember I went like a crazy man from one outpatient department to another," he said. The Florentine newspaper *La Nazione* later reported that Jackson sometimes waited in the car while Baker copped. In his mania, *La Nazione* said, he had even crashed his Alfa into a tree.

Shortly before he opened at Il Bussolotto, Baker drove to a gig in Naples. There, a trunk containing not only his clothes and other belongings but his horn was stolen. "I was a finished man—I could no longer play, I couldn't earn a living," he said, claiming he cried all night after the theft. "I felt alone and abandoned. I had Carol with me, but her words of comfort didn't console me. I had lost my trumpet. I didn't have the money to buy another one."

Sergio Bernardini, who owned La Bussola, saved him by ordering an expensive new horn from America. At the start of June, Baker opened at Il Bussolotto with a trio led by Romano Mussolini. Baker's daily demands for cash advances troubled Bernardini; he didn't want to finance the trumpeter's self-destruction but knew Baker couldn't perform otherwise. Cash in hand, Baker spent his days hunting down Palfium, then arrived for his shows at the last minute. "He started to play like a rocket," said Carlo Loffredo. "It was clearly an effect of the drugs he was taking, which, as you know, dilate time."

At the end of the night, Baker tossed his horn on the piano, like a factory worker hearing the five-o'clock whistle. With no goodbyes, he would rush home to shoot up, his new trumpet sitting there unprotected. During the day, the sun that flooded in through the window of Il Bussolotto made the instrument gleam like gold. Children wandered in from the beach and played with it as if it were a toy, pushing the buttons and blowing into the mouthpiece.

To Bernardini's horror, Baker started missing night after night of work. By now, two doctors were fulfilling his needs. On May 20, 1960, Baker had paid his first visit to Roberto Bechelli, a physician in Viareggio, a large coastal town a few kilometers south of Focette. Having never prescribed Palfium before, Bechelli hesitated—until the trumpeter pressed some money into his hand. Through July 27, he wrote twenty-three prescriptions for Baker.

In the same period, Baker saw Sergio Nottoli, a pediatrician, and reeled off his usual list of ills. Cautiously, Nottoli signed a prescription for the minimum dose of Palfium while insisting that Baker see a radiologist. After two more visits, Nottoli refused to write another prescription. On May 28, Baker responded by sending Giali Giambastiani in his place. Signor Baker was at the *pensione* crippled with pain, Giambastiani explained. Please, wouldn't the doctor show some mercy? Nottoli relented. Because Baker wasn't there, he used Giambastiani's name on the prescription. He did the same a few days later when the innkeeper returned with Jackson, who confirmed Baker's condition. Perhaps knowing the truth and wishing to protect himself, Nottoli agreed to write one more prescription in the name of Aurelio Meliadó, a friend of Giambastiani's.

No one, it seemed, could stand to see Chet Baker suffer, but he rarely returned the sympathy. Gene Victory had left the band some time earlier, losing touch with Baker; when he reappeared—broke, strung out, and sick with tuberculosis, a byproduct of his addiction—he sought out Baker at the Villa Gemma and begged for help. It wasn't a job or a loan he wanted, but Palfium. The trumpeter wasn't pleased. Sitting Victory down in his room, he delivered a stern anti-drug lecture. "With all you've been through, with all you've suffered, do you really want to stay on this road?" Baker asked. "You know very well where it will end." When the drummer persisted, Baker doled out a few tablets, but after several more visits he lost patience. Handing him one last tablet, he told Victory to leave and never come back.

That afternoon, Baker got ready for work, preparing several Palfium-filled syringes for the night. Leaving them on the table, he took Jackson to the movies. Two hours later, he found the syringes empty. "It was Gene," he told Jackson gravely. Baker panicked, for he had no more Palfium. Dino Grilli of *Il Telegrafo* later reported that the trumpeter threw a violent fit in his room, breaking furniture and howling in frustration.

Never had Baker felt so out of control as he struggled to feed a habit that was eating him alive. In July, he went to see another doctor, Enrico Landucci. That day Landucci was away, but his maid, Adua Ghilardi, greeted Baker with motherly compassion. She told him to sit in the waiting room while she stepped away to look up the name of another doctor. Ghilardi left the door to Landucci's office unlocked. When she returned, Baker was gone, along with several of Landucci's prescription forms.

Baker raced to Farmacia Vignoli, a drugstore in nearby Pisa. He presented a prescription from Dr. Enrico Landucci for two boxes of Palfium. The two young women in charge were confused; it was July 15, 1960, but the date was written as 7.15.60, not 15.7.60 in the European manner. Against their better judgment, they gave Baker their only box of Palfium. Their suspicions rose when a young Englishwoman walked in with another improperly dated prescription from Landucci. They turned her away. The owner phoned Landucci, who told her he had never issued a Palfium prescription to a Mr. Baker or a Miss Jackson.

On July 16, the couple arrived late at Il Bussolotto. Baker was so dangerously strung out that he was close to fainting, and Bernardini asked over the microphone if there was a doctor in the house. Through the crowd came Pierluigi (Lippi) Francesconi, director of a small clinic in Lucca, the Santa Zita. Baker confessed his habit to the young doctor, who responded kindly. "Dear Baker, you must face recovery," said the doctor, gripping his hand. "It is a long, difficult cure, but we can try. You must put all your confidence in me, and I, in turn, will have confidence in you." The cure would start the next morning. Baker was worried: his contract with Bernardini had weeks to run, and he needed the money.

Francesconi had a solution. On July 17, Baker checked into Santa Zita. The doctor put him on a regimen of vitamins and a sliding dosage of Palfium. Whenever possible, he drove the trumpeter to work, waited for him to finish, then escorted him back to the clinic to keep him out of trouble. "But I asked myself, how could he stay there?" said Francesconi years later. "I couldn't lock him up, and when he needed to leave to take care of his business, he used to go out. I wasn't there to be his full-time chauffeur."

For all the doctor's efforts, the cure failed as Baker enlisted a series of well-meaning friends to help keep him high. One of them was Joseph (Joey) Carani, a thirty-year-old Italian-American lawyer from Chicago. A jazz lover and amateur musician, Carani adored Baker, whom he had met in the States. Now in Tuscany to see his ailing father, Carani—a slight, nebbishy man with a bow tie and a shock of wavy hair—seemed ready to do almost anything, legal or not, to help his idol. On July 27, he complied with a dangerous request. While still under Francesconi's care, Baker asked Carani and Jackson to accompany him on a ride to the office of Dr. Bechelli. Scared, maybe, of the risk he had taken in prescribing Palfium to Baker more than twenty times, Bechelli had ignored his recent pleas. Now the trumpeter arrived with bait: Carol Jackson, on whom Bechelli had a crush. Thanks to her charms, and another bribe, Baker left with his prescription, made out to Carani.

On Saturday, July 31, 1960, Baker paid his last visit to Bechelli, alone. After scoring more Palfium, he drove to Rimini, a resort town near Bologna, to play a gig. It was a warm, lazy day, the kind that used to send him rushing into the waves at Laguna Beach. But Baker looked like he hadn't seen the sun in years. Chalky and unshaven, with crescent-moon circles under his dead eyes, he could have passed for a derelict stumbling out of a Harlem doorway at 3 a.m.

Late that afternoon, the Lucca police station received an emergency call from a Shell gas station on the outskirts of town. The owner's son reported that a man had locked himself in the rest room and wouldn't come out. The stranger had been heard muttering but wouldn't open up, and now there was only silence. Maybe he was dead, the caller worried.

Minutes later, Officer Neri Gugliermino arrived at the Shell station. He knocked on the washroom door. It swung open. "Suddenly I found a ghost in front of me," Gugliermino said. "He looked like death." Clutching a syringe, the figure stared out like a zombie, standing in front of a blood-spattered sink. His sleeves were rolled up. The veins on his arms looked like "black wire," the officer noticed, and there were reddish puncture marks everywhere. The man stuttered incomprehensibly, teetering as Gugliermino led him out. Now docile as a child, he sat silently in the police car as Gugliermino drove to the station. When the officer's superiors learned that Chet Baker had been apprehended, "there was an earthquake," he said.

Gradually, Baker grew lucid enough to murmur an explanation. He was sick, he said, and had stopped at the gas station to take his medicine, Palfium, prescribed by Dr. Lippi Francesconi. Hands trembling, he had broken two bottles, and by the time he injected the contents of the third, he was too faint to hear the knocking. He was allowed to call Francesconi, who rushed to the station and explained that Baker was undergoing detoxification at his clinic. The trumpeter was released into his care.

The news reports hit the next day: Chet Baker had been found unconscious in a gas station toilet, with blood everywhere. The slightly exaggerated story spread throughout Europe and the United States. Suddenly, a small Italian town where nothing much happened had made world headlines.

A night after the arrest, a reporter from *La Nazione* found him "in a strange state of relaxation." Baker was headed to the cinema to see *La crociera del terrore* (The Terror Cruise) with a friend from La Bussola. "I'm very determined to get better," said the trumpeter, explaining proudly that he now shot up every four hours rather than hourly. "Isn't that great?" he added.

But Francesconi wasn't optimistic, especially when Baker came to him in mid-August and asked to leave the clinic for three days to play a festival in Belgium. The doctor warned him that if he did anything foolish he would destroy the whole cure, but Baker promised to behave. Francesconi measured out three days' worth of Palfium and entrusted it to Jackson and Joey Carani, who accompanied Baker on the trip. Once there, the trumpeter weakened. Before dawn, as Jackson slept, he went to Munich, where he bought all the Palfium he could carry.

He didn't know that a report had been filed by Fabio Romiti, the public prosecutor of Lucca, stating that Baker had committed a crime by appearing in public "in a state of very grave psychological alteration due to narcotics." Romiti was a man possessed. For him this was no mere breach of law; it was a moral apocalypse. Two addicts had been tried recently in Italy, and Romiti feared that drug traffickers were poisoning a sanctified land of Roman Catholic family values.

He launched a frenzied investigation of the local medical community, led by Lucca's *medico provinciale* (provincial medical officer). Joined by a policeman, the *medico* stormed every pharmacy, demanding to see all prescription forms on file. Spotting ambiguous or missing information, he screamed at the terrified druggists. "He was crazy; there was something wrong with him," said Gugliermino, who often accompanied him. The *medico* found twenty-five doctors who had prescribed Palfium for Baker. On August 22, policemen brought an arrest warrant to the Villa Gemma, to which Baker had returned. As they led him off in handcuffs, Jackson burst into tears. "You can't do it—don't take him!" she shouted, according to *Il Telegrafo.*

Two days later, the police arrested Carani, whom Bechelli had named as an accomplice of Baker's. Bechelli, Nottoli, Francesconi, and Giambastiani were arrested for aiding a drug abuser. Investigations began against all the remaining doctors and several pharmacists, who had failed to report their dealings with a junkie, as the law required them to do.

Under Romiti's withering interrogation, Baker admitted smuggling huge amounts of Jetrium from Germany, and to stealing and forging prescription forms. But his revelations didn't end with himself. His ex-drummer Gene Victory, he said, had brought thousands of Jetrium tablets from Munich for both of them. ("Victory knew perfectly well he had committed a crime," Baker later said.) Carani and Giambastiani had copped Palfium on his behalf from Bechelli, he explained. Then there was his wife, Halema, who had transported Jetrium into Italy. Asked where she was, he gave her address in Milan. Pressed further, he began reeling off doctors' names.

Even those who knew him best were shocked to learn that Baker had betrayed the people who had tried to "save" him. Victory escaped arrest, having sold his drums to a young man in Lucca to pay for a ticket back to the States. Others weren't so lucky. "At that time it was very dangerous to have contact with Chet, because the police investigated everyone," said Romano Mussolini. Sensing that Carol was in danger, Baker sent her home to Surrey. But Romiti was more interested in Halema. In an unlawful action that went unchallenged, he drove beyond his jurisdiction into Milan and tracked down the young woman, demanding that she return to Lucca for questioning. Once there, he pressured her into admitting her drug smuggling. She swore through tears that she didn't know she had broken the law, but Romiti wasn't moved. Halema was thrown into a cell in the Penitenziario San Giorgio, the ancient Lucca prison where the accused were held without bail until trial—a reflection of the harsh Napoleonic principle of guilty until proven innocent, which was still in effect. Baker's wife was unlucky indeed: at the time of her arrest, she reportedly had in her purse a plane ticket to America, where she had left her child in the care of her family. Joseph Carani and several doctors, including Francesconi, were imprisoned too.

Francesconi went free in two months for lack of evidence; the other accused sat in jail, waiting. Daily, Baker heard heaving sobs from his wife's cell across the courtyard. Eight months passed before the trial. Near the end of that period, *L'Europeo* paid him to write about his road to destruction. Repeatedly using the word "hopeless," Baker shed tears for just one person. "I don't understand why I'm getting this treatment," he said. "I'm always alone, unable to exchange a word except with the guards. Carani and the doctors are all in the same cell. They can speak, have company, console one another. . . . For eight months I have had nothing but the closeness of my conscience and my fears. . . . Eight hard, frightful months that may have restored my damaged health, but in return have destroyed my heart and my mind." He had no choice, he warned, but to sell his horn to pay his impending legal debt.

Baker's plight touched the heart of Lucca's most powerful lawyer, Mario Frezza, who volunteered to defend him for free. Baker was also approached by Dino De Laurentiis, producer of Fellini's renowned film *La Strada* and, years later, of *Serpico* and *Death Wish.* Seeing movie potential in the Baker fiasco, De Laurentiis allegedly offered him three thousand dollars for the screen rights, with an advance to write the score. The producer suggested delaying the filming until the trumpeter was free to play himself. Baker took the money.

Few movies could top the epic melodrama that exploded on Monday morning, April 11, 1961—the *"processo delle vipere"* ("trial of the vipers"), as the papers called it. This was the most scandalous criminal proceeding in Lucca's history, and practically the whole town showed up for a peek. As mobs gathered outside the *tribunale* (courthouse), paparazzi from all over Italy whizzed up on motor scooters, clunky box cameras hanging from their necks. Shortly before 9 a.m., squad cars pulled up, and out stepped the defendants, escorted by policemen. Each entrance set off a lightning storm of flashbulbs. Some bystanders cheered; others hissed, as if the trial were a hybrid of a Hollywood premiere and the Stations of the Cross. Halema, referred to erroneously by reporters as the "mulatto" or "Negro" wife of Chet Baker, hurried inside, a shadowy figure in a black cape and dark glasses. But Carol Jackson posed for photographers and smiled, modeling her carefully chosen black dress, pearls, white gloves, and lacquered beehive hairdo. Not everyone was impressed; the tabloids had denounced her for breaking up Baker's marriage, and as she approached the courthouse doors, peasant women screamed, *"PUTTANA!"* (whore). "It is beyond discussion," noted Dino Grilli in *Il Telegrafo,* that Halema "could teach Carol about class."

Flanked by three guards, Baker strode in confidently, looking pink-cheeked and healthy. Wearing gray flannel pants, a beige jacket, a white shirt, a skinny tie, and handcuffs, he too smiled for the cameras. Inside the *tribunale,* he played to his fullest Italian house ever. Jazz fans, musicians, students, elderly retired people, and international journalists jammed the benches; others climbed ladders outside and peered through the windows. The paparazzi, barred from the courtroom, stood on nearby balconies and pointed zoom lenses at the open windows.

The Italian judicial system employed no jury; instead, the public prosecutor showed evidence to the president of the *tribunale* and two assistant judges. They questioned the defendants and witnesses, then did the sentencing. Baker's chances looked slim. He was charged with possessing an illegal narcotic, stealing prescription forms from a doctor's office, and forging them to obtain Palfium. Since he had already confessed to everything,

Mario Frezza had to try to prove extenuating circumstances and play on the court's sympathy. The lawyer had coached Baker rigorously, and when President Loria of the *tribunale* called him for a three-hour deposition, Baker looked as calm as "a young farmer from the hills," according to Sergio Frosali of *La Nazione*. As he related various drug-related nightmares, his composure was chilling.

Seated in front of the judge's box and speaking through an interpreter, Baker denied all guilt. His troubles began in Bologna around April, he said, when a pulled tooth triggered terrible headaches. The dentist had prescribed a rare analgesic, Palfium. It was so strong that Baker became hooked, forcing him to seek out all those doctors. The theft of his trumpet in Naples devastated him further. "Tell me, Baker, why are you so desperate for a stolen trumpet?" Loria asked. "You could not buy another? Italy is full of trumpets." Baker looked down sadly, like a little boy whose mommy had taken his prize possession. "But it was a special trumpet, your honor," he explained. "A three-hundred-dollar trumpet. I bought another, your honor, but the sound came out all wrong." Blowing into the horn aggravated his sinusitis and trigeminal neuralgia, the aftermath of two car accidents, he said. Without Palfium he couldn't sleep, eat, or play.

Baker went on to deny nearly every confession he had made earlier, claiming temporary insanity. Asked about the ten thousand pills he had admitted smuggling, he shook his head. "I never mentioned a figure like that," he said. It was Halema who had brought him four hundred pills from Germany, and she hadn't known what they were. "She's my wife, and she does what I tell her to do," said Baker. He retracted his admission of the ten-thousand-lire "payment" to Bechelli, and of stealing prescription forms from Landucci, about whom he played dumb, not too convincingly.

LORIA: Do you know whether Dr. Landucci has his office in the same building as his apartment?

BAKER: My lawyer told me I don't know.

Laughter filled the courtroom. Unfazed, he went on to explain that he had awakened one day at the Villa Gemma to find the forms stuffed under his door, a gift from his former drummer, Gene Victory. The only reason he had lied, said Baker, was to protect Victory. He was straining credulity to the limit, yet Frosali felt waves of sympathy as Baker kept clutching his forehead in a gesture of pain. "There is a clear impression that nobody wants to be very harsh with Mr. Baker," Frosali wrote. It was a tribute to Baker's seductiveness that he melted the heart of Italy's toughest female journalist,

Oriana Fallaci, later known for her savagely confrontational interviews with such world leaders as the Ayatollah Khomeini and Henry Kissinger. Fallaci wrote a passionate defense of Baker in *L'Europeo,* Italy's answer to *Time* magazine, declaring that he had been condemned by a government that had never heard of Louis Armstrong or Charlie Parker, much less "the greatest white trumpet player in the world." The authorities, she wrote, didn't care whether this genius "returned to drugs or barked like a dog or stopped playing that trumpet that sounds at times like a hymn to God."

Throughout the questioning, Halema looked down, doodling on a notepad. Called to the stand, she maintained her innocence. "She's clearly the victim in this situation," reported Frosali, noting the audience's "compassion for her as a betrayed wife." Hearing a swirl of denials, contradictions, and lies, all pertaining to him, Baker remained poker-faced. "What happens around him during the proceedings seems not to be very interesting to him," Frosali observed. "It's very difficult to determine by looking at him whether he listens to the things that are said about him or not."

The coming days were free entertainment for those who packed the *tribunale.* "People were attentive, waiting, maybe, for some incredible scene," reported Dino Grilli. When Dr. Nottoli testified, his many friends, gathered in the courtroom, hooted and clapped as if he were a movie star. When one man tried to start a standing ovation, Loria had him thrown out, announcing angrily, "This is not a cinema!"

Grilli spotted a "roundish and ruddy dwarf" who asked in a low voice, persistently and with utmost seriousness: "But when does he play the trumpet?" He didn't, but afterward, Baker's fans "came to greet their friend the same way they congratulated him after a concert." Giovanni Tommaso fought his way through the crowd and asked Baker how he was. "I'm tired," he answered, sighing. "Last night, thinking about the trial, I couldn't close my eyes."

On Thursday, April 12, Carol Jackson was called to the witness stand. For two hours, Baker's mistress gave the trial its most controversial testimony. Using an interpreter, she refuted almost everything she had said in a previous deposition, claiming repeatedly, "I don't remember." Loria repeated her earlier admission that she had accompanied Baker to Bechelli's office to tempt the doctor into cooperating. "I hated him, and I didn't want to be touched," she had stated at the time, adding, "I had been there twice already and I knew his ways." Reminded of this, Jackson's eyes widened. "I never said anything like this!" she exclaimed.

"Well, did Dr. Bechelli ever put his hands on you?"

"Yes, but he was kidding!"

She then denied her testimony that Joseph Carani had allowed Baker to use his name on a prescription. Loria had her whole deposition read back to her so she could confirm or deny each point. Finally he lost patience, declaring that if she didn't stop "shamelessly" referring to Baker as "my husband," he would charge her with perjury. "There is not very much respect for Carol Jackson," wrote Renzo Battiglia in *Giornale del Mattino*, "especially because the audience realizes that while Halema is in jail, Carol is free." The contempt peaked when Jackson walked up to Baker and planted a lingering kiss on his cheek in full view of Halema, who cringed and turned her head. Cecco Maino recalled how sad he felt at seeing her leave the *tribunale* "crying and alone, with only the company of a group of *carabinieri.*"

As other witnesses, including Sergio Bernardini, testified about his addicted past, Baker seemed to enjoy the attention. Even the damning remarks of Roberto Boni, a radiologist who had x-rayed Baker's face in Viareggio and found nothing wrong, didn't faze him. "The more time passes," wrote Frosali, "the more Baker opens up and seems to be in a good mood." Carani wasn't so upbeat as he faced a possible jail sentence and a jeopardized career. "I had only come to Italy to see my father again and to rest," the shaken attorney told Dino Grilli.

Fabio Romiti, the public prosecutor, was the next to have his say. Finger raised in the air, he delivered a scathing indictment of a man he charged with deriding the law and coldly betraying his friends. "Face of an angel, heart of a demon!" Romiti intoned, glaring at Baker. "Trouble comes to anyone who touches him!" Romiti demanded a seven-year sentence. He denounced Bechelli, Jackson, and Giambastiani, and called for two years in jail for Halema.

In the face of overwhelming evidence, Mario Frezza appealed to the court's pity. He depicted Baker as a man doomed to drug addiction through the bad influence of his pot-smoking father; he also told the apocryphal story of how Crystal Joy had slapped Baker in the face and accused him of killing his best friend Dick Twardzik—traumatizing Baker so much that he was forced to seek comfort in the needle. He hadn't committed any drug smuggling, for Jetrium wasn't on Italy's restricted list; what's more, Frezza argued, a blank prescription form had no value, so theft had not occurred. In any case, drugs had clouded Baker's judgment to the point where he couldn't be held accountable for his actions. The lawyer asked for a blanket acquittal.

On Thursday night, Frezza warned Baker not to feel too hopeful. The next morning, as the judges began final deliberations, teenagers clogged the hallways and staircases of the *tribunale,* eager to learn Chet Baker's fate. At 5 p.m., Loria gathered the defendants in front of the court. The pharmacists were judged not guilty. Carani and Halema were acquitted for lack of evidence. Sergio Nottoli was convicted of the minor crime of falsifying names on two prescriptions; he was fined and let go. So was Giali Giambastiani; though clearly an accomplice, no one could prove he had known that Palfium was a restricted narcotic. Bechelli wasn't so lucky. Concluding that the doctor had accepted a bribe from a drug addict, Loria condemned him to three years in prison and a hefty fine of 300,000 lire, plus the temporary loss of his medical license. Bechelli shuddered; his wife burst into tears and nearly fainted.

Chet Baker was pronounced guilty of drug smuggling and forgery, but acquitted of theft. The judges sentenced him to one year, seven months, and ten days in jail, and a fine of 140,000 lire. Mercy had been shown, said Loria, because of the defendant's drug-induced mental deficiency. Baker just stared. He was bewildered, for he still didn't feel he had done anything wrong. "Self-pity is almost too kind a description of the way he felt," said Ruth Young. "His argument in those self-defense statements was: 'I'm Chet Baker! I'm somebody! And I'm not putting up with this shit. Why're you picking on me? I didn't hurt anybody!' "

Renzo Battiglia was appalled by the mild sentence, even though he agreed that Baker was psychologically lacking: "You cannot consider a man like this normal when he lets photographers take pictures of him in the courtroom in an almost smug way, hugging his lover just two steps away from his wife." Dino Grilli spoke with Halema as the courtroom emptied out. "I'm very sorry for Chet," she said tersely, while denying all possibility of a reconciliation. Minutes later, Jackson told Battiglia that she and Baker would wed as soon as he left prison. "He also wants to get married," she informed him, smiling. But according to the reporter, Baker seemed to be having second thoughts. "This is what he said to the people who were asking him about this: 'I won't divorce Halema. Halema is a wonderful woman. She's a great wife.' " Nevertheless she flew back to the States, leaving him utterly lost.

Guards tied Baker's wrists and led him back to his cell, furnished with a straw mattress, a table, and a steel grating for a window. Under happier circumstances, Lucca might have lifted Baker to new lyrical heights. The picturesque town had inspired its native son Giacomo Puccini, as well as Napoleon; Leo Tolstoy began *War and Peace* with a mention of that Tuscan oasis. Twelve miles from Pisa, Lucca was a world unto itself. Encircling the town was a stone wall built in the sixteenth and seventeenth centuries to keep out the treacherous floods of the river Serchio. Everything in Lucca seemed connected to nature or God. The houses, painted in earth tones of yellow, brown, or red, looked as if they had sprung from the soil. Trees grew like pitchforks, with four or five vertical branches reaching heavenward. Churches dotted the streets, and on Sunday, chiming bells seemed to resound from the clouds. Miles beyond the wall, pale green hills faded into the sky.

But the Penitenziario San Giorgio was hardly romantic. It stood in the center of town, a dingy yellow building with black-shuttered windows in front and gratings in back, where the cells were located. In later years, Baker would give sordid accounts of the "horrors" of his prison stay. He called his cell a "damp, filthy, insect-ridden dungeon," the food so rotten that centipedes crawled in it. He lay on a stonelike bed "in a sort of stupor," he said, "shivering and moaning and talking to myself, while the rats and the beetles and the lice and the fleas crawled at leisure all over me." He "nearly went blind" trying to read by the light of a five-watt bulb; his hands turned blue from the cold as he turned the pages.

Yet by all other accounts, Baker managed to get VIP treatment in prison, and he confided the pleasures of prison life to his friends. The Quintetto di Lucca knew the son of the prison director and asked him to take good care of their pal "Chettino" (Little Chet). Baker was given a job in the bookbinding shop with another inmate. With few books to bind, the two men spent their days playing chess and cooking spaghetti on a hot plate smuggled in by a kindly guard.

Another attendant began teaching Baker Italian, but as usual, the trumpeter communicated more profoundly through music than words. When his fellow prisoners saw him walking the halls or courtyard with his horn, they slapped him on the shoulder and made requests: "Eh, Chet, play 'Tintarella di luna.' " *"Si,"* he answered as he played the popular Italian tune. *"Ah, bella!"* they exclaimed, grinning and flinging a hand against their hearts.

The guards allowed Baker conjugal visits with Carol, who stayed in Lucca. Between meetings, he masturbated to the issues of *Playboy* that she brought him. He described their visits as sexual trysts, enacted in the visiting room. "I doubt if anyone can appreciate what a little sex can mean until you've been locked up in segregation for a few months," he said. Baker spent his remaining time working on the score for Dino De Laurentiis, writing twenty-four melodies that Amedeo Tommasi later harmonized. The pianist recalled most of them as mediocre, yet Baker bound them lovingly into a handsome red-leather volume, listing them in neat schoolboy penmanship on the first page. The titles evoked his neediness: "Love Makes the World Go Round," "A Fool in Love," "Blue Carol," "I Could Never Live Without Your Love."

The Quintetto di Lucca tried to cheer him up by gathering outside the back of the prison, shouting, *"Buon giorno, Chettino!"* and serenading him. According to local legend, a sadder sound drifted into his cell: that of a lone trumpeter playing "Il Silenzio" (The Silence), a lament used at Italian military funerals, like taps. The musician was Nini Rosso, an Italian pop star who made the song famous. Baker's own grief flooded from his horn in the summer of 1961; for years to come, nearby residents recalled hearing him play "Someone to Watch Over Me" and "My Buddy." After dusk, when traffic died down and stillness hung in the air, Baker's music, like the ringing of church bells, seemed to float down from heaven. Gusmano Cesaretti, a film producer who grew up in Lucca, never forgot listening outside the prison as a teenager. "It was magnificent, it was almost a spiritual experience," he said. Standing near the jail with a primitive tape machine, the owner of a local music shop created the first of countless Chet Baker bootlegs: an echoey 45-rpm disc entitled *Chet Baker, dentro le mura* (Inside the Walls). The sleeve bore a crude brown-on-white illustration of a window grating in a stone wall, behind which stood an emaciated figure playing the trumpet.

As months passed, Baker gained enormous sympathy. He used it to his advantage when, on September 8, he and Bechelli, accompanied by Joseph Carani, stood before the Court of Appeals in Florence to ask for reductions in their sentences. Baker explained to the judge that he had conquered his addiction and various ills, save for occasional migraines; Carani added that orchestras all over Italy were vying for Baker's services, and that the great Dino De Laurentiis planned to bring his story to the screen. Bechelli voiced his own pleas. In an extraordinary show of leniency, the court authorized the doctor's release from jail, citing insufficient evidence; they also cut Baker's sentence by three months.

In early December, the press camped out near the prison, awaiting his release. It came on the fifteenth. Thanks to good behavior, Baker was allowed to leave a week early, in time for Christmas. He put his trumpet in a bag, collected a release certificate from the prison manager, and walked out alone.

"I had waited a lot for that moment, but I felt nothing," he later told Oriana Fallaci. "I only thought, 'You're free to go, Baker, but where?' " Jail had become his haven; it left him alone with his trumpet while protecting him from his weaknesses. "A black and frightening wall waits for me on the threshold of the prison, and it holds fear, much fear," he had said in *L'Europeo.*

Speaking with a reporter from *Il Telegrafo,* he mourned the fact that no one had come to meet him upon his release. "I don't have any friends in Lucca other than my lawyer Frezza and Dr. Francesconi," he complained. Reading that statement, Cecco Maino was incensed. "It shows what a liar he was," Maino said. "He had been traveling with Piero Giusti and the quintet for months in 1959. Piero, Rudy Rabassini, Paolo Benvenuti, and Antonello Vannucchi all revered him. Everybody had fed Chet, housed him, given him money. Or perhaps he only considered friends those who supplied him with the stuff. Nobody was there when he was released because nobody knew the exact date and hour except Frezza, who by law had to be informed by the jail authorities."

Baker headed to Jackson's hotel around the corner, and the lovers reunited. A few days later, he was called back to the police station. By order of the Ministry of the Interior of Rome, he had five days to leave the country. After the news of his imminent deportation broke, Mario Frezza sprang into action and got the ruling revoked; from then on, Baker could live in Italy freely.

Others involved in the case weren't so lucky. According to Neri Gugliermino, the *medico provinciale* who had hounded so many doctors and pharmacists during the investigation was later arrested for writing himself hundreds of Palfium prescriptions, making them out to his cleaning lady. "What an ironic thing—the one who was persecuting Chet was a junkie himself," Gugliermino said. The policeman explained that the *medico* was thrown in the prison infirmary, where he awaited trial. Alone in his cell at night, he found a way out. His hospital uniform had a belt. Standing on the bed, he wrapped one end around his neck, tied the other to a hook on the wall, and hanged himself.

11

Now that Baker was free, Carol Jackson could adopt the magical name of Mrs. Chet Baker, or so she thought. She didn't know she would have to wait three years to claim that title officially. After two rocky marriages, Baker didn't seem keen to dash into a third; nor did he appear eager to let go of Halema, who took her own time in severing the tie. After living briefly with Baker's mother and father in Inglewood, she found a home in the same town for her and her son. She began dating a man whom she would eventually marry. But tracking down Baker in Europe to start divorce proceedings was so hard that she "completely lost interest," she said. "And I couldn't have afforded it anyway. I had other things to do. I was raising my child. But anytime Chet wanted a divorce, he could have had one."

First he needed to make some money. Upon his release, the Quartetto di Lucca (the Quintetto had lost its guitarist) arranged a "welcome back" birthday concert to raise funds for the trumpeter. On December 23, 1961, townspeople filled Lucca's Teatro Giglio to hail the resurrected Baker, now thirty-two. In his gray suit, white shirt, black shoes, and black tie, he reminded Oriana Fallaci of "a boy making his first communion who is dying of fear." Nonetheless, said bassist Giovanni Tommaso, "the place was packed. It was a big event for the city—articles, pictures. Man, Chet sounded amazing—he was clean, in good spirits, and musically in the best shape I ever heard him. The combination made him sound so big!"

The audience, mostly awestruck young men, were tantalized by stories about Baker's dope habit; many of them had never heard of drugs until he came along. Gusmano Cesaretti even made a trip to the library to research the subject. He was excited to find marijuana growing in his grandfather's yard. "I started rolling it up, smoking the pot, wondering what's gonna happen to my head—it was great!"

That winter, Baker toured Italy with Tommaso, pianist Amedeo Tommasi, vibraphonist Antonello Vannucchi, and drummer Franco Mondini. Now he could talk to them in the Italian he had absorbed in prison. "Chet had learned it by ear in a wonderful way," said Cecco Maino. "He used to make continuous errors of words, phrase construction, and so on, but he sounded like a native Italian; I have never heard a foreigner, especially a North American, sound as Italian as he did."

His recovery was seen as a triumph; once more he was the *tromba d'oro,* the glowing angel of jazz. He was greeted everywhere with hugs and shouts of *"Bravissimo!"* People showered him with gifts; one Italian nobleman gave him a piece of land outside Florence. Pressured by all the high expectations, Baker worried that someone might offer him the wrong "gift." He confided his fear to Tommasi: "Just keep an eye on me and make sure it doesn't happen again, because I don't want to get back into this."

Baker spent Christmas with Jackson in Milan, and on New Year's Day 1962, he headlined at the Olympia, the theater where she had first caught his eye by prancing around in her sexy costumes. After the concert, Baker mused to Nando Latanazzi, the owner, that he would love to have his own nightclub. The impresario led him to an unused lounge in the Olympia, an elegant boîte in velvet and marble, and announced: "Here, Chet, it is yours!" Latanazzi ordered a neon sign that read CHET BAKER CLUB and hung it outside; thereafter the room was Baker's to play in at his convenience.

He didn't get everything he wanted. By now, Dino De Laurentiis had lost interest in making a film out of Baker's life. Despite the money he had earned from the producer, the trumpeter was furious, and went on to call the incident "The Great Movie Hoax." But he cashed in on his prison compositions when RCA Italiana paid him ten thousand dollars for a one-year record contract. The label hoped to capitalize on his notoriety by making him a pop star; to that end, he was asked to cut four vocal sides in Italian with an orchestra conducted by Ennio Morricone, the famed composer of "spaghetti western" soundtracks. The songs came from Baker's red-leather songbook, with words added by Pino Maffei, founder of *Musica Jazz* magazine.

Swaddled in a blanket of strings and voices, Baker crooned of the sweetness of love and of endless nights without his beloved. He sounded more childlike than ever, his soft choirboy's high notes seeming to float from the purest heart. In "Chetty's Lullaby," written for his son, he murmured tenderly: "Sleep, dear, that tomorrow with the sun I will kiss you . . . without you I feel cold in my heart." Chetty was far away with his mother, who was struggling to rebuild her life as a single parent with no help—financial or otherwise—from Baker. She became an accountant, and would remain one for decades. Halema had no desire for her son ever to see his father again, and Baker made little effort to see Chetty anyway. His feelings toward the boy were a tangled mass of guilt, failure, and paternal ineptitude. It was typical of him to express loving concern on a record, then fail to enact it in real life.

Yet on his first LP since prison, *Chet Is Back,* recorded in Rome on January 5, 1962, Baker sounded just the way he wanted to be perceived: bold, strong, confident. At the recording session, he was photographed with arms held wide, horn raised triumphantly, and head cocked back as if he owned the world. Backed by an all-European quintet, Baker played fast, tricky bop by Thelonious Monk, Sonny Rollins, and Charlie Parker that required manly virtuosity but not much feeling. Even in "Over the Rainbow," his mind was on overhauling Harold Arlen's soaring melody, not on surrendering to its passion. Rarely did he fill a ballad with so many notes, but here he gave the sense that all the stark open spaces he normally left were like emotional pits he might fall into.

Still, his playing sizzled with energy and harmonic daring. Trumpeter Roy Eldridge had once attacked him for having a monotonously unchanging tone, but on this album Baker wasn't afraid to set off his quiet moments with fiery blasts, or to sound metallic, coarse, and honeyed within a few bars. Behind him, René Thomas's fingers flew over the guitar strings, plucking out long, graceful lines in single notes. Bobby Jaspar produced a feathery tone on flute and tenor sax; Benoît Quersin's bass lines nearly held up as melodies themselves.

This elegant music-making didn't reflect their lifestyles, though. Jaspar would die fourteen months after making *Chet Is Back,* Thomas in 1974, both victims of drug addiction. Quersin had a habit of his own. As he surrounded himself once more with drug users, Baker's strength faltered. He compensated by straining to act tough. "He had paparazzi around him like he was a big star," said Daniel Humair, the drummer. "At the end of the session, he started to have a star attitude that shocked me very much. I said, 'Can I be paid? I'd like to go home.' He took the money and threw it at me, and it landed on the floor. I said, 'You're gonna pick it up.' He picked it up, because I was ready to punch him in the nose. From that time on there was an animosity, because I didn't play his game. Most of his accompanists were his victims, and he was the master. I didn't want to play that role at all."

Certainly both Baker and Jackson seemed to relish their newfound celebrity. Their love story offered a minor counterpart to a scandal raging in Rome: the expensive and troubled production of the screen epic *Cleopatra.* The whims of its star, Elizabeth Taylor, had driven the film millions over budget, while her torrid romance with her leading man, Richard Burton, had made world headlines. Both stars had other spouses, and the Romans were shocked and titillated by the couple's sinfulness.

When Burton and Taylor weren't around, Jackson and the still-married Baker served as a poor man's Liz and Dick. Jackson seemed to play up her resemblance to Taylor by copying the actress's beehive hairdos and wing-tipped eyeliner. Baker's Italian acquaintances remembered Jackson only as *"una bella ragazza"* (a beautiful girl) who worshipped her handsome boyfriend and adored being seen with him, yet had no real feeling for his music.

For all the time she spent on her makeup, hair, and clothes, few people paid much attention to her. "First of all, Chet was such a charismatic presence that when he was present, nobody looked at his girlfriends," said Cecco Maino. "We all kept silent and waited for Chet to play, or speak, or whatever. Second, Chet's unfounded jealousy made of his girlfriends beautiful, unapproachable, mute statues. Third, Chet did not socialize at all, so he gave little space to anybody who wanted to become friendly with him or his girlfriends, who never left him for a moment."

Jackson got her moment in the spotlight when she gave an interview the next year to the U.K. tabloid *Today.* "Carol Jackson Talks to Gill Preece About Her Love for Chet Baker," went the headline. The article began:

> A slender, sloe-eyed brunette swept her long lashes across her pale cheeks and murmured: "They told me Chet Baker was a big man. . . . I didn't believe them. . . . But right now I'd say he's ten feet tall. His love stirs my soul like the music which pours from his heart. . . . He needs a mother and a mistress, a woman who can give everything and demand nothing. And I know I am that woman. I know Chet's faults, and I alone understand them.

He was so happy in their love, said Jackson, that she was sure his drug days were over.

That winter, she gave him the big news: she was pregnant. Jackson seemed thrilled to be carrying his child, but Baker was no more capable of fatherhood now than he had been in 1957. He cracked that spring when he brought Jaspar and Thomas to Lugano, Switzerland, for a concert. After the show, a dinner party was thrown in the trumpeter's honor by one of his fans, a pharmacist. As guests milled around the living room of his beautiful villa, drinking, smoking, and chattering about how wonderful their star was, the druggist called Baker into his office to give him a dangerous gift. He opened a drawer, and when Baker glanced inside, his eyes popped. There in neat little rows were boxes of the drug that he had spent hundreds of hours scavenging in Italy.

Moments later, Baker took Giovanni Tommaso into the bedroom. "He wanted me to hold the belt around his arm," the bassist said. Refusing, he begged Baker to reconsider, but it was useless. "Don't worry, Giovanni, it's like drinking a sip of whiskey. Just this once, I won't do it again."

Learning what had happened, Jackson became hysterical and began scolding him like a mother. "She was screaming, 'Don't you do this!' and he slapped her hard in the face in front of everybody," recalled Tommaso. He shouted at Baker: "Listen, man, if you do that again, we're gonna have a fight, because I really dislike what you just did!" Baker snapped, "Mind your own business, Giovanni!"

Baker's relapse wasn't immediate. He wanted to stay clean, but that was impossible at the Chet Baker Club in Milan. Admirers dropped by with "presents"; visiting junkies treated him as a guru of dope, pulling him aside after his shows and asking for drugs or tips on where to score. One night between sets he was approached by three young black men in a condition he knew all too well: twitchy, runny-nosed, sweating. Their leader, a tall, skinny man with a mustache, introduced himself as Donald Scott Brown, a drummer. Brown and his friends, a pianist and bass player, had just come from Beirut, where dope was easy to find. But in Italy they had no idea where to cop, nor could they speak a word of Italian.

Baker would later claim that he tried to send them away, but relented when they came back even sicker the next night. After his last set, he explained, he drove them to the Italian-Swiss border, where he sent Brown to the Swiss home of a doctor who had helped keep him high on Palfium in 1960. Baker and Brown's friends waited in the car. Finally Brown rushed back with a paper bag. Once inside the car, he pulled out a bottle of Palfium. Baker explained how to crush the tablets, dissolve the powder in water, then inject the liquid like heroin. When Brown offered him some, he accepted.

Within days he was a junkie again. Brown's friends disappeared, but the drummer stayed at Baker's side for the next year, ensuring that each would keep the other hooked. Brown became Baker's willing slave, carrying bags, flattering him, and most of all scoring the dope. From then on, the trumpeter had little time for nonusers. He fired Amedeo Tommasi, whose anti-drug warnings annoyed him. "There was no room left in his arms or legs to shoot," said Tommasi. By spring, a disgusted Giovanni Tommaso had quit.

Just as Baker began his latest downslide, he got a high-profile chance to show off his famed recovery. That June, the German bandleader Werner Müller, whose recording of "Malagueña" with Caterina Valente had sold millions of copies, prepared to launch his new orchestra at Kongress-Saal, a major hall in Munich. The event would be broadcast on RIAS (Radio in the American Sector), a top German station. Müller wanted to hire a jazz star to boost the night's prestige. Edward Alexander, an American diplomat in charge of music at RIAS, suggested Chet Baker. The choice was perfect, he assured Müller; everyone knew Baker was off drugs and playing better than ever. The conductor agreed, and Alexander tracked Baker down in Milan and booked him for the June 2 concert.

At the end of May, Baker drove with Jackson and Donald Brown from Milan to Munich—a hellish journey, he recalled, that found them stopping again and again to hunt for dope. To Baker's dismay, Germany had added Jetrium to its list of restricted drugs; once more, he had to haunt doctors' offices to beg for prescriptions. His intake had skyrocketed to its old level; whether he had five pills or twenty-five, he shot them all at once, plus any that Brown hadn't used.

They reached Munich on the morning of the concert. Alexander had expected to see the strong, healthy Chet Baker pictured in recent news reports. Instead he encountered a gutter junkie: "thin, sunken-cheeked, hollow-eyed, and nervous," with filthy clothes and shoes. Baker immediately asked for money to buy a new shirt: under his jacket, the trumpeter's sleeves were stained with blood. Alexander handed him fifty marks, fearing he would spend them on drugs and never return. To his relief, Baker showed up at seven-thirty in his new shirt, a clean jacket, and tie, neatly groomed and acting like a semblance of his cool self.

Maybe he wanted to stay clean for the concert, but his composure didn't last. As the sellout crowd waited to see him in his rehabilitated glory, the craving for dope seemed to consume him. He had to see a doctor, he said, or else he couldn't go on. Two employees of the theater managed to calm him, but everyone's nerves were on edge as Baker walked onstage to thunderous applause. Sick as he was, in a supreme act of will he brought forth a mesmerizing twenty-minute performance. Listening at home with a reel-to-reel recorder was Lothar Lewien, a teenage jazz fan who grew up to become a TV director and the author of *Engel mit gebrochenen Flügeln* (Angel with Broken Wings), a reminiscence of Baker. Lewien's tape is the only known record of that concert. In "When I Fall in Love," Baker poured out a sequence of spare, sweet-toned phrases that moved Alexander to tears. "But Not for Me" found Baker racing through chorus after chorus with the gunfire precision of Dizzy Gillespie. He sailed over the quick-changing chords in Sonny Rollins's "Airegin" and navigated a complex big-band arrangement of Dave Brubeck's "In Your Own Sweet Way" with almost no rehearsal.

Backstage, Müller rushed to congratulate Baker, making plans to meet him at a nearby restaurant to discuss a tour. Baker never came. After collecting his four-hundred-dollar fee from Alexander, he set off on a frantic night ride through Munich to find drugs. A sleepy doctor allowed Baker inside his home and listened to his pleas for Jetrium, but refused to help. On the way out, the trumpeter grabbed some prescription blanks and stuffed them in his jacket. Filling them out hastily, he drove to an all-night drugstore. He gave the pharmacist a wrinkled slip of paper forged in an unsteady hand. "Not knowing German I had to tell the druggist a cock-and-bull story about my being American and that for this reason the doctor had made out the prescription in English," he later said. "It could never have worked." He got his Jetrium, but as soon as his car sped off, the pharmacist phoned the police. A half-hour after returning to the Bayrische Hof, the elegant Munich hotel Alexander had picked for him, Baker was arrested.

The next morning, Alexander was awakened at six-thirty by a call from the police. Baker had requested Alexander as his representative and interpreter. The diplomat hurried to the station. "Chet was totally disheveled and incoherent as I tried to ascertain from him what had happened," he said. As the police listed Baker's crimes—narcotics violation, theft, forgery—Alexander was enraged. He wasn't alone. Baker had shattered almost everyone's hopes for him, even as he took advantage of their interest. But he always found someone to help undo the damage. After a night in jail, he was sent for a physical. The young doctor was a fan, and after hearing Baker's latest hard-luck story, he persuaded the authorities to transfer the trumpeter to a top clinic while he awaited trial.

A few days later, Alexander defended Baker in court. He argued that Baker belonged in a hospital, not in jail, and displayed the musician's recent reviews as proof of his contribution to Europe's cultural life. Thanks to

Alexander, Baker returned to the clinic. He was joined there by Donald Brown, who was busted on June 14. Later that month, both men were deported from Germany. A press release spread the news: "The great trumpeter had ruined his chance at a comeback; promoters will never again book him after what he has done."

A German policeman drove him, Jackson, and Brown to the Swiss border. They proceeded to a friend's apartment in Zurich. On July 4, Baker was arrested for forging another prescription. Told to choose between deportation or a term in a mental hospital, he picked the latter. But Switzerland, too, decided it wanted nothing more to do with him, and on July 18, Baker was thrown out of the country.

He tried returning to Italy, but in light of this newest crime, he was denied entry. By now he was nearly penniless. Baker sent Jackson to Milan to borrow money from a friend. She returned with the cash, and they headed for England, one of the last countries in Europe that would have him.

In August, Baker reached London, a city filled with out-of-work jazz musicians. Despite his fame, he was worse off than they were: supposedly to protect the local players' territorial rights, the British Musicians' Union barred foreigners from working in England until they had lived there a year. But Baker was determined never to go back to the States. He hated the American press and legal system for what they had done to him.

With their child due in four months, he and Jackson went to Surrey to live with her parents. In typical English fashion, their house was so chilly and damp that Baker awoke in the morning with frost on his upper lip. The Jacksons were as unsophisticated as Chesney and Vera: Gladys was a dutiful housewife, Albert a handyman and part-time inventor. Baker remembered him as "a little cockney guy who had never seen a dope fiend in his life."

Into this simple existence came a proper English couple's nightmare: their twenty-two-year-old daughter, pregnant by one of the most notorious drug addicts in Europe—a married one, no less—who was now living in their home. They tried to be supportive, but Al's patience was strained to the limit, especially when a paparazzi photo of him and Gladys appeared in a tabloid article about Baker. Naïvely, the Jacksons lectured him about heroin. "We tried to tell him how bad it was, but what could one do?" said Gladys.

Baker was lucky to land, by special permit, a one-day job: a cameo in a new film, *Stolen Hours.* A remake of the Bette Davis tearjerker *Dark Victory,* it starred Susan Hayward as an American playgirl dying of a brain tumor.

The film opens at a swank party in her mansion. Leading the band is a stoned-looking Baker, wearing dark glasses and playing cold bebop trumpet. His appearance onscreen lasts one second. Behind him, unseen, are two top British musicians, pianist Stan Tracey and bassist Jeff Clyne, and Donald Brown. Years later, Tracey recalled nothing of the shoot except the ride to the studio. A van picked up the musicians, and Baker kept asking the driver to stop so he could find dope. "Chet went into house after house," said Tracey. "He was so concerned with scoring, he didn't say anything to anybody."

Sniffing out the local drug scene, Brown realized they were in a junkie paradise. In England, addicts could register with the National Health Service, which treated addiction like a disease. For a token fee, they could score a bounty of "D.D." (dangerous drugs, mainly heroin and cocaine) from government clinics. It was all an effort to take hard drugs off the street and put them in a regulated setting, but with so much dope available, junkies were gorging on it, sometimes going from doctor to doctor each day. Since no blood test was required to confirm their addiction, dealers even masqueraded as users to stock up on product. Until the system was repealed in 1967, London was *the* place to get high.

Only a few doctors in London were licensed to dispense D.D. The favorite of junkies was Lady Isabella MacDougal Frankau, a white-haired psychiatrist married to a noted surgeon. Her office at 32 Wimpole Street saw more drug traffic than any alleyway in Harlem. Baker and his fellow addicts lined up there each morning, and although they paid a pittance, there were so many customers that Lady Frankau turned a handsome profit. With all this heroin and coke available, Baker discovered the "speedball," a volatile combination of both drugs. Writer and ex-addict Jerry Stahl adored the sensation: "The coke breaks your mind into a million pieces and sets your heart exploding until you feel like you're going to come, and the smack eases you back down to earth with a cosmic full-body tongue lap. The difference between an orgasmic scream and an orgasmic sigh—but simultaneously."

With almost no income, Baker had to find a way to pay his rising dope bill. He found it: Albert Jackson. The trumpeter arranged for Lady Frankau to send his drugs by taxi from London to Surrey—a pricey cab ride. Albert would answer the door to find a shady-looking man standing on his welcome mat, holding a bag and asking, "Is Chet there?" The older man was left to pay his future son-in-law's drug dealers, and their taxi drivers. Furious, he tried reporting Lady Frankau to the police, who informed him that her practice was fully legal.

As Christmas of 1962 approached, Surrey felt overwhelmingly bleak. One of the most treacherous snowstorms in British history raged, bringing activity to a halt. On Christmas Eve, Carol went into labor. Albert called an ambulance, and the wait seemed endless. Finally it arrived, taking her on a slow, slippery ride to a public hospital. Her husband, apparently, was in no condition to join her. She gave birth the next day. Albert took Baker on a two-mile walk through the snow and ice to visit her. There Baker saw his chubby, strawberry-blond son. Jackson named him after James Dean: Dean Albert Baker. The child's father didn't pay much attention. "Carol and the baby were fine," he noted in his memoir, before making a quick segue back to drugs: "I continued to act crazy around London."

Carol seemed to cling to the hope that Dean's birth, and her devotion to his father, would make everything OK. "I think she thought she could cure him," said Gladys. "Of course, we never knew anything about drugs, and she thought that he would get better. And he just didn't. She was a fool, really, but she loved him, she wouldn't leave him, and that was it."

With his cherubic face, Dean drew admiring glances from strangers. "When we took him out, people used to crowd around, 'cause he was such a lovely boy," Gladys said. His father turned himself into another kind of spectacle. Hungry for cash, he accepted an offer from *Today,* a British equivalent of America's *Confidential,* to exploit his addiction in a three-part article. A ghostwriter came to the Jackson house, and in January 1963, supermarkets and newsstands all over England displayed the Chet Baker story: "30,000 Hell-Holes in My Arm."

"Mine has been a pretty sick and revolting story," Baker announced, and he piled on the details.

> From being the fastest-rising jazzman in the business, I have become the world's best-known junkie. Police, medical authorities, the customs men of a dozen countries, the F.B.I. and the British Home Office. . . . All keep a close eye on me. . . . I have pumped enough dope into me to kill a quarter of a million normal people. . . . A monkey on my back? Man, this was a raging gorilla—it ate away my soul, my spirit; it clawed me into the snake-pit of human degradation. . . . My arms have been punctured more than 30,000 times to get morphine and heroin into my veins. The hands with which I make music are scored, scratched and pitted—unmistakable signs of the chronic "mainliner." . . .
>
> I am nauseated and appalled by my drug madness. I loathe myself

> for my addiction. It is sheer lunacy. I have been within a hair's breadth of death, my body almost turning blue. I'm sick to think of the times I have stood cramped in a public lavatory, making frantic attempts to inject poison into my collapsed veins. . . . I've often jabbed a needle into my arms and hands a hundred times over a period of hours—hours of torture and tension—trying to get a few grains of stuff into my bloodstream.
>
> Why? Why did I, at times, throw up everything I had lived for—success, money, recognition? . . . It wasn't for cheap thrills that I took heroin and cocaine. It was more the result of a masochistic impulse for self-destruction. In the first place I had taken marijuana to kid myself I was a genius. I was able to say to myself: I did it for my music. I had a message for the world. I had plenty of talent. But I wanted to express myself better, and faster. . . . Drugs enabled me to feel things more quickly, more deeply. I was certain that they were a short cut to musical fulfillment. Hadn't Charlie "Bird" Parker, one of the greatest jazz talents America had ever produced, been an addict? Couldn't I, too, be a genius with the intravenal aid of narcotics?

The second installment was called "All That Jazz, All Those Girls, All That Dope! This was the sorrow in my trumpet." Here Baker noted "forty major affairs and hundreds of minor ones, ranging from the sweet innocence of a first love at sixteen to a degrading relationship with a New York call girl." Dope, he said, had "destroyed any chance I had for a happily married life. My relations with women became temporary and sordid. I didn't object when one degraded herself to get money to pay for my drugs."

All this was supposedly a cautionary tale, but it emerged as childish boasting. For the rest of his life, Baker talked freely about his habit—"a little bit too much, I think," said Micheline Pelzer, daughter of his Belgian musician friend Jacques Pelzer. "He was proud of it." To Baker, it was a true achievement to challenge death four or five times a day by shooting a potentially toxic substance into his arm or neck or groin. Few of the would-be rebels of the fifties had dared go where he went. The next year, to illustrate another ghostwritten tabloid article, "The Trumpet and the Spike: A Confession by Chet Baker," he even posed for graphic photos that showed him preparing to fix.

But paranoia lay beneath his bravado, and everywhere he looked, he saw persecution and conspiracy. In one of the pharmacies where he cashed his prescriptions, he met a druggist whom he suspected of having a crush on him. The young man invited Baker to meet him at a bookstore so he could give him a gift—the nature of which he couldn't imagine, Baker later claimed. There, the druggist handed him a cigarette box containing a vial of coke, stolen from the pharmacy. Baker took it eagerly. By 4 p.m., he and two friends had finished it off. The druggist's theft was uncovered, and the frightened youth found himself at Scotland Yard. He ended up signing a statement that named Baker as the recipient of the coke.

The police threw Baker in jail. Once more, Albert Jackson came to the rescue by posting bail, and the trumpeter was released into his custody. But Albert had lost patience. "Look, Chet, this is no good!" he shouted. "What are you doing to yourself? Stop it! Pack it in, or I'll have to do something about it!"

Baker responded by diving back into his habit. Sharing needles on the streets of London, he contracted blood poisoning. For days he lay in a British hospital bed, in a giant room filled with dozens of patients. The heavy medication made him drift in and out of consciousness. One day he opened his eyes to see Giovanni Tommaso smiling down at him. The bassist had come to London, where his fiancée was living, and RCA Italiana, his record label, had asked him to find Baker and deliver a royalty payment. "Oh, *hiiii,* Giovanni," Baker murmured. "Listen," said Tommaso, "I think I have a very nice gift for you." He handed Baker an envelope. The trumpeter came to life when he saw the cash inside.

Tommaso went to his girlfriend's home. Later that day, a detective rang her bell. Due, probably, to the articles in *Today,* police had fixed a movie camera on Baker's hospital bed. His "transaction" with Tommaso was assumed to be a drug deal. The bassist convinced them otherwise, but as soon as Baker went home, the mayhem continued. True to his word, Albert went to the judge and withdrew his bail. "Look," he explained. "The man is sick, and they're all getting at him, and he hasn't got a chance in Hades of getting well. Can you please give him some medication, get him back to normal again?"

By now the police saw no point in further rehabilitation. On a freezing winter day, they threw Baker into a jail cell. Withdrawal quickly set in, and he started screaming and banging on his cell door with his shoe. Guards carried him into the infirmary, stripped off his clothes, and dumped him into an isolation cell to kick drugs. "I didn't mind being in the padded cell or being naked, but it was so cold in there," he complained. After ten days he was driven far outside London to Dover, where the famous White Cliffs symbolized hope. Baker was placed in Pentonville, a major English prison.

On February 15, he stood trial for narcotics violation. "I really couldn't take the whole thing too seriously—all those seemingly pompous fools with their white wigs," he recalled. But after hearing the trumpeter's testimony, His Lordship handed down a grave sentence: deportation, to the country of Baker's choice. On March 27, he, Carol, and baby Dean boarded a ferry to France. "British Toss Out Hipster Hophead," reported a newspaper in the United States, where reports of Baker's misdeeds were now so common that they rated only an inch or two of space.

Paris welcomed him as a common criminal. In the week he arrived, Baker was arrested again—this time unjustly—along with a horde of other suspected addicts. They included David "Fathead" Newman, Ray Charles's longtime saxophonist, and pianist Kenny Drew. Examined by a doctor, Baker was certified drug-free. "Understand me, man, there were sad faces among the cops," he said. They granted him a temporary work permit, with the stipulation that he submit to regular urine tests to make sure he stayed clean.

After moving his family into an apartment in Montmartre on the Right Bank, Baker went to work at the Blue Note, a low-ceilinged boîte on the Champs-Elysées where American jazz stars—Jackie McLean, Johnny Griffin, Kenny Clarke—were treated like kings. The air was thick with the pungent sweetness of Gauloises cigarettes, while at the bar and tables, aloof-looking Frenchmen wore the beret-and-goatee look adopted by American beboppers fifteen years earlier. The Blue Note was owned by one of the oddest couples in Paris: American ex-GI Ben Benjamin, a roly-poly gay man, and his wife, Etla, a Frenchwoman whom various acquaintances described as "ugly," "nasty," and a "bitch." (In 1986, Liliane Cukier played her in the film *Round Midnight,* set in a facsimile of the Blue Note.) The Benjamins had a *mariage blanc,* the French term for a marriage of convenience. Ben had moved to Paris after the war, hoping to start a nightclub. In order to obtain working papers, he needed to marry a French citizen. He chose Etla, who became the Blue Note's business manager. Baker noticed how she talked to her husband "like a dog and kept the club in a state of bad vibes."

But in Paris, the Blue Note *was* modern jazz, thanks largely to its star attraction: Bud Powell, known on two continents as the greatest living pianist in bebop, and the most troubled. When he moved from New York to Paris in 1959, Powell was so weakened by alcoholism, tuberculosis, and crippling emotional disorders that a doctor had given him two months to live. At thirty-six, he had spent years in and out of hospitals. His playing, famous for its speed and dexterity, was now severely hindered.

His French fans worshipped Powell (who would die in 1966) no matter how bad he sounded. They considered him an authentic jazz giant, which to them meant American and black. France was known for "rescuing" gifted Negro artists, among them Josephine Baker and James Baldwin, from a seemingly mercenary and uncaring America. But when Baker returned to Paris in 1963, few people besides other musicians accepted him. Aldo Romano, an Italian drummer who lived there, saw the problem when he joined Baker's quartet: "I loved his playing right away, because he had the qualities I like in music: melodic sense, romance, and at the same time a very strong feeling of time and swing. But for the young kids, he didn't mean a lot, because to them jazz meant Negro, and a certain kind of music, quite hard. Chet Baker was handsome, white, playing another style. People didn't agree with the total image. I don't think he had a lot of success."

After his rhapsodic welcome in Italy, Baker fumed at the cold shoulder he felt in Paris. "It's idiotic to say that blacks created jazz," he told two French journalists, Jean-Louis Ginibre and Jean Wagner, from *Jazz* magazine. "At the moment when jazz was established in New Orleans, there were musicians everywhere, working in every country, who played like the blacks and became famous in spite of them." But insecurity took its toll. Out went the pretty ballads and vocals, replaced by "cover" versions of Miles Davis's trademarks: "So What," "Bye Bye Blackbird," "Milestones."

Having scorned trumpeters who only wanted to play "high, fast, and loud," Baker started to do just that. "My playing has settled in," he explained to *Jazz*. "It's become a lot more complex, and at the same time harder, more aggressive." But strain showed on his once-placid face. His tone grew thinner and shriller; his pitch faltered. Lowering the horn from his lips, he looked exhausted. He invited unkind comparisons to Davis, who himself wasn't too generous when he came to the Blue Note on a night when Baker was playing. Years later, Baker told Ruth Young of how Davis sat at a rear table and glared at the stage. After the set, Baker timidly approached his table, trying to offer his hero a cool greeting. Davis spat out his response: *"You suck!"*

But Baker's aura of little-boy-lost meets sexy juvenile offender still had its charms, especially in a three-minute feature made for French TV in 1963. It opens in his hotel room in Paris, where Baker lies in bed, bare-chested and unshaven, biting into an apple and wearing a "don't fuck with me!" expression. He scowls as he lights a cigarette, blowing a dramatic plume of smoke for the viewing audience. The film cuts to the Blue Note stage, where he sits on a stool looking pained. The anonymous filmmaker lets his camera linger on Baker's chest, his lips, his fingers as they fly over the buttons of his horn, saliva dripping from his mouthpiece.

He attracted his share of groupies: "mostly drug people, and women—many women," said Romano. Jackson showed no doubt about her own allure. "I don't think Chet will ever leave me," she had declared to *Today.* They hadn't even married, though, when he had his first "extramarital" affair in 1963, only months after Jackson's interview. It was at the Blue Note, he recalled, that he met Bobbi Parker, a black vocalist who sang there often in a Billie Holiday style. "She was very sexy-looking—tall, beautiful," said saxophonist Johnny Griffin, a Blue Note regular. "A lot of people had the hots for her—movie stars, great pianists." But Baker, apparently, won out. With Jackson at home looking after Dean, he began an affair with Parker, he said. Jackson apparently didn't know. Baker remembered that "very attractive black lady" fondly for the rest of his life.

His stay at the Blue Note ended abruptly. The Benjamins had insisted he stand for the first set each night and wear a tie. Stubbornly, he defied them. Etla finally marched in front of the bandstand during a show and said: *"Stand up!"* Baker motioned for the band to stop playing. That was his last night there.

He was quickly hired by a rival club, the Chat Qui Pêche (The Fishing Cat), a Left Bank cellar whose hard wooden benches and whitewashed walls gave it a Bohemian feel. The club was owned by Madame Ricard, a Frenchwoman who looked so small and delicate that people likened her to the "Little Sparrow," Edith Piaf. According to legend, Ricard had become a heroine of the French Resistance by informing against the Nazis. As she floated through the club she was all maternal warmth, however, calling the musicians *"mes enfants"* and housing them in an apartment she kept over the club. The Bakers lived there for months.

The trumpeter had managed to stay clean, and when Michel Delorme of *Jazz Hot* interviewed him on a night off, he saw one of the last glimmers of the sweet, boyish Chet Baker. As the star and two of his bandmates—bassist Luigi Trussardi and trombonist Luis Fuentes—drove through the Paris streets, Delorme jotted down thoughts in the backseat. "Chet is happy with life; he is in perfect health physically and morally, he gives free rein to his boundless imagination," wrote Delorme, adding, "He likes to do whatever he wants at the moment he wants to." Baker proved it by suddenly shouting: "Stop the car, I saw a candy shop!" He ran in, then returned carrying several large bags of bonbons. "Hey man, I need to blow," he said, and they headed for the Chat. They stopped at Fuentes's house so he could pick up his trombone. After a few moments of waiting, Baker stuck his horn out the window and blew a screeching military call, annoying the neighbors. "Chet is impatient . . . Chet is tired . . . Chet is hungry," noted Delorme.

Late that night, they sat in a diner while Baker wolfed down a meal. Delorme asked him if he thought the jazzman's life was a sad one. "Without a doubt," Baker said. "But creating music compensates a hundred times for the troubles this life can bring." When Delorme told him that Freddie Hubbard, a rising young black trumpeter, had called Baker his first big influence, Baker seemed genuinely touched. Asked what he thought Hubbard heard in his playing, he reflected a moment, then answered: "Honesty, maybe."

But away from his trumpet, he didn't seem to know what honesty was; deception had been second nature to him since childhood. He later declared that he had stayed off drugs a whole year in Paris; in fact, he was only there eight months, and resumed his habit in about three. Once the authorities stopped testing his urine, he knuckled under to temptation, which was everywhere. Acquaintances he had referred to Lady Frankau were coming to the Chat Qui Pêche to bring him "tastes" of the heroin and cocaine she had sold them. When Dexter Gordon came to Paris, Baker scored dope for both of them.

As his habit accelerated, he claimed his trumpet was stolen from the club's kitchen. Given his tendency in the latter half of his life to pawn his horns for dope, his charges of theft were hard to believe. But a French musician rescued him by loaning Baker a fluegelhorn, a warmer-toned brother of the trumpet. Its wide bell and larger air capacity gave it a mellow sound, and he played it for years.

A month before Christmas, Baker left the Chat Qui Pêche to finish out the year at the Club Jamboree in Barcelona, Spain. The booking didn't make much sense; the Spanish didn't know him, and most of them ignored him on their way upstairs to see a troupe of flamenco dancers and guitarists. Luckily, the club had provided him a small apartment, which enabled Jackson to invite her mother and one of her sisters to spend Christmas with them. Any hopes she may have had of showing them a happy home life were probably dashed by Baker, an obvious junkie. In Spain, as in England, addicts could register as such and receive drugs legally. But the Spanish system was tightly monitored, and Baker had to resume courting doctors for Palfium. When a jazz-loving surgeon dropped by the Jamboree, Baker told him how hard it was to inject into his tattered veins. The doctor returned with a set of extra-fine stainless-steel needles from Germany, useful for hitting the tiny veins in the back of the hand. In a photo from that period, Baker cradles Dean in his arms; with a puffy, scab-covered hand, he holds a milk bottle to the baby's lips.

On the long drive back to Paris, he worried about his dwindling stash of Palfium. As he approached the French-Spanish border, he shot the last of it. Panicking, he stopped in nearby Toulouse and put Jackson and his son on a train to Paris. Then he embarked on a frantic hunt to redeem a prescription blank he had stolen in Barcelona, then forged. Finally he found a drugstore. Baker gave Lisa Galt Bond a dramatic account of what happened next. Standing nervously at the counter, he watched the pharmacist turn around and pull a box of Palfium from a tall stack on the shelf. Baker took his small dose and checked into a *pensione* for the night.

After shooting up, he lay awake, haunted by the sight of all that Palfium. Well past midnight, he got out of bed, dressed, and walked the deserted streets of Toulouse through a thick fog. Reaching the drugstore, he tapped on the glass door to see if anyone was inside. Hearing nothing, he kicked the door in. Sprinting over shards of glass, he stuffed his overcoat with every box of Palfium in sight. He vanished back into the fog, and left the next morning for Paris.

There he got word that another Blue Note club, this one in Berlin, wanted to hire him. Though banned from Germany, he went anyway. Immediately he began making the rounds of doctors. In his desperation, he brought prescriptions from two different doctors to the same pharmacy. The druggist phoned the police. A night later—January 22, 1964—Baker was arrested at the Blue Note. At the station, he admitted to having copped Jetrium from six doctors in Berlin by claiming a phony kidney ailment. The police threw him into the isolation ward of a sanatorium for forty days. This time there would be no second chance. His worst nightmare had come true: Germany was deporting him to America. "The career of the man with the golden trumpet has come to an end in Berlin," announced a local newspaper. By now his crimes were such old news that the reporter treated them like a joke: "The doctors say he can bring his trumpet to the hospital and give a concert. 'We have a lot of musicians and singers, and they can have an orchestra.' "

Baker was now unwanted in Germany, Italy, Switzerland, and France; his reputation was tarnished all over Europe. The United States had no choice but to take him back. By now he had lost contact with his main accomplice, Donald Brown, who later killed himself. To musicians who had known the young, boundlessly promising Chet Baker, his self-destruction seemed just as suicidal. It was the ultimate act of rebellion, a loud "fuck you" aimed at every door his looks and talent had opened. Still, he made no apologies. "I never bothered anybody," he would soon tell jazz critic Ira Gitler. "I never sold any drugs to anybody. Everything I did was for myself."

On March 4, 1964, he was brought to Frankfurt's Rhein-Main airport and put on a Manhattan-bound plane. Jackson wasn't with him; lacking a U.S. visa, she had returned to Surrey with Dean. In a few hours, Baker stepped into John F. Kennedy International Airport. He was welcomed home by two federal narcotics agents, who searched him for drugs and grilled him at length. Later he claimed he had only forty cents in his pocket, which wasn't hard to believe; nor was his story about calling Gerry Mulligan from a pay phone and asking for a loan, which Mulligan declined to give. One of the officers took pity on him, Baker said, and offered him a ride to New York. Before he left the airport, a reporter from the *Daily News* asked him if he was still on drugs. It was hard to tell whether his response indicated pride or despair. "No, I haven't had anything for forty days," he said. "I'm cured."

Paris, October 16, 1963. Courtesy of Ruth Young

12

To Chet Baker, America hadn't changed much in his absence: it was still a land of "bullshit," devoid of justice or good taste. He soon learned that the *Today* interviews he had done in Britain for a few quick bucks had cost him dearly. *Hush Hush,* an American scandal rag, had recycled his quotes into an exposé entitled "The Tragedy of Chet Baker: From Top Jazz Man to Number One Junkie!" When the FBI got hold of his confessions, a heated investigation was launched into his criminal past. Memos flew back and forth between Washington, D.C., and Interpol; detectives even knocked on his parents' door in Inglewood, questioning a terrified Vera.

The city of New York denied his application for a cabaret card, thus barring him from working in Manhattan. As a result, the Village Vanguard canceled his "comeback" engagement. *Time* magazine, which had once proclaimed him the shining hope of jazz, now devoted a column to the news that Chet Baker was "down and out." In *Down Beat*'s International Jazz Critics' Poll of 1964, he got almost no votes. For Baker, New York was a place of burned bridges, and few people felt he was worth another chance.

As he stood at a pay phone, Baker could find no one willing to take him in. He was rescued by a man he hadn't seen in years: Tadd Dameron, the bebop arranger-composer who had gone from writing for Dizzy Gillespie and Count Basie to leading the band at the addicts' hospital in Kentucky. Hours after reaching Manhattan, Baker moved into the West Seventy-second Street apartment that Dameron, who was black, shared with his new wife, Mabel, a white, English-born nurse. "The next thing we knew, he was off to the pawnbroker to pawn his fluegelhorn," said Mabel, known as Mia.

"Of course he was using," she noted—this only hours after he had told the *Daily News* he was clean.

For six weeks, he slept on the sofa of a man whose life had been stunted by dope. In 1961, after three years at Lexington, Dameron had moved into a series of cheap New York hotels while trying to make a comeback. But the musician who had helped revolutionize big-band jazz—and whose intricate torch song "If You Could See Me Now" had been recorded by dozens of singers, notably Sarah Vaughan—found himself nearly forgotten. In *Down Beat,* John S. Wilson had attacked his recent album, *The Magic Touch,* as "pretentious" and "ponderous." Dameron pressed on, working day and night at his piano and dreaming of composing film scores. But in the spring of 1964, self-abuse caught up with him. Visiting the bandleader Count Basie backstage at Basin Street East, a prestigious jazz club on Manhattan's East Side, he blacked out and was rushed to the hospital. Doctors suspected a coronary, but the X-rays revealed that, at forty-seven, Dameron had terminal bone cancer. "He came out of the hospital, and if he could have turned white, he would have," said Mia. Her husband would grow skeletally thin, and die in less than a year. Before he did, the Damerons were evicted from their apartment for nonpayment of rent.

Though he had yet to learn the diagnosis in the weeks Baker lived with him, Dameron was already depressed, and spent much of his time drinking, snorting some heroin, and commiserating with Baker. Both men felt left behind in an age when the violent sounds of "free jazz" were exploding all over America, echoing the struggle for freedom. The civil-rights movement had hit a frenzy, with the militant Malcolm X and the pacifist Martin Luther King Jr. struggling to awaken blacks to the oppression they were suffering.

That furor bled over into free jazz. Pianist Cecil Taylor's crashing atonal lines, with their blunt shifts of rhythm and volume, threw listeners constantly off balance. Ornette Coleman, the sax player and trumpeter, honked and screeched without written chords while defying all conventions of proper intonation. "There is no end to pitch," he explained. "You can play flat in tune and sharp in tune."

The movement's greatest visionary was John Coltrane. Once a straight-ahead bebop tenor player, he now packed thousands of harsh, squealing notes into solos that sounded like prolonged cries of anguish or ecstasy, depending on how one heard them. "It was like he was possessed when he put that horn in his mouth," said Miles Davis, his ex-employer. To Davis, Coltrane's music "represented, for many blacks, the fire and passion and rage and anger and rebellion and love" that were bursting out of them. "He played what they felt inside and were expressing through riots—'burn, baby, burn'—that were taking place everywhere in this country during the 1960s. It was all about revolution for a lot of young black people—Afro hairdos, dashikis, black power, fists raised in the air."

They wouldn't have seen much relevance in Chet Baker, who insisted on "creating music that's beautiful" and "keep[ing] it very simple." Baker loathed free jazz; for him it was just noise, "without soul." Coltrane offended Baker with his habit of taking a single short phrase and milking it dry for most of a show. "Forty-five minutes is a long time to be blowing; a lot of people get bugged," Baker told Ira Gitler in *Down Beat.* Having barely heard of Martin Luther King Jr. or Malcolm X, he hadn't much time for the new music of drummer Max Roach, whose *Freedom Now Suite* made an impassioned plea for black equality. In one section, Roach's wife, singer Abbey Lincoln, howled out wordlessly in rage and pain—a catharsis of which Baker was incapable, at least in his music. He "wasn't impressed at all" by the new band of Charles Mingus, then in a historic engagement at the Five Spot. The bassist's rough, impressionistic pieces of group improvisation had made him a "giant of immeasurable stature," according to Leonard Feather, but to Baker, Mingus's music sounded "ragged." The trumpeter known for spurting blood all over an Italian gas station toilet clung to a vision of beauty, in music if not in life. "Whether prettiness is useful or not, that's another story," he admitted.

In his interview with Ira Gitler, entitled "Chet Baker's Tale of Woe," the trumpeter claimed that everyone was out to get him, through no fault of his. "It just seemed like a field day for the police department whenever Chet Baker came to town," he explained. "I really believe it's the fault of the journalists and the newspapers in those countries." In Lucca, he said, he had stopped at that gas station to take his "medicine," not to do anything wrong. He had "just finished and put everything away" when the police came knocking and took him to the station. "In fifteen minutes I was gone," said Baker.

"The man was pissed off that he got a bad rap for making a mess in the bathroom," observed Ruth Young. "Shooting illegal heroin—that wasn't the issue. 'They said I left blood on the walls!'—now that to me is the most adorable insanity you're ever gonna get."

He accused RCA Italiana of cheating him out of his royalties—money Giovanni Tommaso had delivered to him in the hospital. Meanwhile, he said, the young English pharmacist had forced him to accept that vial of stolen coke. Baker went on to complain that he had "suffered greatly" at the hands of the U.S. legal system, which abused addicts horribly. In America, he felt so ostracized as a white man that he would have flown back to Europe in a minute. "If I were a colored musician, with a halfway decent name, any name at all, that's where I'd go to live, to get out of this mess over here, because you certainly don't run into it over there."

Baker's "cool" façade was in tatters, and no amount of heroin could soothe him. He raced through the streets of New York in his car, breaking the speed limit, running red lights, screaming "ASSHOLE!" and "MOTHERFUCKER!" at anyone who got in his way. Years later, he boasted of having more than 2,500 unpaid speeding tickets, which he collected in a pillowcase.

His rage went on view during a two-night engagement in April at the Cork 'n' Bib, a jazz club in the suburban town of Westbury, Long Island, where a Manhattan cabaret card wasn't required. Needing a trio fast, he borrowed the rhythm section of trumpeter-bandleader Maynard Ferguson, who had just finished a run there. Baker showed up for the gig with no music, no set list, just his hostility, which he vented on pianist Mike Abene, bassist Ron McClure, and drummer Tony Inzalaco, all in their early twenties. Walking onstage before a half-filled house, he started calling out bop tunes the trio didn't know, such as Sonny Rollins's "Doxy." Abene was thrown: "He said, 'It's based on 'It's a Wonderful World,' Come on, let's go—one-two-three-four . . .' I was like, 'Oh, man!' "

Fans expecting the prince of cool saw a fire-spitting demon instead. "We'd get halfway through the chorus of a tune, and he'd turn around and say, 'No, no, no, NO!' " recalled McClure. "He'd go over to Mike and say, *'That's not how it goes!'* and sit down at the piano and start showing him changes. He couldn't play the piano, and it would take him a good minute and a half to find the voicing of the chord he wanted. It was ridiculous. He had an agenda, clearly, and that kind of intimidated me." Ira Gitler nevertheless wrote a kind review in *Down Beat:* "Although he seemed a bit uncomfortable with his sidemen, Baker sounded very good."

A month earlier, Baker had made what he would come to regard as the biggest mistake of his life. At Dameron's urging, he had signed with the arranger's manager, Richard Carpenter, an ex-accountant known for taking on strung-out black musicians and getting them to surrender their record royalties and the rights to their compositions. A grossly fat man from Chicago with café au lait skin, a huge bull neck, and a round, double-chinned face, Carpenter spouted street-hipster double-talk and exuded menace—especially toward whites, whom he hated. "He had the air of a gangster, like he'd kill you in a second," said Hal Galper, a young pianist from Salem, Massachusetts, who joined Baker in April. Indeed, stories were told of Carpenter threatening to break people's legs—and worse—if they didn't give him what he wanted.

Ostensibly a jazz lover, Carpenter approached downtrodden black artists as a "brother" who would protect their business affairs from the thievery and exploitation of the "whiteys." The ploy worked: in the fifties and sixties, his client list included saxophonists Lester Young, Gene Ammons, and Sonny Stitt; trumpeter Howard McGhee; and pianists Elmo Hope and Duke Jordan, all top East Coast jazzmen. Immediately after the Damerons' wedding ceremony on January 29, 1964, Carpenter took them to a notary. "We were signing stuff that we didn't understand," Mia said. "I thought, 'Tadd knows what he's doing, he's signing so I'll sign.' " As part of a "management" agreement, the couple relinquished rights to all of Dameron's tunes. Earlier that month, Dameron had sold his record royalties to Carpenter for fifty dollars. Every contract was notarized, making it incontestable. "He robbed everybody that ever came near him, I think," said Mia.

Such practices were rampant in the bop era, but no one had perfected them like Carpenter. He owned several publishing firms—Richcar Music, Charrich Music, Mabreeze Music, Music Royalty Corp.—and would pay needy musicians twenty-five or fifty dollars for their compositions, which he then owned outright. Often Carpenter, who couldn't write a note of music, claimed authorship. The best-known case involved his client Jimmy Mundy, a once-renowned arranger-composer for Benny Goodman and Count Basie. After Mundy's death in 1983, Don Sickler, a trumpeter and music publisher who handled Dameron's catalogue, found the copyright certificate at the Library of Congress for a tune originally called "Gravey." Mundy was believed to be the composer, although some would argue it was Gene Ammons or Miles Davis. The title had been partly erased; "Walkin' " was written over it and Carpenter's name inserted as composer. The song became a jazz standard; Carpenter gets credit for it to this day. He profited even more handsomely when he acquired the song "Evil Ways" from its composer, Clarence "Sonny" Henry, in 1967; three years later it became a top-ten hit by Santana. Most of Carpenter's clients learned the truth too late. "Richard Carpenter's a motherfucker—don't go near that guy, he'll burn you," said Sonny Stitt to Phil Urso, who left his home in Denver to rejoin Baker in the spring of 1964.

It was rare for Carpenter to sign a white musician, but he sensed a cash cow in Baker. Assured by his friend Tadd that Carpenter was a godsend, Baker didn't hesitate. For the manager's services, plus the sum of one dollar (the minimum compensation needed to bind such a contract), Baker signed over his future royalties on March 16. In an interview with Burt Korall of *Melody Maker,* Carpenter announced: "Chet has a unique singing quality and we intend to fully expose this side of his talent so as to invade the pop field. There is no doubt in my mind that he can hit it big."

It seemed like a good deal to Baker. "Richard had the connections to get him records, and he managed the band and took care of him," said Hal Galper. "He paid Chet's rent, and gave him an allowance every week for groceries and dope. It was fine with Chet. The less responsibility he had, the better. Let Richard have all the money—he couldn't have cared less. As long as the rent was paid, all he had to do was shoot up and get high and play the gigs."

A decade later, when Ruth Young would try to untangle Baker's finances, she found his notarized contract with Carpenter, whom he then detested. True to form, Baker denied all responsibility, swearing the paper was forged. "I said, 'Now wait, Chet, come on—a notary is standing there between you and Carpenter, how does he forge your signature?' " argued Young.

In mid-April, Carol Jackson left Dean temporarily with her mother and joined Baker in New York. Carpenter found the couple an apartment two floors below his in a housing project on Ninety-seventh Street and Central Park West. When he wasn't busy terrorizing his pretty wife, Betty, who called him "Big Daddy," Carpenter kept Baker on a tight leash. Every morning he made the white boy squirm for his daily twenty-dollar dope allowance while bragging about all the "turkeys," including Phil Urso and Hal Galper, whose tunes he had bought for fifty bucks.

Baker was equally vulnerable, as anyone could see in July when he played the Newport Jazz Festival. He appeared as Stan Getz's guest on three tunes—a comedown for the former number-one trumpeter in America. "He came on stage hesitantly, looking gaunt, anxious and much too pale," wrote *Jazz Journal.* "But when he started to play there was nothing hesitant about his music. Despite the many years' absence and his various troubles, Baker if possible sounded better than ever."

But his style seemed passé. "It was the old laid-back, behind-the-beat bebop groove, the junkie beat," said Galper. Baker let the pianist hire two energetic young players, bassist Michael Fleming and drummer Steve Ellington. After their first show together, Baker pulled them aside. "You know, uh . . . I'm gonna ask you guys to do something for me," he told Fleming. "Would you just . . . *play simple*?" One night he ordered Ellington off the stage and gave him a drum lesson before a stunned audience. "He was one of the great fascist bandleaders," said Galper. "He'd embarrass you on the bandstand if you weren't doing the things he wanted. That's the way he did it—fear, intimidation."

Nonetheless, Galper said, "I was learning, and Chet was a great teacher. A master improviser, a master line player. Great tone, great time, great dynamics, great drama. He was an absolute master at controlling the music, just with his voice, his horn. I learned so much from him about listening to the whole sound of the band, about playing soft especially. God, he was on my ass about playing soft."

On his U.S. "comeback" LP for the small Colpix label—grandiosely entitled *The Most Important Jazz Album of 1964/65*—Baker wore an uncharacteristic grin on the cover, and played the kind of mellow bop his fans were grooving to in the fifties: swinging tunes with catchy hooks, melodic ballads. Except for "Walkin'," the songs were all unknown pieces by Dameron and Hal Galper that Carpenter owned. Phil Urso wove his lyrical tenor around Baker's lines; the trio (Galper, Art Blakey's ex-bassist Jymie Merritt, and the bebop drummer Charlie Rice) played with the restraint Baker demanded.

But in a season filled with dazzling new sounds—John Coltrane's inspirational, Grammy-winning LP *A Love Supreme; Getz/Gilberto,* a teaming of Stan Getz with João Gilberto and Antonio Carlos Jobim, the fathers of the latest rage, bossa nova—Baker's album title was an invitation to trouble. "It's difficult to get excited over the Baker crew's rewarming of old hash," wrote Pete Welding in *Down Beat.* "What Baker and colleagues are saying here has been said countless times before, with far greater force and conviction."

Sales were poor. A few months later, Baker tried going a little more modern on *Baby Breeze,* the first album of what Carpenter hoped would be a long association with Limelight, the Mercury label's new jazz division. Finally Baker was ready to experiment a little: in Galper's "One with One," written in the modal scale of the avant-garde, he came as close to free jazz as he ever would. "Chet was playing a lot of long lines—long flurries of intricate, connected notes, very creative," said Fleming.

Only years later did Baker learn what emotion that album had stirred in Diane Vavra, the drummer and saxophonist who would become the last great love of his life. "I was very excited when I played that record," she said.

"It had a lot of fire and energy in it. It was all very spontaneous, the way he played. When he recorded 'One with One,' there was no rehearsing beforehand. He doesn't know the changes, so he anticipates them before he starts to play. You can hear him waiting for the chord to sound, and he's playing chromatically. He's going up in half-steps, very careful to pick just the right notes. After he told me that, I listened to it again, and I realized what a genius this guy was."

Baby Breeze also marked his full emergence as a jazz singer. In "You're Mine, You," a misty-eyed vow of eternal love, Baker glides over Kenny Burrell's guitar chords, improvising lyrically and tugging gently at the song's rhythm, just as if he were playing it on trumpet. In *Down Beat,* Harvey Siders commented on how Baker "lavishes loving care on words and phrasing. . . . Baker's critics still complain about the lack of virility in his singing. What they overlook too easily is the wealth of feeling he projects."

Nevertheless, Siders summed up *Baby Breeze* as a "fine, but not spectacular album," and soon it ended up as a bargain-basement cutout. On Baker's second album for Limelight, he and Carpenter tried a more commercial project: a big-band tribute to Billie Holiday, with famous tunes and lots of singing. *Baker's Holiday* didn't sell either—even after Don Nelsen of *Down Beat* hailed Baker for the "delicacy with which he interprets melody. He is most sensitive to the lyrical, to the tender-sad connotations of a ballad. He is the best kind of romantic."

That notion seemed ludicrous to Hal Galper, who saw how easily Baker could switch the romance on and off. "Chet was an absolute realist," said Galper. "He knew exactly what was going on. He didn't have a romantic bone in his body, or a naïve one. He played all the games. He was a pro." Galper's visits to Baker's "love nest" on Central Park West revealed a domestic hell. "He'd just gotten up, but he'd be in the kitchen shooting up, trying to find a vein. There'd be blood all over the kitchen floor. He'd say, 'I'll be right with you in a minute, Hal!' " The pianist learned to demand his pay nightly, lest his salary end up in the boss's arm. "Him and Getz and Frank Morgan and Art Pepper—all the great junkie personalities, it became a part of their image. They played on that a lot. All Chet really cared about was getting high. He would hang with people who were assholes, just to get high. People didn't mean that much to him. It was hard to tell who he really cared about, because Chet was such a user. You let him use you for a fee." When Hersh Hamel moved to New York in 1965, he found his old buddy "all hung up with looking for dope" and indifferent to his presence. "Art

Pepper was my friend no matter what—dope or no dope," said Hamel. "But Chet was very aloof."

Baker's itinerary was a shadow of what it had been in the glory days of his quartet. Only a handful of gigs lay ahead, including the Jazz Workshop (Boston), Shelly's Manne-Hole (Hollywood), Baker's Keyboard Lounge (Detroit), and the Plugged Nickel (Chicago). "His reputation was shot from not being dependable," said Michael Fleming. "So I think he was out to prove himself." Baker once had three days to get from Boston to Hollywood, a marathon he vowed to make by car. "Three days is unheard of for that trip!" said Fleming. "No ordinary person would have tried it."

On a Sunday morning, Baker, Jackson, Urso, and the trio piled into the new Dodge station wagon Carpenter had provided. Baker shot up, then took his passengers on what Fleming called a "hell ride" that convinced the bassist that his boss was insane. "We'd be going so fast you'd think the engine was gonna burst," he said. "At the end of the road would be a hill, and a line of about twelve cars. We're number thirteen. Now we're number six, we're number five. There might be something coming over the hill, you can't see. Sure enough, here comes a car. You're saying, this isn't happening!" With a *whoosh,* Baker sped past the car, missing it by inches. As he repeated the stunt over and over, Galper and Steve Ellington started cheering him on—"YEAH, CHET, GO!" Fleming sat beside them with a newspaper over his head: "I wanted to grab them and choke their tongues out, that's how frightened I was." Jackson sat in frozen silence. "She didn't dare open her mouth," said Fleming. "At his worst he had a very violent temper, and he had her trained. When we'd stop and have something to eat, she was very quiet."

But Baker didn't want to stop, except to buy dope. Cruising through some seedy neighborhood, he would peer at every alley and doorway until he spied "the man." Then he would roll down the window and beckon the dealer over. First he would ask for a "taste" of the "stuff." He'd dip a finger in, then stick it in his mouth. "CHRIST ALMIGHTY!" he shouted once, tasting some bogus substance. "It's a wonder he didn't run the guy over," Fleming said.

Eventually he would find what he needed and race off again. As they passed through the Rocky Mountains of Denver, the car flew so fast that all Fleming heard was a high-pitched, almost supersonic hum. "It was pitch-black out," he recalled. "We're going down through a series of hairpin turns, and there are ice patches, and here he goes again, gunning the engine. All you can see is the top of the pine trees. Now, if these trees are at the bottom and we're looking at the top, how high are we? And there's nothing over the side—you hit the rail, that would be it."

But Baker had "very quick reflexes, no matter how stoned he was," said Galper, and on the afternoon of the opening, he got them to Shelly's Manne-Hole, one of the last straight-ahead jazz clubs in L.A. It was the first time in years that Baker had seen its owner, drummer Shelly Manne, who had taken a road far different from his. Settled into a beautiful home in Hollywood, Manne had earned a fortune as a studio musician and now divided his time among playing choice gigs, breeding show horses, and running the Manne-Hole.

Baker, by contrast, was a tarnished golden boy, forced out of L.A. seven years earlier by a narcotics officer. For two weeks, curious fans filled the club. Baker played well, but his star quality looked faded. "He was a shy person, but between the shyness and the nodding off, sometimes I couldn't tell which was which," said Fleming. Away from his trumpet or car, Baker seemed "boring as hell" to Galper. "We didn't communicate on an intellectual level at all. He talked about people being jive this, jive that. If he ran out of dope, we'd stop at some Howard Johnson's and wait while Chet drove around to find a doctor to give him some pills. Six hours at a Howard Johnson's in the middle of nowhere."

He certainly wasn't attending to his family. "Carol was having a terrible time, moaning and groaning about not having enough money," said Hersh Hamel. The couple's relationship looked "quite often antagonistic" to Galper: "She used to be so jealous of him. Chicks would just fall backwards over Chet. I remember in Chicago, some chick came up to the bandstand and just lifted up her dress, and she had no panties on. He was so helpless, they wanted to mother him."

Jackson was impatient to make their union legal, and with their son well past infancy, Baker had little choice. More than four years into the relationship, her goal to become Mrs. Chet Baker was finally in view. Now that Baker was home in America and easier to trace, Halema served him with divorce papers. Passing through Reno later in 1964, he and Jackson located a justice of the peace and exchanged vows while best man Phil Urso looked on. "Chet did what he thought was the right thing," said Jack Simpson. But his divorce wasn't final, and the next year they had to repeat the ceremony in Las Vegas—this time with Chesney Sr. as best man, and with Carol expecting another child.

Vera had already written to Baker from Inglewood, urging him to put his wife on birth-control pills. If Carol was her rival for her son's affections, Vera knew how to use guilt to gain the edge. Every day, she told him, she put on a smiling front at W. T. Grant's, when in fact she was heartbroken at how badly he had disappointed her. She was so depressed, she said, that she had withdrawn into a shell, and everyone at the store wondered what was wrong with her.

Other troubles were weighing Vera down. Chesney, then fifty-eight, had lost his last job, making her the sole breadwinner once more. Meanwhile, Chesney Aftab, whom she saw often, was suffering from mood swings and fits of anger—all because his father wasn't there, she informed Baker. She added shame to the guilt by asking him not to phone her at the store; she didn't want anyone to know who her son was. She even worried that the FBI might be tapping her calls. The letter suggests where the trumpeter had learned his skills of manipulation.

Baker knew only one escape. He and Phil Urso took a cab each day to 157th Street in Harlem, where they met their connection, "Slim." It shook Baker to hear that Bill Evans was spending seventy dollars a day on heroin. For a moment, Baker caught a chilling glimpse into his own future. "Bill is self-destructing, man—*I'm* not gonna self-destruct," he vowed to Urso. The next day, he was back on the same street corner.

Sensing that Baker was headed for disaster, Carpenter rushed to squeeze as much product out of him as possible. In August 1965 he booked a Manhattan studio for three afternoons, intending to record Baker until he dropped. This time the trumpeter was surrounded by four black beboppers whose playing recalled the group Miles Davis had brought to Birdland in 1954—the one that had made Baker and his trio feel like white-bread phonies. Baker had never forgotten the sting of that episode, and in 1965 he may have been trying to prove himself once more in the eyes of the "brothers." George Coleman, a Memphis-born tenor player, had recently left Davis's quintet after appearing on the group's acclaimed album *Seven Steps to Heaven.* Bassist Herman Wright and drummer Roy Brooks, both from Detroit, were Baker's sympathetic neighbors on Central Park West; pianist Kirk Lightsey, also from Detroit, had provided funky accompaniment for Dinah Washington and Aretha Franklin.

Carpenter was happy to hire them all, largely because they agreed to work cheap. ("The money we made was ridiculous," said Brooks.) In the manner of the quickie bop-record dates of the fifties, when albums were done in a day with hardly any rehearsal, Baker and his group showed up at each session and basically winged it. Jimmy Mundy sat in the control room, anonymously churning out songs for which Carpenter took credit. "He was writing the next tune while we were recording the tune before," said Lightsey. Carpenter had brought along a bundle of Tadd Dameron's music, plus a few Sonny Stitt pieces on which he claimed coauthorship. Only a few standards—"Have You Met Miss Jones," "Fine and Dandy," "Stairway to the Stars"—were used, so Carpenter wouldn't have to pay too many composer and publishing royalties.

In three days, Baker recorded thirty-two songs with a group that challenged him like no band since Charlie Parker's. "Cherokee," the theme song of swing-era maestro Charlie Barnet, catches the spirit of those sessions. Brooks opens it at one of the fastest tempos Baker had ever attempted, and the trumpeter makes a shaky entrance. Wright steps in with a furious walking bass line, Coleman with a torrent of notes fueled by breath control that seems endless. Baker springs to life with a furious bebop solo. "I had no idea he could play like that," said Coleman, who knew him mainly as a crooner. "His placement of notes—I was very excited about that. And when he had to go up high, he could do that too—not extremely high, but higher than you would expect from a guy who played like he did, in the middle register." He and Coleman improvised harmony and counterpoint lines "like they'd been doing it all their lives," said Lightsey. If the band brought him fire, Baker gave them tenderness. Sadness pours out of him in "Lament for the Living," an elegy by Dameron, spare as a dying man's last words. "Chet was strung out, but we didn't care," said Brooks. "It didn't make any difference; everybody was glad to be there with Chet. There were no mistakes. Tempos didn't drag or nothin'. There was nobody to say do this here, do that there, because nobody knew the tunes."

Carpenter sold the tapes to Prestige, which spread them out over five albums. The company marketed Baker as a Miles Davis clone by using a set of titles *(Smokin', Groovin', Comin' On, Cool Burnin', Boppin')* that mimicked a Davis series on Prestige *(Walkin', Cookin', Relaxin', Workin').* Record-store browsers skimmed through liner notes that tagged Baker as a burnout trying to salvage his wasted talent. On *Groovin',* Jack McKinney noted Baker's "return from the dead" after a "decade of frustration found at the point of a hypodermic needle. . . . Those of us who have known and loved his work pray that Chet Baker hasn't sacrificed his life for death on the junk pile." To Bob Porter, who annotated *Comin' On,* the "aging horn man" (then thirty-five) had finally made good after the "terrible hoax" of his early popularity, when "his faulty intonation, lack of vocal variety, and the essential sameness of his material were of little import to his fans."

But Harvey Pekar considered it a lost battle. "Baker's use of fluegelhorn doesn't come off," he wrote in *Down Beat.* "His tone is muddy. His solos lack assertiveness and don't build too well. . . . He improvises some attractive lines but falls back on too many stock figures, some derived from Miles Davis."

The Prestige albums, like most of his others, became collector's items. Baker's year ended with little work and new pressures. On November 11, 1965, Carol gave birth to their second son, a dark-haired boy she named Paul. A month later she was pregnant again. Carpenter had no desire to subsidize the growing family, especially since he had already lost interest in Baker. His plan to "invade the pop field" with Baker and "change his professional image"—for a big-money reward—had failed. Two weeks after Paul's birth, the Bakers returned from out of town to find themselves evicted from their apartment. Carpenter hadn't paid their rent in months.

At first Baker refused to believe he could have been had so badly. He kept phoning Carpenter, and no one answered. He made the doorman buzz him over and over—nothing. Later the IRS audited Baker and charged him thousands in unpaid taxes. He blamed Carpenter, but couldn't shake the ugly realization that he'd walked into a nightmare, blinded by a fog of his own making. "If I hadn't been sick at the time, it never would have happened," he told reporter Richard Williams years later. For the rest of his life, he raged over never having made a dime from the eight albums Carpenter had produced. It was probably true, if one didn't count the cost of twenty-one months of rent, food, and dope money, paid against records that didn't sell and gigs for which Baker couldn't command much of a fee. But Carpenter got his payoff in years to come by collecting untold royalties from several of Baker's labels.

For the rest of his life Baker would despise Carpenter, who spent his last days in an expensive home in Scarsdale, an upscale suburb of Westchester County, New York, before dying in 1996. Baker even talked of wanting to kill Carpenter, and no one doubted he meant it. The whole mess had left Baker worse off than he was on his first day back in New York, and more determined than ever to stay high. But for now, he saw only one option. Packing Jackson, three-year-old Dean, and one-month-old Paul into the station wagon Carpenter had given him, he headed home to Mother.

San Jose, California, 1970. Courtesy of Diane Vavra

13

With Christmas approaching, Vera and Chesney Baker made room in their apartment for a cumbersome "gift": their grown son and his whole family. Life at 129 West Hillcrest Boulevard in Inglewood was already strained. Chesney had somehow found a new job as a security guard in a construction firm—an encouraging sign, were it not for the fact that he was often drunk, and now carried a gun. Vera feared the worst.

Nearly sixty, Chesney had only failure to look back upon. At night, in front of the TV, he complained in a boozy drawl about his son's music, his bad habits, his mistakes. Sometimes Chesney gave him advice on how to play the trumpet. Confronted with his father's failure, Baker had every reason to see himself as a loser too. The "West Coast Sound" now meant the Beach Boys, and most of his buddies from the Haig days had deserted the dwindling club scene to become well-heeled studio musicians. Baker couldn't even keep a roof over his family's heads. At thirty-six, he looked like an aging James Dean, stuck in an endless loop of *Rebel Without a Cause.* On December 27, 1965, less than a month after his return to L.A., he was busted in Hermosa Beach for drugs. He wound up with three years' probation.

Broke again, Baker phoned his original cash cow, Dick Bock, who had recently gone corporate. Heeding the advice of the Maharishi Mahesh Yogi, whose teachings he recorded and lived by, Bock had sold his faltering World Pacific label to a large outfit, Liberty, which recorded Cher, Gary Lewis and the Playboys, and other pop stars. He had stayed on to run World Pacific as a salaried employee, but was now under pressure to keep sales high. Searching for a way to repackage his jazz artists commercially, he tapped into the craze for Muzak—the bland "mood music" piped into elevators, supermarkets, and dentists' waiting rooms. Late in 1965, Bock produced *Michelle,* a Bud Shank album of top-forty rock tunes in treacly string-and-choral settings. Boosted by its title song, a Beatles hit, *Michelle* made the easy-listening charts. Jazz fans scorned him for selling out, but the flutist had little choice: "Remember that by this time jazz records were not selling. Jazz musicians weren't working in jazz clubs. It was a matter of survival. It kept my name alive."

Rather than handing Baker another "loan" he would never repay, Bock had placed his former star trumpeter in the backup band of *Michelle.* "He showed up late and wanted to borrow twenty dollars," said Shank. "Past that, everything was all right. He did exactly what he had to do and did it well."

Encouraged, Bock signed Baker to his own deal. He knew he needed a gimmick to revive Baker's sales, and he stole one from the hottest new trumpeter in pop: Herb Alpert, whose pseudo-Mexican Tijuana Brass records—including "Spanish Flea" (the theme of TV's *The Dating Game*) and "Lonely Bull"—were making millions. Bock tried cashing in with *A Taste of Tequila,* the first of four albums by "Chet Baker and the Mariachi Brass." Playing "Speedy Gonzales" and "La Bamba," the so-called Miles Davis clone turned into a Herb Alpert wanna-be. The arrangements smothered him in imitation Mexican guitar, a stiff trumpet section playing the tune in unison, and pounding tambourines; Baker struggled to find a crack here or there where he could insert an anemic phrase. He played so carelessly off-key that he later denounced those albums as "outrageous, terrible." Herb Alpert agreed: "It was desperation—he probably needed money and they gave him some. But wow, I was saddened by that. Oh, those records stunk."

They helped destroy what was left of Baker's reputation. A *Down Beat* critic called *A Taste of Tequila* his worst ever: "He sounds as if he's on the point of collapse; his solos are mumbling meanderings, devoid of feeling or fire." Don Nelsen gave *Hats Off* a no-star rating in the same magazine, calling it "a loser" and "a wipeout." Baker also made two "mood music" albums, *Quietly, There* and *Into My Life,* with the soporific Carmel Strings. The songs included "Cherry Pink and Apple Blossom White," a tune requested of him by the Italian peasants in jail. "Rarely . . . has Baker sounded as flaccid as he does against the keening strings and choral ooh-ings and aah-ings of these performances," wrote Pete Welding in *Down Beat.* "He's a shade out of tune, too, for added drama."

With his self-respect gone, he needed more than ever to blot out the

Fleeing a suffocating mother and a drunken, abusive father, Baker joined the army at sixteen. Courtesy of Ruth Young

Stationed in Berlin, Baker sails on Lake Wannsee with sergeant and fellow musician Howard Glitt, 1947. Courtesy of Howard Glitt

Private Chesney H. Baker, seventeen but looking twelve. Courtesy of Paul Martin

With no musical training at all, Baker (top row, second from left) outblows the other members of the 298th Army Band in Berlin. Courtesy of Paul Martin

It was easy to spot Baker in the Redondo Union High School orchestra, shown here playing for a student production in 1948. His friend Bernie Fleischer, whom he eventually scared off with his reckless behavior, is the saxophonist standing. Courtesy of Bernie Fleischer

Hollywood cool: Gerry Mulligan, Larry Bunker, Chet Baker, and Lee Konitz at The Haig in 1952, a *film noir* soundtrack come to life. Photo by William Claxton

Baker meets Miles Davis and Swedish trumpeter Rolf Ericson at the Lighthouse, Hermosa Beach, California, 1953. In his memoir, Davis attacked his white rival as sounding "worse than me even while I was a terrible junkie." Photo by Ray Avery

The "Great White Hope" in the shadow of his mentor, Charlie Parker, at a concert in San Bernardino, California, October 1953. The bassist is Carson Smith. Courtesy of Carson Smith

On tour with America's number-one trumpeter in 1954: pianist Russ Freeman; Baker's wife, Charlaine Souder; Joan (Mrs. Carson) Smith; and Marion Raffaele, fiancée of drummer Bob Neel. Courtesy of Carson Smith

In record-store windows nationwide, Baker gets star treatment. Author's collection

Visiting NBC's *Today* show in 1954, Baker and his crew—Russ Freeman, Carson Smith, and "boo-bam" player Bill Loughborough—entertain millions while host Dave Garroway looks on. Photo by Carole Reiff; © Carole Reiff Photo Archive

“To me, there is a sadness about jazz,” Sammy Davis Jr. told *Down Beat.* “Chet Baker has it, for example.” Davis dropped in on Baker and Gerry Mulligan at a club in 1955. Photo by Russ Freeman

Baker was never prouder in those days than when he had Liliane Cukier, his thrill-seeking French girlfriend, on his arm. Photo by Russ Freeman

Baker's fans flock to him after a concert at San Jose State College. According to bassist Jimmy Bond: "Some of the women who chased after Chet were gorgeous, unbelievable. He would leave with three or four." Photo by William Claxton

"Just because Chet was a poll winner didn't mean we didn't play some real dumps," said Russ Freeman. Onstage in Cleveland, left to right: Bob Neel, Phil Urso, Freeman's successor Al Haig, Baker, and bassist Bob Whitlock. Courtesy of Bob Whitlock

The first beefcake model in jazz, photographed by Herman Leonard in 1955

Baker in a less glamorized moment.
Courtesy of Russ Freeman

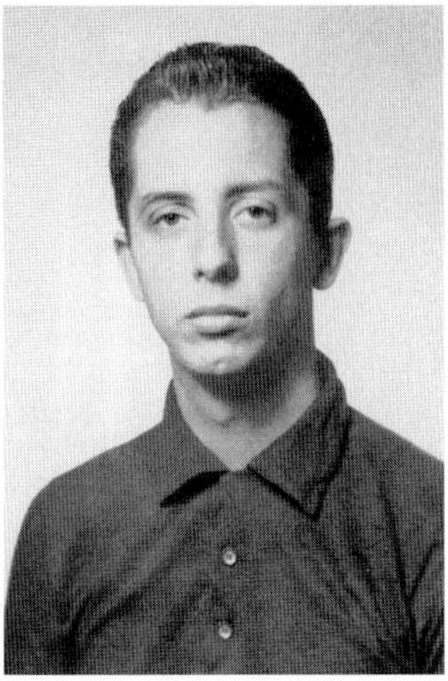

In 1955, Baker met the soulmate of his dreams: Dick Twardzik, a troubled, addicted pianist from Boston. Cherry Vanilla, who worked on the Baker documentary *Let's Get Lost,* reflected: "Maybe Chet loved him in a way we don't even know about."
Courtesy of Crystal-Joy Albert

September 10, 1955: the conquering hero sets off on his first European tour. "He was trying to act cool," said his friend Charlie Davidson, "but deep down I think he was in stark terror." Photo by Carole Reiff; © Carole Reiff Photo Archive

Baker and Dick Twardzik make a smash European debut at Amsterdam's Concertgebouw on September 17, 1955. A month later, Twardzik would be dead. Ed van der Elsken; courtesy of Nederlands Fotoarchief

Adoring Italian musicians crowd around Baker at the RAI-TV studios in Rome, January 1956, but he and promoter Adriano Mazzoletti (far right) only have eyes for Liliane. Courtesy of Liliane Cukier Rovère

Short-lived bliss: the newly addicted Baker and his second wife, Halema Alli, then twenty-one and "terribly naïve," as composer Bob Zieff remembered her. Photo by William Claxton

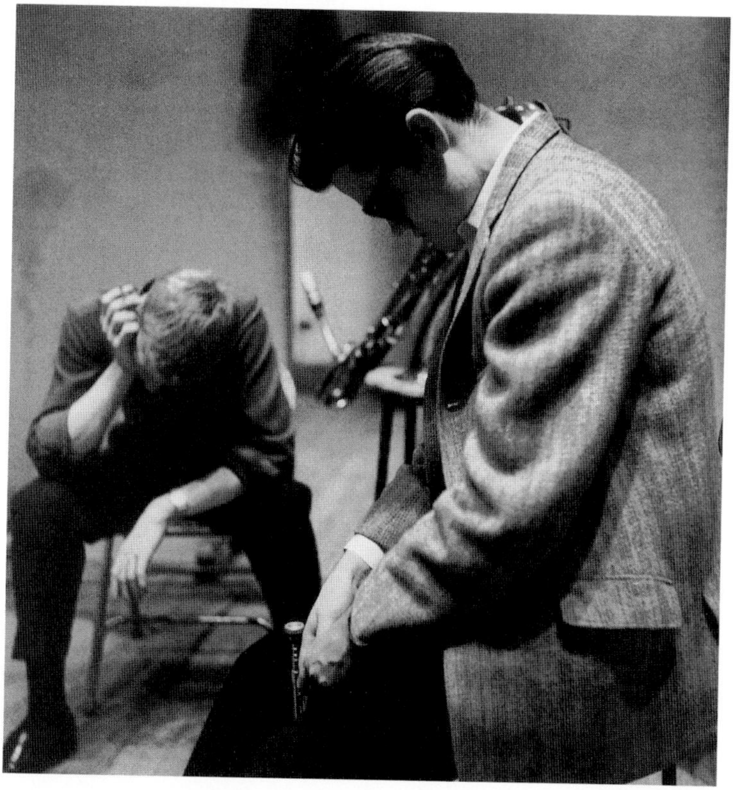

In 1957, Baker and Gerry Mulligan tried to recapture the old chemistry on an album, *Reunion*, but only their mutual contempt remained. "Music requires discipline, and he once had it," said ex-junkie Mulligan of his hooked partner. Photo by Carole Reiff; © Carole Reiff Photo Archive

April 1961: on trial in Lucca, Italy, for drug possession and forgery of stolen prescriptions, Baker denies everything.

En route to the Lucca *tribunale.* Photos by F. Ercolini; courtesy of Archivio Circolo del Jazz, Lucca/Francesco Maino

LA LEGGE E UGUALE PER TUTTI

"Face of an angel, heart of a demon!" declared the town's public prosecutor of Baker. Courtesy of Thorbjørn Sjøgren

For Halema, who was charged with smuggling illegal drugs for her husband, the trial was a nightmare.

For his new English mistress, Carol Jackson, it was a photo op. Halema inspired sympathy; Carol, disgust. Photos by F. Ercolini; courtesy of Archivio Circolo del Jazz, Lucca/Francesco Maino

An incarcerated Baker signs an autograph; at times, his trial felt more like a Hollywood premiere. Photo by F. Ercolini; courtesy of Archivio Circolo del Jazz, Lucca/Francesco Maino

No one worshiped Baker more than Jacques Pelzer, a musician and pharmacist from the Belgian town of Liège. In 1963, the year after Baker's release from prison, they join their friend, saxophonist Jean-Pierre Gebler, in a pub. Courtesy of Jean-Pierre Gebler

Baker leaves the Munich-Haar clinic with Carol on June 27, 1962, after his latest doomed attempt at rehab. Photoreporters

Barred from working in New York clubs because of his drug convictions, an embittered Baker plays Boston's Jazz Workshop, 1966. Photo by Lee Tanner

In the seventies, Baker was relearning to play the trumpet without the aid of heroin after a dope-related beating cost him his upper teeth. Singer Ruth Young, whom he called his "new beginning," helped ease the way. "My Drug Is Now Called Ruth," read a headline in an Italian tabloid. Photo by Lamberto Londi

Baker takes his adoring young protégé, Bob Mover, to Holland for the International Jazz Festival Laren, August 7, 1975. Photo by Pieter Boersma

"I'm not up there to win any beauty contests," Baker informed Ruth Young, whose blue velvet pants he liked to wear onstage. Photo by Pieter Boersma

Ruth and her "Picasso" rehearse at the Musikpodium in Stuttgart, Germany, January 16, 1979. Photo by Hans Kumpf, Germany

Before the year ended, Baker was a heroin addict again. On September 14, at Centro Civico Mirabello in Pavia, Italy, the death mask emerges. Photo by Carlo Verri

Baker's youngest child, Melissa, in her waning days of innocence, c. 1979. Courtesy of Ruth Young

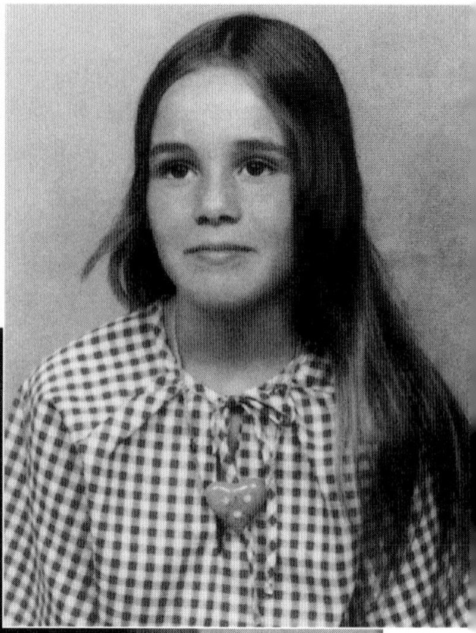

Her father in the New York offices of Artists House Records, an independent label he helped drain dry, May 1980. Photo by Francesco Maino

Baker is honored at the Arkadia Club in Florence, Italy, for his "Thirty Years of Body & Soul," April 7, 1980. Left to right: bartender Tullio, Baker, his Italian agent Rita Amaducci, Rudy Rabassini, unidentified well-wisher, and drummer-turned-business-tycoon Giampiero Giusti. Photo by Francesco Maino

Baker reunited with his old rival, Stan Getz, in 1983 for a European tour that left them loathing each other more than ever. Södra Teatern, Stockholm, Sweden, February 18. Photo by Leif Collin

One of the "angry young men" of British pop, singer-songwriter Elvis Costello, hired Baker for a recording date in 1983. "It was a cash deal," said Costello. "He just came in; it may well have been the next day." Photo by Keith Morris; courtesy of Elvis Costello

Even in middle age, Baker and his last great love, Diane Vavra, reminded some people of teenage lovebirds. Göteborg, Sweden, September 1983. Photo by Dan Kjellman

Children without a father, a wife with no husband: Dean, Carol, and Paul Baker at home, speaking to Baker through the camera of filmmaker-photographer Bruce Weber. Stillwater, Oklahoma, 1987. © Bruce Weber

Bruce Weber was famous for photographing handsome boys in Calvin Klein underwear, but he also "loved beauty that looked kind of destroyed," according to his assistant, Cherry Vanilla. Filming the Baker documentary *Let's Get Lost* in 1987, Weber brought the trumpeter, his friend and disciple Nicola Stilo, and Diane Vavra to the Cannes Film Festival. © Bruce Weber

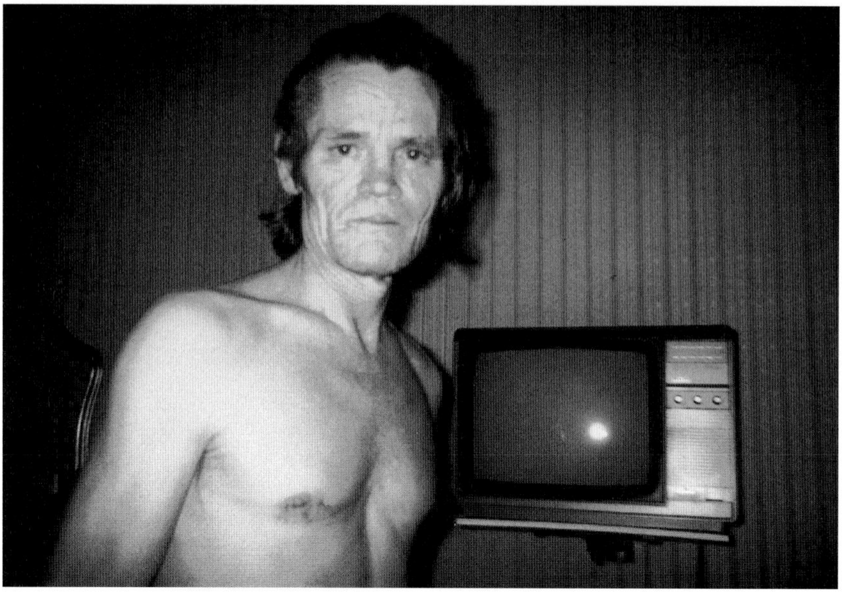

Just before escaping from her violent lover for good in February 1988, Vavra snapped this picture of him in a Santa Cruz, California, motel room.

With drummer Fabrizio Sferra, pianist Enrico Pieranunzi, and bassist Enzo Pietropaoli, but without Diane, a tortured Baker records in Recanati, Italy, March 1988. Photo by Carlo Pieroni

In his last days, Baker's most devoted caretaker was Micheline Graillier, the daughter of his best friend, Jacques Pelzer. Record producer Paolo Piangiarelli (with cap), filmmaker and photographer Bertrand Fèvre (foreground), and Fabrizio Sferra (behind Fèvre) walk with them on a street in Paris, March 15, 1988. Photo by Carlo Pieroni

At Paris's New Morning club on May 6, Fèvre caught this last, sad glimpse of Chet Baker. © Bertrand Fèvre, Paris

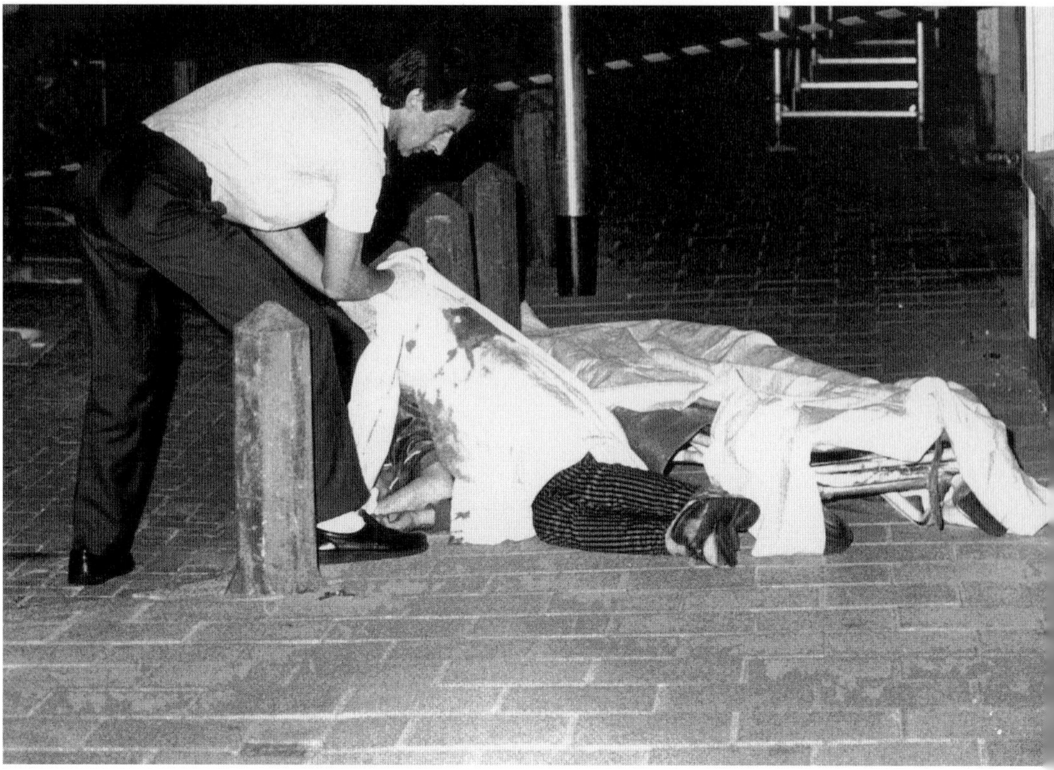

The end of the road: Amsterdam, May 13, 1988. Courtesy of ANP/Netherlands

Baker at peace alongside a shattered Jacques Pelzer, Uitvaartcentrum, Amsterdam, May 18. Barbara Walton/Associated Press; courtesy of Micheline Pelzer

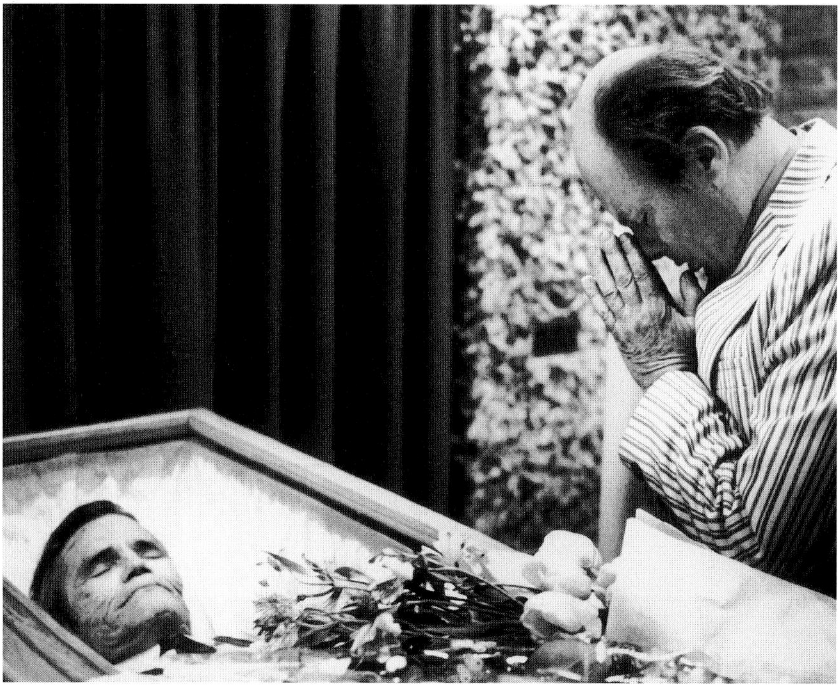

truth. So, apparently, did his wife. The couple had moved to a cozy-sounding street, Spreckles Lane, in Redondo Beach, but life there was grim. For Carol, the strain of being Mrs. Chet Baker seemed to be taking its toll. Migraines plagued her, and she looked pale and frazzled. One by one, Baker's friends learned something that Carol, years later, would swear was untrue: that she, too, was using drugs. "She told me she had a bigger habit than Chet," recalled saxophonist Bob Mover, who would join Baker's band in 1973. "She said, well, if you can't beat 'em, join 'em." Jacques Pelzer gave his daughter Micheline the news in the midsixties, after he returned from a U.S. tour with Baker. "When my father went there, she was already hooked," Micheline said. "And when she stayed in our house in 1977, she was on methadone."

Baker would tell Ruth Young that he had started Carol on heroin to ease her headaches. "He said he always hit her in the same place," Young recalled; according to Baker, this created a diamond-shaped scar on the crook of her arm. The phrase "hit her" had a violent ring, one he made clearer to Sandy Jones, Bill Loughborough's girlfriend and, in 1970, Baker's too. "Chet told me the reason he turned her on to heroin was because he absolutely could not stand her being a bitch any longer," said Jones. Baker didn't like it when women made demands, and Carol had plenty: she wanted a monogamous marriage, a stable family life, and a home, even if she had made a ludicrous choice of provider. Her willingness to share her husband's addiction seemed like a sad attempt to solidify their shaky bond; certainly it made her that much more dependent on him.

With hardly any income, he had two children to feed plus other financial needs. "I think he considered himself the breadwinner," said Bob Whitlock. "Except the bread was heroin. Chet would leave early in the day, maybe not come back until the wee hours of the morning. Poor Carol was alone with those children an awful lot of the time." Laying eyes on Baker for the first time since the fifties, Whitlock saw a creepy Dorian Gray image of a dark soul. "I couldn't believe it," Baker's old roommate said. "Chet had aged thirty years. I remembered him from ten years earlier, looking like a kid, then all of a sudden he had all these deep creases in his face. It was scary."

Whitlock's luck had taken its own plummet since his days as the original bassist in Gerry Mulligan's quartet. He remained a highly skilled musician, but his drug use had cost him a prestigious job with pianist George Shearing. In Paris, Whitlock had acquired a taste for French heroin, whose strength had killed Dick Twardzik. L.A.'s street heroin couldn't compare in potency, so Whitlock took large amounts of it to feed his "jones." Virtually unemployable, he settled into professional junkiedom like his friend Chet, staying hooked until 1976. "The music was just another means to get some money," he said. "I didn't think we'd ever see that day when we were youngsters."

The two men embarked on a crime spree devoted to scoring dope, or the money to buy it, however they could. Baker later told Bob Mover that he became a "second-story man": a thief who scaled homes and broke in through an upstairs window. He was also a master at picking locks. None of this surprised Mover. One night in the seventies, the saxophonist, broke at the time, found himself evicted from his apartment. Remembering Baker's casual remark about knowing how to break and enter, Mover called him. Joined by Stan Getz's pianist Albert Dailey, Baker came to the rescue. He climbed up the fire escape like a cat, opened Mover's window, and crawled in. "He handed the stuff to me and I handed it down to Albert, who put it in Chet's car," said Mover. "We robbed my apartment together."

In 1966, Baker and Whitlock drove from one doctor's office to another, wangling prescriptions for morphine derivatives—Dolophine, Dilaudid, Numorphan—that could serve as heroin substitutes. "We'd run around complaining of kidney stones," said Whitlock. "They'd ask us to give a urine sample. We'd have a little teeny vial of blood in our pocket, dip our finger in, and put a little spot or two in the urine. Damn near invariably you could get a Dilaudid prescription. Frequently that would work up to half a dozen times on one doctor. Then we had this other scam going, telling them we had trigeminal neuralgia, which is very difficult to prove you don't have, I guess." Baker also stole prescription pads, along with any drugs within reach. At the same time, he and Whitlock kept scoring real heroin, and as the veins in Baker's forearms withered he began shooting into his neck, his groin, even under his fingernails.

His FBI rap sheet grew. He was arrested in Culver City, California, for forging prescriptions in January 1966, then in South-Central L.A. for driving under the influence of narcotics. He ended up with more probation and no jail time. The next year brought four arrests, one for burglary. In 1968 came another for driving while stoned. Along the way, he wrecked the car Halema had bought for Vera. No matter what he did, Baker escaped prison.

How he managed that was no mystery to Clifford Solomon, an L.A.-based tenor saxophonist who displayed his versatility with everyone from Clifford Brown to R&B singer Johnny Otis to the Monkees. Solomon had a grim memory of Baker from 1955. Unbeknownst to him, Baker had apparently been nabbed by the police for drugs. He had recently spent time with

Solomon, who found him friendly enough—until the day when Baker showed up at Solomon's door with the cops. "He'd made a deal with the police to target some people at random, to help himself out," said the saxophonist. "There were quite a few people doing that in the fifties and sixties. It was a survival thing."

Art Pepper bitterly related the story of a day when a drug-dealer friend of his got a call from Baker requesting an "appointment." The dealer invited him over—not knowing that Baker was phoning from a police station. He opened the door to find Baker accompanied by two narcotics officers. "I thought it was just common knowledge that Chet was a career police informant," said Pepper's wife, Laurie.

Clearly, the thought of returning to jail frightened Baker, but Pepper had no sympathy; to ex-cons like himself, there was nothing lower than a rat. "It was like pulling teeth to get Art to talk about Chet," Laurie said. "I think these guys really believe it's bad karma to talk too much about rats." In *Straight Life,* he dismissed Baker in one cold paragraph, giving him a pseudonym.

> Billy Wilson plays like he is. When I knew him, when he was young, he was a real warm, sweet, loving person. And he plays just that way. But if you listen to his tone, it never was very strong; it's pretty and kind of cracking. It's weak. And when he was faced with prison—because he got busted for using drugs—he couldn't stand it. He couldn't go because he was afraid, and when they offered him an out by turning over on somebody he couldn't help but do it. He's a weak person. That's the way he plays. That's the way he sounds.

Work for Baker was drying up fast in 1966, but that summer he scored a plum gig at the Trident, a charming glass-walled nightclub on the bay in Sausalito, just past San Francisco's Golden Gate Bridge. Carmen McRae, Bill Cosby, the Kingston Trio, and other top attractions performed on a sunken stage, in front of a picture window that gave a romantic view of boats sailing in the moonlight. For June, the Trident had booked a trio led by the Brazilian pianist-composer João Donato, a star of the bossa nova. Although he then lived in L.A., Donato wasn't known in the States, and after a week at the club, he was asked to add a name musician to the bill to boost attendance. Donato was thrilled to learn that Chet Baker, one of his idols, was available.

A few phone calls, and Baker was there. He brought Carol, who was eight months pregnant, and their sons. At the Trident, Donato played bossa-nova hits like "The Girl from Ipanema" and sang them in Portuguese; Baker offered a few Brazilian standards and some of his vocal trademarks. Ralph J. Gleason, jazz critic for the *San Francisco Chronicle,* called that haphazard engagement "the best thing that has happened to Baker in years. . . . Although there were the usual first night gremlins and nervousness, it was obvious that the group can, with very little woodshedding, become a lyric jazz attraction of the first magnitude."

Even Gleason's rave didn't fill the room, but Baker's attention was elsewhere. One day he took Dean for a drive. Lou Ganapoler, who ran the Trident, was headed to a bank when he saw the four-year-old wandering the street alone. "Where's your dad?" he asked. "He just left me," answered Dean. Ganapoler brought Dean home. Later he learned that Baker had gone to a nearby drugstore to scam for pills. Soon afterward, Carol took both children back to Redondo Beach, where she prepared to give birth to a third. Baker stayed in Sausalito, and each night after the late show he would race to San Francisco to score. He had found a dealer at a seedy hotel in the Fillmore district, a rough black neighborhood that white locals fearfully called "the pits." But that didn't faze Baker.

On July 22, 1966, Carol delivered a daughter, whom she named Melissa. The *New York Times* carried a short Baker news item on Tuesday, August 9, but it wasn't about the birth. The headline read: "Jazz Trumpet Player Beaten on West Coast." It reported that Chet Baker was at home in Redondo Beach recovering from a vicious assault that had taken place in San Francisco in the midnight hours of the previous Friday. According to the *Times,* Baker had just gotten out of his car after leaving a performance "when five Negro youths attacked him." He claimed to have run into the middle of the street, begging help from a passing vehicle. "I tried to get in a car with five white guys, but they pushed me back out. There were lots of people on the street, but they didn't help me at all."

With that report, one of the most mysterious episodes in the Chet Baker story came to light, if only partially; he would tell dramatized versions of it for the rest of his life. The gist—that five young blacks had beaten him up to get his dope money—never changed. But the other details—the location, the date, the cast of characters, the aftermath, and most of all the cause—varied wildly and suspiciously in ways few people ever bothered to question.

In interviews, Baker couldn't decide whether he had been attacked in the Fillmore district or, as he told *Melody Maker,* in Sausalito, where he was "walking home" after dark: "I was just trying to get a taxi, when five guys surrounded me and started to beat me up. Ironically it was two colored guys who'd saved me after I'd tried to escape by getting into the car with four or five white kids who just threw me back in the street. The hoodlums beat me some more until these two colored guys told them to stop and took me to the hospital. It was like a nightmare."

In a 1973 *New York Newsday* interview, the "four or five white kids" became "some older white guys"—this in a scary and deserted neighborhood where whites of any age seldom ventured. He gave a more preposterous account to *Down Beat.* A band member had driven him to Fillmore (he didn't say why), and upon arriving, Baker inexplicably stepped out of the car to hail a cab home. As soon as his friend drove off, five blacks pounced on him. He told Brian Case, another *Melody Maker* writer, that he had gotten into a skirmish with his dealer at the hotel. "Guy tried to rob me and I didn't go for it, so he put these five guys on me the next day to teach me a lesson," he declared. In *Let's Get Lost,* he introduced a new character, a shady-looking thug whom he passed in the stairwell on his way upstairs to meet his connection. Smelling trouble, Baker stuck a hand in his pocket to mimic squeezing a gun and went on his way. That was the man, Baker insisted, who set the "five young black cats" after him.

In any case, the results were the same. "They battered my gums in," he explained, and kicked him in the groin over and over until he was a "bloody mess." His upper lip was smashed and a tooth was broken; he was also kicked in the ear. When found, Baker was allegedly covered in his own vomit.

Having told the *New York Times* he had needed six stitches over his right eye, he informed Rex Reed of the *Daily News* in 1973: "I had stitches all over my face." He did little to refute a claim that would take a high place in his own mythology: that his assailants had knocked out all his teeth. (In truth, as he sometimes admitted, the pummeling had created so much pain that he had to have the upper ones pulled.) Even the date was unclear. Baker began informing the press of the assault on August 8, saying it had happened two days before, but Carol swore it had occurred two weeks earlier, just after Melissa's birth. "The day that Chet was beaten up—I remember it clearly," she told Thorbjørn Sjøgren, Baker's discographer, in 1992. "Our youngest daughter was born on July 22, 1966, and it happened the day I came home from the hospital, July 25, 1966." Why, then, would her husband have delayed reporting the crime, then falsified the date?

All the accounts had a single common thread: Baker was attacked by the "colored guys" and rejected by the "white guys." The episode became an allegory of the racial discrimination he had felt his whole adult life.

After leaving the hospital, he told *Newsday,* "I just got on a bus and headed for home." But in 1997, João Donato remembered him showing up at the Trident one last time, late for work and with a handkerchief tied around his bloodied mouth. "Three black guys beat me up," he said. Baker tried to play the first set but found it impossible, Donato recalled, and that's when the trumpeter went home to Redondo Beach.

Whatever had really happened on that early morning in Fillmore, few of Baker's friends bought his explanation. When Bob Whitlock heard about the "five black guys," he laughed: "You sure it wasn't fifty? Christ, I wouldn't bet fifteen cents on any of those stories!" Jack Simpson, Charlie Davidson, and Micheline Pelzer doubted them too. To Ruth Young, the tale was a prime example of how Baker distorted the truth in order to "milk sympathy from any and all who would listen." It was a tendency that strained her love for him to the limit. She had her own theory of the facts: that the beating was a mafia-style payback to Baker after he had tried to mess with a drug dealer. "He finally got caught in his own game—something he never in a million years thought would happen," said Young. "Obviously the characters at large were wise enough to realize that the best punishment for an arrogant, oh-so-confident trumpet player was to damage the only part of his body that was really worthwhile to him. Once it was realized that good old Chettie was hardly the innocent, that he had ripped off a very intolerant dealer, a plan was put in motion. It was an ordered hit to get this guy to learn the rules of the game. They were trying to say: look, you little white-ass loser, all you are is another fucking junkie."

Instinctively, she came closest to the likely truth, hinted at when Baker started reminiscing with Bob Mover on a long train ride in the seventies. "He told me he'd like to write a book but nobody would believe it," Mover said. "He talked about ripping off a drug dealer in California. He said he and a friend masterminded this beautiful crime, and then somebody found out about it. Nobody was kicking the shit out of him just for fun. He was set up." To Whitlock, who knew Baker's duplicity as well as anyone, this explanation "made all the sense in the world."

The damage to Baker's mouth was obvious in his attempts to record throughout the rest of 1966. Around September, he tried to play on a Bud Shank album, *Brazil Brazil Brazil.* The results were so painful that he wound up appearing on only one track, "Summer Samba," blowing so faintly he could barely be heard. A proposed album with Donato yielded a set of unusable tapes. That fall, Baker made one more Mariachi Brass album, *In the Mood,* a tribute to the swing bandleader Glenn Miller. Struggling to practice beforehand, he sought the help of Bob Zieff, who had recently moved to L.A. "He was so out of shape playing-wise, it was ridiculous," said Zieff. At the session, Baker was handed simple written parts, but "he just couldn't get through anything." Another trumpeter in the orchestra had to sub while Baker added whatever weak fills he could.

After a lifetime of playing with little effort and less thought, Baker couldn't accept the apparent loss of his gift. Hearing that Jimmy Rowles had opened at Donte's, a jazz club in the San Fernando Valley, Baker arrived with a fluegelhorn. It was a depressing moment for the pianist, whom Baker used to visit, trumpet in hand, when he was eighteen and full of fire. Sitting in at Donte's in his late thirties, he produced just a few rusty honks. "I didn't want to see him like that," said Rowles. "I wanted to remember him the way I knew him. I felt bad for him, because I really loved this guy. He had a big heart for music—a natural genius." In France's *Jazz* magazine, Jean-Louis Ginibre made sad mention of that night. "The musicians ended their set as quickly as possible and took a long break. But Chet wants to play at any cost, and often the result is pitiful. Chet is lost to jazz."

Janet Bicker, Dick Bock's wife and secretary, still hadn't met Baker, knowing him only as the dreamboat who had made Pacific Jazz famous. Seated at her desk one day, she saw him walking up the hallway toward her. "He was more like a wraith than a real person—very frail and tenuous, almost ghostlike," she said. "Really wasted." Baker had come to ask Bock for money to have his upper teeth replaced with dentures. Bock agreed, and the operation was performed. Once back home, with dentures in place, he blew into his fluegelhorn—and nothing came out. "Not even a sound," Baker told Rogers Worthington. A man so quick to call life "hopeless" now truly felt he had no reason to live.

With a family of five to support, Baker was forced to apply for welfare. He received $320 a month plus $130 in food stamps. "We got by," he said. For a couple of days, he tried supplementing his income by working in a gas station outside Redondo Beach. Later he would enjoy telling interviewers that he labored there "sixteen hours a day for almost two years"—a claim denied even by Carol, who normally stuck by her husband's stories. In various accounts of that dark time, Baker reported not having played "for almost three years": from 1968 (the year he gave for the San Francisco beating) to 1973. The wildly inconsistent chronology, like most of his distortions, went unchallenged. In fact, he was inactive musically for less than a year, roughly late 1966 through late 1967.

During that period, he was sought out by Arthur "Artt" Frank, an obsessive fan who invited the Bakers to dinner at the Culver City house he shared with his wife, Earla, an aspiring jazz singer. Thin, wiry, and hyper, Frank was an occasional drummer who also claimed to be a "script writer," "bit actor," and "welterweight prizefighter"; later he would call himself a "street minister," decorating letters to Baker and others with religious symbols. "The word of God is my lite," he explained. Around the time Baker met him, Frank was actually on welfare himself, and would spend many years painting houses for money. But after the trumpeter's death, Frank would introduce himself as Chet Baker's drummer "for well over twenty years." They were "like brothers," he said. The only truth in this, said Ruth Young, is that Frank "was as in love with Chet as any woman."

Frank offered to help him in all sorts of ways, and the trumpeter was never one to refuse free labor. In return, Frank got to enjoy a lot of his idol's company. One night in 1967, when Baker came to visit, Frank taped a bogus "radio" interview with him. It gave a dismal portrait of Baker's life as an unemployed "family man." Asked if he had any creative outlet besides music, he drawled in a flat, woozy voice: "armed robbery." Carol appeared, listing her domestic woes. It was no surprise when Baker admitted he would rush back to Italy if he could. Soon he would write to Giovanni Tommaso asking for help to do just that.

Times were bad in Inglewood, too. Chesney Sr. had lost his job as a security guard, and Vera knew no one would ever hire him again. On July 6, 1967, he died at home of a heart attack. Chesney was sixty-one. Both he and his son had wound up in the same black hole, in which the pain of failure was so excruciating that they could hardly face a waking moment sober.

His father's early death did nothing to make Baker clean up his ways; instead, it convinced him that his own time was limited, so he may as well keep self-destructing. More arrests piled up, most of them in the toughest black sections of South-Central L.A.: Gardena, Hawthorne, South Santa Ana. One day Bob Whitlock got a hysterical call from Carol, whom he had never met. She was at a police station. "Chet had been bopped and was in jail downtown and she didn't know what the hell to do," he said. "She was strung out, and could I help her?" Whitlock drove to meet her. "When I got there, here was this very pretty but very hooked woman with these kids in tow. I really felt sorry for her. He was a total mess, and she was too. She had that icky pneumonia look, washed-out and nervous and oppressed. . . . It's unmistakable." Whitlock recalled her asking him to pay her husband's bail of eight hundred dollars—steep at the time, and proof that the LAPD did not want Chet Baker to go free. Whitlock didn't have it, so he went to Shelly Manne, who generously gave him the cash, plus a little extra. "I remember us going out and scoring right after he got out," the bassist said.

Baker had seemingly lost all hope of playing again, but Carol and Artt Frank kept urging him to try. The trumpeter was afraid; with false teeth, the job of building a new embouchure was impossible, or so he thought. But gradually, the drive to do what he considered to be his only reason for existing took over. He began the painful process at home. Over and over he forced air into his horn, trying to produce a thread of music. He persisted for months, struggling to play the scales and intervals he had breezed through in high school. He practiced holding long notes, starting softly, building the volume, then lowering it. Slowly he warmed into a semblance of the old Chet Baker.

The first tentative "unveiling" came at the end of 1967, when Dick Bock hired him for a Bud Shank album of Beatles songs, *Magical Mystery.* On a few tracks, a fluegelhorn peeps through, vaguely identifiable as Chet Baker. The trumpeter was still persona non grata to many in L.A., but Steve Allen generously invited him to play on the June 5, 1968, episode of his TV variety show. Baker was no stranger at the studio, recalled Paul Smith, Allen's house pianist. "You'd feel this hand on your shoulder, and the minute I felt that desperate grasp, I knew who it was. He'd say, 'Hey, they're gonna shut my electricity off if I don't come up with some money for the bill.' "

Allen tried to pump up Baker's prestige, introducing him on air as "one of the men who's done an awful lot for the trumpet" and holding up his recent albums, most of them already unavailable. Out came Baker, looking like an aging Elvis with his long sideburns, hair slicked up into a fifties-style pompadour, and powder-blue jacket over a bright blue T-shirt. Next to the six-foot-tall Allen, Baker looked slight, and wore a pained smile. But when he played a song he knew well, "These Foolish Things," he embarrassed no one. His lyricism had mostly returned, although he had to focus with all his might to make it safely to the next note, like a child taking his first steps. With Vietnam War reports following on the eleven-o'clock news, Baker's performance seemed like a quaint trip back to an era of taffeta prom dresses and kisses stolen inside Dad's Chevrolet.

Allen brought Baker back a month later to sing and play an adolescent torch song he had recorded in the fifties, "Forgetful." Singer Mark Murphy, another guest, greeted him backstage and got a lengthy hard-luck story. "I asked him how he was," said Murphy, "and his answer was like: 'Oh, gee, on the way here I saw an old lady get run over by a car. Then I crossed the street and I saw somebody die of a heart attack on the sidewalk. And then . . .' This man carried a black cloud with him wherever he went."

Subsequently Baker phoned Allen and asked for a "loan" of five hundred dollars. "Wouldn't you feel better about it if you worked for the money?" asked Allen. "You'd still have the bread, but you would have accomplished something in getting it." He arranged for Baker to record a dozen of the hundreds of original songs that had placed Allen in the *Guinness Book of World Records* as most prolific songwriter. Allen sent him a bundle of lead sheets and demos. Weeks later, Baker came to the session stoned, minus his trumpet and completely unfamiliar with the music. As a band member scrambled to find him a horn, Allen and Paul Smith tried teaching Baker the songs.

The album, *Albert's House,* was a disaster. Baker fumbled his way through it as though semi-conscious, playing out of tune and cracking like a first-year trumpet student. Allen paid him, but thereafter regarded Baker with pity. "When Chet started out, he had everything," said the host. "He was handsome, had a likable personality, a tremendous musical gift. He threw it all away for drugs. To me, the man started out as James Dean and ended up as Charles Manson."

If less historic than Manson's, Baker's rap sheet was longer, and it kept growing. Near the end of 1968, he and Whitlock broke into a doctor's office near Long Beach and stole a prescription book. Driving from one pharmacy to another, they felt like kids in a candy store. "We were flying high there for a while," Whitlock said. About a month later, he was arrested and sentenced to three months in jail and five years' probation. Baker panicked, certain the same was about to happen to him. Whitlock soon learned just how paranoid his friend was. In the middle of the night, Baker confided, he had driven to the drugstore where he had filled his phony prescriptions. With a can of gasoline, he doused the pharmacy and burned it down. "He was terrified that they were gonna find the scrip," Whitlock said.

Baker often made his darkest confessions with a hint of childish pride, the kind he had felt as a teenager when he siphoned gas out of cars. It was easier for him to play the junkie outlaw than to rebuild a career no one seemed to care about. But Artt Frank was determined to make him a star again. Frank made the rounds of L.A. jazz clubs, trying to sell them on the comeback of the great Chet Baker. Nobody was interested. Finally, Frank convinced a joint on the Sunset Strip, the Melody Room, to give Baker a few nights in February 1969, with Frank on drums. At the time, the club was overshadowed by its across-the-street neighbor, Whisky A Go Go, the launching pad of Jim Morrison and the Doors. The Melody Room would gain its own notoriety years later when it became the Viper Room—the last stop of the young film idol River Phoenix, who OD'd on the sidewalk out front on Halloween night of 1993. From then on, the press would dub the Viper Room "drug den of the stars."

But in 1969, the Melody Room served as a shrine to a fallen angel of melody. Baker's albums with the Carmel Strings and the Mariachi Brass hung on the wall near the bar as red lights cast an eerie glow throughout the room. Pianist Frank Strazzeri accompanied him on a spinet that had been pummeled into near-tunelessness by rock bands. Baker's group performed on a platform surrounded by a wraparound bar, where customers looked at them as at a circus sideshow. "People came to watch him like a specimen," said Jimmy Rowles. They saw a ruined pretty boy, toothless, washed up, and on welfare at thirty-nine—just the kind of disaster story Hollywood loved. Audiences were mostly small and peppered with dope dealers, who lurked in the shadows, waiting to approach him as he left the stage.

Yet tapes of his shows reveal just how hard Baker had worked to play well. Slowly he was forming a new style out of the wreckage of his beating. His youthful bravura gone, he now sounded slow, careful, intense. In "If You Could See Me Now" he pared his lines down to a minimum, meditating on each note before he played it. He had no upper range and only enough endurance to spin out short phrases. He compensated by giving each one a rhythmic punch that carried the tune along. Strazzeri took long solos that gave Baker time to rest.

Looking out at his listeners, the trumpeter saw pity and ridicule. Frank recalled hearing Baker say that the pressure was unbearable; he was sure everyone was there to see him fall on his face. He nearly did. Frank customarily picked him up at home to drive him to the club, but one night he found the trumpeter passed out from an OD. He and Carol frantically stripped Baker and put him in a cold bath, Frank said, then shaved and dressed him while he was still semi-conscious. Sitting him in the car, Frank sped to the club, where Baker somehow managed to get through his sets.

Despite the problems, Leonard Feather reviewed the trumpeter kindly in the *Los Angeles Times:* "At times Baker seemed to falter or lose the thread of a melodic line, but for the most part he was as sensitively self-expressive as ever."

The engagement led to nothing. He was broke again, and Frank took him along on a couple of house-painting assignments. The drummer also helped get him a job as houseboy for Nicky Blair, a bit movie actor and the name-dropping owner of a Sunset Strip restaurant, Stefanino's, that was frequented by the luminaries of sixties Hollywood. The sight of the great trumpeter in shabby clothes, sweeping floors and running errands with a sad face, broke Blair's heart. "I gave him clothes and money, but I didn't want him to feel it was a handout," Blair recalled. "I said, 'Chet, I've got so many fucking clothes, take these.' "

But all the efforts to help him seemed fruitless. On August 29, 1969, he was busted again for forging a prescription. Baker ended up in the L.A. County Courthouse Jail, facing a five-year minimum sentence. Visitors like Frank saw Baker staring out at them glumly from behind a heavy glass panel, as if he were a leper.

His wounded look devastated the judge, a former college trumpeter and fan of Baker's who didn't feel the musician belonged in jail. On September 10, he sentenced Baker to ninety days in the Chino Institute for Men, a rehabilitation center in Chino, California. The center tried to coddle addicts back to sobriety, but Art Pepper, who had just left, called it a "wasted experience." Patients enjoyed "nice visits with picnic lunches," Pepper said, and gathered for friendly group counseling: "The whole idea was to get people to rat on each other, to try to expose people so they would 'learn' and do better," he explained. "People *informing* on each other!"

Baker stayed mostly silent. He responded better to the detoxification process. Junkies were weaned off heroin with methadone, a synthetic liquid opiate that, when taken in proper amounts each day, prevented withdrawal and helped determined addicts to clean up. The major side effect, drowsiness, gave patients the look of nodding junkies, but it enabled them to lead fairly normal lives.

And that's what Baker tried to do. In early 1970, he left Chino and rejoined his family, who now lived with Vera in Milpitas, the town near San Jose where she had relocated after Chesney's death. After years of upheaval, Vera wanted some order, and her home reflected it. Sandy Jones, Bill Loughborough's girlfriend, recalled it as "a little ticky-tacky house" with a pool out back, all tidied compulsively by Vera. "Everything was clean and well-made and not lived in," said Jones. "She was a strict person; you really couldn't tell anything about her. She didn't have any soul, man, none of that." Yet once more Vera bore the responsibility of providing for her son's family, buying clothes, shoes, and food.

Nerves were frayed, partly because, as Baker would later tell Ruth Young, his mother "hated" Carol for not working to support the children. "She was so offended that Chet had a wife who was spitting out kids that she was ultimately gonna have to take care of," Young said. Vera seemed no happier to have a competitor for the role of her son's maternal savior. "Don't forget to put on your scarf, Chettie!" she would tell her nearly forty-year-old son. "Mom, I'm a grown man!" he would complain. She nagged him about his straggly hair and sideburns. "Chettie, why don't you get your hair cut like Tom Brokaw?" she whined, referring to her favorite TV news anchorman. According to Artt Frank, Jackson fussed over him just as much: "If he drooled, she wiped it off."

"Normal" life was driving Baker crazy, but it didn't last, as he returned to dope. His friend Jack Simpson, who lived in nearby Los Gatos, visited the Bakers often. "Chet used to say Carol had a bigger habit than he did," Simpson recalled. "There was this interchange between the two of them, what they would sacrifice to get more, and it became this kind of domestic addiction." Meanwhile, Baker faced constant reminders of how he had failed. "Carol wanted him to be rich and famous, and she wanted a nice place, not living with his mother," said Sandy Jones. "He ended up leaving her home with the kids most of the time. I think he probably thought of kids as something that mommies raise and schools teach."

Much of his time away from home was spent with Jones. They had met at the San Francisco apartment of her boyfriend Bill Loughborough. Baker's former boobam player now divided his time between doing medical research and managing an improvisational comedy group, the Committee, under the name Bill Love. Loughborough enjoyed experimenting with the newest hallucinogenic drugs, including LSD, and had recently "put a hex" on the rock group the Lovin' Spoonful for implicating him in a marijuana bust. "And it worked," he said. "The group broke up."

Loughborough shared his apartment with Jones (alias Sandi Love), a blonde topless waitress and the mother of his infant son, Fillmore Love. In her spare time, Jones hung out with the Cockettes, a phenomenally popular local drag troupe who paraded onstage in beards and mustaches, feathery costumes, and exposed genitalia. The group's leader, Hibiscus, lived in the basement of Loughborough's building with his roommate Harlow Harlow, one of the Plaster Casters, a group of young women who made casts of "rock cock"—the erect penises of rock stars. Another tenant, a health-food salesman, was reputed to drink blood.

Into this menagerie of hippiedom came Chet Baker, who knocked on Loughborough's door hoping to get some dope money. A bony figure in a dark trenchcoat, he seemed to weigh "about ninety pounds," according to

Jones. "You know when someone's been down for so long that everything is gray, there's no color, emotion, nothing?" she said. But after Loughborough slipped him some cash, said Sandy, "Chet disappeared out the door and came back a half-hour later, very happy!"

Chemically restored, he finally noticed Jones, who shared his addiction. "I remember looking him right in the eyes, he looked me right in the eyes, and we recognized each other," Jones explained. She and Loughborough had an open relationship, and he didn't seem concerned when his girlfriend and his pal of fifteen years became sex partners and needle buddies. On many weekends in 1970, Baker drove to San Francisco to see her, often bringing his horn. "He loved to play music," she said. "Oh God, I remember the first time he opened up that case and pulled out that trumpet that sang. Oh, man, I was just googoo-eyed! There was something Chet had about his touch, in his music, or if he put his hand on your back. The way he sang in my ear. And his cunnilingus!"

Every time he came to visit, something in the house disappeared: a camera, a radio. But Jones didn't mind. She introduced him to her friends, a Bohemian crowd who were thrilled to meet him—"particularly the gays," she said, "who knew exactly who he was and remembered his music."

She and Baker spent much of their time together getting high and taking long drives. As he jammed his foot down on the accelerator and hit the highway, the sheer speed seemed to release a torrent of pent-up rage. "He was incredibly bitter," she said, "losing his teeth with a bunch of black people beating the fucking shit out of him. After all he'd done for jazz. And his father beating the shit out of him too—kids don't forgive that." He spoke admiringly of Carol as he remembered her from 1960—a beautiful young virgin—but that fairy tale had turned sour too. He seemed racked with guilt over his role in her drug use, as he was about his treatment of Halema and Chetty. He longed to see them again, maybe to undo some of the damage, but of course it was too late.

Bringing Jones to the house in Milpitas, Baker introduced her as Loughborough's lady friend. How much Jackson knew about her husband's philandering wasn't clear, but the three of them had other concerns. "All of us were shooting up heroin," said Jones, who recalled forming a light friendship with the Englishwoman, now thirty. Apparently Jackson had nowhere else to turn—especially on a day when, according to Jones, she phoned in a panic to say that Baker was taking frightening amounts of barbiturates. "She said he was trying to kill himself on pills," Jones recalled.

He didn't, but he began to crack in other ways. Starting with his mother,

Baker's feelings about women had always been violently ambivalent: he needed them, yet hated them for it. Jones became his latest victim. Years later, she recounted the time "Chet tried to kill me." In fact, it happened twice, although she never understood why. One day he came to the apartment with "a whole outfit full of the darkest stuff in the world." He shoved her into the bathroom, cooked up the dope, tied her arm, and plunged in a needle. "I got weak in the knees," she said. "A couple of days later I came to." She learned that Baker had walked out, leaving her on the floor—"blue, blue, blue!" Jones recalled, laughing. Luckily for her, two friends in the apartment saved her life. "I guess they did mouth-to-mouth and walked me back and forth for six or eight hours or something until the breathing apparatus could do it on its own," she said.

Still she couldn't resist his charms, although a heavier price lay in store. Sometime after he gave her the overdose, Baker picked up a sweaty female junkie and informed Jones that all of them would fix together, using his only needle—first him, then the woman, and finally Jones. "I didn't like the scene at all," she said. "I didn't want to use the same needle. But I did."

A few days later, Sandy made a cameo appearance in *Palace,* a short documentary about a Cockettes stage show. She and another actress stripped naked and painted themselves yellow. "Mary, I'm turning lots more yellow than you are, and it's the same paint!" said Jones. She came down with hepatitis so severe that it confined her to her apartment, where she had to have her heroin delivered. When Baker came to visit, he found her writhing on a mattress on the floor, nearly delirious. He looked down at her and said hello. "That's the first thing that broke through to my spirit and made me smile," she said. "Oh man, I loved him!"

With no prospects, Baker spent hours wandering alone through the hills of nearby San Jose, deep in thought. That spring he reached a decision. Finding a music shop, he picked out a battered trumpet to replace the last one he had pawned. Then he drove around looking for a place to play. He found Ricardo's, a pizza parlor that held Monday-night jam sessions with a jazz trio. As they played on a raised platform in the back, dinner orders blasted through the music: "PIZZA NUMBER FORTY!" But no place else in the area offered straight-ahead jazz, and even Lee Konitz, a star alto saxophonist who had worked in the original *Birth of the Cool* band, was reduced to playing at Ricardo's. One night the noise grew so deafening that he walked into the corner and blew his horn to the wall.

As soon as Baker walked in, he noticed a hippie-ish woman at the drums.

Diane Vavra wore no shoes or makeup, and her long brown hair hung down plainly. But she seemed totally immersed in the music, and that caught Baker's attention. Vavra had recently separated from her husband, a part-time bass player with a drug habit. Now twenty-nine, she shared a small home with their son, Ronny, who was Dean's age. She had heard that Chet Baker, the man whose *Baby Breeze* album had changed her life, was seen in town buying a trumpet. Now here he was, sitting on a chair near the bandstand, horn in his lap, watching her intently. "He was all golden, like a Greek Adonis," she recalled. "Just gorgeous." Between songs he asked her name. "You play very well, Diane," he said. She was struck by how gentle he seemed, contrary to all the horror stories. "He was very shy, very refined in the way he spoke, very slow," she recalled. "Later on he would tell people about our first meeting, and he would always bring up the fact that I was playing with my shoes off."

Baker introduced himself to Don McCaslin, who played electric piano, and asked if he could sit in. He was out of practice, and the results were grating. But Vavra's heart melted as she saw him struggling to play well in a pizza joint full of screaming teenagers, none of them listening to him. He came back every week, determined to get his chops back at any cost. Word spread, and local musicians began showing up with their instruments, hoping for a chance to sit in with Chet Baker.

They all got their turn, but the only player who really interested him was Vavra. He offered to pick her up before the gig and help her carry her drums. That schoolboy gesture began a love affair that would last three years, then resume in 1982 and continue until the year Baker died. To her he was a classic beauty, a father figure, and a god of jazz rolled into one; she fell hopelessly in love with him.

As she began to tell him about her life, he marveled at how similar they were. Vavra had shown the same childhood prowess that he had. On February 5, 1953, the *Mayfair,* a San Jose newspaper, published the following: "GIFTED—twelve-year-old Diane White, daughter of Mr. and Mrs. E. M. White, can play a familiar tune by ear and then, according to her teachers, she can write out the tune, note for note, as do highly trained scholars of music." Her father loved jazz too—he played piano and sang—but drank to excess and belittled away her confidence, she said. "Whenever I came home, he'd be on the floor. So I'd step over him and I'd go in my room and put this record on—Charlie Parker's *Relaxin' at Camarillo.* It was a wonderful revelation!"

After studying saxophone, clarinet, and several other instruments, she married a bassist and began playing drums with him locally. Finally she settled on sax, first alto, then soprano. Taking a lesson from Lee Konitz, she dazzled him by reproducing a difficult solo by Phil Woods note for note. Vavra would impress Baker so much that for years he tried to get her to perform and record with him. But she never felt worthy. "I just wanted to feel good by playing music," she explained. "I didn't dream of stardom or anything like that."

Sensing he had found a soul mate and a fresh start, Baker showed Vavra off to Simpson, Loughborough, and Sandy Jones, who was now dating a doctor. "He was so proud, like a rooster," Jones said. "He was so happy he'd met somebody who could do something musically." Vavra rhapsodized to her friends about her new romance with a genius of jazz. Otherwise, their affair remained covert: when Baker left Milpitas to see her, he told Carol he was visiting Terry, Vavra's platonic male roommate.

So much about Baker seemed inscrutable to Vavra that she attempted to make her laconic new lover open up. "I'm doing some soul-searching, I'm trying to find out what's going on in my life—how about you, Chet?" she asked. Slowly there emerged a portrait of complete frustration, much of it centered on Carol. "She doesn't understand a thing about my music," he grumbled. "Her favorite singer is *Elvis Presley*!" Yet he didn't have the nerve to divorce her; Vavra wondered why.

His career seemed as dead as his marriage, thanks now to "fusion," the electric jazz-rock that had blasted the remnants of straight-ahead jazz out of the marketplace. The movement was spearheaded by Miles Davis, whose rage had hit such a peak that he traveled with a set of brass knuckles. *Bitches Brew,* his first gold album, was the musical equivalent of a cold-steel swipe across the face. Released in 1970, it found Davis rejecting everything he had stood for—melody, lyricism, intricate harmonic progression—and replacing it with sheets of electrified sound that couldn't be termed song. The rock generation discovered him for the first time, but his older admirers were disgusted. "I think Miles enjoys doing things that upset people," Baker told Jerome Reece. The fusion craze worried him: "You know, some of those tunes, I can't hear them," he told Vavra. "I don't know where they're going."

But Baker's drive to play his own way kept growing. Braving humiliation, he called scores of local bars and clubs and asked to play a night or two. "Most of the jazz places wanted him," said Jack Simpson, "but a lot of them didn't advertise, because they didn't want to stir up any dust." Put another way, the police had their eye on him. Since coming to Milpitas, he had gotten arrested again for driving under the influence of narcotics. Simpson accompanied him to court. "Chet had such a rap sheet, they said, if you come here again we'll throw away the key," he recalled.

Performing around northern California, Baker had to stay almost incognito. In May, he played one night at the New Orleans House, a jazz club in Berkeley, with a local trio. He was still too rusty to be judged by a music critic, yet Baker found himself facing one of the most important ones in jazz: Ralph J. Gleason, the scholarly, pipe-smoking columnist for the *San Francisco Chronicle.*

Three days later, he read the most devastating review of his career: a full column, ominously titled "A Few Came to Hear Chet Baker." The critic sat in a near-deserted room and watched a "bad dream" unfold as Baker shuffled in with his crew-neck sweater and trumpet case. Gleason had raved about the stunning newcomer Baker had been in 1952; now he wrote that the trumpeter looked "like an aging football player coming to a class reunion." The "ravages of time and frustration and the demons of insecurity" were etched all over his face, Gleason noted, as Baker and the band went through the motions, lifeless. His "old tinsel and make-believe pretty songs" now seemed empty, ludicrous. "It was other-earthly, spooky, like a horrible time machine gone wrong," the critic concluded. "A musical play by Kafka. A musical tragedy."

Baker later claimed that after reading the review, he went to his mother's home and punched out all the windows. Then he went to Vavra's. She and her father tried to comfort him, but he seemed inconsolable. His family bore the brunt of his turmoil, as Vavra saw when he brought the children to her house. "The verbal abuse he gave them was really mean," she said. "He would just be very nasty—'Don't pay any attention to them, they're just little idiots.' " One night he shocked her by announcing: "Man, I just hit my mother." She learned he had also been hocking Vera's possessions, including her TV, for drug money. Yet every time the young woman felt like running for her life, he drew her back with some heartrending gesture of sensitivity, such as crying when they made love.

Ultimately she realized how self-obsessed he was. She decided to get him high on LSD—"so that he could get past his narcissism, maybe see the connection between himself and the world." She gave him the drug, then they took a long ride in his car, the place he felt the least inhibited. There in the driver's seat he turned into a goofy child, giggling so hard he couldn't drive. Vavra had to take the wheel. The fact that he needed a hallucinogenic drug just to make him laugh indicated how deeply repressed his sense of joy was.

When the high faded, he returned to his somber self. Friends kept rallying on his behalf. Artt Frank had been pushing for someone to produce a new Chet Baker album, one on which Frank might play. At his urging, Nicky Blair appealed to a friend of a friend, the least likely producer to sign Chet Baker: MGM records president Mike Curb, the twenty-five-year-old "Mr. Clean" of pop. In an age of sex, drugs, and rock and roll, Curb set out to sanitize the business by announcing his plan to fire all substance-abusing MGM artists. He replaced them with such white-bread acts as the Osmond Brothers and his own antiseptic chorale, the Mike Curb Congregation.

Curb didn't know much about Baker, but as a personal favor to Blair—so the restaurateur claimed—the producer signed the most notorious living junkie in jazz for one album in 1970. *Blood, Chet and Tears* required the trumpeter to play AM-radio hits by Blood, Sweat and Tears ("Spinning Wheel," "You've Made Me So Very Happy"), Bobby Sherman ("Easy Come, Easy Go"), the Archies ("Sugar, Sugar"), and the like. He recorded with a rhythm section of high-school rock-band quality; afterward, the tracks were slathered with saccharine horn playing and twinkly bells. Not surprisingly, Baker sounded as if he were half asleep. Artt Frank wasn't asked to play, but he did get to write the liner notes; he called the album a "sheer treasure, like searching for gold and finding uranium." Baker pocketed the cash, and *Blood, Chet and Tears* went unnoticed.

That year, Jack Simpson became the latest friend to try and "save" him. Simpson had taken a job as an eighth-grade art teacher, but the semester had ended, and he volunteered to try managing Baker. He rounded up four young musicians, who spent several weeks rehearsing with Baker in Vera's basement. It excited Simpson to hear Baker's chops returning, and he tried his hardest to keep the trumpeter off dope and to see that he ate properly. But Baker's discipline vanished when he found himself a new drug connection. Soon he and his band were spending their rehearsal time getting high.

Simpson was encouraged when El Matador, a top jazz club in San Francisco, agreed to book the new Chet Baker Quintet. Two days before the opening, the *Chronicle* heralded the engagement with a tiny photo that looked like a junkie's mug shot. It showed Baker unshaven, greasy-haired, and sunken-cheeked, with long hippie sideburns pointing down at his black mesh T-shirt.

Before the first show, John L. Wasserman, the paper's young entertainment writer, came to El Matador to interview Baker. The trumpeter wasn't available: he was locked in a small back room, "anesthetized," said Simpson. Wasserman reviewed the show anyway. Baker sounded "excellent," he said, but somehow "stopped in time, and the time is not today. . . . As the band gets together and Baker's physical problems dissolve, it will be interesting to see what evolves."

Nothing did. The engagement ended in a week. "He got his first check, and that was the last we saw of him for about four days," said Simpson, who was furious. "That was the only gig we got, because when Chet did that, word got out real quick."

Baker was losing the will to keep trying. Echoing his 1953 interview with *Melody Maker,* he told Simpson he wanted to buy a boat, forget about work, and sail away, taking him along—and a lifetime supply of "shit"—for company. Failing that, he had an alternative. "He tried to get me strung out," Simpson said. "That's where we parted ways. I woke up one morning, went to his house, and said, 'I know you're not gonna change—goodbye.' "

Subsequently, Baker and Carol knocked on his door in Los Gatos. "I just hocked my horn, so we can go to the movies tonight," Baker said. Simpson felt no sympathy. "If you pawned your trumpet, I don't have any respect for you," he said. "Who are you trying to impress? You know you'll get another one." He turned them away.

By now Jackson knew of Diane Vavra's existence, although she didn't seem to realize that her husband and Vavra were lovers. "I would take care of the kids sometimes, and they'd go to San Francisco to get high together," said Vavra. One day she got a frantic call from Carol, who blurted out that Baker had taken a huge amount of Seconal and that she couldn't handle him. Vavra drove to Milpitas and picked him up. "I saw Carol, and she had a couple of black eyes," remembered Vavra. The young woman took Baker home to San Jose for three days of hysteria. "At one point he took all his clothes off and ran around in the front yard," she said. Finally, the soft-spoken Vavra let out the angriest outburst she could manage: "You have the nastiest disposition of anybody I've ever known!" He burst into tears and fell into her arms. "Honey, can't you see how frustrated I am?" he said, sobbing. "Yes . . . I can," she whispered as he drew her back into his web.

Baker didn't have the guts to tell Carol the truth about Vavra; in his passive-aggressive way he let her find out for herself. In 1971, he got his first job offer in some time, a gig in Boise, Idaho. He went alone by car, and upon arriving, he sent Vavra a plane ticket. They stayed together in a motel, then drove back together. Soon thereafter, Baker wrote her a note. Carol knew about the affair, he said; apparently she had found Vavra's ticket stubs in his coat pocket. Unable to confront his wife's rage honestly, he tried to explain that "a man can love two women at the same time." He warned Vavra to expect a nasty phone call from Carol, but nothing could have prepared her for the ugliness that followed: "She called up my mother, raving over the phone, *'She's a homewrecker! A whore!'*" Ruth Young later heard about the incident from Baker: "Carol was so out of control, the mother nearly had a nervous breakdown. Carol wouldn't get off the phone. And Chet never did anything to stop her." The months that followed were "pretty bad," said Vavra.

Before anything could change, there was something Baker had to do. In 1972, he joined the Methadone Maintenance Program. According to Baker, so did Carol; he later told Young that this was the only way he felt he could make her independent, and ultimately free himself of her. The next year, Baker decided to move back to New York—but with Vavra, not his wife. They could get a nice apartment together and live with her son, Ronny, he explained, while Carol and his own children stayed in Milpitas. "Although I said yes, I knew I could never do this," Vavra recalled. "I wanted to provide a stable home for my little boy. But I couldn't let go."

Roosevelt Hotel, New York City, 1974. Photo by Sy Johnson

14

After a year on methadone, Baker was clear-headed enough to see a path to the future. In June 1973, it led him to New York. He stopped in Denver first to see his trusted friend Phil Urso. The two men had shared some hellish times, but the sax player, like Baker, was finally heroin-free. Married and awaiting his first child, he worked as a music teacher for the Denver Department of Education. Urso took Baker to a local club to hear Dizzy Gillespie, who effusively introduced his old rival from the stage. He did the same with Urso. Both men stood to a round of applause.

After the last set, Gillespie took them back to his hotel room to play poker. "What are you guys doing here, anyway?" he asked. Urso explained that Baker was off to New York to make a fresh start, and that he might go too.

"Oh, in other words, you're out of work?" said Gillespie. He told them he had just played the Half Note, a posh new jazz club in Manhattan. Gillespie immediately dialed the owners to tell them that "Chettie" Baker needed a job. A half-hour later, one of them phoned back and asked for Baker. "Guess what, Phil!" said the trumpeter as he hung up. "We've got two weeks in New York!"

Baker's elation gave way to fear. He was set to open in three weeks, but he knew he wasn't ready. Earlier that year, he had joined Jack Sheldon and a trio led by Dave Frishberg, a witty, intellectual pianist-composer, to record some standards. Baker still sounded so ragged that the tapes were shelved. He thought it would ease his nerves to have Vavra join him in Denver, and he sent her a plane ticket. Once they were together, he announced his plan to take her to Manhattan, put her son in school there, and live as if they were married. Vavra knew the idea was preposterous, but she didn't refuse at first. "I was kind of addicted," she said. "I was just trying to get strong enough to break free." During a fight, he cracked one of her ribs. Devastated, she flew home, leaving him and Urso to make the trip to New York without her.

Baker hadn't worked there since 1959. With Urso, he checked into the only place that felt like home: the Bryant Hotel, where he had lived in his Birdland days. But the Bryant was now a fleabag, and Birdland itself had closed eight years earlier. Acid rock and funk blasted from every other car that passed by; "Bad, Bad Leroy Brown" was zooming toward number one on the charts. Baker's peers were struggling to "get with it," but he hated most of the sounds of the day.

So, apparently, did the Half Note's owners, three siblings named Mike, Sonny, and Rosemary Canterino. Only months before, they had moved their club uptown from SoHo, soon to become a trendy art capital. Now the Half Note occupied a costly site on West Fifty-fourth and Sixth Avenue, near the theater district. Clutching at the past, the family tried to create a dressy, old-fashioned supper club, with plush banquettes and a galaxy of jazz veterans—Gillespie, Stan Getz, Sonny Rollins, Bill Evans—on double bills. The Canterinos' taste was admirable, but the new Half Note struck some people as a wax museum of the fifties.

"It was kind of bizarre," said bassist Michael Moore, who joined Baker there in November. "You walked into the place, and there was Sonny Canterino in a tuxedo at the door, and his wife, Judi, all dressed up in a sequined gown, charging a whole lot of money with this kind of desperate look in their eyes." The club would close the following year.

In July 1973, though, no one captured the room's sense of doomed nostalgia like Chet Baker. The married vocal duo of Jackie Cain and Roy Kral opened the bill. Despite having started out years before he did, Cain and Kral looked and sounded like eternal spring. Then came Baker. The last time New Yorkers had seen him, he was near his peak of beauty. Now his chalky, wrinkled cheeks were caved in from the loss of his teeth; his eyes were two black hollows, surrounded by arching crow's-feet that seemed to chart every wrong turn he had ever taken. They were framed by hippie sideburns and the thick brown hair of a teenager, slicked back Elvis-style. Gone were the dark suits and skinny ties that had once looked so cool on him; now he wore a loud red blazer, clashing burgundy trousers, and cowboy boots, like an Okie at a high-school reunion.

For the middle-aged audience, it was profoundly unsettling to see the shining jazz prince of their youth reduced to a near-cadaver. A bigger shock came when the music started. With Urso at his side, Baker tried to play the old bop standards—Charlie Parker's "Donna Lee," "If You Could See Me Now"—that he had once sailed through like a bird. Now, according to Richard Williams of *Melody Maker*, many of the notes emerged as "empty, whistling air." The rhythm section, led by a young bop pianist named Harold Danko, moved as gingerly behind him as if they were helping an old man across the street.

Between sets, Baker vanished into a bathroom in the musicians' lounge upstairs. Some assumed he was getting high; in fact, he was gluing his dentures back in place. Through sheer willpower he got through each night, but John S. Wilson of the *New York Times* belittled his effort: "His playing is still laconic to the point of listlessness, delivered in a stark, rather unshaded monotone."

Curiosity kept the club full, and the Canterinos booked the trumpeter for a third week, to start July 23. Near the end of the second, a blonde of twenty-two stopped outside the Half Note, stunned to see flyers touting the return of the jazz icon whose records her mother had played for her. Ruth Young, née Youngstein, had just come from her latest argument with her father, a millionaire film mogul. She dreamed of becoming a cool jazz singer like Anita O'Day and Baker, two of her idols. But she felt no support from her parents in anything she did, and insecurity crippled her; her near-genius IQ was no help.

Still in tears from the confrontation, she went inside. Young wasn't a beauty—she had a birdlike face with a sharp nose, surrounded by a mass of hanging curls that made her look like a Berkeley hippie. But she had charisma, and as she sat at the bar in her short red dress, coolly puffing a cigarette, eyes shifted to her. Young's were fixed on Baker, as she tried to figure out what had gone so horribly wrong with the dreamboat she knew only from his Pacific Jazz records of the fifties. Now she stared at "a tormented soul" braving rejection, fiercely intent on salvaging himself from ruin. She found the spectacle deeply moving. "I felt like I was watching somebody get up off the canvas after he had done eight rounds with Muhammad Ali," she said. "He was standing there in a red jacket and burgundy pants, looking absolutely ridiculous. But still he had this peculiar charm. Chet had incurred every disaster in his life that one could possibly imagine, but still he managed to find within himself the knowledge of what he was put on this earth to do. To see this man completely revealing himself, looking and sounding so terrible but trying so hard—that was the moment I connected with him."

And he with her. After the show, he took the next barstool, attracted, he later said, by her big blue eyes and glowing smile. She improvised a compliment: "Hey, I've got to tell you, it's really great to see you. I think you're doing a hell of a job." When he invited her upstairs to his dressing room, he discovered her quick, barbed sense of humor—pianist Phil Markowitz would call her a cross between Lauren Bacall and Cruella De Vil—and her knowledge of jazz. "So don't be a stranger," said Baker offhandedly in parting, a typical passive-aggressive command.

Young obeyed. They had met on Friday the thirteenth—her "lucky unlucky day," she said. It launched a ten-year relationship of staggering codependency. She came to see Baker as her Picasso, a needy child, and a protector; he would treat her as a mommy, a sex object, and occasionally as a whipping post, subjecting her to all his conflicted feelings about women. "My drug is now called Ruth," read a headline in an Italian tabloid. Young felt the same way. "It took about twenty seconds to get hooked," she said. "And from that time on, my life was hell on wheels."

Ruth Ann Youngstein was one of four adopted children of Max Youngstein, a partner and vice president of United Artists pictures, and his wife, Mae. Raised in a series of luxury apartments in New York and in the affluent gated community of Bel Air, California, Young had lived in a Hollywood-style haze of unreality. Stars like Warren Beatty, Jane Russell, and Marilyn Monroe passed in and out of the family living room, making it hard to tell where cinema fantasy ended and reality began. With her family moving every two years or so, Young switched from one cushy private school to another, making it hard to maintain friendships. In place of roots, her mother and her workaholic father gave her a "megabucks little trust fund," as she called it. But the money didn't last long, particularly after she met Baker. "I was like the millionaire," she said, "writing checks to everybody. What's your name? Joe . . . spell it for me. How much, six thousand? Here. I had no idea what life was about, none. When you grow up with money, you don't understand what anything means. Until you don't have any."

Moving into an apartment on West Seventy-second Street, Young went in search of an identity. Around 1970, in the heat of the acid-rock era, she sought to become a fifties-type jazz singer like Julie London or June Christy.

Adopting the glamorous stage name Jessica Shayne, she showcased in a couple of New York clubs, revealing a cool, wispy style. But terror and self-doubt plagued her, and she began getting "all whacked out" on amphetamines and starving herself into anorexia. One day her dealer came to the apartment and offered her heroin along with the pills. She bought some out of curiosity, then tried it after he left: "The next thing I know, I'm perched on my ledge on the eighth floor, looking down at the street and considering suicide more lucidly than I ever had in my life."

Somehow she found her way back inside, and didn't touch heroin again for years. But like Baker, she stayed poised on a precarious edge between survival and disaster. Her intellect and humor saved her. "Ruth lived by her wits," said Charlie Davidson. "I think Chet was fascinated by her. She was an interesting diversion—this wacko, brilliant Jewish chick and this little Oklahoma farm boy. In her years with Chet, he was more civilized than I ever saw him."

Early on, she loved Baker's gentleness. "He was a lot more vulnerable at the time than he later became, because he was on the rebound of his own career, and he was feeling incredibly insecure," she observed. "A man of his stature—who'd ever imagine he could become even more fragile as time went on?" Baker dreaded telling her he was married. "He had to painfully explain: 'Oh, by the way, this woman, my wife, the children—uh-oh, I have to get them here.' "

"What?" said Young.

"Yeah, well, we'll talk about that tomorrow."

Gradually he offered a few cryptic details. "Look, I gave her nine good years," he said, referring to Carol coldly as "the mother of my children." She slept in her makeup, he said, and had no friends. Most of all, he voiced his common complaint about her indifference to his music. "She's in love with Elvis Presley," he said, adding: "It's not like having three kids, it's like having four."

Baker's neediness and fear of being alone compelled him to try juggling several women at once. He promised Carol he would fly her and the children to New York as soon as he could afford it. Meanwhile, he begged Vavra to come back. Addressing one letter to "Diane Vavra-Baker," he apologized tersely for their scuffle in Denver and told her he couldn't live without her. Vavra hesitated, but agreed to meet him in Chicago that October. When she phoned his hotel room beforehand to confirm, Baker was there with Young. "I'm sorry," he said coolly into the receiver. "That's just not possible right now."

Baker's comeback had caught the eye of the press, who saw its tabloid appeal. "He was up against big negative gossip, and he knew it," said Young. Over the next few years, "Loser" became his middle name. "In that vast union of losers, Chet Baker had overpaid his dues and then some," observed *Playboy.* To Alan Weitz of the *Village Voice,* Baker now played "for all the losers and suckers, for all the hustlers and hustled, for you and me." Writers had a field day comparing him to "a vulnerable, aging Mafioso" (Paul Nelson, *The Village Voice*) and "an emaciated Jack Palance" (Rogers Worthington, *Detroit Free Press*).

Ruth Young was incensed at how fast critics were to dismiss his quarter-century of nearly uninterrupted productivity. "How dare they say what more he might have done?" she said. "Fuck all these people! Have they made a hundred and fifty records lately?" But Baker knew the marketability of his addiction, and supplied writers with a treasure trove of scandal. Syndicated columnist Rex Reed gave him his first big newspaper profile in years, titled "Jazzman Chet Baker Is Back from His Bad Trip." Wrote Reed: "The story of Chet Baker is an American tragedy, so sordid and sad it makes Billie Holiday's life and 'Young Man with a Horn' seem like Disney cartoons. At 44, he's still a little boy lost, with 20 years down the drain in a hypodermic needle."

Baker still portrayed himself as a victim, "kicked through life" yet struggling to hang on. "My whole life for the past 15 years has been a nightmare, going from one fix to another," he told Reed, launching into his familiar "tales of woe" about horns stolen from him, Harlem dope dealers who "tried to burn me, rip me off on rooftops and in alleys." He hauled out his oft-told stories about Lucca, London, and San Francisco. Now, as he explained to Bob Micklin of *New York Newsday,* he was nearly destitute: "After I paid my hotel bill last week, I had only $8 left in my pocket. I can't get enough money together to bring my wife and kids here from California."

After seventeen years of near-continuous addiction, he truly believed this comeback was his last chance. "I think he was totally pressured, and he wanted to do what people expected," said Young. He got a nasty dose of reality every day at Roosevelt Hospital. Addicts on Methadone Maintenance lined up to swallow a dose of red syrup that tasted like poison, even though the nurse mixed it with Kool-Aid. Methadone offered the promise that, with gradually diminishing doses, the craving might fade. "You substitute one addiction for another, but this one only costs two dollars a week, and it isn't illegal," he explained to Reed. "I think I'll eventually get off it altogether." But Baker's so-called unaltered state was a fantasy. He kept himself high on pot, snorted coke, tried angel dust, even stockpiled methadone. "He was always ahead of schedule, so at the end he could take some extra to get high," said Harold Danko. Only "reds" (barbiturates) scared him, with their power to send him into dementia, and he warned Young to keep him away from them.

In late July 1973, he flew Carol and the children into town. Still on welfare, the family moved into his hotel room at the Bryant. Bob Mover, a twenty-one-year-old alto player from Boston who replaced Phil Urso that fall, was struck by how cynical the kids seemed at seven, eight, and ten years old. Carol herself dreamed of a bright new start. She too had joined Methadone Maintenance in New York—"They were both on the program together," said Mover—but her true compulsion remained her husband. "There were no real friends," Mover explained. "She was just Chet's wife to everybody."

Baker still didn't know how to explain Ruth Young to Carol. In junkie style, he resorted to subterfuge. Taking the advice of Phil Urso, he identified Young as his new manager and arranged for her to escort Carol to the Half Note. On a sticky summer night, Young knocked on the door of Baker's hotel room. When it opened, she beheld a would-be replica of Elizabeth Taylor as Maggie "the Cat," the aggressive, sexpot wife of *Cat on a Hot Tin Roof.* Carol's blue-black beehive hairdo had a chiffon scarf running through it; her white dress was so tight that in a few minutes the zipper popped before Young's eyes.

Changing into another dress, Carol talked nonstop. "She really needed it," said Young. "She took me in completely as her ally, no suspicion." Hard-luck stories tumbled out of Carol, who blamed Richard Carpenter for destroying her happy home life. "She never said, 'How did you meet Chet?' or 'Gee, it's great that you're trying to help my husband,' " Young recalled. "Not a curiosity in hell." As they headed to the Half Note, Carol startled her by admitting: "And now we're both hooked on this shit." The musicians were equally surprised to see wife and girlfriend walk into the club together and share a ringside table. Everyone knew the truth except Carol. Even after her husband's affair with Vavra, she seemed too confident in her own charms to imagine that her husband could be in love with a woman like Ruth Young.

Meanwhile, Baker was passionately wooing Young, whom he called "Roofie" or "Roofs." He sent big floral arrangements and signed his letters "Papa Bear." In coming years he wrote her longingly whenever they were apart, rhapsodizing about their love as passionately as if he were Ira Gershwin or Lorenz Hart. Baker called this romantic fairyland his "new beginning," and he saw Young as often as he could sneak away from Carol.

For the rest of the seventies, as they drove from country to country and gig to gig, she lay in the front seat with her head in his lap and asked questions, determined to probe the myth of Chet Baker. "How had a man with a T-shirt and a soft-spoken voice ballooned into this totally inept depiction of a person?" she wondered. "I was doing my Dr. Joyce Brothers routine, asking him anything and everything I could. I think it was as important for him to tell as for me to ask. Finally he could shed layer upon layer of this hideous duplicity, this gargantuan burden to live up to a lie, some of which he created and some he didn't."

Physically, she didn't find him as enticing, but he was insatiable. Boasting that drugs hadn't impaired him sexually, he set out to prove it day and night. "He was practically a pig," she said. "There were missed trains, buses, planes, wrong stops, detours, lots of extra money laid out for tickets as a result of this guy." His tender love songs weren't enacted in bed, though; he didn't even like to kiss. "Sex was sex to him, it wasn't romance," she said. "In the beginning it was like being with a sixteen-year-old who was getting his first taste and went out of his mind. Oh, my God, what that turned into. The poor guy could get on you and off you while you were asleep, and you didn't even have to wake up for it. But he did give great head, being a trumpet player. In the years I knew him, he went from being an F-minus to a B-plus in the sack. How could you not love a guy like that?"

To Young, this was a man straining to prove his masculinity. He often referred to males he disliked as "faggots," and he grew "paranoid," she said, "if I got anywhere near his ass." She came to feel he had latent gay urges that terrified him. "I believe it was a totally repressed thing in his case," she said. "He was just so homophobic from the get-go." His attitude about masturbation was harder to fathom. He liked telling his musicians, in a self-consciously macho tone, that he had "just enough time to eat, jerk off, and go to the gig." But when Young brought up the subject, he was taken aback. "I *never* touch myself!" he swore. Speaking with Jerome Reece in *Jazz Hot,* he described Art Pepper's autobiography as "disgusting," giving one example: "all that shit about how good-looking he was, his peeping into bathroom windows . . . masturbating."

But in 1973, his greater fixation was learning to play again. Coping with the impediment of his false teeth, he fought to repair all the cracks and rough edges in his delivery. In the meantime, he developed his voice as a second instrument. Through scat singing—improvising with wordless syllables—he expressed the ideas he couldn't play, holding the mike as if it were a trumpet. "Scatting is so much fun," he told Les Tomkins in *Crescendo.* "You can really extend yourself, and try to come up with some interesting lines that fit in the harmony and chord progressions, but still swing and still have a meaning. . . . It's nothing that's worked out or thought about beforehand; it's completely spontaneous—and very risky."

For all his effort, demand for his talents was low. Once the novelty died down, his appearances were mostly nonevents. Baker had three agents: Jack Whittemore, who also booked Dizzy Gillespie; Jack Tafoya, a New York promoter; and Ruth Young, who wrote letters, placed calls, and negotiated contracts on his behalf. She learned that Baker could seldom command more than a hundred dollars a night; often he took fifty. "Listen, Ruth, I gotta work," he said testily when she scolded him for selling himself so cheap.

Among his few substantial bookings in 1973 and 1974 (the Village Vanguard in New York, the Jazz Showcase in Chicago) were many more one- or two-nighters at places like the Town Crier in East Islip, Long Island; Dave's Cabaret in Wallington, New Jersey; and Sergio's Restaurant in Hartsdale, New York. Because he was earning so little, he often hired second-rate and inexpensive local musicians. Meanwhile, he let almost anyone, professional or amateur, sit in, largely because it gave him time to rest. Often the clubs were half-full, yet Baker seemed grateful that anyone remembered him at all. "He was very cordial," said Harold Danko. "He always took the time to sign autographs. If you brought a record from 1952 and you wanted it autographed, he'd make you feel good about the fact that you did that. It was kind of touching."

The women in Baker's audience had aged along with him, and their interest in him wasn't as lustful as before. "I think your trumpet sounds like the call of paradise," wrote Harriet Wilder, a fan from Brooklyn, New York, in a letter. "You have beautiful blue eyes. I wanted to give you a kiss and tell you how much I love your work and admire it. However, you look so skinny to me, even though you have a nice physique. Please try to eat a mashed potato once in a while and maybe a plate of chicken livers."

As usual, Baker leaned on everybody for help. His old charts were a tattered mess, and he kept misplacing the book. It fell to the even-tempered Danko to hold things together. A Scientologist and a piano player of mathematical precision, he made business calls and hired sidemen. Ruth Young attended to Baker's every need, even washing his underwear in hotel bidets and checking that he bathed. Wolfgang Lackerschmid, a German vibraphonist who joined the band later in the seventies, recalled hearing her ask Baker in exasperation: "But why can't you take a bath *without* bubble bath?"

"Because it's boring," he replied.

She saw him at his nonchalant best in Toronto, where a customs agent stopped them at the border and let loose a drug-sniffing dog in the car. Young remembered the large bag of pot stashed behind a hidden panel of the dashboard. "Uhhh, Chet, sweetheart," she murmured through clenched teeth, "what about the . . . you know?" He didn't answer. She panicked. "The *dog* is in the *car,* Chet! He's gonna sniff—" Baker cut her off. "*No.* He's not." He stared hard at the dog, and it walked away benignly. "That sums up Chet's attitude," Young said later. "What, it's on fire? That's OK."

At forty-three, Baker still thrived on the outlaw life. His standard getup—blue jeans, fringed leather jacket, cowboy boots, cigarette dangling against a scruffy beard—made him look like a redneck. He ate greasy omelets and fried eggs in roadside diners; enjoyed *Scruples,* Judith Krantz's best-selling sex potboiler (the only book Young ever saw him read); watched Bruce Lee kung-fu movies or his special favorite, *Dirty Harry,* the tale of a vigilante cop looking to blow a murderer's brains out. "It's very funny," thought Bob Mover. "I'm playing black music, but I feel like a cowboy."

To Baker, the "system" in all forms was the enemy. During a visit to Munich later in the seventies, he and Mover stood together in a train station. A uniformed German porter drove by in a luggage wagon, swerving so close to them that Mover fell down. *"What the fuck is wrong with you?"* screamed Baker at the porter. *"Don't you see where you're going? You fucking idiot!"* He and the German yelled at each other in their native languages, neither understanding the other. "Finally," said Mover, "Chet looked at him with such anger and hatred and said, *'I hope you have to ride that fucking thing until your ass rots!'* The German guy just knew he'd been defeated. He looked at Chet and realized that whatever Chet had told him was some terrible reality about his life."

The people Baker respected most were those who spit at the establishment. One of his best friends was Jack Freeman, a reformed addict from Queens who worked as a top-dollar shoplifter. Stealing was fine, Baker thought, if the underdog robbed the rich, powerful, and controlling. The trumpeter dodged the IRS by refusing to have a bank account or credit card and by demanding all payments in cash. He expressed more contempt in his latest car, a Mustang convertible with towels stuffed in the broken windows. Cruising down the highway, he cut off other drivers, then gave them the finger. All the while, he sneered about how America was "just one big hillbilly farm town."

Baker dispensed other worldly wisdom in what Harold Danko called "grandmother's platitudes":

"He who hesitates is lost."

"If you can't carry it, don't bring it."

"If you wanna get it done, do it yourself."

And his favorite: "Life is full of disappointments."

Yet his words, like his music, were so muted and spare that every utterance seemed profound. "You'd feel like you were full of shit if you tried to make small talk with him, if you made a comment about his shirt or something, because you knew he was really taking in who you were," said Danko. Baker's taste in singers was undoubtedly hip. He liked Billie Holiday ("because she never raised her voice," he told Danko), and he played the 1963 album *The Concert Sinatra* over and over. But he didn't care for Ella Fitzgerald's renowned scatting. "It's so kindergartenish," Baker said. "It's all worked out ahead of time and every time she sings that tune it's the same." Most of all, he hated the "hillbilly and rockabilly crap" popular in his hometown. "It's this pickup-truck, rifle-in-the-back-window mentality," he told interviewer Leonard Malone. "For a good time, to have to go out on the weekend and drink beer until you're drunk and get into a fistfight is not my idea, you know, of the hippest kind of . . ."

His seeming confidence was envied by Young, who froze whenever he tried to coax her onstage. "I was nuts with insecurity," she said. "Stand next to Chet Baker and sing? Who am I?" In the midseventies, just before her first TV appearance with him in Italy, she downed a fifth of Cutty Sark, then threw up. He was concerned enough to make a confession that had probably never passed his lips before: "Now, listen, Ruth. I'll tell you this once and only once. You'll never meet anyone more insecure than me." When that didn't work, he tried another tack: "Listen, baby, just remember one thing. Nobody knows what the fuck we're doing. So if you remember that, you'll be fine." Later, at an Italian record date for the album *The Incredible Chet Baker Plays and Sings,* he commanded her to sing two ballads with him, "Whatever Possess'd Me" and "Autumn Leaves." She was terrified. But once the tape started to roll, she fell under his spell, and ended up sounding like his cool, sexy alter ego.

Baker's recording career had fizzled after *Blood, Chet and Tears,* but John Snyder, a young producer who idolized him, vowed to change that. An ex-trumpeter from North Carolina, Snyder had a baby face and a soft Southern accent; he had put aside a legal degree to make a rather idealistic foray into the record business. One of his early missions was to get Chet Baker back on his feet. Snyder brought some recent live tapes of the trumpeter to his boss, Creed Taylor, the owner of CTI, the hottest fusion label in the business. Taylor thought the trumpeter sounded too shaky to record, but Snyder was so persistent that, in mid-1974, CTI produced the latest Chet Baker comeback album.

True to his image as a relic, *She Was Too Good to Me* was pure nostalgia, a fifties make-out album in an age of free sex and fallen innocence. Baker crooned romantic chestnuts—Irving Berlin's "What'll I Do," Rodgers and Hart's "With a Song in My Heart"—in his still-dewy voice. A string section, arranged by Don Sebesky, cushioned him in spun sugar. But when a set of pictures taken for the jacket came back from the photographer, Snyder and Taylor saw the truth. "Chet looked so dissolute, it was shocking," Snyder said. "I argued for keeping it like it was, because to me it looked like an Okie, *The Grapes of Wrath,* and that's who he was."

With an abstract painting, instead, on the cover, *She Was Too Good to Me* hit stores at the end of 1974. Sales were disappointing, but the record did confirm to those who cared that Chet Baker was back. "He has almost no voice—it's all silences, slides, whispers, yearning in its purest form—but his phrasing can be superb, the romantic impact devastating," wrote Paul Nelson in the *Village Voice.* A proud Baker lovingly inscribed his first copy of the album to Ruth Young, whom he had brought to the sessions.

Sensing his progress, he became more driven than ever, and filled his weeks with fifty-dollar gigs all over New York. His headquarters from 1974 through 1977 was Stryker's Pub at Eighty-sixth Street and Columbus Avenue. On Mondays and Tuesdays, anyone could walk down a few steps into this tiny saloon, long and narrow as a railroad car, and see Chet Baker for the cost of a drink. He sat, legs crossed, on a folding chair against the left wall, facing a bar and a few scattered tables. "The smaller the joint, the better—Chet loved playing to thirty people," said Bob Mover. Eyes closed, Baker rested the bell of his trumpet on his knee, as if he hadn't the strength to hold it aloft. An electric keyboard, bass, and drums were beside him. The mood was somber. "It seemed like it was always raining," said John Snyder.

To some, Baker made Stryker's feel like a dreamworld, everything slow and hazy. Bassist Jon Burr noticed how quiet the music sounded. "Instead of sending energy out to people, the band was sucking it in," he said. Few who heard it could forget Baker's version of "The Thrill Is Gone," which he counted off at a tempo so slow that the music seemed to float in space. "This is the end, so why pretend . . . ," he sang, pulling listeners into the black hole of desolation where he seemed the happiest. Then came a trumpet chorus so drawn out and full of silence that it felt as though he were groping through the dark for the next note.

Using a revolving company of musicians—alto saxophonist Mover, pianists Danko and Richie Beirach, trombonist Ed Byrne, bassists David Shapiro and Cameron Brown, drummer Jimmy Madison, baritone saxophonist Roger Rosenberg—Baker turned the club into a workshop. At a time when jazz was as loud and shrill as rock, he schooled his young sidemen in his own lyrical vision. For Mover, then in his early twenties, Baker would become an oracle on drugs, women, survival, and most of all music. "I started out reading *On the Road*," he explained, "and Chet was definitely my Dean Moriarity." Inspired by Charlie Parker and Sonny Rollins, Mover made a fiery counterpart to Baker—sometimes excessively so. "He once told me: 'You know, Bob, this is not a research la*boratory*,' " Mover said. "Like, we're playing for people. It was a good lesson, because I *was* getting self-indulgent."

Beirach, a classically schooled musician, marveled at Baker's ability to direct the band with almost no technical vocabulary. "Miles would say, 'Don't play the bottom so much,' or 'Play less notes in your voicings,' but Chet didn't know to explain those things. He'd say, 'You're playing too loud,' or 'Play smoother, less choppy.' Beyond that, he didn't think it was his place to tell you what to play. It was your offering."

The greatest lesson Baker imparted was how to listen. Unlike Stan Getz, who often stood in the wings smoking his cigarette or checking his watch while his musicians soloed, Baker shut his eyes and focused intently on his sidemen's every note. They, in turn, absorbed his Zenlike process of eliminating everything but the essential from his playing. All the while, he strove to make the most beautiful sound possible, pouring his heart into it more nakedly than he had ever done in his youth. "There wasn't a note, good or bad, that wasn't felt," said Danko.

But Baker still clung to his safe fifties formula of ballads and light bebop, and his musicians tried to bring him up to date. Danko brought him some of the prettier tunes by two stars of fusion, pianist Herbie Hancock and saxophonist Wayne Shorter, along with one of his own songs, "Tidal Breeze"; Beirach wrote him an intricate ballad, "Broken Wing." "Chet wouldn't have sought out anything on his own, because he was one of the laziest human beings in the world," said Mover. "He just wanted to dream and be left alone."

The spell wasn't all musically induced. Between sets, he and Mover drove to midtown to score pot. "To Chet, this was an adventure, like *Dragnet,*" Mover explained. "He'd be in his car. He'd say, 'I'll circle the block three times. Here's the money. Go in, you should have about two minutes of conversation, the elevator should take a minute and a half.' " At the end of the night, they made another transaction with the bartender at Stryker's. The owner, Olivia Stryker, gave him the job of handing out the musicians' salaries; on the sly, he sold coke. "He'd pay Chet and me, then we'd pay him because he was dealing the blow," recalled Mover. "We got fifty a night, and the blow was fifty a night. After a while, money stopped changing hands."

By working constantly, Baker saved enough money for a down payment on a modest house in Dobbs Ferry, a middle-class Westchester County suburb. Finally Carol had the home she had always wanted; the children happily filled it with dogs and cages of white mice. "I have to give Chet a high mark for effort at that time," Mover said. "He was trying to make his family life happen, he tried to be as straight as he could be."

Yet he spent more time at Ruth Young's apartment than he did in Dobbs Ferry, while "lying through his teeth," said Young, to both women. He kept assuring her that as soon as Carol was off methadone he would leave her, but that seemed to be taking forever. When he left town without her to play a gig, Young wrote him an emotional letter. "I feel so helpless and alone," she said. "Please, Chesney, please make the dream come true. . . . I want to share your troubles, lighten the burdens you face, help you in any way I can." Baker accepted the offer. Within a couple of years he had drained her trust fund considerably. Meanwhile, she was reminded of Carol's presence every time she opened her medicine cabinet. Inside was a bottle of methadone printed with the name Carol Baker; Baker had grabbed it by mistake one day on his way to Young's.

By 1974, the truth about his affair with Young had become too obvious for Carol to ignore. One night he brought his wife to Stryker's and told Young to come too, probably seeing this as a way to resolve a matter he lacked the nerve to tackle directly. "He said, fuck it—you wanna come, you come," Young recalled. She came.

Throughout the sets, Carol glared at her rival, who sat defiantly at a front table. When the last set ended and the club was mostly empty, Carol made her move. She lunged at Young from behind, jabbing her with a fork and shoving her into a wall as objects from the table went flying. The bartender jumped out from behind the bar to restrain Carol. Moments later she fled, with Baker trailing behind and scolding her in a limp voice: *"You hurt her!"* Carol considered it a moment of triumph, and told the story for years. But Ruth saw the incident as pathetic: "I thought, who did you do it for? Him, me, yourself? It was a very sad, ineffectual, embarrassing moment for her." Baker's pianist at the time, Hod O'Brien, took Young home and let her sleep on his couch.

From then on, it was war. Carol denounced Young as the "bitch" who had wrecked her happy home; Young thought otherwise. "I did not put a chain on the man and take him away," she said. "Nobody leaves for no reason. You can't blame everything on somebody else." Baker kept showing up on Young's doorstep complaining of Carol's harangues. One day he made the heated announcement that he had just pushed her out of the car as they drove down Central Park West. "He was gloating about it," Young said. " 'I kicked her ass out of the FUCKING car, I've had enough of her FUCKING shit'—that's how he talked." Young was shaken, having had no idea he could be so violent. Soon she discovered it firsthand. "When I told him I'd had an affair with a piano player before I met him, he belted me across the face," she said. "How dare I let anyone else touch me before him? It was the Madonna-whore syndrome. He was insanely jealous."

Petty resentments raged in him, notably the ones he shared with Gerry Mulligan. It annoyed Baker to still be tagged as Mulligan's discovery, while the saxophonist bristled every time a fan asked him: "Do you ever see Chet Baker? Think you guys'll ever get back together?" With neither man at the peak of his career, they couldn't refuse an offer, made by the producer (not the pianist who had played for him in 1957) Don Friedman, for a grand reunion concert at Carnegie Hall. Slated for Sunday, November 24, 1974, the show would also feature Stan Getz, the third titan of West Coast Jazz. Once the deal was set, John Snyder scrambled to arrange a live album on CTI.

If Baker looked like a shriveled cowboy, Mulligan, with his bushy beard and shaggy gray hair, now evoked an aged Jesus Christ. He had tried running his career with a fittingly godlike hand. On record he had teamed himself with the greatest soloists in jazz, including Getz, Ben Webster, and Johnny Hodges; in the sixties, he led his scholarly Concert Jazz Band. "I spent a lot of years building up a place for myself," he explained. "I wanted to play in orchestra halls and places that were built for music, with audiences that were nicely dressed and aware. I had no intention of playing in sewers, which is what Chet did. Anybody that hired him, he'd run off and record. No sir—not me."

Hearing what Mulligan thought of Baker, Ruth Young was furious. "It's not sewers anywhere," she argued. "It's called working for the people. It's getting an audience that wants to be there, instead of a sea of faces that you couldn't possibly know what's going on in the heads of. Gerry wanted the fabulous Hollywood version of jazz. All he did was date, consecutively, Judy Holliday, Georgia Brown, Sandy Dennis—what does that tell you?"

One thing it meant is that he had the clout to get what he wanted, and he took control of the Carnegie Hall concert. Unwilling to revive the pianoless quartet, he brought his current electric band: keyboard player Bob James, bassist Ron Carter, drummer Harvey Mason, and trombonist Ed Byrne. Baker loathed the sound—electric keyboard, he said, sounded like a "toy"—but more than that, he hated Mulligan's bossy attitude. On the afternoon of the show, Carnegie Hall turned into "the zoo of all zoos," said Young. "It was the only time I ever saw Chet nervous in all the years I knew him." Even Mulligan was jittery, and barked an order at her to get him a double Scotch.

Each of the three former boy wonders seethed like children over the attention the others were getting. "There are people who say Chet played much better when he was older," Mulligan noted years later. "I say they're crazy. His chops had gotten very weak, and everybody went out of their way to cater to him. He smothered that concert in an aura of negativity." Baker sneered at his ex-partner's jealousy, and enjoyed telling the story about the police raid on their house in 1953, when Mulligan tearfully led John O'Grady to the stash. "Chet loved to gloat about the fact that Gerry was such a pussy," Young recalled. Getz didn't seem too pleased about being third on the bill; Baker later described him as an egomaniac who "sees everything as a competition." Already signed to Columbia, Getz alone went unrecorded that night.

As the concert began, Young stood in the wings, dressed in a flamboyant leopard coat and crying because Carol—who had grown "as big as Wyoming," said Young—sat with the children in the front row. The show should have been a triumph for all three stars, but it proved something less. Mulligan and Baker's chemistry was now a distant memory. They had grown in opposite directions: Mulligan toward an ever-finer precision, Baker toward a newfound depth of feeling. "Getz and Mulligan didn't have Chet's heart, they had polish," Young thought. "Both of them were very intelligent men, but there was an emptiness in them. There wasn't a submission of themselves in their playing, a here-I-am, this-is-my-life. They withheld."

Baker didn't. At the start of "My Funny Valentine," he flubbed a phrase; it made him sound all the more vulnerable, and the solo that followed drew the warmest applause of the night. Twenty years later, Mulligan would recall Baker's performance sourly: "When he got onstage, the guys were all walking on eggshells, and he blew his ass off. He came off sounding like roses."

John S. Wilson called the show a "nostalgia parade" in the *New York Times.* Proclaiming Mulligan "a jazz virtuoso of the very first rank," he brushed off Baker as a faded Mulligan sideman who had missed reaching his potential. Baker took a further blow when CTI released a double LP of the concert. Mulligan got top billing, along with three long solo tracks; Baker had one. He would later complain that Mulligan got all the royalties. "It was *my* record company. . . . I was the one with the contract," he grumbled to writer Les Tomkins. "They release the album, and he arranges it; so, of course, the album is in his name, and I'm a sideman . . . somehow it just doesn't seem right."

It was only now dawning on Baker that for years he had sold himself cheap to the likes of Richard Carpenter, and that few people respected him. Then there was the matter of his personal reputation. Baker could never resist telling the press about his misbehavior, and most of the publicity surrounding the Carnegie Hall concert had portrayed him as a dope fiend and a jailbird. His neighbors in Dobbs Ferry were not pleased. Three months after he had moved to the suburbs, children began riding by on their bikes shouting "JUNKIE!" and pelting the house with food. They called Carol a whore, and harassed the Baker children so badly that they were afraid to go to school.

Jack Kleinsinger, a lawyer and jazz impresario who came to their aid, later recalled hearing from Carol that Baker had exaggerated the details. But to Baker, the attack was an indictment of everything wrong with America. Look what happens, he concluded, when you try to play by the rules. "The civilized world we live in is a lot of crap," he railed to Jerome Reece. "People think I'm some kind of scum, so I just gave up the whole idea."

He asked Kleinsinger, who worked as assistant attorney general of New York state, to help him get his money back on the house. Baker moved out in the dead of night to avoid attracting the neighbors' attention. Assisted by Bob Mover and trumpeter Tommy Turrentine, he packed up the wreckage of his home life. As the house emptied out, he soared on angel dust.

Homeless once more, all he wanted to do was escape. But his family needed a place to stay. He accepted an offer to move in with Artt Frank, who now lived on welfare in Maine but hoped to fly high on the wings of Chet Baker. Earlier that year, Frank had sent him a letter begging for screenplay rights to his story. He sat at the typewriter composing long tributes to Baker, planning to develop one into a book. America had done Baker wrong, Frank wrote, stressing the reverse-racism angle. His wife, Earla, fantasized about making an album with Baker. Life there, for the few weeks it lasted, proved unbearable to Baker, and he became more determined than ever to flee the country for Europe.

His hatred of America, particularly New York, was leading him to blow one chance after another. "Whenever we had a big concert, he'd find a way to fuck it up," said Mover. George Wein, president and founder of the Newport Jazz Festival, had given Baker a spot in an all-star gala, the Schlitz Salute to Jazz and the American Popular Song, to be held at Lincoln Center on July 1, 1975. Hosted by comedienne Phyllis Diller, the show would be broadcast on National Public Radio. Baker chose two Rodgers and Hart standards, "With a Song in My Heart" and "Have You Met Miss Jones?" He only half-knew the latter, and backstage he had singer Margaret Whiting coach him in the words, to little avail. Baker walked onto the stage of Philharmonic Hall carrying Mover's tattered fake book. He set it on a wobbly music stand, then put on his glasses. "Don't you think the book might be too heavy for the stand?" Mover whispered nervously. "You worry too much," answered Baker. Midway through the song, the stand tipped over, sending pages flying. Baker fumbled his way through the rest of the tune as the audience, and his musicians, watched in embarrassment. The same summer, Jack Kleinsinger presented Baker at New York University as part of his concert series, *Highlights in Jazz.* Arriving in old jeans and tattered moccasins, Baker gave an indifferent performance that disappointed everyone.

His mood brightened when a dream he had voiced to Giovanni Tommaso in 1967 suddenly came true. Alberto Alberti, an Italian jazz promoter who had booked the trumpeter in 1956, came to Manhattan and dropped by Stryker's. Alberti now worked with George Wein's company, Festival Productions. Baker asked Alberti if he could book him abroad. Within days, Baker was set to play two festivals: one in Pescara, on the Adriatic coast of Italy, the other on the French Riviera.

Leaving Carol behind with the children, Baker took Young, who looked forward to the adventure of her life. "Every young girl has to see Europe," he said, thrilling her. Carrying his trumpet case and one small bag, he arrived with Young in Pescara on July 13. If America considered him a stumblebum, Italy welcomed him as a returning hero. "He really was a star there, in a tabloid kind of way," said Harold Danko, who played for him on that trip. "The attention was very little on the music." Baker's physical decay shocked fans who remembered him as "the angel," yet it led the Italian press to romanticize him glowingly. Journalist Costanzo Costantini hailed Baker as "the Rimbaud of jazz, often defeated but every time rising . . . the sweet and fragile boy grown in the slums of New York . . . a bird whose wings are always broken, the defenseless victim of every violence in the wild city."

At Pescara, a hodgepodge of American jazz stars was thrown together for jam sessions, a sloppy format that Baker loathed. Held in an outdoor stadium, the concerts were plagued by rain and bad sound, and boos erupted. Baker was sure people were heckling him—a sign of how insecure he was—yet he emerged as the favorite, and Roberto Capasso wrote that whatever Baker lacked in technique, he made up for in "feeling and determination."

At two-thirty in the morning, Costantini spotted Baker leaving the Esplanade Hotel with Young after another jam session. In her flowing white dress, she looked to Costantini like the ghost of Chet Baker: silent and fleet of foot, floating through the night like a spirit "from the moon." He took them to an outdoor café, where, as Baker picked at his grilled ham-and-cheese sandwich and talked, his mood grew as black as the sky above. Even after the kind reception he had gotten from the press, he was depressed over his rusty playing.

But his preoccupation, in all his Italian interviews that month, was his hatred of America. "Texas, Arkansas, Arizona—the people are just stupid," he told Marco Molendini. "There's no culture. The social relationships are awful. Nobody looks you in the eye. Nobody speaks. Even in jail, nobody says a word to each other. It's hard to have friends. At night you can't go out. Everyone's afraid. Of the violence, of everything." Another journalist, Giulio Palumbo, heard all about how Chet's daughter, Melissa, had been mugged on her way to school. "A black guy held a knife to her throat and tore a watch off her wrist that I had given her for Christmas," Baker said. "It was worth four dollars. But today they go to New York to kill a man for ten dollars."

By contrast, Europe felt exhilaratingly free to him. He relished the chance to look as sloppy as he wanted, defying every American critic who had ridiculed his recent looks. He let his hair grow into what looked like a fright wig, and resisted Young's efforts to comb it for him. "I'm not up there to win any beauty contests, Ruth!" he said testily. Often he didn't bother to bathe: "This is Europe, Ruth. I don't have to take a shower, it's not that dirty over here."

On July 17, they flew to Nice for the Grande Parade du Jazz, an eleven-day festival whose starry lineup included Dizzy Gillespie, Milt Jackson, Zoot Sims, Eddie "Lockjaw" Davis, and Clark Terry. A representative of Festival Productions had promised him he could obtain methadone in Nice, as he had in Italy. But once there, Baker learned that the drug was unavailable for a hundred kilometers, and he was livid. When Bob Mover arrived on the second day, he heard about the consequences. "Oh boy, your man Chet's got problems!" said Sonny Rollins's drummer, David Lee. "He's being completely crazy. Everybody wants to kill him."

The night before, Kenny Drew had joined Baker, Sims, bassist Larry Ridley, and drummer Ray Mosca for a televised jam session, held on a mountaintop stage before thousands. As trees swayed in the summer breeze, fans awaited a freewheeling night of jazz. They saw Baker open his trumpet case and take out a pile of music. "What, are we gonna have a rehearsal?" asked Sims. "Fuck you, man!" snarled Baker. Then he glanced at Drew. "I don't wanna play with *him,*" he announced inexplicably. "Well, later for you!" said the pianist as he and Sims walked off.

That left Ridley and Mosca to accompany a strung-out Baker for several tunes, including "Stella by Starlight." Nervous and sweating, Baker tore through some of the most manic eighth-note runs he had played in years. Afterward, he left the stage and flung his horn over the edge of the mountain. Hundreds of feet below, a *gendarme* found it and carried it back up, whereupon Baker hurled it to the ground and stomped on it. In the days to come, he raged against Festival Productions for misleading him about his methadone, snarled about Zoot Sims ("He's nothing but a goddamned drunk!"), and terrorized Young. He spotted her patting Alberto Alberti's knee during lunch, and as soon as they returned to their hotel, he started screaming: "Nobody makes a fool out of me—who do you think you are, anyway? That's it, you're on the next plane out of here!" Young was petrified. "This guy was obsessed with being fucked over," she said. "He was convinced that every woman was gonna two-time him."

The next afternoon, they attended a huge party on the beach at Juan-les-Pins for the musicians and their friends. As they sipped cool drinks and clowned on the sand, Baker thought he saw her eyeing a handsome lifeguard. He slapped her across the face in full view of his peers, including Gillespie and Sims. By the next day, when he and Mover played a jam session with Sims, Davis, and pianist Gerald Wiggins, nearly everyone loathed Chet Baker. Before another huge audience, Sims called out an opening tune, Dizzy Gillespie's "Groovin' High." "I don't wanna play that," said Baker, pouting. Sims blew up. "Oh yeah? You don't wanna play that? Well, what *do* you wanna play, Chet?"

"I wanna play 'Four.' "

"You know what? We can play 'Four.' We'll play what *you* wanna play. Because you're a fucking baby, Chet. You were a fucking baby in 1955, and you're still a fucking baby. Now we'll play what the baby wants. One-two, one-two-three—"

The musicians were so stunned that no one took the first solo. As Mover jumped in, he heard Sims and Baker arguing behind him: "Yeah, well, *fuck you!*" "Fuck you, too!" Davis turned around: "Gentlemen, what is the matter? What is going on here? This is a performance!"

"Fuck it, *fuck all of you!*" shouted Baker as he stormed off, disappearing into the woods. Mover went after him. "Chet, come back!" he pleaded. "The magazines are gonna write that you stomped off the bandstand—it's not good for you to do these things!"

"Would you shut the fuck up? You worry about everything!"

Mover followed him all the way to ground level. Baker kicked him in the seat of the pants as George Wein looked on. "Now, I'll have no one here raising a hand to anyone else!" announced the impresario. "I didn't raise my hand, I raised my foot!" argued Baker.

After Mover rejoined the session, the trumpeter fired him for disloyalty. Wiggins tried to console Mover by saying that if he had smashed his sax over Baker's head, every musician at the festival would have chipped in to buy him a new one. Only Benny Carter, the veteran saxophonist and arranger, saw the real problem: Baker didn't have his medicine. "All I hear you people doing is putting this man down," he told a group of musicians. "I haven't heard anybody with any compassion at all."

Later, Baker tried to redeem himself to Young by listing all the temperamental greats he had known. "He said, 'You can't be a total asshole and play like a genius.' I said, 'No, Chet, I don't agree with you. Yes, you can. You can just be a gifted motherfucker.' "

However he behaved, Baker found complete acceptance at the Belgian home of Jacques Pelzer, where he spent the rest of the summer. Pelzer divided his time between playing alto and flute and running a pharmacy out of his house in Liège, a manufacturing town on the river Meuse, an hour from Brussels. To "Jack," as friends called him, Baker was a musical god and the guardian of life's profoundest secrets. Hoping to uncover some of them, Pelzer, then forty-nine, queried Baker in a French accent thicker than Maurice Chevalier's.

For jazz lovers in Liège, Pelzer himself was royalty, the closest they had to a homegrown Charlie Parker. Round-faced, with an Arabian skull cap pulled over his prematurely bald head, Pelzer reigned over a small group of Belgian musicians—notably Bobby Jaspar and René Thomas, by then deceased, and Benoît Quersin—whose reputations had spread throughout Europe. But Pelzer was tied to Liège on account of the pharmacy, which he had reluctantly inherited from his father. "All the medicine was in a kind of disaster," said his son-in-law, pianist Michel Graillier. "He was a confused person." With his time for music limited, Pelzer's playing lost some of its youthful polish. But, as Giovanni Tommaso found, "you could always play with Jack, even if it was not the greatest. Because he had feeling. He knew the jazz language."

His home was his sanctuary: a two-story town house in Thier-a-Liège, a charming hilltop neighborhood lined with shops and trees. Behind a nondescript redbrick façade, Pelzer played host to a parade of jazz giants, including Dexter Gordon, Stan Getz, and Elvin Jones. They relaxed in the rear parlor amid shelves full of old bebop records, or played Ping-Pong in a garden perfumed by magnolia trees. The kindly Pelzer gave guests free run of Pharmacie du Thier, with its rows of amber bottles labeled in big letters. The house specialty was his homemade codeine syrup, a sweet-tasting brew invented by his father. But some people, including Young, preferred the morphine suppositories. "Oh, God, they were to die for!" she said.

Baker kept a key to the house, which became his refuge for the rest of his life. "When he was there, it was his place," said bassist Jean-Louis Rassinfosse. "He had the best room to sleep in. They cooked what he wanted. Everything revolved around him." It seemed a jazzman's paradise, yet by the time of her last visit in 1982, Young would dub it the House of Death. "The stuff that went on in there—forget *Dynasty,*" she said. "It was more like *Die Nasty.* Live through this and you'll get a medal."

Pelzer looked around and saw ghosts. His wife, Andrée, a beautiful young pharmacist who played classical piano, had taken her life in 1961 following a decade-long heroin habit. A few years earlier, the son born to her and Pelzer had died in infancy. Heroin had claimed Pelzer's two best friends, Jaspar and Thomas, whose music and laughter had resounded through his house since the fifties. No wonder that, for all Pelzer's fatherly bonhomie, Bob Mover considered him one of the saddest men he had ever met. "These people all had a trail of despair running through them," he said. Like Baker, they smothered their pain in dope and jazz. "Jack was always stoned out of his mind," said Young. "If he just went to the store for a roll of salami, he'd come back through the pharmacy and take a whiff from one of those bottles, like, five times an hour." Sometimes, she recalled, he fixed himself a codeine cocktail in the morning and sipped it all day.

Along came Chet Baker in 1975, with his power to weave beauty out of sheer hopelessness. For all the conflicted creative souls around him, Baker offered, by example, a promise of redemption: if he could turn chaos into poetry, maybe the alchemy would rub off on them.

Few found him more fascinating than Pelzer's daughter, Micheline. Then twenty-five, she had never forgotten sitting on Baker's knee at age five, nor the sight of him shooting up in the bathroom. When Baker came to Belgium in 1963, the pubescent Micheline was even more enticed by the handsome trumpeter. "He was very sweet, but he had a big voice, and he could be really mean," she said. "I was scared of him. Even if I couldn't understand English, I could feel the vibrations."

Micheline was a warmhearted party girl with a gentle spirit; her round face, framed by dark, straight hair parted in the middle, made her look "like a Belgian Janis Joplin" to Young. But Micheline had inherited her father's big, sad eyes; hers, like his, had seen too much. She recalled a visit Stan Getz made to the house in the midsixties. Late at night, after jamming with Getz, Pelzer had gone to bed, leaving his houseguest alone with Micheline. He awoke minutes later to find his daughter staring down at him. "Daddy," she said, "your friend is turning blue."

Her mother had died when Micheline was eleven, under ambiguous circumstances. According to Micheline, Pelzer had taken a mistress, and the woman had vengefully confronted his wife by phone. Soon after that Andrée committed suicide. "I think she took some caps of mercury, or something very heavy," said Micheline. "But I'm not sure. It was too hard to talk about that with Jack. I didn't ask. I didn't want to know." Bob Mover recalled Pelzer's telling him that his wife had died of a brain hemorrhage related to her habit.

Whatever the case, Andrée's death had left Pelzer with overwhelming guilt. Micheline was so traumatized that she barely spoke for two years. Then, in 1965, she heard John Coltrane play "My Favorite Things" on a rainy night at Comblain-la-Tour. "I just stood in front of the stage and boom, I had goosebumps, like a revelation," she explained. With that, jazz became her reason for living. She learned to play drums so well that Wayne

Shorter, the famous American saxophonist, invited her in 1969 to come to New York and appear on his next album, *Moto Grosso Feio,* alongside the fusion star, pianist Chick Corea. Talented though she was, she would play only sporadically in years to come.

In 1972, she moved in with Michel Graillier, a Frenchman who would become one of Baker's favorite pianists. Graillier was depressive and prone to drink, while Micheline, who had vowed never to touch heroin, developed a habit. But by the time Baker came to Liège in July 1975, she was heroin-free and trying to stay that way. In her father's house, where she spent much of her time, sobriety wasn't easy. Bob Mover, who had reconciled with Baker after the Nice fiasco, arrived first. "While you were away," he told Baker, "I got into this stuff, morphine."

So did Young, although no drug could quell her insecurity. The Pelzers took to her instantly—"She was smart and hip, so we dug her," said Micheline—but she frequently hid in the upstairs bedroom. With or without her, the others spent hours around the piano. In rare moments of levity, Baker amused everyone by imitating tenor Mario Lanza's braying rendition of his schmaltzy, pseudo-operatic showpiece "Be My Love." "There was a charming person there too—less than the other side of him, but it did appear, and that's why we forgave him," said Young. "When he was the best part of himself, it was impossible to hold anything against the guy."

But when Mover started questioning him privately about his life, the mood turned grim. "I was like you," said Baker. "I had hope once." Why, asked Mover, did he use drugs?

"Because things are fucked up."

"To him," Mover observed, "what could go wrong would go wrong, people were not worth trusting." Baker had a seething animosity for many people from his past. He called Gerry Mulligan a "motherfucker." Lee Konitz, who had fumed at him for botching a potential duo tour, got the nickname "fuck-face." The trumpeter was sure that Stan Getz, among others, was out to get him.

When he played a festival that summer in Laren, Holland, Baker was once again ready to snap. A member of his entourage cornered singer Sheila Jordan, who was also on the bill, and asked desperately if she had something—anything—to "medicate" Baker. All she could offer was a Valium. Baker managed to give a compelling performance, and in *Down Beat,* Dan Morgenstern praised him for "the emotional quality that we associate with the late Billie Holiday." Mover wanted that feeling too, and thought morphine was the key. Playing the wise father, Baker warned him not to exceed a modest dose of fifteen milligrams per day. Mover ignored him, doubling then tripling his intake. "All of a sudden the world was quiet," he said. "I understood what Bird was hearing, I understood Chet's concentration on the bandstand." Drifting above reality, he found he could listen to Thelonious Monk's groundbreaking foray into the avant-garde, *Brilliant Corners,* with complete understanding.

Soon he began waking up sick to his stomach. "See?" said Baker. "What did I tell you? Now you have a habit." He explained that Mover could either quit that day or get high again. Mover chose the latter. "You feel good now, don't you?" said Baker. "Well, enjoy it, because you know what's gonna happen? Pretty soon all you're gonna feel is normal. You'll run around and spend all your money and time to feel normal. Is it worth it to you? It's not gonna help you play, man."

The warning cut through Mover's fog, and for the next two weeks he lay in the basement kicking. As a reward, Baker introduced him to Florence Thomas, the beautiful daughter of René Thomas. She and Mover embarked on an idyllic romance. "Chet was so happy," said Mover. "He had actually done something good." Baker even slipped him some cash to spend on his new love.

Back in the States, Mover found an apartment for himself and Florence in Greenwich Village. Baker's children helped him paint it. As he stood around watching his protégé's love nest unfold, the trumpeter grew nostalgic. "I did this once, I brought a girl over from Europe," he reflected.

"Oh, really?" said Mover. "What happened?"

"I made her get out of the car on the highway at three o'clock in the morning. I told her to get the fuck out of my life."

Mover's spirits sank. "I thought for once he was gonna be optimistic and bright. I thought, give me something beautiful, like the way you play! No, it's not the way you play. It's fucking ugly. That was the paradox."

15

Baker still hoped he could lead a contented life without heroin. But as he raced back and forth between Europe and America with no real home, and with wife, girlfriend, children, friends, and hangers-on all tugging at him, he was on shaky ground. Guilty over his domestic obligations, he moved his family into Ruppert Towers, a high-rise on Third Avenue and Ninetieth Street. With its parquet floors, modern kitchen, and several rooms, the apartment was so expensive that much of the time they couldn't afford a phone. Renting such a place "was some kind of blind positive thinking on Chet's part," Harold Danko said.

Yet Baker still spent most of his time with Young, and Carol was growing angrier. Her ire was confirmed by Kay Norton, the Bakers' neighbor. Norton ran the jazz division of United Artists Records, a company founded by Young's father. Not knowing at first that she lived directly above Chet Baker, Norton was mystified by the trumpet playing she heard through her bathroom vents, along with the rantings of a woman she dubbed the Screaming Meemie.

The children's lives were in chaos. By now all three had been shuttled from school to school, leaving gaps in their education. Their father's neglect stung, but still they seemed to adore him. John Snyder recalled Dean, in his early teens, as a "sweet, quiet kid" with his father's melancholy air. Dean escaped into his own small universe, breeding tropical fish, riding his bike, and playing with his ham radio. Trying to emulate his dad, he began studying fluegelhorn at school. He learned a few songs, but the process ended abruptly. "Dad lost his horn somewhere and borrowed mine," Dean said. "That was the last I ever saw it."

Most American critics felt that Baker was playing with just a shadow of his former brilliance. The opinion made him seethe. He was ashamed to think of all the polls he had won over such virtuoso trumpeters as Kenny Dorham; only now, he felt, had he really mastered his horn. Yet he kept embarassing himself in public. On August 27, 1975, CTI showcased some of its artists in a Central Park concert, for an audience of thousands who wanted to party. The funk-jazz guitarist and singer George Benson worked them up, and Baker followed. For his second song, he counted off a snail-like tempo and started murmuring *"My . . . funny . . . valentine . . ."* as if it were midnight at Stryker's. "People started booing us, and hissing," said Bob Mover. "I believe I saw a few things hurled at the stage." The band left it in humiliation.

Yearning to stay on the run, Baker accepted anyone's offer to find him work, preferably far away in Europe. He never hesitated to sign multiple "exclusive" deals with managers and agents; it was hard to sue him for breach of contract, because once they'd tracked him down, he was gone. Wim Wigt, a powerful Dutch agent, knew better than to try to bind him to a written agreement. A cool, calculating businessman with a wide roster of American jazz stars—Dexter Gordon, Ben Webster, Art Blakey, Charles Mingus, Dizzy Gillespie—and the best connections in Europe, Wigt knew Baker needed the work, and kept him employed almost nonstop in the eighties.

For now, though, Wigt focused on getting him back to Germany, where lucrative opportunities abounded. Baker was still banned from the country, but somehow, in March 1976, he was booked there anyway. German police promptly arrested him in the Bavarian town of Burghausen. While their heads were turned, the trumpeter swallowed a large chunk of hash hidden in his trumpet case. He was jailed for the night. When Danko visited his cell with the bail, Baker stared out with glassy eyes and a little smile. "Everything's *okaaaay,* Harold!" he drawled. "See you tomorrow!"

He spent the summer with Young in a warmer place: the Music Inn, a jazz club that served as the Roman headquarters of Bill Evans, Johnny Griffin, Art Farmer, and Baker, among other top musicians. A subterranean cave near the Tiber River and the Vatican, the club evoked all of Rome's ancient charm, and Baker played there regularly until the year he died. He would carry his horn through the rotting wooden doorway at Largo dei Fiorentini 3 and descend a flight of stone steps, humid air engulfing him. There in the bowels of the city was a cavern of stone whose arched passageways, candle sconces, and concrete pews suggested an early Christian church.

The Music Inn was owned by Pepito Pignatelli d'Aragona Cortez, a prince from one of the noblest families in Europe. Pignatelli, whose ancestry included at least one pope, was an unrepentant black sheep—a hard-drinking, pot-smoking, womanizing, lovable smart aleck who resembled Humphrey Bogart. His playboy father had blown the family fortune early on, but Pignatelli didn't seem to care. He loved playing the drums and living a "crazy life," as his friend Giovanni Tommaso said. The prince's aunt controlled some inheritance money due him, and when she told him he had to start behaving himself first—"especially give up playing the drums, and the dangerous jazz music," explained Tommaso—he told her to go to hell.

Even after he tossed away his silver spoon, Pignatelli's pedigree gave him entrée all over Italy. Years before *La dolce vita,* he lived like a Mastroianni-type dandy, romping through Rome with a stunning Swedish model and snorting coke. In the early fifties, when he was about nineteen, he was thrown in jail on a drug charge—an outrageous scandal at a time when princes were considered as sacred as bishops and cardinals.

In years to come, he would try various schemes to make money, even becoming a chicken-broth salesman. All he really wanted to do was play the drums, but musicians cringed at his wooden timekeeping, and hardly anyone would hire him. So in 1973, with financial help from Tommaso, Amedeo Tommasi, and other friends, he opened the Music Inn. There he could sit in with some of the greatest stars in jazz, who tolerated it out of their fondness for him.

Pignatelli was almost as inept at business as he was at drumming, but his wife, Julia (known as Picchi), a lovely, soft-spoken brunette who ran the club with him, did her best to prevent disaster. The couple adored Baker and Young, and let them manage the club for the whole summer of 1976. Young greeted people at the door in a sixties Italian movie-star look, with big dark glasses and long straightened hair tumbling down her shoulders. She collected the admission fee in lire, which she couldn't count properly, and stood behind the bar with no ability to bartend. "It was like a botched bank robbery," she said. "But it was so much fun—we had a ball that summer." Baker used Hal Galper on piano, along with an Italian bassist and Pignatelli on drums. He soon fired the owner, then the bassist. That left him and Galper. "I thought, try and fire me—I'm your band!" Galper said.

Night after night Baker recorded his shows, then studied the music in his car or hotel room, deciding what had gone right or wrong. He still rarely practiced; that process took place in his head and in performance. "Eighty percent of the time he made the shit happen," said Bob Mover. "People may amplify the stories of when he was pathetic on a certain night, but you try working as much as he did." On November 5, 1976, Baker played a concert in Bordeaux, France, with Jacques Pelzer, pianist Michel Herr, conga player Alex Serra, and Jean-Louis Rassinfosse, a hulking Belgian bassist with a handlebar mustache and a dark, beefy tone. "It was amazing to see how fast Chet could set an atmosphere," said Rassinfosse. "He just sat in a chair, and there it was."

Baker wrapped himself in a cocoon onstage: eyes closed, head and shoulders curled in, utterly withdrawn from the audience, whom he barely acknowledged. Only the most pained and fleeting smile ever crossed his lips as he visited some hazy inner place. Having regained the mastery lost with his teeth, he had taken a new leap forward. For a man who smoked heavily, he could spin out the softest threads of melody with uncanny control.

As always, he knew that less was more. "He used space in a great way," said pianist Phil Markowitz, who joined him in the late seventies. "In a piece by Mozart, if you take out one note, it will destroy the line. Same thing with Chet. There was such a conciseness and clarity to what he played." More important, said Rassinfosse, "he showed me what music is all about—to express emotion." The Europeans saw Baker as a wise old poet, reflecting on life through his horn. Basking in their adoration, he saw less reason than ever to go home.

Whenever he did, he faced the cold reality of the bottom line. Despite his recent flurry of publicity, Baker's U.S. record sales remained poor, and CTI had lost interest in him. The label itself was in trouble. Owner Creed Taylor's lavish overbudgeting—huge orchestras, costly overdub sessions—was catching up with him as fusion faded in popularity, replaced by disco. Truckloads of overpressed CTI albums, including Baker's, began to fill dime-store cutout bins. John Snyder had left the company in 1975 to start his first big producing job at Horizon, the new jazz division of a major label, A&M. He rushed to record his old heroes, including Paul Desmond, guitarist Jim Hall, Ornette Coleman, and the Thad Jones–Mel Lewis band. But when he asked A&M's presidents, Herb Alpert and Jerry Moss, for permission to sign Baker, they had an allergic response: "Jerry said, 'He's old hat.' Even Herb, who loved Chet, thought, what can you do with him?"

They gave in on the condition that Snyder "do something commercial." Thus began what would be Chet Baker's last big chance to make good in the American record market. Snyder tried to retain at least half of his integrity by planning a double album; one disk would be fusion and funk, the other straight-ahead jazz. Arranger Don Sebesky was hired to make Baker sound current. He set the trumpeter in a jungle of Moog-synthesized bass, electric piano, and funk rhythms, with strings to be tacked on later. The band included such fusion hotshots as guitarist John Scofield, saxophonist Michael Brecker, flutist Hubert Laws, and Tony Williams, whose mentor, Miles Davis, called him "one of the baddest motherfuckers who had ever played a set of drums."

They recorded in Manhattan for three days in February 1977. At a time when young players were becoming as concerned with business as they were with music, record dates weren't so casual anymore, and Snyder felt a machinelike chill at Baker's sessions. "There weren't a lot of good times, slapping on the back, telling stories," he said. "It was kind of like, everybody in their own world." Only the rhythm section recorded "live," with everyone present at once; the trimmings were added piecemeal—an increasingly common practice that yielded a "perfect" but often sterile product. "It was a matter of paint-by-numbers," said Snyder. "Everybody had their parts. They just had to play what was written."

Into this scene of slick young "cats" came Baker, forty-seven and complaining about his dentures. But when the tape rolled, his sidemen were astounded at how quickly he picked up the bluntness of jazz-rock. For a funk treatment of Cole Porter's "Love for Sale," with a synthesized bass line and a backbeat, he threw aside his long-lined gracefulness and played in hard, percussive bursts. In Sebesky's "El Morro," a pseudo-Spanish original that sounded like the score of a Hollywood bullfighting epic, Baker dueled with Laws and Brecker, then tore through several solo choruses. "It's the most shockingly modern thing Chet's ever done," exclaimed Richie Beirach, another band member. "He plays the most intense, burning solo. It sounds like Miles! It's an indication of what Chet could have done."

Yet Beirach sensed how uneasy Baker felt. "He was most at home playing music that touched him," the pianist said. One tune did: "You Can't Go Home Again," a piercingly sad ballad that Sebesky had adapted from Rachmaninoff's Symphony No. 2 and named after a Thomas Wolfe novel. He picked that title with Baker in mind—"He was trying to come home again," Sebesky said.

At Baker's side for that song, along with several standards, was Paul Desmond, his champion from the Presidio days. Now fifty-two, the saxophonist had contracted terminal lung cancer after decades of smoking. Bald and gray, he shuffled around the studio, a drink in his hand and a Pall Mall hanging from his mouth. His cool horn lines, though still lovely, had grown frail, and it shook Baker to see Desmond reduced to a shell of his youthful self, just as Baker himself was. Desmond never recorded again, and would die three months later. "Paul had just about given up," Sebesky said. "He only had about three takes in him. And at the end he said, 'I've got no more.' " Standing at the microphone together, Baker and Desmond made a poignant duo: two middle-aged friends who looked like old men, guiding each other through Sebesky's elegy for lost youth.

Hearing the tapes, Herb Alpert vetoed Snyder's plan for a double album, ordering him to produce one LP of the flashier tracks. Entitled *You Can't Go Home Again,* it hit stores in the fall of 1977, when Baker was in Europe. He and Young heard it for the first time on the car cassette player. "We looked at each other and said, 'What happened?' " she said. The thick overdubbing of strings and percussion and the exaggerated presence of Ron Carter's thumping bass disgusted Baker, who had liked the music before all this "sweetening."

"All of a sudden a big label was telling Chet what to do," said Bob Mover. "Even with management and promotion, there was something in him that rebelled against that, that wanted to be the maverick outside the system, making music on the fringe and playing in that idealized romantic way."

Reviewers took the record seriously, though. "*You Can't Go Home Again* indicates that [Chet] has come a long way," wrote *Playboy.* "The arrangements by Don Sebesky help considerably; they're both intelligent and exciting. . . . [Baker's] tone, the only reservation we ever had about his playing, has put on weight. We like it—and the album—very much." But *You Can't Go Home Again* sold no better than his other recent records, and Alpert, who had dictated its commercial tone, dropped Baker, then fired Snyder. The small-group tracks would go unheard until the late eighties, when A&M issued them after Baker's death.

Snyder went on to pursue his real dream, founding a small but serious jazz label, Artists House. Hoping to right some of the wrongs committed against his idols, Snyder planned to pay them generously, and in some cases let them own their master tapes. But the junkies on his roster drained his resources.

He pinned down Baker for only one LP: *Once Upon a Summertime,* a straight-ahead quintet date. The producer spent the rest of his time trying to help Baker's family, who were in desperate straits. Dean seemed totally lost, and Snyder hired him to run errands. When the young man expressed interest in chess, one of his father's favorite games, Snyder offered his own set as a gift. He also began corresponding with Melissa, who seemed to need a friend. Her poems and letters broke his heart; like the rest of the family, she lived for the moment her father would come home to stay. "She was such a messed-up little girl," said Snyder. "Chet had hurt them all so badly, not paying them any attention. He was never going to be what they wanted him to be. And they didn't know that."

In an effort to befriend Carol, Snyder gave her numerous advances for albums her husband would never make. She in turn confided her frustrations to him. "I think she felt Chet was her only hope," he said. "I guess the option would have been to go out and get a job, get an education, get a life. Or take Chet to court. But how could you expect her to metamorphose into some rational being? Were she that, she wouldn't have gotten herself into this in the first place."

Baker was happy to let Snyder deal with his family problems, but now he faced a familiar one that the producer couldn't solve: paying the rent. The phone and gas had been cut off at Ruppert Towers, and by the summer of 1977 the family was homeless again. Eager to leave New York for good, Baker opted to move them to Belgium. Arriving with them in September, he thought he could put the kids in an American school in Brussels. Once he heard the price of tuition, he abandoned the idea and installed them at Jacques Pelzer's house instead.

But first, Pelzer had to clear out his other houseguest, Ruth Young, who was awaiting Baker. Off she went to stay with Lou McConnell, a young Belgian-American tenor player, while Baker got his family settled at Pelzer's. He seemed acutely uncomfortable with Carol. "I think she could never take the fact that he didn't want to be with her anymore," said Micheline. Seated in the parlor, Carol lost herself in reveries of the early sixties, when she and Baker seemed glowingly in love. "Oh, Chet, do you remember on the beach, when we . . . ," she asked. "Yes, Carol," he said quietly. "Yes. I remember."

Whenever he wasn't around, recalled Micheline, Carol turned angry. On October 7, after he had left her there and taken Young back to America, Carol wrote him a letter complaining of how unwelcome she felt in the house, and how bored. She begged him to call, promising to forgive all his deceptions if he would only come back to her. He didn't, and with nowhere else to go, she took the children to England.

Baker spoke casually about the situation to Paul Fisher, a Toronto DJ. New York was just too dangerous a place to raise kids, he explained, but he didn't know where else to put them. "It'd be all right if they could stay in the building all the time, but they have to go on the street, and they have to go to school. . . . So I sent 'em to Europe, but I think I'm probably gonna have to bring 'em back and maybe send 'em to Oklahoma, where I grew up."

Poorly though it sold, his A&M album brought him work all over the States. That fall through the spring of 1978, Baker toured North America with another group of musicians in their twenties. Pianist Phil Markowitz was one of the "new breed of studious and together cat," according to *Melody Maker;* Jon Burr, a baby-faced bass player from Long Island, was praised in the *San Francisco Chronicle* for his "exceptionally beautiful tone." Jeff Brillinger, Horace Silver's former drummer, impressed Jean-Louis Rassinfosse as "fantastic, because he could give a lot of creation and energy with low volume. And that was perfect for Chet." Baritone saxophonist Roger Rosenberg added an "appealing and welcome sound," wrote the *New York Post.*

On that tour Baker did little to promote *You Can't Go Home Again,* an album he basically loathed. Instead, he reverted to the familiar: "If You Could See Me Now," "Old Devil Moon." The band played a spotty itinerary of clubs—the Lighthouse, the Village Vanguard, Blues Alley in Washington, D.C. Although *Billboard* called the Lighthouse crowd "anxious and electrified," Baker's group also "played places that were almost empty," Rosenberg said. "I didn't feel like we were on the cutting edge of anything."

When the trumpeter played Baker's Keyboard Lounge in Detroit, he and Young looked forward to seeing Halema's friend Alice, an adorable pothead who called herself Alicia Sinatra in honor of her idol. She too fancied herself a rebel, and the couple loved hearing her tell of her recent stint of jury duty, during which she slipped LSD into the water cooler. In a letter, Alicia mentioned that Halema had come for a visit with Chesney Aftab, who was nineteen and living outside Chicago with his grandmother. "He's over *6 ft.* and a nice (good looking) kid," Alicia reported. According to Halema, the young man had an even lovelier singing voice than his father, but he never put it to much use. Being mentally challenged, he remained introverted and unfocused, a loner who related best to his dogs. He would drift from place to place, hitchhiking and repeatedly seeking out his father, who was seldom home. "Chet described that kid with the most sincere emotion and approval," Young said. "I think he felt that of all the kids he fathered, this is the boy he related to—the one who had the difficulty, who was different."

That winter, with Young in New York, Baker went to San Francisco to play a new club, Keystone Korner. This was his first trip to the city since the early seventies. In the opening-night audience was Diane Vavra, whom he hadn't seen in more than four years. She and Baker approached each other shyly before the first set. They tried to play it cool, but the spark was still there. Vavra found herself gazing at him in enchantment, as if the broken rib and cruel words had never happened.

At the end of the night, they drove back to her home in Los Gatos. Vavra was thrilled. But her spirits sank the next day as she took him back to San Francisco, where Carol, now home from England, was planning to meet him. That didn't stop Vavra from returning to Keystone Korner on two other nights, and the ex-lovers planned one more tryst. The appointed time came and went. Vavra waited for hours, unwilling to believe Baker had stood her up. Alone, she ended up throwing a glass at the wall and sobbing.

Ruth Young had never stopped yearning for the day she and Baker could live together, and finally it came. By the spring of 1978, Carol and the children were living in an apartment in Flushing, Queens, outside Manhattan. According to Baker, she was drug-free at last. "Chet felt that now that she was on her feet he could go," recalled Young. In one suitcase he took the few possessions he cared about—old pictures, his *Down Beat* award plaques—and moved into Young's new brownstone apartment at Seventy-first Street off Central Park West. A long, narrow studio with a sleeping loft, it was cluttered with LPs, a baby grand piano, keepsakes galore, and lots of Chet Baker memorabilia. Young had covered one wall with a huge collage of Baker photos and concert posters. She hung them around a foot-long, Shirley Temple–style baby portrait of herself, with a cardboard cutout of blood-red lips underneath.

Even this relative freedom did little to ease Baker's Jekyll-and-Hyde tendencies. One day, Young heard muttering coming from the bedroom and went to investigate. There lay Baker, cursing angrily in his sleep: *"Motherfucker! Cocksucker!"* If he couldn't hide his hostility, he did a fair job of concealing his marital status. As Ruth's domestic partner, he hardly ever mentioned his legal wife to musicians or acquaintances; mail came to Seventy-first Street addressed to Chet and Ruth Baker. The children left Carol's apartment to live there too, and soon the thirty-six-by-fifteen-foot studio housed two adults, three youngsters, two cats, a dog, and a cageful of birds.

Father and children were together again, but in many ways Dean, Paul, and Melissa were strangers to him, and he faltered in his attempts to guide or even talk to them. He tried encouraging the shy Dean, sometimes giving him a little hug, but his rage was never far below the surface. "Those kids were scared shitless of him," observed Young. "And they had every reason to be. This was not a family."

A pattern of abuse that had begun with Chesney Sr.'s stepfather had been passed down another generation. Young remembered hearing Paul confide: "My father's been pounding on me for years." Now thirteen, Paul had grown into a handsome young man, with Carol's dark hair and a face as sweet as his father's had once been. But Young saw him as the most tormented of the children. "He was nowhere, he didn't know what the hell life was about," she said. "He just wanted things to be normal." She helped him find a job in a supermarket, and arranged for her dentist to fix his teeth, which badly needed repair.

Young also befriended Melissa, who at twelve was a portrait of innocence, her long, straight hair framing a pretty face that smiled trustingly. The two spent hours playing cards and sharing girl talk. Besides writing poems, Melissa loved to draw, and in one sketch she placed the words "Chet-n-Roofie 4 ever" inside a big heart surrounded by smaller hearts and a sunburst. In another, she wrote "Ruth Young—World's Nicest Person" in triangular form.

Despite these hopeful images, Young believed that all the children had inherited their father's anger. She remembered Dean smashing his bicycle helmet aggressively on the piano as he came in, while Melissa broke things in the apartment—not by accident, Young suspected. When Baker described his children as "very much like me—inside and out," Young knew what he meant.

Nothing could have struck such fear in his heart as the thought of a new child, as she learned when she told him she was pregnant. After a frozen pause, he gave an equally cold response. "I'll help you as much as I can," he said. "OK, thanks," said Young. "I'm glad I asked." She scheduled an abortion. "Nail him with a kid—anybody could have figured out his stance on that," she noted. It wasn't her last pregnancy, though. "The second time was forced by him. He knew I did not have any protection, and I was practically raped. That meant, 'I just have to have some, I don't give a shit.' Lovely. And I paid the price for that."

Once Baker went back on the road, he lost contact with the kids, who returned to their mother. His letters to Carol were mostly businesslike; sometimes he included token sums of money, but more often he made excuses for sending none. In one scrawled note, he explained how busy he would be in Europe until well into the coming year. Maybe then he could afford to support her and the kids a little better. Hug Dean for him, he wrote.

In truth, his income was still low, forcing him to resume his custom of hiring cheap local players from town to town. The music suffered. "That's the difference between Chet and Miles," said Richie Beirach. "Chet couldn't see far enough to realize that the quality of the sidemen makes all the difference." Yet he had no patience for their shortcomings. "If there were any musical problems," recalled Jeff Brillinger, "he could get paranoid very easily and think that guys were trying to mess him up, and he'd explode." As another European tour approached, Harold Danko couldn't face the prospect of more chaos. Gigs were getting canceled at the last minute; the repertoire was stagnating; and with Baker using bigger-name pianists on most of his albums, Danko knew the job wasn't advancing his career. He accepted an offer to join the Grammy-winning Thad Jones–Mel Lewis big band. At the end of his last night, Baker bid him a frosty goodbye: "Well, good luck."

Roger Rosenberg left too, appalled at Baker's irresponsibility toward his children and frightened by his outbursts. Late one night in New York, the trumpeter drove him home after a gig. When another driver sideswiped them on the West Side Highway, Baker began chasing the car madly through the menacing streets of Spanish Harlem. Rosenberg stared at his crazed employer in disbelief. "We're gonna get killed," he said. Somehow they escaped harm, but Young, whose worst moments of terror with Baker were still to come, knew her lover was a potential maniac. "The guy could kill anybody," she said. "He had that anger in him."

In the fall of 1978, he was pleased to gain readmission to Germany, thanks to the yearlong efforts of John Snyder and Erich Kremer, a German lawyer and the father of Stefan Kremer, a young drummer who had played with Baker. They had managed to convince the authorities that Baker was drug-free and an asset to the country. Further help came from Gabrielle (Gaby) Kleinschmidt, a German agent who had met Baker through Snyder. Eager to book him, Kleinschmidt allowed her name to be listed along with his at every German border, thereby sharing responsibility should he be nabbed for drugs.

Immediately she arranged a long tour of every club that would have him. On November 1, Baker entered Germany with Phil Markowitz, Jeff Brillinger, and bassist Scott Lee. Bob Mover, who joined them on certain dates, found the tour numbingly disorganized—"Austria Monday, Switzerland Tuesday, Wednesday back to Austria, twenty-five kilometers from where we were the first day." He and Baker snorted coke to stay awake. For Baker, though, work itself was the drug; he had to keep moving, far from responsibility and perhaps, Young supposed, from guilt over the people he had hurt. "I think he cared, but not enough," she said. "I think it was just easier to keep drowning in a sea of oblivion than to face caring, because if you cared, you had to do something." She asked him about the friends he had left behind. "What do you mean, my friends?" he said. "I don't have any friends. You're my only friend." His musician pals from the fifties had let him down, he said—"They were all behind me until I made it"—and now they scorned him for his choices. "A friend is someone who knows everything about you, good and bad, and yet doesn't judge or condemn you," he declared.

Young was exasperated. "The word 'friend' to him meant patsy—somebody who could take his shit. How could he have a friend, with all he demanded?"

Baker continued to accept help from anyone who promised it, and that year he signed an American management deal with James Felds, a used-car salesman. But that didn't stop him from booking himself wherever possible, and his itinerary was a shambles. Sometimes he scheduled two jobs on the same day, or hired two pianists and no drummer.

Nobody involved could forget a concert that Rita Amaducci, his Italian agent, had booked for him outside the Castel St. Angelo, a monument near the Vatican. Before the date, Baker had boldly decided to quit methadone—an attempt, maybe, to prove he was in complete control. Accompanied by Jacques and Micheline Pelzer, Young, and Michel Graillier, he drove from Liége to Rome in the pharmacist's old Peugeot. The trip felt like a roller-coaster ride as a strung-out Baker kept gunning the accelerator. Worried about his car, Pelzer made a remark from the backseat. Eyes wild, Baker yelled: *"You wanna drive the car instead of me? Fuck you!"* Slamming on the brake in Tuscany, he stormed out and vanished, barefoot, into the wilderness. Ruth and Micheline spent the next two hours trudging through the woods, calling "CHETTIE! CHETTIE!" With Baker nowhere in sight, they returned to the car. Now late for the concert, Pelzer sped faster than Baker had, and when they reached the outdoor stage, where hundreds had gathered, the Peugeot squealed to a halt, then burst into flames. Everyone leapt out. *"Get the trumpet!"* shrieked Micheline as her father ran around yelling "AGUA, AGUA!" "That's how the concert starts," Micheline remembered.

No piano had been provided for Graillier, so the three other musicians—

saxophonist Gianni Basso, bassist Lucio Terzano, and drummer Giancarlo Pillot—played without him. Afterward, everyone headed to the Anglo-Americano, Baker's favorite Rome hotel. Michel and Micheline found him there, lying in his bed. He had walked through the woods for a few minutes, then hopped a train to Rome, arriving before they did. He demanded to see the rest of the band. "Why did you play without my permission?" he asked them. "You're fired!"

Lacking his methadone, Baker was nearly crazed. In one northern Italian town, he antagonized so many taxi drivers outside the train station that he and the band had to walk to the concert, wheeling instrument cases over cobblestone streets. On a seemingly endless drive through the French Riviera, he refused to let Young make a rest stop. As she squirmed in her seat, Baker told her to "squat down there and do what you gotta do." Having no choice, she took a soft-drink cup and filled it up, then flung it out the window. A fierce wind blew the contents into the backseat, dousing the face of Jacques Pelzer, who sat there wearing headphones, "rolling one of those cone-shaped jumbo hash cigarettes," Young recalled. "He was so fucking stoned, he didn't bat an eye. He just said, 'Oh, a little rain here? That's all right, it rains all the time in fucking Belgium, man.' "

Baker's own mellowness seemed all but gone. As he approached forty-nine, fears of aging and death consumed him. He could still do fifty push-ups as easily as he had in the army, and his upper torso reminded Young of Michelangelo's *David.* But he was haunted by memories of his father's fatal heart attack at sixty-one, and when Jack Freeman, his shoplifter friend from Queens, died prematurely of drink- and drug-induced heart complications, Baker was sure he was the next to go. His paranoia doubled when he began feeling pains in his abdomen. He decided his Fasteeth denture glue was collecting in his colon and poisoning him. "That shit could kill me, Ruth!" he hissed—a worry he had never expressed over heroin. Baker started giving himself enemas, and when they didn't work, he poked his abdomen with his fingers. His self-diagnosis: stomach cancer.

Baker wrote a dramatic farewell letter in Milan, aimed to all who knew him. Death didn't scare him, he declared. He went on to attack his enemies, notably Richard Carpenter, and to praise John Snyder as a hero. Through his music, Baker concluded, he had given the world all he could.

Soon thereafter, on a train headed from Norway to Germany, he rolled onto the floor in agony. As a snowstorm raged, the conductor had to stop the train and call an ambulance. At the hospital he was diagnosed with kidney stones. "No wonder," he grumbled later to Young. "All that greasy fucking meat and potatoes that Carol always put on the plate. Never a fucking vegetable, never a fucking piece of fruit." Once the stones had passed, he received a clean bill of health—one confirmed in Italy by Dr. Lippi Francesconi, who examined him at Young's urging. All the drugs and cigarettes hadn't touched him; Baker, Young found, "had the constitution of an ox."

But other pressures were wearing him down. He was reminded of them in a letter Artt Frank sent him that month. Frank reminded Baker that he'd visited him in the L.A. County Jail in 1969, then gotten him a contract to record *Blood, Chet and Tears* when nobody else cared about him—a life-changing favor, done purely out of love, Frank noted. He begged his imagined soul mate to repay him by getting him a record deal with Snyder, and to play on the album. But he wasn't above scolding Baker, in another letter, for never writing to his children, who, according to Frank, thought their father didn't care if they vanished off the face of the earth; for deserting his wife; and for disappointing Vera until she was reduced to tears.

Carol herself was on the warpath, having discovered, among Baker's things, an envelope of nude Polaroids that Young had sent to keep him company while they were apart. The incident provoked a letter from his mother, who at sixty-seven had retired and moved back to Yale, where her brother lived. Her sweetness exhausted, Vera spewed out a lifetime of resentment at the son who had let her down so badly. Much of her venom was for Young, who, she said, looked like a beast and acted like a whore. Vera accused Baker of spending all his money on drugs for Young—who had no habit—while his children walked around in rags.

Silently, Baker handed the letter to Young. As she read it, he explained that Carol and Vera had always hated each other but were now allies, united against him. "I can't deal with this shit," he muttered.

That December, after a brief separation, he flew Young to Holland to join him for his birthday and Christmas. When they met at the airport, she found him practically "psychotic," full of accusations that she had betrayed him. Once he closed their hotel-room door behind them, the cause of his behavior became clear: he was strung out. He pulled out a bag of heroin and sniffed it in front of her. She was shaken, but still naïve enough to think his snorting would lead no further.

The effects of the drug were clear in a broadcast of a concert he had just given in Ludwigsburg, Germany, with Phil Markowitz, Scott Lee, and Jeff Brillinger. Every tempo had slowed to the "junkie beat" of his 1959 album *Chet,* made at the peak of his early addiction. Now, with his responses similarly dulled, the songs drifted on for fifteen minutes or more, not ending but subsiding. The concert set the tone for his final decade of playing. Brillinger knew something was wrong when he joined Baker in Paris on December 28, 1978, to record the album *Broken Wing.* Baker kept starting his takes before the engineer gave the signal; he sounded vague and lackluster.

On New Year's Eve, he, Young, Micheline, Pelzer, and a French record producer gathered in the Hotel California near the Champs-Elysées to celebrate. Up in Baker's room, the Frenchman asked his companions if they wanted a snort of heroin. Baker accepted. "I feel like getting high," he said. "Me too," said Micheline. She had avoided the drug for about three years, using methadone instead, but this seemed like a good chance to bond with Baker, with whom she had fallen in love. "We really found each other that night!" she said.

Baker took Young to Italy, leaving the band stranded in Paris. Brillinger waited in a hotel for several nights at his own expense; finally he went home, as did Markowitz. Later in New York, Young fought to get Baker clean again, and set him up with a sympathetic drug counselor. Before the appointment, Baker phoned Young from a booth outside the clinic. "I just can't do it, baby," he said. And this time she knew he meant it. "In his heart, I don't think he gave a fuck anymore," she said. "He was smart enough to know there was no reason to put any energy into it. He said, 'Nobody'll ever agree on anything. It's all a big fucking mess.' "

16

January 1979 found Baker home briefly in New York. Since Young had sublet the Seventy-first Street studio, he used Jon Burr's apartment in Queens. For the moment, Baker limited his heroin intake mostly to sniffing; Young, his constant companion, wouldn't see him inject until months later. Sniffing brought only a fraction of the usual high; Jerry Stahl observed that if mainlining felt like a rocket blast, snorting could be compared to an elevator ride. Such moderation wasn't typical for Baker, but he seemed determined to prove he was in command, and resumed taking his methadone on schedule.

No synthetic drug could give him the guts to face his family, though. Carol was trying to support herself and three children as a secretary in a Manhattan real-estate firm. On the job she was a model of efficiency, typing and filing with robotic precision. But her letters to Baker suggested a woman verging on collapse. She continued to suffer migraines, perhaps aggravated by seeing her home life in ruin and her husband engaged with another woman. Melissa's teeth were full of cavities; Paul used a sleeping bag because he had no bed. There was no help in sight from Baker, yet Carol couldn't seem to imagine life without him.

Whenever mail arrived with her writing on it, he frowned and handed it unopened to Young. "Here, you read it," he would grumble. "What's that one say?" Once he listened stone-faced as Young recited Carol's bizarre account of how eight drunken youths had tried to break into her apartment. Her front door, she explained, was worthless, so she opened it and let them in. Baker wrote her from Europe and urged her to move at once. If she needed money, he said, ask John Snyder. Meanwhile, she should get herself

Göteborg, Sweden, September 1983. Photo by Dan Kjellman

a shotgun. Young ended up phoning her mother in New York and asking her to forward Carol five hundred dollars from Young's trust.

Baker could always aim the sympathy back at himself. On January 17, he flew to Stuttgart to tape a broadcast session with a big band led by Erwin Lehn, a veteran German conductor. The trumpeter poured his despair into one of the most poignant solos he ever played. "Once Upon a Summertime" was a mournful waltz that Michel Legrand, the French pop and film composer, had written in the fifties as "La Valse des lilas" (The Waltz of the Lilacs), a portrait of lost love and youth. Baker was drawn powerfully to the melody, whose phrases elegantly dip and pirouette against a minor background. Joe Gallardo, a Texas-born trombonist who played with Lehn, had arranged the song dramatically, with the brass section blazing into big, passionate crescendos. Amid them stood Baker: a quiet, stricken voice, paring down Legrand's baroque lines into what sounded like the last reflections of an abandoned old man. All the same, his tone had stayed so pure and untainted that in some ways he still seemed like a child.

The paradox fascinated Rene Magron, a journalist who reviewed Baker at the Ankel Pö, a jazz club in Hamburg. The room was packed beyond capacity, and Magron observed the viewers on the edge of their seats, staring at this "very skinny, sickly-looking man" with closed eyes hidden behind huge tortoiseshell glasses. His music "went right into the center of the audience's hearts," wrote Magron. "I see it on their faces, everyone is feeling it. . . . It's a broken, lonely, but at the same time endlessly sweet and emotional sound. . . . This is obviously a torn, abused man, someone who has gone through many hells."

No matter where in Europe he played—and in 1979, his schedule included Germany, Austria, France, Belgium, Italy, Denmark, Norway, England, and Switzerland—Baker was treated like an angel from above. At an outdoor concert near Monaco, he and his touring partner, guitarist Doug Raney, performed on an elevated platform. The trumpeter so magnetized his audience that people were climbing the scaffolding to get close to him. Raney thought he had stepped into a Fellini film. Indeed, Baker's mystique fascinated some of Europe's most famous actors. In Rome, Marcello Mastroianni showed up night after night, studying Baker from his table. Jean Seberg swept into a club in her mink coat and passed him a request for "My Funny Valentine." Despite his decrepit appearance, love letters kept arriving from both sexes. A handsome Italian man sent a Polaroid of himself in a bathing suit, inscribed with the note: "If you like, write to me sometimes . . . a little kiss from Fabio."

More spellbound than anyone were the young jazz musicians of Europe, who flocked to Baker as fanatically as the American players had to Charlie Parker. Bringing him new songs and challenging him musically, they helped Baker achieve an outstanding year of music-making. After his session with Erwin Lehn, he stayed in Stuttgart to record a duo album, *Ballads for Two.* His partner was Wolfgang Lackerschmid, a young German vibraphonist and composer whose shoulder-length hair, beard, and glasses gave him the same Christlike look as Gerry Mulligan. Long before the vogue for new-age music, Lackerschmid wrote pieces in that floating, otherworldly style, playing them with an icy shimmer. He could also give standards the breezy lift of Baker's early work, and he and the trumpeter liked weaving lines in counterpoint.

But joy was an alien emotion to Baker, and it never lasted long. Gloom pervaded the session for *The Touch of Your Lips,* one of the more acclaimed albums of his later years. He recorded it in Copenhagen that June with Niels-Henning Ørsted Pedersen, Denmark's most celebrated jazz bassist, and the talented Raney, who played in the spare, single-note style perfected by his father, guitarist Jimmy Raney. Baker came to the studio sick from withdrawal. Immediately he asked Raney, who lived in Copenhagen, if he knew a place to cop. Raney didn't, and the session proceeded tensely, with the fragile trumpeter turning his fading strength into some of the gentlest playing of his career. He pressed his horn to the mike as if it were the listener's ear; ballads like "Star Eyes" and "Autumn in New York" had rarely sounded so intimate. The French jazz critic Laurent Goddet of *Jazz Hot* proclaimed the album a monument to "beauty and truth," adding: "The ideas are of an absolute freshness, the phrases are delicate and unsettling, the tone is one of the sweetest and clearest in existence. . . . The music on this album remains hung in the night sky like a star."

Nowhere did Baker seem more divine than in Italy. Late in 1979, he was approached at the Music Inn in Rome by Nicola Stilo, a bearded, hippie-like flute and guitar player from a small town in southern Italy. Then twenty-three, Stilo had fallen in love with jazz upon discovering Miles Davis, but when he heard Chet Baker, he had a true epiphany. Baker was "so close to the spirit," he felt, that he had to be near him. The promising young musician began following Baker to gigs and recording sessions, everywhere staring at him in rapturous melancholy. Carrying his guitar, Stilo dropped by the Hotel Anglo-American, hoping for a chance to play for the master and to share a few words in Italian, his only language at the time. He told

Baker of having lost his beloved *padre,* who had encouraged him to go into music. Now, it seemed, Stilo had found the ultimate surrogate father. He thought it was a "dream" when the trumpeter took him along on a tour of Italy in 1980. "I was so happy the nights that I played a little well—when I was able to take a good solo and Chet liked it," he said. "You didn't need more than one little look from his eyes to know if he was happy or not. Man, each time with Chet Baker was a lesson of ear training. And simplicity." Stilo hoped to become as much like his idol as he could—a longing that would have certain dangerous results.

Baker started the year by touring with a group led by Enrico Pieranunzi, a composer-pianist whose dark suits, glasses, and neat mustache gave him the look of an Italian businessman. Listening to Baker, Pieranunzi believed he had unearthed the key to the mystery of jazz: that "improvisation is an unlimited land, the land of our innermost reality." With that in mind, he wrote a set of ethereal compositions that he felt captured the trumpeter's soul. These pieces, with such surreal titles as "Animali diurni" and "Brown Cat Dance," formed the basis of *Soft Journey,* an album Baker made in Rome with Pieranunzi's band.

The other members—tenor saxophonist Maurizio Giammarco, bassist Riccardo Del Fra, and drummer Roberto Gatto—would go on to create distinguished careers in Europe. But in 1980 they sat at Baker's feet. Giammarco, a former player of fusion and free jazz, saw something Zenlike in Baker's ability to wend his way through a song purely by instinct. "While I was always thinking about the changes I was playing," said Giammarco, "he led me to discover that there is a higher point, where you forget all the changes and you just go from note to note, knowing exactly where you're going." Del Fra's coke-bottle glasses and boyish face belied his experience with Art Farmer and the prestigious RAI-TV orchestra; *Musica Jazz* had already named him the best bassist in Rome. Yet he was dazzled by the profound meaning he heard in Baker's every phrase. He felt his art rise to a new level as he accompanied a man who he felt could look into his soul.

But reality set in, especially when Baker kept them waiting weeks for their pay. Del Fra saw how the trumpeter and his circle relied on drugs to escape every problem. On his first visit to Jacques Pelzer's home with Baker, Del Fra complained of chest pains. Pelzer offered him a pill, which he swallowed unquestioningly. The bassist slept for twenty hours. When Baker left, Pelzer gave him his usual going-away present: dropper bottles of codeine, ready to be sprinkled in coffee. Entering Baker's "unlimited land" of sensitivity seemed to require numbing oneself to all feeling. "Most of the time he was so quiet, the way he talked," said Micheline. "People didn't know how much smack he would need to be like that."

Not everyone who flocked to Baker had such pure intentions. In the swirl of notoriety that surrounded him, many perceived a cash cow. When his habit was in charge, he welcomed anyone who promised easy money. "Chet was a pigeon," said a dismayed Ruth. "He was great pickin'. All he truly cared about was his drug, and he would do anything to get it. So that became his reputation to a group of bloodsucking people."

For years, many had urged him to write a book. He finally tried in the late seventies. Sitting in hotel rooms and on trains, he began transcribing memories on lined yellow paper. He recalled his childhood in Yale, Oklahoma; the army; his glory days with Gerry Mulligan; his own early quartet; and various misdeeds through 1964. At that point he lost interest. "Who'll give a shit?" he told Young. Baker certainly didn't. His reflections sounded lifeless, without a trace of insight. "Chet thought he was gonna see some money—period," Young explained. The unfinished manuscript lay in the hands of James Felds, his American manager, who had high hopes of selling it to a publisher or to Hollywood. But Felds had no contacts in either field, and nothing happened.

The project came back to life in Rome, where the trumpeter met Tom Baker, a celebrity-obsessed former actor from New York. Back in 1967, Tom's raven-black hair, blue eyes, and chiseled face had interested Andy Warhol, who cast him as the lead in his early feature film *I, a Man.* But despite his full nudity in the last reel, the actor revealed no star quality, and Warhol never used him again. When his acting career fizzled, Tom tried filmmaking, but wound up with only aborted documentary projects and unproduced scripts. As drugs turned him haggard and bloated, he tried to dazzle people with name-dropping gossip, much of it concerning his friend Jim Morrison of the Doors.

His boasting didn't impress Nesya Blue, a New York filmmaker whose husband, the actor and rock musician David Blue, had known him for years. Nesya met the ex-Warholite at One Uni, a trendy Greenwich Village club. Learning she was his friend's wife, Tom made a pass at her. "He was revolting," she said, "a greaseball, sort of a hustler on the decline. One could see that he had been a beautiful young man. And he still liked to think of himself as a seducer of all. But he would disappear and return sweaty and glassy-eyed and very agitated, stoned out of his mind."

Seeking new opportunities in Rome, Tom pursued Chet Baker with promises of using his "connections" to secure a big-money book or film deal. The trumpeter signed a contract giving him rights to his story for six months. Once home in New York, Tom obtained a copy of the autobiography from James Felds. In his loft apartment on Fourteenth Street, he sat at the typewriter revising away, all the while hypnotized by the voice of his new idol singing "My Buddy" on the phonograph. Tom phoned Carol with overtures of friendship. Apparently starved for attention, she responded, and they began meeting in New York. He pumped her for information about Chet Baker; she implored him to tell her absentee husband to write or call.

By now, Baker and Young had been a couple for seven years. With all the complaining he had done about Carol, he had made no move to end their union. "Look, Ruth, I can't keep going from marriage to marriage," he snapped. Finally she persuaded him to file for a quick divorce through Jacoby & Meyers, the low-cost legal firm that advertised on subway posters and late-night TV. He gave her the money for a deposit, then sat down with a sheet of paper and composed a harrowed "goodbye" letter to Carol. How, he wondered, after all her efforts to save their marriage—to the point of enduring a marathon of vile behavior that would have sent any other wife packing—could he make her understand that he had to break away? Apparently he felt he couldn't, for the letter went unmailed; the divorce petition was dropped. When Young tried to press the issue, she saw how guilt-ridden he was. "I've already kicked her in the teeth," he said. "Now do you want me to kick her in the ass?"

He was even more tortured over how he had treated his children. Carol informed him by mail that Paul was turning angry and rebellious. Now fourteen, he hadn't gone to school in months, she said. His father's neglect was taking its toll.

When Baker complained to Young that his children never wrote to him, she urged him to reach out to them, if only to ease his conscience. In the winter of 1980, he composed a letter to Paul. It began with a pained acknowledgment of how deeply he had hurt the boy with his absence. He was sure, he said, that Carol had badmouthed him as a worthless junkie. Baker tried to claim he had too little work to send them any money, but the excuse sounded so feeble that even he seemed embarrassed by it. In a rare flash of self-insight, he wrote that he wished he could have sat them all down and explained why he had left, but he just didn't have the guts. He couldn't even face having an honest conversation with them, he said.

His admissions proved so painful that he never mailed that letter either. He did send one to Dean, though, offering some strained fatherly advice to the seventeen-year-old as he approached manhood. After making excuses for forgetting his son's birthday, he took on the generic tone of a school guidance counselor, urging Dean to join the air force or learn computers and to live as an upstanding young citizen. He added that he wouldn't be there to help, for he expected to die soon. Dean read his father's words and said nothing, noted Carol curtly in her next letter to Baker.

That year, the trumpeter announced plans to buy a house outside Rome, his favorite city, for himself and Young. It never happened, but he continued to bask in the idolatry of the Italians. On March 19, he was welcomed back to Lucca by the Circolo del Jazz, who presented him and Young in an emotional concert at Casina Rossa, a dance club. In the packed audience, Baker saw faces he remembered from jail; they looked back at him adoringly. In the years since his imprisonment, Baker had achieved mythic status in Tuscany. He was treated grandly by Giampiero Giusti, the former drummer with the Quintetto di Lucca and now one of the richest men in the region, thanks to the huge success of a paper-and-cardboard factory he had founded in 1969. Whenever they were in the area, Baker and Young stayed at his sumptuous home in Florence. The basement was a fully equipped music room, perfect for hosting jam sessions in which Giusti got to play drums behind Baker and other celebrity musicians.

On April 7, the Italian Social Democratic Party honored the trumpeter at the Arcadia Jazz Club in Florence. With reporters and a TV crew on hand, as well as a proud assembly of local politicians, musicians, even the former director of the Lucca jail, Baker accepted a plaque with the inscription: THIRTY YEARS OF BODY AND SOUL FOR JAZZ: TO THE GREATEST WHITE TRUMPETER, CHET BAKER, FROM HIS FLORENTINE FRIENDS. He also received two shiny award cups, one of them "for his help in the fight against drugs." Cecco Maino photographed Baker holding the cups aloft like a champion prizefighter.

All was forgiven for an interview he had given recently to RAI-TV. When a crew came to his room at the Hotel Anglo-American in Rome to film an interview, he couldn't resist the chance to scandalize the country anew. Young was still in bed, and Baker had avoided telling her about the appointment until a knock was heard at the door. Panicking, she scrambled for her clothes. "Ah, fuck it, baby, stay in the bed," he drawled. "Keep my shirt on, put the covers over you, what are you getting excited about?"

Italian viewers were shocked to see *l'angelo* chatting casually on the edge of his bed while his girlfriend lay beneath the sheets reading a magazine. Baker hauled out his favorite stories of prescription forgeries, arrests, the loss of his teeth, and his fictionalized two-year stint as a gas-station attendant. "He was having a delightful time that day," said Young. The only honest note came when he was asked why drugs and music were synonymous for him. "There are a lot of pressures," he explained. "Pressures from what I try to play, pressures from the people who come to hear me, of being called the best trumpet player in the world, which happened to me in 'fifty-four and 'fifty-five. The people who come are 30 to 40 percent musicians, so it's a lot of pressure."

Before that interview, Baker had eased the strain with heroin scored from his new Italian dealer. And he took it through his arm, not his nose. The drug had become much more common in Italy since Baker's arrest in 1960, and the Music Inn crawled with pushers whenever he played there. "All around the world," said Nicola Stilo, "if Chet was not looking for heroin, heroin was looking for Chet. Because everybody knew."

The most aggressive pusher was Giuseppe, a young Italian who supported his own habit by selling. Late in 1979, he had invited Baker and Young to the seedy Roman apartment he shared with his wife and their baby, who lay on the floor screaming. Baker had mostly avoided the needle that year, but when Giuseppe prepared a syringe and handed it to him, he gazed at it more romantically than he had at almost any woman. As he held the needle before his face, eyeing it from every angle, Young became hysterical. "Chet, you're not gonna do this!" she pleaded, putting her arms around him. He ignored her. When she tried to grab it out of his hands, his eyes flashed like a mad dog's as he shoved her to the floor. With both Young and the baby sobbing, Baker said offhandedly, "Well, I haven't done one of these in a long time." Moments later, he was flying.

From then on, Giuseppe came to the Anglo-American almost daily. Young was heartsick. "You might as well marry him," she told Baker. "You're not in love with Carol, me, or anybody, you're in love with Giuseppe!" She continued to agonize over his drug use, but he didn't. "Chet felt, OK, if I can do this and still function, what's the big deal? And ultimately that's the attitude I adopted. Because if this person could create something so unique, and go through the crap required to do it, then he should be left alone."

Self-abuse had not agreed with Pepito Pignatelli, the owner of the Music Inn. Constantly drunk in later years, the once devilishly handsome prince now looked like a near-skeleton. His physical decline mirrored Baker's, but not his constitution, and he died of a heart attack in bed next to his wife, Picchi. The core of her life suddenly gone, she was devastated, and never fully recovered. She struggled to keep the Music Inn alive, but it seemed much emptier without Pepito's horselaugh and cartoonlike Italian machismo.

Undaunted by the death of one more self-destructive friend, Baker moved on to Paris, a dangerous city for him. This was the town whose heroin had proven lethally pure for Dick Twardzik in 1955; now, Baker found it easier to score high-quality dope here than anywhere else in Europe. While playing Le Dreher, a jazz club on the Right Bank, he stayed with Young at the apartment of a wealthy young Baker groupie, Denis, in the fashionable district of St-Germain-des-Près. Micheline Pelzer and the American actor Joe Dallesandro, a fan of Baker's, were Denis's other houseguests. Dallesandro's career as the comically vapid boy toy in several Andy Warhol films had ended years earlier. Broke, but with a drug habit to support, the handsome actor relied on the generosity of friends and strangers. After Micheline pawned some of her gold jewelry to make him a "loan," she never saw him or the money again.

Throughout his two weeks at Le Dreher, Baker kept arriving late and in poor shape. On one of his weaker nights, the French movie producer Léon Terjanian made a concert film, *An Evening with Chet Baker.* The band, at least, was top-notch: Maurizio Giammarco; Riccardo Del Fra; the American drummer Donny Donable; and Dennis Luxion, a pianist from Springfield, Illinois, who had come aboard after moving to Liège. Thin and artistic-looking, with longish brown hair, glasses, and delicate hands, Luxion had a classically inspired touch that reminded Baker of Twardzik. But the group could compensate only so much for its leader, who sat in a chair with his head down and played with hardly a trace of energy or inspiration. "He didn't pick up his horn when he wasn't working," said Luxion, "so if he hadn't been playing for a couple of weeks, he could sound pretty horrible." After each solo, Baker let out a huff of exhaustion, dropping the trumpet to his lap as though it were a heavy burden.

The film came to life only in the middle, when Baker was interviewed offstage by Liliane Cukier, by then an established actress in France and the wife of Gilbert "Bibi" Rovère, a French bassist. Twenty-five years after their affair, she and Baker still ogled each other as lustfully as they had at Birdland. Their chatter about the club and the sidemen turned from the innocuous when Liliane spied something sticking out of Baker's shirt. "What is that you've got in your pocket there?" she asked. He gave a little smirk.

"That is a syringe that I use to, uh . . . oil my trumpet," he explained. "That's the only use I have for a syringe these days." They giggled like naughty children. Baker removed the needle and manipulated the stopper. In the film's most memorable image, he rested it atop the trumpet in his lap, as though the two items were interchangeable parts of his being.

The Dreher film pointed up the growing inconsistency of his performances, which too often hinged on the need for cash. His musicians were appalled at some of the conditions he worked in. At the Domicil, a jazz club in Munich, Giammarco lost his cool. "We were playing three sets, really badly paid, and there were all these big drunk Germans shouting all the time. I had an argument with Chet—I told him something like, 'How can you play here? You're a master! You're a great musician!' He said, 'Gigs are gigs. We have to play.' "

Around 1980, mediocre Chet Baker LPs began to flood the market: cheaply made live albums, issued on small European labels, of songs he had recorded better elsewhere. The amateurish cover photos, usually shot in performance, signaled the inferiority of the music inside. On weekends in most clubs, Baker played three sets, making it easy to record a lot of music in one shot. One uninspired night at the Subway Club in Cologne yielded three albums; the same thing happened at Copenhagen's Jazzhus Montmartre and at Le Dreher. The format on nearly every track is the same: Baker plays listlessly for as long as his chops hold out; scats a little; then turns the spotlight to his sidemen, who take turns playing chorus after chorus.

The albums made at Le Dreher particularly upset the drummer, Al Levitt, an American who lived in Paris. One night he had noticed recording mikes and equipment at the club. Baker assured him that Rudolf Kreis, who owned the small Circle label, merely wanted to make a "test" tape for a possible future album. Months later, Levitt found *Night Bird* in a shop. He listened in distress to a badly recorded, dreary performance, released without payment to any of the sidemen. Levitt wrote an indignant letter to Baker and another to Kreis. The producer responded with a copy of a contract Baker had signed on June 26, 1980, the day of the recording, and the information that Baker had promised to pay the musicians himself.

Imported into the United States, most of those albums served only to confirm his decline. *Just Friends* consisted of two songs, "Doodlin' " and the title tune, each of which filled a whole side of an LP. Pete Welding of *Down Beat* called them "shambling efforts in which Baker, alternately, beguiles one with snatches of excellence, then stultifies with long stretches of aimlessness."

That spring, during a lull in his European schedule, Baker took Young back to New York. His return after an absence of more than a year went unnoticed by almost everyone except Lisa Galt Bond. A young Bohemian who lived in the East Village, Bond gave poetry-and-jazz presentations of her original verse, interviewed jazzmen, and worked as a hostess and waitress in several clubs. At that time she greeted customers at Jazzmania, a new club on East Twenty-third Street where she did some booking.

Hearing that the great Chet Baker was home in New York and unemployed, she persuaded the club owner to give him two nights. She knew the risks of even such a short booking: Baker was known to demand half his pay in advance, then to show up late, in bad shape, or not at all. But when he told Bond he needed half of his eight-hundred-dollar fee up front "for music paper," she arranged it, knowing he would come to work if only to pick up the balance.

On a chilly spring day, Baker rang Bond's doorbell to collect his advance. As he walked in, she heard the clip-clop of his sandals, which he still wore because of his feet, more swollen than ever from injecting between his toes. But her eyes were drawn to the "worn, leathery skin on the bones of a once magnificent, now shriveled face," Bond said. Then she felt "the soft, mesmerizing effect" of his voice. "Don't forget how he could use that voice," she explained. "It was an instrument of seduction. He had the charm of the devil. I thought, this man is a presence—something you don't meet often in your life."

Once she had handed him the money, Bond asked if she could interview him. As he sat in her parlor nibbling on a turkey sandwich he had brought along, they had the first of several frank talks. "He felt a lot of frustration about not being respected as a serious musician," she recalled. Bitterly, he commented that other people would probably make a lot of money off him after he died. But for all Baker's anger, Bond saw a man living in fear. This alleged "free spirit" had no choice, she realized, but to live on the run. Scared that the IRS would nab him if they tracked him down, he used a jumble of mailing addresses—Young's, Carol's, Jacques Pelzer's, those of jazz clubs and hotels. Yet he worried that royalty checks sent through the mail would be traceable by the government. That may be why he resisted Young's attempts to hire a lawyer to untangle his finances. "I'm not gonna spend any fucking five hundred dollars an hour to get nothing at the end," Baker grumbled. He continued to demand cash up front for all work—then to complain about getting ripped off by record companies.

Baker despised no one more than Richard Carpenter. After so many years away from him, the trumpeter was sure his former manager would take big revenge if he ever tried to cause trouble. "Chet feared for his life," Bond said—especially when he learned that Carpenter had moved to West Seventieth Street, almost around the corner from Young.

Before leaving Bond's apartment, Baker stared into a mirror near the door. "It struck me that this was a man who stayed high so he would not see who he was," she said. "He could look in the mirror and still see beauty. I saw a corpse."

Jazzmania was packed on both nights he appeared. The crowd included a sprinkling of downtown celebrities, including Joe Dallesandro and writer-humorist Fran Lebowitz. Even in America, Baker hadn't lost his underground appeal. "Chet was part of an elite group of long-term junkie survivors," Bond said. "When he was on, he was still magic." After the show had started, she was confronted at the door by a woman who had walked up the five flights to Jazzmania in stiletto pumps. With her elaborately coordinated, ill-fitting outfit from the sixties and her thick makeup, she was a matronly figure in that hip crowd.

"*I'm* Mrs. Chet Baker!" she announced angrily, perhaps suspecting that Young was inside. Bond directed her to a spot far from Young's table. "Carol was sitting at the bar, glaring at the stage," said Bond. "And Chet's next song was 'Just Friends.' I remember thinking of the irony of that moment, watching this woman watching him. Her glare could have pierced the wall."

Carol had moved from Flushing to a slightly better apartment in Astoria, another section of Queens, but the family remained in trouble. In a letter to Young, Melissa, known as Missy, mentioned that Dean stayed locked in his bedroom, seldom emerging except to eat and go to the bathroom. Then thirteen, Missy was a year behind her seventh-grade classmates, and with her tiny frame, she looked even younger than her age. Given her girlishness, Missy's accounts of life at home—which she wrote in her school notebook, then shared with "Roofie"—were hair-raising.

According to Missy, Carol was doing her best to turn the children against their father and "douchebag," her name for Young, whom she accused of siphoning away their money. When Missy phoned her in tears after one of Carol's tirades, Young took notes. Carol, said Missy, had called Young a "whore" and a "dog" who took her clothes off in front of musicians and used up every cent Baker earned—funds that could have paid for the new clothes Missy wanted. The torrent of rage continued. Their father didn't care one bit about them, and even if he did, Young kept him so stoned he didn't know what he was doing.

The fact that he had always returned to them sooner or later, or promised to, gave Carol the illusion that someday he might come home for good. "But what kind of a reality is that?" Young wondered. "You just sit there waiting for a crumb to be thrown your way? Neglect and blatant abuse and denial of your existence, avoidance of your company, you call that a marriage? Then he might as well be beating the shit out of you. My Lord!"

Carol's words clearly shook Missy. All she wanted was to escape, she wrote to her father and Young. On the back of the envelope, she printed the words "Chet" and "Roofie" entwined amid branches and hearts.

Her desperation shook Baker, who with Young figured out a short-term solution. In the spring of 1980, he sent Missy a letter inviting her to join them in Italy that July for her fourteenth birthday. His invitation thrilled the girl, but not Carol, who seethed at the prospect of that "interfering bitch" vacationing with her husband and daughter. The coming weeks were a nightmare, reported Missy, as Carol taunted her that her father would never keep his promise. To Missy's delight, Baker wrote her in June to say that her tickets were ready. Carol had no choice but to relent, but she warned Baker not to let Missy see him engaged in passionate congress with Young. Missy certainly never witnessed it between her parents, Carol noted.

The child joined her father, Young, and Rique Pantoja, a twenty-four-year-old keyboard player and composer from Brazil, as they toured Italy by car. Pantoja's band, Novos Tempos, had just made an album with Baker, who performed the Pantoja song "Arbor Way" for the rest of his life. The young Brazilian looked forward to a whole summer with the master. "He had such a sweet spirit," said Pantoja. "He would say things like, 'For me, an improvisation is like telling a story. You have to start your solo as if you're telling a story to a kid. You can't just say a whole bunch of words they wouldn't understand; you've got to start with a simple phrase, then develop it.' "

Trying to apply that logic to actual fatherhood, Baker arranged a holiday at a house by the beach. Missy swam almost every day and rejoiced in the company of her dad, who promised to take her to a dentist to have her teeth fixed. He also gave her permission to smoke. In a letter to her friend Ronda, Missy wrote that she wished she could stay there forever. But even at fourteen, she lived with low expectations.

Indeed, the vacation turned sour. For the first time, Young and Missy clashed bitterly, and Pantoja was appalled. He felt such anger in Young that he couldn't imagine why she had stayed with Baker. "Probably she didn't know what she was doing in that relationship," he said. Then one night in a hotel, Missy looked under the sink and found her father's works, tied with a rubber band. With Young looking on, she thrust them in front of him. "Hey, Dad—what's *this*?" she asked. *"What do you think it is?"* he blurted, yanking them out of her hand and taking them into the bedroom, slamming the door shut.

Off they went to Rome, where they stayed at a Holiday Inn for several days. At the end, Baker opted to walk out on the $1,500 bill. "How can we do this?" asked Young, trailing behind as he hurried to the exit. "Look," he said, "if a guy could build a place like this, the son-of-a-bitch doesn't need *my* money!"

Soon thereafter, he put Missy on a plane home. Baker was losing patience with almost everyone. He expected his musicians to be ready on a few hours' notice to leave the country and tour; if they couldn't, he fumed at their inability to "make the road." A six-week itinerary could stretch into months as he tacked on whatever extra gigs he could find. "I said, Chet, you cannot work all the time, because then your price goes down," recalled his agent Gaby Kleinschmidt. "And this is what he didn't understand." Sometimes he lost her neatly typed schedules, forcing the band to check the newspaper to see where and when they were playing. They found themselves pleading to be paid; Baker even tried to borrow money from them. Del Fra went on strike, missing an important job in Paris and threatening to skip others if Baker didn't pay him. "All the money he was making at that point was going into his arm," said Dennis Luxion, who noted his disappointments in a postcard to his girlfriend Christiane. "I don't like this life," he wrote. "I never have any money, the music often isn't good, and I'm not improving." When the trumpeter asked him to come back for another tour, Luxion refused—"because he didn't get his money and things are too disorganized for him," Baker groused to Young. "Another boy living in a dream world."

Tom Baker was in a dream world too, with his fantasies about the power of Baker's name and what it could bring him. But he had gotten nowhere with the biography or any of his other projects, so Baker enlisted Lisa Galt Bond to take over. On March 4, 1981, she signed a contract with him to co-author his memoirs. Prepared by Charles Neighbors, Bond's literary agent, it gave her 15 percent royalties upon publication, along with various other rights. Bond began working on the manuscript, which had not, she felt, benefited from Tom's tinkering. She also interviewed the trumpeter further to try to fill in the gaps. Believing his life nearly over, he wanted a few things memorialized. "Listen, kid," he told her. "Put this in the book—how wonderful it was the first time I got high, how it was one of the most wonderful experiences in my life." For the title, he chose a double entendre: *Hold the Middle Valve Down,* a paraphrase from "The Music Goes Round and Round," a swing-era hit about the trombone.

The possibilities excited Bond, especially when Marvin Worth, the producer of hit films based on Lenny Bruce *(Lenny)* and Janis Joplin *(The Rose),* showed interest in Baker's story, too. But when Neighbors began sending the manuscript to publishers, in came the rejection letters, dismissing Baker as an unsalable has-been. "I just don't feel that Chet Baker is a big enough name for this to be as successful as I'd like," wrote an editor at Putnam. Another, at Macmillan, declared that he found Baker's life "too much of a downer to make a commercially successful book." Only in 1997 would Carol publish Baker's first version of the manuscript, with editorial tinkering and numerous misspellings, under the title *As Though I Had Wings*—a quote from "Like Someone in Love," a standard Baker had recorded in the fifties. It earned mixed-to-negative reviews, like that of Peter Pavia, who in the New York *Daily News* called it a "wisp of a book" that "doesn't offer a shred of reflection or self-awareness."

A more scathing notice appeared in May 1981, during Baker's first engagement at Fat Tuesday's, a jazz club on lower Third Avenue in Manhattan. Manager Steve Getz, the son of Stan, booked the trumpeter there until 1986, despite slow midweek business. "We never made much profit from Chet, just a little bit," he said. Don Nelsen's review in the *Daily News* bore the headline "Baker Drops Egg": "He grimaced his way through some five tunes with what appeared to be angered resignation. . . . He looked like he was forcing every note." Most of the songs, Nelsen wrote, "just lay on the air, nearly comatose. What a waste."

All most listeners wanted, complained Baker, was a trumpeter who performed loud musical acrobatics. He vented his frustration to Michael Zwerin of the *International Herald Tribune:* "It's kind of depressing to realize that so much of what I'm trying to do and say is going by completely undetected. It's really very complicated, but it looks so easy, I'm sure that ninety-five percent of the audience is unaware that I've said anything unique or that there's more depth to it than there was twenty-five years ago." The subject came up again when he talked to Danish interviewer Ib Skovgaard: "It's true, I don't jump around the stage and dance around and joke like Dizzy . . . you know, that's just not my way. Maybe I should make more faces, I don't know." Privately he was less tactful, lashing out at other people—even higher powers—for destroying him. When Bob Mover asked him if he believed in God, he growled: "Yeah, I hope there's a God, so I can grab him by the fucking throat!"

Baker spent the summer of 1981 on a U.S. tour booked by his new agent, Linda Goldstein. In New York that September, he reunited with Donald Frankos, his dealer in 1957 and his cellmate on Rikers Island. In and out of prison ever since, Frankos was now free, and had taken a job dealing heroin and coke in a Manhattan drug ring headed by John Gotti, the Gambino crime family boss. One afternoon, Frankos drove to West Forty-eighth Street to meet a trio of customers. The weather was warm, and all of them wore short sleeves, revealing arms dotted with track marks. "One guy looked familiar," he said. "I recognized him to be Chet Baker—an *old* Chet Baker." Frankos stepped out of the car and introduced himself; Baker smiled and threw his arms around him. "I don't know if he hugged me as friends would do after not seeing each other for a long time, or whether he knew he'd be able to score now," Frankos observed.

Prices had gone up since 1957, of course. Baker had $2,500 in his pocket, but Frankos sold an ounce of pure heroin for $10,000, a "cut" one for $3,500. For old times' sake, he gave Baker a free ounce of the latter, certain he had a steady customer. Frankos never saw him again. Later, speaking with Jerome Reece in *Jazz Hot,* Baker reminisced about the good old days, when a twenty-four-hour supply of high-quality dope cost only a few dollars. "It's so expensive now that no one can afford it," he complained. "And if you're depending on jazz to make money—hah—you can't earn enough money."

He found a short-term solution, witnessed by his friend Jim Coleman, who owned the Audio-Video Salon, a high-end stereo shop on Manhattan's East Side. Coleman recalled spending evenings with Baker in jazz-club dressing rooms around the city. "I met a lot of interesting people, because the top musicians in the world, like Art Blakey, would come in to see Chet," he said. "You know why? He owed them money." Much of the time, Baker turned to Ruth Young for quick cash. In 1981 she gave him another five thousand dollars from her dwindling trust fund. Unsatisfied, Baker had taken to forging her checks, making them out to himself and cashing them at Colony Music, a large midtown shop. On August 25, Baker got a note in the mail from an employee, informing him that two of his checks, totaling $212, had bounced. Unless he reimbursed the store, the evidence would be posted on the register for all to see. Since Baker had no intention of paying Colony a dime, Young went in with the cash.

That year he hired one of his most slavish disciples: Leo Mitchell, a thirty-six-year-old drummer who had moved to New York years earlier from his hometown of Jacksonville, Florida. "Leo was a wonderful cat," said Bob Mover. "You talk about soul, you talk about a person loving music, wanting to play all the time—that was Leo. He loved to play, and he loved to get high. He could swing, and he didn't get in your way. Chet liked that a lot, because he was not really playing off the drums that much. Chet had more of a melodic conception."

Mitchell, who was black, lived on West Twenty-first Street with his mate, Diane, a white public-school music teacher whose devotion to him knew no bounds. Diane willingly supported the scuffling drummer, but at the same time she was determined to keep him out of trouble, and didn't hesitate to lecture or scold him if she saw bad influences creeping in. She went along to his debut with Baker at Struggles, a jazz club on a dark, deserted street in Edgewater, New Jersey. Diane saw Baker's acolytes fawning over him as if he were a cult leader. The trumpeter told her what wonderful things he had heard about her, but Diane wasn't charmed. "I felt the evil force the minute I met him," she said. "The music was great, but Chet's motivation was not the music. Chet's motivation was to get money to buy drugs."

Her mistrust was confirmed a few days later when she, Mitchell, Young, and Baker met for dinner at Young's apartment. Early in the evening, Baker announced that he and the drummer were going out for cigarettes. They didn't come back for hours. From then on, Mitchell became Baker's willing lackey and needle buddy, often scoring for both of them. "The guy would have done anything for him, and that's all Chet cared about," said Young. "He had gotten so lost in himself it was disgusting. He trampled on good people, bad people. He didn't make the distinction anymore." Mitchell was utterly seduced by Baker, especially when the music started, but the trumpeter's seeming vulnerability didn't touch Diane. "It was just something he could do," she said. "It's like pressing a button on a tape machine. All those love songs! If you only knew the guy."

Young felt the same dread as she looked upon a growing trail of corpses that in some way pointed back to Baker. Lou McConnell, his occasional tenor saxophonist from Liège, died there of an overdose on November 11, 1980. He was thirty-three. In Paris, Baker had gotten friendly with a drug-addicted nurse named Philip, the best friend of Baker's sometime host Denis. The trumpeter was interested to hear of Philip's plan to fly to India and score a large supply of pure heroin. He boarded a return flight with the dope stored in a balloon inside his rectum. Had it broken, Philip would have OD'd at once, but he made it home safely and proceeded to party. Within twenty-four hours he was dead of an overdose. Giuseppe, Baker's Roman connection, OD'd less than a year after he and Baker had met. "Talk about a jinx!" said Young. "These people all had habits, but they were fine until Chet came into the picture. Then they were dead."

To Diane, Baker was the "devil incarnate," and she drew pictures of him surrounded by satanic imagery. She pleaded with Mitchell to keep his distance, but he was sure Baker was his friend. Young had long since passed the point of logic in her obsession with Baker. "Chet kept these women strung out, just like they were on dope," said Lisa Galt Bond. "And they all wanted it. He had willing victims—the Brides of Dracula. It wasn't like they didn't know about his bullshit. He put it out there, and they bought it anyway."

Young couldn't shake the memory of a recent drive through France. As they approached the Italian border, Baker spotted two policemen. In a split-second reflex, he tossed a handful of heroin-filled glass vials at her and ordered her to stash them in her halter top. Young obeyed, but she was petrified, for the vials rattled with her every move. "Don't worry, honey, nobody takes a fall for me!" he assured her. Recalling Halema in the Italian prison, her blood ran cold.

The cops checked their passports and waved them through, but scarier moments awaited Young. In the dead of winter, they stayed at the European home of an admiring gay couple. The two men were happy to refer Baker to a dealer, and after they had gone to sleep, he met the connection on the street. Learning that the dealer was a junkie too, Baker invited him upstairs to fix. Minutes later, his guest hit the floor, dead. *"Take his feet!"* hissed Baker to Young. "Come on, come on, we gotta get him outta here!" Dazed, she helped him carry the heavy corpse down several flights of stairs and down onto the dark street, where Baker dumped it behind it a bush. Only later did she recall the rumor that he had abandoned Dick Twardzik at the moment he OD'd, rather than risk facing the blame. Now when he paid her his favorite compliment—"Nobody can handle the road like you!"—the words had a morbid ring.

Twardzik, Phil Urso, Tadd Dameron, Bob Whitlock, Sandy Jones, Jacques and Micheline Pelzer, Leo Mitchell, Carol—all these figures in Baker's life shared a common trait. "If you didn't end up relating to him through drugs, you didn't last long," said Young. Almost inevitably, she started "chippying" in 1981. "I was curious," she said. Baker discouraged her at first, but she persuaded Leo Mitchell to shoot her up. When she started experiencing chills and fever—the early signs of addiction—she vowed to quit. "No more stuff for me," Young wrote to Baker on March 22, 1981.

She later changed her mind. In Italy, Baker invited Larry Nocella, a tenor saxophonist, to join them in their hotel room. The trumpeter broke out the "smack." Any resolve he may have had to keep Young clean had vanished. In the past, Baker had used the needle as a weapon against women, notably Carol and Sandy Jones, and now it was Young's turn. He shot her such a potent dose of heroin that she OD'd. He knew he had to take her to a hospital, yet worried that if he was seen carrying her out of the elevator, he might be reported to the police. As she turned blue, he and Nocella dragged her into a back stairwell and down eighteen flights. "He figured he had to get me there fast or he'd have another stiff on his hands," she explained.

Young awoke in bed with intravenous needles sticking out of her. Nurses hovered in their black-and-white nun's habits, and Baker stood nearby. As soon as she came to, a nun asked her what drug she had taken. Still woozy, she began to tell them the truth. Then she felt Baker's eyes on her, and she murmured that she had used too much Valium. Young survived, but Larry Nocella wasn't so lucky. Within a year, he had died of an overdose.

Gradually it dawned on her that she too was headed for disaster by always putting Baker's needs, no matter how hazardous, before her own. Then she found a letter he had started writing to Carol, promising her that on his next tour, she would be at his side. Young wasn't pleased. "I knew he was playing a game with me now," she said. "He was keeping her on a string." When Young confronted him, Baker said matter-of-factly: "She told me she'd kill herself if I left." Subsequently he showed her a draft of another letter intended for Carol. In it, he informed his wife that if she went ahead and reported him to the IRS, he could wind up in jail for years—two, he thought, for every year of unpaid taxes.

"You're explaining to her how to fuck with you, just in case she didn't have it worked out!" Young warned him. He never mailed the letter; typically, he chose to ignore the situation rather than deal with it head-on. But his mistrust of Carol persisted, and he vowed not to let her get his money. On February 25, 1981, he handwrote a statement declaring that Young should receive any income from an autobiography or film about his life. On March 27, he signed a release (which he later had notarized) granting her power of attorney. The next year, he sent letters to CTI label owner Creed Taylor and to the Blue Note club in New York, instructing them to pay sums owed him—three thousand and one thousand dollars, respectively—to Young.

Starting in 1981, he no longer had Gaby Kleinschmidt to handle his business for him. The agent, whose duties had extended to buying him Valium and denture glue, had booked him in Bremen, Germany, following a date in Austria. Baker planned to drive to the concert with his band while Kleinschmidt traveled by train. He asked her to hold his trumpet case and wallet for safekeeping. At the German border, police stopped the train. Marching up and down the aisles, they inspected everyone's passports, checking them against a government list of criminal offenders. Kleinschmidt's name was there as the representative of Chet Baker. The officers escorted her off the train, then set loose a pack of drug-sniffing dogs. The animals circled her and walked away. After hours of waiting and being questioned, she was allowed to board another train. Slumped in her seat, Kleinschmidt murmured a prayer of thanks. Then a thought occurred to her. Opening Baker's wallet, she found seven envelopes of cocaine inside. Apparently the dogs had been trained to detect only pot and hash. "I would have been in prison for years!" she said. Outraged as she was, her fear of Baker prevented her from ever confronting him. "He didn't know anymore what is right and what is wrong," said Kleinschmidt, who left him a few months later. "My ulcer couldn't take it anymore," she explained.

In February 1982, Baker returned again to New York, where he stayed through December. For the moment he had no formal agent in Europe, and little American work. In a foul mood, he arrived at the apartment of Leo and Diane Mitchell, who had invited him to stay there awhile. Moments after he walked through the door, Baker tossed a pocketful of francs on the table and ordered Diane to exchange them for dollars. "Fuck you!" she said. Baker left in a huff and changed the money himself. "For four days," Diane recalled, "all he did was go out to get drugs. Take the drugs. Sleep. Go and get more drugs." By the end of the four days, the money, of course, was all gone.

"Cool" certainly didn't describe his mood as he fumed over his lousy luck. "I came in with nothing, and I'm going out with nothing!" he told Diane, who showed no sympathy. "That was his personal vendetta, like he got cut a bad pass or something. But he'd had all the gifts you could ever dream of! And he destroyed them. I think that maybe Chet couldn't deal with it. Maybe getting all this attention made him hate people more.

He once made a comment that he didn't like people who didn't take care of themselves, like fat people. I thought, look in the mirror—you love yourself?"

One day she came home to find the bathroom occupied, as it often was when Baker lived in the apartment. Angrily she flung open the door to find him before the sink, in a T-shirt Leo had given him. Jockey shorts around his knees, he jabbed at his bloodied groin with a needle, staring down in the same trance he entered when he picked up his horn. He didn't even seem to notice her. Disgusted, she grabbed her camera and started taking pictures. As the flashbulb popped over and over, Baker went about his "work" as nonchalantly as if it were 1953 and William Claxton were in the Pacific Jazz studios, photographing him in song.

Later, Diane thrust the pictures under Leo's face. "See?" she demanded. "You know why I took these? Just remember this!"

Most people forgave Baker almost anything when they heard him play. That winter, Matthias Winckelmann, owner of the German jazz label Enja, paired him with the vibraphonist and composer David Friedman. *Peace* was the ironic title of an album of originals by Friedman, most of which had a sinister, tiptoeing-in-the-night quality. Inviting Friedman to Young's apartment, Baker greeted the young man in his bathrobe. "Oh, *hiiiiii,* Dave," he said, glazed. Friedman proceeded to sit at the piano and play the songs. "Oh, that's really nice," drawled Baker. Friedman suggested that he get out his trumpet. "I don't have a trumpet at the moment," said Baker, explaining that Winckelmann would buy him a new one. Friedman left, expecting the worst.

At the first of two sessions, he waited for nearly two hours with bassist Buster Williams, drummer Joe Chambers, and Winckelmann. Baker never came. Winckelmann and Young went searching for him at his usual drug haunts. They found him at Fifty-second Street and Ninth Avenue. "Oh, *yeeeah,*" he said when they reminded him about the record.

Now Baker had one afternoon to make a whole album of difficult music he didn't know. In the studio, Friedman nervously ran down the tunes for him. With all the bravado he had shown at twenty-one, Baker picked up his horn at each take and dazzled Friedman with his improvisations. Not knowing the peculiar chords, he responded to them all in the moment, totally by ear. For years thereafter, Friedman, a schooled musician, avoided reading chord changes himself, convinced that Baker had shown him the true light of jazz.

For the rest of 1982, though, the trumpeter aroused mostly disappointment. In June he played the Blue Note, a new Greenwich Village jazz club that soon rose to international fame. Joined by Sal Nistico, a passionate tenor player who had worked with Count Basie, he received a warm notice in the *New York Times,* and attendance was strong. Closing night was the Fourth of July, and tourists packed the club. Between sets, Baker and Leo Mitchell left to cop in the East Village and never came back. The rest of the band had to go on without him. So ended Baker's one and only engagement at the Blue Note.

A subsequent tour of California and Texas was even messier. The dates had been arranged by Luis Gasca, a talented trumpeter whose career had short-circuited due to drugs. Needing money, Gasca endeavored to book and manage Chet Baker. He enlisted the help of his girlfriend Lesley Mitchell, a young singer whose uncle, bassist Red Mitchell, had worked with Baker in the fifties. "Chet was always helpless, or seemed to be," she said. "He had been a junkie for so long that his soul was gone. The only time you could perceive it was in his playing. There was such a duality there, because he was a coldhearted, almost demonic figure. It was very hard to understand where the beautiful music came from."

Early in the tour, he worked in At My Place, a Santa Monica club. When he failed to show up for the first set, Gasca and Mitchell went to his hotel room. There they found him propped against a wall semi-conscious, a heavy wool sweater hanging on his bony frame and a needle stuck out of his arm through the sleeve. "We woke him up and said, 'Chet, don't you think it would work better without the sweater?' " Mitchell recalled.

Nonetheless, business was excellent; there, in the town of his original triumphs, he was a minor legend, even if the fascination bordered on the macabre. "I think most people felt he was on his last legs," said Mitchell. "There was probably a blood-lust element, where people wanted to see if he would fall down, like Judy Garland." He didn't, but when Russ Freeman came to the club to see Baker for the first time in years, he found the club dark; the trumpeter had never shown up.

Further dates in San Diego and Texas, Mitchell explained, "were a big long nightmare," capped, she said, when Baker invited his son Paul to travel with him. His latest attempt at fatherhood shocked Mitchell. "Chet never said one word to that boy that I saw on the whole trip," she remembered. "And when it came time that he wanted the kid out of there, he told me to send him home from Texas on a bus. It would have been a distance of hundreds of miles. So I flew the kid out on my own money. It was very sad."

Young's relationship with Baker was also crumbling fast. More and more he traveled without her, and when he announced, inexplicably, that Carol wanted to take over her continuing efforts to book the band, Young panicked. Her fragility was obvious in the letters she wrote him that year. "Please help Chettie," she pleaded. "I want to be strong for you but it seems as if you don't need me anymore. . . . It's so true that I'm miserable without you. I'm so afraid. Every time I'm in New York I feel this way and I don't know how much more of the terror I can take." His response summed up the pressure he had felt since childhood: *"Don't hang your life up on me!"* Years later Young had to conclude: "He couldn't stand women. He hated them all. Including me."

Despite the failure of the book project, Lisa Galt Bond had grown close to Young, and she worried that her friend might be verging on a breakdown: "Her depression was immense. She wasn't leaving the house. And she was very dependent on me. I felt that she was in trouble, that she needed to save her own life." Bond tried to coax her out of her apartment to hear some music or to hang out in the East Village. All the while, she kept urging her to break free of Baker. "You want to live, you don't want to go down this hole," she said. "This is death."

Bond later reflected: "Chet probably saw me as a bad influence on Ruth. I was trying to help her to be independent. Ruth was defying him. And he resented it." All his life Baker had done the leaving; now he seemed determined to show Young she couldn't escape him. "No woman tells me to go away," he would later tell Micheline Pelzer. One day Young found the courage to lock him out of her apartment. That night when she came home, there sat Baker. Trembling, she asked him how he had gotten in. "Oh, that's a piece of cake," he said lightly.

In coming weeks her belongings began to disappear, hocked for dope money. Turning a corner onto St. Mark's Place and Second Avenue, Bond saw Baker on the curb, selling his own albums and tapes along with others he had stolen from Young. "Hey, kid, you're allowed to look at the stuff!" he said, to Bond's horror.

Her trust fund now dried up, Young could hardly pay her rent or phone bill. Still Baker demanded money. When she refused, he pointed at a silver plate on the wall and insisted she hand it over. She said no, and he turned into an animal before her eyes. As she cowered in tears, he began tearing down the wall collage of Chet Baker photos she had lovingly assembled. By the time his rage had boiled out of him, remnants of the great trumpeter lay scattered in shreds.

The violence had only begun. One day, during one of their nastiest arguments, Young reached for the phone to call the police. Baker grabbed the cord and looped it tightly around her neck. For several terrifying moments, she was sure he meant to kill her. Finally he let her go. A few minutes later, he was calm again. "If I wanted to kill you, I would have killed you," he said blithely. She couldn't accept the convenient notion that dope had turned him into this monster. "Don't tell me you can't think through the fucking drugs!" she said. "Depending on the strength of your character, heroin is no different from any other drug that accentuates who you are to begin with."

As Missy kept visiting regularly, a darkness seemed to be emerging in her that recalled her father. The change was evident in a photo of herself she gave Young. It showed her standing in a liquor store in Astoria waiting for a rainstorm to pass. Posed against rows of bottles, she glared into the camera with cold defiance. At sixteen, Missy remained a confused, impressionable child, caught in a war between two strong women who were battling over her father. Now she rebelled. "I think Melissa envied the position Ruth was in with her father," said Bond. "Traveling with him, being with him, which Melissa was not. I think she was jealous of the material things Ruth had that she didn't."

Late that summer, Young returned to her apartment to find it ransacked. Everywhere she looked, things were gone: a sealskin jacket and other clothing, jewelry, an Oriental scroll, a radio and cassette player, Baker's award plaques and family photos. The trumpeter surprised her by rallying to her support. With her help, he made a list of the missing items and prepared to call the police. Her plumber, he decided, was the culprit.

Baker was wrong. In 1989, at a screening of *Let's Get Lost,* Young would learn the truth. Bruce Weber had filmed an interview with Carol and the children in Oklahoma, where they were living. Young saw Melissa, seated on a sofa between her mother and brothers, proudly reveal herself as the thief. She had gone to Young's apartment to see her father, she said, not knowing he had left town. Peeping through the window, which was slightly open, she saw no one inside. She pried it open and climbed through, whereupon she gathered up all the plaques and other possessions Baker had brought there. "I also got her back for a few things she'd said to me and done to me too," said Melissa in her newly acquired hillbilly twang. "And I don't feel guilty about a bit of it either." When Weber asked for specifics, she said she had stolen from Young "what would hurt the most," notably her jewelry. "She had some *sexxxxy* clothes I liked too," Melissa added, drawing out the word with a mixture of scorn and country-girl envy. What had she done with the jewelry? "I hocked it," she said, smiling. "All of it. For ninety dollars." As Melissa spoke of the theft, Carol giggled and prodded her on.

"These people chill the blood," said Bond. "Chet swam in the middle of that ocean of sharks. He played every side."

By 1982, Carol had filed a complaint against her husband with the Queens Family Services, which summoned him to a hearing for nonpayment of support. He never showed up. Life in New York had become impossible for her, and she moved the family to Stillwater, Oklahoma, near Vera's home in Yale. Finding a job there as secretary to the dean at Oklahoma State University, Carol was finally able to place the children securely in school. Around that time Baker wrote to Mario Andriulli, an Italian trumpeter friend, explaining that his kids just couldn't get a decent education in New York. The classrooms were too chaotic, he said, and overrun with blacks.

On one of their last trips to the Pelzer house, Young answered the phone to hear the voice of Carol, asking to speak to her husband. He was out, so Carol left the terse message that Dean had been hit by a truck in Oklahoma and was in serious condition. As soon as Baker came home, Young gave him the news. "Oh, shit," he murmured, as usual too frozen to react. "He couldn't deal with it," she said. "Or, rather, he chose not to deal with it." Carol's call went unreturned. Although Dean survived, the emotional scars from the accident remained, and he lived at home with his mother for years to come.

Tom Baker had continued to "hang his life" on the trumpeter, even though all their would-be collaborations had died. His idol stayed friendly with him, mainly because Tom's Fourteenth Street loft was a convenient place to fix after an East Village score. Tom, who was still a junkie himself, was proud to have the famous Chet Baker shoot up in his home. By now he had a roommate, Legs McNeil, a journalist and editor who chronicled the punk-music scene of the seventies. McNeil first met Baker in the kitchen. "Chet had his balls in his hand and was shooting up in his uppermost thigh," he recalled. "Tom said, 'Oh, this is Legs.' "

On September 2, 1982, the apartment became unavailable for further visits. That was the day Tom shot the speedball that killed him at forty-two.

Young's relationship with Baker was equally doomed, yet that month she tried one last scheme to revive it. With his consent, she booked a romantic vacation for two to St. Croix in the Virgin Islands. As the departure date drew near, Baker vanished. At the last minute, Young invited Bond to go instead. All week long, Young phoned the apartment, praying in vain to find him there. On September 17, she came home. As soon as she opened her door, she felt his presence. She called out his name. He didn't answer. She found him in the bathroom, oblivious to her as he searched for an uncollapsed vein to hit.

"I walked away, talking to him," she said. "He was not listening. I suppose I was really talking to myself, hoping he would hear." Young left the apartment and wandered down Columbus Avenue, sobbing hysterically. She walked into a small Mexican bar. It was nearly empty except for an employee. Immediately he befriended her, offering to let her stay with him for as long as she needed. Every day Young dialed her number, now hoping Baker wasn't there to answer. Over and over he was. She hung up each time, knowing that just a few words from him would break her resolve.

Baker had other concerns. On September 25, he placed a call to San Jose. "Is this the beautiful and talented Diane Vavra?" he asked in his most charming voice. "Yes!" said the excited woman on the other end. "Is this Chet Baker?" He was heading her way soon, he explained, and wondered if he could see her. Gleefully she agreed.

After three weeks, he had stopped answering Young's phone, and she decided it was safe to go home. She unlocked the door tentatively and peeked inside. The first thing she saw was an empty space on the floor where her piano had been. In the apartment she found a deed in Baker's writing, claiming ownership of the instrument along with the right to sell it to Sheila Ditchfield, a woman on the East Side, for four hundred dollars. She phoned Ditchfield, who wouldn't return the piano. "That was the price I paid to leave him," Young said.

In years to come, she would try to analyze what had kept her tied to an ultimately destructive relationship for so long. "All artists are in their own little world," she said. "Carol Baker fused herself into his life—as did I, and Diane Vavra, and anybody who was with him, because of this allure of fame and importance and mystique. But it isn't real! There is no life behind the celebrity, 99 percent of the time. At least I managed to figure that out, which is why I left." For all this hindsight, Baker's pull on her lingered, and she would write to him often, hoping for a reconciliation that didn't happen.

Shortly after the breakup, she was surprised to receive a call from Vavra, whom she had never met. "It went something like: 'Hello, Ruth? This is Diane. I just thought I would call, 'cause now that you're not together, is there anything I ought to know about that I missed the first time around?' "

For about twenty minutes, Young said, Vavra interviewed her about Baker: "Did Chet do this. . . . Is he still doing . . . should I . . ." Young called that chat "probably the strangest moment of my life."

An odder one awaited John Snyder. With debts from his Artists House label in the six figures, it seemed as though his producing days were over. His wife had departed too, taking the children and the furniture. The phone in his East Side apartment had been turned off, along with the electricity. At night he ran an extension cord down the hall and plugged it into an outlet so he could use the lamp and TV. He slept on a foam-rubber mattress on the floor. "I never left the house," said Snyder. "I didn't bathe for weeks. I just lay there. It was a nightmare." Soon he had no choice but to go back to North Carolina. Prior to that, however, his doorman rang with the news that Chet Baker was downstairs. "Send him up," said Snyder, puzzled. He hadn't seen Baker in a long time. When Snyder opened the door, Baker shuddered. "You look worse than I do," he said.

"Well, yeah, Chet, I'm not doing too good. What is it, what can I do for you?"

"You got any money?" asked Baker.

"Chet, I've got fourteen dollars."

"Can I have half of it?"

"I said, 'Chet, you want seven dollars?' He said yeah. I gave him seven dollars. And he left. I think that was the last time I saw him."

17

In the five years since her last encounter with Chet Baker, little had gone right for Diane Vavra. Now forty-two, she had recently earned a master's degree and was teaching music part-time. But self-doubt so crippled her that she was neglecting her own talents as a soprano saxophone and clarinet player. Much of her free time was spent trying to help her teenage son, whose drug problem had sent him repeatedly to jail.

But with one phone call from Baker, her whole world seemed to brighten. She came home one day to find him standing in front of her house, holding a huge bouquet of flowers. Her heart soared. So did her son's. The young man was inside with his friends, and he boasted to them about his mother's boyfriend, this famous trumpeter who had been a junkie since the fifties. "He's a god, man!" Baker heard her son exclaim. He took advantage of the moment by asking the teenager to find him some dope. "I crumbled inside," said Vavra. "It hurt me. But my joy in seeing Chet overrode everything."

Over the next three weeks, they filled each other in on the details of their lives apart. Baker was much more forthcoming than she remembered. "He was bitter, angry . . . *very* angry," she said. Still, it pained her to say a temporary goodbye to him in December, when he flew to Oklahoma to pay a brief Christmas visit to his mother and family before heading to Europe for several weeks' work. Around that time, he resumed contact with Young. Guilty, perhaps, for having sold her piano, he went out of his way to help her singing career, playing her demo tape for promoters and recommending her for gigs. Writing her in 1983, he voiced utmost admiration, and urged her never to give up singing.

For the moment, he had no woman to take care of him, and in his desperation he turned to the daughter of his best friend. Micheline Pelzer had recently wed Michel Graillier after a decade of living together, but her infatuation with Baker wasn't a secret. Near the start of 1983, when the pianist left their home outside Paris to tour, Micheline took the opportunity to pamper Baker. Standing at the kitchen stove, she gleefully cooked him a big dinner. He walked up to her from behind and touched her. "Micheline, would you be nice to an old man?" he asked.

A "love" triangle soon emerged, involving a carnivorously needy master and a married couple who were as beguiled by him as they were by each other. Having fallen off the wagon by snorting heroin with Baker on New Year's Eve of 1978, she had since resumed shooting it as well. The exact date was vague in her mind, but not the location (Paris) or the circumstances. At first she was reluctant, she recalled. "It was Chet that pushed me a little bit. He said, 'You're a sissy,' and I didn't like that too much. I said, 'I'm not a sissy, go ahead!' So he started shooting me." The same happened with Michel. "I was scared," he said. "Finally I went in the bathroom, I asked Chet, 'Please, do it for me, because I can't find the spot.' He did it for me—marvelous each time." Neither of the Grailliers blamed Baker for their habits, though. "It's up to you to take it or not take it," said Michel.

Now bonded to Baker at the deepest level, they traveled with him all over the world. His journeys accelerated in 1983 when he reunited with Wim Wigt, the Dutch agent who had booked his abortive German comeback of 1976. Now, with all restrictions lifted, Baker could enter any country. He wanted to work nonstop, and Wigt would keep him on a treadmill until he died. With his curly graying-blond hair, glasses, monotone voice, and aloof manner, Wigt had a steely businessman's air, and Baker's friends found him cold and mercenary. The trumpeter took to calling himself and his musicians "Wim Wigtims" as they followed madly zigzagging itineraries for months on end. "Sometimes he was so tired," said Micheline, "because Wim had him work one day in Paris, then the next day down in the south of Italy, and the next day in the north of Germany. I think that's why he needed more and more smack, just to be able to do it."

But nobody forced Baker to take all these jobs, or to jam his schedule further with every last-minute gig and record date he could find. No venue was too small. Whenever he had a few free days, he would play Le Petit Opportun, a stone cave, cozy as a living room, on the Right Bank of Paris. Side trips in search of dope occupied many of his remaining hours. Just to find him was a chore. But rarely had he known such diligent troubleshooters

Montmartre club, Copenhagen, Denmark, February 28, 1985
Photo by Thorbjørn Sjøgren

as Wigt and his wife and partner, Ria, who were experts at delivering difficult artists to their engagements no matter what. Booking Chet Baker, the couple found, was much like baby-sitting. It involved making a battery of calls just to track him down, phoning his hotel hourly to make sure he left for work on time, calming frantic promoters *("Where is he?")*. Baker would call the Wigts at all hours: he had lost his car keys. He had thrown away his plane tickets. Sometimes at the last minute he would inform Wigt that he was leaving for America, forcing the agent to cancel weeks of European dates. Then came the inevitable message announcing that he was back in Europe and needed to start working tomorrow. A musician known for his flawless rhythm "had no sense of day and time anymore," said Wigt.

The tours were held together by the Wigts' road manager Peter Huijts, whom Hal Galper called "the king of the roadies." A soft-spoken family man with glasses and salt-and-pepper hair, Huijts tended patiently to every crisis. One night he phoned Wigt from a concert hall in Nice to announce the safe arrival of Baker onstage. He didn't see what happened next: after a few rusty honks, a disoriented Baker had stormed off, muttering that he had to oil his trumpet. Huijts was horrified to find the stoned musician attempting to lubricate his horn with Fasteeth. Grabbing the trumpet, Huijts pulled out the valves and tried to rub off the glue, but it had already dried, and when Baker blew into the mouthpiece, only air came out. Furious, he threw the horn into a corner. *"Where's my money?"* he snapped. "Chet, we don't get any money, the people are leaving!" said Huijts. "Well, good!" said Baker. "I'll never play in *this* place again!" Time and again, though, he could switch on the charm so meltingly that promoters took him back, whatever the risk.

Since the early fifties, Stan Getz had regarded him as a brat and a nuisance, so he didn't welcome Wigt's proposal to reunite him with Baker for a tour of Europe. Getz was doing fine on his own; what's more, having quit heroin and joined Alcoholics Anonymous, he wanted nothing more to do with the chemically dependent. For all his self-abuse, Getz's career was in stellar shape; recently he had played at the White House, and he was making albums of a high and adventurous level. Unlike Baker, he knew the value of keeping a steady band, and employed three superior New York jazzmen: pianist Jim McNeely, bassist George Mraz, and drummer Victor Lewis.

A tour with Baker was a guaranteed moneymaker, and the trumpeter consented immediately. Getz agreed to it only under a firm set of rules. He refused to pass through customs with Baker or to use his musicians, and reserved the right to "fire" him if he misbehaved. Wigt said yes on all counts, then hurriedly booked more than thirty concerts in Holland, France, Denmark, even Saudi Arabia.

Getz smelled trouble the first day, when Baker showed up for a six-week tour wearing a soiled trench coat and carrying only a brown paper bag and his trumpet case. The saxophonist's temper flared at the opening concert, held in the Singer Concertzaal in Laren, Holland, on February 10, 1983. The two stars shared the stage for most of the show, trading solos and playing an occasional duet. Getz hadn't counted on the extraordinary devotion European audiences felt for Baker. "Chet was getting much more applause than Stan," recalled Irv Rochlin, a pianist from Chicago who lived in Amsterdam and attended that performance. Getz looked like a grouchy suburban grandfather; he shuffled onstage in a pink sweater, sky-blue pants, and white tennis shoes, and frowned throughout. Baker, by contrast, seemed so worn-out and sad that he touched the heart.

They remained a musical mismatch. Baker's stamina may have declined, but that only made him sound more poignant. Getz's playing had all the icy-smooth perfection of his youth, but it was as guarded as ever and, according to his former bassist Jon Burr, far from spontaneous. "Stan had a limited arsenal of licks," said Burr. "The craft he engaged in was the quality of his sound. Whereas Chet was not only into the sound, he was dedicated to finding a new way through the music every night." The biggest ovation of the show always went to Baker, after "My Funny Valentine."

Getz played it cool onstage, but over the next three weeks, he placed an angry series of calls to Wigt. The saxophonist was trying to control George Mraz's drinking, and he complained that Baker had bought the bassist a Cognac. Meanwhile, according to Getz's biographer, Donald L. Maggin, Getz himself had succumbed to both alcohol and coke by the second week. This latest cool-school reunion was starting to seem more like a remake of *Romper Room.*

The tension exploded in late February, when the group reached Saudi Arabia. Baker had copped a supply of "stuff" before the flight and was planning to take it into a country whose anti-drug laws were among the fiercest in the world. When Getz found out, he flew into a rage; according to Victor Lewis, he seized the dope and flushed it down a toilet. With that, he phoned Wigt and declared: "It's him or me." The agent assumed that Getz was mainly jealous. So did Baker when Wigt called him and broke the news, offering to pay him full salary for the remaining shows. Baker took the money. Later he snarled to Guy Masy, a tenor saxophonist from Liège, that he wished he could put the same curse on Getz that he had once cast on John O'Grady.

A short tour was thrown together in place of the canceled Getz shows. Baker worked in duo with Michel Graillier, whose playing combined the elegant harmonic language of Bill Evans with florid touches of French impressionism. Graillier felt like a child at the feet of some wise old seer. But when the pianist's drinking resulted in flubbed chords and sloppy time, Baker turned nasty. "If you are wrong during the music, you are doing a very big violence to the man," explained Nicola Stilo. Baker responded in kind. When Graillier fumbled the changes to "My Funny Valentine" at a cathedral in Sicily, Baker put down his horn, walked to the piano, and shoved Graillier off the bench with one hand, angrily pounding out the chords with the other. Graillier always forgave. "To me Chet was not just a friend, he was like a spiritual father. I think I could stay with him so long because I accepted everything he was doing. Oftentimes it was just not right, really."

Diane Vavra had joined Baker in Europe after the breakup of the Getz tour, and the trumpeter was relieved to have her back. He considered her his alter ego, a woman who seemed to understand his art better than he did. In public, the couple—he now fifty-three, she forty-three—cuddled and held hands like teenagers in love. Unavoidably, Baker's inner circle would become a hornet's nest, as everyone vied for the top spot in his affections. The Grailliers were sure that Vavra resented their closeness to Baker: "She was getting jealous every time Chet and me would go to cop," said Micheline. "But we didn't see her taking him to the middle of the Seine for three hours to wait for the man, you know?" Nicola Stilo's constant presence caused more tension. "He was always with us, always," Micheline recalled. "And sometimes when Diane was not there and I wanted privacy with Chet, that was a drag." Vavra felt the same way: "Nicola and I didn't get along at all, because he was jealous of me and I was jealous of him. It caused a lot of problems."

Baker was too wrapped up in his own worries to notice. In a TV interview during a tour of Spain that year, Baker, seated with Vavra in a hotel lounge in Barcelona, answered questions testily. The trumpeter looked exhausted; his hair hung down in greasy strands that hadn't been cut in weeks, and he needed a shave. His black T-shirt read JAZZ in big letters. "If I don't play I don't eat!" Baker hissed. "That's the only money I've got. . . . I've made over a hundred albums in my life, and I've never made a *penny* royalty from one of them!" Asked why he avoided using drummers, he got even angrier: "Because they make too much goddamn noise, that's why! I don't need anybody to keep time for me!" Poking his brow, he said: "I've got the time locked up *right in my head*!"

Opinions divided sharply over his music-making of the eighties. To many musicians and fans, especially in Europe, he sounded more poetic, expressive, and rich of tone than ever. "I learned so much from him," said Rocky Knauer, a Canadian bassist living in Germany who played with Baker on and off from 1979 through 1988. "Even if it was a bad night, there was still something happening that was good. When things were on, man, it was like a magic carpet ride."

Yet serious problems had set in. Baker felt increasingly sick, and his dentures caused daily pain. His life had become a blur of plane and car rides, gigs and record dates ("They're all running together; I've done too many of them," he said in his last conversation with Ruth Young). Stopping at the Pelzer house, he usually went straight to bed. "There was no life," said Irv Rochlin. "It was the gig, and it was boredom, compensated for by drugs." Now when people stared at him, he felt revulsion in their eyes. Drummer Kenny Washington, then in his early twenties, recalled running into Baker at a hotel diner in Holland. Over breakfast they chatted amiably about gigs and the road. A few tables away sat a man reading a newspaper. He seemed to recognize Baker, and every once in a while he glanced over. The trumpeter kept talking to Washington in his soft, caressing voice: "I'm going to Italy, I've got a tour there . . ." Suddenly he turned toward the curious customer nearby and shouted through a near-empty room: "WHO THE FUCK ARE YOU LOOKIN' AT?" The man slumped in embarrassment and hid behind his paper. "Then he went on talking to me just as if nothing had happened," said Washington.

Baker still had enough confidence to think that after thirty years he could play without warming up. But he wasn't so young anymore, and the first number in most concerts was marred by ugly squeaks and gusts of dead air. Scowling, he would tear the horn from his lips and shake it up and down, as though some gremlin were stuck inside.

"I think at this time of life he was just too tired and depressed to play very well," said Vavra. "Too little sleep, too many drugs—it kills your creativity. His time was wonderful, he got a groove like no one else, but Chet had a bunch of licks, and he just rearranged them. He wasn't reaching for anything. Inspiring musicians inspired him, but he used mostly second-rate guys." On the Getz tour, the presence of Victor Lewis, she felt, had shown what Baker could achieve with superior backing: "The drummer's kicking his ass, saying, come on, man! That's why he didn't want to play with drummers; he was too exhausted to be creative."

Coke and cigarettes had made his once-dewy singing voice sound as pinched and nasal as a kazoo. Delivering songs he had performed hundreds of times, he threw away the words and "blew" on the tunes, impressing musicians but conveying little of his early sweetness. Evert Hekkema, a Dutch trumpeter with whom he lived in the mideighties, sensed Baker's dissatisfaction. When Hekkema praised him after a show, Baker grumbled: "Nah, I didn't play shit tonight!" Onstage he wore a pout, rarely speaking to the audience or even glancing at them.

Frequently he stopped in mid-song to berate the sound man for "twisting the dials"—an attempt to give him some volume. Jean-Louis Rassinfosse witnessed it often: "He would jam the trumpet bell against the mike and make the sound distort on purpose, and say, *'This is what you're doing to me!'* He always had problems with the sound engineers, because they didn't understand what he wanted. Of course I have to admit that he didn't give much information. He would expect people all over the world to know what he wanted the trumpet to sound like." At the end of a concert, Baker would say a few brisk words—"Thank you very much, we hope you enjoyed the music"—and walk off.

But even at his worst, he had a sound that moved people; with just a few notes, he could rivet an audience. For that electric charge, his European fans endured anything. Such was the case at New Morning, a cavernous jazz and world-music club that became his Paris headquarters in 1983. New Morning was run by Madame Eglal Farhi, an Egyptian-born ex-journalist whose charm and refinement masked a shrewd business sense. "The people knew that he might come and not be fit for playing," she said. "They didn't mind. The public was always there." But Farhi, like so many before her, had "the unhappy feeling sometimes that they came like you do when you go to a circus and you expect the trapeze artist to fall. They always thought that it would be the last time."

Only drugs could quell Baker's own fear. One night he and Vavra watched a musician playing at Jazzhus Montmartre in Copenhagen. "You know, if I got up there right now, I would just be shaking all over, because I'm not loaded," Baker revealed. Vavra understood his terror. Whenever he pleaded with her to join him onstage with her horn, she froze, rarely ever complying. "Chet did everything he could to help her," said Micheline.

With few usable veins left on his body, Baker had started shooting into the arteries of his neck. He stared coolly into the bathroom or rearview mirror for hours, probing his bloodied throat with a needle. By now his favorite place to score was Amsterdam, a city with an unmatched permissiveness toward drugs and sex. There, he said, "people are not so uptight about *petty* things as they are in other countries." The French, he felt, were "arrogant" and "insincere," the Germans "boring," but Amsterdam, he told an interviewer, had "a twenty-four-hour party going on." Tourists flocked to cafés like the Grasshopper, where they ordered various forms of pot and hash from a menu. Heroin was illegal, but the city had taken a semi-lenient stance toward it, even supplying addicts with clean needles to reduce the spread of disease.

The junkie utopia was Zeedijk, a winding side street near the train station and the city's notorious red-light district of porno shops and storefront brothels. Unlike most streets in that area, which branch off at several points, Zeedijk was a nearly closed pathway from beginning to end, thus offering privacy to dealers and their customers. Nik Williams, an American artist who lived near Zeedijk in the eighties, remembered the "wall-to-wall" drug activity on the street. "You couldn't go down Zeedijk at night without someone propositioning you to buy," he said. "There was a lot of knife play in that area too." Once they scored, some customers hopped onto boats in the nearby canals and shot up onboard.

Baker became such a regular on Zeedijk that some dealers called him by name. But he found a more discreet way to score when he met Robert, his latest "Dr. Feelgood." A Dutch physician who liked jazz, Robert tended patients in his huge house on the outskirts of Amsterdam. Baker met him through Irv Rochlin, who rented a room from the doctor. Robert was so much in awe of Baker that he supplied him with all the methadone and barbiturates he wanted. The "downers" were far more hazardous to Baker than heroin. Under their influence, he lost all control, driving treacherously and suffering fits of paranoia. Vavra begged Robert to stop giving Baker the pills, but to no avail. "They made Chet completely crazy," she said. "Boy, it was scary."

Heroin remained his drug of choice, however. One day he persuaded a reluctant Rochlin to drive him to Zeedijk. A former addict who had years ago gone to jail on a drug charge, Rochlin waited nervously in the car while Baker scored. On the way back to Baker's hotel, the pianist stopped at his apartment to do an errand. He left Baker alone there. "Chet, don't do up," he said. "I'll take you to your hotel in a few minutes."

Rochlin returned to find his guest standing nude, "shaking like a leaf," and clutching the edge of the kitchen sink. Baker had stripped down to find a vein, then shot a near-lethal dose of heroin, the rest of which lay in a pile on the table. Spotting Rochlin, Baker ordered him to prepare a saline injection, a way for junkies to dilute the heroin and possibly save themselves from death. *"Hit me in the neck!"* gasped Baker. "Put a tourniquet there." Rochlin prepared the syringe, then froze. "I can't, Chet!" he said, handing him the needle. Baker stuck it into his jugular, then sat down, still nude. "He was out for quite a while," Rochlin said.

Finally he stood up, dressed, and scooped his dope into a bag. Rochlin drove him to his hotel. Once there, Baker asked the pianist if he would come upstairs and sit with him. As they talked casually, Rochlin had a question: "Hey, Chet, don't you ever get tired of this shit?"

"He thought I meant getting guys for the gigs, traveling, the usual things a jazz musician has to do. I said, 'No, man, I mean using shit.' "

"Oh, I never think about that."

Determined to make Amsterdam his home, Baker had phoned Rochlin in the spring of 1983 and asked if he knew of a car for sale. As luck had it, he did: Rochlin had a trumpeter friend, Evert Hekkema, who wanted to sell his Peugeot. That day, Baker was sitting at the wheel beside Hekkema, giving the sports car a test drive. Hekkema was surprised at Baker's slovenliness: the matted gray hairs blowing wildly as he sped around the block, the unclipped toenails protruding from his sandals. But Baker flattered the younger musician by asking all about his life in Amsterdam, and Hekkema ended up in such awe that he sold the car at a bargain price. And when Baker said he was looking for a place to stay in town, the Dutchman innocently offered a room in his apartment for only a hundred guilders (approximately sixty-five dollars) a week. Hekkema had a large four-room walkup in a lovely central location near two intersecting canals. But Baker was more interested in the building's proximity to Zeedijk, which was just minutes away.

After settling in, he delighted his host with outrageous autobiographical tales. One involved a train ride he and Leo Mitchell had taken from Amsterdam to Paris. First-class tickets in hand, they entered a cabin occupied by a well-to-do American couple. The two jazzmen looked as though they had been sleeping in an alley, and Baker, who often doused himself with Paco Rabanne cologne in lieu of bathing, made the couple's noses wrinkle. After a few minutes, the man whispered to his wife: "I can't stand that smell!" Baker responded by sliding open the window, letting an icy gust of air into the compartment. "Would you please close the window?" said the man. "We're catching a cold!"

Glaring, Baker said calmly: "The window stays open till the smell is totally gone."

After another heavy silence, the passenger pleaded: "We'd like to have a pleasant trip!"

"Listen, asshole," said Baker. "If you fuck with me, you'll have the most unpleasant trip you ever had!"

Later that night, Hekkema began one of his own. Lying in bed, he became aware of someone in the room. He saw a stoned Chet Baker, nude except for a red T-shirt, standing doubled over and as motionless as a statue. Hekkema stared for several uneasy minutes. Finally Baker opened his eyes and saw where he was. Embarrassed, he tried to turn the moment into a joke, mimicking an old, hunched-over cowboy shaking his cane.

Usually, though, his actions were too bizarre to be funny. Because his body chemistry was so out of whack, simple sensations like hot and cold didn't always register. In his bedroom he turned the heater up to the max, then lay perspiring in bed, the room strewn with clothes and papers. Often he would sleep for fifteen hours or more. He could switch from docile to hostile in a flash. One day a friend of Hekkema's called and heard an unfamiliar voice on the other end. "Who is this?" the friend asked.

"What difference does it make who this is?"

Startled, the friend asked, "Well, I don't know."

"Well, fuck you, then!" said Baker, slamming down the phone.

However capricious his moods, his junkie know-how seldom failed him. Soon after moving in, he left his house keys inside his car, then forgot where he had parked. He rang the bell of a downstairs neighbor. "Hello, my name is Chet Baker," he said politely. "I live upstairs, and I forgot my key." With her permission, he walked through the apartment to the back alleyway. The neighbor watched, astonished, as Baker scaled the rear balconies up to Hekkema's apartment, entering it through the kitchen door. "She said he really went up like a cat," the Dutchman recalled. "He was up in a few seconds. Some people here, they look down, they get dizzy."

Luckily for Hekkema, Baker was away much of the time. He spent the early months of 1984 touring with Michel Graillier, Riccardo Del Fra, and Nicola Stilo in Italy and France. In the spring he traveled through Scandinavia with a trio led by the Swedish pianist Åke Johannson. To Baker's distress, Vavra wasn't with him; a family crisis had sent her home to California.

Ignoring her plight, he bombarded her with letters insisting she drop everything and return to his side. His love for her surpassed any he had ever known, he assured her.

Without Vavra, he turned once more to the Grailliers, who were living in Paris and in a funk of their own. Work was slow for Michel, and the couple were broke and fighting violently. They wanted to stay high, though, and so did Baker. Short on heroin, he gulped a few barbiturates, washing them down with gin. He shared the pills and liquor with the couple, and soon everyone was delirious. Micheline passed out on the bed, and her husband beat her in the face with a magazine until she bled. Seeing what Michel had done, Baker knocked the small man to the floor and began kicking him so savagely that Micheline thought she was about to become a widow. *"You don't know how to treat a woman!"* Baker screamed. With that, he told Micheline to get dressed; they were leaving for Italy. "I took my jewels and all my things with me," she said. "Of course, everything went on the street."

They stayed together for three months. Jacques Pelzer was furious when he learned of his daughter's "elopement" with Baker; it sparked his only serious fight with the trumpeter. Yet Micheline was thrilled to have Baker to herself at last, and accompanied him from concert to concert, sometimes playing the drums. She even carried his stash across borders. Once, in the Alps between Italy and France, police inspected the car and strip-searched Baker. Miraculously, they ignored Micheline, who had ten grams of heroin in her pants. She was a picture of calm. "I was cool, because I was high," she explained.

So was Baker. Micheline watched him mesmerize customs officials to such a degree that he could enter countries with no passport. "He would do a show," she said. "He was a good actor. He would start to talk to the people in French. I didn't know he could do that!" She and Baker laughed a lot, despite the disasters they attracted at every turn. On the highway in Naples, they trailed behind the roadie who transported Baker's trumpet and Riccardo Del Fra's bass. Cars whizzed by at eighty miles an hour, the Italian speed limit. Up ahead, a driver spotted an accident by the side of the road and slowed down to look. Within seconds, dozens of cars had crashed into one another, creating a pileup so thunderous it sounded like an earthquake. Baker's hair-trigger instincts saved him, and he swerved out of harm's way at the crucial moment. But the roadie's car exploded. *"The trumpet!"* screamed Micheline. Grabbing the instruments just in time, they drove off, leaving behind a mess of steel, smoke, and injured bodies.

A greater crisis occurred in Rome when they ran out of drug money. Baker knew what to do. He stopped by SIAE (Società Italiana degli Autori ed Editori), Italy's version of ASCAP, while Micheline waited in the car. He returned with a million lire (about $650) as an advance against royalties for his old prison compositions. "How did you do it?" asked Micheline, astounded. Baker said he told them he had bronchial pneumonia and needed emergency treatment in Switzerland. "We got it, Micheline!" he exclaimed. "Let's get high!" They raced to a dealer, who gave them a sample "taste" of his stuff. It was so pure, Micheline recalled, that they were "high for twelve hours." They spent the whole sum and went on their way. In the car, Baker used Micheline as his tester. She stuck a finger in the bag and touched the powder to her tongue. "Chet, it's salty!" she said. Soon she realized they had spent a million lire on Alka-Seltzer. Baker couldn't accept it, and he insisted she keep experimenting. "Every fifteen minutes he was telling me, 'Try it again!' Up until Milano he made me shoot Alka-Seltzer."

All this struck her as a fabulous lark, but the mood turned serious when she made a revelation to Baker. "I've got a little problem," she said. "I'm in love with you." Baker answered calmly: "I don't want you to be in love with me, because I don't want you to suffer." But it was he who was in agony. Vavra's absence, he felt sure, was proof that she had found another man. After Micheline returned to her husband, Baker reunited with Vavra as well. The accusations started at once: she was sleeping with Evert Hekkema, drummer Aldo Romano, Nicola Stilo. All parties swore it wasn't true; Micheline didn't believe it either. But with every one of his outbursts, Vavra's spirits dipped, until she shared his black cloud of despair. Observers noticed how similar they looked: the same dejected eyes, the mouths that turned down at the corners. However often she fled, she always came back. "I was in turmoil," she said. "I couldn't think straight, I was confused. It was obviously an addiction."

Vavra had never heard the term "codependency," but in 1986, author Melody Beattie would revolutionize pop psychology with her mammoth best-seller, *Codependent No More.* Beattie defined codependents as individuals who were "obsessed" and "tormented by other people's behavior," particularly that of substance abusers, who needed a savior. Codependents, she wrote, gave "until they were angry, exhausted, and emptied of everything." They obsessed over their loved ones' flaws, yet "couldn't see themselves. . . . And they didn't know what, if anything, they could do to solve their problems."

As the only non–heroin user in Baker's inner circle, Vavra had begun to feel left out. Riccardo Del Fra was sniffing at the time, and she asked him how much heroin one could inhale without getting hooked. Vavra tried it and hated the results: she kept nodding off, and complained to Micheline of leg and stomach pain. In a few weeks she quit. From then on, she escaped to California whenever she couldn't stand the pressure. As soon as she left, Baker would revert to an abandoned little boy. He would sleep in Hekkema's room for comfort, and as usual, phoned Vavra twice a day: "Please come back, come back!" Drugs gave him his only solace. "He had different doctors everywhere," said Stilo. "It was not just a problem of heroin or cocaine; he was taking pills, everything." The combination and strength of all these chemicals were inducing hallucinations. One wintry day in early 1985, while Vavra was in California, Baker decided that Hekkema had hidden her in the house. Running into the attic, he yelled: "DIANE! DIANE!"

"No, Chet, she's not here, she's in the States!" said Hekkema.

Baker wouldn't listen: *"You know where she is! Tell me where she is!"* Barefoot and wearing only jeans, he ran downstairs and into the cold street. Eyes darting, he bolted to the other side of the canal and screamed at the windows: *"Diane! I know you're there!"*

Soon she returned to Europe, of course, to join him for another cycle of chilling flare-ups and sober apologies. Life without her was impossible, he admitted to several friends, and he tried to prove it in the sincerest way he knew. In February 1985, Baker proudly told her he planned to record an old hit from 1927, "Diane (I'm in Heaven When I Look in Your Eyes)." Baker's version appeared as the title cut of a duo album he made in Copenhagen with Paul Bley, a Canadian pianist who had worked briefly in his quartet thirty years before. For sheer hypnotic atmosphere, *Diane* had few equals in Baker's career, its ultra-languid tempos allowing him to spin out his most luscious tone. "It's great to play in a car after midnight in a city you don't live in," Bley said.

With that musical valentine in stores, Baker tried to make the sentiments come true. He told journalists he intended to buy a dream house for himself and Vavra in Luxembourg, Rome, Paris, San Jose. A man in his midfifties who had never had the discipline to lay down roots was now imagining how nice it would be to stay in one place for a while. "He was envious of people having homes," said Jean-Louis Rassinfosse. "But the project was always delayed. The money was like an igloo in the Sahara."

Moreover, his traveling soon sped up into another blur. From January through October 1985, he toured heavily in a trio with Rassinfosse and Philip Catherine, a Belgian guitarist known for his fusion playing with such leaders as Jean-Luc Ponty, the French jazz-rock violinist. Baker, Catherine, and Rassinfosse created a form of chamber jazz notable for its airy delicacy, yet marked by all kinds of colorful effects. Catherine challenged Baker with everything from bursts of flamenco-like strumming to the starkest minimalism, while Rassinfosse plucked lovely countermelodies on bass.

The music was tender and romantic, and as with the *Diane* album, it seemed to arouse the same feelings in Baker. Before leaving for a concert in Corsica, France, with Vavra and the two musicians, he decided to turn the trip into a lovers' getaway for all of them. He invited Rassinfosse to bring his wife, and the couple, who had just become parents, left their baby with her mother and flew off for a second honeymoon.

Off they went to Corsica, a large, fragrant island in the Mediterranean Sea between Italy and France. Once there, Baker sank into a foul mood. Crazy from barbiturates, he picked fights with everyone around him. Catherine left immediately after the show, but Rassinfosse and his wife took the hotel room next to Baker's. Past midnight, they heard a fight erupt in the next room, followed by Vavra's anguished cries for help. Baker stormed out. Once he was gone, Rassinfosse went next door. He found Vavra in a daze, her face bruised and covered with tears. "I'm going to the police!" she cried. "He can't do this to people—I want him in prison for the rest of his life!"

Rassinfosse drove her to the hospital, where she was x-rayed. There were no broken bones, and after her wounds were treated, she and the bassist returned to the hotel. They worried that Baker might be waiting there, but he wasn't, and Rassinfosse insisted she stay with him and his wife. All of them lay sleepless, knowing Baker would return. Hours later, they heard him enter the next room. Finding it empty, he pounded on the bassist's door, shouting, "DIANE! DIANE!" Rassinfosse advised the women to lock up behind him, and went outside. "WHERE'S DIANE?" shouted Baker. Rassinfosse was just as enraged: "Did you see what you did to her face?" Baker only got madder. "You're a fucking asshole! She's not your old lady. This is my problem. *Give me the keys!"* But Rassinfosse, who towered about eight inches above Baker, refused to budge. The trumpeter finally left and boarded a plane to Belgium, leaving Rassinfosse with two hotel bills. "That was our lovely vacation," he said.

He flew himself, his wife, and Vavra to Belgium. "I'm fed up with this now," said Diane through sobs. "It's finished. It'll never change." Days later, she allowed Baker to visit her at the hotel where Rassinfosse had put her. "When I opened the door and he saw my face, he was startled. He didn't remember any of it. He started crying." She fell into his arms.

On June 30, 1985, Baker regained everyone's sympathy when he taped a TV special, *Candy,* at a castle in Stockholm with Rassinfosse and Michel Graillier. He closed the show by sitting at a piano and chatting with his old Hollywood crony, bassist Red Mitchell, long a Stockholm resident. With all the enthusiasm Baker had lost, Mitchell demonstrated some new chords he had devised for Rodgers and Hart's "My Romance." Baker played a chorus, then set his horn down. "I think I'm a little too tired," he said, sighing. "I've got to play at midnight. And I've got to catch a plane at seven-thirty in the morning."

"Everybody was going, 'Oh, the poor little thing,' " Vavra observed. "But it was true. He *was* tired. He *was* in misery. I don't think he was just saying it to . . . Oh, who knows. Maybe he was."

After more than two years of having Baker as a houseguest, though, Evert Hekkema had run out of patience. One night in July, Baker and Vavra awakened him repeatedly with their fighting; finally he left to sleep at his girlfriend's house. The next day he confronted Baker. "I had to cancel two students and a tennis match," Hekkema complained. The trumpeter was unmoved: "So you think your tennis match is more important than our friendship?"

"Well, if you think friendship is making a mess out of the house, I don't," said Hekkema. "You really have to leave now. It's about time." Baker's last hours there were tense. He packed silently, then handed Hekkema the keys and headed out. Before leaving, he shouted, "Fuck you, and don't ever talk to me again!" He slammed the door behind him.

A week later, Hekkema ran into him at Bim Huis, a jazz club in Amsterdam. Baker hugged him. "I can understand why you did it," he said. Thereafter, Baker periodically dropped by the apartment, which remained a handy place for him to shoot up. Hekkema recognized Baker's impatient staccato ringing of the buzzer—"so then I knew not to open the door."

One of Baker's last musical adventures took place in August 1985, when he made his Brazilian debut at the country's first Free Jazz Festival. Sponsored by Free Cigarettes, it took place in São Paulo and Rio de Janeiro. The Rio concerts featured a host of big-name American players—Sonny Rollins,

McCoy Tyner, Phil Woods—but Baker was chosen as the closing-night star attraction.

To many of Brazil's greatest musicians and singers, his name was hallowed. The original *Chet Baker Sings* had made its way there in the fifties, traded among such pioneers of the bossa nova as Carlos Lyra, Roberto Menescal, Nara Leão, Oscar Castro-Neves, and João Gilberto. All of them were young and eager to create their own sound, to break from the animalistic samba rhythms and teary crooning of the past. It was Francisco Pereira, a Brazilian photographer of the day, who invited them to his home to hear *Chet Baker Sings.* They were enthralled by the featherweight delivery, the light jazz pulse, the coolness—qualities found in another American album loved in Brazil, *Julie Is Her Name,* which featured the come-hither vocals of singer-actress Julie London, accompanied gently by guitarist Barney Kessel and bassist Ray Leatherwood.

Zuza Homem de Mello, the Free Jazz Festival's program director and a broadcaster and music historian, explained Baker's appeal in Brazil. "Chet's singing was flat, no vibrato at all, almost talking—like a musician should sing," he said. "And economical—a very important word for the bossa nova. If you listen to João Gilberto's songs, they are played through only once, not twice. Chet sang only what the song asked for, without any kind of overemoting."

In 1958, the bossa nova emerged—an equivalent of fifties West Coast Jazz, soft as the breeze that blew off Copacabana beach. Amid the hundreds of new tunes written by Menescal, Lyra, Antonio Carlos Jobim, and others, Baker's songs remained beloved. Gilberto learned "Like Someone in Love" from Baker and sang it in his thick accent; Leão, the movement's wispy-voiced sweetheart, recorded "But Not for Me" and "My Funny Valentine" in Portuguese translations; Leny Andrade, a swinging Brazilian jazz singer, added "There Will Never Be Another You" to her shows. Singer-songwriter Caetano Veloso, a Brazilian musical and political hero starting in the late sixties, called Baker "one of my biggest influences"; he told the *Folha de São Paulo* that he used to imitate Baker while Gilberto Gil, another titan of Veloso's generation, played guitar.

Keyboardist and composer Riqué Pantoja, who had moved back to Brazil after his stint with Baker in 1980, led the trumpeter's group at Free Jazz. Pantoja and everyone else suspected that time was running out for Baker, and the Rio concert sold out so quickly that another was booked for São Paulo. When Baker arrived with Vavra at Rio's Teatro do Hotel Nacional on August 11, de Mello rushed up. "We are very proud and happy to have you here!" he said. Baker just stared. Quickly, de Mello explained what Baker had meant to the bossa nova. "Really?" said the trumpeter. "I've never heard that. Are you sure?"

That night's audience, which included Veloso and Leão, was startled to see the current condition of the sprite from the cover of *Chet Baker Sings*. He walked onstage as effortfully as an old man, then eased himself into a chair, barely moving from then on. "He would play a couple of notes and turn to me and say, 'Yeah, solo,' " recalled Pantoja. "If you'd waited your whole life to see Chet Baker live, then you go see him and he's sleeping in a chair, just spaced out, with messed-up sandals . . . it was just very depressing." Baker gave them his standard set, ignoring the songs they wanted to hear, such as "My Funny Valentine." Reviewing the show in *Jornal do Brasil,* José Domingos Rafaelli praised Pantoja, Nicola Stilo, bassist Sizão Machado, and drummer Larry Wyatt, while commenting tactfully on the star: "Chet Baker's music reflected his introverted personality exactly . . . in that respect, he is virtually unbeatable."

Before leaving for Rio, Baker had only one worry: he had used up all his methadone, a drug unavailable in Brazil. Monique Gardenburg, the festival's manager, attempted a solution. She hired a doctor friend of Pantoja's, Walter Almeida, to accompany Baker to São Paulo, giving him just enough of a methadone-equivalent drug each day to prevent withdrawal. Staying in an adjacent room at the Maksoud Plaza, a large tourist hotel, Almeida tried to keep an eye on him. But when Baker got his full day's dosage in the morning, he shot it all at once, then fought with the doctor for more. Almeida refused, infuriating him. But Baker found others who were eager to "help." Pantoja was giving late-night shows at Jazzmania, a club in Rio. The trumpeter sat in, delighting everyone—especially some local musicians, who rewarded him with lots of cocaine. Mixed with the drug Almeida was dispensing, it was almost as good as a speedball, Baker's new favorite.

The doctor was powerless to stop Baker. All Almeida could do was sit in the hotel room with Vavra and peek occasionally into the bathroom to make sure Baker hadn't died. When he saw the once-golden-voiced musician poking his neck with a needle, Almeida turned pale. "Oh, Jesus!" he said to Vavra. "I'd better order some whiskey! He's really close to the carotid artery, and if he hits that, it's all over!"

A capacity audience of two thousand filled São Paulo's Palace Theatre on August 21 for Baker's show. Paulo Albuquerque, who helped curate the festival, had revamped the repertoire to include songs from *Chet Baker Sings,* and fans were pleased. But Almeida found the spectacle depressing: "He was not playing the way he used to anymore. My impression is that he was a sad, physically decayed man."

Late that night, Albuquerque lay sleeping at the hotel when a festival producer knocked on his door and told him to come to Baker's room at once. He found the doctor trying to revive Baker, who had OD'd on a mixture of morphine, coke, and possibly amphetamines. "His eyes were staring and he was sweating; I remember the doctor had to slap him," Albuquerque said. "I thought he would die. It is amazing that one of the most sensitive musicians I've ever met was committing suicide little by little."

At fifty-five, Baker seemed to be surveying the damages of his life. He caught a disturbing mirror image of himself when he returned to the Nice Jazz Festival that year. There in her last live performance was June Christy, a beloved singer second only to Anita O'Day in the fabled "cool school" of fifties jazz vocalists. Christy had been among the first to encourage Baker to sing, but she herself was terrified of performing, and had drunk heavily to calm her nerves. At forty she had entered semi-retirement; now, at sixty, the onetime "breath of spring" (as singer Rosemary Clooney called her) had aged even more dramatically than Baker. Onstage in Nice, Christy was so scared that the words flew out of her head; each time she started a verse she went blank. Her husband, saxophonist Bob Cooper, was in the band, and he tried whispering the lyrics to her and playing phrases softly in her ear. Nothing worked. She burst into tears, and finally he led her off. Backstage, Baker and Diane Vavra saw her sobbing hysterically. "Aren't you going over to say something?" Vavra asked. "No," he said, turning his head away. "I'd rather remember her the way she was."

In the years since his own prime, Baker had lived hand to mouth with nary a thought about tomorrow. Contracts meant nothing to him, as Jeanne de Mirbeck, who owned a small jazz record label, Carlyne, found when she issued an album of a Baker concert she had produced at Paris's Théâtre de la Ville. "He would never have signed a contract with a percentage," she said. "Poor Chet, he didn't even have a bank account. He wanted immediate money, in cash."

Visiting Houston, Texas, in the fall of 1985, he accepted his usual buyout fee to make an album of originals by Joe LoCascio, a local keyboard player. Later, at Jacques Pelzer's house in Liège, Baker received a contract in the mail from Candee Christoforides, the producer's representative. Per their agreement, she wrote, he would get no royalties, and would pose for publicity pictures and give interviews to promote the record.

He seemed to view that letter as the last straw in a lifetime of ripoffs.

After getting high, he sat down and scrawled angry notes all around the margins, his writing growing wilder and wilder until it became illegible. Baker informed Christoforides that he could have asked ten thousand dollars for making this album, which, given his name value, might sell a half-million copies. This contract, he thought, was just another piece of "fraudulent bullshit" designed to "screw me once again." On the signature line he wrote "But Shaker [sic]."

As it happened, the record, called *Sleepless,* wasn't even noticed. Baker fumed to Peter Huijts that when he got too old to play, he would take a gun and shoot all his agents and producers in the knees. But he was his own worst victim, as he showed when he broke up one of his best groups. In November 1985, after Philip Catherine pulled out of a Paris concert on short notice, Baker fired him. Then Jean-Louis Rassinfosse got a call from Wim Wigt, informing him that Baker would be using another bassist from then on. No explanation was given. Riccardo Del Fra took over the job.

More reminders of his failures awaited Baker in Oklahoma, where he flew at year's end to see his family. This time he brought Vavra, who stayed in a motel. She met Vera, who welcomed her with surprising warmth, maybe sensing some kinship. Vavra confided her grief over Baker's violence; Vera shared her own disappointments. "Chet could have been a celebrity!" she said.

She wouldn't have been proud to see him at his New York headquarters, Fat Tuesday's, during his last engagement there in January 1986. "He was not in good shape," said manager Steve Getz. "He was struggling to play the trumpet. He was staggering, nodding off on the bandstand. He had a drink by the stool, and he kept knocking it on the floor with his foot." Yet as he sang his boyish songs of unrequited love—*"Will I ever find the girl in my mind . . ."*—he stared out at a roomful of middle-aged mother figures, all gazing at him as dotingly as Vera. "Every time he'd sing, they'd swoon," said Getz. "They were in love with him still. It was sort of touching. Even when he looked like he was ready to fall over and die."

Such gruesomeness intrigued Richard Avedon, the renowned portrait and fashion photographer. While on staff at *Harper's Bazaar* in the forties and fifties, Avedon had lifted haute couture to new heights of urban chic, never more so than in his famous picture of Dovima, a favorite model of his, posed regally against a row of elephants. But his portraits revealed a cold, morbid eye that emphasized physical deformities. Traveling to the catacombs of Sicily in 1959, he photographed rotted cadavers in lifelike poses; nearly thirty years later, he took a formal shot of Ronald and Nancy

Reagan that focused on the couple's age-spotted hands. Chet Baker was an obvious subject for Avedon, and his assistant began relentlessly phoning Leo Mitchell's apartment, where the trumpeter was staying.

Hearing that cash was involved, Baker went to Avedon's studio on January 16, accompanied by Mitchell. The results, published posthumously in the French magazine *L'Egoïste,* depicted a ghastly vision of death in progress. The harsh black-and-white close-ups gave Baker the appearance of a man lying on the operating table, light blazing down on him. Avedon homed in on Baker's toothless mouth and vacant eyes, connected by lines that looked chiseled in stone. In the accompanying text, French writer Philippe Adler glorified this image of ruin: "The European public is stricken with a profound, sensitive and respectful love for this eternal wanderer, this voyager without any baggage except his trumpet case. . . . At twenty, he was as beautiful as an angel, with fragile, childlike features, a vulnerable air, sweet, romantic." With Gerry Mulligan, noted Adler, Baker had achieved "instant glory, triumphant tours, front pages of magazines, gold records. The whole planet succumbed to the lethal charm of this airy music." Years later came tragedy: "teeth broken, jaw fractured, trumpet vanished . . . on a deserted beach in California." But it was all worth it, Adler concluded. "From the damaged lips of this broken, defeated, skinny, pathetic man emerges, night after night, a music sublime, luminous, and lyrical. From his voyage to the ends of hell, Chet Baker has resurrected, in the day, the blue diamonds of jazz, the blue vapors of his trumpet."

Only a short "resurrection" was in store for Leo Mitchell, after so many years of addiction. "Leo had made some friends in Europe too, and he was starting to work more on his own," said Diane Mitchell. "He said he was fed up with Chet's shit." The drummer finally quit heroin, but it was too late. Diagnosed with bone-marrow cancer, he would die in New York City on New Year's Eve 1990.

A rare glimpse of a heroin-free Baker came in March 1986, when he made his first tour of Japan. Huijts couldn't believe how excited Baker was; the child in him that had seemingly died long ago reappeared. "We could have gone to Tokyo with a big band," recalled Huijts. "Everyone he met—in Paris, everywhere—he said, 'Hey, man, we're going to Japan, want to join me?' " He ended up taking Michel Graillier and Riccardo Del Fra. Warned about the strictness of Japan's drug laws, Baker packed a three-week supply of methadone, and the trip sailed along. "Chet was taken care of like a king—very nice concerts, beautiful hotels," said Huijts. "So he was happy. He was socializing, he was another Chet. I never knew him like this."

Neither had Graillier: "There I heard Chet like I never heard him before, and never after. He was playing faster than Miles Davis. So much energy—fabulous." Journalists vied to speak with him, and he seemed to love the attention.

His joy didn't last. As soon as he left Japan, he flew to Amsterdam, then London. There on June 6, a stoned and glum Baker taped a TV special, *Chet Baker at Ronnie Scott's,* with Graillier and Del Fra. For a younger generation who never got to see him in person, that show, released on video, became a defining document of Baker. The filmmakers, Stephen Cleary and Robert Lemkin, had arranged an appearance by Elvis Costello, one of the "angry young men" of British pop. Costello had been fascinated by Baker from the time he heard the old Pacific Jazz recording of "The Thrill Is Gone." The eeriness of that performance had so haunted Costello that he wrote and recorded a ballad inspired by it, "Almost Blue," that Baker later sang. In 1983, Costello had hired him to add a rueful solo to a recording of "Shipbuilding," an original ballad of protest against a threatened war in the South Atlantic. Now, as Baker's guest, Costello tried his hand at some standards: "You Don't Know What Love Is," "I'm a Fool to Want You," "The Very Thought of You."

Costello showed up for rehearsal with Van Morrison, the raspy-voiced Irish singer-songwriter of such "blue-eyed soul" hits as "Gloria" and "Domino." When Morrison asked if he could sing too, the producers were thrilled. As the cameras rolled, he snapped his fingers and bungled his way through "Send in the Clowns," making numerous gaffes even as he held the sheet music in front of him. Baker had never heard of Morrison, and couldn't believe he was a professional singer. "He's not singing, he's shouting!" Baker told Del Fra.

But Costello's reedy, nasal voice had a lot of feeling, and Baker respected him. "He's a very talented man, Elvis," the trumpeter told interviewer Ib Skovgaard. Throughout the video, Baker was shown reminiscing warmly to Costello about his Oklahoma boyhood and other familiar topics. In performance, he was photographed artfully on a stool center-stage, big cowboy boots in clear view, energy so low that at times he seemed to be sinking into the floor. But the innate drama of this disintegrated beauty entranced the audience; the camera picked out misty-eyed young women who, with a few changes in hair and clothes, could have been his Birdland groupies of 1954.

Stars also shone in the eyes of Nicola Stilo, Baker's ultimate disciple. After their concerts together in Brazil, the flutist had stayed there a year. He and Baker reunited near the end of 1986. By now Stilo, who had just passed thirty, was a heroin addict himself. Initially Baker discouraged him. "He tried, but I wanted to do it," Stilo explained. "Then, of course, we became closer."

Diane Vavra had a chance to feel closer to Baker too when he went with her to Santa Cruz, the Northern California beach town where she had moved. The occasion was her mother's funeral. There he played an unaccompanied version of the bittersweet standard "For All We Know," that touched her and the other mourners deeply. He liked Santa Cruz, and talked of settling down there with Vavra. For now they borrowed her brother's rented cottage on the ocean. As they left one morning, Baker tossed his cigarette in the wastebasket. They returned hours later to find the house half burned down. The firemen had come and gone. With Baker, even a temporary dwelling couldn't last. "My home is in my left arm," he told Michel Graillier bitterly.

Playing or singing, he was still "looking for the melody," as David Friedman had said. But his attempt to find some kind of order in his life had failed miserably. He would sing the tenderest songs of romance, then beat up the woman he professed to love. In 1946, he had fled his father's rejection and his mother's disappointment; forty years later, he was still on the run. His only refuge lay in ever more extreme highs like speedballs.

Vavra's friends worried about her, none more so than Gary Howe, who owned La Bohème, a jazz club in nearby Saratoga. Baker played there several times while staying at Howe's home with Vavra. At La Bohème, she met Robert Ockeloen, a marketing manager for an electronics company and an aspiring jazz guitarist. One night he and his wife invited her to share their table. She needed to talk, and confided how afraid she was to go home with Baker. Spying the conversation, the trumpeter confronted Ockeloen at the break. "He acted very aggressive with me—'You take my girlfriend away and I'll kick you in the face,' stuff like that," said Ockeloen. "We calmed him down, and in the end, she went with him anyway."

When Baker flew alone to Los Angeles for a day, Howe pleaded with Vavra: "You can't stay with this guy anymore!" Baker was expecting her to drive him home from the airport, but by the time he phoned that evening, she had vowed to say her last goodbye. Heart pounding, she forced out the words: "Chet, these last few years have been too much. I can't go on with you anymore, I *can't* pick you up at the airport." Baker made a veiled threat of suicide, but somehow she found the strength to ignore it. After she had hung up, Howe came into the room. "Gary, I did it!" she exclaimed. "I'm so proud of you!" he said, giving her a hug. They left for a celebratory dinner, where he toasted her freedom.

On the ride back, though, Vavra grew nervous. "Gary, I've got a really strange feeling," she said as they parked in front of the house. They went inside, where Howe retired to his bedroom.

She opened the door to hers. In the darkness, she saw the outline of a man. She gasped. A moment later, Chet Baker's face appeared. As he advanced toward her, she backed up into the living room. "I'm so sorry I've been such an asshole," he said, putting his arms around her. "I'll never get high again."

"We both knew he was lying," Vavra recalled. "I thought to myself, 'Oh, my God, it's starting all over again!' And all I could do was hold him."

18

In November 1986, with his last, disastrous Fat Tuesday's appearance not far behind, Baker got his final chance to play a New York club. Whippoorwill had just opened in a basement on West Eighteenth Street near Fifth Avenue. The room reminded Baker's friend Jim Coleman of an upscale bordello; never before had he seen a jazz club with gold-plated handles on the urinals. Whippoorwill went way overbudget in booking such stars as the Modern Jazz Quartet and Stan Getz; soon it was gone.

Baker's first night there drew just a handful of fans, some of whom were amazed to learn he was still alive. But to his girlfriend of 1953, Joyce Tucker, who now lived in New York, the trumpeter was still a dazzler. Divorced from her first husband, Marvin Koral, and from an actor, Al Latieri, Tucker was at loose ends, and decided to try managing her ex-flame's U.S. career. The effort failed; Baker was rarely in the States anymore, nor did he wish to be. But the sight of "Chettie" still made her starry-eyed, even if he himself felt like a fossil. "People say I play the way I sing," he told Marc Puricelli, a young pianist who accompanied him at Whippoorwill. "Now I'm starting to play like I look."

Jon Burr, his bassist from the late seventies, had rejoined him after years of accompanying such stars as Tony Bennett and the French jazz violinist Stephane Grappelli. Along the way Burr had conquered a heroin habit, but in the mideighties, it had taken hold of him again for a few years. He visited Baker at his temporary quarters, the notorious Chelsea Hotel on West Twenty-third Street. Patricia Morrisroe, in her biography of onetime tenant Robert Mapplethorpe, called the Chelsea "a psychedelic Coney Island for creative geniuses and freaks." Andy Warhol, who collected both, had used it as the shooting site of his 1966 epic *Chelsea Girls,* in which the stars of Warhol's Factory do drugs, hallucinate, and fall apart for a voyeuristic camera. Eviction from the Chelsea didn't happen easily, unless you were Chet Baker. The problem began when Burr saw a huge abscess on Baker's hip, caused by repeated injections. "Junkies get 'em—it's like a monster zit," explained Burr. Baker's was open and raw. Sickened, Burr headed for the elevator. When the door slid open at the lobby, there he was, out cold. The management wasn't pleased. That night at Whippoorwill, Baker gave him the news: "Thanks a *lot,* Jon. You got me thrown out of the hotel!"

Feeling guilty, Burr let the trumpeter move into his apartment on West Ninety-sixth Street. No matter how broke he claimed to be, Baker always managed to score a lot of dope, and the house, said Burr, turned into "junk heaven." Soon Baker found a new source of cash. On the first night of his return engagement at Whippoorwill in December, a limo pulled up outside the club. Out stepped a man with a graying beard, a big black overcoat, and a bandanna around his head. He looked like Santa Claus, but his "elves" were a clinging entourage of beauties, male and female, from the fashion world.

This was Bruce Weber, the photographer whose homoerotic images for Calvin Klein and Ralph Lauren had launched a new age of sexual permissiveness in advertising. At forty-one, Weber was a top celebrity in his field, charging up to twenty thousand dollars a day. His subjects were emblazoned on billboards and in the pages of *Interview* magazine: athletic yet sensitive all-American youths, sprawled out casually in white underwear. They bore more than a passing resemblance to the T-shirted Chet Baker of the fifties, and in fact, Baker was one of Weber's obsessions. Years earlier, Weber had come across a copy of the 1955 album *Chet Baker Sings and Plays with Bud Shank, Russ Freeman and Strings.* "That's sort of the way I always wished I had looked, or I wished I had known somebody like that," he explained. "I grew up in a farm town in Pennsylvania, and I heard a sound on that record that was beckoning me to go west. It was that sound you felt when you listened to the ocean, when you were at the beach late in the afternoon. It was almost like you feel when you look at a surfing magazine, you know?"

At the time he met Baker, the photographer was finishing *Broken Noses,* a documentary about Andy Minsker, a sexy boxer who he thought was the spitting image of the young trumpeter. Weber had been chosen for the upcoming Biennial at New York's Whitney Museum, spotlighting the work of the hottest figures in contemporary art. He hoped to include a picture of Baker, as well as to record him crooning the poignant torch song "Blame It on My Youth" for the soundtrack of *Broken Noses.*

On the afternoon of Baker's opening, Weber sent his employee Cherry Vanilla to Whippoorwill. A punk singer, poet, and rock groupie with hair the color of a cherry Popsicle, she strolled up to Baker at the soundcheck. "Pop stars will instantly get uptight, like, 'What are you doing here?' " she noted. "Chet just looked at me like, 'Oh, hi, how are you?' I said, 'Hello, I'm Cherry Vanilla.' Of course he got off on that." Flirtatious and charming, she relayed her boss's proposal, offering a thousand dollars. Baker accepted. Later on, Bruce Weber arrived with his camera. At the trumpeter's request, Weber took a photo of him with Vavra. It showed Baker—now nearly fifty-seven and looking twenty years older—in Vavra's loving embrace, head pressed to her breast and the same childlike neediness on his face that he had shown in his old Claxton portrait with Liliane. "Bruce had this term he liked to use: 'destroyed,' " said Cherry. "He loved beauty that looked kind of destroyed. That was a big turn-on."

The photographer and his friends went back to the club every night. Each Baker "fix" left him more hooked, and he arranged to shoot a three-minute film at Jon Burr's apartment. On Sunday, Weber, his cameraman Jeff Preiss, and an assistant entered a purgatory of junkie squalor, with cigarette burns in the mattresses, clothes and papers scattered all around, and ashtrays overflowing. "I remember Bruce had a check for me," said Burr. "There was a check-cashing joint around the corner, and I remember going to cash the check. Then I said, 'Bruce, do you mind if I run downtown a second?' "

Weber dressed Baker in a crisp white shirt and filmed him leaning against a wall, staring out in anguish with fingers clutching his temples and neck. Afterward, everyone piled into Weber's van and headed down to Whippoorwill. The photographer proposed a documentary then and there, he said, adding that Baker flung his arms around him in gratitude. "He was just so wonderful!" Weber remarked in *Interview.* "I think his beauty was so much about his openness to people he liked. That's what I think engaged you about him at first—that easiness, pretty much like all great lovers have."

According to Cherry, though, the decision to move forward came as she, Preiss, and Weber's representative and live-in companion, Nan Bush, lay with the photographer on his bed and screened the footage. The silent black-and-white film looked like a cinema verité relic of an old junkie's private hell. It fired the imagination; anyone viewing it could concoct his own scenario of what had turned Baker from dreamboat to scarecrow. "Bruce, this guy is fifty-seven years old," Cherry remembered saying. "The way he lives, who knows how much longer he's gonna be around? And you love him. Why don't you make a movie on him?"

After that, things moved quickly. In January of 1987, Baker signed a contract with Weber for a project entitled "Documentary Film." The clauses were typical of such release forms; they also echoed the kind of deals Baker had been making for decades. For $4,400, he granted perpetual and unconditional rights to his "name, likeness, voice, story" for use in a film, album, play, book, merchandising or advertising campaign, or any other medium. Baker would "reserve no rights with respect to such uses," the document stated. Cherry was sent to obtain his signature. "He goes, 'Is this OK?' I said, 'Yeah.' He signed it. Think Chet read this? No way!" Soon after that, Weber phoned William Claxton and asked to visit him in Beverly Hills and see his Baker photos. Claxton recalled the dialogue that followed: Weber said he had just met the trumpeter in New York and had decided to make a film about him. "What did you think of him?" Claxton asked. Weber cooed like a starstruck boy: "Oh, he sounds wonderful, and he looks wonderful!"

"He *looks* wonderful?"

"Well, he's a little tattered, but yes, he looks as wonderful as ever."

Claxton thought: "Do I have a madman on my hands?"

If not a madman, Weber had a knack for rearranging real life to suit his fancy. He inhabited a romantic bubble—one filled with the beautiful young jocks he photographed, the idealistic love songs of Joni James and Doris Day, pet golden retrievers romping happily, and a comfortable domestic relationship with Nan Bush, whom he presented as his wife. Born in Greensburg, Pennsylvania, in 1946, he had moved to Manhattan in the sixties to study film and theater at New York University. With his preppy handsomeness, Weber found work as a model of the "retro-collegiate" look—the "crew-neck sweaters, the penny loafers, the little shirt collars sticking out," explained Cherry Vanilla, who met him on Fire Island.

But Weber was a bland presence on camera, and he decided to try taking pictures rather than posing for them. His progress was slow until 1973, when he teamed with Bush, a former representative of Francesco Scavullo, the eminent portrait photographer. In a business full of pushy hawkers, Bush seemed like a gentle soul, with long graying hair and a voice that exuded intelligence. But she was tough, and knew how to get what she wanted. Weber had his first solo exhibition, *Body Builders,* in 1974; soon he acquired Calvin Klein and Ralph Lauren as clients and became a fashion star in his own right.

His subjects—masculine but sexually ambiguous, unselfconsciously nude or semi-nude in outdoorsy settings—gave his work the flavor of fifties "physique" photography: a safe form of gay erotica, done at a time when pornography was illegal. Peggy Moffitt, the model who married William Claxton in 1959, saw a link between Weber's work and that of her husband. Aside from Claxton's pictures of Baker, Weber loved his shots of Steve McQueen, one of which showed the movie sex-symbol in white briefs. "Before Bruce started shooting guys in their underpants," said Moffitt, "nobody would have looked at Chet Baker and thought, 'Ah! Fashion!' That's Bruce's talent—he saw something that wasn't related to fashion and related it to fashion and caused a whole big thing. Bruce did it, but Bill inspired it."

In 1985, Weber began work on *Broken Noses.* This "wet dream" of a documentary, as one critic called it, celebrated Andy Minsker, a young boxer and former Olympic contender who taught his sport to pubescent boys in Portland, Oregon. In the opening sequence, the camera lingers on their bare chests as Weber photographs them one by one; between shots, a stylist primps them into perfect Weber specimens. In the background, Joni James sings innocently of puppy love in "Too Young" and Baker croons "Blame It on My Youth."

There wasn't much ambiguity in Cherry Vanilla, whose own creative efforts included an essay about masturbating with a hairbrush. Superenergetic and likable, the former Kathleen Anne Dorritie lived by her wits. Before Weber hired her to research music for the soundtrack of *Broken Noses,* Cherry had worked on a phone-sex chat line; later she turned her dialogues into a nightclub act. In years past, she had done everything from producing radio and TV commercials on Madison Avenue to writing a gossip column for the rock magazine *Creem* ("Cherry Vanilla with Scoops for You"). In 1971, while starring in *Pork,* a play produced by Andy Warhol in London, she met the budding glitter-rock singer David Bowie. For three years, she served as his publicist. "I knew he was a star from the moment I met him," she explained. "I mean, I basically did my PR by telling everybody what a great fuck he was, at the same time that everybody else was saying he was a homosexual. So it created this controversy. Publicity is publicity." She won some glory of her own by recording as a punk singer for British RCA; on tour, her opening act was a then-unknown rock group, the Police. Most of the time, though, she had to scuffle to survive.

Now, as researcher, interviewer, and all-purpose girl Friday on the new film about Chet Baker, Cherry sailed on the wings of Weber's latest fantasia. "Here was Bruce, this very romantic, corny guy," she said, "and here was Chet, who sang these lovely ballads and who used to have a face like a little angel girl. I guess Bruce had the hots for him."

The captivated photographer would admit to spending a million dollars of his own money on the film. The goal, ostensibly, was to learn the truth of what lay behind Baker's shattered beauty. But as Weber told David Hershkovits in *the paper,* "I love the idea of fantasy and reality coming together." To him, Baker was an eternal beach boy, a womanizer, a heartbreaker, a fashion plate, and a kindred spirit wrapped up in one. "I think one of the reasons we connected so well was because I'm on the road a lot," he informed the magazine *7 Days.* "I live in hotels a lot, too—of course a lot more comfortably than Chet—but I know what it's like to be kind of disconnected."

Before anyone had done a bit of research, Weber, Cherry Vanilla, and Jeff Preiss were flying first-class to L.A., where they filmed Baker in two staged recording sessions. Emie Amemiya, the young Asian woman who worked as line producer on Weber's films, booked Sage & Sound, an old-fashioned Hollywood recording studio. The photographer reserved a penthouse suite for Baker and Diane Vavra at the Shangri-La, an art-deco hotel in Santa Monica whose panoramic view of mountains and sea evoked the lazy summer days of Baker's youth.

Weber rushed to William Claxton's home, where he pored over old prints and contact sheets. "I want every picture you've got of Chet Baker!" he said. All the while, recalled Peggy Moffitt, "Bruce asked Bill endlessly: 'Tell me what Chet thought of clothes.' Bill said, 'Chet thought nothing of clothes.' And Bruce wanted it to be more."

With that in mind, he ordered a wardrobe for Baker from Agnés B, a Paris designer whose clothes—a sleek black pinstripe suit, a shiny leather jacket with an oversize black zipper—were a couture version of the French beatnik look. A makeup artist (Bonnie Maller), hairstylist (Didier Malige), and dresser (Tonne Goodman) fussed over the cast members, many of them hired for decoration. Posed throughout the film were Lisa Marie, the beautiful teenage model from Weber's ads for the Calvin Klein perfume Obsession; Baker's supposed look-alike Andy Minsker; Flea, the sexy bassist of the

Red Hot Chili Peppers; and rockabilly heartthrob Chris Isaak, who, like Minsker, reminded Weber of the young Chet Baker. When the photographer met an exotic-looking Italian woman at the Shangri-La, he put her in the movie. "I always liked the way the Italian directors from the thirties, forties, and fifties just threw people in their films for no reason," explained Weber. Frank Strazzeri, a crusty, chain-smoking West Coast pianist of Baker's generation, led the trio at the recording dates.

Into this glamorized Bohemia came Chet Baker. He hobbled through Sage & Sound like an old man, pulling out his dentures then sticking them back in. For the filming, Weber wanted to focus on his crooning, but Baker kept fumbling the words to several standards he didn't quite know, including "Ev'rytime We Say Goodbye" and "My One and Only Love." Vavra sang them for him, but even after he mastered the lyrics, his voice sounded pinched and flat, his playing rusty. "He'd get angry and say, 'I don't like that!' and he'd stop," recalled Claxton, whom Weber had invited. "Bruce was saying, 'It's gorgeous, don't worry about it, it's gonna be great.' "

Claxton and Baker hadn't seen each other since the seventies, and Weber planned a sentimental reunion on film. He instructed Claxton to hide in the next room, then make a surprise entrance, camera around his neck. "And now, Chet, look who's here—here's Clax!" exclaimed Weber. Baker just stared. "Oh, hi, Clax," he said flatly, just as if he had seen him yesterday. The footage was shelved.

In the months to come, Cherry Vanilla got to witness the ultimate beatnik in action. "Chet had absolutely no concept of holding on to ten cents for tomorrow," she said. "All these two-hundred-dollar shirts Bruce bought him—he just left them behind or gave them away. He'd have on a T-shirt that he got at a radio station or something, and some old corduroy pants that were encrusted with blood from the abscesses he had all over his body. He would wear them every day until the next set of clothes came along. He would leave California and get on a plane to Holland or Paris in the winter with no money in his pocket, no coat, no trumpet. Talk about Zen! He had it more than anybody. I envied it. I wish I could be so cool, so free. But of course he had the monkey, which was the heroin habit."

Later on, said Weber, "people would ask me: 'Did you guys get high with Chet? Did you ever score drugs for him?' I said, 'If we had, Chet would never have shown up.' I think he liked it that way, he liked that we were a bunch of squares, in his terms." But according to one accounting log, on March 5, 1987, Baker received $10,000 "for additional recording and filming"; on April 13, $1,000 more; on April 25, $1,500. Anyone who saw Baker in the film—eyelids sagging, slurring his words, all but drooling—could guess where the money went. Unless he got what he needed, Cherry said, "he wouldn't have sat still a minute for us."

Between the Sage & Sound recording dates, Baker, dressed in a luxurious white Agnès B sweater, gave his first interview for the film in his room at the Shangri-La. Cherry shared the questioning with Weber. "That was my job—to get this guy to talk about himself, can you imagine?" she said. "It wasn't easy. He had to be stoned on junk first, then I would get him stoned on marijuana, give him a glass of wine, whatever, and I would make goo-goo eyes at him. We were passing back and forth these big fat joints for hours, right? I remember I was so stoned, it was hard for me to say Twardzik."

Much of the time, a bored-sounding Baker told tired stories by rote: his early days on the L.A. jazz scene, the Charlie Parker audition, the San Francisco beating. The more revealing moments came in flashes. Asked about his wives, he spoke the most warmly of Halema. "Beautiful lady," he said wistfully. In passing he mentioned "an English girl I met in 1959," adding flatly: "We're still married." His few comments about his children betrayed his distance from them. "They're not really into music," he said, sighing. The exception was Chesney Aftab, who had "a very nice voice," he had heard. Baker perked up when Weber asked him to name his favorite high. "Ohhhhh . . . the kinda high that scares other people to death," he explained with a little smile. It was called a speedball. "That first rush of coke is, um, devastating feeling. I mean, scary."

The crew and anyone else who happened to be present wrote questions on slips of paper and passed them forward. "I'd be embarrassed to death at some of the things I was asking him," said Cherry. One of her more painful moments came when Weber made her show Baker, on camera, a book of nudes by André de Dienes, a Rumanian photographer who took pictures of voluptuous California girls in the forties and fifties. Cherry flipped the pages with Baker. "I felt like we were giving him a homosexual test for the army or something," she said. Giggling nervously as she groped for words, Cherry asked if he had known women like these in his West Coast beach days. "He could have said, 'What the fuck are you showing me this for? What has this got to do with my life?' But Chet would never be rude when he wanted to charm someone, and he wanted to charm me. He'd look at me and say, 'Wow, you look . . . *reeeally* something today, Cherry.' I knew I was being manipulated. But I liked it, just like all the women in his life liked it."

During the interview at the Shangri-La, Baker recited, from behind wisps of cigarette smoke, the lyrics to "Deep in a Dream," a 1938 hit he had been singing ever since his Palfium-addicted days in Italy. Jimmy Van Heusen's words tell of the nirvana a man enters when he settles into his armchair, cigarette in hand, and drifts off to sleep: "The smoke makes a stairway for you to descend / You come to my arms, may this bliss never end. . . . Then from the ceiling, sweet music comes stealing / We glide through a lover's refrain. . . ." His cigarette singes his fingers, awakening him to the same old "pain in my heart"; only by sinking back into dreamland can he make that rapture live again. No song better captured the lust for escape that had ruled Baker all his life. As usual, though, he didn't care to elaborate. "Nice words," he said.

For Cherry, finding any information on him at all wasn't easy. In her hotel room, she got on the phone in a mad scramble, hunting down old articles, archival photos, and film footage. Lining up interviewees was another headache. Feeling he had almost no friends, Baker suggested only Jack Sheldon and Ruth Young. "Ruth's a great girl," he told Cherry. Charlaine was now married to a lawyer and living in L.A. By some reports, she was drinking excessively, and in a phone conversation with Weber she sounded barely coherent. He never filmed her. Halema, who now lived in the affluent community of Bel Air, California, with her second husband, refused to speak; so did Liliane Rovère and Jacques Pelzer. Micheline said no, too, bewildering Baker, who couldn't imagine how she could pass up the chance to make some easy money. Cherry did get the cooperation of Joyce Tucker and Hersh Hamel, and began a campaign of calls to Carol, who responded warily. Emie Amemiya located but couldn't pin down Chesney Aftab, a perpetual drifter.

Most of everyone's time was spent heeding the whims of Chet Baker. After the second recording date at Sage & Sound, Weber filmed a celebratory dinner at a Mexican restaurant. Baker sat at the head of a round table surrounded by the adoring cast and crew. With tequila flowing and the air thick with cigarette smoke, Cherry clung to him like a true groupie, while Andy Minsker asked dopey questions. Payment aside, all this was a giant ego rub for Baker. "Chet was the center of the universe!" said Amemiya. "He was loving every moment of it."

In footage used as the movie's motif, Baker sat in the back of an open Cadillac convertible that George Dorritie, Cherry's nephew and the production's chauffeur, drove up the Pacific Coast Highway. Vavra, Cherry, and Lisa Marie took turns making out in the backseat with a stoned, grinning Baker while Preiss filmed them from the front. "That's the way we sort of fantasized about Chet, and that's the way he fantasized about himself," Weber noted. It was harder to explain a scene shot at the Santa Monica Pier, where he asked Baker and Vavra to ride around in a bumper-car rink. "It's a metaphor for his life?" Vavra wondered. "He doesn't seem to get anywhere? Who knows?"

Reality descended in February, when Baker left on a European tour with Jon Burr and two of Burr's friends, pianist Rob Schneiderman and drummer Mike Clark. Burr and Baker spent endless moments waiting for "the guy," palms sweating, before gigs. "Like it or not, Chet played his best when he was full of good shit," said Burr. "The rest of the time he'd be kicking, he wouldn't feel like playing. It's like having a bad case of the flu. Everything aches, all your muscles are tight." After "the guy" came, Burr marveled at Baker's transformation: "I remember there being a ferocity and a joy to the music, and Chet's playing was unbelievable. Chorus after chorus, he would just keep blowing." The tour turned disastrous when Baker stopped at the home of Robert, his Amsterdam doctor, for a supply of Seconal. "He could not fucking stand up after he took them," Burr said. One night Peter Huijts had to beg the trumpeter to leave his hotel room and come to the show. Baker threatened some promoters with nonappearance if they didn't find him a dealer. Many jobs fell through. At New Morning in Paris, Burr recalled, Baker was carried out of the dressing room and placed in a chair onstage. "He'd try and play a couple of notes, end the set quick. I remember seeing incredible lines at the New Morning. That's their convoluted notion of romance."

Every time Baker left, Weber's team worried they might never see him again. "It was like sending someone off to war," said Amemiya. "Everybody became a part of that lifestyle, living on the dark side." Locating him was as usual a trial, but Nan Bush prided herself on her psychic abilities, which she believed had helped her make Weber a success in the seventies. "I always knew when Chet was gonna call," she explained. Sometimes before leaving the office, she informed her staff: "Oh, Chet's gonna call today. When he does, please have the call forwarded."

Once their project got under way, the spirits were with them. RCA Records offered Weber a $70,000 advance for the soundtrack album, and he was delighted with his interviewees. Everyone, it seemed, was as enraptured with Baker as he was. William Claxton described his first sighting of Baker in 1952; he was so mesmerized that he snapped picture after picture, oblivious to the other musicians. Eyes twinkling, Joyce Tucker reminisced about her whirlwind affair with Baker. "We got lost on a sailboat in Balboa Bay, and we loved it!" she raved. Jack Sheldon spoke with unashamed envy—and outrageously smutty humor—of his teenage buddy, who could excel at anything with no effort.

The informant whom Weber coveted most was Ruth Young, who had fascinated him ever since Cherry had unearthed the 1977 Baker-Young duet, "Whatever Possess'd Me." "I thought, who is this magical woman singing this song?" said Weber. It took months to track Young down in St. Thomas, where she was living on a boat with her new boyfriend. Weber flew her to Manhattan and gave her star treatment, filming not just an interview but a record date, which he hoped to release as an album.

Cherry met her at the session. "I remember Ruth warning us: 'Not everything that I have to say about Chet is nice.' That, of course, whet our appetites even more, especially Bruce's. Then he really wanted her. And she knew that. She's smart." Vamping on her cool, breathy delivery in "Whatever Possess'd Me," Weber groomed her into a fifties-style "chick singer," complete with a skimpy black cocktail dress, dangle earrings, and a disheveled blonde chignon. He filmed her sashaying around the studio with one hand on her hip and the other holding a cigarette. "I want smoke," he instructed.

Before the interview, Weber helped loosen her up. "The first thing he asked me was 'What do you like to do? Vodka, Scotch, coke?' I said, 'OK, I'll take some Absolut and the coke, that sounds great." When the film rolled, she was as funny, salty, and articulate as he could have hoped. She recounted her first glimpse of Baker at the Half Note; her heart broke as she saw him "completely reveal himself—to look so horrible, to sound so terrible, but to be standing there and trying." Baker was clearly the love of her life, but bitterness welled up as she recalled watching her "Picasso" lie, steal, and manipulate.

Young sang a snippet of "My Foolish Heart" that for her summed up Baker's whole duplicitous allure. "Love and fascination . . . you said it, baby," she added. "That's the mystique. But that isn't necessarily real. And that's what takes a long, long time to figure out." Her segment ended with the film's most quoted sound bite: "I'm just lucky that those years that I did spend weren't fruitless, finally. Because my ears were open, my heart was open, and my head was open. Well, my legs were open too once in a while!"

Weber and Bush dreamed of making Young a star. "At one point all I could think about was doing a feature and having Ruth as an actress," the photographer said. Meanwhile, he planned a Chet-and-Ruth double album, filled with his favorite songs. "Bruce always had really great ideas about selecting music," said Bush. One lapse occurred when he tried persuading Baker to sing "Jersey Girl," Tom Waits's sendup of old fifties doo-wop love songs. Weber knew it from a Bruce Springsteen record. Cherry Vanilla was aghast: "I said, 'Bruce, these are not jazz chords!' And he'd say, 'But I can't understand it. Bruce Springsteen can sing it, and it's my favorite song. Why can't Chet sing it?' " Baker refused, and Young ended up doing it instead, with a gender revision by Cherry, who changed the line "Go in the bathroom and put your makeup on" to "Go in the bathroom and take off your T-shirt." Young's performance didn't make the final cut of the film, but a comment from Frank Strazzeri did: "Don't forget the doo-wahs!"

Emie Amemiya became one more surrogate mommy for Baker. Often she awoke in the middle of the night and phoned him "to make sure that he didn't OD." He left messages for her in a barely coherent moan: "*Heeeeey,* baby, where are you, I wanna talk to you . . ." If she didn't respond immediately, he phoned again, lapsing into baby talk: "You *saaaaid* you would call me right *baaaack* . . . where *aaaare* you?" A few minutes later: "*Awww,* baby, where the fuck are you? I don't *feeeel* good!"

There was nothing funny about his mood at the Cannes Film Festival, where *Broken Noses* premiered in May. Weber took Baker, Vavra, and the crew to France. He planned to film the trumpeter in performance at a lavish outdoor party for the screening and at a recording studio in Paris. Nicola Stilo was there, glued to Baker's side and matching his drug consumption. "Maybe I made the choice just to live the same life he was doing, you know?" said Stilo. "We were like brothers, maybe sometimes fighting, but really taking care of each other." Their musical rapport was strong, and Stilo's flute and guitar playing became a fixture of Baker's shows. Stilo gave his friend a souvenir from Brazil: "Zingaro" (Portrait in Black and White), a slow, haunting bossa nova by two Brazilian masters, Antonio Carlos Jobim and Chico Buarque.

Baker and Stilo recorded it together at Studios Davout in Paris, a site the trumpeter chose himself, according to Bruce Weber. "His main reason was it was near a place where he could get drugs," Weber told Andrew O'Hehir in *S.F.* [San Francisco] *Weekly.* "And the studio had a real bad feel to it. Some of the musicians were fighting amongst each other, provoked by Chet." Weber would use a moment from that session to open his film. As Baker rehearsed Elvis Costello's "Almost Blue" with Stilo on guitar, he picked a fight over the chords: "I see a lot of fucking attitude's going on here!" He had even less patience with the pricey hotel Weber had picked for him—no improvement, he thought, over the more modest Anne de France, which he loved. "Why doesn't Bruce just put me where I want to be and give me the rest of the fucking money?" he hissed at Cherry. She understood: "When it came to money, Chet could get very angry and dark. Because money meant dope."

His hostility peaked in Cannes when he and Stilo ran out of smack and couldn't find any more. Baker refused to leave the hotel room, and Cherry went to check up on him. She found him pacing tensely while Stilo lay on the bed, sweating and hyperventilating. They grew sicker by the hour. The two men somehow made it to their show, but the invited audience of models, movie figures, and paparazzi talked throughout. Jeff Preiss filmed Baker's disgust afterward, as he fumed about how rude everyone had been. One day, as he and Vavra walked down a street, he suddenly screamed at the top of his lungs: "ALL OF FRANCE IS A PIECE OF SHIT!"

Even at their quietest, this middle-aged couple, who showed each other off like two kids at the high-school prom, seldom failed to get attention. "They were always very mushy, lovey-dovey," said Cherry. "Chet would kiss her on the neck, and Diane was like a little girl who totally lived her life for him and nothing but. It was sweet and sad." One day he squeezed Vavra so tightly she could hardly breathe. "I'll be holding you like this when you're a little old gray-haired lady!" he assured her.

Interviewed for the film in her hotel room in Cannes, she dipped back dreamily into the seventies, when she met her "Greek god" and fell under his spell. "He was very gentle, very sweet, very charming," she said in her girlish voice. "I guess that's what it was. The mystique about him." The fog cleared when he started beating her, conning her, breaking his promises to quit drugs. Her concluding remark revealed a woman living in a sorry state of compromise: "You really can't rely on Chet. And if you know that, then you can pull through."

Back in Stillwater, Oklahoma, Carol Baker was surviving on her own, if barely. She and the children—ages twenty-five, twenty-two, and twenty-one—shared an apartment in an attached two-story house. Carol couldn't shake the hope that her husband would come back and make her life complete. "This is a woman who only had Chet," said Bob Mover. But Vavra concluded otherwise after picking up the phone one day and hearing the voice of Carol, who had called looking for Baker. "I was very civil with her," Vavra explained. "I thought that we were sort of friends." Carol, said Vavra, surprised her by mentioning a romance she was having with a teacher from the university. Vavra recalled hearing her say, "But you know, those professors are so la-di-da!" Maybe Carol was starved for a chance to reinforce her desirability; perhaps she merely hoped Vavra would carry the news, true or not, to Baker and make him jealous. Such a ploy would never have worked. Insanely jealous in his other relationships, Baker showed no sign of this with Carol; instead, he seemed to hope she would forget him and find someone else. But the moment with the professor came and went. "She was so adamant—'Chet is my only man, he'll always be the only one,' " recalled Mover.

In one of their interviews, Weber had asked Baker what sort of legacy he wanted to leave his children. Totally drugged, he turned philosophical as he explained the secret of life he had hoped to impart: "Find something that you really enjoy doing, and then learn to do it better than anybody. And you won't have any problems." If he thought the kids might learn from his singlemindedness, it wasn't apparent from the scene that confronted Weber's crew in mid-1987, when they flew to Stillwater to interview the family. The realities of their lives were a world away from the Norman Rockwell fantasy Weber had envisioned: "I pictured them living on this little farm, the kids working on the farm, Carol cooking, the sons are repairing the fence. We got there and it was totally different. They didn't have ice water in the icebox. We were kind of shocked and stunned."

He arrived bearing a six-hundred-dollar honorarium for Carol (a higher-than-normal fee for a documentary appearance), payments for the children, and the promise of a fond cinematic tribute to Chet Baker. Carol had warned him that the kids had nothing to wear, so he brought various items of clothing: a cowboy hat for Melissa, a leather bomber jacket for Paul. None of this appeased Carol, who was "nervous and a bit suspicious," Weber recalled. "They were kind of angry at everybody, everybody kind of did them in."

To Cherry, they seemed like a welfare family—"bitter, all of them, that they had nothing, and that people all over the world were making money off their father's music. Bitter about their father not sending them money. But they had their TV and their soda pops and beers and pizzas, and surprisingly, they seemed relatively happy to me."

During the three-day shoot, Weber brought Vera and the family to a nearby tennis court and filmed them happily swatting a ball around. They seemed to love getting some attention at last, especially Paul, who strutted shirtless, dressed and coiffed into a facsimile of his dad. Like Dean, he had toyed with the idea of playing the trumpet, but had never followed through. When he later expressed an interest in modeling, Weber and Bush paid to have portfolio shots taken of him in New York. Paul went to the session, then never bothered picking up the finished prints.

Still affected by his near-fatal hit-and-run accident of 1982, Dean stared vaguely, saying little. The most outspoken child was Melissa, who now spoke like a hillbilly and, according to Cherry, wrote country-western song lyrics for fun. But she refused Weber's request to go barefoot and don the cowboy hat, choosing instead a pair of white hip-hugging slacks. She was filmed bounding into the house with a bag of groceries in her arms, grinning at the camera with a mouthful of decayed teeth. "Imagine how that affects a young girl," Cherry said. "Your daddy is a famous jazz musician with all these albums in the bins, and you can't get your teeth fixed." Weber asked her where she would like to go if her father took her on vacation. "Prob'ly be a cruise, because he couldn't get off the ship," she said with a tough laugh.

Vera, now seventy-seven, sat on the sofa in her Sunday-best white jacket and lace blouse and answered Cherry's questions. She recalled the prodigal son who, she noted, had always preferred her to his father. As she described his childhood brilliance, Weber handed Cherry a question. It made her cringe. He later overdubbed himself asking it. For all Baker's talent and acclaim, had he let her down as a son? Vera froze, then stammered: "Yes. Mm-hmm, yes. But . . . let's don't go into that." She forced a smile. Later she took Weber aside. "You're not gonna show this film here, are you?" she asked, worried about what the neighbors might think.

Weber interviewed Carol himself. He seated her in a lawn chair in a huge field of weeds, giving the striking sense of a woman lost in the middle of nowhere. In an exchange that he used to open her segment, he asked if there was some special moment she could share from her early life with Baker that might evoke the thrill of those days. Carol, who normally dwelled so much on the past, stared blankly. After a few moments she shook her head. "I can't think of anything," she said. Her further comments were just as short on insight about the man who had obsessed her for twenty-seven years. When they met, she exclaimed, "he looked so young, he was good-looking—and he could play!" Then Weber mentioned Ruth Young, and Carol's face hardened. "You mean you interviewed that bitch?" she said. This was her chance to strike back in public, and she grabbed it. "That was his downfall, let me tell you," she declared. "*That* was when he started taking drugs. She was a very, *very* destructive force in his life." She punctuated her monologue with disclaimers—"You'll edit this out"—yet in Emie Amemiya's view, Carol "knew exactly what she was doing."

Worse vitriol came when Weber sat Carol and the kids together on the living-room sofa and had them talk some more. Melissa eagerly gave her long account of climbing through Young's apartment window, stealing all the jewelry and "*sexxxy* clothes," then hocking everything for ninety dollars. She, her mother, and Paul laughed vindictively. When Nan Bush saw the footage, she was so appalled that she offered to have one of her employees scour the local pawnshops to see if any of Young's belongings remained. She and Weber couldn't understand why Baker had never divorced Carol. When Bush asked him, he said casually: "Oh, I never got around to it. I only go to Oklahoma to renew my driver's license."

As darkness fell on the last day of shooting, Weber placed the children in his expensive rented car and asked if there was anything they wanted to tell their father on camera. With crickets chirping in an otherwise silent, empty night, they called out their messages. "I love you, Dad!" said Paul. Melissa chimed in: "Stay in touch. Don't be such a stranger!" Dean spoke up from the backseat: "We can use some financial help, Dad!"

Carol and the children weren't the only ones who had used the film to say things to Baker that they couldn't tell him to his face. But the trumpeter knew nothing of the content of these interviews, and never would. That year he spoke proudly to Dutch journalist Jeroen de Valk, mentioning that Weber had interviewed his kids and Vavra. "Chet thought Bruce was great," said Vavra. In a letter to Weber and Bush, Baker wrote: "You all are certainly a big hit with me. . . . I love you Nan, Bruce, Cherry."

At the close of May, Baker embarked on his second tour of Japan. He brought Harold Danko, the veteran Dutch drummer John Engels, and the young bassist Hein Van de Geyn, also from Holland. As before, Baker didn't dare defy the country's strict drug laws, and for three weeks he relied on methadone and a little cognac. Onstage and off, he was so lucid that Engels had trouble accepting all the nightmarish tales about him. For a TV special taped on June 14 at Tokyo's Hitomi-Kinen-Kodo hall, Baker wore an immaculate dark suit, hair combed back as neatly as it was in the fifties. His singing voice sounded reborn, and he played with a silky tone from top to bottom. On "Beatrice," a bop tune by Sam Rivers, Baker amazed the trio with his trills and fast runs, unmarred by heroin.

Instead of vanishing into his hotel room after the shows, he and the band went to jazz clubs and jammed for hours. Fans brought him roses and lined up with stacks of LPs for him to sign. He hugged Danko and posed for pictures, smiling and even laughing. Baker announced that he wanted to come back the next year with a new band, the Love Notes, led by him and Vavra.

But the pressures of a drug-free life were eating away at him, and he fought viciously with her. "Boy, those Japanese tours, you better stay out of his way, because that's when his temper would really flare," Vavra said. "Oh, man, it was terrible." On June 17, they left Japan. As they waited at the airport, Peter Huijts raved about the tour, trying to help Baker see how beautiful life could be without dope. "Yeah," growled the trumpeter. "I can't wait to get to Paris and get *fucked up*!"

Helsingborg, Sweden, February 2, 1988. Photo by Roland Bengtsson

19

By 1987, Baker's friends were noticing his growing preoccupation with death. Writing Lisa Galt Bond, he mentioned how many loved ones he had lost. Death, he observed, could happen so unexpectedly. Over breakfast in Japan, he had gravely told Peter Huijts, "Peter, I hope you remember me when I'm gone." He seemed intent on tying up loose ends, and in July, while visiting the States, he rented a motorcycle and drove it to Oklahoma to pay what would be a final visit to his family. Perhaps as a last-ditch attempt to "provide" for them—and assuage his guilt—he urged Carol to take out a life-insurance policy on him. As a parting gift, he gave Dean the motorcycle.

Baker had been warning people of his imminent demise for so long that it had come to sound like just another of his sympathy ploys. No matter how much of a wreck he appeared to be, he seemed to possess magical regenerative powers. "One night you thought he was dying," said Riccardo Del Fra. "Then you saw him the day after, and you looked terrible and tired and he was fresh as a flower."

But he could no longer hide the decay from himself. Dropping by Evert Hekkema's, he took a small mirror off the living-room wall and carried it into another room. Staring at himself, he recited:

> Mirror, mirror on the wall
> Who's the fairest of them all? . . .
> Not you, motherfucker!

He was compelled to show other people the truth as well. Having torn down Ruth Young's idolatrous wall collage in 1982, he now tried to "correct"

Diane Vavra's view of him. One day he grabbed her copy of *Baby Breeze*—the album that had fixed him in her mind as a "god"—and broke it over his knee, throwing the pieces at the wall. Late in the filming of the documentary, he told Bruce Weber and Cherry Vanilla that he thought he had an infection, and he pulled down his pants to show them. "We almost died," said Cherry. "His body was covered with abscesses. He wanted to see what we thought, 'cause one of them was oozing."

For all this cruel self-exposure, he couldn't stand to be thought of as pathetic; his abscesses, like the ravages in his face, were his battle scars, and he wore them with pride. Weber touched a nerve in his last interview with Baker in France, when the trumpeter was at his most strung out. "I know, Chet, you've run out of your methadone," said Weber in the patient tone of a priest addressing a juvenile delinquent. "You're feeling sick, and desperate . . . it's been so painful to see you like this."

Weber's comments made Baker seem pitiful, and this was more than he could handle. Glaring at Weber with cold eyes, he took a long puff on his cigarette while trying to regain his dignity. "Well, Bruce . . . you want me to level with you and tell you the truth. But in doing that, it only creates pain on your part. This is a big drag, and completely unnecessary, because, uh . . . I *am* fifty-seven years old."

Seeking a pat on the back, Weber asked Baker whether he would look back fondly on their time together. "How . . . the hell else . . . could I see it, Bruce?" said Baker in a drugged-out stammer. "It was so beautiful . . . it was a dream. Things like that don't happen . . . just to very few."

"Chet was a hooker to the end," observed Cherry, who'd been seated at Weber's side. "Of course he was gonna say that. The next month he was gonna be in jail in California and call Bruce and Nan to get him out, and hit them up for another thousand."

It happened at a Number 9 Motel in the San Jose area. Fighting there with Vavra, Baker had hurled the TV through the window. When the owner had him arrested, he called Nan Bush to post bail; of course she agreed. Later, when Weber phoned the jail to speak to Baker, the policewoman who answered said, "Boy, he's sure getting a lot of phone calls!"

"Well, we're bailing him out," explained Weber.

"*Everybody's* calling to bail him out!" she said.

Once back in New York, Weber faced the challenge of turning ninety hours of raw footage into a documentary. His editors, Marvin Levinstein and Angelo Corrao, fashioned a rough cut that ran over three hours. Her role in the project nearly finished, Cherry Vanilla was overcome by sentiment. "I loved the guy," she said of Baker. "He was one of those people that it's exciting just to be around, and you don't know why. If I was in my twenties and he was in his thirties, boy, I would have been madly in love with him too. Probably shooting up heroin with him. Knowing he was a total con artist." For almost a year, Weber had taken her on her all-time joyride: "You were living on somebody else's money, traveling in limousines, Didier was cutting your hair daily, a snip here, a snip there. I flew on the Concorde. It really was a dream, like Chet said. I'll never take that away from Bruce—he did provide us with a little dream."

It ended nastily. Living as much in the moment as Baker, Cherry had never bothered signing a contract with Weber. When he finally sent her a release, she found her onscreen credits limited to those of cast member and researcher—far less than the writer-producer billing she claimed he had promised her. They ended up communicating through lawyers. Years after the video of Weber's film had gone out of print, Cherry seethed over how he had grabbed "all the credit." Nan Bush, in turn, dismissed Cherry as a "big disappointment" who had done a sloppy job; Weber commented as little as possible. One more tempest swirled around the memory of a glassy-eyed, slow-motion trumpeter who, for a while, had obsessed them all.

The struggle to escape from him was still consuming Vavra. When she hid in a women's shelter near her home, Baker grew frantic. Somehow he found her, and booked a gig in San Francisco, trying to lure her back. It worked. When she knocked on the door of his motel room, a Chicano drug dealer welcomed her in. Baker called out from the bathroom: "Oh, hi, honey! I'm getting high. I'll be with you in a few minutes." She glanced inside his trumpet case. There she found a brief message he had written on a sheet of notebook paper. In it, Baker claimed he had been trying to kill himself for a month, speedballing in potentially lethal doses. He was losing weight rapidly. Vavra's rejection of him, he said, had destroyed his will to live; only his music enabled him to hang on. She was sure he had meant for her to find the note, but were its contents just another manipulative ploy?

As the potency of his speedballs increased, so did his paranoia and hallucinations. In October 1987, the couple stayed at the Paris apartment of a handsome coke dealer named François and his girlfriend Sylvie. It wasn't long before Baker started accusing Vavra of sleeping with François. The taunts grew so unbearable that she snuck out and slept at Micheline Graillier's before flying back to Santa Cruz the next morning. Having lost his passport, Baker was sure Vavra had stolen it. On November 5, he wrote a letter in Rome, aimed at no one in particular. Diane, he believed, had altered the passport so that François—who he felt sure was plotting his murder—could use it to flee with her to the States. Baker entrusted the letter to Nicola Stilo's girlfriend Simona, asking her to give it to the American consulate in Rome should he die or disappear.

Once more terrified at being alone, he called Ruth Young and proposed a reconciliation. "I can't take this shit anymore," he said, asking her to call Vavra and tell her the relationship was over. "I know you know how to handle this," he assured Young. She turned him down. Meanwhile, Micheline took him to the American Embassy in Paris to verify his identity so he could get a temporary passport.

By mid-November, Vavra had returned to him. Throughout their relationship, she had used her trips to the States as occasions to get tested for HIV—an obvious threat in a relationship with a junkie. Admittedly, whenever Baker shared needles, he made a point of shooting up first; and as for the risk of infection through sexual contact, his womanizing days were long behind him, and he had probably stayed faithful to her. Still, he took a cavalier attitude toward the disease, as if no bug were any match for him. "I keep all those motherfuckers in there so stoned they can't get to me," he told Harold Danko. Vavra was uninfected, suggesting that Baker, her sole sexual partner, didn't have the virus. But she pleaded with him to have the test. He never did, and when she pressed the issue, he snapped: "If you really loved me, you wouldn't care if I had AIDS! You'd get it from me, and we'd die together!"

As Baker's obsession with Vavra grew ever more violent and twisted, a young Frenchman made a film that glorified the trumpeter as a god of romance. A graduate of the Conservatory of French Cinema, Bertrand Fèvre had worked as an assistant director on several films; soon he would start directing French pop-music videos. Late in 1986, Fèvre tuned in to a radio station in Paris, where he lived, and heard Chet Baker singing "The Touch of Your Lips." He ran to a shop to find the record; after listening to it he hurriedly bought five others.

When the trumpeter returned to New Morning, Fèvre was there. "I had the impression of being in front of a poet, a universal voice," he said. "This is the first time I met a man who was giving himself so deeply into his emotions. And this for me is very risky. That is what makes an artist—to go very deep in your emotion, and then to express it in the most beautiful way." With that in mind, Fèvre produced *Chet's Romance,* a nine-and-a-half-minute encapsulation of the French vision of Chet Baker.

His budget was small—only the musicians got paid—but so were his production needs. On November 25, Fèvre filmed Baker singing "the perfect song for him"—"I'm a Fool to Want You," which sounded to Fèvre like the cry of a man desperately addicted "to a person, love, music, or drugs, and the suffering behind it." The setting was a studio in Paris that had the sinister look of a deserted old soundstage. Fèvre directed Baker to enter dramatically across a catwalk in the rear of the studio, then to descend a staircase before sitting on a platform in front of Riccardo Del Fra, pianist Alain Jean-Marie, and George Brown, an American bebop drummer who lived in Paris. Before the music began, a hand reached into the frame and lit Baker's cigarette. As smoke curled around his head, the man who saw himself as the ultimate victim luxuriated in his suffering. "Pity me, I need you," he moaned in a pinched, slurred voice, as the high-contrast black-and-white photography turned his face into a skull. The tempo matched the movement of the camera, which panned and circled Baker with a hypnotic slowness that suggested a junkie's dim sense of time.

Chet's Romance went on to win a César award (the French Oscar) for Best Short. The Italian jazz photographer and critic Carlo Pieroni called it "a genuine masterpiece" to compare with *Jammin' the Blues,* photographer Gjon Mili's arty 1944 short of saxophonist Lester Young. A few months after the shooting, when Fèvre screened his film for Baker in Paris, the trumpeter was mostly silent. "I didn't realize I had so many lines," he said. Fèvre had included a snippet of an interview he had taped in the dressing room. "I'm definitely a romantic," Baker insists. "I don't think life is really worth all the pain and effort and struggling if you don't have somebody that you love very much."

The sentiment gave voice to one of his recurring delusions. In December, Fèvre drove Baker and Vavra to look at an apartment in Paris's ninth arrondissement, once filled with music halls and poets. Baker spoke wistfully of settling down with his love. He imagined traveling half the year; the rest of the time he would write music, teach, and practice with her to boost her confidence. By the time Fèvre took them home, Baker's black cloud had returned. No landlord would ever grant a lease to someone like him, he said ruefully.

On the twenty-third, Baker turned fifty-eight. According to Wim Wigt, the trumpeter had grossed over $200,000 in 1987—more than he had ever made in one year. But with his drug habit now costing him hundreds per day, his finances were still a mess; as always, scoring was his top priority. Bassist Rocky Knauer, who toured with him that month, was the only clean member of a band that also included Stilo and Michel Graillier. "We were in Rome for a couple of weeks," said Knauer, "and on our days off, we were supposed to go play in Poland. Instead, we ended up hanging around, because Nicola said: 'Let's not go there, let's stay here, I can get some good stuff.' I would have to get the whole fucking band out of bed. I'd run downstairs, go get cabs, and say, 'Hey, guys, let's get out of here!' They'd say, 'No, we wanna sleep!' I'd say, *'We're going!'*"

Given Baker's eminence in Europe, some found it pathetic that he would spend New Year's Eve playing one of his old haunts, De Kroeg (The Tavern), a shoebox-sized bar on a canal in Amsterdam. Mainly a Rasta and reggae club, De Kroeg stank of beer and hash; when filled to its capacity of about sixty, it became stiflingly hot. The owner, Tom Mandersloot, could only pay musicians a token fee, but he let them stay in a crash pad above the club. A steep flight of stairs led to a single large room with a kitchen, a table, a couple of chairs, and mattresses on the floor. The place was infested with mice, and Knauer, who had toured in style with Benny Golson, Art Blakey, and Freddie Hubbard, was revolted; he quit a week before the gig.

Baker, Vavra, Stilo, the Grailliers, Del Fra, and a black drummer from the States lived together in that squalid room for several days, with no work until the thirty-first. "It was complete chaos," said Vavra. "Everybody was fighting and getting loaded, everybody was filthy, heroin was everywhere." Baker, who was speedballing and downing handfuls of pills, lapsed into frightful hallucinations. Micheline watched, frozen, as he stood at the window and challenged an imaginary foe in a tree: *"Come out! Come out, I dare you!"* Del Fra still regarded Baker as a father, and it shook him to tears to see the hellish decline of a man who had influenced him so profoundly. "Riccardo was hiding," said Micheline. "He was scared."

Around 10 p.m. on New Year's Eve, patrons began drifting into De Kroeg. The only promotion for the event was a flyer tacked up outside that read CHET BAKER PLAYS AULD LAND SYNE, but a crew from VPRO-TV, a Dutch station, was on hand. As Graillier played an untuned piano, Baker performed some rather intense songs for a party night, including "I'm a Fool to Want You." Sweat poured down his cheeks and welled in every crevice before dripping onto his lap. Customers hovered with flash cameras, photographing him as if he were a monument ready to collapse. They gave him a loud ovation after every song, and Baker seemed pleased. Just before midnight, he thanked them humbly. "Well, ladies and gentlemen, it's about that time," he said. "We played five days at a very big club, and you could hear a pin drop. I'm not playing well enough for that tonight. But I don't know, you guys have more enthusiasm. Yeah . . . I don't understand it. But anyway, I want to take this opportunity to wish you all a very happy New Year."

"AND YOU TOO!" they cheered, as Baker and the band launched into "Auld Lang Syne." VPRO mingled that footage with excerpts from an interview Baker had given that day. "Nineteen eighty-seven continued to bring me a very wonderful gift, and that is . . . that I got through it," he said wryly. "I managed to survive. And of course I've had Diane with me all this year, and that was another gift that a man can really appreciate. And, uh, I've had a lot of success all over Europe this year." He smiled. "It doesn't have to get any better, if it just stays as good as 'eighty-seven, it'll be fine."

The band rang in the New Year in their favorite fashion. "I think everybody got a lot of coke that night," said Micheline. Upstairs, the mood turned ugly when Baker's drummer began fighting with him over the pay. Disgusted and wired, the trumpeter threw the whole band's money at him and yelled, *"Take it all! I don't care!"* The drummer shrieked about these "motherfuckin' white people" who were trying to rip him off. Then he turned to Vavra with a warning: "He'll just take you down with him, Diane. You better get away from that motherfucker!"

With that, he scooped up the cash and stormed off to Central Station to grab a train to Paris. A few minutes later, when Micheline recalled that the keys to Baker's Alfa were in the drummer's pocket, she and Baker bolted down the stairs and began a mad fifteen-minute dash to the station. Panting, they searched everywhere; apparently he was gone. Baker told her that they may as well go cop on Zeedijk; he knew a dealer who would "advance" them some dope on credit. There, in the middle of Zeedijk, was the drummer—"surrounded by a hundred dealers!" said Micheline.

Reclaiming the keys, she and Baker went back to the apartment. There they had their first fix of a year that, indeed, showed no sign of improvement over the one before.

No city comforted Baker like Rome, and he spent much of January 1988 at the Music Inn with Stilo, Del Fra, and Enrico Pieranunzi. That month he made one of his most eccentric and memorable albums, *Chet on Poetry,* in which he read and sang the verse of Maurizio Guercini and Gianluca Manzi, two Italian poets who had befriended him. The poems were dark, cryptic reflections on failed life and love, set to music by Stilo. Baker's acerbic delivery enhanced their hopelessness. *Chet on Poetry* was just as much a showcase for Stilo, whose music ranged from slick Europop to funk to a graceful jazz waltz. He accompanied Baker lyrically on flute and guitar, and improvised a chilling flute solo as Vavra and Baker took turns reading verses from an abstract poem by Guercini, "Waiting for Chet."

Cocky though he was in his youth, Baker had long shown an endearing humility about his gifts. But he knew that his heartfelt brand of playing was going out of fashion. Looking into the future of jazz, he saw the art form turning cold and robotic. In an interview with French journalist Gerard Rouy, Baker gave an accurate prophecy of the nineties, when "smooth jazz"—the repetitive, shapeless background music epitomized by soprano saxophonist Kenny G, soon to become the biggest-selling artist in jazz—would take over the field. "The average person isn't interested in trying to think about the music too much," Baker said. "That's probably why jazz will sooner or later become a lost art. Everything will go electronic and people will make records by themselves with a synthesizer."

Talking with Jeroen de Valk, he commented on the new generation of jazz trumpeters. "They sound pretty much alike, like they all went to Berklee," he said, referring to Boston's famed music school, whose jazz department turned out impeccably schooled but often faceless musicians. To Dutch reporter Maarten Derksen he praised Tom Harrell, a trumpeter with a lyrical ease: "He has it completely—ideas, musical imagination, and a wonderful mind." Otherwise, he heard steely young technicians who could "run the changes" but had no heart or depth. He had a particular distaste for Wynton Marsalis, the most commercially celebrated jazz trumpeter and pedagogue of the eighties, nineties, and beyond. Marsalis had the facility to mimic any style, but his playing, in Baker's view, had "a lot of technique and no soul."

He turned all this reflectiveness inward on January 29, 1988, when he was profiled on the Danish TV series *JazzMasters.* Leonard Malone, the show's American host, took him at nightfall to a lovely setting: Ny Carlsberg Glyptotek, an art museum in Copenhagen with a lush interior garden. Surrounded by greenery, Baker and Malone sat together on a bench. TV lights illuminated a nearby set of white statues, making them glow like saints and angels. The trumpeter, though, looked like he had just awakened from a bad night: his long hair was matted and greasy, his energy low. Still, he gave Malone his full attention, answering the host's thoughtful questions charmingly and modestly. The topics ranged from his Oklahoma childhood to his artistic milestones to his philosophy of life. "I was very lucky," he said of himself at twenty-two. "I happened to be in the right places at the right time."

Malone wondered if he really believed the title of his trademark song,

"You Can't Go Home Again." Baker took a long pause. "I still have some hope that that may not be true," he said. "But on the other hand, I seem to be getting further and further from what I call home. And my desire is really not too strong to go back, you know. Oklahoma is really a cultural wasteland, and most of the states around it . . . I'd rather be in Europe anytime." Gently broaching the topic of addiction, Malone asked him why he thought drugs and jazz were so entwined. "I think maybe it's an attempt to put your head in a different place, in order to block out a lot of things," said Baker, without naming the "things"—anger, responsibility, guilt—he had tried to erase. "I'm not sorry," he concluded firmly. "And I don't apologize for anything. I've never done anything to hurt anyone. And, uh, I don't think I've hurt myself too much. I'm fifty-eight years old, I'm still here, and I'm still playing."

He left Denmark and went on the road with Nicola Stilo, making quick stops in Norway, Sweden, and Germany. "Musically, that period was very, very important for me," said the flutist. "Chet played every year better and better. Each night was a spiritual thing." But Diane Vavra could take no more. On February 14, she flew to Santa Cruz, saying she had to make an insurance payment on her car and to see her family.

Depressed as he was at her exit, Baker kept working. That month he joined Enrico Pieranunzi to play several concerts in Italy, produced by Paolo Piangiarelli, an impresario from the northern Italian town of Macerata. Piangiarelli owned a small jazz label, Philology, named after one of his idols, saxophonist Phil Woods. But nothing could outweigh his obsession with his "friend-brother-father-son Chet," his "favorite person" and the jazz artist he most revered. He clamored to preserve Baker's every note on tape, and between February 29 and March 2, Piangiarelli recorded two albums with him and Pieranunzi: *Little Girl Blue,* a trio session; and *The Heart of the Ballad,* an achingly sad duo album of standards.

Vavra had been gone only two weeks, but Baker was racked by loneliness. It infused every phrase of "The Thrill Is Gone," a song he had sung on his first album. As he wallowed in the song's theme of love turned tragic, Pieranunzi's stark, tolling chords signaled approaching doom. Years before, while recording *Soft Journey,* Pieranunzi had tried to lighten Baker's gloom with a bright, assertive style; now he succumbed to the darkness, and it changed his whole attitude toward the piano. "He forced me, silently, to use less notes, to choose the notes with care, to build melodies," Pieranunzi said.

Baker phoned Vavra constantly, whimpering for her return or demanding it: "I want you here *now*!" She agreed to come, but Baker didn't believe her, and he tried another tack. On February 29, he mentioned through tears that he had just recorded "The Thrill Is Gone" on a new album. "Chet was very devious, you know," she explained. "I said, 'Are you trying to tell me something, Chet?' He said, 'Oh, it's the way that the melody went, it reminds me of us.' "

On March 1, he wired her nine hundred dollars to pay for an immediate flight to Italy. She never came. Certain she was living with another man, Baker enlisted the help of Bruce Weber, who sent a California friend to Vavra's apartment to spy on her. The friend knocked on her door, pretending to bear a message from the photographer. There she was—"living totally alone, broke, with nothing to her name," Weber said.

Baker wasn't convinced. Deranged from speedballs and barbiturates, he began writing a poisonous, diary-like letter in Paris, finishing it at Jacques Pelzer's. In a crazed hand, he branded his girlfriend a "sick bitch" who was "turning tricks all over Europe." Meanwhile, the calls continued. He tried every scheme he knew to get her back, including veiled threats of suicide. "I know how to do it—you know what I mean?" he told her.

Life in the Pelzer house had darkened since November 1987, when the pharmacy closed after thirty-eight years of business. "He completely mishandled it," said his friend Jean-Pierre Gebler, a Belgian tenor saxophonist in whose home Baker stayed several times. For years, Pelzer had given paracodeine without a prescription to his friends, notably Jon Eardley, Baker's original replacement in the Gerry Mulligan Quartet, who now lived in Cologne. The shop had escaped close legal scrutiny thanks to Pelzer's brother-in-law, a local official. But in the mideighties, the son of a rival druggist became inspector of pharmacies, and he ordered an examination of Pelzer's records. The codeine handouts were all uncovered. Pelzer was fined, but the pharmacy survived. By 1987, however, profits had dried up, and he began selling his antique furniture to stay afloat. Only when it was too late did Pelzer—who had never kept more than half an eye on his business—learn that Popol, his trusted assistant, had been stealing.

The musician was heartsick, but his daughter was immersed in another looming catastrophe. Watching Baker's spirit fade before her eyes, she clung to his side, determined to save him. When he rose in the middle of the night to go score, she went too. Sometimes on the way home, Baker was so stoned he nodded off at the wheel. Micheline shook him, insisting they stop and get coffee. When he fixed a dangerously strong dose of heroin for them both, she suspected he had a double suicide in mind. "I'm not gonna die with you, forget it!" she said. But she was willing to pay almost any other price to stay with him, even as Vavra consumed his every thought. All the way through Madrid, Frankfurt, Paris, and Rome he kept calling her, begging her to come back and losing a little more hope each fruitless time.

On April 1, Baker and Nicola Stilo played a prestigious festival at Theaterhaus Stuttgart. German TV broadcast their concert. The angelic vision in white that had graced Comblain-la-Tour in 1959 had decayed into a near-cadaver. Baker appeared in a rumpled white suit and shirt, stringy uncombed hair hanging below his collar and withered flesh sagging off his cheeks and neck. Angry and distracted, he sang a painfully off-key "I'm a Fool to Want You," forgetting many of the words. The engineer raised the volume, creating a feedback whistle. "PLEASE don't play with it while I'm singing this tune!" shouted Baker. He wrenched the mike out of its stand and stood up, turning his back on the soundman. Gudrun Endress, now the publisher of the German magazine *Jazz Podium,* cringed at what she saw. "The music is the only thing that kept him alive," she said. "I didn't even dare to approach him. He seemed so broken and so sad."

Soon after leaving Stuttgart, Baker stopped in Amsterdam with Micheline. At Evert Hekkema's apartment, the trumpeter called Vavra. Before dialing, he asked Micheline to sit by his side. "You know women—tell me if she's for real or not," he said. Vavra answered. Baker pleaded with her once more to come back, then silently passed the phone to Micheline, who listened as Vavra promised weakly to do so. Once Baker had hung up, Micheline told him she didn't think Vavra was telling the truth. As she later realized, this was the moment when he gave up. "I couldn't blame her, myself," Micheline said.

Baker's despair was overwhelming, and everyone around him was drowning in it. On April 7, he began a short run at the Music Inn. Picchi Pignatelli was struggling to keep the club in business, but she suffered continual harassment from the Mafia, who demanded payoffs she couldn't afford. For the next few years, the Music Inn would keep closing and reopening, always on the verge of demise. Giovanni Tommaso lived in an apartment directly below hers, and one day in 1994, a neighbor told him she smelled gas. Tommaso had saved Picchi from an earlier suicide attempt, but this time he didn't make it upstairs soon enough. At fifty-five, she was dead.

After the engagement, Baker stayed briefly in Rome, bonded to his strung-out friends. Whenever he scored methadone, he shared it with Stilo and the Grailliers. He once told Stilo: "I don't have too much, and I know Micheline is sicker than you are, so it's for her." Micheline tried to help everyone by phoning Amedeo Tommasi, who had known her all her life.

Explaining that she was flat broke, she asked if he would take her out to eat. Tommasi, who made a comfortable living as a film composer, agreed. When he drove out to meet her, he found Baker and Graillier there too. The pianist treated them all to dinner, then brought them back to his home, which contained a recording studio. Sitting at the piano, he played "Ballad for Micheline," a song he had written when she was a child. Micheline burst into tears. But Baker's mood was darker. "I'm tired of living," he grumbled. "Life after you're fifty doesn't seem to make sense." He mentioned how nice it would be to drive his car full-speed into a wall. When they got up to leave, he asked Tommasi for cash, and got it.

No sooner had they bade Tommasi a sentimental goodbye than Baker and his friends went out to score, leaving them broke again. "We were deep in the shit," said Michel Graillier. His wife proposed a solution: "I'll go on the street. I'm gonna be a prostitute!"

Michel had a better answer. On Via del Corso, in the center of town, he set up a battery-operated keyboard and began to play. Passersby gathered to listen. Baker joined in on trumpet, then along came Nicola Stilo and his bassist friend Lillo Quaratino to round out the band. The mob swelled to more than a hundred. After a half-hour, Baker passed his hat among the cheering crowd, collecting change. The take amounted to about a hundred dollars in lire. "We used it to pay the dealer," Micheline said.

Within days, Baker went from playing for tips to starring in the most splendid showcase of his life. Kurt Giese, a producer with Nord Deutscher Rundfunk (North German Broadcasting), had idolized Baker since boyhood, and dreamed of re-creating the 1954 album *Chet Baker with Strings.* Giese masterminded a concert that would surround his hero with both the NDR big band and its symphony. The show would be aired from Grosser Sendersaal, a venerable hall in Hannover, Germany, on Saturday, April 29.

Giese picked songs from Baker's early days of glory, including "I Get Along Without You Very Well," "There's a Small Hotel," and "My Funny Valentine." Among the sixty-two musicians were two of his old West Coast buddies, saxophonist Herb Geller and pianist Walter Norris, both of whom had lived in Germany and worked with the NDR for years.

Five days of rehearsal were to precede the concert. Monday passed, then Tuesday, with no sign of Baker. The Wigts started receiving angry calls from the NDR: "If there is no rehearsal, there is no gig!" Baker, said Ria, "didn't want to do it, he didn't want to rehearse, he didn't want to do anything. He said, 'No, I'm going on a little vacation with Micheline.' " Late on Wednesday afternoon, Baker phoned Giese from his hotel room in Hannover. He had come to the hall, but the doorman had taken one look at him and turned him away, even after Baker pointed to a big sign with his name on it and said, "That's me!" By the time Giese cleared things up, the musicians were leaving. In the trumpeter's absence they had prerecorded their accompaniment, and he practiced by playing along with the tapes. Giese called the results "magic," but Baker couldn't keep his dentures in place, and Walter Norris thought he sounded dismal. The next morning, Norris heard a German engineer snarl: "What is this? He has ruined his health—how can someone with such a great talent destroy himself? He looks like he's seventy-five years old!"

Two hours before the concert on Saturday, Norris had coffee with a despondent Baker. His application for a new driver's license had been rejected, Baker said, and in a few months he wouldn't be able to drive. His lower teeth, which he had kept, were deteriorating, and his gums were causing him such pain that he was sure he wouldn't be able to play much longer. "Everything was closing in on him," Norris said. "He knew this."

That night, tension was high. "We were all holding our breath," said Herb Geller. Baker sat in a chair onstage amid a sea of musicians: the string players on one side, the big band on the other. He seemed determined to prove himself one last time. With every defense shattered, he lived the songs with a painful intensity. The concert peaked with an epic nine-minute performance of "Valentine." Baker opened it with a trumpet chorus backed by guitar only, a chillingly stark musical skeleton; from there, his hollow, otherworldly singing drifted on a cloud of strings. In a roaring arrangement of "Look for the Silver Lining," he rode the big band with calm authority. "All Blues" and "Summertime" nodded to Miles Davis, who had made Baker's style possible. Archie Shepp, a tenor saxophonist, told journalist Peter Niklas Wilson that Baker "had become what he always wanted to be . . . he was actually playing more like Miles Davis than Miles Davis."

Baker knew he had done well. So did his fans, many of whom would remember that show as one of the most moving experiences of their lives. They were eager to congratulate him, but minutes after leaving the stage, Baker jumped into his beat-up Alfa and sped off to Zeedijk. Then he joined Nicola and Micheline in Liège for what would prove a harrowing stretch of days. "Chet was a complete chaos mentally," said Stilo, who listened in horror as Baker streamed nonsensical talk. The trumpeter had received thousands of dollars in payment for the Hannover concert and other appearances, and in a more lucid moment he spoke again of buying a heavenly French oasis for himself and Vavra. But he didn't think he'd be around long to enjoy it. Hallucinating again, he phoned Bruce Weber with a warning: "I just want you to know that if something happens to me, you know, that there are these guys who have been after me."

But the only one poised to destroy Baker was himself. He lost a packet of heroin at the house, and vowed to lock himself in his car and set it on fire unless the "thief" came forward. Micheline found the dope in his pants pocket, but he nearly carried out his threat anyway. Knowing Baker couldn't stand to be alone, Stilo was sleeping with him in the same room. One night Baker dozed off with a cigarette. The flutist woke up to find his friend's pillow ablaze and the air thick with smoke. "Hey, Chet—*Wake up, wake up!*" he hollered, then dragged a nearly comatose Baker off the bed. "In that moment," said Stilo, "Chet took my hand, and I saw two tears from his eyes." Micheline ran in and tossed the burning pillow out the window, then, with Stilo's help, managed to smother the flames before they set the wood-frame house on fire. Baker had come close to razing the only home he had. Afterward, there wasn't much to say. "He was a man completely lost, you understand?" said Stilo. "Asking somebody to show him a minimum reason to live."

Saxophonist Guy Masy came to see him. "He's upstairs," said Pelzer. Masy found the trumpeter lying in bed, staring at the ceiling. "I saw death in his eyes," said Masy. "He was awake, but in another world. You could see that he was suffering physically, morally too. I was so emotional I couldn't say a word."

He seemed to be reflecting on his many failures. Micheline recalled him gazing out the window and saying: "I'm gonna die one day, and my kids won't even know who I am." The damage was irreparable, but Baker saw a chance to tie up at least one loose end. In Amsterdam, he told Irv Rochlin about Richard Carpenter, the man he hated more than anyone else on earth. "What do you think would be the best way to take out a contract on somebody?" Baker asked.

"Are you serious, man?"

"I'm *very* serious," said Baker, who figured that the pianist, having once done time for a drug rap, must know "some guys" who could do the job. Rochlin was stunned at the suggestion. He said goodbye to Baker for the last time.

Accompanied by Nicola, Micheline, and Jacques Pelzer, Baker drove to Paris, where he checked into the Anne de France prior to playing the New Morning on May 4 and 5. Hein Van de Geyn, his bassist on those nights, saw how frail Baker had grown since Japan: "It was like the difference between a well-kept car and one that's ready to go to the junkyard." Liliane Rovère watched in sadness from her table. "He came out of the dressing room, he was *so* high I couldn't believe it," she said. She thought he wouldn't be able to play at all, but he touched her more deeply than ever with "My Funny Valentine." A small muffled sound came out of his horn like a groan of pain, each phrase splintering at the end.

The audience was rapt, but this time there were many empty seats. After the show, he sat with Rovère and mourned the loss of Vavra. Suddenly he asked his girlfriend of the fifties to come back to the hotel and spend the night. "Chet, are you kidding?" she said. "After thirty-five years? It's very flattering that you would still consider, but . . ." She sensed that what he really wanted was company—"someone close, arms around him." Worried, she asked Jacques Pelzer to come along to the Anne de France. In his room, she was terrified by how much dope he shot. The man whose lips had rarely parted in a smile stood there like a zombie with his mouth hanging open.

After he had signed out of the hotel, Micheline checked his room and found a pile of blood-soaked clothing. She gathered it up and burned it. "He was trying to kill himself, but he couldn't do it," Vavra said later. "The gods didn't want him to go yet, I guess."

The next night, *Chet's Romance* was to premiere at a cinema in Paris. Bertrand Fèvre had notified Baker, and looked forward to having the trumpeter at his side. But as the lights dimmed, the young filmmaker sat next to an empty seat. Heartbroken, he went afterward to the New Morning. Finding Baker in the dressing room between sets, Fèvre asked why he hadn't come. He glanced up from the joint he was rolling on his trumpet case. "Why didn't you wake me up?" he asked wearily.

Onstage for the late show, Baker sank into a chair with hardly the energy to lift his horn. Weakly attempting humor, he announced, in an ancient cowboy drawl, that "the old man is having problems with his dentures." People were too disturbed to laugh. "Before Chet left the stage, most of them quietly went away," Fèvre said.

Attended by Stilo and Pelzer, Baker returned to Liège. "He asked me to stay with him," said Micheline. "I was his last nurse." Late on the night of the sixth, after she had gone to sleep, Baker walked out of his bedroom and descended the stairs in the darkness. He passed Michel Graillier. "Michel . . . ," said Baker. He paused. "Never mind," he said. Before departing for Zeedijk, he left a present for Micheline: all his remaining methadone.

On the morning of Saturday, May 7, Baker made the hour's drive from

Amsterdam to Rotterdam to play a night at Jazzclub Thelonious, a theater-like venue with a curtained stage and seating for more than two hundred. A seaport town, Rotterdam was a drug-dealer's paradise; dope was smuggled in by ship from other countries, and according to witnesses, it was readily available at Thelonious. The lure of ready drugs attracted many star musicians, but non-user Hein Van de Geyn, who played there with Baker, couldn't bear the sleaziness. Thelonious was isolated in a graffiti-ridden underground mall of shops, all closed during the club's business hours. "It was the most depressing place I've ever seen," recalled the bassist. Baker was expected to pack the house, but only seventeen customers came. Miserable, he sounded as frail as he had at New Morning. After the shows, Baker was paid only a fraction of the promised fee. Around 2 a.m., when nearly everyone had left, Van de Geyn put his arms around him. "Take care of yourself, Chet," he said. "We need you."

Leaving the club, Baker and Stilo walked up a concrete stairway and stood on a dark, empty street, both unable to remember where Baker had parked his Alfa. After a futile search, they boarded a night train for Amsterdam, then hurried to Zeedijk. On Sunday morning, Baker stocked up on barbiturates from "Dr. Feelgood." He and Stilo spent the next thirty-six hours in an Amsterdam hotel.

There, the flutist watched his friend speeding toward oblivion. Baker shot pure cocaine in terrifying quantities. Jerry Stahl had done the same, and knew the consequences: "Man, it makes you crazy and depressed, and the high lasts less than a minute so you're constantly fixing, a dozen, two dozen times an hour, until your veins are gone and you're a bloody wreck looking for a place left to jab. The crash is beyond anything you can imagine. Every cell is screaming."

The coke, combined with barbiturates, pushed Baker past the brink of insanity. "The cocaine is absolutely the thing that caused the worst problems," said Stilo. Stumbling out of the bathroom, Baker peered out the window with crazed eyes. A lifetime of stifled fear seemed to explode from him all at once. *"Nicola, save me!"* he yelled. "There's a man out there that wants to shoot me!" Then he remembered his missing passport, and another wave of paranoia rushed over him. "Nicola, I'm afraid! I have to go downstairs and get the police, because somebody stole my passport!"

The delusions lasted for hours, "with blood everywhere," Stilo recalled. At one point Baker lurched for the window. "He thought he saw a door there," said Stilo, who had to grab him by the hair to keep him from jumping. In between trying to restrain his friend—who still had the force of a bull—Stilo had to reassure the desk clerk, who kept knocking on the door to complain about the noise.

Finally, the flutist couldn't take any more. On Monday, May 9, he boarded a train to Liège to pick up his guitar. Before leaving the hotel room, he grabbed Baker by the shoulders. "Chet, look at me," he said. "I'm not with you anymore. You're gonna be alone for two, three days. Please, man. Like always, keep strong."

At the Pelzer house, Stilo recounted for Micheline the events of the last few days. "I'm going back to Italy," he said. "I don't want to stay with Chet, because he's going crazy." When he explained that Baker was shooting only coke, with no heroin to buffer the physical shock, Micheline panicked. "He's gonna have a heart attack!" she said. After thirty-two years as a junkie, Baker knew the effects of nearly every type of drug, and she was sure he wanted to die.

Baker stayed alone that night. He likely returned to Zeedijk to score more heroin, which may have alleviated the strain on his heart. Then he went to Rotterdam to find his missing Alfa. On Tuesday, May 10, the Wigts received a late-afternoon phone call. "Hello, this is the Rotterdam police department," an officer said politely. "I have here a Mr. Chesney H. Baker." He explained that Baker had lost his car and had come to them for help; the trumpeter gave Wim Wigt's name as his contact. Certain that Baker was carrying drugs, Wigt called the one person he knew who could probably rescue him in a hurry: Bob Holland, a former Wigt roadie, who lived just minutes from the station. Even though Wigt had fired him years ago, Holland obliged.

Baker didn't know him, but nearly every jazz musician who had passed through Rotterdam did. Holland had worked at Thelonious as a bartender, host, and adviser; he also sold cocaine. He had adopted the Americanized name of Bob Holland, but his tortoiseshell glasses, mustache, and nervous laugh made him easy to spot.

Holland had taken into his home a series of addicted American jazz stars on their last legs. One of them was Philly Joe Jones, who died of heart failure in 1985 after years of self-destruction. When he met Baker, Holland already had two houseguests: Frank Wright, an avant-garde tenor player; and Woody Shaw, a bop trumpeter of the seventies and eighties who was currently touring Germany. The "Reverend" Wright, as he called himself, lived with Holland on and off until 1990, when at fifty-four he died of a heart attack, probably related to his coke habit. Shaw met a sadder fate. Nearly blind from a retinal condition, he had also contracted AIDS. Holland tried nursing him for much of 1988, but finally sent him home to Newark, New Jersey, to live with his parents. Shaw didn't want to go—"He was afraid, ashamed," said Holland. One night in May 1989, after hearing Max Roach at the Village Vanguard, Shaw went alone to Brooklyn, possibly to score heroin. He fell in front of a subway train and lost his arm, dying soon after.

Some thought Holland the Angel of Death, but on May 10, 1988, he was Baker's savior. Arriving at the police station, he found the trumpeter in a pair of striped trousers and his "Jesus Christ sandals," as Holland called them, worn over soiled white socks. "What's going on?" he asked.

"I lost my car," said Baker. "I parked it somewhere on Saturday."

"Well, we have to look for it," said Holland, who knew how to play it cool. An officer took them on a friendly drive through the streets near Thelonious, but they found nothing. The policeman asked Baker where he was staying, promising to continue the search and to phone with any news. Holland gave his own number, and the officer drove them home. "Well, Bob," cracked Baker as they went upstairs, "is this the first time you've been brought home by the cops?"

They entered a large apartment with a dingy white piano in the living room and blowups of Holland's jazz friends on the walls. Baker found himself facing a picture of Philly Joe Jones. He stared, then burst into tears. Holland recalled his words: "Soon I'll be with you, man!"

Baker took off his socks. One held two grams of heroin, the other two grams of coke. "Jesus Christ, Chet!" said Holland. "Standing in the police station with that stuff in your socks!" Unconcerned, Baker dashed off to a drugstore to buy needles. Upon returning, he closed himself in a bedroom, leaving Holland and Wright in the parlor. After a half-hour, Wright became nervous and urged his host to check up on Baker. Holland found the trumpeter seated on the edge of the bed, struggling to find a hit. "Shit, these needles are too small!" he said. The Dutchman was stunned to learn how much dope Baker used: six grams a day—three or four times the intake of a typical junkie—combined with lots of coke. Baker filled the syringe, then held it up. "You could kill a bunch of cows with this," he said. He plunged the needle into his scrotum. "The man was a walking corpse," said Holland. "He was only living for the stuff. Music was the last resort to get it."

For once Baker wanted no sympathy. "Bob, I'm fifty-eight years old," he said, just as he had in response to Bruce Weber's pity in Cannes. "I've used this stuff for thirty years. You can't help me. I'm too far out." Should anything happen to him, said Baker, he wanted his horn to go to Woody Shaw, who, unlike most black musicians, had treated him with warmth. A picture from 1985, taken by photographer Elena Carminati in Verona, showed them with their arms around each other's shoulders, embracing like brothers.

Minutes after his fix, Baker was worrying about the next one. Not knowing Rotterdam, he asked Holland to score for him. Baker pulled out a fistful of lire, guilders, French and Swiss francs, and deutsche marks, spreading the bills all over the table. Holland estimated the total at six thousand guilders, or about four thousand dollars—all the money Baker had in the world. But with heroin priced at one hundred fifty guilders a gram, it wouldn't go far. He gave his host some of the cash, asking him to hold the rest. Holland hid it under a typewriter.

Baker had hardly eaten in days, and Holland took him and Wright to a Chinese restaurant. Baker could swallow only half an eggroll; what he really craved was a chance to play. Off they went to Jazzcafé Dizzy, a neighborhood bar that featured jazz on Sundays and Tuesdays. That night Dizzy was presenting Bad Circuits, a Dutch fusion group led by a young keyboard player, Rob van Bavel. When Chet Baker walked through that dark room and stepped onstage, people cheered. "The great Chet Baker popping in like that and starting to play with youngsters—everyone was flabbergasted," said Holland. Baker managed two tunes, "Rhythm Changes" and "Green Dolphin Street."

"You could see he was finished," said Holland of what would be Baker's last performance. "But he played with so few notes, expressing so much. That was the magic of the man."

After midnight, Holland took his guests to a seamy neighborhood known for its drug activity. They found a dealer with three grams of heroin, but that wasn't enough, and Wright took Baker home while Holland stayed behind to try and locate more. At three or four in the morning he returned to the apartment, empty-handed.

Holland would later tell Rudie Kagie of the Dutch newspaper *Vrij Nederlands* (Free Netherlands) that Baker stayed in the apartment until Thursday morning, when the police phoned to report the discovery of his car. Borrowing the keys, Holland went to pick it up, and to try once more to find a dealer. It wasn't easy. Thursday was Ascension Day, and most Dutch—even pushers, apparently—were out of town.

Around noon, Baker placed a series of frantic calls to Peter Huijts. "*Where is that motherfucker?*" he demanded, certain Holland had run off with his money and his car. Desperate for dope, he said he was about to take a train to Amsterdam. Huijts begged him to stay put, assuring him that

Holland would return. The trumpeter had an important concert in Laren that night, and Huijts didn't want to take any chances. Baker ignored the plea. Taking the rest of his money from beneath the typewriter, he boarded the 1:32 p.m. train.

Holland told Kagie of arriving home an hour later with the car and the drugs. But in 1996 he would make a few confusing and unexplained changes in his story. It was on Tuesday night, he now said, that Baker's car was found. Holland had wanted to pick it up right away, but Baker insisted on going to Dizzy first. The next morning, Holland went to retrieve the Alfa and score more heroin, and by the time he returned at noon, Baker had gone. This version leaves a full day, Wednesday, when Baker was supposedly alone in Amsterdam, engaging in mysterious activities. "I tell the truth and nothing but the truth," said Holland, but his facts, in this case, were vague.

"The truth" meant so little to Baker that Vavra didn't know what to think when he phoned her on Wednesday afternoon. Calmer now, he announced that he couldn't go on without her, and wouldn't be calling for a while—an ominous warning, but not an unfamiliar one.

On the evening of Thursday, May 12, one of the most popular musical radio shows in the country, *Sesjun,* was to have its jubilee concert, a live broadcast from Singer-Konzertsaal in Laren. Baker was slated to share the bill with Archie Shepp, a fiery avant-garde saxophonist, and Annette Lowman, Shepp's vocalist. Wim Wigt, who had booked the show, knew Baker would have to stop at Zeedijk before he could even think of performing, so he put the musicians up at the nearby Memphis Hotel. At six-thirty, a van would take everyone to Laren. But at six, when Ria Wigt phoned the hotel to confirm Baker's arrival, he wasn't there. Peter Huijts was less worried than annoyed. "This had happened before," he said. "Most of the time, Chet would call you and curse you out and blame you for his mistakes."

The other musicians proceeded to Laren without him. The 8 p.m. sound check went ahead with no sign of Baker. Sighs of relief greeted the approach of his Alfa Romeo outside the hall, but instead of Baker, out stepped Holland; Wigt had ordered him to drive the car to Laren to have it ready when the trumpeter appeared. With showtime minutes away, the promoters "were just going nuts," recalled Lowman. Per his contract, Shepp had prepared only a half-hour of music; pressured to fill Baker's slot, he refused. Shepp and Lowman performed their short set, then went downstairs and sat in her dressing room. "It was really a weird silence," the singer recalled. "We just sort of sat there looking at each other. Peter Huijts is a miracle man; for

Peter not to be able to round Chet up and get him there, we knew something was wrong."

Moments later the producers appeared, threatening to withhold Shepp's pay because he hadn't cooperated. War broke out. "There was this unbelievable screaming and yelling where the dressing rooms were," said Lowman. Shepp hollered that he had done his job, and they had better give him his goddamned money; Wigt, who stood to lose his piece of it, blamed Holland for not keeping a closer eye on Baker.

Home in Wageningen, the Dutch town where she and her husband lived and worked, Ria was equally frazzled. "Chet always showed up someplace," she said. "If there was a problem, finally he always phoned." She began an all-night marathon of calls to the train station, to hotels and hospitals all over Amsterdam, even to the police there and in Rotterdam, but to no avail. She suspected the worst; so did Micheline and Nicola. They all knew that Baker had always kept someone nearby when he fixed, especially in recent years, when his gluttonous mixing of coke, heroin, and barbiturates sent him "out of his mind," as Stilo said. Baker's disappearance alarmed his friends. "He knew that if he was alone, nobody could help him, and he would just follow through with any delusions he might have," explained Vavra. "He told me that."

Having heard the news, Micheline, who was staying with friends in Normandy, went for a walk alone on the beach. Suddenly a terrifying premonition overwhelmed her, and she began to wail: "CHET! CHET!" Hysterical, she raced back to her friends' house and phoned Vavra in California. *"Chet's going to kill himself!"* she screamed. "You're the last one who can save Chet tonight. You've got to do something! You've got to find him!"

"I can't find him, I'm here! What can I do?"

"Call Wim Wigt!"

Vavra rang the agent. "What's happening?" she asked. Wigt admitted he couldn't find Baker anywhere, and promised to call when he knew something.

Everyone waited. Unknown to any of them, Baker was in room C-20 on the third floor of the Hotel Prins Hendrik, in the busy commercial hub just off Amsterdam's Central Station. A cheap "convenience" hotel, commonly used for overnight stays, the Prins Hendrik gave junkies a handy place to shoot the dope they had scored on Zeedijk, just steps away. Baker and Micheline had checked in a few times for that purpose, as had Woody Shaw. With most hotels full on account of Ascension Day, perhaps Baker chose the Prins Hendrik as a last resort. Or maybe it was his desire to be alone that night that made him avoid his usual hotels, the Victoria and the Crest, where his friends might have located him.

Sometime on that balmy spring afternoon he had shown up in the Prins Hendrik's small lobby. A female employee spotted him there, carrying his trumpet case. "I thought, 'Oh, my God, what an old man!' " she said. "I didn't know it was Chet Baker." The desk clerk found him "a little nervous" as he registered. Baker settled into a tidy room with bright yellow walls, a double bed, a night table, and a TV. The two windows, which started at knee level, looked out onto a winding network of streets surrounded by hotels and restaurants. Trolley cars whizzed through, and the chiming of bicycle bells filled the air. Baker locked the door behind him.

He stayed hidden away until approximately 3:10 a.m. on Friday the thirteenth. At that time, a man leaving a bar on Zeedijk saw a body on the narrow sidewalk in front of the Prins Hendrik. It lay curled in a fetal position under a full moon. The passerby banged on the door to the lobby, which was dark; at night the entrance was locked, and guests needed a key to enter. According to a police report filed later, the sole clerk on duty was in another part of the hotel and didn't hear the knocking. But an American guest did. He went downstairs, but when he saw the agitated figure at the door, he assumed a drunken vagrant was trying to get in. The guest went back to his room.

Moments later, the police at Warmoesstraat, a street in the adjacent red-light district, received a phone call, probably made by the man who had discovered the body. Officers arrived at the Prins Hendrik minutes later. What had looked like a passed-out junkie or wino proved a grislier sight up close. The man lay next to one of the short concrete posts that lined the streets, his face covered in blood and his skull bashed in. He wore a short-sleeve shirt and a pair of pinstripe trousers, caked in blood. Beside him were a pair of spectacles and a heavy steel pin of the kind used to prop open Dutch windows. Finding that, the police concluded that he had fallen from one of the hotel rooms and struck his head on the post. The corpse was wrapped in a white sheet and delivered to the morgue on Warmoesstraat. Lacking any identification, the body remained anonymous. Its face was obscured by dried blood, but the condition of the body led police to think they had picked up a thirty-year-old man.

On Friday morning at about eight, Rob Bloos, a young inspector, arrived for work at the Warmoesstraat station. Learning about the new corpse at the morgue, he wasn't too concerned. "It was just like the other ones," he said. "At that time we had in this neighborhood a lot of junkies—German guys, Italian guys. The heroin is much stronger here. They used a lot too much. And died."

Nevertheless, he brought two colleagues to the hotel and began a meticulous investigation. His report, which filled more than thirty pages, included a diagram of the room, a complete inventory of its contents, and interviews with hotel staff. Checking the registry, Bloos saw the signature of Chet Baker, a name he had never heard. He found the door to the empty room locked from inside, indicating that no one else had been there. Nor was there any sign of a disturbance. A glass containing traces of heroin and coke, and another with a needle in it, were on a table, along with less than a gram of heroin. The only luggage was a trumpet case, later rumored, inaccurately, to have been found beside the body on the street. In it were a trumpet, a watch, fifty guilders, a bracelet, a cigarette lighter, and a piece of paper with the name Chet Baker on it.

From a databank that listed registration information for every hotel in town, Bloos learned that Chet Baker had stayed at the Capitol Hotel on May 9 and 10. But when he compared the signature on file at the Capitol with the one at the Prins Hendrik, they looked different to him. Bloos concluded that a junkie had robbed an American, forged the victim's name at the Prins Hendrik, checked in, and somehow fallen out the window—a drop of about thirty feet.

All the while Ria Wigt had kept phoning the station, begging the help of anyone who answered. As late as Friday morning, she was assured that no one who fit Baker's description had turned up. Peter Huijts finally called them himself and happened to reach Bloos. Huijts explained that he was looking for a friend, an American musician named Chet Baker, who might be in trouble due to his drug addiction. The inspector said that a young man with a trumpet case had been brought to the morgue the night before. Told what was inside the case, Huijts knew he had better go to the station. When he saw a familiar pair of glasses, he murmured, "Oh, shit." Huijts looked through the case and found a slip of paper listing his own name and phone number. He was brought to the morgue. There, at last, he found Chet Baker.

At around 10 a.m. California time, he phoned Diane Vavra. "Are you prepared?" he asked. He gave her the news. "I just went numb," she said. But once the shock had worn off, she felt a strange sense of relief. "I was addicted to him," she said. "Now that he was gone, I was free." Later Huijts called Carol. "She was rather quiet—not very excited," he recalled.

By Saturday, the news had hit the wire services, and photographers and reporters swarmed the Prins Hendrik. Bruce Weber and Nan Bush were in a Manhattan editing room working on their documentary when word arrived of Baker's death. At that moment he was on their projection screen, talking and playing just a few months before. "When you watch the film, he's right there with you," said Bush. "It was devastating. As much as we were not fond of Carol—I mean, Chet never liked her that much—we immediately called her."

For the next six days, the body remained in Amsterdam pending completion of a battery of forms. An autopsy revealed that Baker's cheek and skull had been smashed on impact with the pointed post. Blood had filled his cranial cavity, and his ribs were broken, creating hemorrhaging in the chest. Track marks dotted his arms. The cause of death was listed as brain injury, although conflicting information emerged about the circumstances. Klaas Wilting, a police representative, issued a statement: "Maybe he started acting funny. . . . He was alone and shoved the window open himself and either fell or jumped out. . . . All we know is that there was no criminal activity involved." Another spokesman, Leo Detering, was quoted in the *Village Voice:* "We performed a special examination of his blood and found no drugs." But in 1997, Bloos reported just the opposite.

All this uncertainty led to wild speculation: A stoned Baker had sat on the windowsill and nodded off. He had opened the window for some fresh air on that warm night and fallen out. Both theories are preposterous, for the window slid up only about fifteen inches, making it difficult, if not impossible, for a grown man to fall through accidentally.

Many people decided that Baker had lost his room key and tried to scale the front of the hotel and reenter through the window, falling in the process. Certainly he had proven his cat-burgling ability, but the Prins Hendrik stood in the most public spot in town, with traffic streaming in and out of Central Station and the red-light district at all hours, and he could hardly have attempted the feat unnoticed; moreover, the building's flat surface would have been nearly impossible to climb.

Bob Holland heard two more theories. One of them incriminated Carol Baker in a scheme to kill the trumpeter for the insurance money; the other, devised by Woody Shaw, implicated the Prins Hendrik. Shaw held that the staff had found Baker dead in the room of an overdose and had dumped the body on the street—a common practice, Shaw alleged, in a hotel rife with junkies. "Of course the police in that area knew what happened in that hotel," Holland claimed.

By far the favorite assumption was that Baker had been murdered by a dealer he hadn't paid, and that his body had been stuffed out the window or dragged onto the sidewalk. Because the police had found no hint of crime, many concluded they had done a sloppy job—an idea reinforced by Carol Baker, who insisted her husband couldn't possibly have killed himself. In a *Village Voice* report titled "Jump, Fall, or Push?" she angrily told Richard Linnett: "It wasn't suicide, it was foul play. . . . Chet deserves a proper investigation." The murder theory gave a crowning touch to the portrait she would offer for years to come: "my husband," as she called him, was a tragic victim in life and in death, killed for what little money he had and snatched from her forever. "People were always dramatizing Chet," said Hal Galper. "They were going to find the most dramatic cause for his death."

But the notion of homicide was rejected by Micheline Graillier, Nicola Stilo, Peter Huijts, and Diane Vavra, the four people closest to Baker in 1988. Bertrand Fèvre spoke for all of them: "Chet had strong hands, strong shoulders—he was able to defend himself, even under drugs. You would have seen traces in the room; he would have fought. He was not the kind of weak person that you can just throw through a window. I think that Chet knew he was going to die—when, he would decide. Taking speedballs the way he was, I think he was trying to escape from himself or from life." The implication that he had committed a sort of passive-aggressive suicide—opening a window and letting death come to him—perfectly fit the profile of a man who, by his own admission, had never had the courage to confront tough decisions.

Baker, it seemed, had died willfully of a broken heart. It was an ultimately romantic gesture on the part of someone who at times had seemed demonically inhuman.

Galper didn't view the death too sentimentally. "Everybody says, oh, cluck, cluck, cluck, what a shame. I said, 'You gotta be kidding. This guy beat the devil by twenty years!' He was a survivor. He should have overdosed, somebody should have shot him, he should have killed himself in a car."

Newspapers worldwide gave him more attention than he had ever received in life. The coverage ranged from a cold obituary in the *New York Times*—"He sang sometimes and seemed to appeal to female audiences"—

to a rapturous eulogy in the Belgian magazine *Pourquoi Pas?* "Chet, my friend: What tragedy, your life, but also what poetry!" wrote Marc Danval.

> For years, we never stopped trembling for you, the number-one junkie of the century. Heroin was your heroine. . . . Outraged but clear-headed, fatalistic but formidably intelligent, you knew too well that these two bitches would end up having your skin. I learned of your death in plain nature, facing a yellow field of golden buttercups and surrounded by woods where the does did a ravishing ballet. The opposite of your infernal universe!

Bruce Weber called Carol and offered to arrange the cremation that Baker had once said he wanted. But Carol demanded a burial, recalled Weber. He, Wim Wigt, and the American Embassy would share the cost of flying Baker to Inglewood. Vera gave her son the plot she had purchased for herself, hoping he could be buried deeply enough so that, in time, she could be lain on top of him: her last Oedipal dream. Weber declined a rather morbid request from Carol that he film the funeral, but he did pay for the whole ceremony, as well as the costs of flying the family in and putting them up at a hotel.

In Amsterdam, a wake was held on Wednesday, May 18. For the viewing, Huijts and Wigt had wanted Baker in jeans and a casual shirt, just as his European fans remembered him. But Carol, said Huijts, had demanded a three-piece suit, so there lay Baker looking ghoulishly waxen and elderly in an outfit he never wore. His hair had been cut short and pasted back, and makeup covered his bruises. With his records playing over the PA system, hundreds filed past the body, surrounded by floral arrangements from fans, some in the shape of trumpets. A distraught Jacques Pelzer was photographed kneeling over the coffin, head bowed and hands folded in prayer. A month later, he would have a heart attack.

On Thursday, Huijts accompanied Baker's remains on a passenger flight to Inglewood. Carol, Vera, and the children arrived the same day. Emie Amemiya, who was coordinating the funeral, met Vera at the mortuary; there Baker's mother would take a final look at her son. "Oh, I'm very nervous," she kept mumbling in a frail voice. Amemiya advised her to wait outside for a moment. Alone, the young woman entered a cold, dark room lit by only the flickering of two floor-standing candelabra. Between them, on a raised pedestal, lay Baker in his coffin. The upper half of the lid was open. "It was *really* creepy," said Amemiya. "He was in scary condition. They had obviously kept him longer than they should have. The discoloration was shocking." Baker's once-alabaster face "was turning bluish-purple, and some parts were pale gray. Then you had these little burn marks." The decay reminded her of Kaposi's sarcoma, the cancer lesions associated with AIDS. The marks had probably resulted from his fall and from the jostling of the body in transit.

Rejoining Baker's mother, Amemiya told her, "I think it's better that you remember Chettie as you've always known him." Vera started crying. That night, Huijts met the family at their hotel. He arrived with albums, pictures, and warm memories of a man they had hardly seen in years. Huijts was struck by how emotionless they seemed.

When Carol learned that Vavra had also been flown in for the funeral, to be held the next day at Inglewood Park Cemetery, she was livid. Weber decided against going, fearing "it would be a circus." It was, and matters only got worse when Huijts presented Carol with a release to sign. Wim Wigt had wanted to stipulate that future royalties from the sale of Baker's albums on Timeless, Wigt's label, would be divided between her and Vavra. "We felt Diane should be included," said Wigt. "To us, she was more his wife than Carol was." The furious widow refused to sign.

After the funeral, everyone headed to Ports o'Call, a restaurant in nearby San Pedro, for a dinner Amemiya had arranged. Lawrence Trimble drove the Bakers; Vavra went with Amemiya and Andy Minsker. "We made sure we stayed in another section of the restaurant in order to keep Diane from being harassed," Amemiya said. Jack Sheldon entertained and reminisced about Baker, but the event was hardly festive. Amemiya was surprised when Paul Baker came to her table and apologized for his family's behavior. She recalled his words: "I just need to get away. I can't fly back with them." He gratefully accepted her offer to buy him a single bus ticket to Oklahoma, she said.

As she, Minsker, and Vavra waited for their car, Trimble drove past them with the family. Vera sat in the back, looking small and sad. Out from the front window came a cloud of cigarette smoke, followed by a woman's hand. It belonged to Melissa, who raised a middle finger as the car pulled away.

In death, Baker lay close to the site of the Trade Winds, the jazz club where he had played with Charlie Parker in 1952. In a sense, he *had* gone home again. And his final resting place was as drab as his roots. The flat, generic marker depicted an open book, on the left page of which appeared the words:

SON HUSBAND & FATHER
CHESNEY H. BAKER JR.
CHET
1929–1988

The right page remained blank, waiting for the death of Vera. Weber had wanted to buy his idol a fitting tombstone, but the funeral home required a release from the widow. Carol didn't comply. Amemiya tried phoning Vera, who spoke in a trembling voice. "I'm not supposed to talk to you anymore, you'll have to talk to Carol," she said. Asked why, she broke into tears. "Please," she begged, "don't make me have to talk to you, because I'm not supposed to."

When Carol learned that Huijts had taken a necklace of Vavra's from the trumpet case and given it to her, she threatened to sue. Her anger was understandable. Not only had Baker left his family no money or likely royalties; he had also failed to prepare a will. His estate was taken over by the state of Oklahoma. In order to start a new one from scratch, Carol would have to pay off a substantial tax debt. "I don't have any property or a bank account," Baker had said not long before his death. "I'm sure I'll die flat broke, and that's OK, because that's how I came into this world."

EPILOGUE

In March 1989, Bruce Weber's black-and-white valentine to Chet Baker, *Let's Get Lost,* premiered in New York. The movie was a far grander "wet dream" than *Broken Noses,* his amateurish portrait of Andy Minsker, and in the press kit Weber added another touch of fantasy. "Everyone asks me why I made a film about Chet Baker," he wrote. "Why a film about 'love and fascination' and jazz? It all started many years ago when I first met Nan. Over a bottle of wine during our first dinner together we discovered that our favorite record was an old Chet Baker album from the fifties called *Let's Get Lost.* I ordered two more bottles of wine and we fell in love."

Jeff Preiss was so attuned to the photographer's style that the film looked like a Weber picture gallery. "Surfaces are everything in *Let's Get Lost,* but they are gorgeously stylish surfaces," wrote Janet Maslin in the *New York Times.* Baker cruises along in a big Cadillac convertible, model-type girls pawing him as silvery palm trees sway against the sky. ("He was bad, he was trouble, and he was beautiful!" gushes Cherry Vanilla on the soundtrack in a sound bite written by Weber.) Wrecked but super-cool, primped and designer-clothed, Baker swaggers along the penthouse deck of the Shangri-La, sad music pouring from his horn and floating out to sea. An orgy of Baker photos erupts across the screen: William Claxton contact sheets, early album covers, paparazzi stills from Europe. The camera mimics Weber's eye, so excited it doesn't know where to look first.

For fifties-style atmosphere, the photographer inserted a number of sequences with no apparent relation to Baker. Cherry Vanilla, Flea, Lisa Marie, and Andy Minsker clown on the beach, scat-singing and talking about Dizzy Gillespie; Jeanne Moreau and Jean-Paul Belmondo are shown in newsreel footage flitting through Cannes; puppies frolic on a sunny street in Venice, California. Baker's crooning is the thread. "His stoned, introverted tonelessness is oddly sensuous," wrote Pauline Kael in *The New Yorker.* "He sings very slowly, and the effect is dreamy." As the film cuts back and forth between images of the boyish and the ravaged Baker, both are so seductive that Weber seems blinded to the difference.

Yet no conventional documentary could have lit up so much of the truth buried in the drug-dimmed chaos of Baker's life. Weber showed the cool trumpeter as the eye in a hurricane of backbiting and jealousy, all of it subtly manipulated by Baker himself. The interviewees emerged vividly and realistically as they told of how he had dashed their hopes. Vera's boy wonder had fallen off the pedestal she placed him on; Carol's junkie Prince Charming couldn't be tamed into a loving husband and father; Diane's "Greek god" had deceived and abused her. As Weber explained to Lynne Tillman in *Elle:* "We take into our own lives what the people we admire give us and we fantasize about it. Sometimes that fantasy is so far out of reach that when we meet that person he can't live up to it."

Among the press, *Let's Get Lost* evoked the same kind of ambivalent fascination as Baker had himself. Janet Maslin called the film "a succession of ghostly, indelible images that are at once hauntingly beautiful and desperately sad." Sheila Benson of the *Los Angeles Times* condemned it as "a phony Valentine, an exploitation of the ruined old junkie that Baker had become, done with the complete complicity of Baker himself." In *7 Days,* Francis Davis complained about Weber's self-indulgences but admitted: "Even when you're staring at *Let's Get Lost* in disbelief, you can't take your eyes off it. . . . The movie is finally as much about Weber's Chet Baker fixation as it is about Chet Baker."

Those who had seemingly known him best couldn't reconcile their memories with the grim portrait in the film. "The work is very good, the photographer is nice, but the image of the artist is not complete," said Nicola Stilo. "It's a lot of the dark side of Chet Baker. And I remember, he had a lot of hours where Chet was more normal. In just a few minutes, Bertrand Fèvre gave much more truth than Bruce Weber." Jacques Pelzer called the movie "a piece of shit"; Micheline Graillier said she "hated it, because it's not Chet"; Diane Vavra found it "pretty dishonest." Diane Mitchell felt otherwise. "It was so real, it was horrifying," she said. "It was like watching *The Exorcist.* I never wanted to see it again." Hal Galper laughed through the whole film: "I thought it was great, because it was so jive. Everybody's lying, including Chet. You couldn't have wanted a more honest reflection of him."

Despite arguments that Weber had ignored Baker's playing (if not his singing) in favor of scandal, the soundtrack album proved extremely popular, introducing a new generation to Baker's music. *Let's Get Lost* enjoyed smash runs at the Film Forum, the Carnegie Screening Room, and the Quad Cinema in New York; it earned an Oscar nomination for Best Documentary, and won the Critics' Prize at the Venice Film Festival. The Chet Baker revival was on, and the battles over him would rage as violently as they had when he was alive.

Of all the women in *Let's Get Lost,* Carol Baker emerges the least flatteringly, and she detested Weber and everything to do with the film. "She was totally pissed off," said Cherry Vanilla, who had bonded with her in a mutual loathing of the photographer. "She thought Bruce had hurt her and everybody else, she was gonna sue him, he had tricked her into cooperating." For years, Carol tried to prove that Weber had violated her rights and her husband's. He hadn't; every participant had signed an ironclad release. But she stayed on the warpath. When Chip Stern of *Rolling Stone* noted the film's depiction of a family "seething with resentment that Baker can't stop shooting dope long enough to get them some bread, let alone visit," Carol wrote an incensed letter to the editor. Denying they had ever been resentful at all, she fumed at how Weber had trampled on her husband's goodness in a film that, according to her, had almost nothing to do with the truth.

The photographer disagreed. "When people who are in the film—maybe Carol, maybe Diane—say this wasn't like it was, it *was* like it was. I felt we were responsible as filmmakers. I think everybody was treated pretty well. We made this film with not too many people caring about it, or not too many people close to Chet wanting it to happen. They didn't feel he deserved it. And I have to tell you that never once did any of these people ever in the simplest way say thank you to anybody who worked for us. The only person that did was Ruth. Maybe I haven't hated somebody that much in my life that I never wanted something OK to happen for them. This film is one of the few things in Chet's later life that was OK."

Nonetheless, Carol set out to spread her own version of reality. "Girls pursued him—he didn't pursue them," she told John Hiscock in the London *Daily Telegraph.* For the book *Chet Baker: His Life and Music,* author Jeroen de Valk interviewed her at length by phone. "Her information was often inaccurate," he found. "She told me again and again that Chet was an angel, that his girlfriends were all 'whores' and all the record companies were led by 'crooks.' " In 1990, the TV news show *Oklahoma Magazine* visited her at home. Fondling Baker's trumpet, Carol raved about how "handsome" her husband was. Their monogamous idyll, as she described it, lasted until he left for Europe in the midseventies. "I guess, like a lot of artists, you sacrifice your family in order to follow your talent," she explained. "And I understood that. His children understood it. And, um, we learned to adjust to it and live with it." Melissa sat at her mother's feet in a long T-shirt. Then twenty-four, she looked closer to twelve as she poked at a toy keyboard. Asked who had taught her to play, she giggled. "My dad," she said.

She and her two brothers had stayed in rural Oklahoma. Melissa drifted through a series of small jobs; Dean continued to live with Carol. Paul worked as a carpet layer and raised two sons, Chad (the name of the Baker-inspired character in *All the Fine Young Cannibals*) and Chet. With Paul's help, Carol devoted her time to the angry pursuit of her husband's money. Once his tax debt was paid, royalties poured in from a bumper crop of CD reissues and from the use of his music in films and TV commercials.

She and Paul went on to establish a Web site, but it was hardly a tribute to Baker's art. In December 2000, the site opened with the greeting MERRY CHRISTMAS, followed by a long "hit list" of record companies whom they branded bootleggers—ignoring the fact that Baker had struck buyout deals with so many labels for quick cash and no royalties. "Without those producers, Chet never would have survived until 1988," said Archi Bechlenberg, a German graphic designer and Baker fan.

Wanting more of that money for herself, Carol founded a record label, CCB (Chet & Carol Baker), releasing live tapes of a few flawed Baker performances. One CD featured their wedding picture on the cover. In a merchandising fury, she offered Chet Baker T-shirts and reproductions of old paparazzi shots of herself and Baker, priced from three to five hundred dollars; "authorized" posters and other items were promised for the future. The site railed against "people selling poster's that have never payed a dime in royalties to Chet or his Estate and are Knowingly violating the right's owned by the Chet Baker Estate [all sic]." Carol and Paul even tried auctioning off the film rights to Baker's story on eBay for a minimum bid of five million dollars, plus royalties. The vengeance threatens to go on forever, no matter how much cash comes in.

Diane Vavra lived with her own disappointments. Baker had once told her he never wanted her to worry about money again, but he had made no provisions for her future. Her part-time job as a music teacher barely supported her, and life was a struggle. Years after Baker's death, his clothes still hung in the bathroom of her one-room apartment, which she filled with other mementos of their relationship. Asked in 1995 to recall a fond, loving moment with Chet Baker, she couldn't think of one.

A brighter legacy survives among his musical protégés. Micheline Pelzer and Nicola Stilo quit heroin after Baker's death; they, along with Michel Graillier, Riccardo Del Fra, Enrico Pieranunzi, Bob Mover, Phil Urso, Ruth Young, and countless others, remembered him in the most romantic terms. "Each time I play, Chet is on my shoulders," said Graillier. "Forever. I don't know if he changed the lives of people, but he made all the deep things appear." On May 13, 1999, a bronze memorial plaque was hung on the Prins Hendrik. Below an image of Baker blowing his horn, a caption read: "Trumpet player and singer CHET BAKER died here on May 13th, 1988. He will live on in his music for anyone willing to listen and feel."

No one felt his last impact more profoundly than Jacques Pelzer, who lived by the advice Baker had given him: "Play simple and strong." By 1994, though, the saxophonist had turned frail. Friends found him home much of the time, staying as high as he could. "Twice, three times a week he called me saying he felt old, that his pals had died, and that he was lonely," said Jean-Pierre Gebler.

On Saturday, August 6, of that year, Pelzer made plans to drive to a jazz festival with Guy Masy. He spent the afternoon playing Ping-Pong in the garden, as he had for years. It was a very hot day, and the game exhausted him. Returning to the parlor, Pelzer slumped in front of the TV set and asked his daughter, who was in the house, to call Masy and cancel; he didn't feel so well. Worried about his heart, she insisted on taking him to the hospital. Reluctantly, he agreed. But he needed to go to the bathroom first. Micheline escorted him there. "How do you feel?" she asked. "Very weak," he said, closing himself inside.

A moment later she heard a thud, followed by choking sounds. Opening the door, she found him slumped over. Micheline had taken up Buddhism, and she held him in her arms and started chanting, her own heart pounding like a drum. As he stared at her in fright, she tried to comfort him: "You're gonna play your sax again, don't worry!" Hands shaking, she phoned the doctor. He arrived one minute after Pelzer, then seventy, had succumbed to his second heart attack.

Before her eyes, death erased the ravages of time from her father's face.

"In three minutes he looked forty years old," she said. It was easy now to understand how Chet Baker's body could have been mistaken for that of a man half his age.

Pelzer's death was front-page news in Liège. But Baker became a worldwide myth. The original *Chet Baker Sings* album held a mystique for all generations. So did the glamour he embodied: that of the beautiful, self-destructive rebel who lived on the run, avoiding responsibility, rejecting convention. "Chet was the anti-Rockwell, and all the more so 'cause he had the face of a prairie angel," said Jerry Stahl. Baker's "cool" mannerisms had entered the collective unconsciousness starting in the fifties, and they would be reincarnated decades later in a whole school of young Hollywood actors: Brad Pitt, Leonardo DiCaprio, Johnny Depp, Matt Damon, Ben Affleck, Luke Perry. The trumpeter's way of balancing prettiness with manliness, of acting profound and unknowable, became a popular pose for young people everywhere who wanted to be taken seriously. Pitt, DiCaprio, and Jim Carrey were all reported to be interested in playing Baker onscreen, and in the 1999 film *The Talented Mr. Ripley,* Matt Damon briefly did. As a seductive psychopath of the fifties with a flair for assuming other people's identities, Damon uncannily mimicked Baker singing "My Funny Valentine."

DiCaprio's mammoth following of teenage girls inspired *New York Times* journalist Maureen Dowd to explore the phenomenon in a 1998 column titled "Prettier Than Barbie." Never, she wrote, had "the object of girlish affection been so, well, girlish." Amy Pascal, then the president of Columbia Pictures, described him to Dowd in words that had once applied to Baker: "He's incredibly sexy because he's so beautiful and so troubled and he seems like he has a wild streak."

In the jazz world, a growing number of young trumpeters shadowed Baker's look, feel, and sound. The most successful was Till Brönner, a German musician, born in 1971, whose lyrical playing and singing, plus his teen-idol looks, made him the sweetheart of German jazz. Brönner's passion for Baker was such that he posed for a replica of William Claxton's "Chet and Halema" photo; in 2000, he released his best-selling album, *Chattin' with Chet.* "It was a really big moment for me to hear a guy who just played melodies," Brönner said. "To me, the old trumpet players all tried to play as high and loud as possible. All of a sudden this guy comes along and does the total opposite. Probably his trumpet playing came as close as possible to the human voice. It's so touching. Chet Baker was such a romantic guy, and I think he must have been suffering a lot. He must have been on a constant search for love and understanding; otherwise I can't imagine how he could have played like that."

The debating over Baker's every thought and motive went on endlessly. "I don't think he'd appreciate any of this crap," said Ruth Young. "Chet's aura is overcelebrated. Somehow his lack of personality became his personality. The *tromba d'oro* and the good looks and all that crap—if Chet had looked like Mickey Mouse, we would not be having this conversation. The guy did not want to do anything other than play his horn and sing and hopefully leave behind something of musical merit. There's so much goodness to be seen in his effort. To sit here and discuss why he did this, and why didn't he do that, and what more could he have done—what is this? I know what he'd be saying: 'What's all the talk about? Everybody makes mistakes. What are mine, so much worse than anyone else's? Leave me alone!'

"Most people don't take chances, they don't reach, they don't live. Chet did—liar, cheater, son of a bitch that he was. A zillion people on Wall Street are walking into the bathroom and getting high in their three-piece suits and doing it with far less relevance to anything in their own lives. It's the lack of soul versus the soul. And that is why people gravitated to him. He really was spiritually knowing in his path. Chet was free-spirited, which means he was in touch with his spirit." And if he was shackled by addiction, when he played he escaped so far inside himself that "he transcended, he soared," according to Lisa Galt Bond. He took many of his listeners with him.

Michel and Micheline Graillier managed to rise above their own troubles. Stormy as their union had been, they remained fiercely devoted to each other, and in 2000 they renewed their marriage vows. Every few weeks, though, Micheline left their one-room apartment in Paris and returned to Liège. Years after her father's death, she held on to his house in all its friendly disarray. At the entrance to the parlor hung a painting of Pelzer in his fez, saxophone raised like a mighty sword. His treasured Bird and Coltrane albums were covered in dust, while the stacks of cassettes he had made on his pocket recorder had sat untouched for so long that they were stuck together.

Upstairs in Baker's old bedroom, an armoire revealed a bloodstain that wouldn't wash off—one of the many souvenirs of his presence. The house was full of ghosts: Bobby Jaspar, René Thomas, Dexter Gordon, Chet Baker, and, of course, Pelzer. Micheline felt them watching over her like guardian angels. But the air seemed awfully quiet. "It's sad," she said. "There's no more music in the house."

ACKNOWLEDGMENTS

To everyone quoted in this book, my deepest thanks for your time, candor, and insight. For kindly sharing photos, recordings, and other materials, or for providing useful contacts, more gratitude goes to Crystal Joy Albert, Gary Alderman, the late Steve Allen, Santo Arico, Jeff Atterton, Roland Bengtsson, Ian Bernard, Sandro Berti-Ceroni, Janet Bicker, Lars Bloch, Lucy Bonnington, Charlie Bourgeois, Mark Cantor, Warren Chiasson, Pete Christlieb, Jim Coleman, Leif Collin, Elvis Costello, Michael Cuscuna, Gene Davis, Greg Dawson, Edvard P. Deckers, Eddie de Haas, Jeroen de Valk, Alan Eichler, Donald Elfman, Gudrun Endress, John Engels, David Finck, Bernie Fleischer, Artt and Lisa Frank, Russ Freeman, Will Friedwald, Jean-Pierre Gebler, Stu Genovese, Maurizio Giammarco, Howard Glitt, Maurizio Guercini and Virginia Kay, David Hajdu, Jim Harrod, Gordon Jack, Dianne Jimenez, Sandy Jones, Brooks Kerr, Delphine King, Matthias Kirsch, Karl Emil Knudsen, Eric Kohler, Wolfgang Lackerschmid, Fran Landesman, Herman Leonard, Phil Leshin, Peter Levinson, Betty Little, Christopher Loudon, Bill Loughborough, Dennis Luxion, Paul Martin, Pierre Martin, Guy Masy, Adriano Mazzoletti, Loonis McGlohon, Richard Merkin, Pierre Michelot, Jeanne de Mirbeck, Diane (Mrs. Red) Mitchell, Lesley Mitchell-Clarke, Audrey Morris, Jacqueline L. Mosher, Bob Mover, Romano Mussolini, Zé Nogueira, Andrea Palazzo, Micheline Pelzer, Mario Petroni, Enrico Pieranunzi, Ross Porter, Jess Rand, Liliane Rovère, Pat Sheinwold, Jack Sheldon, Kent Sherwood, Don Sickler, Joel E. Siegel, Jack Simpson, Carson Smith, David Smith, René Sommer, Gilbert Sorrentino, Jerry Stahl, Nicola Stilo, Lee Tanner, Ingo Thouret, Amedeo Tommasi, Giovanni Tommaso, Joe Urso, Cherry Vanilla, Steven Watson, Arnold Weinstein, Larry Whitford, Bob Whitlock, Matthias Winckelmann, Bruce Weber and Nan Bush, and Ingo Wulff.

For graciously allowing me to stay in their homes as I traveled through Europe and the United States, I am indebted to Lars Bloch, Martine Couchoud, Zuza Homem de Mello, Carole Fèvre, Micheline Pelzer, Evert Hekkema, Gaby Kleinschmidt, John and Linda Knipe, Lothar Lewien, Ercilia Lobo, Harry Locke, Giorgio Martinazzo, Ian Shaw, Nicola Stilo, Corina Teunissen van Manen, and Lucy Chase Williams. To Giangi Zucchini, thanks for showing me your home town of Lucca through your eyes.

Several multilingual friends gave me valuable help in translating articles from other countries. Thank you, Archi Bechlenberg, Zuza Homem de Mello, Lothar Lewien, Susannah McCorkle, Bob Morrison, Robert Ockeloen, Andrea Palazzo, Francesco Pini, Corina Teunissen van Manen, and most of all Luigi Santosuosso, who gave me so many hours of his time. To Rossana Braga and Daniele Protti of Rizzoli Publications in Milan, Leif Collin of Dragon Records in Sweden, Klaus Gottwald, Ellen Hansman of the Deutsche Press Agency, Rima Kabbani of IPC Media, Leslie Lambert of Little Bear Productions, and Enrico Pieranunzi, thanks for jumping to my aid at the eleventh hour. A special thank you to several marvelous photographers from around the world—Roland Bengtsson, William Claxton, Dan Kjellman, Herman Leonard, Lamberto Londi, Carlo Pieroni, Lee Tanner, Carlo Verri—for their remarkable kindness.

I can't imagine what I, or anyone in the New York area who writes about jazz, would do without Dan Morgenstern and the Institute of Jazz Studies at Rutgers University. Thank you, Dan, for your endless knowledge and your readiness to share it. Similar appreciation goes to Marije Nie, Herman Openneer, Tanya Wijngaarde, and the late Pim Gras of the Nederlands Jazzarchief of Amsterdam; Janice Clark at the Yale, Oklahoma, Public Library; and to Jean-Pol Schroeder and the Maison du Jazz in Liège. Ingo Wulff, editor of the remarkable photographic history *Chet Baker in Europe 1975–1988,* inconvenienced himself numerous times to help me. Harvey Bloomfield, creator of the Web site "Chet Baker—Lost and Found" (chetbaker.net), and Lee Mergner, publisher of *JazzTimes,* were exceedingly thoughtful in their announcements of my book. My fellow Chet Baker biographer, Jeroen de Valk, showed me a very thoughtful willingness to help. To the members of Lucca's Circolo del Jazz—Paolo Benvenuti, Giampiero Giusti, Gianni Paganini, Rudy Rabassini, and above all my Italian angel, Cecco Maino—*grazie di tutto cuore;* I could never have told the story of Chet in Italy properly without you.

To my parents, Viola and Jack: thank you for your patience and for believing in me always. Patricia Morrisroe's biography of Robert Mapplethorpe was the blueprint for this project; brava, Patricia, for doing such a magnificent job. Much appreciation goes to my lawyers, Mark Sendroff and Eric Goldman, and to Jon Fine and Bette Graber of Random House, who have all worked hard to keep me out of hot water. Retired NYPD detective Chris Reisman helped me fend off two psychos: a valued service, and one I'll probably have to ask him for again. To my editor at Knopf, George Andreou, thank you for honing the text so astutely and for helping guide this dream of mine into the light. To George's assistant, Robin Reardon, thanks for giving me so much expert and sympathetic help. Knopf's art department is unrivaled; my enormous appreciation to Carol Devine Carson and Peter Andersen for their superb job in designing this book.

For their encouragement and cheerleading throughout the years it took me to complete *Deep in a Dream,* I am beholden to Steven Bach, Archi Bechlenberg, Rosemary Clooney, Baby Jane Dexter, Tom Evered, Harry Gittes, Peggy King, Marla Kleman, Jackie and Roy Kral, Phil Leshin, Arthur Lubow, Mark Murphy, Rebecca Parris and Paul McWilliams, Frank Rich, Robert W. Richards, Liliane Rovère, Donna Shore, Jerry Stahl, Tom Toth, Joe Urso, John Wallowitch, Margaret Whiting, and the late Susannah McCorkle, whom I miss very much.

There are others who went so far out of their way to help me at every turn that I can never repay them. To Charlie Davidson, Bertrand Fèvre, Micheline Pelzer, Stephen Holden, Richard Lamparski, Lothar Lewien, Grange Rutan, Thorbjørn Sjøgren, and Zuza Homem de Mello—I hope I have vindicated your faith in me. Joseph Marcoux made the end of the ride much brighter; I hope he sticks around. Lisa Galt Bond's innumerable kindnesses include suggesting I call this book *Deep in a Dream,* and providing a lot of crucial handholding. Thanks, Lisa—I couldn't have done this without you. To Diane Vavra, who took me into a difficult past with remarkable frankness and courage: thanks for trusting me, Diane; I hope you're pleased with the results. And to Ruth Young, whose insightfulness, archival instincts, and sense of humor are unsurpassed, thank you for your heartwarming generosity in helping me seek out the truth.

NOTES

Unless otherwise credited in the text or below, all quotations are drawn from the author's interviews.

PROLOGUE

3 "one of the most beautiful cries": Marc Danval, "Dernière lettre à Chet Baker," *Pourquoi Pas?* (Belgium), May 26, 1988.

4 "phenomenal luck": "Chet Baker, Jazz Trumpeter, Dies at 59 in a Fall," *New York Times,* May 14, 1988.

"It wasn't suicide": Richard Linnett, "Jump, Fall or Push?" *Village Voice,* August 16, 1988.

"I'm looking down": Frank Strazzeri to Bob Rusch, *Cadence,* September 1995.

"It was as though": Colin Butler, liner notes for Jeri Southern album *When I Fall in Love,* MCA MCL 1791, 1984.

5 "singing corpse": J. Hoberman, "The Cool and the Crazy," *Village Voice,* April 25, 1989.

"withered goat": Julie Salamon, "Film: Sweet-Looking Jazzman Whose Life Turned Sour," *Wall Street Journal,* April 25, 1989.

"hollow-cheeked, toothless": Charles Champlin, "Searching for the Appeal of Baker, 'Let's Get Lost,' " *Los Angeles Times,* April 1989.

"unreliable, conniving": Lee Jeske, "Louse with a Horn," *New York Post,* April 19, 1989.

"bloodsucker": Chip Stern, "Drowned in a Sea of Love?" *Rolling Stone,* May 4, 1989.

6 *"Not now!":* Recalled by Emie Amemiya.

CHAPTER 1

Baker family history drawn from interviews with Lisa Galt Bond, Baker's partner on the unfinished memoir published in edited form under the title *As Though I Had Wings;* from autobiographical notes made by Baker for the project; and from U.S. census records. Other family background, including that of Grandpa Beardsley, from a letter written by Vera Baker to Chet Baker, July 2, 1964. History of Yale, Oklahoma, drawn from *National Register of Historic Places Inventory,* U.S. Department of the Interior; *The Oklahoma Petroleum Society,* by Kenny A. Franks (University of Oklahoma Press, 1980); and *A Survey of Yale Oklahoma,* by Billy Heilmann and King Cacy Jr., 1955.

8 "I had a very": Chet Baker in conversation with Lisa Galt Bond.

10 "World's Greatest Athlete": Brochure, *Jim Thorpe Home,* Oklahoma Historical Society; date unknown.

12 "My old man and his pals": Chet Baker, "The Trumpet and the Spike: A Confession by Chet Baker," magazine and date unknown.

"They were almost": Chet Baker, "La droga è la mia condanna," *L'Europeo* (Italy), 1961.

"I don't know how": Chet Baker to Jerome Reece, "Les Confidences de Chet Baker," *Jazz Hot* (France), November 1983.

14 "Yes, mother . . .": "La droga è la mia condanna."

15 "dreadful quarrels": Ibid.

"He would never admit": "The Trumpet and the Spike."

17 "drag": Chet Baker in conversation with Ruth Young.

19 "Never again, never again": Chet Baker in conversation with Lisa Galt Bond.

"my first pussy": Ibid.

CHAPTER 2

Background material on Baker's army experiences drawn from interviews with Lisa Galt Bond, from Baker's memoir, from his autobiographical notes for Bond, and from interviews with his fellow soldiers Paul Martin and Howard Glitt.

24 "lived like packed maggots": Chet Baker, *As Though I Had Wings* (New York: Buzz Books, 1997), p. 5.

25 "My kind of guy": Chet Baker in conversation with Lisa Galt Bond.

26 "Be-bop cut us off": Gilbert Sorrentino, "Remembrances of Bop in New York 1945–50," *Kulchur,* Summer 1963.

27 "Everything changed": Chet Baker to Les Tomkins, *Crescendo International* (U.K.), 1979.

28 "I'd love to": *As Though I Had Wings,* p. 14.

"She didn't really care": Chet Baker, "All That Jazz, All Those Girls, All That Dope! This Was the Sorrow in My Trumpet," *Today* (U.K.), March 30, 1963.

29 "pretty boy": Jimmy Rowles to James Gavin (JG).

32 "In high school": "*Playboy* Interview: Miles Davis—A Candid Conversation with the Jazz World's Premier Iconoclast," *Playboy,* September 1962.

33 "those crazy, sick": Miles Davis to Quincy Troupe, *Miles: The Autobiography* (New York: Touchstone Press, 1989), p. 14.

"big singing sound": Ibid., p. 62.

"founding the next": Ross Russell, *Record Changer,* date unknown.

"White people": *Miles: The Autobiography,* p. 119.

34 "I didn't really": Chet Baker to Leonard "Skip" Malone, *JazzMasters* TV interview (Copenhagen), produced by The Jazz Masters Partnership: TV Team (Poul Henning Olsen, co-owner), Meta-4 Productions (Terry Carter, President), and Leonard "Skip" Malone. Taped January 29, 1988.

"I readily agreed": Chet Baker, "30,000 Hell-Holes in My Arm," *Today* (U.K.), February 2, 1963.

"Everything becomes beautiful": Chet Baker, "La droga è la mia condanna," *L'Europeo* (Italy), 1961.

35 "I wanted to do": Mike Nevard, "Mulligan's on a 'Worship' Kick Says His Multi Wonder-Man—Chet Baker," *Melody Maker* (U.K.), June 6, 1953.

37 "The women dressed": Art and Laurie Pepper, *Straight Life* (New York: Schirmer Books, 1979), p. 41.

39 "one of the biggest": *As Though I Had Wings,* p. 35.

"spaced-out guy": Ibid.

40 "badge": Red Rodney to Ira Gitler, *Swing to Bop: An Oral History of the Transition in Jazz in the 1940s* (New York: Oxford University Press, 1985), p. 282.

"fear as the liquid": Chet Baker, "La droga è la mia condanna."

"I threw up": Chet Baker to Rex Reed, "Jazzman Chet Baker Is Back from His Bad Trip," New York *Daily News,* July 8, 1973.

41 "sharp-looking blonde": "All That Jazz, All Those Girls, All That Dope!"

"She loved being": *As Though I Had Wings,* pp. 37–8.

42 "I don't know what": Chet Baker in conversation with Lisa Galt Bond.

CHAPTER 3

Background on Baker's Presidio days and his marriage to Charlaine drawn from interviews with Lisa Galt Bond, from Baker's memoir, and from his autobiographical notes for Bond.

45 "He had such": Chet Baker to Les Tomkins, *Crescendo International* (U.K.), 1979.

46 "dynamite grass": Chet Baker in conversation with Lisa Galt Bond.

47 "Hermosa Beach": Chet Baker, "Rebel Without a Pause," *Spin,* February 1990.

48 "Four out of five": Fran Kelley, *Metronome,* June 1955.

48 "a buoyant": Bob Bach, liner notes for Shorty Rogers's album *Cool and Crazy,* RCA LPM 3138.

"The jazz out of": Teddy Edwards to Bob Rusch, *Cadence,* April 1994.

"the same old clichés": Miles Davis to Nat Hentoff, "Miles," *Down Beat,* November 2, 1955.

"get pretty funky": Ralph J. Gleason, liner notes for Quincy Jones album *Go West, Man,* ABC-Paramount ABC-186, 1957.

49 "in those all-night": Shelly Manne to Ralph J. Gleason, ibid.

"hard-hitters": Edwards to Rusch, *Cadence.*

"one of the first": Leonard Feather, *The New Edition of the Encyclopedia of Jazz* (New York: Bonanza Books, 1962), p. 310.

50 "jazz concerts": "Mulligan's Blast Was Just an Act: Rumsey," *Down Beat,* June 3, 1953.

"I was beginning": Edwards to Rusch, *Cadence.*

51 "pitch black": *Hoop,* VPRO-TV, Netherlands, January 10, 1988.

52 "He treated me": Brian Case, "The Price of a Golden Horn," *Melody Maker* (U.K.), April 14, 1979.

"I can see now": Chet Baker to Mike Butcher and Tony Hall, 1955; quoted by Alun Morgan in *Jazz Monthly* (Australia), June 1963.

"snorting up": Brian Case, "The Price of a Golden Horn."

53 "You got nothin' ": Chet Baker in conversation with Ruth Young.

"like magic": William Claxton, *Young Chet* (Munich: Schirmer Art Books, 1994), p. 20.

54 "thought he had": Joyce Tucker to Donald Goddard, *Joey* (New York: Harper & Row, 1974), p. 130.

"DON'T EVER DO": Recalled by Bob Whitlock.

"GO FUCK YOURSELF!": Ibid.

"No sooner did I": Martin Abramson, "Cool Cats Listen as Mulligan Plays," *Telegraph* (city unknown), November 20, 1959.

55 To Baker, he was more: Interview for tribute to Lars Gullin, Sweden, April 6, 1983.

"The junk had": Abramson, *Telegraph.*

"To have an instrument": From liner notes for Pacific Jazz PJLP-1, *Gerry Mulligan Quartet.*

56 "I've never been around": Gerry Mulligan to Les Tomkins, *Crescendo International* (U.K.), October 1987.

58 "fantastically clear": Peter Schickele, *New York Times,* December 27, 1999.

59 "a sound reminiscent": *Metronome,* April 1953.

"I wanted to play": Chet Baker to Leonard Malone, *JazzMasters* TV interview (Copenhagen), January 29, 1988.

"fantastic, fugue-ish": Ralph J. Gleason, "Swingin' the Golden Gate: Mr. Mulligan Has a Real Crazy Gerry-Built Crew," *Down Beat,* October 22, 1952.

60 "every creative": Norman Mailer, "The White Negro," *Advertisements for Myself* (New York: Perigee Books, 1981), p. 301.

61 "In comparison with": "Counterpoint Jazz," *Time,* February 2, 1953.
"morning, noon, and night": Jane Russell to Leonard Feather, *Down Beat* Blindfold Test, June 2, 1954.
62 "You're here to": Recalled by Carson Smith.
"The next pretty note": Recalled by Harold Danko.
63 "bored into you": Chet Baker in conversation with Lisa Galt Bond.
65 "Says Gerry Mulligan": *Down Beat,* July 25, 1956.
"Gerry Mulligan is a": Mike Nevard, "Mulligan's on a 'Worship' Kick Says His Multi-wonder Man—Chet Baker," *Melody Maker* (U.K.), June 6, 1953.
66 "the dream of": John O'Grady, *O'Grady: The Life and Times of Hollywood's No. 1 Private Eye* (Los Angeles: J. P. Tarcher, 1974), p. 48.
"Mine was not": Ibid.
67 "ball-busting Sergeant O'Grady": Ibid., p. 52.
"I set out": Ibid., p. 51.
"I ran Charlie": Ibid., pp. 51–52.
68 "I've been on": Gerry Mulligan, "Hot Lips Bopster, Aide and 2 Wives, Jailed; Nab Dope," *Los Angeles Mirror,* April 14, 1953.
69 "the most overrated": Ralph J. Gleason, "Ralph Mulls Mulligan, Finds Overrated Child," *Down Beat,* September 23, 1953.

CHAPTER 4

71 "Aw, I don't know": Recalled by Carson Smith.
"Oh, thank God": Recalled by Arlyne Brown Mulligan.
"How much more déclassé": Ibid.
72 "Son, you don't want": Ibid.
73 "What key?": Recalled by Herb Geller.
"see things I've never": Mike Nevard, "Chet Baker Says: I'm Quitting Jazz," *Melody Maker* (U.K.), November 21, 1953.
74 "the scent of": Jerry Stahl, *Permanent Midnight* (New York: Warner Books, 1995), p. 140.
"You don't exactly": Ibid., p. 141.
76 "I practice": Chet Baker in conversation with Liliane Cukier Rovère.
77 "He's full of shit": Brian Case, "The Price of a Golden Horn," *Melody Maker* (U.K.), April 14, 1979.
78 "charming theme": *Down Beat,* May 6, 1953.
79 "Our suspicions": *Down Beat,* July 29, 1953.
"a little annoyed": "Club Files Claim Against Getz," *Down Beat,* November 4, 1953.
"Naturally I liked": Mike Nevard, "Mulligan's on a 'Worship' Kick Says His Multi-wonder Man—Chet Baker," *Melody Maker* (U.K.), June 6, 1953.
80 "cool, clever, and bloodless": *Down Beat,* 1954.

81 "I find strings": Chet Baker to Paul Fisher, CRQI-FM radio interview (Toronto), 1978.
"to get away": "Listen to Those Zsounds," *Time,* February 1, 1954.
82 "It was apparent": Richard Bock to Will Thornebury, liner notes, *The Complete Pacific Jazz Studio Recordings of the Chet Baker Quartet with Russ Freeman* (Mosaic MD3-122).
"Gerry's so pissed off": Jerome Reece, "Les Confidences de Chet Baker," *Jazz Hot* (France), November 1983.
"largely soporific": *Down Beat,* January 14, 1954.
84 "Anita, you've got": Anita O'Day with George Eells, *High Times, Hard Times* (New York: G. P. Putnam's Sons, 1981), p. 13.
"Tell me something": Claxton, *Young Chet,* p. 88.
86 "sounded like two": Ibid., p. 55.
87 "He sounds like": Richie Beirach to JG.
"There was a very": Richard Williams, "The Man Who Came Back from the Dead," *Melody Maker* (U.K.), July 21, 1973.
"Criticizing Baker's 'singing' ": Mimi Clar, *Metronome,* August 1959.

CHAPTER 5

90 "This was a generation": Lisa Phillips, "Beat Culture: America Revisited," *Beat Culture and the New America: 1950–1965* (Whitney Museum of Modern Art, 1995), p. 30.
92 "This young man's rise": John McClellan, Storyville broadcast, March 16, 1954 (issued on Uptown UPCD 27.35, *Chet Baker, Boston, 1954*).
"For our next tune": Chet Baker, ibid.
93 "challenge the edge": Kevin McCarthy in *Montgomery Clift,* a documentary by Claudio Masenza, 1983.
94 "You had the feeling": Howard Goodkind in *The Fifties,* a History Channel documentary, 1997.
"Mr. Baker": Recalled by Carson Smith.
96 "He lacks the ability": Nat Hentoff, *Down Beat,* March 7, 1956.
"Brownie has really": Nat Hentoff, *Down Beat,* 1954.
"If conditions had been": Max Roach to Barbara Gardner, "The Legacy of Clifford Brown," *Down Beat,* October 12, 1961.
97 "that Chet Baker ballyhoo": Nat Adderley, *Crescendo* (U.K.), September 10, 1962.
"About Chet Baker": Roy Eldridge, *Down Beat* Blindfold Test, 1956.
"It puts a pressure": Chet Baker to Rogers Worthington, "Chet Baker, Back from the Dead, with Beauty," *Detroit Free Press,* November 23, 1975.
"Both him and me": Miles Davis to Quincy Troupe, *Miles: The Autobiography* (Touchstone Press, 1989), p. 167.
"dirt": Ibid., p. 180.
98 "I guess it was": Ibid., p. 141.

"the second coming": Ibid., p. 156.
"worse than me": Ibid.
"One passionate note": Martin Williams, *Down Beat,* date unknown.
99 "He can't be": Nat Hentoff, *Down Beat,* June 2, 1954.
"I can't stand": Nat Hentoff, "Even Mynheers Turn to Silver," *Down Beat,* October 31, 1956.
"wholly alive, stimulating voice": Nat Hentoff, *Down Beat,* June 2, 1954.
"I really wasn't ready": Baker to Worthington, *Detroit Free Press.*
100 "young black cats": Chet Baker in conversation with Lisa Galt Bond.
"Bird was all": *Miles: The Autobiography,* p. 175.
"I go to this": Steve Voce, obituary for Walter Bishop Jr.; Internet posting, February 1, 1998.
101 "Chet Baker? Who's that?": Recalled by Carson Smith.
102 "She likes the white": Recalled by Liliane Cukier Rovère.
"She was different": Chet Baker, "All That Jazz, All Those Girls, All That Dope!" *Today* (U.K.), March 30, 1963.
103 *"I'm gonna kill":* George Avakian to JG.
105 "tightly constructed": *Down Beat,* December 29, 1954.

CHAPTER 6

108 "overwork": Bill Brown, liner notes, *Chet Baker Sings and Plays with Bud Shank, Russ Freeman and Strings,* Pacific Jazz PJ 1202, 1955.
"anemic singing": Bill Coss, *Metronome,* August 1955.
"flat, dead voice": John S. Wilson, *The Collector's Jazz: Modern* (New York: J. B. Lippincott Co., 1959), p. 32.
"drag": Recalled by Carson Smith.
109 "watered-down Miles": Teddy Charles, *Metronome,* May 1955.
"Chet is above Miles": Douglas Hague, "Cool and Hot," *Jazz Journal,* May 1955.
113 "Honey, please never": Dick Twardzik to Crystal Joy, letter, Baltimore, c. 1955.
"disastrous": Bill Coss, *Metronome,* July 1955.
114 "beatnik brigade": Maya Angelou, *The Heart of a Woman* (New York: Bantam Books, 1981), pp. 3–4.
"I didn't know this": Recalled by Liliane Cukier Rovère.

CHAPTER 7

119 "Sorry, but": "Chet Baker Letters Tell Europe Successes," *Down Beat,* May 2, 1955.
"thunderous ovation": Pieter Sweens, "Chet Baker—triomf van de tristheid," unknown Dutch newspaper, October 1955.

119 "a bit nervous": Piet Pijnenborg, "Jazz-poezie van Chet Baker," unknown Dutch newspaper, September 19, 1955.

"Chet Baker, Trumpet Wonder": C.W., unknown Dutch newspaper, September 17, 1955.

"Modern Music": Bob Leenart, unknown Dutch newspaper, September 19, 1955.

"Jazz Poetry": "Jazz-poezie van Chet Baker."

120 "Perhaps it's": "Chet Baker—triomf van de tristheid."

"CHET'S VOCALS": Henry Kahn, *Melody Maker* (U.K.), October 8, 1955.

122 "He had to break": Rogers Worthington, "Chet Baker, Back from the Dead, with Beauty," *Detroit Free Press,* November 23, 1975.

124 "There was a lot": Chet Baker, "30,000 Hell-Holes in My Arm," *Today* (U.K.), February 2, 1963.

"With Chet": Bill Coss, "Eulogy for Twardzik," *Metronome,* January 1956.

"Practically from" . . . "Of course he was": Chet Baker to Peter Clayton, BBC radio interview (U.K.), March 20, 1981.

"I let him": "30,000 Hell-Holes in My Arm."

"Dick's overdose": Jerome Reece, "Les Confidences de Chet Baker," *Jazz Hot* (France), November 1983.

125 "His first words": Mike Nevard, "Young Man Without a Horn . . . ," *Melody Maker* (U.K.), October 29, 1955.

"We're a little bit": Broadcast tape from Odd Fellow-Palaeet, Copenhagen, December 11, 1955; issued on *Chet Baker in Europe, 1955* (Philology 42–2).

126 "In a hall": Mike Nevard, "Chet Plays in Britain," *Melody Maker* (U.K.), November 12, 1955.

CHAPTER 8

129 "I always had": "*Playboy* Interview: Miles Davis—A Candid Conversation with the Jazz World's Premier Iconoclast," *Playboy,* September 1962.

130 "The history of": Martin Williams, *Down Beat,* February 19, 1959.

"This may well": Nat Hentoff, *Down Beat,* April 4, 1957.

"attractive colored girl": Chet Baker, "30,000 Hell-Holes in My Arm," *Today* (U.K.), February 2, 1963.

131 "It is always": Chet Baker, "La droga è la mia condanna," *L'Europeo,* 1961.

136 "Judging by": John Tynan, *Down Beat,* August 22, 1957.

137 "The next couple": Chet Baker, *As Though I Had Wings* (New York: Buzz Books, 1997), p. 79.

CHAPTER 9

139 "one of the most": Nat Hentoff, *Jazz Is* (New York: Random House, 1976).
"a city where 'pushers' ": "The Junkies," *Time,* June 25, 1951.
141 "I didn't even bother": Chet Baker, "All That Jazz, All Those Girls, All That Dope!" *Today* (U.K.), March 30, 1963.
"If Gerry Mulligan": Chet Baker in conversation with Ruth Young.
"You take that car": Recalled by Bob Zieff.
"You foreign-looking bastard!": Ibid.
142 "Jack, that's where": Jack Simpson to JG.
143 "That little-boy-lost": Clive Davis, U.K., publication unknown, c. 1995.
144 "fiasco": Jack McKinney, "Chet Baker: A Major Talent Diminished," *Metronome,* October 1960.
"When it isn't": Martin Williams, *Down Beat,* 1958.
145 "the most devious": "Alton Prince" to Fern Marja and William Duffy, "Drug Addicts, USA," *New York Post,* January 10, 1958.
"After two weeks": "All That Jazz, All Those Girls, All That Dope!"
"sharp hustler": Ibid.
"I had all": Ibid.
146 "Can you carry": Martin Williams, *Down Beat,* January 8, 1959.
147 "Is that a singer": Dinah Washington to Leonard Feather, Blindfold Test, *Down Beat,* April 30, 1959.
148 "superb lyricism": Douglas Watt, New York *Daily News,* June 7, 1959.
"Baker picks his way": *Down Beat,* July 9, 1959.
149 "If you turned": Jerome Reece, "Les Confidences de Chet Baker," *Jazz Hot* (France), November 1983.
150 "a devil's mix": Donald Frankos, *Contract Killer* (New York: Pinnacle Books, 1992), p. 82.
"I was fighting fit": "All That Jazz, All Those Girls, All That Dope!"
151 "could fill a room": John Fordham, *The Guardian,* 1999.
"lackluster": Bill Coss, *Metronome,* December 1959.
"stillborn": Jack McKinney, *Metronome,* October 1960.

CHAPTER 10

Valuable background for this chapter comes from Paola Boncompagni and Aldo Lastella's 1992 book, *Chet Baker in Italy* (Rome: Nuovi Equibri,), a collection of interviews with Baker's Italian friends and colleagues. Details on Baker's arrest, trial, imprisonment, and release were drawn from the Italian newspaper articles cited below, most of which were supplied by Francesco Maino and the Circolo del Jazz, Lucca. These include: Sergio Bindi, "Baker è ormai guarito e suona un'ora al giorno," newspaper unknown, November 25, 1960; Nicola Bosio, "La 'tromba d'oro' Chet Baker martedì davanti ai giudici lucchesi," newspaper unknown, April 9, 1961; A.A., "Il trombettista Baker si discolpa e narra come divenne tossicomane," *Corriere della sera,* April 12, 1961; Renzo Battiglia, "Poco favorevoli a Chet le risposte della ballerina Carol Jackson," *Giornale del Mattino,* April 13, 1961; Renzo Battiglia, "Sette anni di reclusione per Chet Baker," *Giornale del Mattino,* April 14, 1961; Renzo Battiglia, "La triste infanzia di Chet," *Giornale del Mattino,* April 15, 1961; Sergio Frosali, "Chet Baker è stato condannato a un anno e sette mesi di carcere," *La Nazione,* April 16, 1961; "Chet Baker è colpevole perchè voleva drogarsi," *Il Telegrafo,* September 8, 1961; "Chet Baker e i 'Quattro di Lucca' in un concerto al 'Giglio,' " *Giornale del Mattino,* December 20, 1961; Paolo Benvenuti, "Eccezionale concerto jazz con la partecipazione di Baker," *Giornale del Mattino,* December 22, 1961; "La tromba di Chet strappa applausi al Giglio di Lucca," *Il Telegrafo,* December 24, 1961.

153 "CHET EST ARRIVÉ": Jean-Pol Schroeder, *Histoire du jazz à Liège de 1900 à 1980* (Brussels: Editions Labor, 1985), p. 178.

154 "bullshit": Chet Baker to Gudrun Endress, Ludwigsburg, Germany, December 8, 1978; interview published in *Jazz Podium* (Germany).

off to a shaky start: Roberto Capasso, "Festival a Fregene," *Musica Jazz* (Italy), October 1959.

155 "a man . . . meets the woman": Oscar Valdambrini to Salvatore G. Biamonte, "Chet Baker in Italy," *Musica Jazz* (Italy), December 1994.

156 "He looked like": Carlo Loffredo, quoted in *Chet Baker in Italy,* p. 20.

"both the haven": Aldo Santini, "La magica tromba di Chet Baker è caduta nella fossa delle vipere," *Il Tirreno,* August 4, 1960.

157 "We made that film": Lucio Fulci, quoted in *Chet Baker in Italy,* p. 32.

158 "The most reassuring": Carlo Loffredo, quoted in *Chet Baker in Italy,* p.17.

"He became somebody else": Ibid., p. 15.

159 "lethargic": Don DeMichael, *Down Beat,* 1960.

"Signor Baker": Chet Baker, "La paura mi aspetta alla porta," *L'Europeo,* April 1961.

"I need you": Ibid.

160 "We lived together": Ibid.

"I was into": Chet Baker in conversation with Jack Simpson.

"I lived in a nightmare": Chet Baker, "La paura mi aspetta alla porta."

161 "scantily clad ladies": Chet Baker, *As Though I Had Wings,* unedited manuscript.

162 "As a man": Oscar Valdambrini, quoted in *Chet Baker in Italy,* p. 30.

163 "Something went wrong": Chet Baker, "La paura mi aspetta alla porta."

"Sinusitis?": Ibid.

"I've already tried them": Ibid.

164 "They put in my hand": Ibid.

"I remember I went": Ibid.

"I was a finished": Ibid.

"He started to play": Carlo Loffredo, quoted in *Chet Baker in Italy,* p. 15.

"It was clearly": Ibid., p. 17.

165 "With all you've": Chet Baker, "La paura mi aspetta alla porta."
"It was Gene": Ibid.
a violent fit: Dino Grilli, "Oggi si apre a Lucca il 'processo delle vipere,' " *Il Telegrafo,* April 11, 1961.
166 "Dear Baker": Chet Baker, "La paura mi aspetta alla porta."
167 "in a strange": A.V., "Dramma per Chet Baker," *La Nazione,* August 1, 1960.
168 "in a state": From transcript of sentencing, April 15, 1961; courtesy of Associazione degli Industriali della Provincia di Lucca and Rudy Rabassini.
"You can't do it": "Chet Baker arrestato a Marina di Pietrasanta," *Il Telegrafo,* August 22, 1960.
169 "Victory knew": Chet Baker, "La paura mi aspetta alla porta."
Baker's wife was: Renzo Battiglia, "Sette anni di reclusione per Chet Baker richiesti dalla pubblica accusa," *Giornale del Mattino,* April 14, 1961.
"I don't understand": Chet Baker, "La paura mi aspetta alla porta."
170 *"processo delle vipere":* Dino Grilli, "Oggi si apre a Lucca il 'processo delle vipere,' " *Il Telegrafo,* April 11, 1961.
171 "a young farmer": Sergio Frosali, "Chet Baker disintossicato e tranquillo racconta ai giudici la sua storia di drogato," *La Nazione* (Italy), April 12, 1961.
"Tell me, Baker": Oriana Fallaci, "Dove andrai Bakerre?" *L'Europeo* (Italy), January 1962.
"But it was": Ibid.
"I never mentioned": Renzo Battiglia, "Chet Baker guarito in prigione afferma che la sinusite lo ha abituato alla droga," *Giornale del Mattino,* April 12, 1961.
"She's my wife": Frosali, "Chet Baker disintossicato."
"Do you know": Battiglia, "Chet Baker guarito in prigione."
"There is a clear": Sergio Frosali, "L'amica di Chet Baker in tribunale mette in difficoltà i difensori," *La Nazione,* April 13, 1961.
172 "the greatest white": Fallaci, "Dove andrai Bakerre?"
"She's clearly the victim": Sergio Frosali, "Sette anni per Chet Baker chiesti dal pubblico accusatore," *La Nazione,* April 14, 1961.
"People were attentive": Dino Grilli, " 'Nessuno sapeva che ero intossicato nemmeno mia moglie' dice Baker," *Il Telegrafo,* April 12, 1961.
"This is not a cinema!": Dino Grilli, "La bella Carol Jackson smentisce piccanti rivelazioni su un medio," *Il Telegrafo,* April 13, 1961.
"I'm tired": Grilli, "Nessuno sapeva."
"I don't remember": Dino Grilli, "La bella Carol Jackson."
"I hated him": Ibid.
173 "shamelessly": Dino Grilli, "Sette anni chiesti per Chet Baker, 'faccia d'angelo, cuor di demonio,' " *Il Telegrafo,* April 14, 1961.
"There is not": Frosali, "Sette anni per Chet Baker."
"crying and alone": Letter from Francesco Maino to Alexandra Kuhl, posted on chetbaker.net, June 16, 2001.

173 "The more time": Frosali, "L'amica di Chet Baker in tribunale."
"I had only come": Grilli, "Sette anni chiesti per Chet Baker."
"Face of an angel": Ibid.
174 "You cannot consider": Renzo Battiglia, "Chet Baker condannato a 19 mesi di carcere," *Giornale del Mattino,* April 16, 1961.
"I'm very sorry": Ibid.
"He also wants": Ibid.
175 "damp, filthy": Chet Baker, "Only My Trumpet Kept Me Sane," *Today* (U.K.), April 6, 1963.
"in a sort of stupor": Chet Baker, "The Trumpet and the Spike: A Confession by Chet Baker," magazine and date unknown.
"nearly went blind": Chet Baker in conversation with Lisa Galt Bond.
"Eh, Chet": Ibid.
"I doubt": Chet Baker, *As Though I Had Wings.*
177 "I had waited": Fallaci, "Dove andrai Bakerre?"
"A black and frightening": Chet Baker, "La paura mi aspetta alla porta."
"I don't have": "Ridotta la pena a Baker Bechelli e Carani assolti," *Il Telegrafo,* September 9, 1961.

CHAPTER 11

Background on Baker's post-prison travels through England and Germany drawn from interviews with Lisa Galt Bond, from Baker's memoir, and from his autobiographical notes for Bond. Information on London's 1960s drug scene provided in part by Bobby Wellins. Baker's arrest history drawn in part from his FBI file. Other articles consulted: Mike Hennessey, "Bud Powell Today," *Melody Maker,* July 29, 1961; "Henry Kahn Does the Rounds of the Jazz Clubs," *Melody Maker,* December 16, 1961; "Chet Baker Told to Hit the Road," New York *Daily News,* June 16, 1962; P.C., "Chet Baker en pleine forme," *Jazz Hot* (France), May 1963; "Chet Baker Told to Stay Out of Germany for 3 Years," *New York Post,* June 1963; "Chet Baker Put in Isolation," New York *Daily News,* February 9, 1964; Eddie Rogers, "The Archer St. Scene," *Crescendo* (U.K.), January 1965; John Hiscock, "Jazz Star's Diaries Reveal Society Doctor Who Kept Him High," London *Daily Telegraph,* 1997.

178 "a boy making": Oriana Fallaci, "Dove andrai Bakerre?" *L'Europeo* (Italy), January 1962.
179 "The Great Movie Hoax": Chet Baker in conversation with Lisa Galt Bond, 1980.
181 *"una bella ragazza":* Pierluigi "Lippi" Francesconi to JG.
"Carol Jackson Talks": *Today* (U.K.), March 30, 1963.
184 "Not knowing German": "The Trumpet and the Spike: A Confession by Chet Baker," magazine and date unknown.
186 "Is Chet there?": Albert Jackson to JG.

187 "Carol and the baby": Chet Baker, *As Though I Had Wings* (New York: Buzz Books, 1997), p. 101.
"Mine has been": Chet Baker, "Only My Trumpet Kept Me Sane," *Today* (U.K.), April 6, 1963.
"From being . . . 'mainliner' ": Chet Baker, "30,000 Hell-Holes in My Arm," *Today* (U.K.), February 2, 1963.
"I am nauseated . . . bloodstream": "Only My Trumpet Kept Me Sane."
188 "Why?": "30,000 Hell-Holes in My Arm."
"forty major affairs": Chet Baker, "All That Jazz, All Those Girls, All That Dope! This Was the Sorrow in My Trumpet," *Today* (U.K.), March 30, 1963.
189 "I didn't mind": Chet Baker, *As Though I Had Wings,* p. 104.
190 "British Toss Out": Newspaper unknown, March 29, 1963.
"Understand me, man": "The Trumpet and the Spike."
"like a dog": Chet Baker in conversation with Ruth Young.
191 "It's idiotic": Jean-Louise Ginibre and Jean Wagner, "Chet l'exile," *Jazz* (France), July 1963.
"My playing has settled": Ibid.
"You suck!": Chet Baker in conversation with Ruth Young.
192 "I don't think Chet": "Carol Jackson Talks to Gill Preece About Her Love for Chet Baker," *Today* (U.K.), March 30, 1963.
"very attractive black lady": Chet Baker in conversation with Lisa Galt Bond.
"Stand up!": Ibid.
"Chet is happy": Michel Delorme, "Chet Baker sur le vif," *Jazz Hot* (France), July–August 1963.
194 "The career of ": Unknown newspaper, Berlin, January 24, 1964.
195 "I never bothered": Ira Gitler, "Chet Baker's Tale of Woe," *Down Beat,* July 30, 1964.
"No, I haven't": "Baker, Musician Expelled from West Germany, Back," New York *Daily News,* March 5, 1964.

CHAPTER 12

Background drawn from Baker's autobiographical notes and interviews with Lisa Galt Bond and from the trumpeter's FBI records. Richard Carpenter's history supplied in part by Don Sickler of Second Floor Music.
197 "down and out": "Back from the Dark Side," *Time,* April 17, 1964.
198 "pretentious": John S. Wilson, *Down Beat,* September 27, 1962.
198 "It was like": Miles Davis to Quincy Troupe, *Miles: The Autobiography* (New York: Touchstone Press, 1989), p. 223.
"represented, for many blacks": Ibid., p. 286.
199 "creating music that's beautiful": Chet Baker in conversation with Lisa Galt Bond.

199 "without soul": Burt Korall, "Chet Makes a Comeback," *Melody Maker,* July 18, 1964.
"Forty-five minutes": Ira Gitler, "Chet Baker's Tale of Woe," *Down Beat,* July 30, 1964.
"wasn't impressed at all": Ibid.
"giant of immeasurable stature": Leonard Feather, *The Encyclopedia of Jazz in the Sixties* (New York: Bonanza Books, 1966).
"ragged": "Chet Baker's Tale of Woe."
"Whether prettiness": Michel Delorme, "Chet Baker sur le vif," *Jazz Hot* (France), July–August 1963.
200 "Although he seemed": Ira Gitler, *Down Beat,* May 21, 1964.
202 "Chet has a unique": Korall, "Chet Makes a Comeback."
"turkeys": Chet Baker in conversation with Ruth Young.
"He came on stage": *Jazz Journal* (U.K.), September 1964.
203 "It's difficult to get": Pete Welding, *Down Beat,* October 8, 1964.
204 "lavishes loving care": Harvey Siders, *Down Beat,* March 25, 1965.
"delicacy with which": Don Nelsen, *Down Beat,* November 4, 1965.
207 she put on a smiling front: Letter, Vera Baker to Chet Baker, July 2, 1964.
209 "Baker's use of fluegelhorn": Harvey Pekar, *Down Beat,* December 29, 1966.
"invade the pop field" and "change his professional image": Korall, "Chet Makes a Comeback."
"If I hadn't been sick": Richard Williams, "The Man Who Came Back from the Dead," *Melody Maker* (U.K.), July 21, 1973.

CHAPTER 13

Background on Baker's arrests drawn from his FBI file.
212 "outrageous, terrible": Richard Williams, "The Man Who Came Back from the Dead," *Melody Maker* (U.K.), July 21, 1973.
"He sounds as if": *Down Beat,* date and reviewer unknown.
"a loser": Don Nelsen, *Down Beat,* August 25, 1966.
"Rarely . . . has Baker sounded": Pete Welding, *Down Beat,* December 1, 1966.
215 "Billy Wilson": Art and Laurie Pepper, *Straight Life* (New York: Schirmer Books, 1979), p. 112.
216 "the best thing": Ralph J. Gleason, "The Best Chance for Chet Baker," *San Francisco Chronicle,* July 1, 1966.
216 "walking home": "Chet Baker Beaten Up," *Melody Maker* (U.K.) August 20, 1966.
217 "some older white guys": Bob Micklin, "A Magic Trumpet Comes Back," *New York Newsday,* July 23, 1973.
a more preposterous account: "Chet Baker Beaten in San Francisco," *Down Beat,* September 22, 1966.

"Guy tried to": Brian Case, "The Price of a Golden Horn," *Melody Maker* (U.K.), April 14, 1979.
"They battered my gums in": Susan Barnes, *San Francisco Bay Guardian,* February 2, 1978.
"bloody mess": "Chet Baker Beaten in San Francisco."
"I had stitches": Rex Reed, "Jazzman Chet Baker Is Back from His Bad Trip," New York *Daily News,* July 8, 1973.
"The day that Chet": Carol Baker to Thorbjørn Sjøgren, *Chet: A Discography* (Copenhagen: JazzMedia ApS, 1993), p. 97.

218 "I just got on": Micklin, "A Magic Trumpet Comes Back."
"Three black guys": From an interview with João Donato conducted for this book by Zuza Homem de Mello, October 1997.

219 "The musicians ended": Jean-Louis Ginibre, *Jazz* (France), Summer 1968.
"Not even a sound": Rogers Worthington, "Chet Baker, Back from the Dead, with Beauty," *Detroit Free Press,* November 23, 1975.
"We got by": Williams, "The Man Who Came Back from the Dead."
"sixteen hours a day": Jerome Reece, "Les Confidences de Chet Baker," *Jazz Hot* (France), November 1983.
"for almost three years": Case, "The Price of a Golden Horn."

220 "script writer": Fred Bouchard, *Down Beat,* October 1979.
"The word of God": Letter, Artt Frank to JG, 1995.
"for well over": Web site: "Artt Frank: Bop Drumming Legend," www.arttfrank.com.
"like brothers": Bouchard, *Down Beat,* October 1979.

223 "drug den of the stars": Joshua Mooney, "Johnny Depp's Den," *Movieline,* May 1995.
"At times Baker": Leonard Feather, "Trumpeter Chet Baker at the Melody Room," *Los Angeles Times,* February 11, 1969.

224 "wasted experience": Art and Laurie Pepper, *Straight Life,* p. 318.

225 "Don't forget": Ruth Young to JG.

229 "I think Miles": Reece, "Les Confidences de Chet Baker."

230 "A Few Came to Hear": Ralph J. Gleason, *San Francisco Chronicle,* May 27, 1970.

231 "excellent": John L. Wasserman, "A 'New' Image of Joan Baez," *San Francisco Chronicle,* July 17, 1970.

CHAPTER 14

237 "empty, whistling": Richard Williams, "The Man Who Came Back from the Dead," *Melody Maker* (U.K.), July 21, 1973.
"His playing is still": John S. Wilson, "Chet Baker Comes in from West Coast," *New York Times,* July 13, 1973.

238 "My drug is now": "Ora la mia droga si chiama Ruth," *2000* (Italy), August 1, 1977.

239 "Diane Vavra-Baker": Letter, Chet Baker to Diane Vavra, August 15, 1973.
240 "In that vast": *Playboy,* May 1978.
"for all the losers": Alan Weitz, "Blue-Chip Blues," *Village Voice,* August 2, 1973.
"a vulnerable, aging Mafioso": Paul Nelson, "Chet Baker, American Hero," *Village Voice,* March 3, 1975.
"an emaciated Jack Palance": Rogers Worthington, "Chet Baker, Back from the Dead, with Beauty," *Detroit Free Press,* November 23, 1975.
"Jazzman Chet Baker": Rex Reed, New York *Daily News,* July 8, 1973.
"kicked through life": Ibid.
"After I paid": Bob Micklin, "A Magic Trumpet Comes Back," *New York Newsday,* July 23, 1973.
"You substitute one": Rex Reed, New York *Daily News,* July 8, 1973.
242 "new beginning": Recalled by Carson Smith.
"disgusting": Jerome Reece, "Les Confidences de Chet Baker," *Jazz Hot* (France), November 1983.
243 "Scatting is so": Chet Baker to Les Tomkins, *Crescendo International* (U.K.), 1979.
"I think your trumpet": Letter, Harriet Wilder to Chet Baker, November 3, 1975.
245 "just one big": Chet Baker to Les Tomkins, *Crescendo International,* 1979.
"He who hesitates" . . . "Life is full": Recalled by Ruth Young.
"It's so kindergartenish": Gerard Rouy, "Chet Baker Walking on Eggshells," *The Wire* (U.K.), November 1985.
"hillbilly and rockabilly crap": Chet Baker to Leonard Malone, *JazzMasters* TV interview (Copenhagen), January 29, 1988.
246 "He has almost": Nelson, "Chet Baker, American Hero."
248 "I feel so helpless": Letter, Ruth Young to Chet Baker, October 17, 1975.
249 *"You hurt her!":* Recalled by Ruth Young.
"bitch": Carol Baker, interview for *Let's Get Lost,* 1987.
250 "sees everything as a competition": Recalled by Ruth Young.
251 "nostalgia parade": John S. Wilson, "Mulligan, Baker in a Jazz Reunion," *New York Times,* November 26, 1974.
"It was *my* record company": Chet Baker to Les Tomkins, *Crescendo International* (U.K.), 1979.
"JUNKIE!": Chet Baker in conversation with Ruth Young.
"The civilized world": Reece, "Les Confidences de Chet Baker."
252 America had done Baker wrong: Artt Frank, unpublished essay on Chet Baker, year unknown.
253 "the Rimbaud of jazz": Costanzo Costantini, unknown newspaper, Italy, July 17, 1975.
"feeling and determination": Roberto Capasso, "Chet Baker con la grinta anni '50," *Paese Sera* (Italy), July 16, 1975.
"from the moon": Costantini, unknown newspaper, Italy.

"Texas, Arkansas, Arizona": Marco Molendini, "Il ritorno del Chet," unknown newspaper, Italy, July 1975.

"A black guy": Giulio Palumbo, "Divento Italiano per dimenticare la droga," *Paese Sera* (Italy), July 16, 1975.

254 "What, are we gonna . . .": Recalled by Bob Mover.

"He's nothing but": Charlie Davidson to JG.

255 "I don't wanna" and other quotes in this passage: Bob Mover to JG.

258 "the emotional quality": Dan Morgenstern, "Caught . . . International Jazz Festival Laren," *Down Beat,* December 18, 1975.

CHAPTER 15

Background on Pepito Pignatelli supplied by Giovanni Tommaso.

264 "one of the baddest": Miles Davis to Quincy Troupe, *Miles: The Autobiography* (New York: Touchstone Press, 1979), p. 262.

265 "*You Can't Go Home Again* indicates": *Playboy,* May 1978.

266 "Oh, Chet, do you remember": Recalled by Micheline Pelzer.

all his deceptions: Letter, Carol Baker to Chet Baker, October 7, 1977.

"It'd be all right": Chet Baker to Paul Fisher, CRQI-FM radio interview (Toronto), 1978.

267 "new breed of": Brian Case, "The Price of a Golden Horn," *Melody Maker* (U.K.), April 14, 1979.

"exceptionally beautiful tone": Conrad Silvert, "Trumpeter Blends Craft, Maturity," *San Francisco Chronicle,* February 9, 1978.

"appealing and welcome sound": Richard M. Sudhalter, "Cornering Chet Baker at Sweet Basil," *New York Post,* April 8, 1978.

"anxious and electrified": Bruce Bogucki, *Billboard,* March 4, 1978.

"He's over *6 ft.*": Letter, Alicia Sinatra to Chet Baker and Ruth Young, December 14, 1978.

269 "very much like me": Chet Baker in conversation with Ruth Young.

271 Nobody involved: quotes in Castel St. Angelo passage recalled by Micheline Graillier and Ruth Young.

272 "No wonder": Chet Baker in conversation with Ruth Young.

273 Frank reminded Baker . . . on the album: Letter, Artt Frank to Chet Baker, December 10, 1978.

beast . . . whore: Letter, Vera Baker to Chet Baker, April 16, 1978.

CHAPTER 16

275 Her front door . . . let them in: Letter, Carol Baker to Chet Baker, November 26, 1979.

277 shotgun: Letter, Chet Baker to Carol Baker, September 2, 1980.

277 "very skinny, sickly-looking man": Rene Magron, "Ein Wiedersehen mit Chet," *Stern* (Germany), date unknown.
278 "beauty and truth": Laurent Goddet, *Jazz Hot* (France), February 1980.
281 Now fourteen: Letter, Carol Baker to Chet Baker, February 2, 1980.
282 join the air force: Letter, Chet Baker to Dean Baker, January 14, 1980.
283 "There are a lot": Chet Baker, interview for *Galleria,* RAI-TV (Italy), January 1980.
285 "shambling efforts": Pete Welding, *Down Beat,* March 1985.
288 "interfering bitch": Letter, Carol Baker to Chet Baker, June 12, 1980.
Missy certainly: Letter, Carol Baker to Chet Baker, July 22, 1980.
289 "make the road": Recalled by Ruth Young.
"I don't like this life": Postcard, Dennis Luxion to Christiane Rey, March 24, 1980.
290 "I just don't feel": Letter, Ellis Amburn to Charles Neighbors, September 10, 1981.
"too much of a downer": Letter, Frank Wilkinson to Charles Neighbors, September 14, 1981.
"wisp of a book": Peter Pavia, "Let's Get Lost," New York *Daily News,* December 21, 1997.
"Baker Drops Egg": Don Nelsen, New York *Daily News,* May 1, 1981.
"It's kind of depressing": Michael Zwerin, *International Herald Tribune,* November 1981.
"It's true, I don't": Chet Baker to Ib Skovgaard, interview for Danmarks Radio (Copenhagen), October 2, 1979.
291 "It's so expensive": Jerome Reece, "Les Confidences de Chet Baker," *Jazz Hot* (France), November 1983.
298 "Please help Chettie": Letter, Ruth Young to Chet Baker, c. 1981.
300 The classrooms: Letter, Chet Baker to Mario Andriulli, October 30, 1982.

CHAPTER 17

303 he voiced utmost admiration: Letter, Chet Baker to Ruth Young, March 27, 1983.
311 "people are not": *Hoop,* VPRO-TV (Netherlands), January 10, 1988.
"arrogant" . . . "insincere" . . . "boring": Recalled by Ruth Young.
"a twenty-four-hour": Chet Baker, *Hoop.*
315 "obsessed" . . . "couldn't see themselves": Melody Beattie, *Codependent No More* (New York: HarperCollins/Hazelton, 1992), pp. 5–6.
319 "one of my biggest influences": Marcos Augusto Gonçalves, "A requintada 'seita Baker,' " *Folha de São Paulo* (Brazil), August 11, 1985.
320 "Chet Baker's music": José Domingos Rafaelli, "Lírico e intimista num 'show muito seu,' " *Jornal do Brasil,* August 13, 1985.
323 "The European public": Philippe Adler, "Le Jazz en chute libre," *L'Egoïste* (France), 1988.

324 "He's a very talented man, Elvis": Chet Baker to Ib Skovgaard, interview for Danmarks Radio (Copenhagen), March 1, 1985.

CHAPTER 18

327 "a psychedelic Coney Island": Patricia Morrisroe, *Mapplethorpe: A Biography* (New York: Random House, 1995), p. 67.

329 "He was just": Cyn Zarro, *Interview,* February 1989.

332 "I love the idea": David Hershkovits, "The Re-making of a Legend," *the paper,* April 1989.

"I think one of": Jon Bowermaster, "Bruce Weber in Mid-Career Crisis," *7 Days,* May 17, 1989.

338 "His main reason": Andrew O'Hehir, "Let's Get Lost," *S.F. Weekly,* May 31, 1989.

342 "You all are certainly": Letter, Chet Baker to Bruce Weber, reprinted in *Let's Get Lost: A Photo Journal* (New York: Little Bear Productions, 1989).

CHAPTER 19

Some background on Chet Baker's last days drawn from "De Eenzame Dood van Chet Baker," *De Telegraf,* May 19, 1988; Rudie Kagie, "Hij dacht erover zich permanent ergens te vetigen. In Almere was hij al een flatje gaan bekijken," *Vrij Nederlands,* May 21, 1988; and the 1990 documentary *Chet Baker: The Last Days* (RNTV, Netherlands).

349 "a genuine masterpiece": Carlo Pieroni, publication unknown.

351 "Nineteen eighty-seven": *Hoop,* VPRO-TV (Netherlands), January 10, 1988.

352 "The average person": Gerard Rouy, *Chet Baker* (Paris: Editions du Limon, 1992), p. 126.

"They sound pretty much": Jeroen de Valk, *Chet Baker: His Life and Music* (Berkeley, Calif.: Berkeley Hills Books, 2000).

"He has it completely": Maarten Derksen, "Chet Baker is terug: geen junkie meer," unknown newspaper, Netherlands, 1975.

"a lot of technique": Chet Baker in conversation with Ruth Young.

353 "friend-brother-father-son": Letter, Paolo Piangiarelli to Chet Baker, March 21, 1988.

354 "living totally alone": Dylan Jones, "Horn Loser," *The Face,* December 1988.

357 "had become what": Archie Shepp to Peter Niklas Wilson, NDR radio interview (Germany), January 13, 1990.

358 "I just want you": Jones, "Horn Loser."

368 "Maybe he started": Richard Linnett, "Jump, Fall or Push?" *Village Voice,* August 16, 1988.

368 "We performed": Ibid.
369 "It wasn't suicide": Ibid.
"He sang sometimes": *New York Times,* May 14, 1988.
370 "Chet, my friend": Marc Danval, "Dernière lettre à Chet Baker," *Pourquoi Pas?* (Belgium), May 26, 1988.

EPILOGUE

373 "Surfaces are everything": Janet Maslin, "The History of a Musician's Disintegration," *New York Times,* March 24, 1989.
374 "His stoned, introverted": Pauline Kael, "Fascination," *The New Yorker,* May 1, 1989.
"We take into": Lynne Tillman, "White Cool," *Elle,* 1989.
"a succession of ghostly": Maslin, "The History of a Musician's Disintegration."
"a phony Valentine": Sheila Benson, "Documentary Ignores Baker's Music—It's Not Photogenic," *Los Angeles Times,* May 25, 1989.
"Even when you're": Francis Davis, "Obsession," *7 Days,* April 26, 1989.
375 "seething with resentment": Chip Stern, "Drowned in a Sea of Love?" *Rolling Stone,* May 4, 1989.
"Girls pursued him": John Hiscock, London *Daily Telegraph,* March 20, 1999.
376 "handsome": Carol Baker, *Oklahoma Magazine* (TV), November 21, 1990.
378 "the object of girlish": Maureen Dowd, "Prettier Than Barbie," *New York Times,* April 22, 1998.

BIBLIOGRAPHY

All books quoted are listed under Notes; other volumes that proved useful in my research are noted below.

Avedon, Richard. *Evidence 1944–1994*. New York: Random House, 1994.
Broecking, Christian, and Matthias Kirsch, et al. *Jazz in Berlin*. Berlin: Jaron Verlag, 1998.
Claxton, William, and Hitoshi Namekata. *Jazz West Coast: Artwork of Pacific Jazz Records*. Tokyo: Bijutsu Shuppan-Sha, 1992.
de Valk, Jeroen. *Chet Baker: His Life and Music*. Berkeley, Calif.: Berkeley Hills Books, 2000.
Feather, Leonard. *The New Edition of the Encyclopedia of Jazz*. New York: Bonanza Books, 1962.
Feldman, Gene, and Max Gartenberg, eds. *The Beat Generation and the Angry Young Men*. New York: Dell Publishing, 1959.
Giddins, Gary. *Celebrating Bird: The Triumph of Charlie Parker*. New York: Beech Trees Books, 1997.
Gottlieb, Robert, ed. *Reading Jazz: A Gathering of Autobiography, Reportage, and Criticism from 1919 to Now*. New York: Pantheon Books, 1996.
Grime, Kitty. *Jazz Voices*. London: Quartet Books, 1983.
Halberstam, David. *The Fifties*. New York: Villard Books, 1993.
Klinkowitz, Jerome. *Listen: Gerry Mulligan*. New York: Schirmer Books, 1991.
Lewien, Lothar. *Engel mit gebrochenen Flügeln. Eine Hommage*. Vienna: Hannibal-Verlag, 1991.
Maggin, Donald L. *Stan Getz: A Life in Jazz*. New York: William Morrow, 1996.
Whitburn, Joel. *Joel Whitburn's Pop Memories 1890–1954*. Menominee Falls, Wis.: Record Research Inc., 1986.
Wulff, Ingo, ed. *Chet Baker in Concert*. Kiel, Germany: Nieswand Verlag, 1995.
———. *Chet Baker in Europe 1975–1988*. Kiel, Germany: Nieswand Verlag, 1993.

DISCOGRAPHY

As any reader who has followed me this far knows, Chet Baker had one of the most unwieldly recording careers in jazz. Only Thorbjørn Sjøgren, the Danish author and historian, managed to sort it all out, in his book *Chet: A Discography* (JazzMedia ApS), one of my bibles in writing this biography. The following is a near-complete list of Baker's albums; it includes catalogue numbers of the last available CD issues, along with the year of recording. For more details, consult Sjøgren's book.

1950s

With Charlie Parker: *Inglewood Jam: Bird and Chet Live at the Trade Winds*
Fresh Sound FSR-CD 17 — 1952
With Al Haig: *Chet Baker: Live at the Trade Winds, 1952*
Fresh Sound FSCD 1001 — 1952
Gerry Mulligan Quartet Featuring Chet Baker
Fantasy OJCCD-711-2 — 1952
The Pacific Jazz Years (4-CD set spanning 1952–57
Pacific Jazz CDP 0777 7 89292 2 2
Gerry Mulligan—The Original Quartet with Chet Baker
Pacific Jazz CDP 7243 4 94407 2 2 — 1952–53
Chet Baker Quartet Featuring Russ Freeman
Pacific Jazz CDP 7243 4 93164 2 3 — 1953
With the Lighthouse All-Stars: *Witch Doctor*
Contemporary OJCCD-609-2 — 1953
Chet Baker & Strings
Columbia/Legacy CK 65562 — 1953–54
This Time the Dream's on Me: Chet Baker Quartet Live, Volume 1

(includes the album *Jazz at Ann Arbor* plus a performance from the Carlton Theater in Los Angeles)
Pacific Jazz CDP 7243 5 25248 2 2 — 1953–54

Chet Baker & Stan Getz: West Coast Live (live at the Haig and Tiffany clubs, Los Angeles)
Pacific Jazz CDP 7243 8 35634 2 5 — 1953–54

Grey December (includes the album *Chet Baker Ensemble* plus four string tracks from *Chet Baker Sings and Plays with Bud Shank, Russ Freeman and Strings*)
Pacific Jazz CDP 7 97160 2 — 1953–55

Newport Years Vol. 1 (TV and radio performances)
Philology W 51-2 — 1953–56

The Complete Pacific Jazz Studio Recordings of The Chet Baker Quartet with Russ Freeman
Mosaic MD3-122 — 1953–56

Let's Get Lost: The Best of Chet Baker Sings (includes the complete album *Chet Baker Sings* plus six tracks from *Chet Baker Sings and Plays with Bud Shank, Russ Freeman and Strings* and a later vocal session)
Capitol/Pacific Jazz CDP 7 92932 2 — 1953–56

Chet Baker, Boston, 1954 (broadcasts from Storyville)
Uptown UPCD 27.35 — 1954

The Complete Pacific Jazz Live Recordings of the Chet Baker Quartet with Russ Freeman
Mosaic MD3-113 — 1954

Out of Nowhere: Chet Baker Quartet Live, Volume 2 (live at the Tiffany Club in Los Angeles and the Santa Cruz Civic Auditorium)
Pacific Jazz CDP 7243 5 27693 2 2 — 1954

My Old Flame: Chet Baker Quartet Live, Volume 3 (from the Tiffany Club)
Pacific Jazz CDP 7243 5 31573 2 6 — 1954

Young Chet (miscellaneous rarities from the Pacific Jazz vaults)
Pacific Jazz CDP 7243 8 36194 2 9 — 1954–56

Chet Baker/Big Band (includes the complete albums *Chet Baker Sextet* and *Chet Baker Big Band*)
Pacific Jazz CDP 0777 7 81201 2 4 — 1954–56

2 Trumpet Geniuses of the 50's: Brownie and Chet (TV and radio performances of Baker plus others by Clifford Brown)
Philology 214W13 — 1954–57

Chet Baker in Europe, 1955 (live broadcasts)
Philology W 42-2 — 1955

With Dick Twardzik: *Chet in Paris: The Complete Barclay Recordings of Chet Baker, Volume 1*
EmArcy 837 474-2 — 1955

Chet in Paris: The Complete Barclay Recordings of Chet Baker, Volume 2
EmArcy 837 475-2 — 1955

Chet in Paris: The Complete Barclay Recordings of Chet Baker, Volume 3
EmArcy 837 476-2 1955–56
Chet in Paris: The Complete Barclay Recordings of Chet Baker, Volume 4
EmArcy 837 477-2 1955–56
With Dick Twardzik: *The Great Lars Gullin, Vol. 1—55/56*
Dragon DRCD 224 1955–56
Cool Way to Florence (live at Conservatorio Cherubini)
Oscar OSC701 1956
Chet Baker & Crew
Pacific Jazz CDP 0777 7 81205 2 0 1956
With Art Pepper: *The Route*
Pacific Jazz CDP 7 92931 2 1956
With Art Pepper: *Playboys*
Pacific Jazz CDP 7 94474 2 1956
Quartet—Chet Baker & Russ Freeman
Pacific Jazz CDP 7243 8 55453 2 0 1956
With Bud Shank: *Theme Music from "The James Dean Story"*
Pacific Jazz CDP 0777 7 95251 2 6 1956
With Jack Sheldon: *Jack's Groove*
Fresh Sound FSR-CD 70 1957
Embraceable You
Pacific Jazz CDP 7 24383 1676 2 1957
With Gerry Mulligan: *Reunion*
Pacific Jazz CDP 7 46857 2 1957
Annie Ross Sings a Song with Mulligan
EMI-Manhattan CDP 7 46852 2 1957
With Stan Getz: *Stan Meets Chet*
Verve 837 436-2 1958
It Could Happen to You
Riverside OJCCD-303-2 1958
Chet Baker in New York
Riverside OJCCD-207-2 1958
Chet Baker Introduces Johnny Pace
Riverside OJCCD-433-2 1958
Chet
Riverside OJCCD-087-2 1958–59
Chet Baker Plays the Best of Lerner & Loewe
Riverside OJCCD-137-2 1959
Chet Baker with Fifty Italian Strings
Jazzland OJCCD-492-2 1959
Chet Baker in Milan
Jazzland OJCCD-370-2 1959
Chet Baker—Italian Movies: Music by Piero Umiliani (soundtrack music recorded by Chet Baker for several Italian films)
Liuto LRS 0063/1 1959–62

1960s

Live in Paris 1960–1963, Nice 1975
France's Concert FCD 123
The Italian Sessions
RCA/Bluebird 2001-2-RB 1962
With René Thomas: *Hallucinations: Live in Cantina/Bologna*
Jazz Birdie's of Paradise J-Bop 049 1962
The Most Important Jazz Album of 1964/65
LP: Colpix SCP 476 1964
Baby Breeze
Verve 314 538 328-2 1965
Baker's Holiday
EmArcy 838 204-2 1965
Lonely Star (this and the two following CDs collect all the material Baker recorded for Prestige)
Prestige PRCD-24172-2 1965
Stairway to the Stars
Prestige PRCD-24173-2 1965
On a Misty Night
Prestige PRCD-24174-2 1965
With the Mariachi Brass: *A Taste of Tequila*
LP: World Pacific WPS 21839 1965
With Joe Pass: *A Sign of the Times*
LP: World Pacific WPS 21844 1965
With Bud Shank: *Michelle*
LP: World Pacific WPS 21840 1965
With Bud Shank: *California Dreamin'*
LP: World Pacific WPS 21845 1966
With the Mariachi Brass: *Hats Off*
LP: World Pacific WPS 21842 1966
With the Carmel Strings: *Quietly There*
LP: World Pacific WPS 21847 1966
With Bud Shank: *Brazil Brazil Brazil*
LP: World Pacific WPS 21855 1966
With the Carmel Strings: *Into My Life*
LP: World Pacific WPS 21859 1966
With the Mariachi Brass: *In the Mood*
LP: World Pacific WPS 21859 1966
With Phil Urso: *Live at Pueblo, Colorado, 1966*
CCB 1225 1966
With Bud Shank: *Magical Mystery*
LP: World Pacific WPS 21873 1967

Albert's House
Par PAR-2007-CD 1968

1970s

Blood, Chet and Tears
LP: Verve V6-8798 1970
Chet Baker—Lee Konitz—Keith Jarrett (a performance for WNYC-TV)
LP: JazzConn JC 113 1974
She Was Too Good to Me
CBS ZK 40804 1974
With Gerry Mulligan: *Carnegie Hall Concert*
CBS ZGK 40689 1974
With Jim Hall: *Concierto*
CTI/Legacy ZK 65132 1975
Seven Faces of "Valentine" (live performances of "My Funny Valentine")
Philology W30-2 1975–87
Chet Baker in Italy (a collection of live performances, for a special issue of *Musica Jazz Magazine*)
Philology W 81.2 1975–88
Deep in a Dream of You (live at the Music Inn, Rome)
Moon 026-2 1976
Once Upon a Summertime
Galaxy OJCCD-405-2 1977
You Can't Go Home Again/The Best Thing for You
Verve 314 543 516-2 1977
With Ruth Young: *The Incredible Chet Baker Plays and Sings*
ANS 12009-2 1977
The Rising Sun Collection (live in Toronto)
JustAMemory RSCD 0010 1978
Live in Chateauvallon, 1978
France's Concert FCD 128 1978
Live at Nick's (Laren, Holland)
Cross Cross CD 1027 1978
Broken Wing
Verve 440 012 043-2 1978
Two a Day (live in Hérouville, France)
Dreyfus FDM 76491165082 1978
Tender Variations: Soundtrack from the Film "Flic ou Voyou"
LP: Decca 6.23969 AO 1979
The Touch of Your Lips
SteepleChase SCCD 31122 1979

All Blues
Arco 3 ARC 102 — 1979
With Duke Jordan: *No Problem*
SteepleChase SCCD 31131 — 1979
Daybreak (this and the two following titles live at Copenhagen's Jazzhus Montmartre)
SteepleChase SCCD 31142 — 1979
This Is Always
SteepleChase SCCD 31168 — 1979
Someday My Prince Will Come
SteepleChase SCCD 31180 — 1979
Just Friends
Arco ARC 112 — 1979
Chet Baker/Wolfgang Lackerschmid
Inak 8571 CD — 1979
With Enrico Pieranunzi: *Soft Journey*
IDA 033 CD — 1979–80

1980s

Chet Baker—Steve Houben
52e Rue Est RECD 019 — 1980
"Live" at the Subway Club Vol. 1 (this and the two following titles from Subway Club, Cologne)
Circle RKCD/2 — 1980
Just Friends
LP: Circle RK22380/27 — 1980
Down
LP: Circle RK22380/35 — 1980
Leaving
LP: Intercord INT 160.154 — 1980
With Ron Carter: *Patrão*
Milestone MCD-9099-2 — 1980
Tune Up (this and the two following titles live at Le Dreher, Paris)
West Wind 2037 — 1980
Night Bird
West Wind 2038 — 1980
It Never Entered My Mind
LP: Circle RK25680/36 — 1980
With Wolfgang Lackerschmid: *Why Shouldn't You Cry: Chet Baker, The Legacy, Vol. 3*
Enja ENJ-9337 2 — 1979–87

Chet Baker in Europe (a collection of rarities and interviews, sold with the book of the same title)
b&w bwcd 001 — 1979–88
With Riqué Pantoja: *Chet Baker & The Boto Brasilian Quartet*
Dreyfus FDM 36511-2 — 1980
Chet Baker Quartet with Special Guest Bud Shank: Live at Fat Tuesday's
Fresh Sound FSR CD 131 — 1981
My Funny Valentine (this and the two following titles live at Salt Peanuts Club, Cologne)
LP: Circle RK 23581/24 — 1981
'Round Midnight
LP: Circle RK 23581/25 — 1981
I Remember You
LP: Circle RK23581/28 — 1981
Chet Baker/René Urtreger/Aldo Romano/Pierre Michelot (live at Théâtre de la Ville, Paris)
Carlyne CARCD 15 — 1981
With Michel Graillier: *Dream Drops*
Owl 026 CD — 1981
With David Friedman: *Peace*
Enja R2 79625 — 1982
With Jim Hall and Hubert Laws: *Studio Trieste*
CTI 63051 — 1982
Out of Nowhere (live at the Nine of Cups, Tulsa, Oklahoma)
Milestone MCD-9191-2 — 1982
The Stan Getz Quartet with Chet Baker: Quintessence, Volume 1 (this and the following title live in Norway)
Concord Jazz CCD-4807-2 — 1983
The Stan Getz Quartet with Chet Baker: Quintessence, Volume 2
Concord Jazz CCD-4858-2 — 1983
Stan Getz & Chet Baker: The Stockholm Concerts
Verve 537 555-2 — 1983
With Kirk Lightsey Trio: *Everything Happens to Me*
Timeless CDSJP 192 — 1983
Jean-Louis Rassinfosse/Chet Baker/Philip Catherine
Igloo IGL 034 — 1983
Mr. B
Timeless CDSJP 192 — 1983–85
With Jim Porto: *Rio*
LP: Siglo Quattro 1019 — 1983
The Improviser (live in Oslo, Norway)
Cadence CJR 1019 — 1983
A Trumpet for the Sky, Vol. 1 (this and the following title live at Club 21, Paris)
Philology W55.2 — 1983

A Trumpet for the Sky, Vol. 2
Philology W56.2 — 1983
Naima: Unusual Chet, Vol. 1 (live European performances)
Philology W 52-2 — 1983–87
With Åke Johannson Trio and Toots Thielemans: *Chet & Toots*
Dragon DRCD 333 — 1985
Chet Baker Live in Sweden with the Åke Johannson Trio
Dragon DRCD 178 — 1983
Chet al Capolinea
Red 123206-2 — 1983
With Duke Jordan: *September Song* (live at New Morning, Paris)
Marshmallow CECC 00216 — 1983
With Duke Jordan: *Live at New Morning*
Marshmallow CECC 00420 — 1983
With Duke Jordan: *Star Eyes* (live at George's Jazz Café, Arnhem, Holland)
Marshmallow CECC 00206 — 1983
Soundtrack: *Le Jumeau*
Carrere 96.251 — 1984
With Warne Marsh: *Blues for a Reason*
Criss Cross 1010 CD — 1984
Live at Buffalo
CCB CD 1223 — 1984
My Foolish Heart
IRD TDM 002 — 1985
Misty
IRD TDM 003 — 1985
Time After Time
IRD TDM 004 — 1985
With Paul Bley: *Diane*
SteepleChase SCCD-31207 — 1985
I Remember You: Chet Baker, The Legacy, Vol. 2 (live at Copenhagen's Café Montmartre)
Enja ENJ-9077 2 — 1985
Chet Baker in Bologna
Dreyfus FDM 36558-2 — 1985
Chet's Choice
Criss Cross 1016 CD — 1985
Strollin'
Enja CD 5005 2 — 1985
Candy
Sonet SNTCD-946 — 1985
With Mike Melillo: *Symphonically*
Soul Note SN 1134 CD — 1985

With the Amstel Octet: *Hazy Hugs*
LP: Limetree MLP 198601 — 1985
Soundtrack: *'Round Midnight*
CBS CK 40464 — 1985
Chet Baker Sings Again
Timeless CDSJP 238 — 1985
Live from the Moonlight (Macerata, Italy)
Philology W 10/11-2 — 1985
Riqué Pantoja & Chet Baker
Warner WH 55155 — 1985
With Lizzy Mercier Descloux: *One for the Soul*
LP: Polydor 827-910-1 — 1985
With Joe LoCascio: *Sleepless*
LP: Pausa PR 7200 — 1985
With Christopher Mason: *Silent Nights: A Jazz Christmas Album*
Varrick CD 032 — 1986
When Sunny Gets Blue
SteepleChase SCCD 31221 — 1986
Night Bird (live at Ronnie Scott's, London)
Essential ESMCD 015 — 1986
Cool Cat
Timeless CDSJP 262 — 1986
As Time Goes By
Timeless CDSJP 251/52 — 1986
Chet Baker Sings and Plays from the Film "Let's Get Lost"
RCA/Novus 3054-2-N — 1987
A Night at the Shalimar Club (live in Senigalia, Italy)
Philology W 59-2 — 1987
Chet Baker in Tokyo
Evidence 22158 — 1987
With Wolfgang Lackerschmid: *Welcome Back*
West Wind 2083 — 1987
With Charlie Haden Quartet: *Silence*
Soul Note 121 172-2 — 1987
The Legacy, Vol. 1 (live broadcast with NDR Big Band, Hamburg)
Enja ENJ-9021 2 — 1987
Chet on Poetry
RCA/Novus PL/PD 74347 — 1988
With Jan Erik Vold: *Blåmann! Blåmann!*
Hot Club HCRCD 50 — 1988
With Enrico Pieranunzi: *The Heart of the Ballad*
Philology W20.2 — 1988
With Enrico Pieranunzi's Space Jazz Trio: *Little Girl Blue*
Philology W21.2 — 1988

With Nino Buonocore: *Una città tra le mani*
EMI 090-7902042 1988
With Archie Shepp: *Archie Shepp–Chet Baker Quintet: In Memory of*
L&R CDLR 45006 1988
Live in Rosenheim
Timeless CD SJP 233 1988
The Last Great Concert: My Favourite Songs Vol. I & II
Enja 6074 22 1988

INDEX

A NOTE ABOUT THE AUTHOR

James Gavin is the author of *Intimate Nights: The Golden Age of New York Cabaret,* a winner of ASCAP's Deems Taylor Award. He is a frequent contributor to the *New York Times* and other publications. His liner notes for *Ella Fitzgerald: The Legendary Decca Recordings,* a CD boxed set, received a 1996 Grammy nomination. He lives in New York City.

A NOTE ON THE TYPE

This book was set in Adobe Garamond. Designed for the Adobe Corporation by Robert Slimbach, the fonts are based on types first cut by Claude Garamond (c. 1480–1561).

Composed by Creative Graphics, Allentown, Pennsylvania
Printed and bound by Berryville Graphics, Berryville, Virginia
Designed by Peter A. Andersen